THE BRITISH SCHOOL OF
ARCHAEOLOGY AT ATHENS

*Supplementary Volume No. 11*

# LEFKANDI I

TEXT

Published with the support of the
Charles E. Merrill Trust, the Marc Fitch Fund, the
Dr. M. Alwyn Cotton Foundation
and a donation by
Mr. C. A. Rodewald

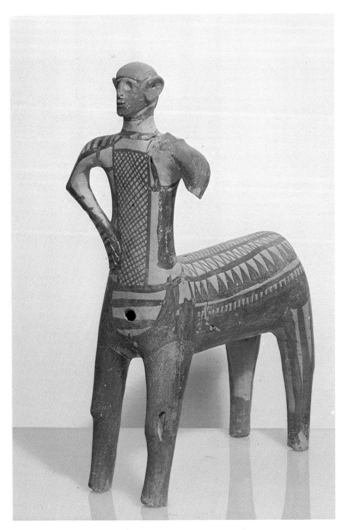

(a) The Centaur (Toumba T1 and 3).

(b) Pendent Semi-circle Skyphos (Skoubris T. 59A, 4).

(c) Jug (Palia Perivolia T. 23, 1).

# LEFKANDI I

# THE IRON AGE

## TEXT

## THE SETTLEMENT

### EDITED BY
### M. R. POPHAM AND L. H. SACKETT
### AND, WITH P. G. THEMELIS,

## THE CEMETERIES

MAIN CONTRIBUTORS
J. BOARDMAN WITH M. J. PRICE
H. W. AND E. A. CATLING
V. R. d'A. DESBOROUGH WITH O. T. P. K. DICKINSON
R. A. HIGGINS
L. H. JEFFERY

THE BRITISH SCHOOL OF ARCHAEOLOGY AT ATHENS

―――――

THAMES AND HUDSON
1980

Printed in Great Britain at the Alden Press, Oxford

FOR
'PETER' AND ELEKTRA
MEGAW
AND
TO THE MEMORY OF
VINCENT DESBOROUGH

# CONTENTS

Appendices

# PREFACE

A brief outline of the excavation of Iron Age Lefkandi and the subsequent research into its history by members of the British School at Athens was given in the general introduction to the PLATES volume; and acknowledgement was there given to the various hands who helped in the production of the illustrations. The full study presented here is equally the work of many hands, those who contributed to the excavation of the site, the study of the excavated material (successively in the mosque at Chalcis, in the Chalcis Museum and latterly at the Eretria Museum), and those who wrote the final report.

The excavations took place in the summers of 1964–6 under the direction of M. R. Popham and L. H. Sackett, joined in 1968 (spring) and 1969–70 by P. G. Themelis, when work was extended to include the cemetery areas. Professor Sp. Marinatos was particularly helpful in making possible this most productive section of the excavations, and in encouraging the extension of a hasty rescue operation into a planned excavation. We are most grateful to him and to the successive Ephors of Antiquities responsible for Euboea in those years for their close co-operation and assistance – to B. Kallipolitis, N. Verdelis, A. Vavritsas, E. Mastrokostas and D. Lazaridis; also for continued help in later years at Eretria to A. Andreiomenou and E. Touloupa. Special acknowledgement is due to the Directors of the British School at Athens, A. H. S. Megaw and P. M. Fraser during excavation, and subsequently to H. W. Catling, for their encouragement, good advice and administrative help throughout. As this was the principal dig of the British School, opportunities were given to students currently in Athens to join the excavations, and the help of those who participated is gratefully acknowledged. A full list of the excavation staff is given below.

Much of the digging was carried out by a hardworking and skilled group of men who came over from Knossos, first with Manoli Markoyiannakis as foreman, and later, after his death, with Antoni Zidianakis. They were assisted by local workers from Lefkandi, Vasiliko and Phylla, but help was also brought in the initial stages from Athens (in 1964), thanks to the generosity of Professor Homer Thompson, and later from Eretria (in 1970). Throughout the years of excavation and later of study, Petros Petrakis cleaned, mended and restored the finds, helped by his wife Eleni. Thanks to them both for patience, skill, speed and good humour.

Lefkandi is a major Bronze Age and Early Iron Age site, and only a very small portion of it has yet been excavated. For the visitor today only the main settlement area excavated at the northeast edge of Xeropolis remains open to view, and what is to be seen there is almost entirely of Bronze Age date. The test trenches of 1964–5 and all the cemetery areas, which were not in purchased land, had to be filled in and have reverted to their original agricultural use. Future work is much to be hoped for in the settlement sites at Xeropolis and on the adjacent hill slopes to the north, and also in the cemetery areas. In the meantime we express our thanks to the landowners, Ch. Koutoulas, N. Koutroularos,

S. Petroyiannis, I. Kakaras, D. Kalfas, A. Skoubris, N. Nikolaidis, G. Neroutsios and B. Frangas for their co-operation in permitting us to excavate in their fields.

The material published in this volume is housed in Eretria Museum where a small selection of the finds are currently on display.

Most of the organisation, cataloguing and photography of the excavated material at the Museum was done by the excavators during study. But special mentioned should be made of the work of Oliver Dickinson at this stage and of Martin Price who made preliminary studies of the Protogeometric and Late Geometric pottery from Xeropolis respectively.

The major contributions to this volume are written by John Boardman, Hector Catling, Vincent Desborough and Reynold Higgins. These scholars have all worked patiently over a number of years with a considerable body of sometimes quite fragmentary material, and have given their enthusiastic support to the successful completion of the whole enterprise.

Other important written contributions have been made by Anne Jeffery in discussing the inscribed sherds, by Nicolas Coldstream in identifying the imported Geometric wares, by Richard Jones on clay and metal analyses, and by Jonathan Musgrave in studying the human remains.

To our other contributors, John Younger, Jill Carington Smith and Glynis Jones, as well as to our numerous helpers and advisors we are most grateful; of these we can mention only a few, Helen Brock, Jim Coulton, and Elizabeth French as well as Allison Wilkins for preparing last-minute charts and plans. Students and scholars patiently attended and made valuable suggestions at a term's seminar on the history of the site at Oxford University.

Sections 1—2, 5—7 and 14 are the joint work of Mervyn Popham and Hugh Sackett; the former was responsible for the initial draft of the Introduction, the account of the Settlement and most of its finds, and the historical conclusions; the latter for that on the Cemeteries and their finds. Throughout, the notebooks and plans kept by the dig supervisors have been our basic sources, while descriptions of many objects, made by Vincent Desborough, Hector Catling and Reynold Higgins, have been incorporated into the catalogues.

In taking on the study of the Dark Age pottery, Vincent Desborough was faced with the greatest and most fundamental task, and to him we owe the essential framework of our stylistic and chronological sequences for this long stage in the history of the site. But this is not all: he read over and carefully revised the descriptive sections on the tombs, pyres and their contents, and with his special combination of meticulous attention to detail and courage to throw out bold hypotheses, became not only a most valuable helper but also an indefatigable promoter of the importance of Lefkandi, giving many lectures and publishing several papers on the subject. He devoted the major part of his study time in his last years to Lefkandi, and handed over his completed text on the Dark Age pottery in June 1978, only shortly before his sudden death in July of that year. We much regret that by his death we were deprived of his immediate advice and criticism when formulating our historical conclusions: he would have enjoyed participating in this perhaps more than all else. He was not able to see and refer to the important Catalogue of the Exhibition in the Benaki Museum of part of the Goulandris Collection (1978) nor to E. Gjertad and others 'Greek Geometric and Archaic pottery found in Cyprus'.

We are sure that Peter and Elektra Megaw will welcome our addition of Vincent Desborough's name to theirs in our dedication of the text part of Lefkandi I and will be pleased to honour with us the memory of a scholar and friend for whom we had the warmest of affection and the greatest of respect.

We are especially indebted to the Committee of the British School at Athens, who gave financial support at all stages of the work, in excavation, study and writing the final report, and who applied on behalf of the excavation for assistance from the British Academy. The Cambridge University Classics Fund, the Craven Fund of Oxford University and Sydney University also contributed towards the cost of the excavation. Especial thanks are due to the Charles E. Merrill Trust for several generous awards; it and the Cotton Foundation also assisted financially the publication of this volume. The cost of printing the scientific results in Appendices C, D and E was generously met by the Fitch Fund with a grant from the University of Bristol. Mr. C. A. Rodewald, also, made a kind donation in memory of Vincent Desborough.

The clay analyses referred to in the text were part of a larger study, not yet completed, and will be published later elsewhere; as, too, will a report on the animal bones, which is concerned with the material from all periods on the site.

With some reluctance we have abandoned our original intention of having an index. The sub-headings at the beginning of each section should make reference to discussion of particular aspects or classes of objects fairly easy. An index to be more useful would have needed to be very full and detailed, involving a delay and expense which we thought unjustified.

The following were the members of the excavation staff in the successive years at Lefkandi:

1964 Mervyn Popham, Hugh Sackett, John Carter, Anne Chapman, Roger Howell, Maria and Martin Price, Norman Postlethwaite, Elizabeth Ramsden, Peter Rhodes, Peter Warren; Vasilios Adamakos, foreman.

1965 Mervyn Popham, Hugh Sackett, Gerald Cadogan, Anne Chapman, Roger Howell, Alastair Jackson, Ken McFadzean, Elizabeth Milburn, Bill Phelps, Maria and Martin Price, Elizabeth Ramsden, Cressida Ridley, Michael Smee, Peter Warren; Manoli Markoyiannakis, foreman.

1966 Mervyn Popham, Hugh Sackett, Anne Chapman, Oliver Dickinson, Roger Howell, Elizabeth Milburn, Ken McFadzean, Peter Warren; Manoli Markoyiannakis, foreman.

1968 Mervyn Popham, Hugh Sackett, Petros Themelis (short emergency excavation).

1969 Mervyn Popham, Hugh Sackett, Petros Themelis, Susan Bird, Richard Chamberlin, Nick Gimbel, Roger Howell, Ken McFadzean, Cressida Ridley, Susan Rotroff, Geoffrey and Elizabeth Waywell, Peter Warren; Andoni Zidianakis, foreman.

1970 Mervyn Popham, Hugh Sackett, Petros Themelis, Susan Bird, Miranda Buchanan, Richard Camberlin, Jeremy Harrison, Ken McFadzean, Cressida Ridley, Susan Sherwin White; Andoni Zidianakis, foreman.

MERVYN POPHAM

HUGH SACKETT

PETROS THEMELIS

# ABBREVIATIONS

## LOCALITIES

| | |
|---|---|
| KT | Tombs in the Khaliotis field |
| P | Palia Perivolia Cemetery |
| S | Skoubris Cemetery |
| T | Toumba Cemetery |

## CHRONOLOGY

SM    Submycenaean (approximately 1100–1050 BC)

EPG   Early Protogeometric

MPG   Middle Protogeometric

LPG    Late Protogeometric

(The whole Protogeometric phase being approximately 1050–900 BC)

SPG   Sub-Protogeometric

(Phase I roughly equated with Attic Early Geometric I approximately 900–875 BC)

(Phase II roughly equated with Attic Early Geometric II approximately 875–850 BC)

(Phase III roughly equated with Attic Middle Geometric I and II approximately 850–750 BC)

LG    Late Geometric (approximately 750–700 BC)

Dimensions of objects are stated throughout in centimetres.

PLATE    refers to illustrations in the PLATES volume.

FIG.    refers to illustrations included in this volume.

## BIBLIOGRAPHICAL ABBREVIATIONS

| | |
|---|---|
| *AA* | *Archäologischer Anzeiger* |
| *AAA* | *Athens Annals of Archaeology* |
| *AD* | See *ADelt* |
| *ADelt (Chron)* | *Arkhaiologikon Deltion (Chronika)* (Athens) |
| *AE* | *Arkhaiologiki Ephimeris* (Athens) |
| *AIARS* | *Acta Instituti Atheniensis Regni Suecial* (Lund) |
| *AJA* | *American Journal of Archaeology* (Princeton) |
| *Alaas* | V. Karageorghis, *Alaas: a Protogeometric Necropolis in Cyprus*. Nicosia 1975 |

| | |
|---|---|
| *AM* | *Mitteilungen des Deutschen Archäologischen Instituts, Athenische Abteilungen* |
| *Analysis* | A. Furumark, *The Mycenaean Pottery: analysis and classification.* Stockholm, 1940 |
| *Ann* | *Annuario della Regia Scuola Archeologica di Atene* |
| *AntK* | *Antika Kunst* |
| *AR* | *Archaeological Reports* |
| *Asine* | O. Frödin & A. W. Persson, *Asine; results of the Swedish excavations 1922–1930.* Stockholm 1938 |
| *Athenian Agora* | *The Athenian Agora: results of excavations conducted by the American School of Classical Studies,* 1–21. Princeton, 1953–76 |
| *B* | Classification of fibulae in *Fibules* (below) |
| *BABesch* | *Bulletin Antieke Beschaving* |
| *BCH* | *Bulletin de Correspondance Hellénique* |
| *Beth Pelet i* | W. M. F. Petrie, *Beth Pelet i (Tell Fara).* London, 1930 |
| *Beth Pelet ii* | J. L. Starkey & L. Harding, *Beth Pelet ii.* London, 1932 |
| *BICS* | *Bulletin of the Institute of Classical Studies,* London University |
| *BMB* | *Bulletin du Musée de Beyrouth* |
| *BMQ* | *British Museum Quarterly* |
| *Boll. d'Arte* | *Bolletino d'Arte* |
| *BSA* | *Annual of the British School at Athens* |
| *Bull. Met. Mus.* | *Bulletin of the Metropolitan Museum of Art* (New York) |
| *CAH* | *Cambridge Ancient History* |
| *CBMW* | H. W. Catling, *Cypriot Bronzework in the Mycenaean World.* Oxford, 1964 |
| *CCO* | J. Boardman, *The Cretan Collection in Oxford: the Dictaean Cave and Iron Age Crete.* Oxford, 1961 |
| *CGA* | P. Courbin, *Le Céramique Géométrique de l'Argolide.* Paris, 1966 |
| *ChO* | *Kharisterion, Studies in honour of A. K. Orlandos,* 1–4. Athens, 1965–8 |
| *Chronologie* | H. Müller-Karpe, *Beitrage zur Chronologie der Urnenfelderzeit Nördlich und Südlich der Alpen.* Berlin, 1959 |
| *Corinth* | *Corinth: results of excavations conducted by the American School of Classical Studies at Athens,* 1 ff. Cambridge, Mass. 1932–75 |
| *CR* | *Clara Rhodos* |
| *CVA* | *Corpus Vasorum Antiquorum* |
| *DAG* | A. M. Snodgrass, *The Dark Age of Greece.* Edinburgh, 1967 |
| *Délos* | *Exploration archéologique de Délos, faite par l'école française d'Athenes,* 1–31. Paris, 1909–77 |
| *Delphes* | *Fouilles de Delphes,* I–V, Paris, 1902–76 |
| *Dialoghi* | *Dialoghi di Archaeologia* |
| *EA* | see *AE* |
| *EGAW* | A. M. Snodgrass, *Early Greek Armour and Weapons.* Edinburgh, 1964 |
| *Eretria* | *Eretria: fouilles et recherches,* 1–4, Berne 1968–72 |
| *Ergon* | *To Ergon tis Arkhaiologikis Etaireias* |
| *Euboean Participation* | V. R. d'A. Desborough, *The Background to Euboean Participation in Early Greek Maritime Enterprise* in *Tribute to an Antiquary, Essays presented to Marc Fitch.* London, 1977 |

FGI           E. Sapouna-Sakellarakis, *Die Fibeln der griechischen Inseln,* Prähistorische Bronzefunde Abteilung XIV, 4. Band. Munich, 1978

*Fibules*       Chr. Blinkenberg, *Fibules grecques et orientales* Copenhagen, 1920

*Fortetsa*      J. K. Brock, *Fortetsa: Early Greek Tombs near Knossos.* Cambridge, 1957

GDA           V. R. d'A. Desborough, *The Greek Dark Ages.* London, 1972

GG            J. N. Coldstream, *Geometric Greece.* London, 1977

GGP           J. N. Coldstream, *Greek Geometric Pottery.* London, 1968

GkO           J. Boardman, *The Greeks Overseas.* London, 1973

*Goulandris*    Ch. Doumas and L. Marangou, *Exhibition of Ancient Greek Art from the N. P. Goulandris Collection at the Benaki Museum.* Athens, 1978

*Greek Pins*    P. Jacobsthal, *Greek Pins and their connexions with Europe and Asia.* Oxford, 1966

CRJ           R. A. Higgins, *Greek and Roman Jewellery.* London, 1961

HandCC        J. L. Myres, *The Metropolitan Museum of Art, Handbook of the Cesnola Collection of Antiquities from Cyprus.* New York, 1914

IstMitt        *Istanbuler Mitteilungen*

JdI           *Jahrbuch des deutschen archäologischen Instituts*

JdI 77        H. Müller-Karpe, *Die Metallbeigaben der früheisenzeitlichen Kerameikos Gräber, JdI* Vol. 77 (1962), 59 ff.

Ker           W. Kraiker and K. Kübler, *Kerameikos: Ergebnisse der Ausgrabungen,* I—XI. Berlin, 1939—76

KrChr         *Kritika Chronika*

LMTS          V. R. d'A. Desborough, *The Last Mycenaeans and their Successors.* Oxford, 1964

MMA Bronzes   G. M. A. Richter, *Greek, Etruscan and Roman Bronzes* (The Metropolitan Museum of Art). New York, 1915

NdS           *Notizie degli Scavi*

*Nouveaux*      V. Karageorghis, *Nouveaux Documents pour l'étude du Bronze Récent à*
*Documents*     *Chypre.* Paris, 1965

PAE           *Praktika tis en Athenais Arkhaiologikis Etaireias*

*Perati*        S. E. Iakovides, *Perati: the Cemetery,* I—III. Athens, 1969 (in Greek).

PGP           V. R. d'A. Desborough, *Protogeometric Pottery.* Oxford, 1952

PGRT          N. M. Verdelis, *The Protogeometric Style of Thessaly.* Athens, 1958 (in Greek).

*PG Style in*   A. Pieridou, *The Protogeometric Style in Cyprus.* Athens, 1973 (in
*Cyprus*        Greek).

PofM          A. J. Evans, *The Palace of Minos*

Pr            see *PAE* above

*Preliminary*   M. R. Popham and L. H. Sackett (eds.) *Excavations at Lefkandi 1964—*
*Report*        *66, A Preliminary Report.* London, 1968

PT            A. J. B. Wace and M. S. Thompson, *Prehistoric Thessaly.* Cambridge, 1912

QDAP          *Quarterly of the Department of Antiquities in Palestine*

RDAC          *Report of the Department of Antiquities, Cyprus*

RM            *Mitteilungen des deutschen archäologischen Instituts, Romische Abteilung*

*Salamine*      *Salamine de Chypre; fouilles sous la direction de J. Pouilloux et G. Roux, 1—7.* Paris, 1969—1977

| | |
|---|---|
| *Samos V* | H. Walter, *Samos V, Frühe Samische Gefässe.* Bonn, 1968 |
| *Samos VIII* | U. Jantzen, *Samos VIII, Ägyptische und Orientalische Bronzen aus dem Heraion von Samos.* Bonn, 1972 |
| *SCE* | E. Gjerstad and others, *The Swedish Cyprus Expedition. Finds and Results of the Swedish Excavations in Cyprus 1927–31, 1 ff.* Stockholm, 1934–72 |
| *SIMA* | *Studies in Mediterranean Archaeology,* 1–51. Lund, 1962 ff. |
| *S–S* | Classification of fibulae in *FGI* (above) |
| *Stele* | *Stele, Volume in Memory of N. Kondoleon.* Athens, 1977 (Greek) |
| *Studies* | C.–G. Styrenius, *Submycenaean Studies.* Lund, 1967 |
| *Survey* | L. H. Sackett and others, *Prehistoric Euboea: Contributions toward a Survey,* BSA 61, 1967, 33 |
| *Thorikos* | H. F. Mussche and others, *Rapport Préliminaire sur la Campagne de Fouilles,* I–VII. Bruxelles/Gent, 1967–78 |
| *Tiryns* | *Tiryns: die Ergebnisse der Ausgrabungen des Instituts,* 1–8. Athens, 1972–5 |
| *Vergina* | M. Andronikos, *Vergina I; the Cemetery of the Tumuli.* Athens, 1969 (in Greek) |
| *Zagora* | A. Cambitoglou, *Zagora: Excavation of a Geometric Settlement on the Island of Andros,* I ff. Sydney, 1971 ff. |

# Section 1

# Introduction to the Excavations

M. R. POPHAM and L. H. SACKETT

## THE SITE

Lefkandi was a small fishing and farming hamlet when we first went to Euboea some 15 years ago. The rusty skeleton of a pier running out into the harbour from a large brick warehouse was all that remained from more prosperous days when it was the loading point for the magnesite (lefkolithos) mined further inland. Brick-making, which had replaced the manufacture of roof-tiles, was its only industry: clay from the rich alluvial soil of the Lelantine plain was brought to two or three factories in a nearby bay where it was moulded and fired in kilns. Periodically caiques anchored in the bay to load and transport the bricks, mainly to islands in the Cyclades.[1]

Now Lefkandi has become a popular seaside resort with restaurants and hotels strung out along its beaches, and every year more and more summer bungalows spring up by the coast or on the slopes of the hill above its harbour, where the ancient cemeteries were found. Industrial development, too, in the area has been substantial, the nearest being a large wood-processing plant in a small bay east of the village where freighters anchor to off-load their cargo of foreign timber.

The ancient settlement was just to the east of Lefkandi on a coastal prominence, now called 'Xeropolis', the arid, or perhaps deserted, town.

Xeropolis, whose ancient name is unknown, lies about half way between the modern towns of Chalcis and Eretria, on the south shore of Euboea, where the sea between the island and the mainland begins to narrow until both coasts nearly touch at the Straits of Euripus by Chalcis (plan at PLATE 2a). The site can be easily picked out on the aerial view at PLATE 1a as a promontory projecting slightly into the sea at the eastern (lower) edge of the dark area which extends either side of the river. This area represents the modern cultivated fields and gardens of a fertile, well-watered valley,[2] known as the Lelantine Plain in antiquity and famous as a point of contention between Chalcis and Eretria, two of the most important city-states in the early Iron Age, whose conflict was one of the first major wars remembered by the Greeks. The site itself is a long, rather narrow plateau, rising some 17 m above sea level with abrupt cliffs facing the sea and with a quite steep incline on the landward side, PLATE 3a. At either end are small bays, that to the west being deeper and larger, and used today as an anchorage for visiting caiques. The other bay is small but may have extended further inland in antiquity where the land is now marshy, PLATES 3b and 4.[3]

1

Xeropolis is a large site, some 500 m in length and 120 m broad. Surface sherds found there on our initial visits suggested it had been occupied from the Early Helladic until the Geometric period. We were later to learn that we were not its first discoverers; it was known to, and visited by, other archaeologists and its existence had been already recorded.[4]

To say a little more about the site we must anticipate some of the results of our excavations. Xeropolis is now fairly flat on the summit but soundings across the hill in two sectors (PLATE 4 plan and sections) suggest that this is the outcome of years of erosion and cultivation, not to mention the centuries of occupation and levelling which preceded this.[5] The soil is shallowest near its highest point: here, in Trials D and IX, we met rock less than 1.5 m below the present surface, and in both trenches the occupation levels were so telescoped that we may conclude it had been the practice in this area throughout the history of the site to clear away the previous structures rather than build on top of them. This is not so in the case of the north or inland face of the hill where the natural incline of the rock must have been much gentler than the present rather steep slope; in Square CC in the main area of our excavations rock lay 8.5 m below the surface and, in Test C, at a depth of 3.5 m. The south edge of the hill, towards the sea, must always have been abrupt, though, no doubt, it has been eroded by the sea during stormy weather: here Tests F and E showed that the Mycenaean buildings projected beyond the present cliff edge though they were probably terraced into a slight natural decline; the accumulated soil in this region, too, was deeper than towards the centre of the hill. The east and west ends of Xeropolis are now fairly gentle slopes and in the former case, at least, this may well reflect its natural configuration, for in Trial Z, well down the eastern incline, walls of the latest occupation were still preserved.

So we may suppose that at the days of its earliest occupation, the flat summit of Xeropolis was a much smaller area, rather less than the present 17 m contour. Towards the sea, the south edge was steep and abrupt, and would probably not require fortification. To north, east and west the slope was fairly gradual but some protection against attack from inland may have been afforded by greater inlets of the sea into the low-lying valley to the north. In general, occupation seems to have been spread over the slopes where buildings perhaps rose in terraces to the summit. Particularly on the landward edge later houses were frequently built over the demolished ruins of earlier structures until the hill assumed a more level surface, a process completed by ploughing, cultivation and erosion after its abandonment.

The water supply was probably always a problem. We found no wells in our excavations, and the pebble conglomerate and sandstone of which the hill is composed preclude the existence of any natural spring. It seems likely that the inhabitants fetched their water from elsewhere.[6] At present there is abundant fresh water in wells just across the valley to the north.

We do not know the ancient name of the settlement. Xeropolis is clearly a fairly recent descriptive name, showing that the local inhabitants knew of the existence of a ruined settlement but that its name had already been forgotten. It is difficult to believe that no record has come down in ancient history or legend of such a large settlement which survived well into the 8th century. Various candidates have been proposed and their claims will be considered later, in Appendix B.

No cemeteries of the Bronze Age occupants of Xeropolis have been located though some intramural burials of its later stages were made within the settlement itself. But Iron Age cemeteries were found some 600 m away, on the hill slopes immediately north of Lefkandi's harbour. These lay both on the ridge near the principal road leading from the plain down to Xeropolis, and on Toumba, a separate knoll a little further west, PLATE 73. Much of this land is cultivated as vegetable gardens or 'perivolia', though buildings are now encroaching more and more, whether for summer residence, chicken farm or restaurant. The rock here is a coarse and quite loose pebble conglomerate with occasional layers of soft marl below the surface, both easy material for the digging of shaft graves. Five separate burial grounds, spread over a fairly wide area, were located in this region, and there may exist yet others.

## THE PURPOSE OF THE EXCAVATIONS

The decision to excavate at Lefkandi arose directly from a survey of ancient sites being made in Euboea. We found that surprisingly little was known archaeologically of the early history of the Island and excavation had been sporadic and insufficient. Historians were intrigued by the ancient references to a war between Chalcis and Eretria at a time when these cities were among the foremost of the Greek colonisers. Archaeology, however, had played little part in the studies dealing with this subject with one notable exception. After publishing pottery from Chalcis and Eretria, Professor John Boardman had suggested that much of the earliest pottery found by Woolley in the Near Eastern trading station at Al Mina was Euboean in character.[7] Hints of the important role of Euboea in early Greek history were becoming an archaeological reality.

With these encouragements, we first chose Amarynthos as the most promising site to excavate but, when this proved impracticable, we turned to Xeropolis, with which we had meanwhile become familiar.[8] A few seasons' work with strictly limited objectives were envisaged, since it was intended shortly to resume excavations at Knossos.

Our objectives were threefold: to establish the date of the abandonment of the site, to define the character of the local Protogeometric and Geometric pottery, and to see whether there had been continuity of occupation through the latest stages of the Mycenaean period into the Early Iron Age, the so-called Dark Age in prehistoric Greece.

As for our first objective, surface sherding suggested that the site had remained virtually unoccupied after the Geometric period and it seemed reasonable to associate its abandonment with the scanty references to a major conflict between Chalcis and Eretria believed to have taken place during this period. The strategic position of Xeropolis made it highly probable that it would have been involved in this conflict and so the pottery belonging to its abandonment might help date the war itself.

Secondly the pottery of both the Geometric and Protogeometric stages had an importance of its own. Boardman's suggestion that many of the earliest sherds at the trading post of Al Mina were Euboean was based on the small amount of comparable material known from the Island itself: a greater quantity would enable its character to be more clearly defined.

Finally surface sherds indicated that Xeropolis had been extensively occupied in Late Helladic IIIC and in Protogeometric times. It seemed, therefore, a good site to produce evidence for the intervening centuries. They were little known archaeologically and, for us, the degree of continuity both of occupation and of culture during the 12th and 11th centuries was one of the most interesting and important problems of Greek history.

Discoveries, both intentional and accidental, made during the excavation, determined that its main aims and its duration should be extended. It was quickly apparent that the site was unusually rich in Late Helladic IIIC remains and that deep, well-stratified deposits were preserved there. A sounding to bed-rock revealed a quite unexpected depth of occupation, 8.5 m, with Early Bronze Age pottery of an unusual character in the lowest levels. So it was decided to investigate both aspects more fully, by uncovering a wider area of the Late Helladic IIIC structures and by excavating one complete 5 m square down to the rock.

In addition, reports of cist tombs, followed later by the destructive but revealing activities of a mechanical excavator and of deep ploughing, led to the discovery on the slopes above Lefkandi of five separate burial grounds. Their partial investigation was carried out jointly with the Greek Archaeological Service as a rescue excavation, which proved a valuable supplement to excavations on Xeropolis, not least in producing evidence for periods scantily represented in the settlement.

## THE COURSE OF THE EXCAVATIONS[9]

The first season, 1964, was spent in exploratory work with the purpose of finding a suitable area with Geometric structures which could be more extensively excavated the following year. A series of test trenches, called Trials A to N, were dug: their placing was largely determined by the willingness of only a very few of the many owners of the hill to permit excavation in their fields. Fortunately it was possible to make a partial section across the hill in two places, PLATE 4.

From these tests it quickly became apparent that in most cases remains of Late Helladic IIIC date were the first to be encountered, a few Geometric and rather more Protogeometric surface sherds being all that survived of any later phases of occupation in the area. The edges of the hill had a greater accumulation of soil, though even here the latest surviving occupation levels were with one exception Late Helladic IIIC. The exception was on the northeast edge where two tests made in the last days of the season found Geometric levels, and in one case, Trial L, produced Protogeometric pottery stratified below the Geometric.

A local report of cist tombs near the village of Lefkandi was investigated and four such graves of apparently Protogeometric date, with a pit burial and cremation, were uncovered before the excavation was stopped as being outside the area defined in the excavation permit.

In 1965, after purchasing the land in the region of Trial L, an area measuring 17 by 11 m was opened up; it comprised six adjacent trenches, each 5 m square (Squares AA to GG; FF was omitted) and these were henceforth our main centre of activity in the settlement (PLATE 9). It was our intention in the first season to complete excavation of this area down to the Geometric levels. These were covered by nearly a metre of surface wash which contained a few Archaic sherds. The Geometric structures were poorly preserved and, since their excavation was finished more quickly than expected, a test was made below them. This revealed an extensive pit filled with sherds of Protogeometric character, and below this again was encountered a destruction level with Late Helladic IIIC vases. As a result, the whole of one trench (Square AA) was excavated to recover as much Protogeometric pottery as possible and to investigate further the Mycenaean destruction level. Here and elsewhere Late Helladic IIIC burials, stratigraphically later than the destruction, were found inside the buildings.

At the same time, another series of tests was made across the hill to the west of the main area, called Trials I to X. In two of these, Trials IV and V, later joined into one area, parts of several rooms were uncovered which had been destroyed by fire, the vases on the floors being Late Helladic IIIC.

In addition, two tests were made on the eastern slope of Xeropolis, Trials W and Z, in the latter of which Late Geometric vases were found on the floor of a room seemingly abandoned or destroyed.

1966, which was to have been the final season, was spent in investigating the IIIC levels in the main area and in excavating one of the squares, CC, to bed-rock which a sounding the previous year had shown to be 8.5 m below the surface. Furthermore the extent of the excavation was enlarged by opening up two further squares immediately to the south, KK and LL; these were subsequently joined to the main area.

Three major building phases were distinguished in the IIIC period and several more intramural burials were found. In the deep sounding, in Square CC, Early and Middle Helladic occupation was represented by 3.5 m of accumulated debris. The earliest buildings, just above the rock, belonged to an advanced stage of the Early Bronze Age, while in a late stage of Middle Helladic was found part of a well-built house with plaster floors through which had been sunk several early Mycenaean burials.

In 1968 an emergency dig, lasting 6 days and carried out in collaboration with the Greek Archaeological Service, investigated tombs in the 'Skoubris' cemetery following disturbance by a mechanical excavator laying a pipe-line for the village water supply. The cist graves and pyres covered a period from Submycenaean into Middle Geometric in Attic terms, our Sub-Protogeometric III.

This excavation was continued in 1969, when a larger area of the cemetery was uncovered. At the same time, a test on a nearby hillock called 'Toumba', which was thought to be a possible location for the Submycenaean and Early Protogeometric settlement, revealed instead another cemetery.

In the same year specific clearing-up operations were carried out on Xeropolis to clarify problems raised in the study of the material already excavated, and to prepare the way for the final report. In the main area, Squares KK and LL were extended 2 m to the south to recover more of the house plans of the final Mycenaean occupation, and Trial IV–V, too, was enlarged with the same purpose in mind for the earlier IIIC stage.

Finally in 1970 a further season was devoted to the cemetery area, where deep ploughing had revealed a third cemetery, 'Palia Perivolia'. The limits of this cemetery were defined and about two thirds of its tombs and pyres were excavated. Test trenches dug as part of this work exposed a separate cluster of tombs and pyres some 20 m to the east, and these we called the 'East Cemetery', PLATE 76a. At the same time trials were made in the Toumba cemetery to define its limits and further tombs were excavated to make the previous tests there comprise a more coherent and representative unit, PLATE 76b.

## SUMMARY OF THE RESULTS OF THE EXCAVATIONS[10]

The results of our excavations and their historical implications, as far as they relate to the Iron Age, will be described in detail later in this volume. However, a brief overall account of the site, from its first settlement to its final abandonment, may be useful as an introduction to the later stages of its history and place the final, important phase of its occupation into a wider perspective. This will involve anticipating conclusions to be drawn in the volume covering the Bronze Age, but work on that is sufficiently advanced to make any major change of opinion unlikely.

It should again be stressed that the area we have excavated is only a very small part of the whole settlement and, that for the earliest periods, we have done little more than make soundings within the main area of the excavation.

The real history of the settlement begins about 2000 BC, towards the end of the Early Bronze Age, with the arrival of a people using a distinctive, 'alien' pottery unrelated to the native Early Helladic wares of the Mainland and of Euboea. They were not, however, the earliest occupants, since a small quantity of Late Neolithic sherds and a few fragments characteristic of Early Helladic II were found on Xeropolis. But, as these occur only sporadically and out of chronological context, they may have been brought subsequently to the site in mud bricks made nearby but not on the hill itself.

This first settlement was large, to judge from evidence of occupation found in widely separated areas (Trials B and X and Square CC). The area excavated was insufficient to recover a complete house plan but the walls were well built and substantial and clay-lined pits were used for storage purposes. Three superimposed building levels in the main area show that these settlers continued to live on Xeropolis for some length of time. Throughout this period their pottery changes little; undecorated but frequently both burnished and wheel-made, its characteristic shapes are shallow plates, bowls and cups of a type which all find their closest parallels in Western Anatolia. Similar pottery has been recognised recently on the nearby island of Kea; some, too, occurs on other islands in the Cyclades and there, also, it seems intrusive if not, as at Lefkandi, dominant. It may be that the evidence now accumulating points to an incursion from Western Anatolia with its route through the northern Cyclades and up the straits of Euboea to Xeropolis and Manika, with elements perhaps penetrating as far as Orchomenos in Boeotia, and even to coastal Thessaly.

In the main trial on Xeropolis, the latest building belonging to these people was abandoned and in its fill Grey Minyan of a formative stage, and frequently hand-made, occurs with a small quantity of decorated wares related to the typical Early Helladic III pottery of the Mainland. The first settlers had been conservative and exclusive; now there are signs of change and contact with other parts of Greece.

The deep Middle Helladic deposits, we found, consisted mostly of household refuse not closely associated with buildings; indeed, the only building of any consequence in the small area excavated belongs to the later stages of this period. Nevertheless, some 2 m of material, rich and well-stratified, give a good overall picture of the development of the pottery throughout the Middle Bronze Age on the site.

There is a general continuity but, within it, several stages of development can be distinguished and defined. The pottery from the earliest stage is particularly valuable in that it is little known; it continues to a considerable degree the traditions of Early Helladic III while moving towards the more classic Middle Helladic, later characterised by ring-stemmed goblets and angular shapes, with the addition of Matt-painted wares. Bichrome pottery, related to that found in the Shaft Graves at Mycenae, is characteristic of the latest stage, to which belonged a house with a thick plaster floor. Throughout the period, imported sherds show some contact with the Cyclades and in the later phases there were close relations with Boeotia and, perhaps, coastal districts of Thessaly.

Widely separated tests indicate that the Middle Bronze Age settlement covered most, if not all of the hill, while surface sherds and other finds make it probable that occupation extended well beyond its limits in the later stages. Xeropolis, from about 1900 to 1550 BC, was probably a Middle Helladic town of considerable size and importance.

Less information was forthcoming about the Mycenaean settlement in its early and middle stages. In the main area, several early burials had been dug down into and near the latest Middle Helladic building. The pottery shows that Xeropolis was in touch with the main trend of Mycenaean developments, probably through connections with the nearby import-ant centre of Thebes, though it would be premature, with the small quantity of material recovered, to define how early and close this relationship may have been or to assess the role of the site at this time.

It is not until the closing stages of the Late Bronze Age that the evidence is at all com-prehensive. It is then quite apparent that Xeropolis was a large settlement, intensively occupied and involved in the events of this period. Lack of evidence, at present, that the site shared in the general catastrophes in Greece towards the end of the 13th century does not necessarily mean that it escaped unharmed. The subsequent Late Helladic IIIC occupants undertook around 1200 BC an ambitious scheme of rebuilding in the course of which much of the earlier remains and evidence was levelled away. An increase in population is certain, and the amount of new building suggests a wholesale take-over, whether or not it was peace-fully achieved.

The earliest IIIC inhabitants may have included foreign elements; at least, a small amount of primitive hand-made pottery of non-Mycenaean type was in use and its shape was probably deliberately imitated by the Mycenaean potters to meet a local demand. The first IIIC houses lasted long enough for some internal alterations to be made before they were destroyed in a great conflagration which may well have devastated most of the settlement. The ruins were quickly levelled and new houses built above them which differ in plan and alignment, and display a novel and unusual regularity. It is quite likely, therefore, that a new people had taken control, but, if so, they continued to use Mycenaean pottery of similar character, except that its earlier dullness is soon enlivened both by a greater use of decor-ation and by an intriguing pictorial style. Xeropolis is abreast of developments elsewhere in Greece though it retains a noticeable individuality.

The second settlement suffered some damage which, though repaired, seems to mark the beginning of its decline. Intramural burials within the houses, one at least a battle casualty, are signs of the unsettled nature of the time. Some lowering of standards and living conditions is apparent in one area where a yet later building superseded that of the second IIIC settlement. The Late Bronze Age appears to end with the partial or total abandonment of the settlement.

A gap in occupation at Lefkandi, after about 1100 BC, seems probable but it cannot have been long. For people were living in the neighbourhood early in the Iron Age, the evidence coming not from Xeropolis but from one of the cemeteries where Submycenaean and Early Protogeometric cist tombs have been found containing cremations. It is uncertain whether these people were all newcomers or, in part, survivors, and we do not know whether their settlement was on Xeropolis or elsewhere. It is not until late in the Proto-geometric period that we can be sure occupation had been resumed on the old site, and by then the inhabitants are prosperous, engaged in bronze working and already using the distinctive type of cup with pendent-semicircle decoration that was to be a feature of early Greek trade in the Near East, and even to reach the West.

However, for the intervening period, say about 1050—900 BC, and later too, the best evidence for the history of the area comes from the cemeteries which span the time from Submycenaean to a stage contemporary with Middle Geometric I in Attica (Sub-Protogeometric III in Euboean terms). Traditional to an extreme in their unusual burial practices and in their adherence to a pottery style which once evolved was clung to for over

150 years, the inhabitants were nevertheless a remarkably enterprising people, in touch with northern Greece, the Islands, Attica, Cyprus and the Near East, as finds in the tomb testify. There is evidence, too, of a prosperity outstanding in the Greece of its day, and it increases markedly in the two generations before some important change took place in the history of our site.

It is hardly without significance that after about 825 BC no burials appear to have been made in any of the investigated cemeteries. This fact, together with slight indications of a destruction in Middle Geometric times, early in our Sub-Protogeometric III phase, and some evidence for a possible decline in the extent of the settlement, might mean that it suffered during some local power struggle or act of aggression. Eretria begins to emerge into prominence as Xeropolis declines, and the same may be true of Chalcis.

However, occupation, if on a reduced scale, certainly continued on Xeropolis, until about 700 BC, when it was destroyed and practically abandoned. Erosion, stone-robbing and perhaps deliberate demolition have all contributed to the sad state of preservation of the Late Geometric settlement. An apsidal house and three circular structures, probably granaries, can be recognised, and the associated pottery is more than sufficient to make clear the type in use at Xeropolis at the time of the disaster. The old persistent Protogeometric tradition has been discarded and is replaced by a fully developed and eclectic Geometric style with a distinctive character of its own, so distinctive, indeed, that there can be no doubt that much of the contemporary pottery at Al Mina is Euboean.

The final destruction of Xeropolis is surely to be ascribed to some major incident in the recorded conflict between Chalcis and Eretria; the pottery would place the event near the end of the 8th century. This time there was no revival, though there are indications here and there to show that the site was not completely deserted during the next 200 years.

# THE SETTLEMENT

# Section 2

# The Geometric and Protogeometric Settlement

## M. R. POPHAM and L. H. SACKETT

## INTRODUCTION

Investigation of the Geometric and Protogeometric settlement was, as we have explained above, our principal interest when deciding to excavate on Xeropolis. The tests made in the first year determined where the main area of our excavations should be; only the two adjacent Trials L and M produced well-defined Geometric and Protogeometric levels, though in some of the other tests sherds of these phases were found in surface soil or in superficial levels. Two of our later tests, those called Trials W and Z, showed that remains of this period were preserved on the east slope of the hill and in Trial Z a small deposit of Late Geometric vases was found.

During excavation we were hampered by lack of knowledge of the development of the local pottery. The Late Geometric was generally easily recognisable; it had already been defined before we started and we became familiar with it from deposits encountered early in the excavation. But the division of the earlier pottery of Protogeometric character into the subdivisions Late Protogeometric to Sub-Protogeometric III, now proposed as the result of later study, were quite beyond us at the time. Consequently the initial pottery classifications made in the excavation records were too broad for subsequent interpretation of detail and in some cases may have led us wrongly to suspect that the contents of a level were mixed in date and not worth preserving. We were, however, working in a little-known sphere and the knowledge we have since acquired should enable future excavators to work with greater precision. Even so, early in the excavation, it was decided both as a safeguard, and so that future scholars might be able to study an unsorted batch of sherds, to retain intact a basket of pottery from each major deposit. A list of those retained from the Iron Age levels is given at the end of the Sections on the settlement pottery.

This conservatism in the pottery has led us, despite our dislike of the term, to apply the description Sub-Protogeometric (abbreviated to SPG) to pottery and events which belong after the end of the Protogeometric period in Attica and before our own distinctive Late Geometric phase begins. Where it has been possible to be more specific and equate this intervening period approximately with the Early Geometric I and II, and Middle Geometric I–II phases in Attica, this is expressed as SPG I, II and III respectively in addition to the more generally applicable terms of Submycenaean (SM) and Early, Middle and Late Protogeometric (EPG, MPG and LPG).

Our permit limited excavation to Xeropolis but surface exploration and chance finds supplied additional information. Modern building operations on the small promontory to the east of Xeropolis produced a quantity of LPG/SPG sherds, and deep ploughing on the north west slope opposite Xeropolis brought to the surface deposits of SPG III pottery, some among burnt material, Trial SL, PLATE 2b. Near the path running parallel to the N face of Xeropolis, too, a hole dug for a telegraph pole produced a few LPG/SPG sherds. To judge from surface sherds, much of this slope to the north of Xeropolis might well have been inhabited at this time. Earlier we had conjectured on similar evidence that the small hill 'Toumba' and its slopes, north of the village of Lefkandi, were also part of the ancient settlement and that some LPG structure existed on its summit. Subsequently a test on the E face unexpectedly revealed a cemetery, but in 1977 a cutting into the N face disturbed a wall associated with LPG pottery.

This spread of sherds of Protogeometric character well beyond the confines of Xeropolis is impressive and suggestive of extensive occupation, though excavation is required to confirm this. There is no such evidence for the final, Late Geometric, stage, and it is possible that the settlement at this period was a small one concentrated on the north east incline of Xeropolis facing the East Bay.

## THE LAYOUT OF THE EXCAVATIONS

The layout of the trenches in the main area is shown at PLATE 9a. Reference to the names given to these trenches during excavation will be avoided, or placed in parentheses, where they have been redefined by architectural areas. Some account, however, of their disposition and the reasons for subsequent enlargements of the original area should be given.

The main area of excavation consisted initially of a grid of six adjacent squares of 5 m with a metre baulk between them (AA to GG). They were laid out 1 metre to the east of the first year's trials, L, M and N and were aligned, as were all the tests, with the grid made for the whole site, PLATE 4. The main extension to this area was the addition of two 5 m squares to the south (KK and LL).

Square AA was extended 1 m to the north to uncover an LG structure (AA N extension); it was also extended 3 m to the east (AA E extension), an area which included Trial L, in order to complete excavation of the 'SPG Pit' found in the eastern half of AA. The south west part of this extension, adjacent to Trial L, was enlarged 2 m to the east to recover more material from the dump of LPG clay moulds; it was subsequently filled in again (L extension).

Square BB was enlarged by 1 m to the north (BB extension 1) to bring it into alignment with AA N extension; it was later further extended by about 1.5 m (BB extension 2), the purpose in both cases being to find more of the architecture of, and pottery from, the LG building. The latter extension was subsequently filled in.

Squares CC and GG were extended 2 m to the west (CC extension and GG extension) mainly to provide a barrow run from the deep sounding in Square CC.

Squares KK and LL were extended 2 m to the south (KK extension and LL extension) to uncover more of the latest Mycenaean structures.

Trench AB, 1 m to the east of Squares AA and BB was intended to link information gathered in the first season from Trials L and M. It was dug to the bottom of the LG levels and then refilled.

Trenches HH and JJ to the south of Square GG were opened to see whether there was LG occupation in that region; none was found and subsequently HH became part of the barrow run from the deep sounding in CC. Trench JJ was filled in.

Squares AA, BB, DD, EE and LL were excavated down to the earliest phase of LH IIIC apart from small soundings in both AA and EE, and a larger test in LL where the LH IIIB levels were investigated. KK was abandoned at the latest LH IIIC levels while GG was dug to the second IIIC phase. CC was excavated to bed rock all over.

Apart from the main area, three series of trials were made, mostly across the width of the hill, shown on PLATE 4. Their original names will be retained in publication. The first two series were given letters of the alphabet, Trials A–G, L–N, S–Z; they were mostly small tests made to try and locate Geometric and Protogeometric occupation and, consequently, were only in a few cases, notably Trial C, dug to any great depth. Trial L was later incorporated into the main area of the excavations.

The third series was given Roman numerals I to X; from them it was hoped to learn more about occupation near the centre of the hill. Trials IV and V, which uncovered part of an LH IIIC house with a destruction deposit, were subsequently joined together and enlarged. Trial X was sunk near the bottom of the hill to investigate Early and Middle Helladic levels of refuse dumped from further up the slope.

All tests except L, M and N were subsequently filled in. For the periods under consideration, only Trials W and Z are relevant apart from the main area of excavation which will be described first. In place of the original trench names it has been divided into more meaningful architectural sectors, PLATE 9b, the numeration beginning with Area 1, which contained the only preserved building and then moving around it from east to west; Area 2 is the eastern part, Area 3 the region to the south and Area 4 that west of the building.

## THE EXCAVATIONS

### The main area

Loose top soil, some 25 cm deep, covered the area and below this was encountered a much harder layer scored with plough ruts, running west to east and showing the accumulation of surface wash since the field was last ploughed some 50 years ago (Section level 1 at PLATE 10). Walls began to appear 40–60 cm below the surface. The task was then to clear away fallen stones and disintegrated mud-brick (level 2) and to find the latest floors which were of earth with occasional patches of small pebbles. Only one or two courses of the stone walls survived and in many cases even these were lacking. It is consequently difficult to decide which of the disjointed lengths of walling were already ruinous during the latest period of occupation and which were part of structures still in use and disturbed subsequently, PLATE 5.

Certainty was, however, possible in the case of one building with its adjacent stretch of walling onto which some circular structures abutted. Vases, all of them smashed but many complete or capable of restoration, were found lying on the latest floor inside the building and show that it was still inhabited at the time of its destruction.

## Area 1: the building (PLATES 7a, 8a and 11)

This building, seemingly oblong in plan with an apsidal end, was poorly preserved. Considerable sections of its walls were missing and attempts to fill in these gaps by detecting foundation trenches or a soil change were unsuccessful. In the case of the W wall, the gap is partly explained by the discovery of a pit, dug possibly for stone robbing; part, too, may have fallen inward with the collapse of its mudbrick superstructure, decayed remains of which were particularly marked in this region. Traces of a similar pit were later detected in part of the gap in the E wall. Modern ploughing, also, may be responsible for some of the damage and for the scatter of stones within the building, though deliberate demolition could well have played a part. The north wall and entrance has probably disappeared entirely due to erosion on the edge of the hill.

In the interior of the building, a more or less square structure (C) on PLATE 11, had been built against its E wall (B), and either side of it were post holes. On a line with its S face and mid-way between the main walls was an ashy area with burnt wood surrounded by stones — possibly a hearth or, more likely, the carbonised remains of a central wooden support for the roof. A line of stones in the NW part of the building on the edge of the excavation may be the face of a corresponding square structure against the W wall (A); it has been tentatively restored on the plan at PLATE 8a.

The latest floor (Floor 1), difficult to trace, was of earth with occasional patches of small pebbles. A small area of pebbles in the gap at the S curving end of the building, together with the rather unusual straight face of the wall where it breaks off, could indicate the existence of a doorway. This would be most unusual, and it seems more likely that the pebbles were washed down later from the pebble floor outside the building to the S. The content of the house floor and, indeed, the Geometric 'soil' in general was markedly grey in colour and this became for us a feature of the Late Geometric levels.

Most of the objects found in the final occupation level were located inside the building: they are plotted on the plan at PLATE 8a. Apart from pottery, there was an iron knife and whetstone (nos. 11 and 86), three stone pounders and grinders (1, 3 and 5), a stone axe (13), a small stone basin (23), two loomweights (39 and 46), a fragementary faience bead (91), a stone disc (10) and a pierced sherd (59). The vases, all LG in style, had been smashed and scattered, apart from nos. 43 and 45, both large coarse ware jars found seemingly *in situ* in the apsidal end of the building, but by far the greatest concentration of pottery lay at the north end. These included LG nos. 1, 4, 9, 14–17, 23–30, 37 (not 38 as on plan), 40, 43 and 45–47. Most are skyphoi, with a few mugs and kotylai, and a cup; two craters, an oenochoe and the handmade, burnished and coarse-ware vases make up the remainder.

Outside the building lay two stone grinders and a quern (4, 6 and 21), a pierced sherd and a misshapen object of bronze (84).

These finds represent normal domestic activity and we may confidently conclude that the building was used as a dwelling house.

That the destruction of the building was accompanied by fire is clear from some of the vases on which burnt and unburnt fragments join. Evidence of conflagration, otherwise, was not marked except towards the N, possibly due to a greater amount of timber construction there. Two fragments of one of the vases in the building were found some distance away, in the yard areas to the S and E indicating considerable later disturbance.

On removal of the destruction floor and its build-up, a hard layer of red earth was discovered some 5–10 cm below. This appeared to be the original floor of the building

(Floor 2); the main walls of the building were resting on it with the exception of the square structure (C) against the E wall, which was at a higher level associated with the later floor and so, presumably, a later addition, PLATE 11.

The original floor contained few features. There were two ashy areas near the middle of the room, one apparently a small pit. the other may have been a hearth and by it was found a quern.

The sherds from the original floor were very scrappy and those contained in the walls even more so: none was clearly later than SPG III. The fill below the building, level 9, also appears to belong to the same stage and may well have been part of the levelling activity more clearly indicated in Area 2. It follows, therefore, that the levelling and construction either took place in SPG III, or in LG provided there was no pottery of that stage in the neighbourhood before construction began, and that Floor 2 was used only during the building of the house and before the occupation proper of it.

### Area 2: the N—S wall, its associated structures and the region to the E (PLATE 8b)

Clearly in contemporary use with this house in its final stage was a stretch of walling, D, some 8 m long running N—S and separated from the building by a passage less than a metre wide. Abutting onto this wall were three circular structures, one to the west, G, and two to the east, E and F. All three share common features: they are more or less circular and have two parallel slots running across them. In the case of the most northerly, E, the best preserved example, some stones lay across the slots, PLATES 6c and 7b. That adjoining it to the south, F, had a thick covering of clay and a ring of stones around its edge; it seemed to have been put to some secondary use, PLATE 6b. The third on the W side of the wall, G, was probably not in use since the layer of pebbles beside it, a yard floor, ran in part over it. Their function will be discussed on p. 24.

On removal of the most northerly structure, remains of what seemed to be an earlier one were found below it, hatched on PLATE 8b. If its plan had been roughly similar to the later structures, then it might once have adjoined the outer wall of the building: it must have been dismantled before the construction of the N—S wall, D, which passes over the area it would have occupied.

A *terminus ante quem* for the construction of the yard wall, D, and for structure F east of it, was provided by the contents of a shallow pit, Pit 3, which lay in part under them: from the sherds in it the LG vase no. 52, PLATE 43, has been reconstructed. LG sherds found inside wall D and its three associated circular structures confirm that this was the date of construction. A very thin level, 2—4 cm thick, of grey soil was noticed below the wall and structure G, when they were dismantled; presumably this represents the soil accumulated between the time the house and its earliest circular structure were built and subsequent dismantling of the latter and the construction of the yard wall and its associated structures. Immediately below this level, a hard red layer was encountered, similar to that on which the house was founded — the top of level 4.

In the passageway between the building and the N—S wall the upper soil, level 3, was similar to that in the open area to the east, grey in colour, loose in texture and containing patches of yellow clay and burnt orange mud-brick, and many sherds, particularly in the N part; the pottery was LG. As to the E, it too cleared down to a hard red layer, level 4. In the open area E of wall D and in the latest occupation level, a concentration of heavy stones was found near the E baulk (PLATE 8b), which continued into adjacent trenches and was apparently not connected with any structure but perhaps dumped there for future use.

A little below the upper and loose textured soil, remains of an LG pebble floor were distinguished over the area generally, especially well defined to the E of the most northern circular structure. Signs of a contemporary earth 'floor' were noticed S of the two circular structures against the N–S wall; below it, the soil was again grey in colour and remained so until the hard red level, 4, was encountered. A small LG pit E of the N–S wall and immediately S of the circular structures had been cut down into this layer, Pit 4. A further shallow LG pit, Pit 2A, which lay further to the E just under the latest floor, contained a small deposit of pottery including the unusual amphora, LG no. 71 (PLATE 44).

The passageway adjacent to the house and the region E of the N–S wall were clearly open areas; the latter seems to have been a yard in which the circular structures had some function; nothing could be seen in the soil above or around them to suggest what this function was though an iron nail (87) and a stone pounder were found in dismantling structure G. The upper loose soil with much sherd and other debris was probably rubbish thrown out periodically, though it may in part consist of disintegrated mud-brick from the building we have considered above and the superstructure of wall D. The hard surface of the underlying red layer indicates that this was the original 'floor' of the yard over which, after some accumulation of refuse, a later pebble and earth 'floor' was made, level 3. A little below the surface of the original floor, a group of post holes with carbon and ash patches was noticed in the north-east corner of the yard, PLATE 8b; it is possible that they are related to the initial use of the yard and with the remains of the earlier presumed circular structure, before the N–S wall and its adjoining structures were built.

The hard red layer was the top of a deposit, level 4, as deep as 50 cm in places. Composed of red-brown earth, unlike the grey soil above it, this deposit seemed to be not a slow accumulation of occupation debris but a fill or dump of material placed there on one occasion for a specific purpose. The need for this was apparent from the underlying stratum (below levels 10 and 11) which was very uneven. Buildings, Mycenaean in date, had weathered after their abandonment so that, while the walls and their collapsed mud-brick superstructures were still standing generally to some height and lay little below the Late Geometric levels, in other places, particularly between the walls, deep hollows still remained. In contrast, the overlying red level had a very even surface and its contents were fairly homogeneous in composition containing much fragmentary pottery; little of it could be reconstructed nor could it be associated with any walls. It thus seems likely that the deposit was placed there with the deliberate intention of levelling the site; the obvious explanation for this operation is that it was preparatory to the construction of the building and its earliest associated structure. This deposit has been named 'Levelling Material', the pottery from which, basically of SPG III character, is discussed at pp. 36ff.

A natural process of levelling had, however, already begun before this, by the wash of material, mostly Mycenaean but containing some later pottery, from further up the hill (levels 10 and 11). At the next stage, the area had been used for dumping refuse; a large depression E of the line of the later N–S wall, seemingly not a natural hollow but a man-made pit, was found filled with stones, bones and sherds of SPG I – SPG II date (level 6, Pit 2), the pottery from which is discussed on pp. 31ff.

This pit, called the SPG Pit, which stretched over much of Area 2 is shown on PLATE 11; it was ill-defined in its upper reaches and it is difficult to decide exactly at what stage it was dug, though it was subsequent to the wash level mentioned above and earlier than the levelling activity. It had been cut down deeply into the Mycenaean levels and its extent is clear where it penetrated and went a further 50 cm below the latest Mycenaean floors.

At this floor depth, it measured some 6 m in length and 4 m in width. A line of stones, sherds and carbon, visible on section D, PLATE 10, seems to mark one stage of its fill, but no time lag was detectable between it and the lower material, level 8; the pottery immediately above and below this line had no noticeable chronological difference. The pit seems to have been largely filled up by the time the whole area was levelled though a looser portion in its centre suggests that it may still have been somewhat of a dip in the ground.

It was not the earliest deliberate dump, however, for this pit had cut into an earlier Iron Age deposit, the fill of what was probably another pit, Pit 1, level 12 (PLATES 10 and 11), though in this case the depression cleared down to an even surface. This earlier dump, which contained an important deposit both of LPG pottery and fragments of discarded clay moulds from a bronze foundry, was situated near the very eastern limit of the excavation. It has been named 'Moulds Deposit': the pottery and moulds from it are discussed on pp. 27f and pp. 93. We were able to make a small extension further eastward to recover more of the material from this pit and to define its extent but could not excavate further to discover whether it was connected with contemporary buildings further down the E slope.

The southern limit of Area 2 has been set at two disjointed stretches of E–W walling, L and M, just to the north of which are the remains of a small, roughly circular enclosure, H, abutting onto a section of thick walling, I. This enclosure, PLATE 6d, had no internal divisions, and resembles the other circular structures only in general shape. An open animal pen or thatched shed are obvious possible conjectures as to its use. Two LG holes which converge to form Pit 5 could be twin post holes, associated with this enclosure, though more recent animal runs, of which there were many on the site, cannot be excluded. The enclosure was in use until the abandonment since it partly overlay a large pit, PLATE 11, Pit 6, which contained among its grey earth fill, a valuable group of LG pottery, Deposit D discussed at pp. 58ff.

It is tempting to link the bit of walling M with wall N and surmise that they were the N wall of an apsidal structure but no trace of a parallel wall was found to the S where the surface and ancient levels are higher. Possibly, walls L, M and N are foundation courses of a terrace wall (which curved abruptly northward at the W) intended to retain a levelling fill of LPG date in Area 3. This would help explain the difference in levels between the PG structure (J–K) and its yard at the S limit of the excavation (in Area 3) and walls L, M, N and R (with its associated floor) in the centre of the excavation, not to mention that of the later LG building further N. If this is so, the LPG/SPG contents of Pits 7, 8 and 9, together with large contemporary sherds found near Pit 9, could be preliminary levelling before the construction of such a terrace wall. As so often, disturbance and erosion make any certainty impossible.

## AREA 3

Erosion was, however, less marked at the S end of Area 3 where a yard floor, on which lay large sherds and a scatter of stones, ran up to the foundations, wall K, of the corner of a building. Wall J seems to be a continuation southwards of the same structure but here the latest LH IIIC building had been preserved practically to the same level and were partly incorporated in the later foundations. Further to the W, however, the Late Bronze Age remains were lower and a considerable fill had been required before the yard floor was laid. This fill, seemingly homogeneous and LPG in date, has provided useful supplementary information on the domestic pottery of this stage. It and the contents of the yard floor together with the SPG sherds found on it are discussed on pp. 44ff. The yard floor and SPG occupation may extend well to the SW since in Trial JJ (PLATE 9) a superficial deposit of pottery including vase 65/P77 (PLATE 25) was found there.

A shallow pit, 10, dug into the yard floor also contained contemporary SPG material. A much later and superficial LG pit was found nearby; the much larger LG Pit 11 further N had penetrated into Mycenaean levels, PLATE 6e, LG Deposit C discussed on p. 58. There was no other sign of LG activity in this southern sector.

## AREA 4

The region W and SW of the LG house had suffered most from erosion, stone-robbing, pits and, in addition, disturbance in Archaic times after the LG abandonment. A patch of pebble floor against the W baulk seems from material above and under it to have been laid in the Archaic period, and some structure must have existed to account for the 6th-century pottery, nos. 344–8, and the roof tiles, PLATE 72, concentrated in this region. No walls could be confidently linked with this phase though wall O is a possibility; it had been deliberately robbed of stone at its N end and erosion had removed any trace of a floor running up to it.

Immediately W of the LG house a large, deep pit, Pit 13 on PLATE 11, had been filled with refuse contemporary with the occupation of the house, containing LG pottery listed under Deposit C on p. 61 and the graffito, find no. 101. A few fragments of PSC skyphoi in its contents may be strays or indicate when the pit was dug; it was cut down into Mycenaean buildings which it had partially destroyed. It had also removed part of a later, crude and roughly square structure, walls P and Q on PLATE 11, of which only the S wall was of decent construction. Again, levels in the immediate area were eroded and disturbed, and there is no more than a probability that it is of SPG date: at least it is later than LH IIIC Phase 2, the date of the underlying building, and earlier than the LG pit which partly destroyed it.

Greater precision is possible in the case of the stretch of E–W walling, wall R, since several relayings of pebble floor ran up to its south face, and both these and the wall itself contained SPG pottery and nothing later.

To the N of it there were patches of a possible earth floor but, in general, disturbance had removed most of the evidence and any other walls of this period there may have been. There was, however, a fill containing SPG pottery immediately over the Mycenaean, PLATE 22E, suggesting that there had, perhaps, been some deliberate levelling activity at that stage, such as was detected in Areas 1 and 2.

Extension of the excavation further to the W might help clarify the sequence of occupation in this region provided it is less disturbed. As it is, only this area and a superficial deposit on the eastern border of Trials IV–V (containing vase no. 343, PLATE 59) provided evidence for occupation after the Late Geometric destruction and abandonment.

## TRIALS ON THE EAST SLOPE

Two trials, W and Z, were made on the slope facing the East Bay to ascertain whether the later settlement had extended in that direction and was still preserved (PLATE 4).

Trial W was positioned on the 13 m contour, some 40 m east of the main excavation. Trial Z, lower down on the 11 m contour, lay some 20 m east of Trial W.

## Trial W (FIG. 1)

Dug in 1965 as a test 3 m by 4 m, the trench was slightly extended in 1969 and 1970 in all directions until the main area measured 4.5 m by 5.5 m. In the lower levels, part of an LH IIIC building of Phase 2 was uncovered, and below this an earlier structure destroyed by fire in Phase 1.

Above, in the upper levels, part of an Iron Age building was found, the walls of which lay just below plough soil, some 30 cm from surface, and, not surprisingly, these had been somewhat disturbed (FIG. 1c).

Best preserved was the north part where two walls, one E—W (wall A) and one N—S (wall B) bounded a hard floor of red earth (floor I) in which rested *in situ* the lower part of a pithos, re-used and mended with lead clamps (pot 1). In it had been placed another vase (pot 2) a large hand-made bowl, for which see p. 48. An extensive pit was found under the floor, filled with earth, many large stones, and sherds, mostly coarse wares; one sherd carried an alphabetical graffito, find no. 102.

Walls A and B make an angle of some 120° where they presumably joined, the slight doubt being due to a small pit which had removed part of wall A; the northern end of wall B had been similarly disturbed. The area excavated was too small to indicate the size of the room or its shape.

There were no signs of deliberate destruction, and the building was apparently abandoned. While the two coarseware pots of the floor deposit are unhelpful in dating this event, the sherds in the fill, discussed at p. 48, were SPG with some earlier material but nothing typical of the Lefkandian LG phase. The pit below the floor contained pottery similar in character, with one vase suggestive of the beginning of the LG stage. So a date near the end of SPG III for the fill of the pit, final occupation of the building and its abandonment is strongly indicated.

When the building was constructed is far less clear. Minor alterations are attested by an earlier, grey floor of earth (Floor II) which ran up to wall B, FIG. 1b: it was ill-defined, however, to the S and may have preceded the construction of wall A and have been associated with the earliest phase of another wall, D, which runs roughly parallel to it. The sherds between the two floors could possibly be as early as SPG I (discussed on p. 49).

The south half of the trench was more disturbed and the pottery was badly worn and suggestive of wash: the overwhelming preponderance of LH IIIC sherds in this region need not mean that the walls are of this period. The underlying structures belong to LH IIIC Phase 2.

Wall C may be a southward continuation of wall B though somewhat thicker. It has already been suggested that the lower courses of wall D, south of wall A, may be associated with the early SPG Floor II to the north.

The poor preservation of the walls and lack of detectable floors in this area make it uncertain to which period should be ascribed several fragments of bronze slag, the spout of a crucible and a whetstone found just east of wall C.

## Trial Z (FIG. 2)

This smaller trial, also made in 1965, was begun as a 2 m square and then extended 2 m to the N and 1 m to the E, making an area 4 by 3 m.

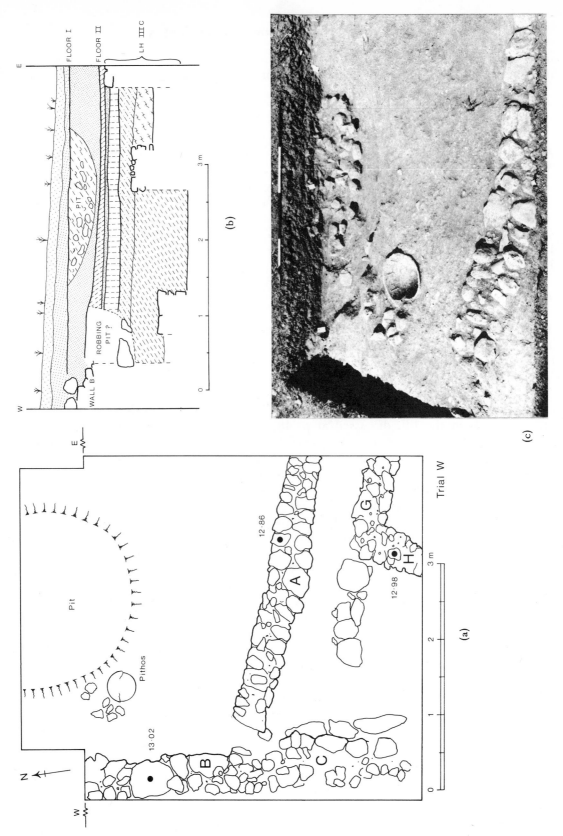

FIG. 1 Trial W: (a) plan, (b) E–W section, (c) view of original trench from the south

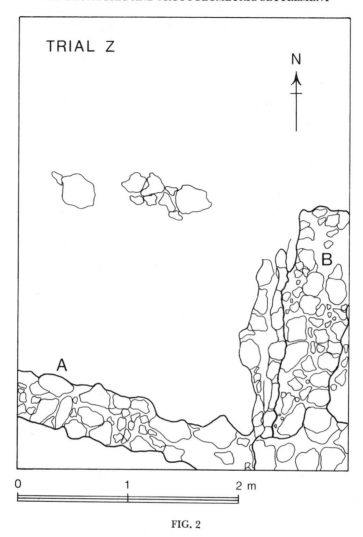

FIG. 2

The main interest of the test was a deposit of fragmentary LG vases clustered around an isolated group of stones in the centre of the original trench, a find which led to the extension of the area without, however, finding any further pots. Instead it uncovered two walls at right angles, one running E–W (wall A) and the other N–S (wall B), the top of the latter being some 35 cm lower than the former but retaining a capping of disintegrated mud brick. They were probably in contemporary use, though wall A may stand on an earlier foundation.

The stratigraphy was straightforward: below some 20 cm of plough soil had accumulated a compacted wash of grey-brown earth about 30 cm deep; this covered a looser grey fill, resembling disintegrated mud brick of the LG type, in which lay the group of isolated stones and the vases. It cleaned down to a pebble floor in the NW corner where Wall B terminates, perhaps in a doorway; elsewhere the floor was ill-defined. A test below this level in the S part of the trench revealed burnt mud brick debris over a grey earth floor which ran under wall B; the sherd content of this debris was LH IIIC.

We may, therefore, conjecture that we uncovered two adjacent walls and a doorway belonging to a house which its occupants abandoned in LG leaving a group of whole vases on its floor. There were no clear indications of deliberate destruction by fire or otherwise, but in a trial of this size and with the architecture badly disturbed, much is inevitably uncertain.

The vases, LG nos. 10, 36, 38 and 44, are discussed on pp. 58ff.

## AREA SL

This was not an excavation but a collection of sherds brought to the surface by deep ploughing.

During the campaign of 1970 we were informed that cultivation on the slopes N of Xeropolis had turned up a quantity of broken pottery but it was not until the last day of the season that time was available to investigate this report. The field was outside the area covered by our excavation permit, and there was not time to do other than make some notes, a sketch plan and collect the surface sherds. The importance of the find was not fully appreciated until the pottery was studied and mended some years later.

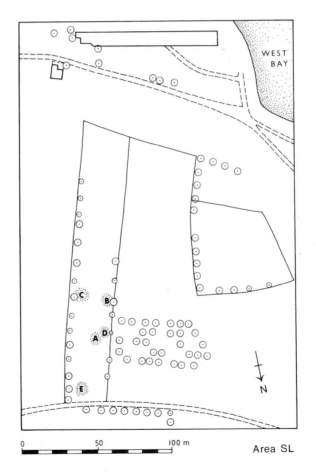

FIG. 3 Sketch plan of Area SL

The field in question lies between the path along the foot of Xeropolis and that parallel to it running along the ridge to the north, PLATE 3. The sketch plan at FIG. 3 shows the location of the field and the areas in it where the sherds were concentrated and collected in separate batches.

The finer and decorated pottery is considered at pp. 49ff; there was in addition a considerable quantity of cooking pot wares. Burnt sherds among those collected in localities A, B and D, the concentration of bowls/cups in B with small amphorae in A and D, and the surprising rarity of fragments of the popular pendent semicircle skyphoi raise problems of interpretation. We may, I think, reject pyres to account for the burning, for we would not expect these concentrations of vase types, a point which seems to rule out rubbish dumps of broken pottery. The presence of Attic imports, moreover, would be inconsistent with another possible explanation, that we have rejects from a pottery kiln.

We are left with the likelihood of a building or buildings in which pottery had been stored before they were destroyed in some conflagration. The curious localisation of certain pottery types in particular areas, and the absence of others, suggests either a very large establishment with widely spaced stores of specialised pottery (and one thinks of the Palace of Pylos) or pottery shops (and Al Mina comes to mind): in neither case would the Attic vases be out of place.

There is no reason to doubt the contemporary nature of the pottery from the various areas in this locality, and the Attic imports would place the destruction, to which they owe their preservation, to MG I, or early SPG III in Lefkandian terms. The significance of this, when coupled with the apparent cessation of burials in the known cemeteries of this date, will be considered in the historical conclusions.

### The architecture (PLATES 5, 6 and 11)
It has been suggested above that walls L, M and N may be disjointed lengths of a once continuous and taller terrace wall retaining the higher ground to the south; its construction resembles that of the LG house and the yard wall (D).

The circular structure just north of it, abutting onto a short stretch of wall (H and I) is not comparable with the three more complex ones discussed below and may simply be the foundations of a yard hut or animal pen. A similar function may be assumed, too, for the apparently rectangular enclosure W of the main building (P and Q) where it looks as though wall P is the re-used remnant of an earlier building.

All too little is known of a building, the corner of which was uncovered in the SE edge of the main area (J and K), and only further excavation could elucidate whether the two walls are contemporary, — LPG/SPG I in construction — and remained in use until SPG II, as the associated pottery suggests. The use of large flat slabs over a double row of edging stones, to be seen in one segment of it, was a feature of the short stretch of wall, containing LPG sherds, investigated on Toumba, see pp. 12ff.

Interest, however, centres on the better preserved structures to the north — the house and the three circular foundations on either side of N/S yard wall.

### The house (PLATE 8a)
Such doubts as we had about its original form have been detailed above in the excavation report. Destroyed in LG, we may be reasonably certain it was constructed earlier in the same period, and, as such, conformed in general with the apsidal plan typical of its day, examples of which are conveniently assembled by H. Drerup in *Archaeologia Homerica* II,0.

Our house is no mean affair, with internal dimensions of near 5 m wide and over 8.5 m long, its preserved but not its full, original length.

The construction of its walls, like that of the yard wall, is very irregular, the general practice being to place larger stones with a fairly flat surface on the outer faces with a rubble and earth fill; there is the occasional header lying the full width of the walls, some 40 cm across. We may assume from the better preserved section of it that it had two stone courses at least, which were capped with mud brick; fallen remains of these were traced near the W wall above the latest earth floor, patches of which were laid with small pebbles.

An unusual feature is the square 'platform' against the E wall, evidently an afterthought since it rested on the second, and latest, earth floor. Constructed mostly of 'pudding' stones and one course high, it was covered in part by a thin layer of red clay — either its surface or disintegrated mud-brick. It is flanked either side by post holes positioned close to the main wall. Evidence for a corresponding structure further N against the opposite, W, wall is slight, and its completion on the plan at PLATE 8a should be regarded as conjectural. Some 1.4 m square seems too small for a bed or couch and perhaps unnecessarily large for an internal buttress. A table or bench is an obvious possible function but positioned inconveniently low.

Initially, a depression with a surround of stones and ashy fill, in the middle of the room, in line with the S face of the 'platform' was interpreted as a hearth and so marked on earlier plans. Subsequently, when we excavated more of the building to the N and found clearer signs of fire destruction, we preferred an alternative, and perhaps more convincing, explanation of it as a post support for the roof where the radial rafters of the apse met. The posts along the walls (and we may have missed one hole against the W wall) could have supported a diagonal cross brace, or else, more simply, carried beams along the walls to support the rafters. If either explanation is correct, we lack a hearth, unless it be the patch of carbon (hatched on the plan) about midway between 'platform' and W wall.

The stones plotted on Plate 8a at the N end of the house, beside the conjectured second 'platform', were in a superficial level, having no obvious association with the building.

The contents of the building are consistent with those of a normal, if prosperous, dwelling, with kitchen activities suggested for the apse with its two stone pounders, knife and whetstone, and two large coarse-ware jars. How did they cook, however?

### The circular structures (PLATES 8b and 11)

Only the most northerly of the three, E, was apparently in proper use at the end and, since all correspond closely in construction and it was the best preserved, we may concentrate on this one example.

The plan and section illustrate its construction. Circular in outline, two slots were left (roughly at right angles to the adjacent yard wall) while the outer faces of the structure and those bordering the slots were built of larger stones with a rubble and earth fill behind. Hence we called them initially 'theta structures'. The northern example was preserved in places for three courses, while two slabs appeared to be in position bridging part of one slot (PLATE 7b).

Nothing in or around the structures suggests a possible use for them, unless account should be taken of the iron nail and stone pounder found in dismantling G. Negatively, the absence of burning or of clearly discoloured soil nearby would seem to exclude ovens or oil (but perhaps not wine) presses. Architecturally two functions are indicated. The slots are for wooden beams to hold some superstructure, which in turn suggests some form of press. Or the slots are for ventilation below a circular wooden (or less likely, clay) floor, which would indicate granaries. In support of the second alternative, we may immediately point to the clay models on the lid of a small clay chest from Athens, interpreted as granaries by Professor Smithson and admirably discussed by her in *Hesperia* 37 (1968) 96ff. If correctly interpreted, not only have we the analogy of circular buildings (with a domed superstructure), but two ground-level openings on both faces of the models as ventilation shafts. This would, moreover, better suit the impermanance of our structures, since F certainly and G probably had fallen into disuse, or rather, in the case of F, it had been apparently put to some secondary use with its covering of clay and circle of surrounding stones (PLATE 7b and plans at PLATE 5 with the stones in position, and PLATE 8 after their removal). So, on present evidence, we may accept them as the foundations of granaries.

Too little of the buildings in Trials W and Z were uncovered to merit discussion beyond that given in the excavation report above. In retrospect, we may regret we did not go on to reveal their full plans.

# Section 3

# The Protogeometric and Sub-Protogeometric Pottery

V. R. d'A. DESBOROUGH with O. T. P. K. DICKINSON

## I   XEROPOLIS, AREA 2 (PLATE 9)

The stratigraphical relationship of the three deposits from Area 2 considered below has been described at pp. 16ff. Basically the earliest deposit, the 'Moulds Deposit Pit 1' was cut into by the digging of a pit which was then filled, the 'SPG Pit 2'; at a later stage earth was laid over the area generally, including Pit 2, to level it up, the 'Levelling Material'.

These three deposits will be considered separately in some detail and, then, in the final section the chronological limits of the pottery in them will be examined.

### Area 2, Pit 1; the Moulds Deposit (PLATES 13—14, nos. 1—89 and 66/P262; PLATE 30)

*Wheel-made*
All the pottery, with the possible exception of a few pieces, is of local fabric. No sherd of Attic origin was identified. About 400 sherds were taken into account.

*Open Vases.* The shapes represented in this deposit are one-handled cups, skyphoi, kraters and kalathoi. Cups and skyphoi are the most common, and it is to them that will have belonged the unattached bases, on the three types of which an explanatory note is desirable at this point. The flat base (about thirty examples) is characteristic of the cup, as can indeed be seen from the surviving body profiles (see below); it is not impossible for a skyphos to have a base of this type,[1] but I know of no example from Lefkandi. The ring base (seven sherds only, see 19 for one) is apparently confined to the skyphos. The conical or flaring foot, finally, of which type about thirty fragments were found (see 36—9, 46—9 and PLATE 30, 21—3), may belong either to a cup or to a skyphos; for the importance of the frequency of these as a possible chronological criterion see pp. 31 and 43.

*The Cup.* 1—18. PLATE 30, 1—6

In all cases, the diameter of the mouth is 10 cm or less. There are two main types, the criterion being the decoration of the outer lip.[2]

(i) A high offset lip with one, or two, rough zigzags on the outer surface. This is by far the most common type: there are thirty-seven fragments, including the four for which a complete body profile was able to be retrieved (2, 3, 12, 14). Apart from the lip, the cups have a single strip handle from rim to belly (nineteen monochrome, two barred — see 18) and a rounded body which is monochrome, with one exception, dogtooth decoration on the upper body (18). Those with complete profile have flat bases, and the unattached bases of this type all most probably belong to this type of cup, as do many, or even most, of the conical feet.

(ii) The shape is the same, and indeed the only difference from the type above is that the outer surface of the lip is monochrome. This is a characteristic SPG, as opposed to LPG, type, and it is consequently of importance that one example only was found of it in this deposit, the restored vase 66/P262 (see also PLATE 30, 6).

*The Skyphos.* 19—35, 40—5, 50—4. PLATE 30, 7—18.

As with the cup, there are two main types that persist throughout this deposit, the SPG Pit, and the Levelling Material; here, however, the distinction between the two lies both in the shape of the lip and in the body decoration.

(i) The lip is straight, overhanging and carinated; the body is curved, and comes down to a ring base — the conventional kind of base for these skyphoi, though only seven fragments were identified in the deposit. The mouth diameter varies between 12 and 16 cm, and the lips, except for one of 1.3 cm, are all high.[3]

Lip, handles, and lower body are as a rule monochrome. There remains the upper body, which contains the feature that is the hallmark of this type of skyphos, the two sets of pendent semi-circles, and I shall normally refer to it as the PSC skyphos. There were eighteen lip sherds with part of the upper body showing the PSC motive (see 20—27 and PLATE 30, 7—11), and one complete profile (19 = PLATE 30, 12), whose semicircles have a triangle filling, a most rare occurrence in the series. Apart from these there are forty-six body sherds which show arcs only, which probably mostly belong to this type.

(ii) The lip is slightly outswung, blending in to the body, which comes down in a gentle curve to the base. In the absence of a complete profile, either here or elsewhere on the site, the type of base is uncertain: a flat base seems from the evidence elsewhere to be improbable, so this type of skyphos will have had either a ring base (but note the scarcity of these in the deposit) or a high conical foot.[4] The rims of only five vases of this type have been recovered, and the mouth diameters vary from 12 to c. 24 cm (see 33—35, 44, 50 and PLATE 30, 16—18) — indeed, the one with the largest diameter (34) almost qualifies as a small krater, but I have classed it as a skyphos on the basis of the lip profile.

As to the decoration, the outer rim is always painted over, and may have a band beneath. For the lower body, there is one instance of supporting bands (33), but evidence is otherwise lacking. The characteristic feature, as with the PSC skyphos, is on the upper body — two sets of circles between the handles,[5] and this will be referred to as the circles skyphos. Of some interest for this deposit is that in four cases

(34, 35, 44, 50) the circles have a central filling — two reserved crosses, one Maltese cross, and one uncertain. There are also two instances of an intervening motive between the circles: 34 (the very large skyphos), some sort of vertical panel, and 35, a cross-hatched diamond.

To judge from the recognisable pieces, there are far fewer of this class than of the PSC type. They reflect the Attic LPG type of skyphos, and their appearance is of great interest, since none has yet been found in any tomb or pyre (though there are fragments in the surface material and fills of the cemeteries).

These, then, are the two main classes; there is a third, represented by three sherds only, but worthy of record, as confined to this one deposit in the settlement. The shape is close in conception to that of the cup, with high and offset lip, and zigzag motive (one, two, or three rows) on its outer surface. These sherds are, however, certainly from skyphoi: in two cases (31, 32) the stump of the horizontal loop handle has been preserved, and in the third (28) the estimated diameter of the mouth, c. 17 cm, is too great for a cup. The body was no doubt monochrome as a rule, but 28 has full circles. There is no complete profile, but the foot was almost certainly of the high conical type, on the analogy of two similar examples from the cemetery, P Pyre 11, 7 and 8 (PLATE 152).

In addition, there are a number of miscellaneous or atypical skyphos sherds, which may be treated individually.[6]

29, 30. Two sherds from the same vase; vestige of a carinated lip, PSC on body flanking a panel of verticals enclosing a zigzag; also a wart. Presumably a skyphos, and if so probably a curious variation on the PSC skyphos.

23. The lip is not carinated, but comes out in a sharp curve; the greatest diameter is at the belly (see PLATE 30, 7). PSC in a narrow zone below the lip. No handle preserved, but presumed to be a skyphos. Perhaps not local: clay brown, clear light brown slip, very dark and slightly lustrous brown paint. See PLATE 276, 969 for a similar sherd.

45. High offset rim, banded; two bands below the handle, body otherwise unpainted.

40. Sherd from open vase (skyphos?) with cross hatching on upper body. Cf. perhaps PLATE 24, 626.

41. Fairly straight rim, with verticals below.

42. Slightly outcurved lip, painted; unclear motive below.

43. Lip with two bands below rim, and zigzags below these.

51. Lip with trace of rough zigzag below.

52. Fairly high offset lip, painted; uncertain below.

53—4. Two sherds from same vase. Heavily grooved high lip; lip and body monochrome. Brown clay, and metallic brown-purple paint, so perhaps not local. Not certainly a skyphos.

The total number of sherds taken into account, about a hundred and forty, is much greater than for the cups, but there were far fewer joins possible. The variety of shapes and decoration is notable, especially when compared with what is known from the tombs. There is a strong feeling of experimentation.

*The Krater.* 55—60, 68, 69. PLATE 30, 19.

This, regretfully, is a small and relatively unrevealing group; apart from several sherds with banded decoration, which were discarded, and one rim which is not illustrated, there remain the eight sherds shown on PLATE 14 (see also PLATE 30, 19 for one).

All one can say is that the kraters of this deposit had squarely offset rims, flat on the top, that a ridge below the rim is possible, that the upper body was decorated with rectilinear motives, panelled or not, that the lower body was dark ground with occasional relieving reserved bands, and that there is one instance (68) of a high flaring foot.

*The Kalathos* 70, 88, 89. PLATE 30, 20.
There are fragments of three vases only. Two belong to the type with impressed triangles, and it may be noted that a sherd of 89 was found in the SPG Pit. 70 is unindented.

### Closed Vases

*Amphorae.* 61–7, 71–7, 79–81, 84, 85. PLATE 30, 25 and 26.
There were just under two hundred fragments, some of which might belong to hydriai or to large jugs or oinochoai, and most of which were discarded as unhelpful. No complete profile was recovered. The following observations may be made.

Lips, handles and bases, so far as one can tell, are such as would suit the LPG period. All the lips except one (77, see PLATE 30, 26) belong to neck-handled amphorae (74–5 and PLATE 30, 25). No fragment of a handle is illustrated: the neck handles had decoration of bars, intersecting verticals, or intersecting diagonals between horizontal bars — just one had two parallel verticals; for the belly handles the paint, as usual, covered the outer surface. No base is illustrated either, but only ring bases were recorded, twenty-seven of them.

Necks were light ground or monochrome, with the exception of two fragments with dogtooth motive (65, 85).[7]

Shoulders often have the conventional semicircle motive, sometimes with central filling (upright and inverted triangle, and hourglass). There are three clear cases of languettes (indented on 84), and 64 has what appears to be a set of diagonal lines, possibly languettes, flanking semicircles. The two thick horizontal scribbles of 63 may be noted. An unillustrated sherd, finally, has a panel motive, vertical lines enclosing a zigzag.

The belly may have full circles or reserved bands (see 71–2, 81). For the body as a whole the impression, based on the mass of sherds not illustrated, is that the scheme was usually a light ground one.

*Jugs and Oinochoai.* 78, 82, 83. PLATE 30, 24.
Only about fifteen sherds could with certainty be assigned to this class, but there may have been more (see above, in the analysis of the amphorae). The general system of decoration, now as later, was dark ground, the only relieving feature being semicircles on the shoulder, a motive found on four sherds.

Three sherds are illustrated. The first, 83, is one of the four with semicircles — the belly, it may be noted, is surprisingly sharply curved. 82 is a trefoil lip; and 78 (= PLATE 30, 24) is the rim and part of the neck (grooved beneath the rim) of a jug with cutaway neck, with light brown clay and black paint, a very rare piece indeed in the settlement. A joining sherd to this last piece, and also a join for one of the shoulder fragments with semicircles, were found in the Pit deposit.

No sherd was able to be assigned either to a lekythos or to a pyxis.

### Miscellaneous
87. Fragment of a ring-stand? Dark red paint. No parallel known.
86. Fragment of a stand with three internal struts? Perhaps a variation on the tripod dish 54, 1?

*Coarse domestic hand-made ware*[8]
I quote from Dr. O. Dickinson's report.

'An orange-red handmade ware of medium thickness seems normal; this is generally smooth on the inside, and may be worn on the outside. A medium-sized wide-mouthed jar or jug seems to be the only shape. There is, however, a relatively fine thinner-walled variety, ranging in colour from fine orange-brown to very dark brown, that is burnished on the outside, showing vertical ripples from the burnishing instrument in the best examples. Some thirty or forty fragments of varying quality could be identified, including jug or jar rims, a very large flat base (d. 13 cm), a small flat base fragment, three flat handles, and what might be part of a flaring foot.'

None of these is illustrated; for the type, however, see PLATE 22A. The shape of the jugs is no doubt much the same as that of the cooking pots found in the tombs of SPG II and SPG III date (see PLATE 269d).

## Area 2, Pit 2: The SPG Pit (PLATES 15–17, nos. 90–249 and 69/P44; PLATES 31–2)

*Wheel-made*
As for the Moulds Deposit, the fabric seems to be overwhelmingly local. The few clearly imported sherds are dealt with separately. There were about 1500 sherds.

*Open Vases.* The same range of shapes is found as in the Moulds Deposit, with the addition of the shallow bowl with strap handles. Cups and skyphoi continue to be the most popular, and it is again to these that one should attribute the unattached bases, or fragments of such. There were seventy-six flat bases, mostly belonging to cups, but in this deposit some will have belonged to shallow bowls, which always have a base of this kind. As opposed to the seven ring bases recovered from the Moulds Deposit, eighty-nine were found in the SPG Pit, and these will most probably all have belonged to skyphoi. On the other hand there were fewer conical feet, about thirty, which will have come from either cups or skyphoi. See PLATE 31, 18–19 for two of these. The difference in distribution from that of the earlier deposit is remarkable.

*The Cup.* 90–4, 98–103. PLATE 31, 1–3
The diameter of the mouth is 10 cm or less. The same subdivisions are adopted as for the Moulds Deposit, but for class II the outer lip more often has reserved bands than the purely monochrome system. The body is invariably monochrome outside; inside, there is usually a reserved band just below the rim, and a reserved circle on the floor. Thirty-three handle fragments were recovered, belonging to either class; three were barred, the remainder were monochrome.
(i) 90–4, 98. There were altogether forty-four sherds with zigzag on the rim, including two with two rows of zigzags (91, 98). Note 93 with the band above the zigzag. The shape has been described above, and see PLATE 31, 1 and 2 for two complete body profiles.
(ii) 99–102. Twelve outer lips were monochrome, thirty-six had one or more reserved bands, a very different picture from that of the preceding deposit. On the whole, the lips tend to be not quite so high as those with zigzag motive. No further comment is needed. Finally, there was one example (103) of a cup of a different type, with gently outcurving lip, and wholly monochrome.[9]

*The Skyphos.* 95—7, 104—28, 140, 149, 150. PLATE 31, 4—24

The two main types are the PSC and the circles skyphos, as in the Moulds Deposit and the Levelling Material. Numerous sherds were found, which could be ascribed equally to either type, and this usually applies to the fragments of handles, of which just under two hundred were recovered.

(i) *PSC Skyphoi.* 108—10, 114—15, 119—23; see also PLATE 31, 4—10, including one complete body profile. Eighty-four lips with traces of PSC below were found. The great majority of these are high or medium, only half a dozen being low (see PLATE 31, 10). Almost all are straight, and overhang the body. The inner monochrome system is normally relieved, as for the cups, by a reserved band below the lip. The outer rim is always painted over, and it is most probable that the same applies to the lower body. The characteristic PSCs occupy the area between the handles; no central filling was noted; in some cases the two sets of semicircles intersect, but for most one cannot tell. The mouth diameter ranges from 12 cm to 20 cm.

(ii) *Circles Skyphoi.* 95—7, 104—7, 111—13, 116—18, 124—8; see also PLATE 31, 11—17. More sherds of this class of skyphos were found in the SPG Pit Deposit than in any other; in addition to the forty-five rim fragments there were other sherds which certainly or possibly belong to it.

Two subsidiary types can be distinguished. The one has an average mouth diameter of 18—20 cm, a gently outcurving rim, painted over and with a band — in one instance two bands — below, and the characteristic circles well down on the body (e.g., 95, 97, 104). The other is smaller, its average mouth diameter being 13—14 cm. The shape of the rim is variable: it can be the same as on the larger skyphoi, but more often it is very low, distinguished from the body by being slightly out-turned. In several instances only a very thin band of paint covers the outer rim, and there is no supporting band; the circles, perhaps because of the dimensions of the vase, come higher than on the larger ones, even touching the rim band (e.g., 111—13, 116—18, 124, 128). This smaller type is the more popular of the two. It should be made clear, however, that the potter did not feel himself absolutely bound by the one type or the other, and there are variations especially in the profile (see PLATE 31, 14—17). 125, indeed, has a carinated lip, as on the PSC skyphoi.

As to the body decoration, the circles are normally unfilled (in contrast to the Moulds Deposit), but three reserved crosses (see 125—6) and one Maltese cross (124) were noted. Other motives are extremely rare: one sherd shows the start of a panel, another (107) vertical lines flanking a set of circles. The lower body can presumably be either monochrome (see PLATE 31, 11) or have supporting bands below the circles, as in one case in the Moulds deposit. Since PSC skyphoi, to judge from examples at Lefkandi and other sites, have a monochrome lower body, one is probably correct in assuming that sherds showing arcs and supporting bands come from circles skyphoi.

No information is available on the type of base.

Finally, there are four sherds which can be listed as miscellaneous, though they have one common feature, a zigzag in a panel.[10]

140. (= PLATE 32,9). Straight rim, gradually incurving body; zigzag in panel, with band above (and below?), between the handles.

149. Similar profile to 140; zigzag in narrow panel below rim.

150. Gently outsurving lip; zigzag between bands in panel well below rim.

PLATE 31, 20. High, well-outcurving lip; trace of rough zigzag in panel in handle zone,

*The Shallow Bowl with Strap Handles.* 137–8, 141–2, 147–8. PLATE 32, 10 and 11.
These are subdivided in accordance with the type of rim: either everted, of which there were twenty-four examples[11] (see 138, 142, 148 and PLATE 32, 11), or incurved, of which there were nine (see 137, 141, 147 and PLATE 32, 10). There is no complete profile, and the shape of the lower part of the vase may then be thought uncertain, but evidence from elsewhere indicates that both types were flat-based and had a monochrome lower body. Mouth diameters range from 12 to 15 cm, and the height from 5 to 6 cm. The everted bowls have either a rough zigzag or bands below the rim, the incurved ones normally have bands.

This shape is not represented in the Moulds Deposit.

*The Krater* 151–60, 162–77, PLATE 32, 1–6.
No subdivision is possible, nor is there any complete body profile. Thirty-seven lips were recorded, and the main variations are shown on PLATE 32, 1–6. In several cases there is a ridge, which may be of the rope variety, beneath the lip. There are at least twelve loop handles — possibly more, but one cannot always distinguish between the handle of a krater and that of an amphora. There were nine ring bases, and at least one high conical foot.

As to the decorative system, the interior is painted over. For the exterior, the upper surface of the rim is either monochrome, or has sets of bars (eleven examples); paint continues under the lip and for a slight distance below. The main decorative motives are confined to the area between the handles (see below), with a supporting band or bands beneath, and the likelihood is that the lower body was normally monochrome.

The motives found in the area between the handles display a fairly conventional variety. The most favoured system is that of circles flanking a panel (for the best example see 156 and 163, with dot-fringed circles). The circles sometimes have a central filling — reserved cross, Maltese cross, wheel spokes. The panels normally consist of vertical lines flanking one of several motives — cross-hatching, zigzag, chequers, hatched and solid diamonds and triangles, triangles set base to base. There are also examples of groups of opposed diagonals, with their interstices filled or unfilled. And there may be one instance of PSC, 155.

Mention must also be made of a sherd (175) which may be from a small krater: it has the combed and incised decoration and black paint associated with the Black Slip ware, but the clay is a light brown.

*The Kalathos.* 133–6, 145–6. PLATE 32, 7.
This shape is divisible into two types: those with impressed-triangle decoration, of which there are four sherds (133–6); and those with monochrome and/or banded decoration, represented by eight sherds (see 145–6; PLATE 32, 7).

*Miscellaneous*
178. Part of a strut with cross-hatched decoration. Light brown clay and slip, black paint. Probably locally made.

*Closed Vases*

*The Amphora.* 161, 201–29. PLATE 32, 15–17, 19.
There was no complete profile. The great majority of the sherds will have belonged to neck- and belly-handled amphorae; other types as well may be represented, notably hydriai, and there are also, as is evident from the cemeteries, exceptionally large jugs and

trefoil oinochoai, the fragments of which would usually be indistinguishable from those of small amphorae.

There were just under a hundred rim sherds, mostly from neck-handled amphorae (see PLATE 32, 15), and only a very few of the belly-handled type (see PLATE 32, 17). The subsidiary ridge on some of these (see 206) seems not to be earlier than SPG: thirteen (see 201, 203, 209) had horizontal grooves, giving a ridged impression to the lip. Most had the lip painted over, but on five (see 201, 208) there were sets of vertical bars on the top of the outer rim.

Seventy-four sherds belong to neck handles, eighteen from belly handles; the neck handles most frequently had intersecting verticals, but several were barred, and one (223) had a combination of both. On the belly handles the paint follows the curve of the handle, and usually continues below it.

All the forty-eight bases were of the ring type with the outer area painted over.

About eighty necks were fragments, most of them unpainted except for bands at the junction with the shoulder and just below the rim. A few were monochrome, and of these the ones with panelled decoration will be discussed below, as a small separate type of their own.

For the body (again excluding the type to be dealt with separately) the general system was normally light ground, allowing for subsidiary decoration on shoulder and belly, these two areas being clearly demarcated by supporting horizontal bands. The shoulder motives included six instances of languettes from the base of the neck (see 202), but by far the most popular was sets of concentric semicircles — between seventy and eighty sherds — usually with no central filling, but there were three with hourglass and two with triangles (see 210, 215, 220). No instance of the use of full circles on the shoulder area was confirmed, though it is known that the Lefkandians, and others in the region, used this motive in the SPG period. The belly decoration includes full circles (one with reserved cross filling), vertical zigzag, cross-hatching in various rectilinear forms, dogtooth and diamond. The design is sometimes in panel form, and there is one case of two zones, but the precise motives are not always entirely clear.

*The Dark Ground Type.* 230–47. PLATE 32, 12.

This class can best be traced in the cemeteries, where it does not seem to precede SPG II, and is therefore a useful stylistic criterion. It involves relatively small- or medium-sized neck-handled amphorae, and trefoil oinochoai — and it thus provides, in this context, a transitional stage to the smaller closed vases. The general system of decoration is by definition dark ground — normal for oinochoai, not so for amphorae — and the vases have a slender shape. The vases also share certain features of individual decoration: on the neck, an hourglass panel (though this need not be present); and on the belly either a zone of zigzag — perhaps more common on the oinochoai — or groups of opposed diagonals with unfilled interstices, for both the motive being usually encased between two encircling bands.[12]

There is no sign of the type in the Moulds Deposit; it appears first in the SPG Pit, and continues strongly into the Levelling Material. It is represented in the SPG Pit by several panelled hourglass sherds from amphorae (230–2, 234–5) and by one from a trefoil oinochoe (233);[13] by one or two instances of belly zigzags from amphorae (see 245), and by six from oinochoai; by twenty-five sherds with opposed diagonals on the belly, ten and fifteen from amphorae and oinochoai respectively. The evidence is thus fairly substantial, and worth stressing.

Four additional points may be made in connection with the groups of opposed diagonals. The distinction between those which belong to amphorae, and those to oinochoai, is not as sharp as I have implied; the possibility should be borne in mind that one or two of the smaller, narrower ones could belong to pyxides rather than to oinochoai, on the basis of the tomb evidence; the groups are often done with a multiple brush; and (arising from the last point) at least two of the amphora sherds belong to a vase of which other fragments were found in the Levelling Material.

Finally, it may be remarked that the best comparative material from the settlement comes from the SL Area, datable to SPG II and to the earlier stages of SPG III (pp. 49ff, and PLATES 28–9).

*The Jug and the Trefoil Oinochoe.* 179–91, 194–9.[14] PLATE 32, 13 and 14.
The trefoil oinochoe has already been, in part, dealt with above. The jug can cover several varieties of shape, which one can not always identify. The following analysis will make the problem clear.

Of the thirty or so rims, eighteen are from jugs, and six of these have thin grooves below the lip, either from jugs with cutaway neck or from tall cylindrical jugs. Six, three with vertical bars on the outer lip, belong to trefoil oinochoai (see 181).

Handles numbered fifteen, either barred or with intersecting diagonals, or a combination of both. One plain handle (179) comes to just below the rim of a large jug which may be an import — its dull red paint does not look local.

There were nine neck sherds, all monochrome (as is the usual system for the smaller closed vases), of which one belongs to the jug mentioned above.

For the body, the shoulder was either monochrome or had sets of semicircles — eleven examples of these, no doubt mainly from trefoil oinochoai. Some of the belly sherds are monochrome, too, but often have a zone of decoration; as well as the opposed diagonals and zigzags, already discussed, two — most unusually — have cross-hatched panelling (191, 199), one has dogtooth (198), and one vertical lines. These, I think, will have come either from trefoil oinochoai or from a shape not yet mentioned, the pyxis — it may be stressed that sets of vertical lines are, so far as is known, peculiar to the latter shape (see below).

Note may finally be made of a fragment (194) which may belong to the rather unusual straight-sided jug.

*The Pyxis.* 184, 185, 187, 192, 200 and 69/P44 (= PLATE 32, 18).
Mention has already been made of the possibility that some of the decorated belly sherds could come from pyxides — and so also could some of the monochrome or reserved-band scraps. There is, however, specific evidence of the shape in the SPG Pit deposit. Alone among the closed vases, the pyxis provides an example of a complete body profile (69/P44, = PLATE 32, 18). It has a globular body, an everted rim and a ring base, and is monochrome except for groups of vertical lines in a wide belly zone (see PLATE 180 for a similar system in the cemetery). This vase seems clearly to belong to the SPG I–II period. Sherds from it were found over a wide area, from the Levelling Material as well as from the SPG Pit.

Five sherds from lids almost certainly belonged to pyxides.[15] Three are identified by their knobs (see 185, 187). Two (184, 192) show part of the lid's rim: they come from different lids, but have the same type of decoration, semicircles, one with triangle central filling, and broad encircling bands above and below.

Apart from this only two body rim sherds (see 200) could with confidence be attributed to pyxides.

*Imported ware*
There were three Attic sherds.
129. Rim and part of body of an EG II skyphos. Multiple zigzigs in window panel.
130. Small sherd of skyphos with multiple zigzag. Probably EG II.
131. Sherd of skyphos with multiple chevron or zigzag. EG II or MG I.

As well as this it is most likely that 132 is an import, though not from Attica; the shape is not altogether certain, but it looks like a flat tray, with cross-hatched? battlement on the outer body, and small concentric circles on the outer part of the base.

There are two other imported pieces (no doubt there were more, unrecognised). One is from a closed vase, probably an amphora, and the fabric is extremely micaceous; it has sets of semicircles, possibly pendent. The other is the jug rim, neck and handle (179), mentioned above, on the basis of its alien-looking paint.

There was nothing demonstrably later than EG,[16] a point of clear chronological significance in view of the considerable quantity of Attic or atticising MG sherds recovered from the Levelling Material.

*Coarse hand-made ware*
No statistics were kept of this material, but there was a fair quantity of it, almost exclusively from jugs. As an example, the sample group 739 contained about a hundred and twenty hand-made sherds, of which under twenty were of the thin-walled type. See 248–9 for two exceptional pieces.

**Area 2: The Levelling Material.** (PLATES 18–21, nos. 250–451 and 65/P64, with PLATE 33; PLATE 22, A, nos. 452–66).

*Wheel-made*
The fabric, once again, is overwhelmingly local. The clearly or possibly imported sherds are discussed separately, in conjunction with such sherds of local fabric which imitate Attic ware in shape and decoration. The total amount of material is rather greater than that from the SPG Pit, but the sherds tend to be smaller and more scrappy.

*Open Vases.* To the shapes previously known, and still current in this deposit, only one can be added, the plate. As usual, cups and skyphoi are the most common, and it is to them that most of the unattached bases will have belonged. There were a hundred and eighteen flat bases (including about twenty with a raised flat base), and these should be assigned either to cups or to shallow bowls with strap handles. Possibly all the ninety-four ring bases will have come from skyphoi. There were, as in the SPG Pit, about thirty conical feet, either from cups or from skyphoi.

*The Cup.*[17] 250–60
The same subdivisions, and to some extent the same comments, can be made as for the SPG Pit. The mouth diameter, however, can be as much as 12 cm, assuming that 253 and 259 are cups. There were also far more fragments of handles (ninety-four), of which only three were barred, the rest being monochrome. Bodies were almost without exception monochrome: note, however, 257, with circles and Maltese cross filling and 254, with

curious confronted solid triangles, which both look as though they belong to cups; also, 256 with dogtooth on the body surely comes from a cup similar to that found in the Moulds Deposit (PLATE 13, 18).

(i) There was one complete body profile (258) and twenty-eight other sherds with one or more zigzags on the outer lip. This is a significantly smaller number than was retrieved from either the SPG Pit or the Moulds Deposit.

(ii) Thirty-six sherds have a monochrome outer lip, and fifty-six have one or more reserved bands (see 259). No particular comment is needed.

One sherd (260), probably from a cup, does not fall into either of the above classes. It has a very sharply everted short lip, and the body profile indicates that the greatest diameter was at the belly; the decoration is a series of horizontal encircling bands, as far down as can be seen. The paint is a good clear brown, and this fragment is perhaps not of local make.

*The Skyphos.* 261—322. PLATE 33, 1—29
The same general comments apply as for the SPG Pit; in this deposit, it may be noted, nearly two hundred and fifty handle fragments were found.

(i) *PSC skyphoi.* 261—96. PLATE 33, 1—5, and 6—28 for profile only.[18] No fewer than a hundred and seventy-three lip fragments with traces of PSC below were recovered, from which the popularity of the type is self-evident. The figures for the height of these lips, based on the sample sector (PLATE 33, 6—28) and on some of the lips from the rest of the deposit, suggest that nearly one half were of medium (1—1.4 cm) height, about a third were low (under 1 cm), and not more than 15 per cent high (1.5 cm or over).[19] The inferences that may be made will be discussed in the general commentary on these three deposits, below.

Apart from this, the general and detailed decorative system is as for the SPG Pit, and it is probable that no other base but the ring type was used. The diameter of the mouth varies, ranging from 11 to 18 cm and mostly between 12 and 16 cm.

There are three atypical PSC sherds.

269. High and well swept-back rim, with three reserved bands on its lower outer surface: no parallel, to my knowledge.

PLATE 33, 4. Rim and upper body unparalleled for a PSC skyphos: note especially the heavily convex curve of the body. The PSC do not intersect; the compass points are well below the upper band, due no doubt to the difficulty in using the dividers on such a sharply curved surface.

PLATE 33, 5. The rim has a gentle outward curve, as in the circles skyphoi.

(ii) *Circles skyphoi.* 297—312
Distinctly less common than in the SPG Pit, to judge from the number of rim sherds, of which there were about twenty-five. There is no way of estimating the number of body sherds.

On the whole one gets the same range of shape, size and decoration as in the SPG Pit, but there is a noticeable drop in the number of those whose rim was covered by a narrow band of paint only, with the circles coming up close to it. Nor can one so readily ascribe those with a band below the rim to a larger type of vase. There are, as in the SPG Pit, one or two sharply out-turned rims.

The decoration of the body is, by definition, sets of circles, and there are at least three instances of a central filling of some form of cross (299, 307—8). There is also one skyphos where the circles are flanked by three vertical lines (307), and it may be noted, in connexion with what has been said above, that although the rim of this vase has two bands beneath it, the diameter of the mouth is only 11 cm.

Nothing can be said with certainty about the decoration of the lower body.

There are also a few sherds, probably from skyphoi, which may be classified as miscellaneous or atypical (for the three atypical PSC sherds, see above).

313. A reserved band on the outer lip. The estimated mouth diameter, 17 cm, means that this is almost certainly a skyphos, and not a cup. It may be of the atticising type (see PLATE 20, 65/P64).

314. The massiveness of this monochrome sherd also suggests a skyphos.

315. The decoration is apparently an hourglass flanked by two vertical lines (panel?): an open vase — skyphos or cup?

317—9. Same vase. Panel on belly with rectilinear design.

316. Rough zigzag on upper body with band above. Very low lip. Diameter of mouth c. 12 cm, so could be either a cup or a skyphos.

320. Panel with rough zigzag on belly, handle stump suggesting loop handle on rim.

321. Out-turned lip, reserved band on outer surface, bands on rim. Horizontal reserved panel on belly.

322 = PLATE 33, 29. Black Slip ware. Combed and incised decoration. D. of mouth 20 cm. Straight rim, similar to P39B, 17 (PLATE 147). Note the two string holes, which would normally suggest a kalathos or pyxis, but the body profile would not suit either.

*The Shallow Bowl with strap handles. 323—28.*

This is the same shape as noted in the SPG Pit, and there is much the same distribution of the two types of rim — twenty-three everted (see 323—5) and twelve incurved (see 327). The decoration is also the same, bands or zigzag below the rim. The mouth diameter ranges from 19 to 25 cm. No complete profile was found.

328 may belong to a bowl of this type, but one cannot be sure; the panelled diagonal cross below the rim is in any case atypical (see PLATE 276, 977).

*The Krater. 337—58. PLATE 33, 36*

There was no complete body profile. Twenty-nine rim sherds were recovered, all fairly heavy, sometimes with ridges below, which are occasionally of the rope type (see 338—9, ?340); all but five have the flat upper surface decorated with sets of bars or solid triangles (see 337, 341—2). There were nine fragments of loop handles, and possibly up to fifteen others. Only three sherds of ring bases seem to have been found, and one that could have come from a high conical foot. There were a fair number of body sherds.

The most substantial piece is 337, drawn on PLATE 33, 36. The top of the rim is barred, there are four heavy grooves well beneath it, and the belly decoration consists of sets of opposed diagonals with unfilled interstices — the curved line at the break on the left is probably part of the handle decoration rather than the arc of a circle.[20] Several other non-joining fragments were found in other parts of the deposit (see 353).

The decorative motives on the body are very much the same as those found in the SPG Pit. There were several further examples of the opposed diagonals with unfilled interstices; apart from this there are circles (with or without central filling), in one case dot-fringed, pendent semicircles, chequers, cross-hatching, vertical and horizontal zigzag, vertical solid diamonds, steep chevrons, and wavy lines — for a selection of these see 342—58.[21]

The usual system is either full circles, or vertical lines enclosing some rectilinear motive and breaking up the surface into panels, or groups of opposed diagonals.

*The Kalathos.* One sherd of the impressed-triangle type, with three tiers preserved, was found: not illustrated. No significance need be attached to its presence in the deposit, nor, perhaps, to the failure to identify any fragment of the monochrome or banded type.

*The Plate.* 329–36.[22] PLATE 33, 30 and 31.
Scattered fragments were found of five vases of this type. The rim may be incurved (329, 331 – see PLATE 33, 31), or slightly offset (330 – see PLATE 33, 30), or slightly offset and separated by carination from the body (333–4). There is one example of double-loop handles (336). The diameter ranges from 14 to 20 cm. The shape as a whole (there is no complete body profile) is surely as for those found in a tomb at Salamis in Cyprus,[23] but 329 may be deeper than usual – and its broad band over the outer rim is atypical. The characteristic decorative motive is PSC.

*Closed Vases*

*The Amphora.* 359–74. PLATE 33, 37–40
The same introductory remarks apply as for the SPG Pit, but there were three substantial joining sherds (359 = PLATE 33, 40) from an amphora of a type not yet mentioned, the shoulder-handled variety. It has an out-turned rim and a short thick neck, both painted over; the handle zone has sets of opposed diagonals.[24] The shape is in principle the same as that in the tombs from SM to SPG I–II, but this is a much larger vase.

The great bulk of the material in any case belongs to neck- and belly-handled amphorae. Of the nearly eighty rim sherds all but a few are from neck-handled amphorae, and eight have horizontal grooves or ridges (see 361–4 and PLATE 33, 38). Almost all are monochrome, but five have groups of bars on the upper rim. Neck-handle fragments numbered sixty-eight, belly-handle nineteen; the same variations in decoration are found as in the SPG Pit, but there was also one instance of a wavy line, and one of a single vertical line. There were about fifty-five bases (some of which could belong to large jugs or trefoil oinochoai), all of the ring type, with the outer area painted over.

The figures for neck sherds – in two or three cases with a slight central rib – are similar to those from the SPG Pit, and so is the ratio of light ground to dark ground. The panelled hourglass motive will be dealt with separately, but note one instance of a rough zigzag in a narrow band at the base (366).

The general system of decoration of the body, apart from the class discussed below, remained predominantly light ground, with the shoulder, belly, and foot demarcated by bands. The lower body was left free of decoration, but shoulder and belly usually have some individual motive or motives, which nearly always find a parallel in the SPG Pit material. On the shoulder the most common design is still the sets of semicircles, and there are no fewer than eight recorded examples of languettes from the base of the neck (see 360, 365); the usual decoration for the belly is circles.

Apart from this there seems very little that can with reasonable certainty be assigned to amphorae, but note may be made of three closed fragments: 367, with a zone of rays and a ?meander above;[25] 368, multiple enclosed squares with crossed diagonals in the centre; and 374, with a panelled motive.

*The Dark Ground Type. 375–83. PLATE 33, 41*

This, as we have seen in the discussion of the SPG Pit deposit, concerns small- or medium-sized neck-handled amphorae, and also certain trefoil oinochoai. In this deposit there are further examples of the panelled hourglass on the neck (see 376–7[26]); for the belly, horizontal zigzags are very rare, but there are far more sherds (over fifty) showing the groups of opposed diagonals with unfilled interstices (see nos 378–83, and PLATE 33, 41).[27] This latter motive is, I think, more common on oinochoai, but quite a few will have come from amphorae.

On the assumption that the Levelling Material is later than the SPG Pit (though containing sherds which are contemporary with, and even join, some of those from the SPG Pit — which makes stylistic analysis a hazardous process), one can probably say, on this evidence, that the greatest use of the opposed diagonal motives comes within the period of the Levelling Material, or at least its early stage of use. This receives some confirmation from the krater sherds and from the amphora with shoulder handles, mentioned above.

*The Jug, the Trefoil Oinochoe, and the Pyxis. 384–401*

There is no evidence for the lekythos, nor indeed for the small shoulder-handled amphoriskos, but this is not of any necessary significance, given the difficulty of identification.

For the pyxis, apart from the fragments of the restored vase (PLATE 16, 69/P44), some of which were recovered from the Levelling Material, there is just one rim fragment, and a sherd from a lid (401). It must also not be forgotten that belly motives of zigzag and opposed diagonals can belong to this shape, but it is possible that this long-lived local, globular, type was by now dying a natural death.

It is altogether likely that most of the sherds come from trefoil oinochoai (one variety already discussed) or from jugs. There were two trefoil lips, a few jug rims, and several where identification was not possible. The same uncertainty applies to the handles and bases, and indeed to the rest of the body.

For the shoulder, sets of semicircles, occasionally with central filling, are still the most popular motive, but note also languettes from the neck base (391), verticals enclosing dots (395), a sherd (396) with diamonds between verticals, flanked by semicircles or circles, and one with herringbone cut by a vertical (394). The belly, apart from the zigzags and opposed diagonals discussed above, was usually painted over — so also can be shoulder area be — but there is one instance of cross-hatched confronted triangles in a panel (397).

The general system of decoration was almost invariably dark ground, but there is one partial exception (384), fragments of what could be a large jug or oinochoe with continuous thick and thin bands, in two instances enclosing rough zigzags — see PLATE 14, 63.

*Attic and atticising fragments.*[28] (402–51, 64/P64. PLATES 21 and 33, nos. 32–35)

These constitute one of the most important features of the Levelling Material. It is sometimes difficult to say whether a sherd is of Attic or local fabric, and it is often impossible to distinguish either between Middle Geometric I and II, or between Early Geometric II and Middle Geometric I. Bearing in mind these uncertainties, the following list can be made out.

I  *Attic*[29]

    403. Pointed pyxis with battlement meander. EG II/MGI.

    404. Skyphos with triple zigzag. MG.

    405. Pyxis base, part of hatched leaf. MG II.

    406. Kantharos, steep zigzag in ancillary panel. MG II.

These may be considered certain; there may be a few more among the atticising sherds listed under section II. The total is in any case considerably smaller than one might expect from the tomb evidence, but it is important to realise that these imported sherds are later than the three from the SPG Pit.

II   In this section I catalogue for the most part the atticising MG sherds found in the deposit. Two fragmentary cups and a handful of sherds, however, belong to LG I, and are discussed in the relevant chapter under Deposit B. In the interests of completeness I mention them, and illustrate most, in this context as well — and I list them before the MG sherds.

(a)  *Late Geometric.* 446—50, and PLATE 43.
PLATE 43, 61—2. Two fragmentary flat-based cups. Reserved bands on inner and outer lip; added white for concentric circles at either side of the handle.
446. Skyphos, circles on the outer lip; panel below unclear. Not mentioned in Section 4.
447. Skyphos, linked circles on outer lip and cross-hatched panel below. See PLATE 43, 55.
448. Skyphos, vertical dashes on outer lip, panel below with cross-hatched butterfly, dot rosette. See PLATE 43, 57.
449. Skyphos, lozenge on body. Not mentioned in Section 4.
450. Skyphos, dotted lattice on outer lip.

(b)  *SPG III: atticising MG.* 407—51, 65/P64, PLATE 33, 32—5.

*Skyphoi*[30]
  (i)  *Monochrome body*
65/P64 = PLATE 33, 32. Complete profile. Reserved band on outer and inner lip.
451. Substantial piece, band on outer lip, reserved band on inner lip. PLATE 33, 33. Profile of a similar skyphos.
These belong within the MG phase, to judge from the height of the lip.
 (ii)  *Multiple zigzags*
407—12. 407—8 from the same vase, probably not local (creamy surface, dark red paint). 412 may be an Attic import: light brown clay, clear light brown slip, lustrous dark brown paint. All MG.
(iii)  *Vertical chevron panel*
413—18. 418 might be Attic. One fragment unillustrated. MG II.
 (iv)  *Meander*
420—26. 425 has dots on the rim, and is MG II. For the others, MG is the safest attribution.
  (v)  *Sets of vertical lines on the body*
433. There are five other, unillustrated, sherds with this motive, and one could be from a cup. It is possible that these are LG,[31] but perhaps MG II should not be ruled out.
 (vi)  *Miscellaneous*
419. Banded outer lip, uncertain motive on body. MG II?
444. Leaf motive: if part of a quatrefoil, LG. Also an unillustrated sherd with quatrefoil.

*Kraters*
  (i) *Meander*
      429–32. 430–2 from the same vase. MG.
 (ii) *Miscellaneous*
      427. Dogtooth in ancillary zone. Hatching and ? in main zone. MG II?
      434. Cross-hatched diamond flanking verticals. Quite likely not atticising.

*Pyxis*
435. Large knob of lid, may be atticising MG.

*Amphorae*
428. Meander. MG.
443. Verticals and ?meander. MG.
445. Steep chevrons with formal zigzag in ancillary zone. MG II?

*Oinochoai or jugs*
  (i) *Multiple zigzags on body*
      436–39. 437 has an ancillary zone of dots between bands. Also an unillus-
      trated neck fragment with this motive. MG.
 (ii) *Meander on body*
      440–42. Same vase. Fabric, slip and paint could be Attic, but draughtsmanship
      not very good; local atticising more likely. MG.

This is a reasonably substantial body of material; the number of atticising pieces, as
opposed to imports, is impressive, as also is the fact that there are imitations of the
MG II phase. The importance of the material in the sequence and relative chronology
of the SPG Pit and the Levelling Material will be considered below.

*Coarse hand-made ware.* PLATE 22A, 452–66.
The fabric is the same as was found in the Moulds Deposit and in the SPG Pit, but there
were fewer sherds of the relatively fine ware. The dominant shape, as before, is the jug,
but some sherds may be from pithoi. Rims are of varying profile (see 453–5), handles are
flat and broad (see 458), and bases may be flat, raised-flat, or of the ring base type. There
are several examples of incised motives on the body (see 456–7, 461–3).

**Moulds Deposit – SPG Pit – Levelling Material: Stylistic Sequence**
The three deposits, the Moulds, the SPG Pit, and the Levelling Material, are stratigraphically
superimposed, the Moulds Deposit being the lowest, and the distinction between this and
the SPG Pit being particularly sharp (see the section on PLATE 10). There is then a strong
likelihood of a chronological sequence in the pottery. How far is this apparent stylistically?
Allowing for some blurring of the picture due to admixture, in unknown quantity, in the
two upper deposits of earlier material — undeniable in view of the number of joins made
between one deposit and another, and in any case clear from the number of Mycenaean
(and earlier) sherds that can turn up anywhere — the evidence in favour can be summarised
as follows, taking into account also the sequence as derivable from the cemeteries.

In the Moulds Deposit: one example only of the cup with monochrome lip, tentative
and experimental treatment of skyphoi, predominance of high lips for PSC skyphoi,
presence of skyphoi with zigzag(s) on the outer lip, large number of high conical feet,
high proportion of kalathoi with impressed triangles, presence of jug with cutaway neck,
absence of shallow bowls with strap handles and of plate, absence of later constructional

details in amphorae, absence of later decorative system on amphorae and oinochoai, absence of motive of opposed diagonals with unfilled interstices.

The material would, on the analogy of the pottery from the tombs, be datable to the LPG and early SPG I periods.

In the SPG Pit: the cup with monochrome or reserved-band lip common (but so also is the 'zigzag' type), no example of skyphoi with zigzag on the lip, for PSC skyphoi an increase in the number of medium lips, and a very few low ones, circles skyphoi relatively popular and roughly divisible into two types, more evidence for later type of kalathos, presence of shallow bowls with strap handles — but still no example of a plate; amphorae with grooved lips and ridge below lip, hourglass on neck and belly zone decoration for some amphorae and oinochoai, use of motive of opposed diagonals with unfilled interstices.

The extreme chronological range of material could be LPG to early SPG III.

In the Levelling Material: cups much the same as in the SPG Pit, though appreciably fewer with zigzag on the lip, most of the PSC skyphoi now with medium or low lip, and very few indeed with a high one, circles skyphoi less common than in the SPG Pit, shallow bowls as for the SPG Pit, presence of plate fragments, amphorae and oinochoai much as for the SPG Pit, but great scarcity of pyxis fragments.

The material could represent all stages from LPG to SPG III, and the development in the PSC skyphos lips, taken with the appearance of the plate, and possibly the relative scarcity of certain other shapes, indicates the presence of a definitely later stage of SPG III than is visible in the SPG Pit.

Alongside all this, however, the most remarkable feature is the continuance throughout of much the same shapes and decorative system, including individual motives. This statement is, I believe, justified, regardless of the inevitable intrusion of earlier pottery into each of the two later deposits.

The evidence is not as strong as one could wish, but it already seems possible to distinguish clearly the Moulds Deposit from the SPG Pit and the Levelling Material, to conclude that it is the earliest of the three (as of course its stratification indicates), and to assign it to a specific period of use. The separation of the SPG Pit from the Levelling Material, their chronological relationship and respective periods of use, are by no means so easy to determine on the evidence presented — strongly suggestive rather than provable.

There remains one section of the pottery which seems to settle the matter, that is to say the sherds of vases of Attic origin, and those where the local potter has imitated an Attic original. The Moulds Deposit contained no sherds of Attic origin, nor indeed any imitating Attic in any form. The SPG Pit produced three Attic EG II sherds; no atticising fragments were found, but this evidence, when taken with the local pottery, is sufficient for us to conclude that the deposit goes into SPG II (roughly contemporaneous with EG II). The Levelling Material included fragments of at least five Attic vases: one of these is EG II or MG I, two belong somewhere within the MG period, and two are specifically of MG II date. Furthermore, this deposit also contained about fifty atticising sherds, almost all certainly or probably imitating either Attic MG I or (the more frequently, I think) Attic MG II. This is an astonishing number, and must surely suggest, when set against the evidence of the other two deposits, that the material covers the whole known span of the SPG III period, even though some of the sherds are earlier. Also, the absence of such MG I—II pottery, both imported and atticising, from the SPG Pit, allows the inference that that deposit is unlikely to have continued long into SPG III if at all — and that it is earlier than, and distinct from, the Levelling Material.

If these conclusions are correct, they are extremely important for our knowledge of the final stages of Lefkandian SPG, since this sector, sealed as it is by some building of apparently early LG date, provides the only evidence anywhere in Lefkandi where one can follow the course of SPG virtually until its supersession by LG (the cemeteries, it will be found, fell into disuse during the first stage of SPG III).

Before congratulating outselves on this conclusion, however, two possible objections have to be considered. First, the Levelling Material contained a few sherds that are of Late Geometric date — does this not affect our whole conception of the deposit? The answer to this is in the negative: the discovery of a little LG could well be due to human fallibility, in the excavation of a highly complex area, and there were also two small pits dug into it during the LG period, to which it could mostly belong (see discussion of LG Deposit B below in the relevant section).

The second possible objection arises out of the removal of the first: if the LG material is regarded as intrusive from above, why not also the MG imported and atticising sherds? The answer to this lies in the known date of the yard floor and structures built over the Levelling Material, which are not earlier than LG, and even if this were not so, the insignificant number of LG sherds would, I think, lead one to reject the possibility.

## II  XEROPOLIS, AREA 3 (SOUTH) (PLATE 9)

**Area 3 South** (PLATES 23, nos. 494–559; 24, nos. 560–652 and 69/P10; 34, nos. 1 and 2).

This is the only sector of the main excavation, apart from Area 2, where there was a stratified sequence with sufficient material to be helpful stylistically. Three divisions are made in the following account. The first is the pottery from the surface down to the earth floor of a yard, and includes the fill of Pit 10[32]; the second is the contents of the yard floor itself; the third, the fill beneath the yard floor, and above the LH IIIC remains, probably a levelling operation preparatory to the laying of the floor and the erection of the stone building (most of which lies in an area still unexcavated) associated with it (see pp. 17–8).

### 1. *Surface to yard floor and Pit 10* (PLATE 23)

The total number of sherds (not recorded) is likely to have been in the region of a thousand. There was some Grey Minyan and Mycenaean, and one Archaic Black Glaze sherd was noted. A selection of the main sherds is illustrated as follows:

*Cups.* 494–8. 494 is a complete profile of a flat-based monochrome cup with everted lip. 495–6 were the only sherds found of the type with zigzag on the outer lip.

*Cups or Skyphoi.* 499–505. Considerable variation in profile. The straight lip with two bands, 503, may be a late feature; 505 has a very sharply everted lip with reserved bands on the outside. All bodies except for 504 are monochrome.

*Skyphoi.* 506–15, 518–25. 506 may be atticising MG II, if this is an attempt to imitate the Attic horizontal chevrons.[33] 507–15 are PSC: note the central filling of 511; and lips 514–15 are atypical, especially 515, which is convex instead of straight and carinated. 518–24 are from circles skyphoi: on 522 the central circle has apparently been painted over, and 523 has an eight-spoke filling. 525 falls into no category: it has a horizontal scribble and bands on the body.

*Shallow bowls with strap handles.* 516—7, ?526—7. Note the close wavy line on 526.

*Kraters.* 534—6. No comment.

*Plates.* 528—9. 528, straight rim; 529, slightly everted rim.

*Pyxides.* 530—3. 530—1, from the same vase, probably belong to a massive straight-sided pyxis with vertical loop handles; the main design is probably a meander.[34] 532—3 may belong together, and are apparently from a large globular pyxis, though it is unusual for the top of pyxis rims to have decoration.

*Amphorae.* 537—40, 543—9, 551. Rims (note the scribble beneath the rim of 538), neck (551, hourglass — perhaps an oinochoe), neck handles, body sherds (543, massive).

*Oinochoai and Jugs.* 541: jug lip. 542: trefoil lip, barred. 550: probably from a straight-sided jug. 552—5: body sherds (including examples of diagonals with interstices both filled and unfilled). 556: from a closed vase, shape unclear.

*Hand-made.* 557—9. The first two show ridges and impressed decoration; 559 appears to belong to a tripod dish.

The unillustrated material includes further sherds of cups of SPG type, PSC and circles skyphoi, kraters, amphorae, and small closed vases. Much of the material could span the period LPG to SPG II; some sherds are unlikely to be earlier than SPG II (strap-handled bowls, neck with panelled hourglass); the plate fragments probably take us into SPG III, and so certainly would the atticising MG II sherd 506, if correctly interpreted as such.

2. *Yard Floor* (PLATE 24, 560—602). About two hundred sherds retained.

*Cups.* No fragments illustrated:[35] there were five monochrome or banded lips of SPG type, but none with zigzag.

*Skyphoi.* 560—2, 566, 573—4: PSC; rims fairly high or medium; note the 'open' semicircles of 561. 565, 570—1, 575—6, 579, 581: circles skyphoi; 571 has small circles and an atypical lip, 575 has an added central panel, recalling Attic LPG, and 579 may be upside down. 578: either PSC or circles. 563—4, 567—9, 572, 577: other types; varying profiles, all monochrome except for 568 and 577 (perhaps from a shallow bowl?)

*Kraters.* 583—6. 585 not of local fabric; 586 atticising, part of a large pedestal base with dogtooth above the lower edge.

*Closed vases.* 587—602. Mainly semicircles and circles, but note the four horizontal rows of rough wavy line (590), the outlined cross-hatched triangles placed alternately above and below a horizontal band (600), and the diagonals (602). There are two neck sherds with decoration, 592 with a ?meander, probably atticising EG,[36] and 593 with panelled hourglass.

On the basis of 593 and of the krater foot 586 it is reasonable to suppose that the floor was in use at least into SPG II.

3. *Fill under Yard Floor* (PLATE 24, 603—52, 69/P10). Also PLATE 34, 1 (= 69/P10) and 2 (= 69/P43). I do not know the number of sherds recovered. All appear of local fabric.

*Cups*

69/P10. Rest. h. 8.7. Max. d. (at lip) 9.2. Local fabric. The restoration of a high conical foot is surely correct; of the two such feet illustrated (627–8), 627 would have been suitable, though does not belong. LPG.[37]

69/P43. H. 9.6. Max. d. (at lip) 12.2. Local. Handle missing. Unpainted; the low conical foot may be a sign of earliness; the vase is surely not later than LPG.

622–5: from cups with zigzag on the outer lip. No evidence of the later type, unless 629 belongs to one (see below).

*Skyphoi.* 603–4, 609: PSC; rims high or medium; the sets of semicircles on 609 intersect. 605–8, 611–14, 618: circles. Of the four lips, three have broad bands of paint with or without supporting band, one (slightly everted) with narrow band at the top and a narrow band below.[38] Note the Maltese cross filling of 612, and the evidence for panelled design on 606 and 613 – the latter exceptionally fine.[39] 610, 615, 617: PSC or circles skyphoi. Miscellaneous: 626, with a rather heavy rim, has a most unusual cross-hatched body;[40] 629 (d. unknown, so not certainly a skyphos) has two bands on the outer lip, recalling 503 above; 630, a fairly high straight lip, and bellying body with a formal zigzag zone; 631 is monochrome; 632 has a horizontal scribble and some other motive; 634, finally, is a complete profile (h. 7.5, d. c. 11.5) of a ring-based skyphos with gently outflaring lip and a wide panel between the handles – two horizontal scribbles and three bands dividng them.[41]

*Kraters.* 619–21, 633. All have circle motives, 621 with reserved cross filling, 633 with eight-spoke filling and two panels flanking the circles.

*Closed vases.*[42] 635–44, 647–52. Thirteen of the fourteen shoulder and belly sherds have semicircles or circles; note the languettes of 639, the ?verticals of 640, and the central filling of 641. The single exception is 651, which has diagonals supporting a zone of chequerboard and what may be a kind of filled zigzag (see 613?). Two handles (647, jug?; 652,[43] amphora) are shown.

*Wheels.* 645–6. Both have their axles pierced, but differ in shape and decoration. They could have belonged to some object like the toy horse from Athens.[44]

What is the date of the material beneath the yard floor? There is no LG, nor any sign of the developments noted above as characteristic of SPG III and SPG II. On the other hand, traces of any pottery earlier than LPG is – as elsewhere on Xeropolis – completely lacking. So the negative evidence suggests that the range lies within LPG or SPG I or both: but that is not enough.

Most of the shapes and decorative motives are current in both LPG and SPG I. Some, however, are far more likely to be LPG. The combination of zigzag on lip and conical foot for the cup, the plain cup 69/P43, the skyphos with scribble zigzags on the body, the central fillings to the circles on skyphoi of this type – and perhaps even more the presence of a central panel, in view of the closeness to the Attic original.[45] And there is a feeling of experimentation which would accord with the end of LPG, visible for the most part on the open vases, but for the closed found only on the amphora sherds 651.

As against this attribution to LPG, there are three sherds which could be later. First, the somewhat sophisticated herringbone decoration of the amphora handle 652: if the idea came from Attica (likely but not inevitable), then it must be remembered that there is no known example of it there before EG I (see n. 12). Second, the cup or skyphos lip with two bands on it, 629: on present evidence, this is probably an SPG I development. Third, the large fragment of a panelled krater, 633: the rather open technique seems alien to LPG, and I know of no example in that period of an eight-spoke filling to the circles.

This analysis is obviously inconclusive, and one must take into account the overall scarcity of the material available, and the nebulousness of the frontiers between LPG and SPG I. My impression is that the three sherds mentioned above, even if no others, could bring the terminal date of the deposit into SPG I, though so many of the others are or could be pure LPG. Whatever the true answer, this is an important deposit, comparable to that of the Moulds Deposit, and also perhaps to that of the lower fill in the North Channel of Palia Perivolia Cemetery.

## III   XEROPOLIS, AREA 1: POTTERY ASSOCIATED WITH INSCRIBED SHERD, FIND no. 103 (PLATE 22F)

The levels in this region were very telescoped and difficult to distinguish. The basketful of sherds, which included the inscribed sherd find no. 103 (PLATE 69c), was thought to come from a defined stratum, and, because of the importance of this sherd and its context, they were all retained and are considered below.

There were about eighty sherds, fairly evenly divided between open wheel-made, closed wheel-made, and hand-made.

The ten illustrated are with one exception (bottom row left, amphora with semicircles) from open vases. The top left fragment is from an atticising MG skyphos with banded lip and narrow zigzag panel below; next to it is another atticising MG sherd — there are two rows of zigzag. Then comes a sherd of a cup with zigzag on the lip, and at the right of the top row a fragment of a very large skyphos with lip 3 cm high. Of the three in the middle row those to right and left are krater sherds, and the centre one is from a cup (or bowl?) with reserved band on what remains of the lip. The bottom row illustrates a PSC skyphos fragment, a krater sherd to its right, and at the end on the right a bowl with unusual wavy lines motive just below the rim.

None of these sherds is as late as LG, but an unillustrated one may be. It is from the lower neck and top shoulder of an amphora: the neck has a horizontal band in added white, and the shoulder has vertical strokes, also in added white. So far as I know, at Lefkandi this technique is confined to LH IIIC and LG.

## IV   XEROPOLIS, AREA 4 (SOUTH), A SAMPLE LEVEL (PLATE 22E)

This region was eroded and particularly disturbed by pits of different periods. During study it was decided severely to select the pottery, the retained sherds of which are discussed in section VII below, under the heading 'Various Areas'.

During excavation, one level was thought to be a pit but may have been a levelling operation such as took place in Area 2. As was the practice, one basketful of sherds was retained intact as a sample of this level (Trench GG, level 4, basket 323) and it is considered below.

The sherds, totalling just over a hundred, were kept in their entirety. There are seven hand-made fragments, from jugs. The rest, all local, are wheel-made: the open vase sherds (in the majority) are mostly from cups and skyphoi, with a small number from shallow bowls and kraters; for the closed vases, amphorae are well represented, jugs/oinochoae are rather scarce.

Of the fourteen sherds illustrated, at PLATE 22E, those to the left are from open vases, two at the top from shallow bowls with strap handles, four from PSC skyphoi (note the low and incurved lip of one), and one, at the bottom left, from a circles skyphos. For the closed vases there is a fine sherd of a jug/oinochoe with semicircles with central filling, three from amphorae showing circles or semicircles, and two amphora rims. Finally, part of the flat handle of a handmade jug is shown in the top row.

There is nothing distinctively LPG, nor on the other hand any LG. The deposit is likely to fall wholly within the SPG period. The shallow bowl fragments are probably SPG II; the low, incurved skyphos lip, rare at Lefkandi, may belong to an advanced stage of SPG III.


## V    XEROPOLIS, TRIAL W (PLATES 22B and 34, 6–10)

The stratification is described on p. 19 above. Three divisions are made here: surface down to Floor I; a pit dug below this floor;[46] and the make-up of the floor.

### Surface to Floor I (PLATES 22B, 467–480; 34, 9 = 468)

The two vases found on the floor are unhelpful for dating — the re-used base of a pithos and the large hand-made and burnished bowl, mistakenly illustrated among the LG pottery (PLATE 42, 51).

Of the 600 sherds or so, such as were datable belonged to SPG.

Of the fourteen sherds illustrated, 467–73, 475 and 480 are from open vases, 474 and 476–9 from closed vases. Three are conventional local, 473 from a high-lipped PSC skyphos, 476 the shoulder of an amphora, 479 with its opposed diagonals, from an oinochoe or pyxis. Local but unusual are the skyphos sherd 472, with curious ribbing effect and slightly sloping lines that do not seem to be PSC (see PLATE 26, 755), the skyphos lip 475, with unclear vertical decoration below, the amphora fragment 474, which shows a panelled belly and possibly the ends of semicircles brought down through the supporting shoulder band, the lattice motive of 477 (also an amphora), and the inverted dogtooth of the krater sherd 480 (see PLATE 26, 702).

The remaining six are as follows:

467. Skyphos. Banded lip; dot rosette and verticals on body. Clay and slip brown; paint red, perhaps not local. Atticising MG II or LG IA.
468. Krater. Multiple zigzag over ?   Atticising MG.
469. Cup. Monochrome; added white band on lip. LG?
470. Skyphos. Panel with chevrons, dots, and? Possibly Attic MG II; otherwise atticising.
471. Skyphos. Multiple zigzag. MG I. Possibly Attic.
478. Oinochoe. Panel with ?meander. Atticising MG?

### The pit below Floor I (PLATE 22C: 481–5, 487; PLATE 34, 8 (= 481))

About two hundred and fifty sherds, those datable suggesting a picture similar to that of the surface to floor group.

The illustrated sherds show the latest datable material, as follows:

481. Pyxis. Rim and body; on body, meander, hatching and chevrons, ?dots below. Neither local nor Attic. MG II.[47]

482–4. Skyphos. Substantial fragments, showing banded lip, and a framework of vertical and horizontal lines and bands on the body. LG I?.[48]

485. Amphora neck, multiple zigzags in panel. Atticising MG.

487. Krater. Rim and body. Top of rim barred; bands, gear pattern, bands, ?meander. Brown clay, rather metallic dark brown paint. Atticising MG II.

**Make-up of Floor I (PLATE 22D: 488–93; PLATE 34, 10 (= 492))**
No estimate made of number of sherds. No trace of LG, or of Attic or atticising MG: sherds predominantly SPG, but some could belong to an earlier stage than those above the floor.[49]

Of the illustrated sherds, 488 is a circles skyphos with Maltese cross filling, possibly not later than SPG I; 489–91 are from kraters — note the butterfly and verticals motive of 490;[50] 492 is from a large impressed-triangle kalathos, unlikely to be later than SPG I; and 493 is from an amphora with 'open' circles.

## VI    AREA SL (PLATES 28, 29, 35)

The pottery discussed in this section was found on the gently sloping ground N. of Xeropolis (see plan, PLATE 2 and pp. 22–23); all came from the surface. There were five main groups or concentrations of sherds, A–E.

*Group C*[51]
This may be disregarded, as there were very few sherds, and these revealed nothing of interest.[52]

*Group B*
Some five hundred sherds were recovered. The emphasis was on open vases, but closed vases were also well represented. Many of the sherds, especially of amphorae, were burnt.

*Open.* Mostly from flat-based cups and shallow bowls with strap handles and slightly everted lip. There were thirty-six everted cup lips, usually monochrome outside, only rarely with a reserved band; and forty-nine handles, most from cups and monochrome. Ninety-two lips belonged to shallow bowls; the fifty flat bases are either from cups or from shallow bowls. PLATE 29A illustrates two substantial fragments of shallow bowls: top left, showing the typical handle zone decoration of two reserved bands; second row right, the underbase and lower body.

In addition, a surprisingly large number of complete profiles of these two shapes were able to be made up. For the cups, eight more or less complete ones were assembled: see 70/P5 and 6 on PLATES 28 and 35.[53] For the shallow bowls there are eleven complete profiles: see 70/P3 and 4 on PLATES 28 and 35.

No cups with zigzag on the lip were found, nor any conical feet. Other types of open vase are rare: only two ring bases such as would be appropriate to skyphoi; no certain instance of a PSC skyphos — just one sherd with arcs that may belong either to a PSC or to a circles skyphos. Krater sherds were also extremely rare (see PLATE 29A, second row left). And there was just one fragment of a kalathos with impressed triangles, PLATE 29A, top right.

*Closed.* Amphora sherds (many joins made) were plentiful, but few of these could be certainly assigned to the belly-handled variety — for example, only two of the fifteen handles, and the rims[54] were those normally associated with the neck-handled amphora. The massive type of amphora was not represented. For decoration, the dark ground system predominated for the lower body and the neck. The range of motives was small, the most favoured being semicircles for the shoulder, and circles for the belly (in such cases belonging to belly-handled amphorae). Notable also are twelve sherds, two or three from the same vase, with belly decoration of opposed diagonals with unfilled interstices, and two sherds showing panelled hourglass on the neck — all characteristic of the medium-sized dark ground neck amphora.

Jugs and oinochoai were relatively few, though it must be remembered that one cannot always distinguish between a medium to small amphora and a fairly large jug or oinochoe. There was no doubt, however, about the two trefoil lips found.

A selection of closed vase fragments is shown on the lower three rows of PLATE 29A. Most belong to dark ground amphorae. Note the very unusual motive on the neck handle, a steep zigzag above horizontal lines; the fine rim with the start of some decoration on the neck which is not an hourglass panel; the hourglass panel next to it; and the combination of semicircles on the shoulder with diagonals on the belly, in the middle row of the three.[55]

### Groups A and D

So closely adjacent that they may be discussed together. As for B, about five hundred sherds, of which only twenty-five came from D. As opposed to B, closed vase sherds (a considerable number of which showed signs of burning) were in the majority.

*Open.* In complete contrast to B, cups and shallow bowls were extremely rare.[56] Nevertheless, a complete profile of one of each shape emerged from the sherds collected. The cup (70/P7, PLATES 28 and 35) came from D; it is flat-based, with a fairly low everted rim; apart from two reserved bands on the outer lip, the vase is monochrome outside. The fragments, mostly joining, of the shallow bowl from A are shown on PLATE 29B, lower right; the design of vertical lines in the handle zone is distinctly unusual — and the same motive continues over the (unillustrated) handle.

As to other open shapes, skyphos sherds were few, but there were three examples of the PSC type. Kraters were also relatively uncommon, but they provided the only evidence at Lefkandi of a virtually complete profile (70/P1, PLATES 28 and 35) — the foot, unfortunately, was not recovered; the shape, and the body decoration (three sets of circles divided by verticals), are similar to those of two kraters from Marmariani.[57] There was also a ribbed conical krater foot (PLATE 29B, top right), probably Attic of EG II or MG I date; and a fine unillustrated body piece with circles flanking vertical diamonds encaged in vertical lines.

*Closed.* Most of the sherds[58] belonged to dark ground neck-handled amphorae of medium size. The situation here is similar to that of Group B, with the probably accidental exception that there were fewer examples of semicircles and circles and more (twenty-two) with opposed diagonals with unfilled interstices. Many joins were made, the most notable resulting in an almost complete amphora with opposed diagonals on the belly (70/P2, PLATES 28 and 35). There was also a fine fragment of rim (ridged) and neck with panelled hourglass (PLATE 29B).

The few belly-handled amphorae were, so far as one can tell, light ground. They include two joining belly sherds showing 'open' circles flanked by verticals (PLATE 29B), and several non-joining sherds from an amphora with double rough zigzag on the belly.

Many sherds may have come from either type of amphora. Some may indeed belong to jugs or oinochoai, but the smaller closed vases were less plentiful: one trefoil lip, a few shoulder fragments with semicircles, and two non-joining sherds of a jug or oinochoe with outlined cross-hatched triangle on the shoulder, and then three supporting bands below this, before one comes to the monochrome belly and lower body.[59]

### Group E

Only twenty sherds were retained. Ten of these, three joining, came from an Attic krater of MG I date (PLATE 29C for six).[60] It has, first, a panelled body zone, with vertical lines and zigzag framing a meander — note the curious variation of vertical and diagonal filling on the arms of the meander;[61] then, either in sequence or below,[62] and set centrally, multiple zigzags (five rows) supported by three horizontal bands, and dogtooth in a narrow zone below these; the whole design is supported by two further horizontal bands, and two others relieve the monochrome area of the lower body. The sherds show signs of burning.

As well as these there are two other krater sherds (one a foot), a low conical foot from a small open vase, five amphora sherds (including one with opposed diagonals, one with circles, and a ridged rim), a jug/oinochoe base, and a rim of a coarse handmade vase.

### Commentary

It seems clear that in all cases[63] we are dealing with settlement material. In addition to the pottery discussed above, the records make mention of much coarse ware or many cooking pot sherds in each group. Other indications are: the presence of krater fragments, the concentration in Group B of cups and shallow bowls (the latter not yet found in tombs), the frequency of amphorae of medium size, and the small number of jugs and oinochoai. This is a distribution which would suit neither tomb nor pyre.

Two of the groups, B, and A with D, have much in common. Each has a number of almost complete, or at least restorable, vases — far more than have been found in any other Lefkandian settlement deposit before Late Geometric. Second, the same types of vase, and of the same style, are found in both. This is particularly clear in the case of the dark ground neck-handled amphora with its characteristic motives. It is not quite so clear for the cups and shallow bowls that are so popular in Group B, but at least A and D contain a near complete example of each shape, which must therefore be typical of the group. These three types constitute the main evidence for homogeneity; other types of vase, not so popular, in no way contradict it. Third, it is worth noting that each group contained many sherds that were burnt, or showed traces of burning.

These groups are not far from each other, and it is reasonable that they should display similar features. Group E lies at some distance to the North, but here as well one can argue for links with the first two, even though it was a small group. The fragments of the Attic MG I krater can be linked with the pedestal krater foot of Group A, also Attic and probably of the same period; and another stylistic connexion is recognisable in the sherd from E of a dark ground amphora with opposed diagonals on the belly. Group E also shares in common with the others a number of burnt sherds and some coarse hand-made ware.

The fact that all this material was collected from the surface, and not a product of systematic excavation, lessens its value unless one can identify a closely corresponding stage within the excavated area of the settlement or in the cemeteries. This can be done to a certain extent. From the settlement on Xeropolis, a range of identical shapes appears in the SPG Pit and in the Levelling Material, but not in the Moulds Deposit, so we can, on present evidence, eliminate an LPG, and probably an early SPG I, stage of occupation. From the cemeteries, although the shallow bowl is altogether lacking, the development of the dark ground amphora would put the stage represented in the SL area not earlier than SPG II; and the closest comparative material is observable in S 59 and 59A, which belongs to early SPG III. It may be deduced that the occupation of the SL area finished early in SPG III; and the presence of Attic MG I is of importance here. There is no material that can be assigned any later date. The surface nature of the finds in an advantage in this instance, for had there been later occupation it is likely that some trace of it would have been recognised.

## VII  XEROPOLIS, VARIOUS AREAS (PLATES 25–7: 653–818, 65/P77; PLATE 34, 3–7, 11–12)

Most of the other levels on Xeropolis contained too little pottery to be useful stylistically, so their sherd contents, insofar as LPG–SPG III is concerned, will be taken as a whole. In general the same vase types, in respect both of shape and decoration, were represented as in the Area 2 material and in the other sectors dealt with separately. I confine myself to a discussion of the small selection illustrated and drawn: some are included because they are fine specimens of their type, others because they belong to a rare shape or have some unusual feature. In addition, the very few Attic sherds, those imitating the Attic style, and the rare sherds which are neither local nor Attic, have almost all been illustrated.

### The Cup
The main types are adequately illustrated elsewhere, and I have therefore not included any sherds in this selection, with the exception of the small conical foot 660. Conical feet 662–3 could also be from cups.

### The Skyphos
Conical foot 661 is probably from a skyphos, and perhaps 662–3 as well (see above). No skyphoi with zigzag on the outer lip were identified.

### PSC skyphoi 653–9[64]
There is the usual variation in the height of the lip. Unusual features are the 'open' semi-circles of 653–4, the hourglass filling of 656 (see P 3,14), and the three sets of PSC of 655,[65] a sherd also unusual in having three supporting bands below the PSC.

### Circles skyphoi 664–76, ?687. See also PLATE 34, 3(= 664) and 7 (= 667).
There are two exceptions to the usual gently outcurving rim: 667, a very large skyphos, has a pronouncedly outturned lip; and 664 has a lip which would be more appropriate to a PSC skyphos. The latter piece, together with 665 from the same vase, is interesting for two other reasons: the circles have reserved cross filling,[66] a feature which when taken with the type of lip suggests an early and experimental vase; and it provides the closest parallel I know of to the skyphos found at Amathus in Cyprus.[67]

Four other sherds with central circle fillings are shown: 670, 672,[68] 675 and 676.

670 is also notable for a central panel, verticals flanking a cross-hatched design;[69] and 673 has a vertical line flanking the circles.

For the lower body, the few instances illustrated (665—6, 668—9) show that it can be banded or monochrome.

I have included 687 as a possible example of a circles skyphos on the basis of the zigzag below the bands, as this is a feature frequently encountered on Attic LPG skyphoi with circles.

*Other skyphoi* 682—6, 689, 755—6, 758—9.
682—3 are of the type with zigzag in a narrow body panel. 684—5, quite different in shape from each other, are monochrome.[70] 686, with its high everted and banded lip, and mono-chrome body, has no parallel known to me. 689,[71] from a fairly large open vase, has a curious design, including a gear pattern which probably puts it late in SPG. 755, with its ribbing and verticals, recalls 472 from Trial W; this and 756 are unclassifiable. The cross-hatched panel of 758 could conceivably come from a circles skyphos, but on 759 the cross-hatching seems too continuous for a panel, and the lip, with its two bands, may suggest a late piece.[72]

*The Krater* 688, 700—24
Structurally, there is nothing unusual in the range of rims except for the multiple ridges of 706; most have the flat square projecting rim. No sherd with moulded ridge below the rim is illustrated, but there were some. One high flaring base, 724, is shown.

For decoration, the most common motive, as elsewhere, was concentric circles, of which only a few examples are shown. Of these, the small circles of 722 are most unusual, and the dotted fringe to the circles of 720 is not at all common at Lefkandi.[73] The circles of 700 have a filling of uncertain type, but there is no doubt about the reserved cross filling on 721.

As to other motives, the zigzags beneath the rim of 701—2 are very uncommon for a krater, and the inverted dogtooth of 702 is rare on any shape.[74] 711 has (presumably) opposed diagonals with filled interstices, and 712 has a lambda ornament.[75] The motives used in panels are mostly familiar enough from other contexts — the cross-hatched rectangles and diamonds, the hatched and solid diamonds, the chequers — but 708—9 and 716 exhibit a most unusual panelled design.[76] 713 has what looks like a battlement motive, and that of 704 could be either a battlement or diminishing rectangles.[77] Note finally the remarkable interlocking semicircles of 723.[78]

These krater sherds add something, but not a great deal, to our existing knowledge.

*The Plate* 677—681
Three varieties of rim represented: incurved (677), straight (678), and slightly everted (679—81). 678 has a reserved band enclosing dots at the top of the inner rim. All have PSC.

*The Shallow Bowl with strap handles* 65/P77, 690—5. See PLATE 34, 4.
65/P77 is complete, of the type with incurved rim and banded panel; 690 (complete profile) is similar. 691—3 have slightly everted rims with zigzag between the handles. 694 is unusual: the lip is high and vertical, with paint round the top (dots along the inside) and a double zigzag on the outside; the monochrome body falls away at a sharp angle.[79] 695 is not a handle, but a body sherd from a shallow bowl of uncertain type, with decoration to which I can find no parallel.

*The Kalathos 696—9*
All of the impressed-triangle type. No sherd of the monochrome and/or banded type was identified.

*The Kantharos 725—7?*
725 and 726 are from the same vase, and the small excrescence rising above the rim of 725 suggests that it could be a kantharos; the motive is a battlement, possibly but not certainly imitating Attic. I have included 727 with these two on the grounds of the similar decoration; the shape is quite uncertain. These are very difficult to date, but early in SPG is possible.

*The Amphora 771, 774—94*
The sherds illustrated (a very small proportion of the whole) provide few surprises. Only one rim is shown (774, with ridges), and no example of base or handle. For the neck, 778—80 have the panel enclosing an hourglass motive (assumed for 780), and 777 is a fine example of a double zone of rays from a really massive amphora.[80] Seven sherds show the shoulder decoration. 776 and 787[81] have full circles; 776 is probably a very late piece — note the slapdash way in which the circles have been drawn, and the possibility that the same multiple brush was used for the wiggly lines. The other five sherds have the more usual semicircles: 784 has no fewer than twenty arcs, nd the two sets intersect over nine of these; 785 has eighteen arcs, but this sherd is remarkable rather for the tantalising object in the upper corner, which looks extraordinarily like the tip of a spear; 782 has an hourglass central filling, and 794 a tongue filling; 775 also has a filling, possibly just two verticals, and certainly unusual.

The ten remaining sherds provide examples of belly motives. There are two fo full circles, 783 and 791, and two of opposed diagonals, 792—3. Four, 771, and 788—90, display cross-hatched rectilinear designs, and the last three are from massive amphorae.[82] 786, with its arrangement of cross-hatching, dogtooth, and diamond, probably also belonged to a very large amphora. There remains 781, a small fragment showing panels of vertical lines enclosing diamonds, with perhaps the start of an arc at one side.

*The Oinochoe/Jug 795—808, 810, and PLATE 34, 6.*
Illustration concentrates on the shoulder area, where subsidiary decoration is usually to be found. 795 and 799 show semicircles with central filling, hourglass for 795, and for 799 a curious and not entirely clear design, not unsimilar to that of 775. 798[83] and 801 have semicircles or circles — probably the former. In the case of 798 the preserved part of the neck is unpainted except for a band at the base and a rudimentary scribble above it. Similar close zigzags or scribbles constitute the shoulder decoration of 796—7 (that of 797 recalling the MPG system), and are also found on what may be the belly of a small closed vase, 807. A zigzag is the subsidiary zone to what may be a meander (both on the belly) of 805.[84] 808 has a formal zigzag with three supporting bands, 804 a cross-hatched motive (probably on the shoulder). 802—3 have dogtooth on the belly, in the case of 803 surmounted by a sort of diagonal chequer design. 810 has an elaborate and unparalleled set of motives on the shoulder, hatched diamonds flanked by panels with butterfly motive, with an intervening feature of parallel horizontal lines on one side, to fill up a gap. 800, the mouth of an oinochoe, is shown because it is not a true trefoil, but just pinched in; 806 is the lower stump of a handle with very unusual decoration of cross-hatching. PLATE

34, 6, finally, shows the flat base and part of a sharply angular body, monochrome, from a jug or oinochoe.[85]

## The Pyxis 764?, 809.

809 comes from a straight-sided barrel pyxis, a type most unusual at Lefkandi.[86] 764 could be from an amphora, but the cross-hatched swastika has a good parallel on the globular pyxis P 47,15 (PLATE 151).[87] It is possible that other instances of belly decoration on relatively small closed vases may come from pyxides (as 805?).

## Incised sherds 813—6

813, perhaps from a vertical-handled amphoriskos, is in the Black Slip ware, with typical combed and incised decoration. 814 is from an open vase: the paint is dark mauve on the outside, black inside. 815, also from an open vase, has light brown clay and worn black paint. 816, from a closed vase, is painted black; the zigzag is slightly indented, with incised grooves above and below.

## Coarse hand-made ware

(a) PLATE 34, 5, 11 (65/P11) and 12. These show, in the order given, a shallow dish and two jugs.

(b) 811—12, 817—18. 811 shows a ?jug with vertical side handle; 812 illustrates a rope ridge. 817—18 are oddities: 817, with its many perforations, could be part of a strainer, while 818, 1.5 cm thick, might perhaps be a fragment of a brick.

No date is assignable, except that they are post-Mycenaean.

## Attic and atticising EG II—MG. All known sherds illustrated.

### Open

(a) *Meander* 728—45. With the exception of the four described below, all are certainly or probably from skyphoi. 737 and 744 could be Attic, the rest are atticising — note the zigzag on the lower limb of 728, and possible instances of a hook meander (e.g. 728—9, 745) which are likely to be MG II rather than MG I.[88] For the four exceptions; the ancillary zones of 731 (multiple zigzags), 732 (uncertain), and 739 (gear pattern) suggest that they are krater sherds — 739 may be Attic; and 738, with dots above bands on the rim, and hook meander, could be from an Attic MG II kantharos.

(b) *Multiple zigzags*[89] 746—9. 746—8 from skyphoi, 748 being probably Attic. 749, with a further zone above the zigzags, may be from a krater.

(c) *Vertical chevrons.* 751—4. All from local skyphoi, atticising MG II.[90]

(d) *Other motives* 750, 757, 760—2. 750 and 757 are from skyphoi; the dots below the lip of 750 suggest MG;[91] 757, with its high banded lip and rectilinear motive on the body (note the rather elementary rosett) is not, I would think, earlier than MG II.[92] 760 might be from a krater; 762 certainly is, and may be Attic.[93] 761 could be from a kantharos: the gadroon motive is first found in Attica in MG I, but as used here is probably later.[94]

## Closed. 763, 765—70, 772—3

These I take in order, as being few. 763 is the rim of a local atticising MG II tankard.[95] 765 may be from the neck of an atticising EG II or MG I oinochoe. 766 comes from a small closed vase; the ancillary zone of close zigzag may suggest an MG date, and clay, paint, and draughtsmanship would permit an Attic origin. 767 is probably from an amphora;

if atticising, the row of dots suggests MG. 768 shows part of a panelled amphora neck; the multiple zigzag could indicate Attic influence, but the total composition is unclear. The system of decoration on the jug sherd 769 recalls that of 768, and both (note the enclosed dot) recall that of 757 above. 770 comes from the neck of an oinochoe, possibly Attic, and the hook meander suggests MG II. 772 is a fragment of the upper body and lip of an Attic MG pyxis.[96] 773, finally, is also from a pyxis, not Attic, but local atticising MG.

## RETAINED LEVELS

Sample baskets of sherds from important levels retained with no, or minimal, sorting. The purpose is explained in the Introduction to Section 2.

Area 2 Pit 2 (SPG I–II)

Basket 746 in box titled 'From bottom of SPG Pit. AA E. Ext levels 7 + 7A'
Basket 739 in box titled 'From SPG Pit. AA E. Ext levels 5B + C + D'

The SPG III Levelling Material. Area 2, section level 4 on PLATE 10.

Baskets 83–4 in box titled 'SPG Levelling Material. AA level 5'
Basket 730 in box titled 'SPG Levelling Material. AA E. Ext level 5A'

Area 4 South, a probable SPG Fill, discussed in Section 3, part IV.

Basket 323 in box titled 'SPG Pit. GG level 4'

# Section 4

# The Late Geometric Pottery

JOHN BOARDMAN with MARTIN PRICE

## 1. INTRODUCTION

The LG pottery from the excavations was initially sorted, selected and catalogued by Dr. Martin J. Price who is also responsible for many of the photographs used here. The final selection and presentation of the material has fallen to the present writer whose firsthand experience of the material is partial and recent.

All the pieces are from the settlement and no LG graves have been found. Inevitably, therefore, the material is very fragmentary with the exception of a number of restorable vases recovered from limited areas of the last floors of the main period of occupation, the 'desertion' deposits. This pottery is listed separately (Deposits A: 1–51). Within LG there were relatively few clear earlier deposits and of these three have been chosen for separate listing (Deposits B–D: nos. 52–102). The remainder of the pottery has been classified by shape in Section 4 and it is here that a general discussion of the pottery from both deposits and elsewhere is given. In Section 4 the treatment is discursive rather than by catalogue. This is in the interests of both economy and clarity since it should prove sufficient to identify and assess the major classes found at Lefkandi. The same classes are better represented in Eretria in the Swiss excavations and further judgement on the full significance of the Euboean LG styles had better wait upon the completion of their excavations and publication. I acknowledge gladly their kindness and liberality in allowing me to see their finds and I owe Angelos Choremis knowledge of some important groups of LG from Chalcis. The fullest recent study of Euboean LG is by Coldstream in *GGP* chapter 7 to which can be added his article on the Cesnola Painter in *BICS* 18 (1971) 1–15 (on the painter see also below, Section 5b), Miss Andreiomenou's publication of pottery from Eretria in *AE* 1975, 206–29 and the preliminary reports and publications of the Swiss excavations at Eretria in *AntK* and in the *Eretria, Fouilles et Recherches* series.

## 2. THE POTTERY: APPEARANCE AND PRESENTATION

Virtually all the LG pottery from Lefkandi is of Euboean manufacture, but it is not yet possible to declare which if any of it was made locally. This is likely to be true of much, since fine clay beds, still in use, lie adjacent to the site in the lower valley of the river Lelas, and analysis has demonstrated the similarity between the clays of these beds and those of the ancient wares of Lefkandi.[1] The quality of the fired clay is very high, comparable with Attic. It is free from obvious impurities, such as mica. Firing at a high temperature produces a good, clean biscuit which varies in colour from a pale yellow-brown, the most normal colour among the LG sherds, to a darker brown, usual in the earlier pottery, to the clear orange-red familiar in Attica.[2]

The paint usually has a somewhat matt finish, which distinguishes it from the best Attic, and the black often has a touch of blue which gives it a metallic look and oxidises to red with the slightest misfiring. When used over a thick slip, as it is commonly in the later LG, the paint tends to peel away rather easily. On earlier pieces the paint looks more Attic with some sheen, often a fairly deep black, and on these the slip is less frequently used.

A robust white or creamy slip is used on many of the finer vases. On the rest it may be thinner and chalky in consistency or amount to hardly more than a pale self-slip. The added white is of different consistency and good colour. 253 and 295 are exceptional for their polished orangey ground.

Details of paint and slip will be given only for the pieces listed from the deposits in Section 3. The dimensions of complete or important vases and fragments is stated. For others illustrated in the Plates the scale is approximately 1:2 or 1:3 unless a scale appears beside them or dimensions are specified in the text (in centimetres).

## 3. DESCRIPTION OF SELECT DEPOSITS

Certain deposits, designated A to D, have been selected for separate listing. A consists of pottery found in desertion deposits, B and D are groups sealed below structures or floors in use at the time of the desertion, and are referred to as 'penultimate deposits', and C is the fill of a pit, possibly still open when the site was abandoned.

A. (1–51) The 'desertion deposits' from the floors of two buildings abandoned in LG. Nos. 10–11, 36, 38, 44 and 50 are from Trial Z (for which see pp. 19–22): the remainder are from the LG house in Area 1 (for which see pp. 13–14 and PLATE 8a where their find spots are plotted).

B. (52–76) Pottery from Area 2 stratified below the latest LG yard floor and immediately above the SPG III Levelling Material — mostly from level 3 on PLATE 10, above SPG level 4. Included with this are the contents of Pits 2A and 3.

Pit 2A (PLATE 10 level 5) contained, with vase 71, LG sherds 54 (3rd sherd), 57, 61, 68 and 334, to which should be added from PLATE 20 nos. 402, 434 and 448 (= LG 57). Since part of 61 was found in the next basket (digging level 5A basket 730) PLATE 20 nos. 449 and 450 from this level, and possibly 446, are probably from uncleared parts of the same pit.

Pit 3 (PLATE 8b), which lay below LG structures, contained vase 52 and sherds 53 and 74.

C. (77–87) The lower fill of a pit, Area 3, Pit 11 on PLATE 11, which may have remained open until the abandonment. The lower fill of a similar pit, Area 4, Pit 13, has not been listed but its contents included nos. 168, 200, 204–5, 227, 251, 281, 295 and 312 as well as PG/SPG no. 772.

D. (88–102) The fill of Pit 6 in Area 2 (PLATE 11), which was covered by LG structures; see p. 17 for discussion.

**DEPOSITS A** (the 'desertion' deposits) (1–51 PLATES 36–42 and 60–1)
1. (PLATE 60) *Skyphos-kotyle* fr. D. c. 11. Red-brown paint on pale white slip. White line within the lip.
2. (PLATE 60) *Skyphos* D. 14.5, H. 9.2. Black paint on white slip. Three reserved bands in lip. *Preliminary Report* fig. 72; *Dialoghi di Archeologia* 1969, fig. 29c.
3. *Skyphos* D. 12, H. 7.5. Black paint on pale grey slip. Reserved band in lip.
4. *Skyphos* D. 14.4, H. 9.3. Blue-black paint on buff ground. Sextuple brush.
5. *Skyphos* D. 16.8, H. 9.4. Black to red paint on white slip. Four reserved bands in lip. Sextuple brush. *Dialoghi di Archeologia* 1969, fig. 29b.
6. *Skyphos* frr. D. c. 15. Orange-brown paint on white slip. Sextuple brush.
7. *Skyphos* fr. D. c. 16. Red-brown paint on white slip. Three reserved bands in lip.
8. (PLATE 60) *Skyphos* D. 15.5, H. 9.3. Black-brown paint on pale white slip. Three reserved bands in lip.
9. *Skyphos* D. 13, H. 6.5. Black to red paint on buff ground. Two reserved bands in lip.
10. (PLATE 60) *Skyphos* D. 15. 3, H. 9.8. Black-brown paint on yellowish white slip. Four reserved bands in lip. Some fragments are burnt. Sextuple brush. *GGP* pl. 41b; *Preliminary Report* fig. 73.
11. *Skyphos* fr. D. c. 15. Black to red paint on white slip.
12. *Skyphos* fr. Black to red paint on white slip.
13. *Skyphos* fr. D. 13.6. Red-brown paint on white slip. White wavy lines on lip and below the handle zone. Three reserved bands in lip and two wavy lines in white lower within the bowl with a reserved band between them.
14. (PLATE 60) *Skyphos* D. 17, H. 8.4. Black-brown paint on buff ground. White for the wavy line on lip, the heart of the dotted oval and the fill of the double diamond. Three reserved bands in lip.
15. *Skyphos* frr. D. c. 15. As the last.
16. (PLATE 60) *Skyphos* D. 12.8, H. 6.5. Red-brown paint on pinkish brown ground. White for the wavy line on lip, and, faintly, for the heart of the dotted oval and the fill of the double diamond. Two to three reserved bands in lip. *Preliminary Report* fig. 74.
17. (PLATE 60) *Kotyle* fr. D. c. 23. Brown-black paint on white slip. Groups of bars on the reserved inner edge of the lip. Butterfly; hatched body of a bird to right with three dots above.
18. (PLATE 60) *Cup* D. 11.2. The foot is missing. Black paint on white slip. Reserved band in lip.
19. *Cup* D. 11.7, H. 6.2. Dull black paint. White lines on the handle, crossing at the top.
20. *Cup* frr. As the last.
21. *Cup* fr. As the last.
22. *Cup* fr. As 19, with three incised lines just below the lip, and all painted, in and out.
23. (PLATE 60) *Tankard* D. 8.5, H. 8.9. Black-brown paint on white slip. Cross on the handle. Unpainted within but for a band in the lip.
24. (PLATE 60) *Tankard* D. 8, H. 11. The handle is missing. Black paint on yellowish white ground. Unpainted within but for two bands in the lip.
25. (PLATE 60) *Deep skyphos* D. 9.8, H. 7.8. Black-brown paint on buff slip. Unpainted within but for five bands in the lip.
26. (PLATE 61) *Deep skyphos* (?) H. pres. 6.1. Black paint on light brown ground. The upper break must be at the lip, with three bands on the otherwise unpainted interior.
27. *Kalathos* D. 22.8, H. 13.5. Black-brown paint on yellow-brown slip; burnt on one side. Pierced by two holes at one side. Three hoops under the plain foot. Seven groups of six multiple-brush strokes vertical on the lip. The upper wall carries eight deep grooves. Painted within. Sextuple brush.
28. *Skyphos-krater* D. 29, H. 25.2. Black-brown paint on white slip. Three to four reserved bands in the lip. Double handles with vertical quadruple wavy lines and lateral dashes beneath them. Panels divided by eight lines; hatched quatrefoil with crossed diamond fill; cross-hatched diamond with corner dots; bird to left with crossed diamond above back, rows of dots below and before body. Bands and plain-painted below.

29. *Krater* D. 18, H. 21.1. Black paint on orange-buff ground. Top of lip and interior painted. Double handles with strap to lip. Five grooves on stem. Sextuple brush.
30. (PLATE 61) *Miniature krater* D. 9.8, H. pres. 5.4. Black paint on cream slip. Reserved band in the lip with groups of seven bars. Single loop handles with a strap, decorated with a cross and bars, to the lip. The base (pedestal?) is missing.
31. *Krater* fr. Black-brown paint on buff ground. Vertical panel lines at the left. A horse to left with a manger, a bird and dots below, an axe above.
32. *Krater* fr. of foot D. 24, H. pres. 15. Black-red paint. Bands and six grooves on the stem.
33. *Krater* fr. of body. Black-brown paint on white slip. A panel with a bird with raised bent wing. In the field dot clusters and a cross-hatched traingle.
34. *Krater* fr. of lip and shoulder. D. c. 28. Black paint on white slip. Vertical bars on the lip. In the panel a wavy line edged with dots and neat dot rosettes with seven-line border.
35. (PLATE 61) *Oinochoe* H. 18.6. Black-brown paint on white slip. Partly burnt. *Preliminary Report* fig. 76; *BICS* xviii, pl. 13f.
36. *Oinochoe* H. 26.3. Black-brown paint on white slip. Partly burnt. The handle is missing. *GGP* pl. 41c; *Preliminary Report* fig. 75.
37. *Oinochoe* H. 24.7. Red-brown paint on buff ground. Sextuple (only five completed) brush lines in the panel on the neck.
38. *Oinochoe* fr. H. 7. Coarsely made and painted. Lip and handle missing. Brown paint, four reserved bands on the body.
39. *Amphora* fr. of neck. H. 12.4. Black-brown paint on pink-buff slip. Axe painted on the plain neck. By the right break graffito *alpha*.
40. *Fenestrated foot* fr. D. c. 9, pres. 4.8. Red paint on yellow-white ground. Banded. Three rectangular (once four?) fenestrations.
41. *Amphora* fr. Red paint on white slip. Added white for wavy line below bands.
42. (PLATE 61) *Lid handle* (?) in the form of a skyphos. H. 4.5, D. 6. The handles are broken away. Burnt. Black paint on white slip. Two reserved bands in lip. Broken from a larger object with a plain interior, possibly a lid but the surface is roughly finished without wheel-marks beneath.
43. (PLATE 61) *Plain jar* H. 30.5. Handmade. Half of the lip and shoulder missing, so it is not clear whether there was a handle. Light brown clay with horizontal burnishing. Triple wavy lines incised at lip and shoulder, and three vertically. Two mastoi on the shoulder.
44. *Plain jar* H. c. 47, D. of base 23.5, max. D. c. 50. Half the upper body and fragments of base preserved. Coarse red-brown clay. Rows of incised crosses at the lip and shoulder, where there are also mastoi. Vertical burnishing on the neck.
45. *Plain hydria* H. 41.5.
46. *Plain amphora* D. of lip 10.5, H. c. 22. Black paint, mainly gone. Handmade with marks of burnishing.
47. *Plain oinochoe* fr. D. of lip, c. 5.5. Handmade, highly micaceous clay. Apparently a cutaway neck.
48. (PLATE 61) *Plain tripod vase* fr. H. pres. 24, D. of base 32. Handmade, brown clay, burnished, burnt within.
49. *Plain cooking jug* frs. Handmade, highly micaceous clay. Several pieces from jugs with plain strap handles, one with finger impression at its base.
50. *Plain jar* frs. From several vessels, none with a complete profile. Decoration includes incised herring-bone up a strap handle; zigzags or crosses just below out-turned lips; and several body fragments, one with a raised flat band, decorated with oblique impressions made by the blunt tips of a comb-like instrument (see 331, 333, 335 for clearer examples).
51. Mistakenly included; it is from an SPG context, see pp. 000–000.

**DEPOSITS B (52–76: PLATES 43–4)**
52. (PLATE 62) *Skyphos* D. 11, H. 6.8. Red-brown paint on cream ground. Reserved band in lip.
53. *Skyphos* frr. with banded lips and panels with bird, crossed diamond and dot rosette; double cross with dots, dots by handle.
54. *Skyphos* frr. with concentric circles on the lip and panels with hatched quatrefoil with dot rosettes; birds with dot rosettes.
55. *Skypos* fr. with linked concentric circles on lip and a cross-hatched panel.
56. *Skyphos* fr. with linked blobs on the lip.
57. *Skyphos* frr. with dashes on the lip, dots by the handles, panel with cross-hatched butterfly.

58. *Skyphos* fr. Black-brown paint. Painted outside, reserved band in the lip. The flaring profile is close to that of the skyphoi with slip-filled ornament (187–197).
59. *Skyphos* frr. of body with panels with birds, hatched butterfly.
60. *Kantharos* fr. Black paint on cream slip. Dots on lip; panels; reserved band in lip. Handle break to left.
61. (PLATE 62) *Cup* D. 12, H. 6.8. Black-brown paint. Reserved bands in and out of lip, painted handle. Added white for concentric circles at either side of the handle.
62. *Cup* fr. of rim and wall, as the last.
63. *Cup* frr. with multiple-brush patterns on the walls.
64. *Krater* fr. Black-brown paint on grey ground. Chequer.
65. *Krater* fr. Black paint on white slip. Cross-hatched diamond; teeth.
66. *Krater* fr. Black paint on white slip. Panel with dotted wheel and star.
67. *Dinos* fr. Lines interrupted by bar.
68. *Krater* fr. Black paint on cream ground. Frieze of alternate groups of upright wavy and straight lines. Sextuple brush.
69. *Krater* foot fr. Ribbed pedestal and part of bowl.
70. *Fr. of open vessel* D. c. 12. Red-brown paint on white slip. Tall straight lip with three reserved bands in. Cross-hatched diamonds.
71. *Amphora* H. 33.1. Black-brown paint on yellow-brown micaceous clay. Slight base ring. A painted crescent 'hangs' from each handle base.
72. *Amphora* handle fr. Black paint on white slip. Barred.
73. *Amphora* (?) fr. Black paint. Slashed raised moulding.
74. *Amphora* or *Pyxis* (?) fr. Red paint on cream slip. Dot rosettes and trailers from the panels, divided by a strip of vertical Ms.
75. *Amphora* (?) fr. Vertical, cross-hatched diamonds between lines.
76. *Amphora* (?) fr. Black paint on white slip. Frieze of linked blobs.

**DEPOSIT C (77–87: PLATES 44–5)**
77. *Skyphos* fr. Black paint on white slip.
78. *Skyphos* fr. Red-brown paint on grey ground. Vertical wavy line at left break, beside panel lines.
79. *Skyphos* fr. Red-brown paint on white slip.
80. *Skyphos* fr. Red-brown paint on cream ground.
81. *Skyphos* frr. D. 19. Black-brown paint on white slip. Five reserved bands in lip.
82. *Skyphos* fr. Black paint on white slip.
83. *Kotyle* fr. Black paint on white slip.
84. *Kotyle* fr. D. c. 10. Black paint. Two reserved bands with white pendent semicircles, out; within, a reserved band and white line.
85. *Kotyle* fr. Black paint. Two reserved bands out; within, a reserved band and white line.
86. *Cup* fr. Brown paint. Two reserved bands in lip.
87. *Krater* fr. Red-brown paint. White wavy line.

**DEPOSIT D (88–102: PLATE 45)**
88. *Skyphos* fr. D. 18. Red paint on buff slip. Brown micaceous clay. Reserved band in lip.
89. *Skyphos* fr. D. 19. Black-brown paint on white slip. Two reserved bands on lip with white crossed diamonds beneath. Reserved band in lip with groups of bars.
90. *Skyphos* fr. Black-brown paint. Very rough fabric and finish.
91. *Skyphos* fr. Black paint. Reserved band in lip.
92. *Skyphos* fr. Black-brown paint on buff ground.
93. *Skyphos* fr. Black-brown paint on cream ground. Reserved band in lip.
94. *Skyphos* fr. Red paint. Three reserved bands in lip.
95. *Skyphos* fr. D. c. 14. Black-brown paint on white slip. Reserved band in lip.
96. *Skyphos* fr. Black-brown paint.
97. (PLATE 62) *Cup* D. 10.5, H. 6.1. Red-brown paint on yellow slip.
98. *Cup* fr. Black paint on white slip.
99. *Krater* fr. Red-brown paint on yellowish ground.
100. *Krater* foot fr. Brown paint. Two reserved bands.
101. *Fr. of open vessel.* Black paint in cream ground. Reserved band in lip.
102. *Pyxis* lid handle. H. 4.5. Red paint on pink ground. Banded.

## 4. DESCRIPTION OF SHAPES AND DECORATION

### Skyphoi (103–97; PLATES 46–50)

The skyphos is the most prolific and significant shape in the Late Geometric from Lefkandi. The classification of the fragments here by the decoration of rims is a matter mainly of convenience although there are some chronological implications too and a tendency for some body patterns to be more popularly employed with particular rim patterns. Some body fragments have accordingly been classed with the basic rim patterns, I–VI, and the others put together under VII, with three distinctive skyphos types kept separate, VIII–X. It is clear that the handles of the skyphoi are usually painted black on the outside, rarely dotted, and that the bases are flat. The quality of the painting on the skyphoi is generally not high and it is noticeable that few have a carefully prepared slip ground and most are satisfied with a light fugitive slip or simple self-slip.

The skyphos-craters (225–30) which bear a general resemblance to the skyphoi in shape and scheme of decoration should also be noticed, and the possibility that some of the fragments considered in this section are from kantharoi.

It can be seen that the dominant decorative scheme of the Lefkandi LG skyphoi is metopal, a Euboean trait which has been noticed before. It is shared with the Cyclades and is to be distinguished from the growing use of such panel decoration in Attic LG I by the regular use of broad multiple-brush verticals rather than the more restrained Attic triple or quadruple lines (as *GGP* pl. 10). The reason for this may be that the use of the multiple brush, on a compass, had persisted to the inception of LG in Euboea and the painter was prepared to go on using the brush with four, six or more members, free-hand, as an easy way of covering the surface.[3] He can use it freely too for some of the motifs chosen to fill the panels (e.g. 117, 145–7) and on the cups, 216–22, he uses it over the whole vase. The scheme encourages a deeper zone of handle decoration on skyphoi with roughly square panels and dividers, and thence a tendency to deeper bowls and proportionately higher lips. It is likely that Euboea, though not necessarily, or even probably, Lefkandi, should take priority over the Cyclades for the development of this style since the greatest variety of lip and body patterns is to be found in the island, and its political and maritime importance in these years is likely to have given it the role of leader in other fields, especially in view of the brisk export of its wares.

We shall see that all skyphos types represented at Lefkandi are matched at Eretria or Chalcis, or both, although there are some variations in frequency which might prove significant, and it is worth noting that the type with a simple zigzag, found at Eretria,[4] is lacking.

### I. Banded lips (103–17)

This is one of the commonest varieties and the bands themselves are not chronologically important. General remarks about shape and body decoration will be found to apply to other skyphos groups. The earliest have a shallow lip, deriving from the MG skyphos, and a comparatively low profile favouring a shallow panel in the handle zone with zigzags, dotted snake or the simplest multiple-brush patterns (103–6). There is a single reserved band immediately within the rim, occasionally with groups of cross-bars, another early trait. The lip becomes higher and straighter. There are several good examples from the penultimate deposits (52, 53). These then attract either more bands, or one thin and one thick (107, 108); the reserved bands within the rim rise in number to two and the cross-bars are dropped. In the last phase, represented in the desertion deposit, the lip has grown taller and straighter, less clearly set off from the rather deeper bowl, if at all, and carries more bands, or broader ones. The complete example, 3, has still only one reserved band within the lip, but we can see from other skyphoi of the desertion deposits, which exhibit the same peculiarities of profile, that there is generally a proliferation of reserved bands in this position and this must be taken to be characteristic of the latest LG skyphoi. After the early shallow panels the usual body decoration is the familiar Euboean metopal with an apparent tendency to increase the number of vertical multiple-brush strokes used to divide the panels. The presence of one or more bands beneath the panels is variable. The scheme with the panels is as that for the skyphoi with other lip decoration. There may be only one panel, which seems a speciality of the simple banded rims (3, 52), two or three. The banded rims owe more to earlier skyphoi and this may explain why they attract the more traditional decoration, as of maeander or key, but they are found also with thinner vertical panels (with a wavy line or hatching, 77, 78). Birds and crossed diamonds are shared with other lip types, but specialities seem to be multiple-brush patterns (114—17), the single or double cross with dots (53, 111), and the dotted panel of 90 may be noted.

Persistence with simple banded rims for skyphoi to the end of LG seems peculiarly Euboean and Cycladic[5] — most other wares prefer some sort of pattern once the early, shallow, banded rim has been outgrown. At Eretria the type is presented with the double cross and dots.[6] characteristic at Lefkandi and it is seen at Chalcis. Farther afield, of Euboean origin or inspiration, it appears for quite advanced LG at Veii,[7] Al Mina[8] and in Cyprus.[9] The distinctive pair of concentric circles in a single panel, on 52, is imitated in a skyphos found at Chiusi,[10] and the cross-hatched diamonds (as on 3) are a particularly popular metope-filler in the west.

## II. Lips with concentric circles (118—30)

The lips are medium to high, with one to three (the usual number) reserved bands within. There are comparatively few with really high lips, like the complete example from a desertion deposit, 2, so we may regard the class as characteristic rather of the early to middle range of LG, and this is supported by the relatively high quality of the painting which appears on the bodies, apart from the fact that the handling of the small multiple-brush compass would not have been chosen by a hack artist. There are regularly three concentric hoops (rarely two, 126), with the centre spot usually dotted with paint. Tangentially linked, like a false running spiral, they appear on one lip fragment (55), but this is a more widely used pattern and basically different from the separate circles which are so characteristic of the Euboean series.

The usual body pattern is of three panels with hatched birds facing the centre, which carries a hatched quatrefoil with dot rosettes. The bird panels may also carry rosettes or dots, sometimes poor. The better examples have four-line dividers. Bodies with crossed diamonds with dots (119, 120), or cross-hatched diamonds, as 2 (compare 3), are presumably generally later in the series, and several of the unassigned body fragments (Class VII) may go with these lips. Occasionally the hatched quatrefoil can display the neat constrast of deliberately thinned hatching with bold outline (128) seen in the comparable patterns of finer large vases.

This is the most distinctive Euboean rim, well represented also at Eretria[11] and Chalcis,[12] with specimens also in Ischia (though few) and Al Mina.[13] Their presence elsewhere is also expressive of the range of Euboean LG interests: Castelluccio,[14] Delos,[15] Naxos,[16] Knossos, Samos,[17] Cyprus,[18] and imitated in Sicilian Naxos.[19]

The pattern appears on other Geometric wares, notably Boeotian and in the Cyclades, especially Naxos, but generally in other positions.[20] As rim decoration it could have been inspired by Cypriot pottery with which the Euboeans must have been acquainted for some time.[21]

*III. Lips with dots or dashes* (131—47)

This is the commonest type of lip decoration, learned from Attic MG. The shallow lips carry dots. As the fashion for higher lips grew the artist preferred to fill the extra height by turning his dots to tall dashes rather than adding or thickening bands. The dashes usually have none or one line above them (rarely two) and two (rarely one or three) below. The most common body patterns with this lip have panels carrying dotted circles, with a star or cross centrally (as 5; circles only on 6), and crossed diamonds (some with double outline) with dots. This is a scheme found with the dashes rather than the earlier dots, which are found with maeander or plain painted (Class VIII). The cross-hatched diamond is a late filler of pairs of panels (4; cf. 12, 145—7) and for another variety see 57.

The type is well represented at Eretria[22] although not, it seems, at Chalcis, which may be accidental, but it is worth noting since it is so very prolific at Lefkandi. There are typical examples at Al Mina[23] and on Ischia with what may be an imitation at Capua.[24] The dotted rims are common enough in Attic but the rows of loose dashes do seem a speciality of the later LG of Euboea, and particularly at Lefkandi.[25]

The way in which the multiple brush is used to supply the dots in the panel corners beside a cross-hatched diamond on a pre-excavation find at Lefkandi is notable.[26] The same expedient is used on other Euboean cups,[27] and may even be resorted to in attempting to dot circles.[28]

*IV. Lips with running blobs* (148—51)

The elegant Cycladic version from a penultimate deposit may be noticed, 88. The Lefkandi examples are comparatively late to judge from the height of the lip, usually with four reserved lines within, and one lower in the bowl on 148, which is unusually well painted and slipped, with a broad panel and confronted birds. The only other body pattern preserved is the ordinary crossed diamond on 149.

In this position the pattern had seemed peculiar to Lefkandi, in Euboea, and rare enough elsewhere until the recent publication of fragments from Eretria.[29]

*V. Lips with hatching* (152—9)

The close cross-hatching on tall lips (155, 156) seems confined to the latest LG and is represented in the desertion deposits (10, 11). Narrower bands of hatching, separated from the boundary lines (157—9), are on medium to high lips, but commonly with four reserved lines within. The preferred patterns for the body panels are dotted circles and hatched crossed diamonds. The single rows of dotted diamonds on the lips, 152—4, also usually have four reserved lines within although the lip height is generally slightly less. All these lip patterns can be taken to fall in the middle to late range of LG.

The type with close cross-hatching is represented at Eretria,[30] also with the dotted circles, and at Chalcis.[31]

*VI Lips with dotted hatching* (160—163)

These are invariably tall lips with two to four lines above the hatching, two or three below and between four to as many as eight reserved lines within. The body pattern seems invariably to be a maeander in a broad panel, with several lines beneath it. There is one example from a penultimate deposit, 81. As Coldstream observes (*GPP* 193) the lip pattern appears with EPC or LG IIb in Attic, and could not therefore have been adopted early in LG in Euboea, which is suggested also by the height of these lips, although not perhaps by the choice of maeander for the bodies.

There are examples at Eretria,[32] Chalcis[33] and Al Mina.[34]

### VII. *Other body fragments* (164–79)

Bird panels may carry as fill diamonds, sometimes crossed or dotted, and dots which approximate to the neater dot rosettes with stems seen in Attic panels (as *GGP* pl. 10c). The other common Euboean panel pattern is the crossed diamond with the corners of the panels carrying one or more dots. The diamonds may also sometimes be flanked by a multiple-brush row of dots, discussed under III, above.

### VIII. *Plain painted* (180–5)

There are a very few examples of skyphoi painted all over, including the one from a penultimate deposit (58). More commonly the rims of medium height (including examples from the desertion deposits, 8, 9) carry a row of dots or short dashes, with one thick or two thin lines below and the bowl plain painted. There are usually three reserved lines in the lip.[35]

### IX. *Black and white* (186)

An example from a penultimate deposit (89) is all black but for white crossed diamonds outside and a reserved band with cross-bars (an oddly early feature) within. 186 has a dotted snake and rosettes, and three reserved lines in the lip. Both tend to the broad conical profile of Class X.

This use of white can be observed further on the next class of skyphoi, and a plain painted example from Chalcis has a wheel painted in white within.[36]

### X. *Bichrome* (187–97)

This is the most original class of Euboean LG skyphoi, employing a style of decoration which is almost wholly confined to this shape (an exception here, the handle 295). In its simplest form the bichromy is simply a matter of added white for a wavy line on the black lip. The most elaborate example, 13, has further lines on the lower bowl and within. The handle zone carries dotted ovals and a crossed diamond, set in free field, without dividers, a dissolution therefore of the old metopal system. With this goes the filled diamond on 189. The lips are usually treated in this way and the only variants are all-black (196) or a row of dots, with the lip alone slipped (195). Most, however, are not content to leave the body motifs in plain black but they are drawn in outline and filled with the white slip laid directly on the clay. The scheme is generally still as on 13, but the oval is white (occasionally with a black heart, 190–2) surrounded by black dots, and the diamond is an outline filled with white. The only other pattern admitted, treated in exactly the same way, is the swastika (187, 188). On some examples the surface is polished to a bright orange (compare 295).

The shape is a broad cone with the lip slightly offset from the bowl (14, 16) but nowhere near as high relatively as the latest of the other skyphoi. Yet it is clear that this is among the latest of the skyphos types, with several examples from desertion deposits, and only 193 from a possibly penultimate deposit. The type must be regarded as parallel to the latest of the skyphoi with the tall lips, already described, and not derived from them (pace *GGP* 191) since both the lip and the whole body shape are different. The freer disposition of the ornament, without the panels, one might almost regard as an orientalising trait; and the shape is close enough to the LG II Attic low skyphoi of the Birdseed type (*GGP* 68, 86 f.) for it to be probable that there is some connection. The Attic are so open as to admit figure decoration within, which is barely true of the Euboean, but notice the wavy lines within 13.

This class is well represented at Eretria where there is often more finesse and variety of pattern. The all-black patterns are found, with white only added over black in wavy lines or with dotted, slipped lips;[37] indeed this style is relatively far commoner there. The slip-filled patterns include the crossed diamond,[38] but also a simpler scheme of three groups of dots on either side, represented in the West Gate tombs.[39] At Eretria too we find at least one example of the slip-filled scheme, applied to another shape.[40]

The most typical varieties of this class have yet to be found at Chalcis, where we find the applied white wavy lines in and out (lip) combined unexpectedly with panel decoration.[41] At Al Mina there is the slipped rim, the typical filled diamonds, but also the same shape with black lip and roughly dotted circles on the body.[42] There are no examples yet from the west, so far as I know.

It may well be that we should regard the slip-filling as the latest phase, the earlier skyphoi bearing only the applied white wavy lines, and the earliest thus represented by the Chalcis fragment which still admits multiple-brush dividers for panels. The probable Athenian origin for the shape has been noted, and the same source no doubt supplied the dotted ovals. The shallow profile meant that the use of multiple-brush dividers would have given triangular, instead of roughly square panels, which may be why they were soon abandoned in favour of the rather unusual free-field system which is so rare on this or any other shape in Attic LG that we might wonder in which direction influence, if any, was passing.[43]

### Kantharoi (198, 199; PLATE 50)

The shape is barely attested at Lefkandi (also 60) but it is very probable that some of the fragments considered with the skyphoi are in fact from kantharoi.[44] Significantly the most substantial fragment, 199, bears a scheme of decoration similar to that of the distinctive skyphoi of Class II, but there is only one reserved band in the lip, with cross-bars.

### Kotylai (200—14; PLATES 50—1)

The decoration which most closely resembles that of its Corinthian models has bands of chevrons with the usual disposition of grouped vertical and horizontal lines, 200. On this the lip is still very slightly out-turned and the same feature is seen where the decoration has degenerated to multiple-brush chevrons or Z's (83, 201—4).

A more characteristic group for Euboea is of all-black kotylai, with a thin reserved band just within the lip and all other decoration in added white (84, 85, 205—7). This may take the form of single pendent semicircles at the rim, recalling the old SPG scheme, 84, 205, 206; or a zigzag, 207. Within the lip there is a single white line, where we might otherwise expect a reserved line, and within 207 there are two additional white lines lower in the bowl.

Other varieties of decoration in the handle zone include a dotted snake, 214, and birds with hatched bodies. One of these has the distinctive Euboean raised bent wing, 210, and there is a pair confronting a strip of diamonds, 213. The strongly Corinthianising wire-birds, which are well represented elsewhere in Euboea, appear at Lefkandi on only one scrap, and this from a reoccupation deposit, 209. The deposits tell little of value about relative chronology, but two pieces with added white (84, 85) are from penultimate deposits, and an example with the hatched bird and butterfly, 17, was found in a desertion deposit.

Black kotylai with added white are found in Protocorinthian but the scheme naturally appealed to Euboeans to judge from their use of added white on other shapes, and they were far more ready than the Corinthian to add a white line within the rim when there was no applied white outside.[45] There are examples of black kotylai with added white at Eretria[46] and Chalcis.[47] Eretria offers a wide variety of other patterns[48] including the wire birds which are conspicuous by their virtual absence at Lefkandi and Chalcis.[49] The bird kotylai, and others of Euboean origin or inspiration, are very well represented at Al Mina[50] and on Ischia,[51] where we also find the white on black patterns of pendent semicircles and concentric circles (compare our cup, 61).

### Cups (215–24; PLATE 51)

There are two main classes of one-handled cup. The commoner has a black body with a strap handle decorated with various simple linear patterns in added white, or with a vertical wavy line between bands. There is also added white decoration on 61 in the form of a pair of concentric circles, of the variety familiar on skyphos lips, set one at each side of the handle. These black cups are so well represented in the desertion deposits (18–22) that we may regard them as typical of the latest LG but not exclusively of this late date.

The second class is of smaller cups, more heavy-walled, and decorated all over with multiple-brush patterns which run vertically or obliquely over the walls, crossing towards the base and often running on to the base itself (63, 216 = PLATE 62, 217–22). These too must be fairly late although they seem absent from the clear desertion deposits, at least in anything like complete examples.

There are other scraps with simple linear patterning of other types on the walls (223–4) and the latter seems to have been quite carefully painted.

All varieties normally have a reserved band within the lip and a flat base.

The black cups are too common a Geometric type to deserve special study here,[52] but the small multiple-brush cups are distinctively Euboean. In the West Gate cemetery at Eretria the type, as known at Lefkandi, is found in children's graves, including one with a side spout, as a feeder, and a small kantharos decorated with the same scheme.[53] Examples from Chalcis[54] and near by[55] have the lower wall painted black, and this is the type found later in Boeotia[56] and on Ischia. The scheme is managed more neatly over the whole body of larger kantharoi in Attica and Boeotia.[57]

### Kraters and dinoi (225–72; PLATES 52–5)

There is considerable variety in the fragments of large open vessels found at Lefkandi but some clear major groups can be distinguished.

Some vessels with tall thin lips are constructed like the skyphoi but are larger, have double handles and the complete specimen from the desertion deposit has a ring foot, 28. This carries the latest scheme of decoration as we know it from skyphoi. The concentric circles on 225 and 226 are also borrowed from the skyphoi but there is more originality in the hatched diamonds of a lip from a penultimate deposit, 70, and the lip with neatly drawn multiple-brush (tenfold) wavy lines, 227. Other fragments, 229, 230, from thin-walled but large open vessels and carrying multiple-brush patterns are probably also from these 'skyphos-kraters'.

The fine fragmentary krater 231 (PLATE 62) stands apart. It has no context, unfortunately, but stylistically it is early LG and is apparently Euboean. Beside the double handles is a star and dots. The main panel has maeander, with double zigzags in the side panels. The general scheme resembles that of the big skyphos in pre-desertion deposit C, 81. The linked dots on the rim, with interspace dots, is an uncommon feature in Euboean LG but appears on the Cesnola Group and will attract further comment below.

The commonest kraters, sometimes quite well painted and slipped, have thick upright lips, normally painted with a row of blobs or dashes and presumably the contemporaries of the middle to late LG skyphoi with the same lip patterns. Where substantial fragments of the lips are preserved it can be seen that spouts were preferred (232 = PLATE 63, 233, 235). The two examples from desertion deposits, one complete (29), the other miniature (30), lack spouts but have handles with a spur running up to the lip and the complete example has a splaying ribbed foot. These must be the latest types, as can also be judged from the crude multiple-brush work of the large example and the shoddy horses on the miniature, who stand facing the centre diamond without panel dividers. The other kraters, represented by fragments only, seem to have had ring feet, not pedestals, but our evidence for this may be incomplete. The lower parts of the bowls were broken by groups of reserved bands between which zigzags, crossed and single wavy lines or battlement pattern in added white regularly appear (234—41). From the handle zone we have panels with a variety of patterns easily matched on the skyphoi. They include varieties of crossed diamonds (233, 235), quatrefoil, birds (232, 234), maeander (235), but also tall panels with cross-hatching (232, 235), dotted snake (34) and dotted diamonds (233). A more unusual pattern is the hatched butterfly on 234. 232 is exceptional in having a human figure in the panel below the broken spout. We see the dot-in-circle head and torso of a warrior. His left hand, with fingers marked, reaches down towards the hilt of his sword, worn horizontally at his waist, and there are traces of a spear running obliquely across his body along the break at the left. There are chevrons in the field beside him. The panel to the right has the head of a bird and part of a filling diamond.

Scraps show that the same krater profile could be decorated differently (242—7) — with dots, running dots or running dots-in-circles, and cross-hatching, and the panel on 242, which has a distinctly shallower lip, has an unusual outlined cross, related to the double crosses of the skyphoi.

Some of the kraters with added white on the lower bowls are from penultimate deposits, and the same is true of what must be regarded as another late phenomenon, the 'dinoi' (67, 248 = PLATE 63, 249, 251—6). These have shallower lips, more triangular in section, and are distinctively decorated. They were probably handleless but may have had flat bases. The shoulder zones are decorated with broad groups of multiple-brush strokes interrupted by broad crosses or an oblique stroke (251), or set close together with only a thick upright stroke between them. On 253 this stroke has a white wavy line superimposed, and the ground is a burnished orange (see on 295).

Of the other fragments the looser decoration on 250 suggests the approach of orientalising schemes[58] while on 257 the panels seem filled by plain painted blobs of uncertain original form which recall the devices on the late or sub-Geometric Euboean grave amphorae. There is one example, 258, with white pendent semicircles painted on the black body in the manner of the decoration of some kotylai. Its lip is squat and thick.

Few of the other fragments from krater bodies deserve special note. 263 carried an unusually elaborate panel pattern with a fringed hoop enclosing linked dots-in-circles and a central star,[59] the most elaborate treatment of the motif which we see abbreviated on skyphoi and a krater fragment (66). It is probably a fringed wheel that we see behind the rosette and bird on 264. 266 is unusual in adding a dash frieze below the panels, and below this the black band carried a white zigzag. The badly worn 265 had a quatrefoil panel and vertical strip of diamonds. 268 may carry the legs of a human figure. 271 shows elaborate decoration under the double handle of a krater, and 270 the bars on a double handle. 272 was a particularly large ribbed foot (cf. 29, 100) The scene on 267[60] is not clear but there is a hint of an animal with raised bent forelegs, like the goats at a tree on the Cesnola Painter's vases (see below, pp. 000ff.) and there is a line of dots where, for a horse, we would look for a solid tail.

The most interesting group are the fragments with figure decoration painted in a good brown black on thick creamy white slip. 260 is from the upright lip of a large krater, like the Cesnola krater. The lip has a zigzag fringe and below it we see the neck of a horse right, a Dipylon shield over its back and two stars. Of the two small fragments one has part of the neck of a grazing horse (261). the other upright strips of cross-hatched diamonds and concentric diamonds (262). The large fragment from a body, 259, is the most informative for this style. Below what was probably a triple zigzag frieze we have a horse with a fringed eight-spoked wheel over its back, dots between the spokes. Beneath its body is a bird, and it is held on a curly guide rope by a small warrior with cross-hatched chest, wearing a sword but with no definition of a helmet. Before him, and with a hand stretched towards him, is a taller warrior whose helmet crest, dot-eye, nose and chin are more clearly defined. He too wears a sword. The fill is of large and small stars and of vertical rows of chevrons. The hand of this, and almost certainly of the other fragments in this style (260–2) which might even be from the same vessel since they were not much scattered, will be further discussed below.

From the desertion deposit comes a fragment (31) with a horse at a hatched manger, double axe above, bird below; and another (33) with the distinctive Euboean bird with a bent wing, dots and a hatched triangle. The poor horses on 30 have been remarked.

42 seems likely to be the skyphos-knob to a krater lid, after the model of the Cesnola krater which uses a miniature amphora, or the Cesnola-inspired krater from Pescia Romana[61] in Italy, where a skyphos is used.

Skyphos-kraters like our 225–8 are not always easy to identify from photographs but they are clearly well represented at both Eretria[62] and Chalcis with either concentric circles or multiple-brush patterns on the lip. It is not possible to be sure whether all had double handles.

The kraters with dots or dashes at the rim, and with spouts, which seem particularly dear to the Euboeans (learned from Athens, GGP 48), are also readily identified at the other island sites,[63] including pieces with added white on the lower walls.[64]

The dinoi with added white on the lips and the very distinctive vertical bars with an added white chain are also well in evidence at Eretria,[65] and include a piece with an added white battlement pattern on the lower wall,[66] like 238. At Chalcis I know only the obliques between verticals,[67] as on 251. There is also a piece from Chalcis with added white concentric circles,[68] a pattern we have met on cups (and cf. 258).

The bar-and-verticals pattern is so popular on these vessels, with or without the added white, that it is worth a moment's attention. It is managed far more neatly in Attic, as on the kantharos, GGP pl.15c,[69] and may derive from the hatched tongue patterns (GGP pls. 10e, 15b; p.50f.) which themselves hail from earlier gadrooning. The later stage of the pattern at Eretria appears on the subgeometric grave amphorae,[70] and note our 257.

The Euboeans of Ischia maintain their interest in spouts for craters, but the proportions of their vases are often different and they may have vertical handles.[71] The added white zigzags are also seen there. Incised wavy lines on dinos lips, like those painted on Euboean dinoi, are seen on Samian vessels.[72]

### Tankards and the like (273–9; PLATES 55–6)

There are few examples of tall tankards. 279 is the most informative, with its high strutted handle, carefully decorated, and the vertical strips of chevrons to either side. 274 is from a very similar vessel. From the straight wall we have part of a horse with chevron fill beneath it, then a row of very neatly drawn linked concentric circles, then multiple triangles with dot rosettes between. 273 may be from the handle of such a vessel, with a dotted snake, and 275, with chequer and an upright strip of dots, from the body of another. They are all characterised by delicacy of painting, far superior to that of the standard skyphoi and kraters.

The shallower tankards, with simple handles and rather like deep mugs, but unpainted within except for one or two bands in the lip, are represented in the desertion deposit. The circles on 23 are neat enough to suggest that it need not be latest LG but the dashes and zigzags on 24 are very like the latest skyphoi. 278 is an example of the shape with the black and white decoration at the lip favoured for other vessels at Lefkandi. It is sadly preserved but there was a white zigzag at the lip, a painted zigzag on the strip beneath, then a tooth pattern. The lip had cross-bars in groups and a broad band within but the interior is otherwise unpainted. Other probable tankard body fragments offer the usual bird panels with star, diamond and dashes fill, over cross-hatched triangles, 277, and a multiple-brush pattern, 276.

With these we may mention the deep skyphoi from the desertion deposits, 25, 26. These too are unpainted within but for bands in the lip, and represent a local late LG variation.[73]

The simply decorated tankards are seen at Eretria.[74]

### Oinochoai (280–308; PLATES 56–7)

The most distinctive variety has a round mouth cut away beside the handle. There are two complete examples from the desertion deposits (35, 36) but the former is of the Cesnola Group so the shape was established appreciably earlier. A fragment from the lip of another is decorated with bars and zigzag in white on black (285), the scheme employed on other shapes. The other desertion oinochoe (36) with cutaway neck carries simple birds and a striped body. This simple decoration of banding is seen on another substantial fragment, 280, and the neck of the other normal oinochoe type, with trefoil lip, 282.

The trefoil oinochoai are also decorated with white on black, lines or zigzag, and there are white chevrons and bars on what may well be oinochoe handles. Of the other handle fragments 291 was from an elaborately decorated vase and 292 is twin-reeded. 295 is the only example of the bichrome technique on a shape other than a skyphos. The black at the top edge suggests that it is from an oinochoe. The ground is a burnished orange colour, like the krater fragment 253, and the filled diamond has black dots added to the white, like the cores added on some of the white ovals on skyphoi. Of neck fragments 287 and another carry concentric circles of the type most familiar on skyphoi: these may be from cutaway mouths. Other decoration is not remarkable but notice the panel with wavy lines on 288 and compare the whole oinochoe from a desertion deposit, 37.

A number of fragments of closed vases may well be from oinochoai, but might also be from amphorae or hydriae with decorated bodies, a type attested in Euboea. Apart from decoration of the range familiar from other vessels the carefully atticising friezes of 297, apparently with a row of concentric circles by the neck, is notable; the birds on 296, 302; and several pieces with chequer pattern (303–5) including some which show that on this shape too the lower body may carry white zigzags over the black bands. 306 has the rare linked dotted circles, hand-drawn, however. In plain black there is a small trefoil mouth (308) and part of the lip and body of a jug with a high uspwung handle of unusual shape, 307.

The distinctive cutaway lip was learned from Thessaly and is represented at Eretria,[75] Chalcis and on Ischia. All these sites also give evidence for the use of added white on the lower body and sometimes on the lips of oinochoai of this or of the more conventional trefoil-lip shape.[76] An oinochoe from Andros (Zagora) which may have had a cutaway lip, has white wavy lines added on the body and is probably Euboean.[77] I also have note of an oinochoe with cutaway neck, LG birds and added white zigzags in Istanbul Museum.[78] A cutaway lip on Ithaca may owe more to Euboea than northern Greece.[79]

## Amphorae (309–17; PLATE 57)

There is only one important group of amphorae, of a shape and style of decoration otherwise best represented in the cemetery at Eretria. The necks flare slightly to a blunt lip (311, 313) and are decorated with thick upright wavy lines. We have the shoulder of one (312) where there are panels with cross-hatched diamonds. The tall foot flares to a blunt toe and is decorated with multiple-brush patterns, 317. To judge from the complete specimens known elsewhere there were double handles at the shoulder.

Although the Lefkandi fragments are few and small they are enough to demonstrate the presence of the amphora type in a settlement rather than a cemetery, where they have hitherto been found.

The earliest of the subgeometric grave amphorae at Eretria have cylindrical necks.[80] The Lefkandi pieces may carry the shape back a little into the eighth century with the familiar scheme of thick, vertical wavy lines on the neck, and with the neck flaring. It is possible, however, that they should rather be associated with a class of latest-Geometric Boeotian grave amphorae, many of which are decorated in a similar manner, and which persist with the flaring necks into the seventh century.[81] One of them,[82] hitherto regarded as Boeotian, has rightly been declared Euboean by Coldstream, for the birds and fill which match the Euboean skyphoi, and it is just possible that the Lefkandi pieces have more or as much to do with Boeotia as with Eretria. The possibly close relationship is demonstrated by an amphora from Euboean Ischia[83] where the goat head and eight-armed swastika in the field look Boeotian.

For the highly eccentric 71, see below, under Imports. The handle 309 with the bold bar and butterfly pattern is possibly not Euboean. The neck with the painted axe, 39, is not from one of the main amphora series already discussed but has a heavy rolled lip and is probably from a storage vase, no doubt Euboean.

## Pyxides (318–22; PLATE 57)

There are pieces from the lids and body of plain painted globular pyxides, 102, 318, 319. The shallower pyxides with concave walls and flanges to take the lids are represented by a fragment, 320, with the cross-hatched diamond and row of blobs familiar on skyphoi, and 321 which has a white on black wavy line on the rim and perhaps part of a bird from the body. 322 is from the plain disc of a lid appropriate to this shape. 74, if from a pyxis, had more elaborate panels perhaps with birds flanked by dot rosettes.

### Bowls (323–4; PLATE 57)

There are three pieces of shallow bowls which appear to have had single strap handles and plain upper walls (323 = PLATE 63) or vertical stripes. There is one fragment of the spur from the loop handle of a shallow bowl or dish, with cross-bars on the spur and rim, 324.

### Aryballos (325; PLATE 58)

There is one banded lip from an aryballos imitating the usual EPC type. Some exotically decorated Euboean imitations of EPC aryballoi are found at Eretria and elsewhere.[84]

### Kalathos

A complete example from the desertion deposit, 27, presents an unfamiliar scheme in the general assemblage. The upper body is black and heavily ridged. One would be inclined to doubt its Euboean origin were it not for the free use of the multiple brush as panel dividers and on the lip, and for the simple crosses in the panels, which can be matched on late dinoi (as 248).

### Imports (326–8; PLATE 58)

The possibility that some of the pottery taken for local was made either not at Lefkandi or not Euboea is considered in the following section. After the amount of Athenian MG pottery which was found at Lefkandi it is rather surprising to find no certain Attic in LG, although 26 and 231 have been suspected of being so, and a very restricted range of other imported pieces.

There is one piece of a Corinthian LG or EPC kotyle, with chevrons in the handle zone, 326. 88 is from a skyphos in micaceous brown clay with reddish paint on a buff slip. The elements of the decoration are seen on the Euboean skyphoi but the fabric and style here are clearly Cycladic, possibly Naxian.[85] The dots at the left are from beside the handle and there is a reserved band in the lip.

The large amphora with concentric circles from a penultimate deposit, 71, is also highly micaceous and probably imported, no doubt from the Cyclades, where the use of large concentric circles, although not the exact shape, is matched on Delos.[86]

There is the lip and neck of a small jug of the class formerly known as 'Argive monochrome' but probably all made in Corinth.[87] The fragment is 3.5 high, in pink, rather speckled clay with a pale surface. Other fragments from a plain small vessel, 327, are in a light yellow-brown clay and have pricked decoration of horizontal and multiple zigzag lines.

328 is from a kalathoid vessel, painted within, in a yellowish-brown clay with pale slip. The general fabric resembles Corinthian but the shape is odd: from the interior it is clear that we have almost the total height of the vessel.

### Coarse vases (329–42; PLATES 58–9)

Since the pottery is from a settlement the proportion of plain wares represented by the fragments is naturally high, but few complete shapes could be recovered. Those in the desertion deposit have been described already (43–50) but fragments from a penultimate deposit are included here (334, 336, 340–2) since their patterning is indistinguishable from that of fragments recovered with other Geometric pottery, and we may be confident that all these wares are LG. They seem to bear no relationship to earlier coarse wares.

All the coarse vases seem to be of local manufacture with the possible exception of one or two highly micaceous pieces. The rest are generally rather crudely hand-made with signs of burnishing on the smaller vessels and a variety of incised and impressed patterns on the larger ones which provide their main archaeological interest.

From the desertion deposits there are substantial pieces of jars (43—4), a hydria (45), as well as fragments of pithoid vessels. The other fragments tell little more about shapes, but the jugs generally have their handles brought close to or on to the lip. There are also pieces of flat, ring and knob pithos bases, of a tripod or fenestrated base (334) and of a sieve (329).

The commonest form of decoration is zigzags, sometimes multiple, rows of crosses or simple cross-hatching; also incised herring-bone pattern, with or without a spine. Raised and slashed rope mouldings are seen, framing zigzags, and decorated raised flat bands. It looks as though an octuple comb was used on 333, septuple on 339, 340, 342, and quintuple on 336. A different type of decoration is impressed with the same comb-like implement (see especially 333 where one implement is used for both patterns) but using just the tip to produce a line of sinkings. The general effect is close to that of the multiple-brush patterns on the painted vases. On 333 they are also used to make a zigzag on one part of the fragment, but elsewhere, and on 50, they are used haphazardly, as on the raised moulding on 335. The only other notable pattern in the incising technique is the triple comb of panels on the desertion jar, 43, which, like 44, also carries mastoi.

The smaller plain vases are commonplace chytrai and hydriae met elsewhere in Geometric Greece. The decorated vases are more interesting. The type is already well attested in Eretria[89] with a variety of stamped and incised patterns and a fondness for fenestrated feet on the larger vases which otherwise resemble the painted grave amphorae but are handleless and have more sloping shoulders. Of the Lefkandi patterns only the impressed comb pattern is remarkable. Outside Euboea only Attica presents a comparable range of Geometric incised coarse ware,[90] and there too the more elaborate relief vases of the islands are lacking.[91]

## 5. SUMMARY AND CONCLUSIONS

### a. Chronology and site history

The only important event for which stratigraphic evidence is available during the LG period, apart from the desertion itself, is the construction of the buildings which seal the penultimate deposit B, and the few other pits which have been described and two of them (C, D) listed with their contents. Only one class of pottery is clearly later than this penultimate stage and this is the group of bichrome skyphoi (187—97). The other penultimate pottery already shows signs of very advanced LG in the height of skyphos rims and patterns, and it is not necessary to assign a long time to the development of the bichrome skyphoi in the Lefkandi finds. Hardly ten to fifteen years need have elapsed between the structures and the desertion.

The absolute dating of these events, or their relative dating vis-à-vis other wares, is less easy. For their shapes the bichrome skyphoi must have started some time within the period of Attic LG II. It is not altogether clear whether the absence of the wire-bird kotylai (see on 209), so well represented at Eretria, should be a chronological indicator or not, since it is always possible that they may prove to be an Eretrian speciality. Coldstream (GGP 194) has discussed the origins of these in early EPC and we would expect the commonest Eretrian imitations to have been current by about 710 (taking EPC as about 720–690 BC). On this score the Lefkandi desertion should have taken place about 710, but possibly later.

The number of decorated vases, including some of quality, in the desertion deposits, indicates some degree of wealth since settlement deposits are not always as well characterised by fine pottery as are cemeteries. The presence little earlier of pieces of fine and large figure-decorated vessels (as of the Vrokastro Group, see below) supports this. So many of the desertion vases were found in a virtually complete state that the settlement must have been abandoned in a hurry, and it is clear that the LG house in the main area of excavation was burnt at that time or immediately afterwards.

### b. The Cesnola Group

Some of the figure-decorated pottery from Lefkandi requires special attention for its relationship to the great Cesnola crater from Cyprus and vases recently associated with it. Kontoleon had argued cogently for the Naxian origin of the krater, followed by Coldstream in *GGP*, who distinguished the hand of the Cesnola Painter and made attributions to his workshop (pp. 172–4). Subsequently, however, he was able to lengthen the lists and make a case for the Euboean origin for the whole group, the argument being based in part of an example of the painter's work which had been found a Chalcis, and the Lefkandi oinochoe, 35, from his workshop (in *BICS* 18 (1971) 1ff.). At the same time Elena Walter-Karydi, publishing pottery from Naxos, restated the case for a Naxian origin in *AA* 1972, 386ff. There are in fact other relevant pieces from Lefkandi and elsewhere and they suggest some further refinement of the lists which could help towards a solution of the problem.

The painter's known works are listed by Coldstream (in the following lists I give in brackets the numbers of his list and reference to his illustrations in the *BICS* article; and I add one piece, no. 3):

1. (1:pl. 1a) New York 74.51.965. Krater from Kourion. Also *AA* 1972, 406–8, figs. 30–2; *AntK* 16 (1973) pls. 25, 26.1.[92]
2. (2:pl. 2a) New York 74.51.838. Oinochoe from Kourion. Also *AA* 1972, 408, fig. 33.
3. New York 74.51.5885. Oinochoe fr. from Kourion; neck and shoulder with decoration as on no. 2. The clay is red, the slip yellowish, as on no. 1.
4. (3:fig. 1b, c) Krater from Delos. Also *AA* 1972, 393, fig. 11.
5. (4:pl. 1b, c) Hydria from Chalcis.

A few of the characteristic patterns can be briefly reviewed. Notable motifs are the goats at a tree and the horse at a manger with bird below and axe above. The horses have high fetlocks. There are grazing birds with raised feathered wings. The fill includes rows of chevrons and folded swastikas (arms bent to near 45°), and the friezes with diamonds or linked circles and discs have dots in the interspaces.

Near the painter's work seem to be:

6. (5:fig. 1a) Lid fr. from Chalcis. *ADelt* 27 (1972) pl. 57B.
7. Oinochoe fr. from Delos. *EADelos* xv pl. 54 Attic 10. This piece seems to have been overlooked yet it too has the goats at a tree, in a fine style close to that of the crater but with open muzzles for the animals.

In the following of the Cesnola Painter are these:

8. (7:pl. 3c) London 1955. 4–22.24. Crater fr. from Al Mina.
9. (9:pl. 2c) London 94.11–1.31. Crater fr. from Amathus. Also *AA* 1972, 394, fig. 12.

10. (10:pl. 2e) Amsterdam 1233. Krater. Also *AA* 1972, 395, fig. 15.
11. (12:pl. 3d) Amphoriskos fr. from Samos. Also *AA* 1972, 408, fig. 34.
12. (pl. 3f) Oinochoe from Lefkandi. Our 35.
13. Krater fr. from Lefkandi. Our 31.
14. Krater fr. from Lefkandi. Our 231.
15. Krater fr. from Lefkandi. Our 267.
16. Oinochoe fr. from Eretria. *BSA* 47 (1952) pl. 3A.8.
17. Krater fr. from Eretria. Ibid., pl. 2A.9.
(The following is also strong in Italy. E.g., from Ischia, *Dialoghi di Archeologia* 1969, fig. 27 below; *Expedition* 1972, 38, figs. 3–4; krater from Pesara Romana, *Dialoghi di Archeologia* 1974–5, figs. 6–7; oinochoe, *Prospettiva* 4 (1976) 27.)

The next group of fragments are, to my eye, related to the Cesnola vases but in a distinctively different style, and they make a coherent series which we might call the Vrokastro Group:

18. (6:pl. 2b) Heraklion. Crater frs. from Vrokastro. Also *AA* 1972, 394, fig. 14, with an important extra fragment.
19. Krater fr. from Eretria. *AntK* 11 (1968) pl. 27.4. The creatures in the lower frieze are lions, not boars; notice their teeth and tails.
20. Krater fr. from Chalcis. *BSA* 52 (1957) pl. 1.32.
21. Krater frs. from Lefkandi. Our 259–262.

There are a number of other pieces imitative of these, but by no means likely to be from the same workshop:

22. (pl. 3e) Krater fr. from Chania, Crete.
23. (fig. 2) Krater fr. from Zagora, Andros. *Zagora* i, figs. 47–8.
24. (11:pl. 2d) London 1955.4–22.26–29. Krater frs. from Al Mina.
25. Krater fr. from Eretria. *BSA* 47 (1952) 5, fig. 7.
26. Krater fr. from Lefkandi. Our 232.
27. Krater frs. from Ischia. *Dialoghi di Archeologia* 1969, fig. 27 top; *AR* 1966–7, 31 fig. 2 top right.
(The list could be extended with other pieces from Ischia[93] and the style is echoed in Boeotia, as on the Paralimni crater, *AR* 1973–4, 19, fig. 32.)

It might first be noted that where the clay of the main series, nos. 1–21, has been described it is called red and that although this can fall within the range of Euboean wares it is not characteristic of them. It may simply imply more careful preparation and rather different firing conditions in a specialist workshop. Thanks to Dr. Bothmer, samples of the Cesnola krater and the oinochoe found with it (nos. 1, 2) have been analysed in the Oxford Research Laboratory for Archaeology. The results match each other very closely but are not a good match for the Euboean wares so far recognised from analysis of Bronze Age, Geometric and later material, including modern samples from Lefkandi.[94] This is not decisive since the practice or even location of a specialist workshop in Euboea might explain it, and no close match for the clay has yet been found (or seriously looked for) elsewhere. For the moment we are left with considerations of style.

If the Cesnola Painter worked in Euboea he was probably an immigrant and his workshop kept itself apart from other Euboean ceramic activity. His goats-at-a-tree theme has a

Euboean distribution (nos. 1, 5, 7, 15?), including Ischia (*AR* 1970–1, 64, fig. 2). Euboean birds have raised wings but they are bent (as our 33, 210; in Ischia and Italy too[95]) rather than raised and feathered, as his (see our 35). Coldstream thought the latter type might indicate Chalcis[96] in view of the find of no. 5 but the bent wing is represented there too (unpublished). The Painter's interspace dots in friezes are extremely rare on other Euboean Geometric (though prominent on the lip of our crater 231, and cf. 306), as is the folded swastika. Given Euboean painters' long devotion to the multiple brush and compass both in the preceding period and in LG (on skyphos lips etc.) it is astonishing to observe that the Cesnola Painter, if he was Euboean-trained, abjures its use — the linked concentric circles on his big crater (no. 1) are all hand-drawn.[97] From provenience and style it would be easy to take the vases listed as near the Painter, nos. 6–17, as pure Euboean, and this would be understandable if the Painter himself had been a relatively independent newcomer in the island. If this is what happened it is in Naxian Geometric that we see most in the way of pattern and figure work to remind us of his style and Naxos might have been his original home, but none of the vases listed here is from the island and this seems to tell against the production of any of them there.[98] The strongest succession to his style is found in Italy; he may have been an inveterate wanderer.

The Vrokastro Group is a somewhat different matter and almost certainly Euboean. The vases are decorated in a fine miniaturist style, precise and with a tendency to exploit the pattern of heavy outline and thinned-paint hatching in ornament and figures[99] (birds, chests, shields). The stables and the goats are gone; instead we have warriors and cavalrymen. The chevron fill is tidy now (no. 18), the birds with feathered wings are flying (no. 18 and cf. 24) — a most original concept. Gone are the interspace dots, the linked circles or discs, the folded swastika. This is a worthy, but highly original successor to the Cesnola Painter's studio. The final phase of Euboean figured Geometric appears in imitations of the Vrokastro Group (as nos. 23, 25, 26), a fine amphora neck from Eretria (to be published shortly by Professor Kahil) and the mourners, *AntK* 3 (1960) 318, fig. 2.8; and much at Ischia, where the horse and manger remain in favour.

### c. Lefkandi and the Euboean cities

The LG period is generally thought to have seen the conflict of the two major Euboean cities, Eretria and Chalcis, in the Lelantine war. Lefkandi's position, with a good harbour, a long and prosperous earlier history (earlier than Eretria for the Iron Age) and the archaeological evidence of its sudden desertion, make it an important site for possible further elucidation of this episode.[100] Unfortunately for any comparative study of the fortunes of the three sites the relevant pottery from Chalcis is still little known and new finds might upset deductions, but a fair range of styles is already represented from casual finds and excavations in Chalcis, not all yet published.[101]

In general the range of styles represented at the three sites is very much the same. Even types and styles which do not appear until the period is somewhat advanced, such as the extensive use of added white on some shapes, or which do not appear until the latest phase, such as the bichrome skyphoi, are represented. And we have noted fairly indiscriminate distribution of the figure-decorated vases of the Cesnola Group and its relatives. This seems to imply no serious or protracted interruptions of communication at the level of pottery trade between the sites in the relevant period. The possibility that all were supplied for much of the time from a single source, probably then in the Lelantine plain, cannot be ruled out. This may well have been true of the earliest vases in use at the new site of Eretria. In these circumstances it is worth provisionally observing nuances of difference in the ceramic record of the three sites in case some prove to be diagnostic of separate centres of production. These must be set against the general correspondence between them in the ordinary wares, already remarked.

It is only with some of the latest styles of LG at Lefkandi that some discrepancies with the other sites might be noted. Three groups, common to Lefkandi and Eretria, are so far poorly if at all represented at Chalcis: the late skyphoi with rows of dashes at the lip, the bichrome skyphoi (but for an early or experimental example), the cups with multiple-brush patterns over the whole wall. And there is one type whose floruit may be somewhat later than those just mentioned, which is common at Eretria but rare (at the least) at both Lefkandi and Chalcis: the wire-bird kotylai. The last is possibly explained at Lefkandi by the prior desertion of the site.[102] The rest show a very considerable correspondence in the ceramic record between Lefkandi and Eretria. The discrepancy, if it is real, between them and Chalcis is not explicable in terms of any positive gap in the record from Chalcis, where a good range of LG has now been found with the pottery continuing into the earliest seventh century. It is just possible then that there was a limited interruption of communication between Chalcis and Lefkandi/Eretria which persisted a little after the desertion of Lefkandi, a circumstance which might then indicate that this desertion was the result of action by Chalcis, and that Eretria, strong and prosperous in its new site, was happy to abandon the town in the plain. Against these hints must be weighed the correspondence between the sites in earlier LG and in most wares of later LG, and it may be premature to draw any such conclusions until Chalcis has been more fully explored and the Lefkandi LG cemetery found.

A point of possibly equal historical importance to the problems of the end of LG and the fortunes of the different Euboean cities is the dramatic change represented by the start of the LG style for pottery, which seems a generally Euboean phenomenon. The potters appear to turn their backs decisively on the lingering SPG tradition of the pendent semi-circle skyphoi, and to devote themselves to a new repertory of shapes and patterns inspired mainly by Athens and the islands. Without the overwhelming evidence of excavation and fabric it might have seemed difficult to believe that the SPG and LG were successive products of the same cities, and the contrast should put paid to any lingering suspicion that, in Euboea at least, SPG could continue through the second half of the eighth century. Its almost total absence from Eretria is a further demonstration of the same point. As well as the new pattern for skyphoi in LG we also see a rash of new shapes, the oinochoe with the cutaway neck is revived, and of all the other shapes discussed here perhaps only the strange kalathos 27 reflects an immediately prior fashion in the island. It is difficult to believe that such a dramatic cultural revolution in such a basic industry is not a symptom of other changes, not necessarily dramatic or violent, which brought Euboeans, who had already long travelled foreign waters, to follow more closely the prime styles of their fellow Greeks who were beginning to compete with them in the west, and, soon, in the east. And since such a change is unlikely to have occurred independently in several separate and competing centres, it may be an added argument for the production of central Euboean wares in one place in the crucial years of the mid-eighth century, when overseas cooperation between the Euboean cities is attested and before dissent between them had erupted into war.

### d. Lefkandi and other sites

When the Euboeans took a leading role in the foundation of a trading post at Al Mina in

North Syria before the end of the ninth century[103] the new city of Eretria had not been created and only Chalcis and Lefkandi stood as major settlements in the Euboean narrows. The Euboean interest in Al Mina continues to beyond the desertion of Lefkandi, into the period of the wire-bird kotylai, and, it may be, into the seventh century if the interruption of life at Al Mina is connected with the destruction of Tarsus in 696. We cannot judge which cities were most active on the eastern routes in LG since the Euboean from Al Mina matches the full range from our home sites, but Lefkandi was still at the receiving end of goods carried on this route, to judge from the Lyre-player seal found there — a type characteristic of earlier LG graves at Ischia where many more were carried by the islanders.[104]

When the Euboeans (Chalcis and Eretria are named by our sources[105]) founded Pithekoussai on Ischia in about 770 (to judge from the excavated evidence) the new city of Eretria had barely been founded and it is questionable whether it is Lefkandi or Eretria that could have taken the leading role. In the west the Euboeans soon began to make their own vases but the imports continued and new developments at home were observed and copied; the spouted craters, some figure motifs from the Cesnola Group (horse and manger, goats at tree), and the wire-bird kotylai which are missing at Lefkandi. In this case it is not possible to assign any special role to Lefkandi, nor is it easy to make comparable claims for Euboean ceramic associations with Greek sites nearer home. Andros, which Strabo (448) lists with Teos and Keos as under Eretrian sway, has several Euboean or Euboean-inspired pieces.[106] The possible role of Naxos has already been observed, as a source for the Cesnola Painter or elements of his style. In Boeotia, over the water, the debt of some of the latest LG and subgeometric amphorae to Euboean styles represented at Lefkandi has also been noted.


## 6. REOCCUPATION DEPOSITS (PLATES 59, 63)

There is little pottery to date the sparse sixth-century reoccupation of the site. 343 is an undistinguished one-handler (its horizontal handle missing) with a broad band at the lip and blotches all over — not closely datable.[107]

Some kotylai of local manufacture (344—8) but Corinthian in scheme of decoration are attested already at Eretria and in Boeotia (Rhitsona) where the contexts are of the middle and second half of the sixth century.[108] Only 345, with its mainly black body, might be earlier.[109] The usual scheme is of simple multiple-brush patterns in the handle zone and for the 'rays', though on 348 there seem to have been real outline rays and the underfoot is carefully hooped. The dot circle on 346 is an odd variant, perhaps inspired by the pattern of East Greek rosette cups which keep the centre point.

The Attic black figure fragment showing a boxer engaging another (missing) over a tripod prize (349) is from a lekythos of little after the middle of the century. His chest is red. 350 is a black Attic kylix, no earlier than the last quarter of the century.


## RETAINED LEVELS

Sample baskets of sherds from important deposits retained with no, or minimal, sorting. The purpose is explained in the Introduction to Section 2.

Area 1, The LG House
Basket 18 in box titled 'Area 1, LG House, floor deposit. BB level 3A'
Basket 123 in box titled 'Area 1, LG House, floor make-up. BB level 3B'

Area 2, The yard to the east of the LG House

Basket 69 in box titled 'Area 2, Make-up of yard floor. AA level 4'

Area 3, Pit 11

Basket in box titled 'Area 3, Pit. DD level 14D'

Area 4, a probable reoccupation pit

Basket 1120 in box titled 'Area 4, Pit. GG ext level 8'

## CONCORDANCE

Of illustrated Late Geometric pottery and inventory (P) numbers. (Supplementary details are given for some pieces not individually catalogued in the Deposit lists, 1–102 in the text.) The numbers 5/, 6/ refer to 1965 and 1966, the years in which the items were catalogued.

Deposits

| | | | | | | | | | |
|---|---|---|---|---|---|---|---|---|---|
| 1 | 6/296 | 13 | 5/6 | 25 | 6/276 | 36 | 5/163 | 47 | 6/1669 |
| 2 | 6/274 | 14 | 6/287 | 26 | 6/291 | 37 | 6/294 | 48 | 6/1670 |
| 3 | 5/197 | 15 | 6/288 | 27 | 6/277 | 38 | 5/175 | 52 | 6/1672 |
| 4 | 6/279 | 16 | 6/295 | 28 | 6/278 | 39 | 5/12 | 71 | 5/162 |
| 5 | 5/14 | 17 | 6/286 | 29 | 6/281 | 40 | 6/299 | 81 | 5/32 |
| 6 | 6/293 | 18 | 5/175a | 30 | 6/285 | 42 | 5/19 | 88 | 5/43 |
| 8 | 5/27 | 19 | 6/275 | 31 | 6/290 | 43 | 5/8 | 89 | 5/42 |
| 9 | 6/283 | 23 | 6/282 | 32 | 6/292 | 45 | 5/10 | 90 | 5/46 |
| 10 | 5/177 | 24 | 6/284 | 35 | 5/4 | 46 | 6/289 | 97 | 6/83 |

Other Pottery

| | |
|---|---|
| 117 | 5/21; D. of lip 11.2, H. 7.6. Black to red paint. |
| 120 | 5/36; H. c. 6. |
| 129 | 6/298; H. c. 9.5. |
| 131 | 5/23; D. of lip c. 15.5, H. pres. 8.5. Fugitive red paint. |
| 132 | 5/34; L. 8. Red paint. |
| 148 | 5/24; H. c. 10. Black to red-brown paint, white slip. |
| 157 | 5/9 |
| 180 | 6/27; D. 12, H. 6. Red-brown paint. |
| 194 | 5/35; H. 5.4. Black to red-brown paint, creamy white slip, orange ground. |
| 195 | 5/36; H. 6. Black to red-brown paint, white slip. |
| 196 | 6/79 |
| 201 | 6/78 |
| 208 | 6/19; D. of lip c. 15. Black paint. |
| 209 | 6/23 |
| 211 | 6/20 |
| 213 | 6/22 |
| 215 | 5/25; D. of lip 11.3, H. 6.6. Red-brown paint. |
| 216 | 5/29; H. 6.8. Matt black paint. |
| 217 | 5/47 |
| 225 | 5/22; H. pres. 13.5. |
| 232 | 6/25 |
| 233 | 5/28; H. pres. 9.7. Light brown paint, cream slip. |
| 234 | 6/251; H. 17. |
| 235 | 6/1671; D. of lip c. 30. |
| 248 | 6/252; H. c. 20. |
| 259 | 5/18 |
| 279 | 5/5; H. 22. |
| 280 | 5/151a |
| 309 | 5/26; H. 17.5. Dark, blue-black paint. |
| 323 | 6/21; D. c. 12. |
| 334 | 6/270; H. 13.5, Th. c. 1.0. Flanged at either side on the back. |
| 343 | 6/112 |
| 344 | 5/17; D. of lip 13.2. |
| 345 | 6/18; D. of lip c. 10. |
| 347 | 6/1673; D. of base 6. |
| 349 | 5/1; H. 4.1. |

# Section 5

# The Other Finds

*Objects of stone, clay, metal and other materials*   M. R. POPHAM with L. H. SACKETT

## OBJECTS OF STONE, METAL AND OTHER MATERIALS

The finds from the settlement, though generally unimpressive, cover most aspects of daily life and are probably typical of activities going on in a town of the early Iron Age. Exceptional are the mould fragments and graffiti, discussed separately at the end of this section, and the seal.

The finds have value, too, in that most were found in stratified contexts though of varying precision, which in some cases enable close dating, changes, and developments to be suggested.

The objects are grouped under the broad heading of the material of which they were made; a catalogue, similarly arranged, is given at the end of the discussion in which, where appropriate, account will be taken of corresponding finds from the cemeteries.

## OBJECTS OF STONE (PLATES 67–8 and 71)

The Late Geometric house and yard were adequately furnished with stone quern, basins (or mortars), pounders and hammers to serve its needs; for the pounders there was a ready supply in the pebble beaches below the settlement. Less readily explained, however, is the concentration of stone impliments in the LG phase and the presence of three tools, two axes and a chisel, which look every bit like Neolithic survivals, PLATE 67k–m. It might well be supposed that these were chance finds from an earlier age, reused after discovery, but we

have no such tools in the earliest levels on Xeropolis. Similar finds on the Pnyx at Athens
have been considered Neolithic too; and perhaps we should note our surprise rather than
suggest the possibility of an unexpected reversion to stone tools in the 8th century.[1]

Metal weapons, tools and knives required frequent sharpening, and, for this, the
Lefkandians in LG used plaques of schist pierced at one edge with a hole for suspension,
PLATE 67i, j; much earlier, two warriors were given whetstones of a different stone for
their burials (T Pyre 8, 3 and P Pyre 16, 3, PLATE 237f, g).

The marbles, or small balls, of white limestone come, in two cases, from an SPG I—II
context and so are later than the two LPG instances in the cemeteries (P 7, 7 ?SPG I, and
P 24, 15), where these objects are found seemingly in multiples of five; the burials are not
obviously of children though pieces for some game is their most ready explanation,
PLATE 237e.

This is clearly true in the case of the two stone dice, PLATE 66q, r, both from mixed
contexts which include Archaic pottery, though Near Eastern parallels do not exclude an
LG date.[2] Interestingly the arrangement of dots on ours for the numerals 3 and 4 are
not standardised.

The most important discovery, however, is the seal (25), PLATE 67u, belonging to the
so-called Lyre Player group, which was found in a penultimate LG level. Popular as offerings
in children's graves at Pithecussae, this is the first from Euboea, though we may suspect that
it was her merchants in particular who carried them to other parts of the Greek world and
to Italy from N. Syria or Cilicia, where Boardman and Buchner have located their place of
manufacture.[3]


## OBJECTS OF CLAY (other than moulds and tiles) (PLATES 64—5 and 70—1)

Most of these fall into two catagories, loomweights and spindle-whorls (or buttons) as they
are usually described. In addition, there are a number of pierced sherds and discs, with a
few other individual finds, a marble, thimble and fragmentary figurines.

### Loomweights
The loomweights, if correctly identified, were nearly all found singly, rarely in pairs,
obviously quite insufficient to equip a loom, but this is not surprising since most are from
pits, accumulated debris and levelling fills. However, these weights may have had several
uses, a conclusion indicated by two individual instances from the cemeteries (P Pyres 29 and
47), unless each was a symbolic offering only.

Four types are readily identifiable, the shapes of which have suggested the analogous
terms of 'doughnuts', 'oranges', 'figs' and pyramidal. The doughnut types (PLATE 70f),
though generally somewhat larger and flatter, seems closely related to the fig version
(PLATE 70a), the difference in shape, though sometimes blurred, being due to the method
of manufacture; in the latter case the large central hole has been pierced with a stick, or
similar object, while the pat of clay was still wet, so forming a distinctive frill or projection
on one surface around the hole. In both cases these weights, of rather coarse clay, gritty
and sometimes with straw inclusion, are often blackened on one side or on the base,
indicating that they may have been made at home and baked on the hearth. The same may
be true of the pyramidal type (PLATE 70l) though on these outer finish is much finer.

The doughnut shape was in use by LPG since several were found in the Moulds Deposit
(Area 2, Pit 1) and sufficient appear in SPG contexts to indicate that they continued in use

throughout that stage: none come from LG levels. The fig version, of which there are fewer, occurred in the SPG I–II Pit (Area 2, Pit 2) and in no certainly earlier level, while none are clearly later than SPG. Three of the four pyramidal weights were found in basically LG contexts; the remaining one could be earlier, SPG III, but may be part of some intrusive LG pits in the Levelling Material in which it occurred.

So there is a presumption that the doughnut version is the earliest, beginning at least in LPG which is the earliest period on the settlement; one of two examples from the cemeteries probably also belongs to this period, while the other is undatable, P Pyres 29 and 47. This type seems to have remained in use, and overlapped with, the fig variety which is first attested in SPG I–II and which could have persisted longer, into SPG III. The pyramidal shape would appear to replace these in LG. The single orange-shaped example, FIG. 70c, in an SPG I–II context may be a variant or an LBA intrusion. It is unfortunate that we cannot go further back than LPG on the settlement, to see whether the earliest type, which is not derived from the LBA, is one of the SM innovations. None published from Greece, of which we are aware, is even as early as ours. Most of the other shapes are simple ones and similar objects in the Near East in much the same periods may be just coincidence.[4] The pyramidal version, however, is an innovation at Lefkandi, and we may be justified in looking further afield both for its introduction in LG at Lefkandi and for its distribution over much of Greece, though elsewhere evidence for its use is generally later than on our site.[5]

### Spindle-whorls, buttons and beads

The smaller, pierced terracottas are usually variously classified as spindle-whorls, buttons or beads. Most of our few settlement examples are pear-shaped, PLATE 71t; their earliest appearance is in the SPG I–II Pit (Area 2 Pit 2) and none was found in later levels, apart from a near surface find (48). Similar ones from Corinth are said to be typical of the well-made Attic versions of the Classical period; ours are of fairly gritty fabric with a finer slip and are certainly much earlier.[6] To the few conical, or slightly concave, and undecorated examples (51 and 51a) may be added three instances from the cemeteries (P Pyre 15, T Pyre 4, 5 and P 3, 30), the two latter cases carrying their date back to LPG when they look related to contemporary incised examples (P Pyre 39, 3 and P 3, 30). The group of six from S Pyre 4 (nos. 19–24), PLATE 222, are each different, ranging from conical to exaggeratedly concave, the latter perhaps an SPG II development. In this case, six appear too many for spindle-whorls; buttons or beads is more likely. The interpretation as elements in a necklace would best suit, too, the circumstances in an LPG tomb, P 3, where the plain conical type were found grouped with undoubted beads. These beads (PLATE 214), with their stroke incisions and impressed circle decoration, exactly correspond in type and variety with others at Athens where they seem equally alien in fabric and are to be compared with the contemporary PG dolly of similar clay and patterning. They have been admirably discussed in detail by Professor Smithson.[7] Clearly the one incised bead from P Pyre 29, no. 3, is from the same source, while another singleton of convex shape, P Pyre 39, 3 is at least related (PLATE 236j, k). The impressed circles on a roughly contemporary bead from Xeropolis (47, ?LPG/SPG I) are the only link with the preceding ones; its careful grooving and superior fabric make it exceptional (PLATE 65o).

### Discs and others

Discs and roundels, pierced or not, shaped from sherds of various sizes, appear on most sites in many periods, so the twelve examples from the settlement and two from the tombs are no surprise (PLATE 65a—m). Unexpectedly, perhaps, most occur in LG levels, though the few from the cemeteries are earlier. Lids, gaming pieces and counters are among suggested uses discussed by Braun in the case of Attic finds;[8] more than one use is likely enough. Toumba 36, 32 is too small to cover the one vase in the tomb, a kalathos, though the example in P 36 could be a lid for the cup with this SPG I child burial. Unusual and curious, however, are the well-shaped small roundels (63—4) each with a groove around the edge PLATE 71w, v; no obvious use suggests itself.

The small clay ball (66) is presumably a cheaper version of its stone counterparts discussed above. The thimble (67) is undoubtedly such, since it bears clear bruises from needle ends which it has been used to push: handmade and from an SPG I—II context (Area 2 Pit 2), it would fit big finger or thumb.

On the two fragmentary figurines (68—9) Dr. E. French has kindly commented:

'Two animal figurines, presumably horses, display characteristics of the early Iron Age. One has a flattened splaying nose/muzzle and pierced eye and the other arched legs with angular section. Each has a pinched mane. There is no evidence whether these fragmentary pieces were attached to a vase or not. The typology of the horses seems more closely related to Attica than Boeotia but, as the main study is of those from the Kerameikos, this impression may not be justified.'

These fragments were not found in conjunction with the two wheels, which in any case had axles of different sizes, but wheeled toy horses are more likely than chariot groups.[9]

## OBJECTS OF METAL (PLATES 66 and 71)

These are mostly everyday utensils, where intelligible, and few deserve particular comment. The occupants of the LG house had a simple iron knife (86); a smaller cutting tool of bronze (76) occurred elsewhere in a superficial level. The objects include a small iron point and several related bronze awls with a small chisel of bronze, from different periods of occupation. Several objects are too misshapen or simple to suggest a use, though two might be identified as a pin or nail head (82) and a lead weight (73). The lead wheel PLATE 66b, is more exotic: they occur elsewhere and are usually termed votive with a later context.[10] Ours appears to be in an SPG level. The back of a fibula with leaf-shaped bow (83) is a useful addition to the relatively small number from the cemeteries, discussed in that section under 'Fibulae'; its context was unfortunately very wide, LG to LPG.

## OBJECTS OF BONE (PLATE 65t—v)

The two bone points and spatula are far fewer than might be expected in this readily available material. This perhaps reflects a poor rate of recovery by us due to the large quantity of animal bones, or kitchen refuse, in all levels.

## OBJECTS OF GLASS (PLATE 71a)

The few fragments of glass beads, too, probably represents a much larger original number of such objects, which quickly disintegrate in settlement conditions. Most are from SPG levels. Such beads are naturally better represented in the cemeteries and are discussed in the section dealing with glass objects from the burials.

## ARCHITECTURAL OBJECTS (PLATE 72)

All but one of the considerable quantity of fragmentary clay tiles come unfortunately from the very confused W. boundary of the main area (Area 4), where in Archaic times there was some reoccupation and disturbance. None were found associated with the LG house and the mass of tiles are no doubt later. Two joining fragments, however, of a rather different type and bearing a non-alphabetical inscription (98), PLATE 69l, were found on the E. edge of the excavation in a level containing SPG and LG pottery but nothing later; nor was there other evidence for subsequent occupation in this region. Most of the tiles were plain but a few were covered with paint ranging from red to near black, while one had additional streaks of applied white.[11]

## CATALOGUE

Digging levels, with chronological ranges, are given since many objects come from small deposits not considered in the general account of the stratigraphy and pottery, though this is quoted where relevent. Positions of objects from the LG House are plotted on PLATE 8a.

### STONE (PLATES 67–8)

**Pounders, hammers and rubbers**
1. Grey-green, crystalline. D. 6.5. Nearly spherical, one side flattened and pocked. On abandonment floor of LG House. Not illustrated.
2. Dark grey, crystalline. D. 5.6. Cuboid, surface uniformly rough. M level 9, basically LG.
3. Red. D. 6. Cuboid, four surfaces smoothed by use. On abandonment floor of LG house.
4. Grey-green. D. 6.5; Th. 4.7. Flattened sphere, one surface smoothed by use. BB level 3A, LG abandonment.
5. Dark grey with red mottling. Oval, 7.7 × 5.9; Th. 4.5. Sea pebble, one side flattened and smoothed by use. On abandonment floor of LG House.
6. Green, crystalline. D. 6.5; Th. 4–5.5. Two surfaces flattened and smoothed by use; broad groove along thickest edge: ?frag. of shaft-hole axe. BB level 4, SPG to LG.
7. Dark grey. D. 7.3–8.3; Th. 4.5. Irregular discoid pebble with one face smoothed. M level 7, LG.
8. Dark red with black flecks. Fragm. 7 × 4.3. One side smoothed. AA surface level. Not illustrated.

**Discs**
9. Green with black mottling. D. 8; Th. 2. Disc-shaped; one surface rough. CC Ext. level 7, mixed to Archaic.
10. Porous white limestone. D. 7.5; Th. 1.9; hole D. 1.2. Pierced disc: ?weight. On abandonment floor of LG House.

**Whetstones**
11. Schist, warm brown. L. 14; Th. 1.2. Flat rectangular slab, perforated at one corner, and uncompleted drill hole at opposite end; burned grey. On abandonment floor of LG House.
12. Schist, dark grey. L. 8.5; Th. 1.2. Flat rectangular slab, perforated at one corner; blackened at surface so perhaps originally from same context as 11. BB level 2, near surface.

**Axes and chisels**
13. Dark red with black mottling. L. 6; W. 2.3. Elongated oval, polished blade blunted by use. On abandonment floor of LG House.
14. Greenstone, granular. L. 6.7. Elongated oval, broad polished blade blunted and chipped by use. GG level 1A, near surface.
15. Greenstone with black mottling. L. 3.2. Triangular; finely polished blade. L Ext level 9, SPG I–II, probably part of Area 2, Pit 2.

**Small balls or 'marbles'**

16. Two examples found together. Both white limestone with D. 2.5. One well rounded; other irregular. Area 2 Pit 2, SPG I–II.
17. As 16, porous. D. 2.8. Fairly regular sphere. DD level 1, surface.

**Pierced, spherical beads or buttons**

18. Black serpentine. D. 2.3. Biconical, polished but worn; traces of incised wavy line on one surface. CC level 2, near surface.
19. Dark grey. D. 3.2. Biconical, smooth but worn. GG Pit X. LH IIIC and SPG.
20. Black serpentine. D. 2.1. Rather conical, irregular, worn and chipped. GG level 5, LH IIIC and SPG.
(see also no. 52)

**Quern**

21. Light grey, crystalline and coarse. Broken on one side; extant L. 19; W. 22; H. 6. Almost flat, smoother and more level on top. On abandonment floor of LG house.

**Basins and mortars**

22. White limestone. W. 14; H. 9.5; depth of depression 2. Rough hewn, rather hemisherical base. Shallow depression with spout, roughly cut, on top. BB level 5A, possibly Mycenaean but could be LPG–SPG.
23. Buff, porous, ?limestone. D. 6.5; H. 4; depth of depression 2.5. Birdnest shape, roughly hewn outside, uneven base. On abandonment floor of LG house.
24. Blue-grey, crystalline. D. 14.5; H. 8.5; depth of depression 3.5. Birdnest shape, well-rounded outside. AA level 2, near surface but perhaps originally as 23.

**Seal**

25. Red serpentine. 1.4 × 1.0 × 0.8. Chipped on one side. Seal of 'Lyre Player Group': a tree with herring-bone trunk and palmette top, flanked on both sides by a bird and ankh. Cf. *JdI* 81 29, no. 63 and 36, no. 128. DD level 2A, penultimate LG 'floor'.

**Dice**

26. White ?limestone, porous and lightweight. Cuboid, 1.8 × 1.8 × 1.4. Flattened, worn and rounded at edges. On opposite faces, dot numerals for 1 and 6, 2 and 5, 3 and 4. The 3 arranged as triangle on its apex, four as a cross and the remainder as usual today. GG Ext level 3; LG but in area with Archaic.
27. As 26. Cuboid, 1.8 × 1.8 × 2. More regular and better shaped than 26. Numerals placed as on 26, but 3 is arranged in a diagonal line and 4 in a square. GG Ext level 5; context as 26.

CLAY (PLATES 64 and 70)

**Loomweights**

*Doughnut type*

28. Brick-red clay with straw inclusion and some grit; buff to red fine slip; one face split away. D. 7.7; Th. 3.5. L level 9, SPG I–II, probably part of Pit 2 Area 2.
29. As 28; fire blackened on one face. D. 7; Th. 3. L Ext level 8; context as 28.
30–1. As 28. Frags about $\frac{1}{3}$ of weight. Area 2 Pit 1; LPG.
32. As 28. D. 7; Th. 3. Area 2 Pit 2, SPG I–II.
33. As 28; fire blackened on one face. D. 7; Th. 3. BB/CC level 5A, ?SPG.
34. As 28; fire blackened on one face. D. 5; Th. 1.7. DD level 4C, SPG and LG.
35. Two pieces as 28 but badly fired and worn; probably doughnut type. D's. 3.7 and 4.2; Th. 2. GG 3D/EE 3, SPG to LG.
36. Condition and context as 35. D. 4.3.

*Orange type*

37. Rather coarse buff clay, self slipped, smooth and burnt black at one edge. D. 7; Th. 4.4. L level 8, SPGI–II, probably part of Pit 2 Area 2.

*Fig type*

38. Fine buff clay and smooth slip, burnt black underneath. D. 6.2; Th. 3. Area 2 Pit 2, SPG I–II.
39. As 38. D. 7.8; Th. 3. BB level 4A ?SPG.
40. Dark brick-red with much temper, smoother slip; darkened underneath. D. 4.8; Th. 2.6. DD level 4B, mixed LPG to LG.
41. Fine buff clay and slip; damaged. D. 5. DD levels 3,4,4B, mixed but mainly SPG.
42. Fine red-buff, burnt black on upper surface; fragmentary. D. 4.5. EE level 2D, mixed to Archaic.

*Pyramidal*

43. Coarse red clay with grit, smoother fine slip; well-made and evenly fired. H. 9.2. M level 7, LG.
44. Yellow-buff rather coarse with smoother slip, burnt black on one face. H. 8. CC/GG Ext level 6, LG to Archaic.
45. As 44 but not blackened; broken at top. AA level 5, basically SPG III but some LG intrusion.
46. Coarse red, blackened on one face, damaged. H. 5. From abandonment floor of LG House.

**Spindle-whorls and buttons**

47. Fine red-buff with smooth light brown slip. Biconical, H. 3.5; D. 4. Incised grooves and stamped circles. DD level 7C Pit III, LH IIIC and LPG, possibly SPG.
48. Fine grey, self slipped. Piriform, H. 3; Max D. 3.8. Half preserved. BB level 2, mixed to Archaic.
49. As 48, blackened on one side. Piriform, H. 3; Max D. 3.5. L Ext level 8, SPG I–II, probably part of Pit 2 Area 2.
50. Gritty dark brown to black clay with fine red slip. Piriform, H. 2.2. Half preserved. Hollowed base, pierced from top with frill below. L level 12, SPG I–II, (not illustrated, as 51a below).
51. Fine red with grey, slightly 'soapy' slip. Conical, H. 2.2; Max D. 3. AA level 5, on edge of Pit 2 Area 2 (SPG I–II) but includes LH IIIC.
51a. Crumbly red, somewhat coarse, smooth slip. Conical, Max D 3.2. Top missing and damaged. M level 4, LPG–SPG with LH IIIC.
52. Stone (included here in error), black serpentine. H. 1.6; D. 2.1. Irregular spherical, worn and chipped. GG level 5, SPG III with much LH IIIC.
53. Fine grey-buff, smooth slip. H. 1.7; D. 2.5. Flattened spherical with one convex surface. EE/GG Pit X, SPG III with LH IIIC.

**Pierced sherds**

54–62. Little point would be served in individually describing these common objects beyond illustration, details of which can be found on the excavation catalogue cards. Most are from LG deposits, and 57 and 59 from the LG House, but the date of the sherds themselves is usually indeterminable. Most are from large vases, with a fairly flat surface, roughly chipped around the edge into a circle; in two cases the single hole (as on all) has been similarly chipped out but generally it seems to have been made with a bevilled drill or awl.

**Discs**

63–4. Both are sherds, slightly convex, very carefully made circular and incised with a neat groove around the edge, ?to hold a thread. Ds. 2.6 and 2.8. BB/CC level 5, ?SPG and LL level 2, near surface.
65. As 63–4 but without groove. D. 2.1. Area 2 Pit 2, SPG I–II.

**Marble**

66. Red, fairly fine, roughly hand-shaped into spherical. D. 2.7. Cf. nos. 16–7 in stone. CC level 2, near surface.

**Thimble**

67. Red-buff fine clay and slip, handmade, uneven outside and in. L. 2.3; D. c. 2.4. Prick marks on tip. AA level 5 = Area 2 Pit 2, SPG I–II but with some LG intrusion.

**Terracottas**

68. Red clay, lustrous paint; bands across neck. Frag. of ? horse figurine; arched legs with angular section and pinched mane. AA level 3A, LG.

69. Buff clay, brown wash paint; head solid painted, neck solid painted on right, horizontally banded on left. Frag. of ?horse figurine; trumpet nose and pierced eye. JJ level 2A, LG and SPG.
70–1. Two wheels both fragmentary and of different sizes, see also PLATE 70 and commentary above. Area 3 South, illustrated as 645–6 on PLATE 24 with associated LPG pottery.

## METAL (PLATES 66 and 71)

### Lead
72. Rectangular plaque, 5.4 × 2.2; Th. .025. AA E. Ext level 3, LG.
73. Small round and conical ?weight. D. 1.9; H. .09; Wt. 15.25 g. AA E. Ext level 8, mostly LH IIIC with some SPG I–II.
74. Seven-spoked wheel with axle sleeve; mould made. D. 3.7; L. of sleeve 1.5. Trial III level 2A, LH IIIC with SPG.
75. Amorphous flat frag. which had 2 tubular projections on one side, now broken off. ?Part of mending clamp for a large vase. 3.7 × 2.0; Th. .02–6. GG level 2, near surface.

### Bronze
76. Small one-edged knife, complete but for end of tang. L. 3.8. DD level 2, near surface.
77. Small chisel, complete but for chip off blade. L. 5.1. Oblong section at head. DD level 5C Pit III, SPG, probably to LG.
78. Awl or drill of near square section, complete. L. 5.4. BB level 4, SPG but probably with LG.
79. Frag. broken at both ends of object similar to 78 with near square section. Ext. L. 5.4. DD level 1, surface.
80. Frag. of awl or nail of square section. Ext. L 5. AA level 3A, LG.
81. Awl, punch or drill, square section at head, round at point. L. 6.8. AA level 5, SPG I–II, Area 2 Pit 2 but with some LG intrusion.
82. Head of nail or pin, mushroom-shaped with socket. D. 2.3. AA level 5, context as 81.
83. ? Bow of leaf-shaped fibula. Pres. L. 4.1. DD level 7A, LPG to LG.
84. Misshapen lump with 'loop' at one end; oval in section. L. 4.1. From desertion floor of LG House.
85. Pierced disc or circlet. D. 2.8; Th. 0.2. AA E. Ext level 5, SPG I–II, Area 2.

### Iron
86. Knife blade, broken at haft, one-edged. Pres. L. 11.4. From desertion floor of LG House.
87. Point of nail or awl. Pres. L. 5.7; max. D. .06. DD S. slot of LG structure G.

## BONE (PLATE 65)

88. Long curved point of round section, fragm. Pres. L. 15.1 + 3.3. Polished surface but worn. GG level 4B, basically SPG.
89. Straight point of oval section, complete. L. 6.4. Sharpened at one end, flattened at other; worn. DD level 4B, SPG to LG.
90. Point, sharpened at one end; point broken. L. 9.3. BB E. baulk level 3, ?SPG III.

## GLASS (PLATES 66 and 71)

91–7. Fragments of variegated glass beads of cylindrical and spherical shapes, in contexts from SPG I–II to LG, and so augmenting and continuing the series after the end of the cemeteries in early SPG III. Details of context and date available on the excavation catalogue cards.

## ARCHITECTURAL (PLATES 69 and 72)

### Tiles
98–9. Many fragments of roof tiles, collected at W. edge of Area 4, a zembil (basket) full, including parts from some 10 pan tiles of 'Corinthian' type (estimated width 24.0) and fewer cover tiles. The area was confused but the tiles appear to have belonged to some Archaic building in that region. Typical fragments are drawn on PLATE 72 under the collective no. 99. Clay is generally light red, gritty with a cream smooth slip.

99. Fragment of flat pan tile (PLATE 69). Pres. L. 21; W. 24; Th. 3.8. Coarse gritty buff clay with red and black inclusions; self slipped. Smooth at the end and upper surface, rougher below where there is a broad, retaining groove. A non-alphabetic graffito in groove (see 110). M level 8, SPG and LG.

## THE GRAFFITI

### Their archaeological context

The graffiti, discussed by Dr. Jeffery below and catalogued with their contexts at the end of this section, are not on intact vases but on fragments. Moreover, all but two shreds are from plain or solid-painted vases which make them practically impossible to date stylistically. So, their stratigraphical contexts, where dependable, only give a terminus ante quem for their date.

The earliest, no. 111, a non-alphabetical graffito, is from an SPG I–II (EG I–II) context and the decoration of the sherd is consistent with this dating. A somewhat later date, SPG III (MG II) for no. 103, also non-alphabetical, is suggested by the fabric of the cup it is incised upon and by its far from decisive stratigraphical context. Perhaps contemporary, no. 102 is certainly alphabetical and scratched on a seemingly non-local vase. No other alphabetical inscription from the site is demonstrably earlier than LG.

To this stage may confidently be ascribed the most important and longer examples, nos. 100 and 101, both from pits exclusively LG in content. It is interesting that both these and the remainder, except for no. 112, are from pre-desertion deposits, though the interval between their deposition and the abandonment of the site could well have been very short; see Professor Boardman's comments at pp. 73 above. (M.R.P.)

### Commentary on the graffiti, with a Note on the Greek use of the long sigma (PLATE 69) by L. H. Jeffery

LH = letter-height. See the Catalogue, after the Note, for fabric, pot shapes, and context.

*Alphabetic inscriptions*
105 LH 1.9.
> Sign now incomplete, but clearly deliberate: a vertical stroke with a hook to L. at the top end. The writer had two tries at the hook, one splayed, one more sharply bent; this suggests that he was inscribing a letter, a pi R to L — we should not invert the sherd and read a lambda L to R, for which the sharp hook would be inexplicable. Nor are retrograde alpha or rho likely, for an unfinished transverse stroke would be odd in either case.

The following three sherds, all in plain wares, bear fragmentary inscriptions which could be simply owners' names, or the start of something slightly longer, as in some of the earliest Attic graffiti (cf. those published by M. K. Langdon, *op. cit.* under 102 below).

101 LH 1.2–2.7. R to L. Αἰσχρι[---]
> Sigma here is 5-stroked, the 'long' sigma which was also used in certain other areas, but has not hitherto been attested in Euboic, a matter discussed in the Note at the end. The letters start small, then increase in size, as in others of our very early inscriptions, e.g. the 'Dipylon Jug'.[12] Possibly our writer started with a 3-stroke sigma (as in 100 below), increased it to the longer form (for whatever reason), and automatically lengthened the following letters to match. Αἰσχ- is certain, with the 'red' chi-form normal in Euboic; Αἰσχίνης, Αἰσχρίων, Αἰσχρυβίων are all attested elsewhere in Euboea,

cf. *IG* xii. 9, Index Nominum. The next vertical could be part of iota, rho, or upsilon; then comes the lower part of another vertical, with (just where the sherd breaks) a possible trace of a branch to L, as for an upsilon. This, if certain, would suggest Αἰσχρυ[βίον]; otherwise, Αἰσχίν[ες] or Αἰσχρί[ον] are possibilities, in the nominative or the possessive genitive. (To read L to R here, -χσία (fem. nom. or masc. genitive) is of course ruled out by the Ionic dialect of Euboia.). Cf. A. W. Johnston and R. E. Jones, *BSA* 73 (1978) 129 n. 30.

100 LH 2.2. ?R to L. Σαμ[---]
Sigma here is the normal 3-stroked type. Part of owner's name? As in 101 above, the Ionic dialect forbids our reading L to R -ίας, either masc. nom. or fem. genit. The third letter is uncertain; mu is suggested here because the names Σάμος, Σάμιος are certainly attested in Euboic; c.f. *IG* xii 9, Index Nominum.

102 LH 1.1. R to L. [---] σα, or L to R, Ἀμ[---]
If it reads R to L (as nos. 100–1, and probably 105 above) we have again a long sigma, though tilted out of vertical, and a retrograde alpha, with a crossbar as normal, sloping down to L. If L to R, we have the normal Eretrian 5-stroked mu (though sloping sharply upwards) and alpha with abnormal crossbar. For the early, curving alpha here and in 100 and 112, see M. K. Langdon, 'A sanctuary of Zeus on Mount Hymettus ' *Hesperia* (1976) 42 and L. H. Jeffery, *JHS* xcviii (1978) 202f., a review of Langdon.

112 LH 2.6. Single curving alpha, with crossbar prolonged down to L. The surface of the sherd is battered and worn, but it does not look as though there were any more letters originally (hardly visible on PLATE 40, no. 39).

108 LH 2.7. This appears to be epsilon L to R, its top part lost (shown upside down in the photograph).

109 LH 2.4. ?Part of an alpha L to R (shown upside down in the photograph).

*Non-alphabetic signs*

103 Lower part of sign carefully incised. Rho or beta might suggest themselves, but here the well-rounded curve is totally unlike the ductus in any of the very early graffiti which show either letter, and the tail is too short for an early rho, and too deliberate for a beta (for a typical tailed beta in 8th cent. graffiti, see Langdon, *op. cit.* 16 fig. 7, 20). Probably, therefore, an owner's mark or the like.

106–7 Arrow-type graffito on each, possibly the same owner's mark?

110 LH c. 1.0. Four signs, apparently meaningless. The graffito may possibly have been scratched on a single sherd at some time after the tile had been broken (see illustration, for the breaks). It suggests the pseudo-script of an illiterate hand, but at least this indicates that others in this society were literate at the time indicated by the stratification.

111 Sherd preserving part of a sign which was heavily ploughed in the clay before firing; it consisted of at least three short vertical lines with a horizontal line scored across them. Probably not an example of xi, for which one would expect a writer to start with the long vertical before putting in the three cross-strokes. Perhaps some kind of tally was intended or a merchant's mark.

104 LH 1.6. This graffito looks deliberate, and might conceivably be meant for a zeta here shown sideways; but it suggests, rather, some simple identification-mark.

Brief though it is, the material from Lefkandi makes an important addition to our other existing examples of very early Greek alphabetic graffiti, since its dating in the 8th century rests fundamentally on stratification-levels carefully observed. The letter-types are characteristic of the local Euboic script; and there is one peculiarly interesting form, the long sigma, discussed in the Note which follows. Alongside the literate writers' graffiti, the non-alphabetic signs are, roughly speaking, of the kind found elsewhere on early Greek pottery, probably by illiterate writers: mostly owners' marks to ensure identification, the sort of thing that Homer's heroes may have scratched on their pebbles (Iliad vii 175—89) when casting lots for the privilege of duelling with Hector.

*Note on the Greek use of the 'long' sigma*
The 5-stroked sigma in 101 appears to be deliberately done and is as yet perhaps our earliest example of the letter (though cf. also the earliest example from Smyrna, discussed below). On the present evidence it would be rash to argue that the script of Lefkandi should belong to early Eretrian, of which we have many examples, rather than early Chalcidic, of which currently we have none earlier than the 6th century. They are basically alike, but the 5-stroked mu of Eretria and her western colonies is as yet absent from Chalcis and hers. It is likely, however, that the script of agricultural, conservative Bocotia — attested c. 700 BC or earlier — was derived from that of her neighbour Chalcis, for it resembles hers rather than that of Attica, the other obvious possibility as a source; and one of our earliest datable Boeotian inscriptions is the dedication by one Mantiklos, in the Boeotian dialect, to Apollo on a large bronze statuette dated c. 700—675; and it does show, among its 4-stroked sigmas, one 5-stroked example. This may be an error, but the whole inscription was cut carefully by the bronzeworker with his tools, which could suggest that at least he was familiar with a 5-stroked form.[13] Possibly, then, this craftsman was aware of the existence of a 'long' type of sigma, though he then turned over to the four-stroked type.

It does not appear that the 'long' letter represented any difference in pronunciation of the sibilant, in Euboea or elsewhere; it seems to have been simply an epigraphic variant, as with the 3- and 4-stroked types of sigma. But there may be some ethnic or geographic pattern evident from the places where it is attested. Its extensive use in Laconia is well known, from the first half of the 6th century onwards through the 5th.[14] It is still un-attested in Arcadian and Elean, which otherwise are close to Laconian; we do not know whether it came into Laconian from elsewhere, as a proper letter-form, or whether, in the small closed circle of Laconian craftsmen, some early letterer elaborated his sigma thus, and the thing caught on. Certainly it seems to have been used there longer and more consistently than in any other Greek state.

Nearer to Euboea, Attica has produced two possible, very early examples. One is the baffling 'Steinsplitter' *IG* i² 484 (*LSAG*, Attica no. 2); I once doubted,[15] but now accept the earlier editors' interpretation of its long zigzags as sigma. The other occurs in the fragmentary painted inscription on a sherd from the rim of a Protoattic amphora (c. 700—650),

[---] ς  :  με [---].[16] Given the height of the complete letters, it is hard to reconstruct the surviving top of the first one as other than a multiple-stroked sigma.

Boeotia, Attica and Euboea cohere on that east side of Hellas whence, in the PG period, bands of emigrants were filtering across the Aegean to settle on the richer coast of Asia Minor opposite; and we note that, whether or not by chance, the long sigma occurs in the Aiolic area (across from north Euboea via Skyros) at Smyrna. A sherd with three surviving graffiti letters, one the zigzag, was found, 'context LG, with some intrusions': a sherd almost certainly of local Ionic fabric.[17] The letter might equally well be a Phrygian or Lydian sibilant (see below), but Smyrna has also produced two clearly Greek examples, both of the 7th century:[18] one a potter's painted inscription round the flat rim of a clay dinos, c. 650–25, naming the producer as Istrokles, and the other a fragmentary dedication incised on part of a greave of a type datable roughly c. 700–650.

It has long been suggested that the Old Phrygian script was derived from an early Greek alphabet, judged by the similarity of its letter-forms to the early Greek ones, especially in those cases where both differ identically from the Semitic practice (e.g., the 'vertical' alpha, and the line-direction, boustrophedon and left-to-right). The long sigma is very common in Phrygian, though the shorter form is also used; both types passed thence into the Lydian script. The occurrence of long sigma at Lefkandi and Smyrna may hint that the Phrygian script was derived from the script of the early Greek settlers in Aiolis. The Greek tradition said that the Midas – or a Midas – of the Phrygian royal dynasty had made a dynastic alliance with Agamemnon the Greek ruler of Kyme in Aiolis, by marrying Agamemnon's daughter Hermodike (var. Demodike).[19] Absolute dates for the earliest Phrygian inscriptions are not yet stabilised, but the latest research[20] on the stratification at Gordion city, and on the objects in the Great Tumulus, suggests that the dates previously proposed for the earliest inscription from Gordion and for the Great Tumulus[21] are too high. If this is right, then our earliest inscribed Greek material should precede in date our earliest Phrygian, and leave us free to hypothesise that the Phrygians could have got their script directly from a colonial Greek source such as Kyme in Aiolis or Smyrna – ultimately, that is, from the Thessaly–Euboea area, whence the Greek settlers in Aeolis came[22]; of which area, only Euboea counted for anything epigraphically at the time. There are as yet no early Greek inscriptions from Skyros, and none before the 6th century from Chios, the two islands which were important stages on this early trans-Aegean route. The 5-stroked sigma has indeed turned up off the coast of Asia Minor, but further south, in the Heraion at Samos, on the flat rim of a clay dinos (c. 600? TAQ of c. 570 BC): an incised verse-dedication in Ionic Greek.[23] What do we make of this (as yet) solitary example from Ionia? Was it taken from the Aiolic into the Ionic script? Or was Istrokles himself Ionic, though his painted dinos was dedicated at Smyrna? Or should the examples from Laconia warn us against seeking to localise the use of 'long' sigma too precisely? Its appearance on both sides of the Aegean, among the Greeks in the area of Euboea and their Asiatic neighbours, Greek and barbarian, does seem suggestive; but the Laconian usage – even allowing for the known archaic links between Sparta and Lydia – is not yet satisfactorily explained.

## Catalogue

Dimensions for sherds and graffiti are not given since the reproductions are scaled or have centimetre scales included. The letter in brackets after their inventory number refers to that given them on PLATE 69.

100(a) Shoulder frag. from large jug/amphora, plain; medium coarse core with fine grit, baked grey, with finer slip, light brown and smooth; hard-baked. Inscription a heavy incision which has splintered the surface. The first stroke is incomplete at top and bottom.

LK/65/50 from AA digging level 3; the yard in Area II, in a basically LG context with some SPG.

101(b) From vertical neck of large vase, plain; lower edge of sherd shows junction with body; coarse red-orange fabric with heavy grit content; slip lighter brown with uneven surface. Sharp incision into the slip. 1st and 2nd letters incomplete at top; 3rd, two left hand strokes incomplete.

LK/65/58 from CC digging level 3A; fill of Pit 13 in Area 4. Associated sherds are LG; see discussion under LG Deposit C above.

102(d) From incurving neck of ?jug, just below junction with lower end of handle; red, slightly sandy clay with considerable small mica; slightly finer, dark red slip; handmade ? Probably an import. Heavily incised with sharp point. 2nd stroke incomplete at top and bottom.

LK/69/74 from Trial W digging level 2A; pit under latest floor. Context possibly SPG III, see discussion at pp. 19 and 48 above.

103(c) From base of cup, solid-painted in and out; red, slightly glossy paint, typical of SPG reserved-line cups, see PLATE 265c. Incised with sharp point. Top of letter incomplete.

LK/69/75 from BB digging level 5. Context possibly SPG III (MG II), see discussion on p. 47 above.

104(e) From lip of solid-painted cup with reserved lip outside and two reserved bands inside, usual local clay with black to brown slightly glossy paint. Profile resembles PLATE 62,97. Second vertical incision incomplete below.

LK/66/194 from GG Extension digging level 7. Context SPG to LG.

105(f) From neck of jug/oenochoe painted black on exterior, plain in; usual local clay with rather lustrous black paint. Heavily incised. Lower stroke incomplete.

LK/66/193 from EE digging level 4A. Context mixed to LG.

106(g) From shoulder of large, rather coarse, plain jug/amphora. Heavily incised.

LK/65/84 from DD digging level 14D; LG Pit 6 in Area 2. For LG context, see discussion of LG Deposit D above.

107(j) Body frag. from large coarseware vessel.

LK/65/15 from DD digging level 2, practically a surface level and without chronological value.

108(h) From large jug/amphora neck, plain; for fabric and context, see 109. Since photographed, two frags. were joined showing that as reproduced it is upside down and its upper edge (as reproduced) is close to the junction of neck with body.

LK/66/140; possibly from same vase as 109.

109(i) From shoulder of large jug/amphora, plain; dark red hard-baked clay with yellow-grey slightly micaceous slip. Could be from same vase as 108. Sherd probably reproduced upside down. Bottom and left hand stroke (as reproduced) are incomplete.

LK/66/139; from L Extension, digging level 5. Context basically LG, nothing later.

110(k–l) Frags of unpainted tile; drawn in section at PLATE 72,7.

LK/69/70; from Trench M digging level 8. Context, LG and SPG.

111(m) From shoulder of large jug/amphora decorated with concentric circles, of micaceous clay, so probably not local. Heavily incised when clay was wet and before painting.

From AA E. Extension digging level 5A + B + C = Area 2 Pit 2 'The SPG Pit'; PLATE 16, no. 171. Context SPG I–II, discussed above.

112 PLATE 40, no. 39. Described under LG Deposits A and under Amphoras in section on LG Pottery above. Right hand stroke incomplete below.

LK/65/P12, from an LG desertion level.                                                                    (M.R.P.)


## THE MOULD AND CRUCIBLE FRAGMENTS — THE FOUNDRY REFUSE

In the fill of Pit 1 Area 2, was a large quantity of very shattered clay objects in a context which is dated around 900 BC, a matter of the utmost importance in any assessment of the character of Greek Dark Age bronze metallurgy.

The material is not as explicit as one would have hoped, but it is absolutely clear on two basic metallurgical points. The evidence of crucible fragments shows that metal was melted

on the site in preparation for casting, while the evidence of fragments of lost-wax moulds
makes it clear that quite sophisticated bronze objects were cast. Unfortunately, these mould
scraps are too fragmentary for it to be clear exactly what kind of object was involved.

Before the brief catalogue of significant fragments that follows it is important to under-
stand the general character of the material. Investment casting (= the cire perdue/lost wax
process) involves the following procedures – first, the construction of a full scale model
in wax of the desired end-product. This model is clad ('invested') in a very fine-textured
clay which completely covers the wax; the clay takes upon itself in negative all the positive
characteristics of the wax original. The finer the investment clay, the more subtly it can
reflect the character and detail of the wax original. In its turn, this investment clay is
enveloped in a thick covering of much coarser clay which protects the finer inner material
and, presumably, in due course, absorbs some of the shock created by the inpouring of
molten metal. When these two stages of investment have been completed and the clays
allowed to dry, sufficient heat is applied to the invested cartoon to melt out the wax completely and bake the investment. Molten bronze is then poured into the mould to replace
the melted wax and left to cool down. This process leaves, at this stage, an invisible bronze
object clad in a relatively shapeless clay envelope. Only by shattering the envelope – the
investment mould – can the founder produce his creation. The smashed pieces of the mould
are of no further consequence, for they cannot be re-used for their original function. (At
a further remove a kind of mass production of lost-wax moulds is possible. A stone or metal
master mould can be created in which the wax cartoons/or components of them may
themselves be cast (instead of being hand-made) and then subjected to the procedures
already described). In an ideal world, it should be possible to reconstruct a lost-wax mould
from its shattered parts. Arguing from the Lefkandi material, there are two major obstacles.
First, many of the parts went astray before the remainder were swept up and deposited
in the pit-filling. Second, the two types of clay tend to separate from each other. On survival
performance, the fine investment clay, (to be seen as a distinct layer on PLATE 12e and
shown black on the sections on PLATE 13a) which alone carries the original appearance
of the wax cartoon in negative, evidently disintegrates if it is separated from the much
coarser envelope clay. There were quantities of fragments of envelope clay with no investment clay adhering, a much smaller number where the two varieties were still united – and
none consisting of investment clay alone.

The consequence was that of more than 350 fragments collected and examined, fewer
than twenty possessed any characteristic that was of any value in establishing their function.
For what follows a description of the two types of clay employed may be of assistance.

*Investment clay.* Relatively fine, well levigated (blows would be disastrous for a cast)
pale brown material which shows a typical bluish-grey tinge at what will have been the
point of contact with the molten metal.

*Envelope clay.* Very coarse indeed, with a laminated structure, dark red at the contact
point with the investment clay (heat induced, presumably), then yellow-buff, then a roughly
smoothed yellow buff surface.

In studying the mass of material, nearly 200 'crumbs' of envelope clay were set aside
initially as uninformative in any way. In addition to these, about sixty larger amorphous
lumps of coarse envelope clay were also set aside as uninformative. The remaining pieces
were divided into two categories – identifiable and unidentifiable. A catalogue of the
former is given below. The latter were further subdivided as follows:

A  A group of flat thick pieces. The material is envelope clay. Eight pieces, the largest 9 × 7 × 2.2. The remainder were 1.5 thick. The inner surfaces were rough and quite unfinished, the outer surface reasonably well smoothed. No trace of investment clay attached to any of them.

B  A group of thick lumps. The material is envelope clay. Forty pieces 2–5 square, 2.5 thick. No trace of investment clay attached, and no suggestion of form.

C  A group of thin fragments of envelope clay. Twenty pieces, varying in thickness 1–1.5. One or two fragments had grey inner faces, suggesting they must have been fairly close to molten metal. No joins could be made, and none of the pieces large enough in itself to suggest shape.

D  A group of thick fragments of envelope clay. Twenty pieces, varying in thickness from 1.5 and above.

E  A miscellaneous residue of fifty various sized fragments, which may have included some crucible pieces, some having blackening marks on one face, presumably from contact with molten metal, as well as fragments showing heat cracking.

## Catalogue of recognizable foundry rubbish (PLATES 12–13)

M.  1  Crucible fragment with metallic waste matter adhering to the side. Extant ht. 7.2. Extant length 13.5. Greatest thickness 4. Two joining fragments. Clay extremely course greyish brown with heavy mixture of grey, surfaces red in patches. (NB this clay is recognizably coarser than the envelope clay described above).

M. 2–3, 5–10 Fragments of *cire perdue* moulds for casting fairly solid rectangular strips decorated in relief. Such strips would have been sturdy enough to be used as the legs of tripod stands or tripod cauldrons, for instance. Different fragments preserve part of the front (decorated) or part of the back (plain) of such strips or legs. The fragments suggest that the mould was broken by blows struck along its narrow face, for this is the line followed by the fracture in most observable cases. It was not possible to join any of the front parts to the back. (In fact, only two joins of any kind could be made among the fragments.) The face of the strip had been decorated with three fairly closely set parallel relief ridges on the central axis flanked either side by a line of linked spirals. A single relief ridge on the outside left and right completed the design. From the centre of one spiral to the centre of the next is 2 cm. The diameter of individual spirals was about 1 cm. At least two strips seem to be represented, to judge from differences in the arrangement of the spirals — in one case, M. 2, the links run from left to right, whereas in another fragment, M. 3, the links run from right to left. A rough idea of the thickness of metal cast in the mould was obtained from careful study of M. 3 and M. 7. In the former, the thinnest point must have been at least .15, the thickest .5 M. 7 presupposes a thickness of at least .65.

The complete mould(s) seem to have been quite neatly finished, with fairly smooth surfaces to the envleope clay, PLATE 12b. The latter is rarely more than 1.5 thick.

M. 2, 5  Part of front of strip. Extant 1. 11. Greatest w. 6.8. W. of cast 5.2. Combined thickness of envelope plus investment clay 2.3. The links between spirals run from left to right.

M.  3  Part of front of strip. Extant l. 8. Greatest w. 7.5. Greatest thickness 2.8. Part of investment clay broken away and lost. The links between spirals run from right to left.

M.  6  Probably part of front of strip. Extant l. 7. Greatest w. 7. Combined thickness of envelope plus investment clay 2.3. Surface of investment clay too much rubbed to identify ornament though traces of the relief ridges survive.

M.  7  Part of back of strip. Extant l. 8. Greatest w. 7.2. W. of cast 5.2. Combined thickness of envelope plus investment clay 2. Faint traces of four very fine relief ridges.

M.  8  Part of ? back of strip. Extant 1. 7.5. Greatest w. 7.2. Thickness 2.1. The investment clay has disappeared; it occupied a space 5 wide.

M.  9  Fragment without investment clay. Extant 1. 5. Preserved w. 6. Thickness 2.

M. 10  Fragment without investment clay. Extant 1 5.8. Preserved w. 6. Thickness 2.4.

M.  4   Part of front of strip, probably of different form from the preceding. Extant 1 7.5. Preserved w. 5.3.
        Th. of matrix clay 1.0. The investment clay is damaged, and only two parallel relief ridges can be
        distinguished. The strip from this mould may not have been flat in section, but the relief surface
        could have been concave.
M. 11   Two joining. Preserved 1.9. Extant w. 5.3. The casting space seems to have been subrectangular
        3.3 × 5 in plan, and undecorated. If the decorated strips already described are in fact legs, then this
        piece of the mould may have fitted the end of the strip (of which, of course, it was an integral
        part) and served as the foot.

**Miscellania**

M. 12   Mould ? Foot. Extant h. 4.8. W. 5. Extant th. 3.8. Envelope-type clay. Possibly the finished mould
        was given feet of this kind on which to stand during casting.
M. 13   'Plug' shaped object. Ht. 3. Dimensions of upper surface 3.6 × 3.2. Very lightly baked orange-red
        clay, with some grit. Function uncertain.
M. 14   Fragments of a shallow receptacle made of envelope clay. Plain rim, ht. 8.1, 1. 11.2. Attached
        separately to a flat disk which composed the floor, of which only a fragment 4.7 wide survives.
        Function uncertain — ? mould for disk ingot.
M. 15   Fragment of a pouring funnel, composed of envelope clay. Ht. 5. W. 4. Th. 1.8.
M. 16   The like. Ht. 5.5. W. 5.5. Th. 1.6.


This material has stimulated much interest since its first discovery, both for what it
tells us of the level of metallurgical achievement in Euboea in the later Dark Ages, the
force of which is undeniable, and really requires no further emphasis; the material speaks
for itself and, in my opinion, serves as a very important corrective to the view that a great
deal of bronze-working expertise had to be reintroduced to Greece as the Dark Age ended,
either from the Orient or barbarian Europe (with which, for the moment, we must include
Italy). This view, of course, runs counter to the view of Dark Age bronze shortage, a factor
which should not be ignored in view of the strength of the case for it.[24]

The more particular question raised by the identifiable mould fragments concerns
the identity of the object of which the casting was to form part. Is this evidence for the
manufacture of tripod stands or tripod cauldrons in Greece at this early date? If it is not,
then what kind of evidence is it? This is not the place for a complete review of the extremely complex question of the origin and development of bronze tripod-making, particularly
of the relationship between the Cypriot production at the end of the Bronze Age[25] and
the major tripod series of Late Geometric Greece. But, despite Professor Snodgrass' dis-
claimer, the Lefkandi find has suggested that there is a stronger case for a continuous
development than at one time seemed likely. I, too, for different reasons, expressed a
dissenting view in 1964 when I said[26] 'The revival of the tripod in Greece depends not on
copying the antique stands that survived from a forgotten relationship with Cyprus, but
on the arrival of fresh ideas from the East. It is with the tripod from Altin Tepe that the
next stage must be related . . .'. I no longer think this assumption can pass unchallenged.
I think the decoration of the Fortetsa Tomb XI tripod's legs,[27] with their lines of linked
spirals, makes a very important link between the Levantine group and the Lefkandi moulds.
The discovery of the Lefkandi moulds, from the other side, reopens the question of the
place of manufacture of such a tripod stand as Fortetsa Tomb XI. Notice that even if it
could be decided where such a stand had been made, it would not necessarily identify
the maker. Given the evidence for foreign contacts at Lefkandi, especially for oriental
contact, we could not exclude the presence there of a bronzesmith trained in the East
working as an itinerant craftsman. What is more, he may well have brought with him the
materials he needed for his work, as well as his expertise.

Before the proposal is rejected that there is a unifying link between Cyprus—Crete—
Euboea and the great series of tripod cauldrons of Olympia and elsewhere,[28] it has to be
explained why the Lefkandi arrangement of parallel relief ridges and running spirals should
appear in almost exactly the same kind of juxtaposition as the ornament of some of the
tripod cauldron legs from Olympia.[29] Almost as close is the decoration of the leg of one
of the Ithaka tripods.[30] To suppose that there is no connexion is surely to abjure the
traditional archaeological arguments. We have already seen that Lefkandi must stand in
some relationship to the Fortetsa Tomb XI tripod. This in its turn must carry with it the
whole Levantine series. To turn the discussion on its head — it would surely require a great
deal of ingenuity to erect a series of hypotheses that could account for these data without
finding any common factor.

# THE CEMETERIES

# Section 6

# The Excavation and Layout of the Cemeteries

M. R. POPHAM and L. H. SACKETT, with P. G. THEMELIS

## INTRODUCTORY

The cemeteries of Lefkandi are situated on the slopes immediately to the north of the village, at a distance of about 600 m from Xeropolis, the main settlement site (see map and air photo PLATES 2b, 73a, b). There are five separate burial grounds. The earliest investigated is that furthest to the north, in the field of A. Skoubris, which has a high proportion of cist graves of the Submycenaean and early Protogeometric periods. Two robbed cists in the field of A. Khaliotis, to the east in the direction of Xeropolis, may be earlier still (and there are reports of others), but this area remains unexcavated. About 100 m to the southwest of the Skoubris field lies the Palia Perivolia cemetery, in the field of N. Nikolaïdis; this contains pyres and shaft graves of Protogeometric and Sub-Protogeometric date, and from the part excavated its total area can be estimated as about 30 x 15 m, containing perhaps sixty burials. A trial trench 20 m to the east of it revealed a small group of contemporary pyres and tombs: this is separate, and is known as the 'East Cemetery', see plan PLATE 76a. About 50 m to the west of Palia Perivolia a further cemetery was identified, on the eastern slopes of the hillock 'Toumba', from which it has taken its name. A smaller proportion of this has so far been excavated, but the burials so far revealed are roughly contemporary with those of Palia Perivolia.

In all, 147 tombs and 80 pyres have been found,[1] the earlier mostly concentrated in the north and east, the later in the southern and western parts (see cemetery plans, PLATES 75, 77, 79).

It is uncertain whether the settlement to which these cemeteries belonged was on

Xeropolis, for although this hill was inhabited from Late Protogeometric times onwards, there is no clear evidence in the small area excavated, nor in the trial trenches, for the earlier Protogeometric or for the Submycenaean phases.

### System of reference to cemetery objects

The following abbreviations and system of cataloguing have been adopted. For the individual cemeteries, Skoubris = S, Palia Perivolia = P, Toumba = T. The East Cemetery is not abbreviated, but the two robbed tombs in the field of A. Khaliotis are distinguished by the letters KT.

Tombs and pyres form separate series, and are numbered consecutively for each cemetery, 'Pyre' being added to distinguish the pyres from the tombs: thus Skoubris Tomb 4 = S 4, Skoubris Pyre 4 = S Pyre 4. The East Cemetery was excavated as part of Palia Perivolia, and the original sequence of numbering has been retained for the four tombs and three pyres found there: thus, e.g. East Cemetery Tomb 42 = P 42. Objects found are also numbered consecutively for each tomb and pyre, e.g. T 26,1 etc.

In addition, the complete or fragmentary vases found in the surface levels of Skoubris are referred to by the letters SF, e.g. S SF3.

### Excavation

The stratigraphy was generally simple (see PLATE 75 section A—A' for Skoubris, PLATE 78 sections A—A' and B—B' for Palia Perivolia). Natural soil or rock was encountered in most places immediately beneath the layer of cultivated topsoil, at a depth of c. 20—40 cm, and tombs and pyres were found dug into this.

The rock is a coarse conglomerate with whitish pebble content and associated areas or veins of rust-red earth; almost everywhere the original hard weathered crust had been removed, leaving an upper layer of loose conglomerate rock very difficult to distinguish from the material used to refill the graves, which has re-compacted.[2] Where there was an intermediate level, as in parts of the Skoubris and Palia Perivolia fields, this consisted partly again of decayed rock from tomb cuttings or cultivation, and partly of silt. In places, too, a sherd, pebble and silt fill was found in rock depressions or gullies (see under Skoubris and Palia Perivolia below).

In a number of cases tombs or pyres were stratigraphically related, when one was superimposed above or partly cut into another. This is a source of useful chronological information which is tabulated below for each cemetery separately; but sometimes the exact line of a cutting in the loose conglomerate could not be followed and the fills could not be distinguished, and in these cases the sequence remains unclear.

Two types of tomb are typical of the Lefkandi cemeteries, the cist and the shaft grave, and in general the one is followed by the other in chronological sequence. Much rarer examples occur of pit graves, built graves of mud brick and urn burials.[3] All these types are considered in detail in Section 8.

Cremation pyres, about equal in number to the tombs in Palia Perivolia, though fewer elsewhere, occur throughout the period of the cemeteries' use,[4] and may in certain cases have subsequently served as tombs also.

### Tombs in the field of A. Khaliotis (PLATE 73a)

No regular excavation was undertaken in this area. The four objects published here were chance finds, although three of them (KT 2—4) were said by the landowner to have come from a cist in his field. This information led to the investigation of two robbed cists, the one at the E edge of the village road, the other about 10 m further SE, in the field; these two are about 50 m from the main area of cists in the Skoubris field. Both were empty. Patches of ash indicated the presence of pyres nearby, and it is possible that a cemetery here extends further E towards the hill slopes directly facing the settlement site of Xeropolis.

### Skoubris Cemetery (PLATES 74–5)

Excavation here consisted of rescue work, test trenches and some later extensions to these. Rescue work became necessary in April 1968 after a slit trench was opened mechanically, for a water pipeline which ran from north to south through the cemetery field (PLATE 74), destroying some graves and cutting through the carbon deposits of several pyres.

Two test trenches had been already dug in 1964 (A, B), and of these only the first was productive; here were found Tombs S 1–5 and the deposit S Pyre 1A (PLATE 80). Trench B appears to lie outside the eastern limit of the cemetery. Seven small tests were dug in the north of the field in 1969, prior to the erection of a building in the field;[5] two of these (K and O) contained cists and pyres (S 26–7, S Pyres 12–18 PLATE 91), but the others found no burials and probably fell outside the limit of the cemetery at the northeast. Very productive however were the extensions made to the trenches in the main area at the S: an opportunity was taken in 1968 to link up the S end of the pipeline cutting with the 1964 trial (see section A–A' PLATE 75); here 21 tombs (S 5A–25) and 11 pyres (S Pyres 1–11) were found. Then in 1969 a larger extension was made (Trenches Xi, Pi, Rho, Sigma), which contained another 40 tombs (S 28–63) and 1 pyre (S Pyre 19).

A total of 64 tombs was excavated (56 cists, 3 shaft graves, 4 pit graves, 1 amphora cremation) and 21 pyres or pyre deposits. Of these, 3 tombs and 9 pyres were damaged by the mechanical excavator and others by cultivation; in addition 5 tombs had been disturbed during the period of the cemetery's use, but still the majority (42 tombs, 11 pyres) were found intact, and where there was disturbance it had not in every case reached the grave offerings.

The extent of the cemetery is not known. Its northeastern limits may run somewhere on a line from Trench K to Trench A, but it could extend over the whole of the unexcavated central part of the field, and beyond the field boundaries to the north and west (where local reports place chance finds in the past). Little extension to the south is likely, since a rocky outcrop rises to the surface here at about five metres distance. It seems possible that the area excavated (c. 175 sq. m) is no more than a quarter of the whole cemetery.

In the extreme SW of the excavated area there was a broad gully in the rock surface running down from the higher slope at the S (see plan PLATE 75). This contained a fill of pebble and sherds some 25–50 cm deep, which covered the area of Tombs 36–8, and extended as far as Tombs 10 and 13 before petering out as a thin scatter of sherds in the sub-surface soil. The sherd material, though it includes some shapes not occurring in graves, such as the krater and pithos, is contemporary with the later period of the cemetery's infrequent use and seems to be connected with it in some way. See discussion of this and the similar fills in the Palia Perivolia and East Cemeteries on pp. 266 and 273 below.

### Palia Perivolia Cemetery (PLATES 76–8)

The excavation of Palia Perivolia was comparatively thorough. The field was laid out in 5 m squares on a N–S grid; first every other square was dug in a checker board pattern to test as wide an area as quickly as possible (Squares A, C, E, G, J, L, N, P, R, T), later some of the alternate squares (F, M, Q and part of B, D, H, K) were dug, and extensions were made to the S (Square V) and to the E (Trenches LL–PP), PLATE 76a.

This made it possible to define the boundaries of the cemetery with reasonable certainty in all four directions. To the S and W there are wide areas of open ground with no graves (Squares E, P, T, R, V), to the E is a barren strip of rock some 10 m wide, revealed in the test trenches MM, NN, OO (PLATE 76a), while to the N a channel perhaps served as a boundary ditch running E—W through the northerly squares (A—E), PLATE 197b. A total of 40 tombs and 47 pyres were found within these limits,[6] the greatest concentration occurring in the central E area (Squares F, G, L, M, Q), thinning out towards each side when approaching the edge of the cemetery (see plan at PLATE 77).

The Palia Perivolia cemetery contained only one cist (P 25B) while the majority of tombs (33 in all or 83%) consisted of rock-cut shafts of an average depth of 1.20 cm. The remaining six tombs were shallow pit graves, cut only 10—45 cm deep in the rock. The pyres had a black ash fill and the surrounding rock or earth was burnt hard and often showed a clear red outline. Their rock cuttings were only of an average depth of 30 cm, but in most cases, if not all, the upper part of both pit graves and pyres had been cut away by the plough.

The orientation of both pyres and graves is far more regular than that in the other two cemeteries; all except four tombs and three pyres run from N to S, some having a slight NE deviation. These four exceptions, the northern group of large shaft graves (P 12, 21, 22) and a child burial (P 35), are oriented approximately E—W, as are P Pyres 7, 8 and 39. Whether or not this represents a distinction in terms of family grouping or status, there is no chronological unity.[7]

The northern boundary of the Palia Perivolia cemetery was formed by a rock channel, 1.0—2.0 m wide and 1.0—1.20 m deep at the centre. It was excavated in three separate squares (A, C, E). The three sectors of channel excavated contained a fairly homogeneous fill of pebbles and silt with much pottery, most of which was apparently dumped there during the period of use of the cemetery. The bottom 50 cm of fill in the Square A sector ('silt' in section B—B′, PLATE 78), were dug separately and contained among other pottery an early (SM) amphora, predating any tomb yet found in the cemetery. In the rest of the fill were included large amphora and krater fragments as well as smaller vases. This fill is discussed separately below, p. 269. The channel seems to have been used as a deposit both for the excess spoil from the digging of graves and pyres — consisting mostly of pebbles from the conglomerate — and for the remnants of discarded pottery connected with the use of the cemetery: grave offerings, markers and perhaps vessels used at the funeral ceremonies.

A separate pit was found in Square T, c. 30 cm deep, cut into the rock (PLATE 77 lower left, and section B—B′ on PLATE 78a). This contained a small amount of MH occupation pottery, homogeneous in character and belonging to the MH II phase.[8] The deposit serves to show the very wide spread of the Lefkandi settlement at this period.

### East Cemetery (P 42–3, 45, 47; P Pyres 48–50) (PLATES 76a, 78b)

In order to establish the eastern boundary of the Palia Perivolia cemetery, a series of 5 × 1 m test trenches (LL, MM, NN, OO, PP) was dug, late in the 1970 season, in the field of G. Neroutsios as an eastern extension of the Palia Perivolia grid. This purpose was achieved in that the tombs and pyres of the main cemetery were seen to end after about 8 m and there followed 10 m of featureless rock surface. However, the test trench was further extended for 7 m and a separate group of tombs and pyres was discovered at a distance of from 18 to 24 m from the original Palia Perivolia grid, both in the line of the tests (Trenches NN, OO, PP) and directly to the N of these. This group forms the East Cemetery.

It was not possible to investigate this area fully, but four tombs were excavated, and three pyres were identified (but not excavated). The tombs were dug into a rock depression or gully, shown as a shaded area in PLATE 76a, and it is clear that they form a separate group, which may well be confined to the immediate area of the gully. Further extension tests to the eastern limit of the field showed that the burials do not continue in this direction. The principal point of interest of this group, as so far dug, lies in the fact that the two larger tombs (P 45 and 47) contained inhumations, unlike any of those in Palia Perivolia.[9]

### Toumba Cemetery (PLATES 76b, 79)

Surface sherds found on the slopes of Toumba and concentrated on the E side in the field of V. Franges, suggested the existence of a settlement here, incorrectly as it turned out. The cemetery was discovered in the summer of 1969 when trial trenches were dug in the hope of finding a Submycenaean or Early Protogeometric settlement associated with the Skoubris cemetery (Trials I and II, PLATE 76b). These trenches immediately hit a complicated series of graves which included T 5 and T 7 close beneath the surface. After a survey of the field undertaken with a Proton Magnetometer by M. Aitken, the trenches were extended principally on the west side (Trenches I—III), and here Tombs T 1—19 and T Pyre I were found and excavated.

In 1970 during a fuller season a grid of five 5 m squares was laid out and excavated (Trenches IV—IX, PLATE 76b). Here were found Tombs T 20—37 and Pyres 2—10.

A total of 36 tombs was dug and one other located (T 37); almost all were shaft graves, but three, possibly four (T 12A, 13, 36, 4?) were constructed in mud brick and set in shallow pits.

No excavation could be made in the adjacent fields to the west, so that it is impossible to estimate what proportion of the whole cemetery has been revealed. The small test trenches towards the N and S edges of the field (B, D, N, PLATE 76b), and the E extension were unproductive, but surface sherds and stone slabs found 50—80 m further W, near Toumba summit, might suggest extension in this direction, or possibly a separate burial ground.[10]

The layout of the tombs so far excavated is interesting, in that they fall into two quite dense groups on either side of an empty strip, possibly a track or road leading up the hill from the harbour area. There is also an unoccupied space of levelled rock at the northwest of the excavated area. One small tomb, T 30, was the only one cut into this rather harder weathered rock surface, and the only other features observed were three shallow rectangular cuttings arranged in a triangular form with outside measurements 1.0—1.20 m, as if for the feet of a large tripod. This levelled area was bounded on the west side by the robbing trench for a wall; it contained some rubble and mudbrick fragments, but few foundation stones remained in position. The dotted line on the cemetery plan (PLATE 79) gives its estimated position. Possible functions of the levelled space in connection with the use of the cemetery are discussed below (p. 214).

## STRATIGRAPHY AND THE RELATIVE CHRONOLOGY OF TOMBS AND PYRES

Although there was a general pattern of movement from the early use of burial grounds at the N and E to a later use of those at the S and W, there is no clear pattern of progression within each cemetery,[11] see plans PLATES 75, 77, 79.

There was a close concentration of tombs within the ground used, and their layout, especially in Skoubris and Palia Perivolia, indicates a general respect for earlier graves and *a priori* a knowledge of their precise position, from some kind of marker. But there were instances where earlier tombs were disturbed or destroyed, presumably after a lapse of sufficient time for the marker to have disappeared. This was especially true of the Toumba field.

The surface levels contained both burnt sherds, probably from disturbed pyres, and also others unburnt, principally amphorae, which may have been set up over a tomb or pyre.

## Skoubris Cemetery

Recent disturbance and cultivation will account for most of the vases and sherds found in the surface level, though others found in the subsurface soil may come from tombs which were destroyed during the period of the cemetery's use; both are included in the catalogue of surface finds (p. 139, see also discussion on p. 265, and PLATE 111).

In considering the extent of possible clearing and re-use of the ground, it is worth noting that the sherd fill in the south gully has most material from the period which has fewest tombs surviving in the excavated portion of the cemetery (SPG I–III).[12]

Too small a proportion of the cemetery is as yet excavated to make it possible to define a chronological pattern in the location of the tombs and pyres; one may say only that the SW corner of the field was in use from the earliest times (SM–MPG), that there is a concentration of pyres in the NW, and that the later (SPG) tombs are inserted sporadically in unused areas (S 5, 21, 25A, B, 33, 45, 56, 59).

The following tombs and pyres were stratified, either where a later tomb lay over an earlier, or more frequently where the diggers of one tomb cut into another and partially disturbed it (the earliest burial is listed first in each case):

S 3 → S 2 and 5 (S 3 was cut into and disturbed by S 2; S 5 partly overlies S 3).
S 4 → S Pyre 1A (S Pyre 1A overlies S 4, and is interpreted as contemporary).
S 9 → S 10 (S 10 cut through part of S 9 and went deeper).
S 19 → S 18 and 20 (S 18 partly overlies S 19; S 20 is close to but at a higher level than S 19, and must be later).
S 21 (cist) → S 25A/B and S 21 (deposit) (S 21 was cut by S 25; the deposits S 25A and B may be later than the cist S 25 itself; the deposit S 21, 1 and 2 are probably a later deposit, outside S 21).
S 35 → S 30 and 31 (S 30 overlies S 35; S 31 is closely adjacent and higher).
S 36 → S 33 (S 33 cut and destroyed the south end of S 36).
S 46 → S 45 (S 45 cut and disturbed S 46).
S 52 → S 62 → S 51 (S 62 cut and partly disturbed S 52; S 51 overlies both).
S 55 → S 54 and 59 (S 54 partly overlies S 55; S 59 cut and partly destroyed S 55).
S 59 → S 59A (Deposit S 59A overlies S 59, and is interpreted as contemporary).
S Pyre 4 (lower) → 5 Pyre 4 (upper) (the one lies directly over the other).
S Pyre 13 → S Pyre 14 (S Pyre 14 partly overlies S Pyre 13).
S Pyre 16 → S Pyre 17 (S Pyre 17 partly overlies S Pyre 16).

## Palia Perivolia Cemetery

The surface soil contained some sherds, principally from pyres, but no tombs had been disturbed by modern activity, and there were few cases of ancient disturbance.

In some cases there were fragments of pottery in the fill of the tomb shafts. Most were scraps, including MH fragments; but when relevant to the dating of the tomb, or of intrinsic interest, they are mentioned in the catalogue of individual tombs, or in the separate discussion of sherd material from the cemetery area (p. 268 below).

The Palia Perivolia pyres and tombs are concentrated into a comparatively small area, but only in seven cases is an earlier tomb encroached on by a later one (P 6, 14, 19, 22, 24, 26, 39A). Five of these were left unviolated, a blocking wall being constructed in three cases (P 19, 22, 24); the other two were found empty (P 14, 26), and might have been robbed. Two further possible instances of disturbance may be noted: the rock cutting labelled P 25A, and a possible destroyed tomb at the west end of P 22 (*qv.*). In five other cases a shaft cutting touched that of an earlier tomb (12/17, 22/19, 23/26, 46/30, 33/34) without, however, penetrating the grave itself.

In a number of cases trenches for pyres were cut above earlier tombs (Pyres 14A, 14B, 24, 28, 33–7, 41); one (P Pyre 20) cut down through the edge of a pit grave. But normally their shallower cuttings did not disturb the much more deeply set burials.

Tombs which are stratified are as follows (the earlier tomb or pyre is in each case mentioned first):

P 14 → P 11 → P Pyre 24 (P 14 is cut by P 11 and partially destroyed; both lie beneath P Pyre 24).

P 16 → P Pyre 14B → P Pyre 14A (P 16 lies beneath P Pyre 14B; both lie beneath P Pyre 14A).

P 19 → P 12 (P 19 is cut by P 12 — blocking wall).

P 24 → P 21 (P 24 is cut by P 21 — blocking wall).

P 25B and 46 → P Pyre 35 → P Pyre 34 (P 25B and 46 lie beneath P Pyre 35; P 46 and P Pyre 35 lie beneath P Pyre 34).

P 32 → P Pyre 33 (P 32 lies beneath P Pyre 33).

P 37 → P Pyre 20 (P 37 is cut by P Pyre 20).

P 38 → P Pyre 36 (P 38 lies beneath P Pyre 36).

P 40 → P Pyre 28 (P 40 lies beneath P Pyre 28).

P 41 → P Pyre 37 (P 41 lies beneath P Pyre 37).

P Pyre 25 → P 6 → P 9 (P Pyre 25 is cut by P 6; P 6 is cut by P 9).

P Pyre 27 → P Pyre 31 (P Pyre 27 is cut by P Pyre 31).

P Pyres 28 and 43 → P Pyre 42 (P Pyre 42 partly overlay the other two)

P Pyre 32 → P 28 (P Pyre 32 lies beneath P 28).

In the following cases where tombs intersect, the sequence is stratigraphically uncertain: 12/17, 21/22, 22/23 (blocking wall), 21/26, 22/19, 23/26, 39/39A, 46/30, Pyres 21/9, 9/39, 37/39.

### East Cemetery

In the area of the East Cemetery the rock surface shelved down to form a gully c. 1.10 m deep, see section, PLATE 123. The principal fill of the gully was a deposit of loose pebbles with dark earth, beneath an upper layer of brown silt. Tombs P 45 and P 47 were both cut down through this fill, and made use of the natural rock edge of the gully to form one side of their shafts. Thus the sherd content of the fill, though limited in quantity, is significant in that it stratigraphically predates Tombs P 45 and 47. P 42 was at one edge of the gully and appears to predate the sherd fill (for discussion of the sherd fill and chronology, see p. 273 below).

No tombs were stratigraphically interrelated.

## Toumba Cemetery

Some of the tombs lay only 20–40 cm below the surface, so that it is fortunate that no deep ploughing had yet been done in this field. The majority of tombs, 22 in number, were found intact; only three had been partly destroyed by the plough (T 4, 12A and 36), and there were no signs of robbing in modern times. The surface soil contained some sherds of interest (p. 275 below), but there were few other finds;[13] no pits or deposits of any kind were found outside the tombs and pyres.

The stratigraphical interrelation of tombs and pyres was more complicated than in the other cemeteries, and there seems to have been less effort to place tombs in fresh ground. However, the existence of grave markers is suggested by the presence of a large stele-like slab in the upper shaft of Tomb 34.

The following tombs and pyres are stratified (the earlier is listed first in each case):

T 1 → T 11 → T 5 (T 1 lies partly beneath T 5 and T 11, T 11 partly beneath T 5).
T 6 → T 4 (T 4 lay partly over T 6).
T 6 → T 14 → T 5 (T 6 is cut by T 14; T 14 lies beneath T 5).
T 3 → T 15 → T 13 (T 15 lies partly over T 3 — blocking wall; T 13 lies over T 15).
T 8 → T 7 → T 12A (T 8 was cut and partly destroyed by T 7, and cut also by T 12A).
T 21 → T Pyre 6 (T 21 lies beneath T Pyre 6).
T 23A → T 23 → T 24(?) (T 23A is cut by T 23; T 24 cuts T 23 and is probably later).
T 26 → T Pyre 4 (T 26 lies beneath T Pyre 4)
T Pyres 5 & 7 → T 29 → T 27 (T Pyres 5 and 7 are cut by T 29; T 29 is cut by T 27).
T 35 → T 31, 32, 33 (T 35 lies beneath T 31, and is cut by T 32 and 33).
T 34 → T Pyres 8 & 9 (T 34 lies beneath T Pyres 8 and 9).
T 34 → T Pyre 9 → T 32 (T 34 lies beneath T Pyre 9; T 32 cuts T 34 and T Pyre 9).
T Pyre 1 → T 17 (T Pyre 1 is cut by T 17).

In the following cases where the tombs intersect, the sequence is stratigraphically uncertain: 2/11, 6/2, 6/11, 14/11, 23/28.

# Section 7

# The Tombs, Pyres and their Contents

M. R. POPHAM and L. H. SACKETT with P. G. THEMELIS

## SKOUBRIS CEMETERY (PLATES 73—5, 80—114)

**S Tomb 1** (PLATE 80). Cist. 67 x 26, depth 26. Intact. Three limestone cover slabs (only 20—5 below the surface). Neatly built with rectangular side slabs of a gritty grey conglomerate with an inner lining of white magnesite at each end. Pebble floor. Light silt fill; no other contents.

**S Tomb 2** (PLATE 80; Contents, PLATE 92). Cist. 86 x 25—30, depth 30. Intact. Four cover slabs; side slabs of blue limestone, end slabs of white magnesite. Pebble floor. Silt fill, with possible trace of ash. On the floor five pots, apparently tipped in at random; no. 2 is burnt and broken. The feeder (3) shows that this was a child cremation.

**Pottery.** Homogeneous, locally made. The quality of the surface has deteriorated, especially inside the open vases; the paint is thinly applied and streaky, with a tendency to flake off. All intact except for no. 2.
1. Pedestal bowl. H. (without handles) 6.5. Monochrome except for reserved foot, and barred handles and rim.
2. Multiple vase, deep bowl type; single section broken off at either side. H. 5, with handle 10.2. The breaks suggest that this was the central section of a triple vase joined longitudinally; they are not precisely opposite, but if this was a circular kernos the diameter would have been very great. Fabric burnt to grey; dull black paint inside and out, much worn.
3. Feeder with basket handle (jug). H. 10.6. The handle is at a little more than $90°$ to the spout. Decorated as shown. Spout and outside of handle monochrome.
4. Shallow bowl. H. 2.8. Two string holes (D. 1—2 mm) below the lip. Monochrome except the underside and a central dot on the floor.
5. Pedestal bowl. H. (without handles) 6. Three handles on the rim. Monochrome except for reserved foot and bands, and barred handles and rim.

**S Tomb 3** (PLATE 80; Contents, PLATE 92). Cist. Length c. 80: partly destroyed when S Tomb 2 was constructed. Two small cover slabs were in position, two others had fallen in; three vertical slabs, including a dressed slab of white magnesite at the south end, were in position. Two pots, apparently *in situ,* were found in a dark silt fill inside the presumed area of the grave.

**Pottery.** Local clay and paint. Intact except for chips, and one handle missing from no 1.
1. Small neck-handled amphora. H. 12.2. The wavy lines on each side are linked by a ring round the root of the handle, which itself has a thin vertical band on the outside. Otherwise banded.
2. Deep bowl. H. 8. Note the dots inside the rim. Decorated as shown. PLATE 256c.

**S Tomb 4** (PLATE 80; Contents, PLATE 92). Cist. 145 × 30. Five large limestone covers, side slabs of magnesite and coarse conglomerate. Pebble floor. Two vases were thrown into the S end of the cist and broken; the jug (2) was burnt, presumably in the cremation pyre. Above the cover slabs was found an ashy deposit, with sherds which may be part of the offerings for this tomb and are catalogued separately as S Pyre 1A (following below).

**Pottery**
1. Tripod. H. 8.3. Intact. Local fabric. There are four tab handles on the rim, one above each leg and a small additional one. Decorated as shown. PLATE 257d.
2. Jug. H. 10.8. A fragment missing where the handle joins the rim. Local fabric, burnt to grey; streaky black paint. Monochrome except lower area.

**S Pyre 1A** (PLATE 80; Contents, PLATE 92). Above the cover slabs of tomb 4. A quantity of sherds making up into four vases, badly damaged by fire, and contained in a loose fill of grey ashy earth, not the thick black carbon deposit such as occurred in the normal pyres of the Lefkandian cemeteries. They must represent the rakings from a cremation pyre, and are separate from the adjacent amphora burial (S Tomb 5). In a number of cases (see p. 201) some offerings were placed inside a cist and others over the closed tomb, and it seems most probable that this is what happened here. This group is then either contemporaneous with, and part of, the funeral offerings of S Tomb 4, or a separate offering placed over it not long afterwards.

**Pottery.** The vases are one half to three quarters complete. Local fabric, from the unburnt fragments; the effect of the fire, however, has been to burn the clay to grey, and to damage the surface so that the paint is cracked and flaking off.
1. Pyxis, straight-sided, with lid. H. of pyxis 14.5, with handles 16. H. of lid 6.8. Both pyxis and lid have been restored in plaster. Decorated as shown.
2. Lentoid flask. D.12. Most of one side preserved, but little of the other, and none of the neck or mouth. Flattened sphere, with hole (d. 9 mm) where the neck joined the body, and a small airhole beside it (d. 3 mm). Decorated as shown.
3. Triple vase. H. 7.8. L. (rest) 16.2: D. (central vase) 5.5. Three joined belly-handled amphoriskoi, decorated as shown. Note that only two of the horizontal side handles have been preserved. The restoration can be taken as certain both for shape and decoration.
4. Cup. H. 5.8. Monochrome except reserved lower area and barred handle. Reserved central dot on the floor.

**S Tomb 5** (PLATE 80; Contents, PLATE 93). Amphora cremation burial, at the S edge of S Tomb 4 and partly overlying it. The lower half of the amphora was in position, set on a bed of rough stones and surrounded and supported by others (five in position); its base was only c. 40 below the surface, and its upper part had been destroyed by the plough. Inside were the undisturbed remains of a cremation: white calcined bone fragments, ashes, and the badly damaged fragments of a macehead, which had been subjected to the funeral pyre. Beside the amphora and overlying the S cover slab of S Tomb 4 was a small neck-handled amphora, lying on its side and probably to be associated with this cremation burial.

**Pottery.** Both vases are of local fabric.
1. Belly-handled amphora, fragmentary. H. (pres.) 28.5: Max.d. 30.5. Decorated as shown. PLATE 267e.
2. Small neck-handled amphora. H. 17.4. Complete, with slight restorations. Monochrome, reserved bands.
*3. Macehead, fragmentary. Largest fragment 5.3 × 3.2. Greatest th. 0.45, to as little as 0.1. Restored l. 13. Shaft d. 4.7. Boss d. 5.4. Six main fragments and two scraps, anciently broken. Parts of some fragments are folded double. Some crusty surface patina. It originally consisted of a cylindrical shaft the swollen central section of which is prominently ribbed. The shaft on either side is picked out with groups of two encircling relief ridges. Made by lost-wax; the inside is rough, and reflects the unsmoothed surface of the clay core. PLATE 239j–k.

**S Tomb 5A.** Cist. 55 × 18, depth 20. Very close to surface, and disturbed by ploughing. Only the upright slabs of three sides remained, and one schist cover slab (30 × 20), found nearby. Pebble floor; no contents.

**S Tomb 6.** Cist. Width 25; partly destroyed by the bulldozer. Three uprights and one cover slab survived, the side slabs protruding beyond the end slab to form an H. The slabs are dressed and of white magnesite, about 10 cm thick. Pebble floor; no contents, but some of the surface finds may originate from this cist.

**S Tomb 7** (PLATE 193d). Cist. 144 × 43, depth 34. Set in a rectangular rock cut pit. Six uprights of limestone, magnesite and schist, roughly shaped and held in place by smaller packing stones. Two large cover slabs, intact. Pebble floor; no contents.

**S Tomb 8** (PLATE 81; Contents, PLATES 93, 208a–b). Cist. 105 × 40, depth 45. The bulldozer had removed one cover slab, but the rest of the structure was intact. It was cut into the natural conglomerate at 1 m below the surface, and had rough side slabs, with smaller round stones above, to accommodate the heavy conglomerate cover slabs. Pebble floor; four vases, two fibulae.

**Pottery.** All four cases intact and of local fabric. 3 is less well fired than the rest, with cream slip and orange paint.
1. Trefoil oinochoe. H. 16.5. The trefoil is barely noticeable. Monochrome except for reserved lower area and bands, and barred handle.
2. Lekythos. H. 11.5. Airhole to right of handle (d. 4.5 mm). Decorated as shown.
3. Cup. H. 8.8. Monochrome except for reserved lower area and bands. Reserved central dot on the floor.
4. Cup. H. 4.8. Shape and decoration as 3, but no reserved band inside the lip.

**Bronze**
5. Arched fibula (B.II.3). L. rest. 5.4. H. rest. 3. Th. of bow 0.25. Stem, much of spring, tip of pin lost. Slim rod of rhomboidal section, one end hammered flat and rolled for catch-plate. Catch to right.
*6. Arched fibula (B.II.1). L. 4.1. H. 3.1. Th. 0.2. Complete, recomposed of fragments. Slim rod of round section and even thickness, one end hammered flat and rolled for catch-plate. Arch of rather more than a semicircle. Spring (one turn) and catch to right. PLATES 238b, 247, 2.

**S Tomb 9** (PLATES 81, 193d; Contents, PLATES 94, 205e). Cist. c. 185 (rest.) × 35, depth 43. The S end had been cut away, probably when S Tomb 10 was dug to a deeper level. The cover slabs had been removed by the plough; the uprights were roughly shaped and of a coarse conglomerate. Pebble floor. The vases were found at the N end; other offerings may have been lost at the time of disturbance.

**Pottery.** Three cases, intact except for chips, and breaks on no. 2. Local clay and slip; paint within the local range, tending to flake off. The surface of 2 is badly worn.

1. Lekythos. H. 11. Airhole at base of neck, d. 3 mm. Decorated as shown. PLATE 257a.
2. Lekythos. H. 12.5. No airhole. Decorated as shown. The handle has vertical lines, crossing at the top.
3. Lekythos. H. 14.3. Airhole to right of handle, d. 3 mm. Decorated as shown. The bars on the handle continue downwards below its base as a ladder pattern.

**S Tomb 10** (PLATES 81, 196a; Contents, PLATES 94, 208c–d). Cist of superior construction. 62 × 24, depth 36. The two cover slabs were revetted to fit closely into place, the depth of the revetting being c. 2.5. The side slabs fitted at the ends with carefully cut insets. The floor was paved with four slabs. A soft yellowish oolite was used, easily worked and showing the marks of the broad cutting chisel or drove (a tool with a rounded edge, see G.M.A. Richter, *AJA* 47, 188f.).

The grave offerings were set out as if for an inhumation burial, with two cups and the triple vase at the 'head', two pins at the 'shoulders' with two fibulae at their lower end, a further pin and fibula, and a lekythos, at the 'midriff', and an amphoriskos at the 'feet'. Some garments were also placed in the tomb, as the iron pins preserve clear indications of cloth on their corroded surface (p. 227).

Three scraps of bone, of a green to white colour, were found (the largest 4 × 7 mm).

**Pottery.** Six vases, five intact or making up complete. Local (paint streaky and flaking off). The amphoriskos 5 stands out as a new unused item among old possessions: it has a warmer buff slip and a more orange brown paint than the others.

1. Cup. H. 6.7. Monochrome, except reserved foot and one band.
2. Cup. H. 5.4. Monochrome except reserved foot.
3. Triple vase. H. 9.5, (with handle) 15.4. Made up of three vertical-handled amphoriskoi linked together in triangular form, each having one handle at the outside. They are held in the centre by a high basket handle which was attached at the final stage, and whose base covers a central vertical hole left at the junction of the three bodies. Paint inside the lips, and also generally on the outer surface, though some areas missed.
4. Lekythos. H. 11.9. Decorated as shown. Four groups of semicircles (from four to seven in number) on the shoulder.
5. Amphoriskos, vertical-handled. H. 11.2. Decorated as shown. PLATE 257c.
6. Jug base fragment. D. 6.2. Not illustrated.

**Gold**
7. Earring. D. 7–10 mm. Wt. 0.3 gr. A single coil of fine wire (th. c. 1 mm), twisted into an elliptical shape; open hoop.

**Bronze**
8. Arched fibula (B.II.1). L. 3.5. H. 2.3. Th. 0.2. Complete. Slim rod of round section and even thickness, one end hammered flat and rolled for catch-plate. Distinct straightened forearm above catch. Spring (one turn) and catch to right. PLATE 247,5.
9. Arched fibula (B.II.3) Pres. L. 3.7. H. 2.8 Th. 0.3. Stem, spring, much of pin lost; what remains in one piece. Slim rod of rhomboidal section, one end hammered flat and rolled for catch-plate. Catch to right.
10. Leaf-bow fibula (B.I.7). Pres. L. 7.2. Est. H. 2.4. Th. 0.4. Spring, pin and catch missing; what remains broken into many pieces. Rod of rectangular section, bow hammered into a flat ellipse. The oxydisation has obliterated any pointillé ornament there may have been. PLATE 239i.

**Iron**
11. Dress pin. Pres. L. 10. D. of head 1.4. D. of swelling 1.9. Lower shaft and point lost. Two fragments

join, a third doubtfully. Evidently once consisted of a long-shafted pin with plain disk head above a spherical or oval boss. Cloth traces.

12. Dress pin. Pres. L. 10. Part of shaft and — possibly — boss. Probably once part of a pin resembling 11. Cloth remains.
13. Dress pin. Pres. L. 10.5. D. not recoverable. Three joining fragments of shaft. Probably part of a pin as 11. Cloth remains.

**S Tomb 11** (PLATE 193d). Cist. 70 × 20, depth 22. Three cover slabs; roughly shaped side slabs of magnesite and grey marble. Floor paved with stones of schist and limestone. No contents.

**S Tomb 12** (PLATE 81; Contents, PLATE 95). Cist. 93 × 29, depth 30. Two large cover slabs of magnesite and conglomerate; limestone uprights; pebble floor. The outside of the S end slab was blackened by the fire of S Pyre 9, which was lit there later. This grave was set quite deeply in its rock-cut pit, so that the top of the cover slabs was c. 15 below the rock surface.

Pottery. Local; the paint is glossy, but thinly applied and streaky. Both vases intact except for chips.
1. Trefoil oinochoe. H. 16.5. Monochrome except reserved bands, barred handle.
2. Cup. H. 6.2. Monochrome except lower area, and one band, reserved. Reserved dot on floor inside.

**S Tomb 13.** Cist. 73 × 35, depth 24. The grave was only c. 25 below the surface. The S and E sides had been destroyed, and only one cover slab survived at the N end. The remaining uprights were of limestone, sandstone and magnesite. Pebble floor. No surviving contents.

**S Tomb 14** (PLATE 193c). Cist. 62 × 24, depth 22. Set in a broad rock cutting which had a stone lining on a different alignment, suggesting that this cist replaced an earlier burial. The long uprights of limestone and sandstone were interspersed with small irregular stones; the three finely cut cover slabs were only c. 4 cm thick. The end slab at the N, and the adjacent packing stones, were blackened by the fire and ash of S Pyre 9 which was set above them. Pebble floor. No contents.

**S Tomb 15** (PLATES 81, 194d; Contents, PLATE 95). Double cist, with a larger and a smaller compartment (15A and 15B respectively). Width c. 30; lengths 53 and 27. Two upright slabs at the NW corner, and the cover slabs, of 15A were missing. Slabs of sandstone and white magnesite. Pebble floor. 15A was empty. Eight objects were found in 15B, and also tiny fragments of brittle white and calcined bone.

**Pottery**
1. Hydria. H. 13.7. Intact except for a break at the rim. Local. Decorated as shown.

**Bronze**
2. Arched fibula (B.II.1). Pres. L. 3. Pres. H. 1.7. Th. 0.15. Part of bow and forearm lost; what remains in several pieces. Slim rod of round section and even thickness. Spring (one turn) and catch to right.
*3. Arched fibula (B.II.3). Pres. L. 2.8. H. 2.6. Th. 0.15. Forearm and catch-plate lost. Slim rod of rectangular section; what remains of the arch symmetric. Spring (two turns) to right. *FGI* no. 157.
*4. Arched fibula (B.II.1). L. 4.5. H. 3.3. Th. 0.2. Complete apart from catch. Slim rod of round section and even thickness, one end hammered flat and rolled for catch. Arch not quite symmetric, for curve alters above catch-plate. Spring (one turn) and catch to right. PLATE 238a.
*5. Arched fibula (B.II.1). L. 5.2. H. 2.8. Th. 0.2. Pin broken; tip, and part of spring, lost. Slim rod of round section and even thickness, one end hammered flat and rolled for catch-plate. Arch of bow low in relation to width. Spring (one turn) and catch to right. *FGI* no. 74A. PLATE 247,4.

*6. Open ring. D.c. 1.3. W. 0.9. Th. less than 0.1. Complete, but broken. Thin hammered strip, widest at centre, with tapering, rounded terminals. Rolled into hoop, now misshapen.

6a. Double spiral pendant. Th. of wire c. 0.1. In four fragments. Part of suspension loop lost. Length of fine wire coiled into three-turn spirals either side of an open suspension loop — possibly part of something else. (Cf. T13, 17, in gold).

**Iron**

7. Fragment. 2 × 1.4. Shapeless. Not illustrated.

**S Tomb 16** (PLATES 81, 194c; Contents, PLATES 95–7, 206–7). Cist. 95 × 42. The cover, sides and floor were carefully constructed of thin slabs of yellow-green sedimentary rock c. 4–6 cm thick, the largest c. 1 m in length. Pebbles were packed in at the top of the uprights to give the two large cover slabs a level bedding. The tomb contained an unusually large number of offerings.

**Pottery.** Twelve vases, all intact except for amphoriskos 7, chipped at base and rim. Many in mint condition, suggesting that they were made specifically for the burial. With the exception of 10 (q.v.), of local fabric. 2, 3 and 9 show slight signs of burning.

1. Bird vase. H. 10.1 L. 14. Small aperture at the beak (d. 3 mm). Eyes represented by a very slight swelling. Decorated as shown. PLATE 254c.
2. Amphoriskos, belly-handled. H. 9.7. Decorated as shown.
3. Amphoriskos, vertical-handled. H. 11.8. Irregular, very heavy at the base. Decorated as shown. Note that the reserved panel shown on PLATE 96 is not repeated elsewhere on the vase.
4. Amphoriskos, vertical-handled. H. 11.6. Decorated as shown.
5. Pedestal bowl, H. 7, (with handles) 8.5. Flat turned-out rim with three ribbon handles. Decorated as shown. On the floor inside, a reserved central dot with a cross painted on it. PLATE 257e.
6. Cup. H. 5. Monochrome except reserved lower foot.
7. Amphoriskos, belly-handled. H. 10.2. There are four groups of four vertical wavy lines on the upper body.
8. Triple vase. H. 8.5, (with basket handle) 11.5. Three belly-handled amphoriskoi, each with one handle, linked together in triangular form, and held by a high basket handle at the centre. This handle is attached to the shoulder and rim of one segment, and ends between the other two in the form of a bird's head. Decorated as shown. The chevrons are in either twos or threes; there is only one example of the cross-hatched triangle.
9. Trefoil oinochoe. H. 6.9. Decorated as shown.
*10. Bird vase. H. 12.2 L. 20.4. Fabric not local; whitish slip with dark rather matt brown paint, thinning to orange on one side. Flaring spout at beak. The small raised plastic eyes are painted and encircled by a band. Decorated as shown. PLATE 254a.
11. Hydria. H. 13. Decorated as shown.
12. Kalathos. H. 3.4–3.7 (with handles) 4.9. Wheel-made, but irregular. Two vertical handles on rim. Monochrome, but underside and floor inside reserved.

**Faience**

13. Necklace in blue faience. Three beads consisting of five connected segments are preserved. d. 2–2.5 mm, string hole c. 1 mm, L. 9 mm. 142 other separate segments in small groups or single. With 45 segments recovered by sieving, a total of 202 was reached (L. approx 37).

**Bronze.** Five rings and eleven fibulae.

14a. Finger ring. D. 2.3. Inner d. 1.7. W. 1. Th. 0.3. Complete, surface covered in crusty oxydisation, by which 14b is permanently attached. Plane-convex section, apparently undecorated.
14b. Open ring. D. c. 1.5–1.6. W. 0.9. Th. 0.2. Complete. Surface oxydisation, by which it is adhering to 14a. Terminals overlap by more than 1.5. Strip hammered flat, ends slightly rounded. Probably undecorated.
*15. Finger ring. D. 2.3. Inner d. 1.8. W. 0.6. Th. 0.25. Complete. Plano-convex section, apparently undecorated. Found with three metacarpals and one carpal.
*16. Finger ring. D. 2.2. Inner d. 1.7. W. 0.7. Th. 0.25. Complete. Plano-convex section, apparently undecorated. Found with a finger bone.

*17. Open ring. D. 1.7. W. 0.7. Th. 0.15. Extended L. 7. Complete. Strip of plano-convex section, with slight medial ridge. No taper to terminals.

*18. Arched fibula (B.II.3). L. 5.1. H. 3.2. Th. 0.2. Complete and intact. Slim rod of rhomboidal section and even thickness, one end hammered flat and rolled for catch-plate. Curve of arch straightens into forearm above catch-plate. Spring (one turn) and catch to right. *FGI* no. 73.

*19. Arched fibula (B.II.1) L. 4. H. 3.5. Th. 0.2. Complete, pin broken. Slim rod of round section and even thickness, one end hammered flat and rolled for catch-plate. Arch somewhat asymmetric; pin out of alignment. Spring (one turn) and catch to right. *FGI* no. 74c.

20. Arched fibula (B.II.3). L. 5.6. H. 4.3. Th. 0.25. Complete and intact. Slim rod of rhomboidal section and even thickness, one end hammered flat and rolled for catch-plate. Arch somewhat asymmetric, and its curve straightens at the forearm above catch-plate. Spring (one turn) and catch to right. *FGI* no. 239.

21. Arched fibula (B.II.3). L. 4.4. H. 3.7. Th. 0.15. Catch-plate chipped, otherwise complete and intact. Slim rod of rectangular section thickening slightly above catch-plate. Arch high. Spring (one turn) and catch to right. *FGI* no. 163.

*22. Arched fibula (B.II.3). L. 3.9. H. 2.6. Th. 0.2. Complete, pin broken. Slim rod of rhomboidal section and even thickness, one end hammered flat and rolled for catch-plate. Symmetric arch, but straightens above catch-plate. Spring (one turn) and catch to right.

23. Arched fibula (B.II.3). L. 4.3. H. 2.6. Th. 0.2. Complete. Slim rod of rectangular section and even thickness, one end hammered flat and rolled for catch-plate. Arch just asymmetric, and straightens above catch-plate. Spring (one turn) to right, and catch to left. *FGI* no. 162.

*24. Arched fibula (B.II.3). L. 3.6. H. 2.2. Th. 0.2. Tip of pin and catch lost. Slim rod of rectangular section, widening to a forearm above the catch-plate (hammered flat and rolled). Shallow symmetric arch. Spring (one turn) and catch to right. *FGI* no. 166.

25. Arched fibula (B.II.3). L. 3.6. H. 2.2. Th. 0.15. Tip of pin and catch lost. Slim rod of square section, even thickness; end hammered flat and rolled for catch-plate. Symmetric arch, straightening immediately above catch-plate. Spring (one turn) and catch to left. *FGI* no. 164.

*26. Arched fibula (B.II.3, but not far from B.II.15). L. 5.4. H. 3.2. Th. 0.25. Complete and intact. Slim rod of rectangular section and even thickness; end hammered flat and rolled for catch-plate. Asymmetric arch, straightening into forearm above catch-plate. Spring (one turn) and catch to right.

*27. Arched fibula (B.II.3). L. 4.7. H. 3.5. Th. 0.2. Complete. Slim rod of rhomboidal section, even thickness; one end hammered flat and rolled for catch-plate. Asymmetric arch, which straightens into forearm above catch-plate. Spring (one turn) and catch to right. *FGI* no. 167.

*28. Arched fibula (B.II.3). L. 4.9. H. 3.6. Th. 0.3. Broken — part of tip and catch lost. Slim rod of rhomboidal section and even thickness; one end hammered flat and rolled for catch-plate. Symmetric arch, straightening just above catch-plate. Decorated with impressed notches on three of the four edges of the bow. Spring (one turn) and catch to left. PLATE 247,10.

**Iron**
*29. Dress pin. Press. L. 9.5. Th. 0.4. Bead on shaft: L. 0.6, d. 0.6. In three pieces; head (and probably tip) lost. Part of shaft of pin, on which is threaded a small cylindrical bead, shown by analysis to be iron.

30. Dress pin, Pres. L. 11.3. D. less than 0.5. Two non-joining fragments, head and tip lost. Possibly a fellow to 29.

## S Tomb 17 (PLATES 82, 196b; Contents, PLATE 97). Cist. 105 x 25. Two cover slabs of limestone, uprights of magnesite or conglomerate, roughly shaped. Pebble floor. A large conglomerate boulder, c. 39 high, was set upright at one end, evidently as a grave marker. Two finger-rings inside the cist; outside the NE corner, a bowl set in an upright position.

**Pottery**
1. Deep bowl. H. 9. Local fabric. Monochrome except reserved lower foot.

**Bronze**
*2. Finger-ring. D. 2.1. Inside d. 1.55. W. 0.7. Th. 0.3. Complete. Plano-convex section; undecorated.
*3. Finger-ring. D. 2. Inside d. 1.5. W. 0.5. Th. 0.3. Complete. Plano-convex section; undecorated. Found with a fragment of metacarpal *in situ*.

**S Tomb 18** (PLATE 82; Contents, PLATES 97, 210a). Cist. 82 × 31, depth 18. Covered by a single large conglomerate slab (122 × 64); side slabs of magnesite and conglomerate. Pebble floor. Partly overlies S Tomb 19.

**Pottery.** All intact except the skyphos no. 2. Local clay, slip and paint (flaking off). Note the pocked surface of the cups.
1. Pedestal bowl. H. 6.9. Monochrome except reserved lower area, band on body, band on rim, and central dot on the floor. PLATE 258e.
2. Skyphos. H. 6.9. Wholly painted inside. Monochrome, reserved bands and foot outside.
3. Jug. H. 12.8. A slight groove remains where the neck was attached by the potter. Decorated as shown. The rim and handle are barred. PLATE 258d.
4. Cup. H. 5.1. Monochrome, except reserved foot.
5. Cup. H. 5.9. Monochrome, except reserved lower body and foot.

**S Tomb 19** (PLATES 82, 195c; Contents, PLATES 98, 203). Cist. 84 × 28, depth 33. Three cover slabs of white magnesite, rougher uprights, with a packing of smaller stones to give level support to the covers. Pebble floor. The bronze dress ornaments were on the floor, with the vases above them, concentrated chiefly at the S end. One fragment of burnt bone (10 × 12 mm) was found, and two sea shells. Partly overlain by S Tomb 18.

**Pottery.** Intact, except for chips, part of the handle of the askos (5), and the basket handle of the double vase (2). All are of local make; the askos (5) and hydria (7) were probably the work of the same potter, who may also have made the amphoriskos (3) and the pyxis (4) — the double vase (2) was so badly made that it might have been the work of his apprentice. The stirrup jar (6) has a darker red clay than the other, is softer fired than they are, and has a buff slip and orange-brown paint.
1. Cup. H. 7.8. Heavily made. Monochrome.
2. Double vase. H. 8. Two belly-handled amphoriskoi crudely joined by a solid core of clay which is pierced horizontally between the two necks and originally rose to form the (missing) basket handle. On the shoulder one side has semicircles with half-moon filling, the other has three horizontal wavy lines with oblique hatching added. PLATE 255e.
3. Amphoriskos, vertical-handled. H. 16. Decorated as shown. Handles barred.
4. Pyxis. H. 7.4. A string hole (d. 2 mm) above each handle. Decorated as shown. PLATE 255f.
5. Askos. H. (without handle) 8.3. L. 17. Simple slit opening for spout. Decorated as shown. It is conjectured that the figures on the one side panel represent animals (horses?), on the other, birds on the wing, and that birds are also shown underneath at the front. PLATE 254b.
*6. Stirrup jar. H. 9.9. Airhole (d. 3 mm) beside the handle. Monochrome, small reserved areas. The disc has a reserved dot on top.
7. Hydria. H. 12.8. Decorated as shown. PLATE 255d.
8. The bases of two cups, perhaps for use as stoppers. Not illustrated.

**Bronze**
9. Earring. D. 1.4 × 1.3. Th. 0.15. Complete. Twist of thin wire of round section, tapering to terminals. Plain.
*10. Asymmetric arched fibula (B.II.15). L. 5.4. H. 3.4. Th. 0.3. Complete and intact. Rod of rectangular section, slimmer on forearm than on bow; end hammered flat and rolled for catch-plate. Spring (one turn) and catch to right. *FGI* no. 242. PLATE 238h.
11. Arched fibula (B.II.3). L. 5.2. H. 4.1. Th. 0.25. Complete. Slim rod of rhomboidal section, even thickness throughout; end hammered flat and rolled for catch-plate. Arch high, straightens to forearm some way above catch-plate. Spring (one turn) and catch to right.
12. Arched fibula (B.II.1/3). L. 3.8. H. 2.7. Th. 0.3–0.1. Formed of a strip of flat plano-convex section, twisted and rolled to form catch-plate. Spring (one turn) and catch to left. *FGI* no. 192. PLATE 247, 6.
*13. Arched fibula (B.II.1). L. 5.2. H. 2.9. Th. 0.3. Complete and intact. Slim rod of round section, even thickness throughout; one end hammered flat and rolled for catch-plate. Low arch, made asymmetric by straightened forearm above catch-plate. Carelessly coiled spring (one turn) and catch to right. *FGI* no. 74B.

*14. Open ring. D. 1.6 × 1.8. W. 0.9. Th. 0.1. Extended L. 7. Overlap of 0.9. Tip of one terminal lost. Flat strip of metal rolled to shape, narrowing slightly at the terminals (which are straight-ended). Found with a fragment of a metacarpal.

*15. Open ring. D. 1.5 × 1.5. W. 1. Th. 0.3. Extended L. 6. Overlap 1 cm. Complete and intact. Flat strip with raised medial ridge, edges very slightly ridged.

**Miscellaneous**

16. Two sea shells. PLATE 203b.

## S Tomb 20 (PLATE 82; Contents, PLATES 99, 209a–b). Cist. 85 × 22, depth 25. Well constructed, with cover and upright slabs of magnesite and schist. Pebble floor. Close to, but higher than, S Tomb 19, and considered to be certainly later.

**Pottery.** Seven vases, all but 6 intact except for chips; 6 broken. All local, though with minor variations in clay, slip and paint; note that 2 and 7, with identical light coffee-brown slip and dark paint, were probably fired together.

1. Jug. H. 8.4. Monochrome.
*2. Bottle. H. 11.6. Decorated as shown. Four groups of three shallow arcs on the shoulder.
3. Amphoriskos, vertical-handled. H. 10.4. Decorated as shown.
*4. Deep bowl. H. 9.1. Four handles: two horizontal, two vertical. Four panels of antithetic triple arcs set vertically. PLATE 257b.
5. Lekythos. H. 13.5. Airhole (d. 5 mm) on shoulder beside handle. Three groups of six or seven hand-drawn semicircles. PLATE 255c.
6. Cup. H. 6.5. Monochrome except reserved foot and band on body.
7. Cup. H. 6.5. Monochrome except reserved foot, band on body, band in side the rim, and dot on the floor.

**Bronze**

*8. Arched fibula (B.II.1). L. 5.7. H. 4.3. Th. 0.3. Complete and intact. Slim rod of round section, even thickness throughout; one end hammered flat and rolled into catch-plate. High symmetric arch, straightening into forearm above catch-plate. Spring (one turn) to left, catch to right. *FGI* no. 71. PLATE 247, 3.
9. Finger ring. D. 2.1. Inner d. 1.8. W. 0.5. Th. 0.15. Part of hoop lost. Flattened plano-convex section, rounded edges. Undecorated.

**Iron**

10. Arched fibula (B.II.3). Estimated L. 5.7. Estimated H. 3.5. Th. less than 0.5. Six fragments, four of which join. Apparently a rod of rhomboidal section. Arch was probably symmetric. Not drawn.

## S Tomb 21 (PLATE 82; Contents, PLATE 99). Cist. Width 34, depth 28. Disturbed at the S end, probably by the construction of S Tomb 25. Two conglomerate cover slabs were found in position on a stone packing above the side slabs. The cist was set in a long rectangular rock cutting (c. 175 × 75) and packed with stones at the sides: original length uncertain. No objects were found inside the cist.

In the disturbed area to the S were found one cooking pot in an upright position and almost intact, and the fragments of a second; both were at a slightly higher level than the pebble floor of the tomb. They need not be associated with S Tomb 21 as grave offerings, and they probably belong to a later stage of activity, along with the stone structure between S Tombs 20 and 22 and the curving wall at S Tomb 24.

**Pottery.** Two vases, not in S Tomb 21 proper, nor likely to be of it.

1. Cooking pot. H. 24.2. Hand-made. Underside slightly rounded and burnt. Broad flat handle. Coarse red fabric with large grits and smooth burnished surface; vertical smoothing marks on neck and upper body, becoming horizontal on lower body.
*2. Cooking pot fragments. D. (rim) c. 15. Not illustrated. Similar to 1.

**S Tomb 22** (PLATE 82; Contents, PLATE 99). Cist. c. 85 × 30, depth 29. Intact; well constructed with dressed slabs of limestone and magnesite; stone packing around the outside. Pebble floor.

**Pottery**

1. Deep bowl. H. 8.2. Local fabric. Monochrome, except reserved foot and dot on the floor inside.

**Gold**

2, 3. Two earrings. D. 7–10 mm. Wt. 0.3 and 0.5 gr. Th. of wire c. 1 mm. Each is a simple coil of wire with ends overlapping.

**Bronze**

4. Earring. D. 1.3. Th. 0.1. Terminals lost. Twist of thin wire of round section. See S 19, 9.
*5. Finger-ring. D. 2.1. Inside d. 1.6. W. 1. Th. 0.3. Complete and intact. Plano-convex section. Probably undecorated. PLATE 241e.
6. Open ring. Pres. d. 1.0. W. of terminal 0.6. Th. 0.05. At least half lost. Flat strip bent to shape. The terminal is 0.1 wider than the centre of the hoop. Probably undecorated.
7. Arched fibula (B.II.7). L. 4.6. H. 2.2. Th. 0.2. Part of bow lost, pin broken. Slim rod of square section, even thickness throughout, tightly twisted (twists c. 0.1 apart). Symmetric bow, without forearm above catch-plate. Spring (one turn) and catch to right. PLATE 247, 15.
*8. Arched fibula (B.II.3). L. 7.7. L. of bow 6.7. H. 5.2. Th. 0.3. Complete, but in three pieces. Slim rod of rhomboidal section, even thickness throughout, one end hammered flat and rolled for catch-plate. Arch symmetric, but springs from a distinct stem and forearm and is accordingly proportionately high. Spring (one turn) and catch to right. Pin protrudes well beyond catch-plate. *FGI* no. 161. PLATES 238e, 247, 8.

**S Tomb 23** (PLATE 82; Contents, PLATE 99). Cist. 66 × 22, depth 35. E of the bulldozed trench. Intact. Three cover slabs and all side slabs of a very friable conglomerate. Pebble floor. One shallow bowl, placed centrally.

**Pottery**

1. Shallow bowl. H. 3.4. Complete, Fabric burnt to grey; paint black to dark-brown inside and out; only the underside reserved.

**S Tomb 24** (PLATE 82; Contents, PLATE 99). In the NE corner of trench Delta was found an irregular line of round stones forming an arc; in the centre of the area enclosed was a disturbed cover slab and other stones, forming part of the fill of a rock-cutting and evidently once part of a cist tomb. About 20 cm lower, at the bottom of the rock-cutting, was found a section of gravel floor, and on it one cup.

It is probable that the cup is from an earlier disturbed cist, and that the circular structure is a later feature — a similar stone circle held the amphora burial (tomb 5) only a few centimetres to the E.

**Pottery**

1. Cup H. 6.5. Locally made. Decorated as shown. Handle barred. Reserved dot on the floor. PLATE 256b.

**S Tomb 25** (PLATE 82; Contents, PLATE 100). A disturbed cist, destroyed at both ends and divided by an upright slab in the centre. Width c. 40, depth 25 at W, 40 at E. Pebble floor. At the W end the rather rounded uprights of S Tomb 25 cut the line of S Tomb 21, but a later disturbance has cut away this end of S Tomb 25 also. This area to the W is designated 25B. One cover slab of white magnesite was found in position here, and there were three vases in this part of the cist. Three others, and two fibulae, were found at the E end, called 25A.

That S Tomb 21 was cut and disturbed by S Tomb 25 is certain, as also is the disturbance of S Tomb 25 at both W and E ends. Groups 25A and 25B seem to be the offerings for two separate burials and 25A should be the earlier. Whether, however, either group was contemporary with the construction of cist S Tomb 25 is perhaps open to question. On the other hand, the depositing of the two cooking pots S21, 1 and 2 is probably a separate activity, and the latest.

**S Tomb 25A pottery.** Three vases of local fabric.
1. Kalathos. H. 4. Two string holes (d. 3 mm). Impressed decoration made by a square-ended instrument; the identations were punched with the right hand, from right to left, starting regular and horizontal, but ending oblique where the hand had to reach further round. Narrow reserved band inside the rim and central dot on the floor.
2. Kalathos. H. 3.8. Two string holes. Monochrome, one reserved band.
3. Kalathos. H. 2.9. Two string holes (d. 2–3 mm). Monochrome except for underside.

**S Tomb 25A bronze**
4. Arched fibula with swollen bow (Variant B.II.1). L. 5.1. H. 3.3. Th. 0.35. Tip of pin and part of catch lost. Rod of round section slightly swollen in centre of arch. One end hammered flat and rolled for catch-plate. Asymmetric, with straightened forearm that extends beyond circumference of arch. Spring (two turns) and catch to left.
*5. Arched fibula with central boss (B.II.14). L. 2.5. H. 1.6. Boss 1.6 x 0.85. From bow to pin, 0.5. Complete and intact. Made by lost-wax. The plano-convex boss is 'threaded' on a bow of square section, whose stem turns into the round section of the pin, while the forearm is flattened into the angular catch-plate. The boss is set off from the bow by two fine fillets on either side. Spring (two turns) and catch to left. PLATES 239g, 248, 15.

**S Tomb 25B pottery.** No. 1 fragmentary, 2 and 3 intact. Local fabric.
1. Cup. H. 5. Made up from fragments; part of one side missing. Monochrome.
2. Kalathos. H. 4.2. Two string holes (d. 6 mm). Monochrome. Single reserved band on inside.
3. Trefoil oinochoe. H. 16. Decorated as shown.

**S Tomb 26** (PLATE 91). Cist. 60 x 20, depth 15. The cover slabs had been removed by the plough; side slabs of white magnesite only 25 below the surface. Pebble floor. No contents.

**S Tomb 27** (PLATES 83, 91; Contents, PLATE 100). Cist. 170 x 45, depth 25. Cover slabs of bluish schist, side slabs of magnesite and limestone. Pebble floor.

**Pottery.** Two vases, intact except for chips. Local fabric.
1. Cup. H. 6.4. Monochrome except lower area. Reserved dot on floor.
2. Jug. H. 7.9. Decorated as shown, but a band 0.5 deep has been omitted inside the lip.

**Miscellaneous**
3. Sea shell. PLATE 237d.

**S Tomb 28** (PLATE 83; Contents, PLATE 100). Cist. 77 x 20, depth 33. Three cover slabs of limestone and magnesite; side slabs of magnesite. Pebble floor.

**Pottery.** Three vases, intact except for chips and the handle of no. 1. Local fabric.
1. Cup. H. 5.9. Monochrome, except reserved foot.
2. Cup. H. 5.8. Monochrome except lower body and foot.
3. Cup. H. 3.8. Monochrome except lower area.

**S Tomb 29** (PLATES 83, 194e; Contents, PLATE 100). Cist. 62 x 26, depth 21. Single cover slab of magnesite, 85 x 45; squared side slabs of magnesite, protruding at the ends. Pebble floor.

**Pottery**. Three vases, intact except for chips. Local fabric. Surface of cups much deteriorated.
1. Cup. H. 5.2. Monochrome except reserved foot and band.
2. Cup. H. 6.6. Monochrome except lower area.
3. Jug. H. 9.5. Decorated as shown.


**S Tomb 30** (PLATE 193a). Cist. 165 × 30, depth 30. The tomb was robbed, and had a fill of small pebbles such as were normally used for flooring; no other contents. Five cover slabs, with two others overlying these — but at least one is missing at the N end. They are thin irregular slabs of limestone and magnesite. Two of the side slabs had collapsed. Pebble floor.


**S Tomb 31** (PLATES 83, 193a; Contents, PLATE 100). Cist. 89 × 30, depth 32. Large cover slabs of sandstone and magnesite; heavy and irregular side slabs of sandstone. The cist is set in a rock cutting with packing of small stones. Pebble floor. Vases and bronze objects all at W end; the ring held a small fragment of the finger bone, in a black and friable condition.

**Pottery**. Intact except for chips. Local fabric. 1 and 2, identical in colour, texture and preservation, were probably fired together. The surface of 3 is very worn.
1. Hydria. H. 12. Decorated as shown. The area beneath the belly handles is unpainted. PLATE 258b.
2. Amphoriskos, vertical-handled. H. 10.4. Decorated as shown.
3. Lekythos. H. 13.1. Painted inside mouth. Three groups of five or six hand-drawn semicircles.

**Bronze**
*4. Finger ring. D. 1.9. Inner d. 1.7. W. 0.4—0.25. Th. 0.1. Complete, cracked. Hoop of irregular width; section very flat ellipse.
5. Fibula fragments. Pres. l. 3.3. Th. 0.15. Two joining fragments. Probably fibula pin from near spring to point. Not illustrated.


**S Tomb 32** (PLATE 83; Contents, PLATES 101, 209c—d). Cist. 98 × 25, depth 25. A single cover slab of magnesite; six long slabs of sandstone and limestone as uprights. The cist was strongly built and had four additional cover slabs on top at the N end. A limestone boulder, 35 × 28, fallen at the NE corner may have been the grave marker. Pebble floor.

**Pottery**. Six vases. 2—6 intact except for chips, no. 1 fragmentary and in poor condition. Locally made; 4 and 5 are a pair, probably made together, and 2 and 6 are also a pair, and are very well preserved.
1. Lekythos. H. 10.7. Poorly fired, and crushed by the shifting of a side slab. Airhole (d. 4—5 mm) to right of handle. Surface mostly vanished, and no decoration survives except for traces of paint on handle and lip, and inside lip.
2. Trefoil oinochoe. H. 12.6. Monochrome except reserved lower area. Note the two bands of paint inside lip.
3. Amphoriskos, belly-handled. H. 13.1. Decorated as shown.
4. Amphoriskos, vertical-handled. H. 11.8. Monochrome except reserved lower area and band, and barred handles.
5. Jug. H. 11.2. Monochrome except reserved lower area and band, and barred handle.
6. Deep bowl. H. 7.7. Decorated as shown. PLATE 256e.

**Bronze**
7. Finger ring. D. 2.3. Inner d. 1.9. W. 0.8—0.5. Th. 0.2. Complete and intact. Hoop of irregular width; section plano-convex. Probably undecorated.

**Iron**
8. Arched fibula (B.II.?3). Estimated l. 5. Estimated h. 2.2. Th. less than 0.4. Pin and catch lost; what remains broken and grossly altered by oxydisation. Probably originally consisted of a symmetric arched bow of constant thickness and perhaps rectangular section. Spring (one turn) to right.

**S Tomb 33** (PLATE 83; Contents. PLATES 101–2). Pit grave. c. 90 x 85, depth 25. The outline of the tomb is difficult to distinguish, since it appeared as only a shallow depression in the rock. Two separate vase deposits were found in the gravelly sub-surface earth, at the N and S ends of the pit respectively, c. 90 below the surface. The pots had been placed in the pit unbroken, and then covered with earth, rock fragments, and stones; they are homogeneous in character, and seem to belong to one burial. No trace of ash or bone found.

**Pottery.** Thirteen vases, broken but made up complete except for small fragments. 1–12 are wheelmade; 3 is very probably an import, and the remainder are of local fabric, though 2, 4, 10, and the lid of pyxis 12 are less well fired, with consequent differences in the colour of clay and paint. The cooking pot 13 is handmade, of the standard type with red gritty fabric fired to a dark brown on the surface and burnished.

(a) *North group.*
1. Skyphos. H. 12.4. PSC with high lip. Reserved central dot on floor.
2. Skyphos. H. 9.5. PSC with medium lip. Reserved central dot on floor.
*3. Flask. H. 12.8. D. 9.4. White clay, flaky brown paint. Probable import.
4. Neck-handled amphora. H. 30.1. Decorated as shown. Two groups of ten semicircles on each side.
5. Neck-handled amphora. H. 20.6. A ridge with double groove at the collar where the neck, made separately, was fitted over the sleeve of the upper body. Much of the body made in two skins — the inner one still intact, but the outer one (th. 2–3 mm) has peeled away in large pieces. Foot made separately and attached later, and has broken off complete. The handles have become detached at all four joins. Monochrome, reserved bands. Handles barred. Paint goes just over inside of rim.

(b) *South group.*
6. Neck-handled amphora. H. 20.8. Well made (as opposed to 5) and well fired. Decorated as shown. PLATE 266a.
7. Cup. H. 4.4. Monochrome except reserved lower area and band inside lip.
8. Pyxis with lid. H. 14.5. H. of lid 4.5. Two string holes opposite each other beneath the rim match two on the lid. Eight panels of decoration on belly. Central reserved dot on knob of lid.
9. Pyxis with lid. H. 15.2. H. of lid 3.6. Two string holes as 8. Monochrome, reserved bands.
10. Pyxis. H. 11.4. No lid preserved. Two string holes as 8. Monochrome, reserved bands.
11. Pyxis, with lid H. 10.2. H. of lid 1.9. Two string holes. Poorly made, asymmetrical with oval mouth. Monochrome, reserved bands.
12. Pyxis with lid. H. 10.8. H. of lid 2.7. Two string holes. Monochrome, reserved bands.
13. Cooking pot. H. 12.2. Vertical smoothing marks. No wear at base, but blackened on one side.

**Small objects.** All with N group, but only 14, 15 and 19 could be recorded on the plan.

**Gold**
14. Earring. D. (head) 6 mm, (wire 1–2 mm. Wt. 2.4. gr. Intact. A half coil of wire fitted at each end with a low conical head. Each cone is solid; the joint is smooth at its flattened underside. PLATE 231a.

**Bronze**
15. Arched fibula (Incipient B.II.19). L. 4. H. 2.3. Th. 0.3–0.15. Pin broken, now lost. Bow of round section, slightly swollen towards the spring, but slimmest at the stem and above the catch-plate. One end hammered flat and rolled for catch-plate. Spring (two turns) and catch to left. *FGI* no. 72.
16. Arched fibula (Incipient B.II.19). L. 3.4. H. 2.1. Th. 0.3–0.15. Catch, nearly all spring lost; separate pin fragment may belong. Bow of round section, swollen off centre towards spring; slimmest at stem and forearm. At least two groups of finely traced encircling bands, on stem and centre of arch.

**Bronze and iron**
*17. Dress pin fragment. Pres l. 1.6. D. of boss 1.2. L. of boss 1.3. D. of pin shaft 0.3. Boss and scrap of pin only. Oval bronze boss threaded on to iron shaft. PLATE 242i.

**Iron**
18. Dress pin. Pres. l. 4.6. Thickness not recoverable. Section of shaft round. PLATE 242i.
19. Dress pin. Pres. l. 25.7. D. of head 2.5. D. of shaft 0.8. Almost complete in joining fragments. Disk head, probably originally flat. Boss below head swollen to unrecognisable proportions. Shaft originally of round section. Cloth remains. PLATES 242g, 250, 7.

**S Tomb 34** (PLATES 83, 195a; Contents, PLATE 103). Cist. 102 × 30, depth 32. Fine construction very similar to that of S Tomb 10, and very likely by the same mason. Three cover slabs, revetted at the sides and one end to fit closely on to the upright slabs, which in three cases have neatly cut insets at the corners to form joints. Four paving stones of the same material, a greyish-yellow oolite. Cuttings can be seen clearly on the worked surface of the stone. See also S Tomb 10, p. 112.

**Pottery**. Two intact vases of local manufacture.
1. Deep bowl. H. 8.2. Monochrome, reserved lower foot and band inside lip.
2. Trefoil oinochoe. H. 13.4. Note the ridge at the junction of foot and body.

**S Tomb 35** (PLATE 193a). Cist. 127 × 25–40, depth 32. Intact, with five cover slabs and paced floor of a soft grey-green limestone, rough-hewn. At the sides, long thin unworked slabs, chiefly of a hard bluish limestone. The S end, which the paving does not reach, is wider; it has an area of pebble floor. No contents.

Stratigraphically earlier than S Tomb 30, which partly overlies it, and than S Tomb 31, which would have been disturbed had S Tomb 35 been cut down after it.

**S Tomb 36** (PLATE 83; Contents, PLATE 103). Cist, destroyed at E end by cutting of S Tomb 33. 105 (est.) × 29, depth 28. One rectangular cover slab 120 × 58, of a grey gritty conglomerate. The side slabs, of conglomerate and magnesite, protrude to form an H at the intact end. Pebble floor. Only the end slab and one side removed at E. Contents robbed or disturbed. Beside the pin, two long bones (pres. l. 25) and several bone fragments, lying haphazardly.

**Bronze**
1. Dress pin. L. 28.5. D. of head 0.5. D. of bulb 0.6. L. of bulb 1.5. Complete in four joining pieces. Small domed head, slim oval bulb, not set off from the shaft in any way. Undecorated. PLATES 242d, 250, 4.

**S Tomb 37** (PLATE 83; Contents, PLATE 103). Cist. 66 × 25, depth 27. A single conglomerate cover slab, c. 10 below the surface, intact over most of the cist, but broken off by the plough at the S end. Side slabs of a coarse gravelly conglomerate, ends of dressed magnesite and oolite. Pebble floor. The aperture left by the breaking of the cover slab was only c. 10 wide, and the contents may then safely be considered intact; the single cup would accord reasonably with a child burial.

**Pottery**
1. Cup. H. 5.6. Intact. Local make. Monochrome. The lower part of the foot is reserved (it was evidently intended that the whole foot should be).

**S Tomb 38** (PLATES 84–5, 194a–b; Contents, PLATES 103, 204). Cist, stone-lined and rectangular, set in a deep shaft. 200 × 75, depth 80–86. The shaft was cut into the rock to a depth of 3.30 m and slightly widened lower down. Large cover and side slabs of a pale blue conglomerate with limestone pebble content. One of the four cover slabs had recently collapsed, probably the result of liberal irrigation above − the cist had been well sealed previously, and there was no accumulation of silt. On the floor was found a fresh layer of grit, c. 1 mm thick, from the decaying under surface of the cover slabs; beneath this was a crust of dried mud c. 1 cm thick, and then a thin layer of blackish earth in which lay the grave goods (some with traces of cloth). Pebble floor on a level rock-cut surface.

**Pottery.** Three vases, intact except for a break at rim of 3. Locally made; note the appearance of large white grits in the clay.

1. Stirrup vase. H. 13.7. Carefully made. Slightly concave top disk, painted over. Airhole (d. 6 mm) beside the false neck. Decorated as shown. Four groups of four (once) or six (thrice) multiple triangles. PLATE 255b.
2. Triple vase. H. 8.3–9, with handle 15. Hand-made. Crude in modelling and decoration. Made up of three belly-handled amphoriskoi, joined in a triangular form. The central cavity at the junction is filled solid from above and below, where a high basket handle is attached. Decorated as shown.
3. Amphoriskos, vertical-handled. H. 8.3. Clumsily made. Monochrome, reserved areas.

**Gold**

4. Earring. D. 8–10 mm. Th. c. 1 mm. Wt. 0.5 gr. Wire coil, badly distorted; one end pointed, the other pinched off. Probably originally a loop-earring with slightly overlapping ends.
5. Earring. D. 0.7–1.2. Plain coil of wire, d.c. 1 mm, flattened at one side, open hoop. One end is cut straight, the other pinched off and sharp.

**Bronze**

6. Dress pin. L. 17.7. D. of head 0.7. D. of bulk 0.6. L. of bulb c. 1.5. In two pieces, complete. Small domed button head, slim oval bulb not set off from the shaft. Undecorated. PLATE 242c.
7. Dress pin. Pres l. 17. D. of head 0.8. D. of bulb 0.5. L. of bulb 1.5. Tip probably lost. The fellow to 6. PLATE 250, 1.
8. Arched fibula (B.II.3). Estimated l. 3.6. Estimated h. 2.3. Th. 0.15. Slim rod of rectangular or rhomboidal section, even thickness, one end hammered flat and rolled for catch-plate. High, slightly asymmetric arch. Spring (probably one turn) and catch to right. *FGI* no. 71A.
9. Arched fibula (remains of) (B.II.3). Estimated l.3. Estimated h. 1.7. Th. 0.15. Part of spring and pin lost; what remains in many fragments. Slim rod of square section, even thickness, one end hammered flat and rolled for catch-plate. Form of arch uncertain. Spring (one turn?) and catch to right. Not drawn. *FGI* no. 71B.
10. Finger ring of 'shield' form (remains of). W. of hoop 0.7. Th. less than 0.1. Bezel remains not measurable. Eight scraps of much oxydised metal. Hoop of thin strip with overlapping ends secured by small rivet. Bezel fragments distinct from hoop, possibly decorated in pointillé. Not illustrated.

**Iron**

11. Dress pin. Pres. l. 14.8. Greatest w. (including oxydisation) 1.5. D. of shaft 0.5. Possibly preserves a small button head and an oval bulb. Shaft originally round. Two small non-joining fragments may belong. Cloth remains.
12. Dress pin. Pres l. 19.7. Greatest w. 1.7. D. of shaft 0.6. Probably incomplete (head seems to be lost), composed of several joining pieces. Probably the fellow to 11. Abundant cloth remains. PLATE 237b.
13. Unidentified. Pres. dimensions 3.5 × 2.2. Th. ± 0.2. What remains composed of four joining pieces. Remains of a small hollow sphere? Decoration of a dress pin? Cloth remains.

**Ivory**

14. Three fragments of ivory. The largest 2.1 × 0.7, and 0.8 thick. Each fragment has one flat surface with traces of red paint surviving. Original shape not recoverable. Not illustrated.

**Found in the upper shaft fill of S Tomb 38**

15. Neck-handled amphora, fragment. Pres. h. 21. D. (rim) c. 14. Large fragments of shoulder and neck, with one neck handle and part of the rim, whose surface has flaked off. Local: fine pink clay, pink slip, dark brown paint, glossy on the shoulder, streaky and flaking elsewhere. Note a shallow indentation at the root of the handle (d. 2 mm, depth c. 1 mm) made after the vase was painted. Decoration as on PLATE 282B; there is a deep band of paint inside the lip.

    This fragment was thrown into the shaft at the time of the filling, and was sealed by a later deposit in the gully above (level 2 in section, PLATE 85). It should then be contemporaneous with, or earlier than S Tomb 38, and may be the earliest object yet found in the Skoubris cemetery. PLATE 282B.

**S Tomb 39** (Contents, PLATE 103). Cist. 149 × 49, depth 54. Cover and side slabs of a course grey conglomerate. Pebble floor. The tomb had been robbed, one cover slab remaining in position. Two bronze objects found in the disturbed earth.

**Bronze**

*1. Finger ring. D. c. 3.2. Inside d. 1.7. W. 1.5. Th. c. 0.6. Complete. Unusually heavy ring; section probably plano-convex.
2. Fibula or dress pin fragment. Pres. l. 1.8. Th. 0.25. Broken at both ends. Round section: could be part of fibula pin, or section of shaft of dress pin. Not illustrated.

**S Tomb 40** (PLATES 84, 193b; Contents, PLATES 104, 205a–b). Cist. 78 × 25. Two cover slabs of limestone and green schist, uprights of yellow oolite. Pebble floor. Offerings concentrated at E end.

**Pottery.** Three vases: 1 and 2 intact, 3 broken. Local clay and slip; 2 and 3, with almost identical decoration and paint, were probably made together.
1. Trefoil oinochoe. H. 12.2. Monochrome except reserved areas and barred handle.
2. Jug. H. 6.9. Decorated as shown. Wavy line on the handle.
3. Cup. H. 8.8. Decorated as shown, with handle barred. PLATE 256a.

**Bronze**
*4. Asymmetric arched fibula (B.II.15). L. 5.8. H. 3.4. Th. 0.2. Complete save tip of pin. Slim rod of rectangular section, rather thinner at forearm, end of which is hammered flat and rolled for catch-plate. Spring (one turn) and catch to left. *FGI* no. 241. PLATES 238g, 247, 13.
*5. Arched fibula (close to B.II.3). L. 5.3. H. 3.7. Th. 0.25. Tip of pin and catch lost; what remains are two joining fragments. Rod of square section of even thickness from spring to forearm, where it widens to catch. Symmetric arch. Spring (one turn) and catch to left. *FGI* no. 165.
*6. Arched fibula, twisted bow (poor version B.II.7). L. 4. H. 2.25. Th. 0.2. Complete save part of catch. Slim rod of rhomboidal section, even thickness, end hammered flat and rolled for catch-plate. Bow loosely twisted (twists 0.3 apart) from above catch-plate to spring. Though badly shaped, this is B.II.7 rather than B.II.15. Spring (one turn) and catch to right. Finger ring 7 threaded on to the pin. *FGI* no. 211A. PLATES 238j, 247, 16.
*7. Finger ring. D. 2.5. Inner d. 2.2. W. 0.8. Th. 0.25. Complete and intact. Hoop width varies very slightly; marked plano-convex section. PLATE 238j.
8. Finger ring. D. 1.8. Inner d. 1.3. W. 0.55–0.45. Th. 0.15. Complete and intact. Hoop width varies; plano-convex section. PLATE 241f.
9. Open ring. D. 1 × 1.3. W. 1.1 × 1.3. Th. c. 0.05. Chips lost. Thin flat strip rolled to an open-ended hoop. Visible terminal tapers and is slightly rounded.

**S Tomb 41** (PLATE 84; Contents, PLATE 104). Cist. 89 × 28, depth 31. Cover and side slabs of limestone. Pebble floor.

**Pottery.** Two vases, local fabric, perhaps made together. Intact except for chips at rim and base.
1. Trefoil oinochoe. H. 10.9. Heavy and clumsily made. monochrome, reserved areas.
2. Deep bowl. H. 8.6. Monochrome, reserved lower body and foot. Paint very carelessly applied; even a splash of paint over the foot.

**S Tomb 42** (PLATES 85, 193b; Contents, PLATE 104). Cist. 64 × 40, depth 34. One limestone cover slab survived, displaced by the plough; at least two others missing. Vertical slabs of limestone or conglomerate on three sides; the S side has been entirely destroyed. Pebble floor.

**Pottery**
1. Cup. H. 5.5. Intact except for chips at rim. Locally made. Decorated as shown, with handle barred.

**S Tomb 43** (PLATES 85, 193b; Contents, PLATES 104, 205c–d). Cist. 71 × 28, depth 25. Constructed with thin rectangular slabs of blue limestone; packing of smaller stones. Pebble floor.

**Pottery.** Four intact vases. Local; note that white grits have caused pock marks on the surface of 1 and 2.
1. Alabastron, three strut feet. H. (without struts) 7.4. Max. d. 11.5. A slight angle at the point of maximum diameter shows that the vase was made in two pieces. The lower sections of the struts have been cut off, so that these have no function. Three ribbon handles from the belly. Decorated as shown. One group of three of four chevrons between each handle.
2. Neck-handled amphora. H. 13.7. Decorated as shown. Three vertical wiggly lines on the shoulder on the side not illustrated.
*3. Deep bowl. H. 7.7. Monochrome, except reserved lower foot, band inside rim, and central dot on floor.
4. Cup. H. 4.4. Unpainted except bands over lip, at junction of body and foot, and down handle.

**Bronze**
*5. Asymmetric arched fibula (B.II.6). L. 5.4. H. 3.2. Th. 0.2. Tip of pin lost, otherwise complete. Slim rod of square section, slightly wider at forearm, end hammered and rolled for catch-plate. Bow twisted (twists 0.2 apart) from spring to forearm. Spring (one turn) and catch to right. *FGI* no. 211. PLATES 238i, 247, 12.
*6. Asymmetric arched fibula with swollen bow (B.II.17/19). L. 3.7. H. 2.7. Th. 0.4–0.15. Catch-plate and pin-tip lost. Asymmetric swollen bow set off from spring and forearm by bead and fillet mouldings of considerable delicacy. Bow of round section, forearm rectangular. Angular transition from bow to forearm. Spring (two turns) to right. PLATES 238k, 247, 18.
7. Asymmetric arched fibula (B.II.15). L. 3.3. H. 2.8. Th. 0.2. Complete – pin reattached. Slim rod of square section, even thickness throughout. End hammered flat and rolled for catch-plate. Arch high; a clumsy piece. Spring (one turn) and catch to right. *FGI* no. 229. PLATES 238l, 247, 17.

## S Tomb 44 (PLATES 85, 193b; Contents, PLATE 105). Cist. 54 x 25, depth 15. Cover and side slabs of grey conglomerate. Pebble floor. One cover slab missing, leaving the S half of the cist uncovered. The feeder found in the NE corner may however represent the sole original offering, as often in the case of a child burial.

**Pottery**
1. Feeder (jug type). H. 9.2 (with handle) 12.1. Intact except for chips at base. Local fabric: note a few large white grits. The high basket handle is not quite at right angles to the spout (about 100°). Decorated as shown.

## S Tomb 45 (PLATES 86, 193b; Contents, PLATE 105). Shaft grave. 90 x 55, depth of shaft c. 105. Fill of earth and stones. While preparing this tomb the diggers hit the S end of S Tomb 46, lifted one large cover slab, and reset it at right angles (in alignment with S Tomb 45), resting it partly on the rock ledge at the S end of 46, and partly on a stone and earth fill. This slab covered only the E end of 45. There were no stone slabs over the rest of the tomb, and any rock ledge there may have been, to receive a wooden cover, has crumbled away.

A cluster of six vases, set upright, was found on the floor in the middle of the tomb, and a gold ring lay underneath the flat dish in the centre; four other vases at N and W sides. The pebbles for the floor were not of the type brought specially for the purpose, as with the cists, but had the coarse pebble content of the conglomerate.

**Pottery.** The handmade cooking pot 5 is made up almost complete from fragments; the rest are intact except for rim chips, and are of local manufacture – the cup 4 has a fine and relatively dark buff clay, thin walled and fired hard.
1. Trefoil oinochoe. H. 16. The neck and handle decoration are as on 2.
2. Trefoil oinochoe. H. 15.1. Decorated as shown.
3. Skyphos. H. 6.9. On each side two set of ten PSC, in one case the semicircles being taken right on to the rim. Reserved band inside rim, and reserved central dot on floor.
4. Cup H. 5.8. Monochrome, reserved lower body, bands outside and inside lip, central dot on the floor, and a small triangle on the upper part of the handle, missed by the brush.

5. Cooking pot. H. 19.6. Handmade. Coarse ware of gritty red to brown fabric. Vertical smoothing marks on outer surface. Slightly blackened on side opposite handle.
6. Dish. H. 3.2. D. 12.5. Two small lug handles at rim, one pierced (string hole d. 2—4 mm). Irregular, heavily made. Monochrome.
7. Kalathos. H. 4.9. Two large string holes, 1.5 apart. Monochrome, reserved band on rim.
8. Kalathos. H. 4.3. Two string holes. Monochrome, reserved bands.
9. Kalathos. H. 3.9. Two string holes. Monochrome, reserved bands.
10. Kalathos. H. 2.8. Two string holes. Monochrome, reserved bands. Underside unpainted.

**Gold**
11. Finger ring or hair spiral. D. 1.4. Wt. 2.9 gr. A triple coil of plain wire with round section, d.c. 1 mm. Open at the ends; the third coil does not quite come full circle. PLATE 230j.

**S Tomb 46** (PLATE 86; Contents, PLATE 106). Shaft grave. 125 × 40—45, depth 105. The shaft is c. 75 wide at the top, but at the depth of c. 70 becomes narrower at a rock ledge which is bedded with stones to receive the cover slabs; it is also longer at the top (c. 180), at least partly due to later disturbance and rearrangement at the S end. Three heavy cover slabs of soft limestone, the southern one out of place (see under S Tomb 45), below these, a fill of earth and stones, probably thrown in when 45 was built. Natural conglomerate floor as for 45. With the exception of the cup, found in fragments in the fill inside the tomb, the grave offerings were protected by the two intact cover slabs.

**Pottery**. Three vases: no. 2 intact, the other two made up almost intact from fragments. 1 and 2 are locally made, the cup having a darker clay, and thin-walled as S 45, 4 above. 3, the dipper juglet, is an import (see below).
1. Cup. H. 6.6. Monochrome, reserved lower body and foot, band on body, band inside rim, central dot on floor.
2. Lekythos. H. 10.6. Decorated as shown.
*3. Dipper juglet, trefoil lip. H. 11.3. Yellow orange fabric with pitted porous surface, and very slight trace of a yellow wash. Imported from the Syro-Palestinian area. PLATE 270b.

**Bronze**
4. Arched fibula (B.II.3). L. 7.1. L. of bow 6.6. H. 4.3. Th. 0.3. Complete, pin broken. Rod of rhomboidal section, even thickness. End hammered flat and rolled for catch-plate. Arch high, symmetric except short straight section above catch-plate. Spring (one turn) and catch to right. Tip of pin projects beyond catch. *FGI* no. 160. PLATES 238f, 247, 9.
*5. Leaf-bow fibula (B.I.8). L. of bow fragment 6.5. L. of pin and spring c. 9. Greatest pres. w. of bow 2.5. Catch-plate and part of bow lost, what remains broken. Bow hammered into a thin oval sheet decorated in pointillé; outlined, medial line, either side of which three triangles on common bases. Positive side uppermost. Spring (two turns) to left. *FGI* no. 31. PLATE 247, 1.
6. Fibula fragment? Pres. l. 2.2. D. 0.15. Broken both sides. Slim rod of round section which could be part of bow or pin of a fine fibula. Not illustrated.

**Iron**
7. Dirk. Pres. l. 22.7. W. at hilt 3.3. L. of hilt 8. Max. th. 0.8. Pommel ears lost; what remains composed of four pieces. Scaled-down version of Type II sword. Handgrip and guard are flanged; junction of grip and guard pinched. No trace of rivets in guard or grip, or of hilt-plates of organic material. Profile of blade narrower in centre, then widens towards tip; blade section apparently elliptical. PLATE 245e.
8. Fibula fragment. Pres. l. 2.3. D. less than 0.3. Broken either end. Spring (one turn) with start of pin and bow; type indeterminable. Traces of cloth. Not illustrated.

**S Tomb 47**. Cist. 175 (est.) × 45, depth 39. Destroyed at both ends. Side slabs and one remaining cover slab mostly rectangular, of a coarse conglomerate. Pebble floor. Robbed, no contents.

**S Tomb 48.** Cist. 56 × 22, depth 20. Two cover slabs of limestone; vertical slabs of cut conglomerate and oolite. Pebble floor. No contents.

**S Tomb 49** (PLATE 85; Contents, PLATE 106). Cist. 48 × 28, depth 24. Single limestone cover slab, side slabs of limestone and white magnesite, with packing of flat stones and pithos fragments as a bedding for the covers. Pebble floor.

**Pottery**
1. Cup H. 7. Decorated as shown, with handle barred.

**S Tomb 50.** Cist. 160 × 20–30. Four cover slabs of limestone and magnesite; an extra slab at the E end could represent a grave marker. Well constructed and intact. Pebble floor. No contents.

**S Tomb 51** (PLATES 87, 195b; Contents, PLATES 106, 210b–c). Cist. 100 × 30–40, depth 22. The cover slabs and one side slab at the N were missing, due to the plough. Side slabs of conglomerate and magnesite. Floor of pebbles and the flat cover slabs of S Tombs 52 and 62 which lay beneath. Compacted earth fill.

**Pottery.** Four vases, in comparatively poor condition due to lack of protection by cover slabs. No. 4 is intact, nos. 1 and 3 have rim or handle breaks, and no. 2, the hydria, is badly cracked and is missing rim fragments and most of the neck handle. Clay, slip and paint are in all cases what one would expect from the locality, but spectrographic analysis indicates that the hydria was not made at Lefkandi. The surface of all except no. 1 has deteriorated badly.
1. Jug. H. 17.7. Decorated as shown.
*2. Hydria. H. 15.1. The area beneath the belly-handles has been left unpainted.

FIG. 4 Confronting archers; shoulder decoration of hydria S 51, 2

The remarkable shoulder decoration, FIG. 4, unique for the period, needs verbal description. There are two elements. The first, to the left of the neck handle, is a multiple zigzag pattern, six rows of zigzag with wolftooth filling above and below, neatly done and marked out with dots before painting, not quite vertical.

The second, to the right of the handle, consists of two confronted archers apparently shooting at each other from a sitting position; in spite of the poor preservation, it is possible to restore the figure at the left fully, and most of the figure at the right. The archers are represented by a simple broad curve with angular legs and arms protruding from the side; the head, connected by a short stalk-like neck, is a fringed circle with central dot for eye. They have strung their bows, and hold them ready without drawing the bow fully. The bows are doubly convex, whether the Cretan type of self-bow or a composite bow (see Snodgrass, *Early Greek Armour* 140ff. and Rausing, *The Bow, Some Notes on its Origin and Development* 98 and figs. 19, 20).

Both motives are astonishing. Whether the archers show continuity of human representation from Mycenaean times (note the 'golliwog' heads), or whether they reflect chance finds from the Mycenaean occupation (and, as we know, there is no lack of figured sherds in the Xeropolis settlement), one cannot tell for sure. The multiple zigzag is equally remarkable in its way, as one would not expect it until well into the Sub-Protogeometric period. PLATE 270d—e.

*3. Skyphos. H. 6.9. Monochrome, reserved lower area, bands on body, band on rim.

4. Pedestal bowl. H. 7. Monochrome, reserved foot, bands on flat surface of rim.

**Iron**

5. Fibula fragments? (a) L. 4. (b) L. 3.7. Th. less than 0.6. Two non-joining fragments, broken away both sides. Could be parts of the bow of a fibula, perhaps rhomboidal section. Traces of cloth. Not illustrated.

**S Tomb 52** (PLATE 87). Cist. 60 × 32, depth 30. Disturbed at both ends. Thin limestone cover slabs; thin side slabs of white magnesite, 2 — 3 cm. thick. No slab at E end, and the W end is built up with small stones. One cover slab, at the W end, was reset by the grave-digger of S Tomb 62, which encroached slightly at this point. Pebble floor. No contents: probably robbed.

**S Tomb 53** (PLATE 85; Contents, PLATE 107). Cist. 78 × 26, depth 26. Two cover slabs of limestone and schist; side slabs of limestone and coarse conglomerate. Pebble floor.

**Pottery**

1. Amphoriskos, belly-handled. H. 12.7. Intact. Local fabric: note a few large white grits left in the clay. Heavy and poorly made, crudely painted. Decorated as shown.

**Bronze**

2. Open ring. D. 1.4. W. 1.2. Th. 0.05. In three pieces, scraps missing. Flat strip of metal rolled into hoop. The straight terminal does not narrow. Oblique fine band of *tremolo* ornament. A metacarpal found in the ring.

**S Tomb 54** (PLATE 85; Contents, PLATE 107). Covered pit grave. 55 × 25, depth 13. Three limestone slabs covered a small roughly rectangular pit, with lining of small stones. Pebble floor. One bronze fibula centrally placed. Perhaps a child's grave. The E cover slab encroaches slightly over the NW corner of Tomb 55.

**Bronze**

*1. Arched fibula, twisted bow (B.II.7). L. 5.3. H. 5. Th. 0.2. Complete; repaired. Slim rod of square or rhomboidal section, end hammered flat and rolled for unusually high catch-plate. Bow slightly twisted (twists at 0.15 intervals) from spring to catch-plate. Arch exceptionally high. Asymmetric as straightens into a forearm. Spring (one turn) to right, catch to left. *FGI* no. 212. PLATES 238d, 247, 14.

**S Tomb 55** (PLATE 85; Contents, PLATE 107). cist. 112 × 30 (est.), depth 30. One cover slab of oolite preserved at N end; slabs of conglomerate and magnesite on three sides; the fourth side and most of the cover slabs were removed by the later cutting for the large shaft grave, S Tomb 59. Pebble floor. The lekythos, no. 1, was *in situ* in the covered N half of the tomb. Some of the fragments of the deep bowl 2 were inside the cist, others in the disturbed fill over S Tomb 59.

**Pottery**

1. Lekythos fragments. H. (rest.) c. 14. Neck, handle, foot, and several very damaged body fragments preserved; much of surface flaked off. Local manufacture. Airhole to right of handle. Decorated as shown. Three groups of hand-drawn semicircles on shoulder. Band beneath rim linking with the vertical strokes on the laddered handle.

2. Deep bowl. H. 7.5. About three quarters preserved. Locally made. Decorated as shown. Note reserved band with dots inside the lip.

**S Tomb 56** (PLATE 86; Contents, PLATE 107). Pit grave at the N edge of trench *Sigma*, only about half excavated, probably oval. W. 60, depth 55. The amphora (no. 1) was found fallen on its side among stones at the top of the pit, c. 35 below the surface; it probably originally stood as a marker, the stones forming its bedding. The other vases were found on the rock floor on the pit.

Pottery. Five vases. Three intact except for chips; 1 and 3 restored from fragments. The clay, slip and paint of 1, 3 and 5 are those customary for the local wheel-made vases; 2 is of Black Slip ware; 4 is hand-made in a red gritty coarse clay.
1. Belly-handled amphora. H. 28.5. The ridge on the neck shows where the potter attached the rim and upper neck to the lower neck. Decorated as shown. Five groups of twelve semicircles on the shoulder.
*2. Trefoil oinochoe. H. 20.7. Black Slip ware, with streaky black paint; note a few white grits in the clay. The vase has the combed and incised decoration (done with the same three-pointed instrument) so common on this ware.
3. Skyphos. H. 9.6. Decorated as shown. Two sets of sixteen PSC on each side.
4. Shallow bowl. H. 3.8. D. 14—15.5. Hand-made, oval. One string hole. PLATE 269c.
5. Kalathos. H. 5.7. Two string holes. Monochrome, reserved bands.

S Tomb 57. Cist. 50 × 22, depth 25. Limestone cover and side slabs. Pebble floor. Intact, but no contacts.

S Tomb 58. Destroyed cist. c. 60 × 34. Nothing of the stone structure remained *in situ*, but a rectangular area of pebble floor was found below a tumble of slabs. No contents.

S Tomb 59 (PLATES 88, 195d; Contents, PLATES 108—10, 224—5). Shaft grave. 230 × 80, depth 155. A series of large cover slabs of marble and limestone were set on a rock ledge at a depth of c. 110 in the shaft. Slabs collapsed at both ends; at the centre the cover slabs were thick, of grey marble, and intact, one of them overlaid by a large dressed lime-stone block, cut to a rectangular shape with square section (80 × 33 × 33).

The group of pottery and other objects catalogued as S Tomb 59A was found in the earth fill above the cover slabs. All most probably represent offerings related to S Tomb 59 and placed over it after it was closed. The vases are homogeneous, and the same potter was in certain instances probably responsible for pots both within the tomb and above the cover slabs (e.g. 59,9 and 59A,7; 59,8 and 59A,2). 59A,1 and 6 *in situ* on the cover slabs; joining fragments of 59A,1 and 2 were found inside 59, presumably as a result of the collapse of some of these slabs.

The tomb proper, catalogued as 59, was partly filled with earth and stones; some of the fill had fallen in later, but some seems to have been thrown in with the deposit of grave offerings (principally the kalathoi 59,8, 9, 11—16) which were heaped up along the E side. On the floor was a layer of black earth, 2—6 thick, containing one fragment of burnt bone, the small finds, and certain vases.

### S Tomb 59A finds

Pottery. All restored from fragments, and all have the local pink to buff clay, with pale buff slip. Most have brown paint, but the lid of pyxis 5, the inside of kalathos 6, and kalathos 8 have a brighter, orange-brown, paint.
1. Amphora, neck-handled. H. 37.5. Decorated as shown. The groups of diagonals on the belly and of vertical strokes on the lip done with a multiple brush.
2. Kalathos, openwork. H. 10.9. Two string holes below the rim. The cut-out triangles rather irregular in shape and size, and the relation between the two tiers not consistent: sixteen triangles in upper tier, fourteen in lower. The struts are easily broken and some are missing. String lines at top and bottom of each tier. See 59, 8.

3. Skyphos. H. 7.1. Decorated as shown. Two sets of nine PSC on each side. Area beneath handles un-painted. Reserved dot on floor.

4. Skyphos. H. 9.9. Decorated as 3, but fourteen PSC in each set. PLATE 265b.

5. Pyxis with lid. H. 12.6. H. of lid 2.9. Two string holes beneath rim, diametrically opposite each other and matching two on lid. Decorated as shown. Battlement motive carelessly done, with one crenel-lation improvised where the design came full circle. Top of lid knob unpainted. PLATE 267a.

6. Kalathos. H. 5.3. Two string holes close together. Monochrome, reserved bands.

7. Kalathos. H. 4.5. Two string holes as 6. Banded; see 59, 9.

8. Kalathos. H. 5.2. Deep conical shape, flaring rim. One string hole survives. Monochrome, underside reserved. Not illustrated.

9. Miniature Kalathos. H. 1.6. D. 4.9. Hand-made. Shallow conical, painted inside and out. Two string holes close together. The diameter corresponds closely with that of the lead scale pans 11 and 12 (s.v.), and this vase was found very near them.

### Bronze
10. Fibula fragment. Pres. l. 1.6. D. of spring 0.7. Spring and pin of very small fibula, type indeterminable. Spring (perhaps two turns) to left.

### Lead
*11. Small scale-pan. D. 5. Greatest th. 0.55. Edge chipped, otherwise complete. Well preserved. Slightly concave, of plano-convex section. Four evenly spaced suspension holes at the circumference, d. 0.1. Very finely traced lines joining opposite holes form a cross on the floor of the pan. PLATE 246f.

*12. Small scale-pan. D.5. Th. 0.5. Complete save chip lost at one suspension hole. Well preserved. The fellow of 11. PLATE 246f.

## S Tomb 59 finds

**Pottery.** All intact except for small chips on four; most in mint condition and probably unused before the burial. No. 3, a cup, is hand-made. The rest are all wheel-made, and all except the Attic pyxis no. 4 were locally made. It is noteworthy that the clay of the Attic vase looks very similar to that of the local vases. A group of four, nos. 5 and 6 (pyxides), 9 and 14 (kalathoi) have a similar treatment of equally spaced horizontal bands — perhaps by the same hand?

1. Trefoil oinochoe. H. 19.9. Decorated as shown. The neck motive is an hourglass framed in a rectangle. Handle barred. PLATE 266e.

2. Skyphos. H. 6.7. Decorated as shown. Two sets of ten PSC on each side. Reserved dot on floor. PLATE 265a.

3. Cup. H. (without handle) 7.4. Hand-made. Light red micaceous fabric with a few grits, self slip. Heavily made.

*4. Pyxis with lid. H. 10.6, with lid 16. Two pairs of string holes about 2 cm apart, diametrically opposite, matched on the lid. The inside edge of the flange painted, but not the top surface. Decorated as shown. Attic. PLATE 272d.

5. Pyxis with lid. H. 7.8, with lid 10. Two string holes nearly opposite each other, matched on the lid. Monochrome, reserved bands. Reserved dot on top of lid knob.

6. Pyxis with lid. H. 7.9, with lid 10.2. The lid has two diametrically opposite string holes, with a scratch on the underside joining them (and extending to the edge on one side), apparently as a guide line. The process of matching these on the pyxis was hardly competent: there are five holes on the flange, including the two which match perfectly. Decorated as shown. Cross on the underside. Top of lid knob unpainted.

7. Miniature lekythos. H. 4.7. Monochrome.

8. Kalathos, openwork. H. 9.7. D. 18.4. Two string holes. Intact. Shape and decoration as 59A, 2, prob-ably by the same potter. Sixteen cut-out triangles and one narrow cut-out rectangle in upper tier, twelve triangles and a broader rectangle in the lower tier. PLATE 265d.

9. Kalathos. H. 6.9. Two small string holes close together. Banded. Reserved central dot on floor.

10. Kalathos. H. 4.5. String holes as on 9. Vertical marks beneath rim (done with a bone tool?) give the appearance of rouletting. Monochrome.

11. Kalathos. H. 4.8. Monochrome.

12. Kalathos. H. 5.7. Monochrome. Reserved dot on floor. Underside unpainted.

13. Kalathos. H. 3.9. Pronounced rouletting. Monochrome. Underside unpainted.

14. Kalathos. H. 4.8. String holes as 9. Monochrome, reserved bands on body and inside rim. Reserved band inside rim. Underside unpainted.
15. Kalathos. H. 4.3. As 14, but no reserved bands on the body.
16. Kalathos. H. 4.4. As 15.

**Gold.** 17—25 intact and in excellent condition. Of the finger rings, 19—23 (ribbed) have retained their shape, 24—5 (plain) are bent.
17. Earring. D. (head) 9 mm, (wire) 1—1.5 mm. Wt. 1.2 gr. A half coil of wire, thickening at each end, is fitted into a small socket beneath each head. The head consists of a thin disk pushed up at the centre to form a pointed cone or 'Chinaman's hat'. PLATE 231a.
18. Earring. D. (head) 9 mm, (wire) 1—1.5 mm. Wt. 1.2 gr. The twin of 17. Position in grave not recorded: found in sieving.
19. Finger ring. D. 21 mm. W. 8 mm. Wt. 1.0 gr. Broad ring with six ribs. Made from thin foil, turned over at the outside edges. Closed hoop. PLATE 230i.
20. Finger ring. D. 17 mm. W. 5 mm. Wt. 0.8 gr. As 19 but with four ribs.
21. Finger ring. D. 17—18 mm. W. 5 mm. Wt. 0.5 gr. As 20.
22. Finger ring. D. 17—18 mm. W. 5 mm. Wt. 0.5 gr. As 20.
23. Finger ring. D. 17 mm. W. 5 mm. Wt. 0.5 gr. As 20.
24. Finger ring. D. 18—19 mm. W. 8 mm. Wt. 0.6 gr. Plain ring with slightly curved section, formed from paper thin foil. Closed hoop. The foil is too fine and fragile to have been used on its own; it would originally have had a stiffening core of a different material (wood or ivory?) since burnt or decayed. PLATE 230d.
25. Finger ring. D. 16 mm. W. 8 mm. Wt. 0.5 gr. As 24.
26. Gold foil, two fragments. L. 5.1, 4.7. W. 7—10 mm. Wt. 0.5 gr. Bent and damaged at the edges. Fragments practically identical, square at one end, rounded at the other. Plain surface. Perhaps from a diadem.

### Gold with iron
27. Gilt iron pin, three fragments, joins uncertain. D. (head) 12 mm, (shaft) 5 mm, (lower sleeve) 4 mm. L. (pres.) 10.2. One fragment preserves the head, which is button shaped, and the start of the shaft, round in section; gold foil preserved on the head and c. 10 mm of the shaft. A second fragment preserves a sleeve of gold foil, l. 2.8, terminating at each end in a wire ring, c. 0.5 mm thick, which has held its shape against the oxydising process. Traces of cloth on the shaft near the head (weft-faced type of weave).
28. Gilt iron pin, three fragments, joins uncertain. D. (lower sleeve) 4 mm. L. (pres.) 7.1. As 27, but the head is missing, and the only feature with gilt surface preserved is one end of the lower sleeve.

**Bronze.** Of the eight fibulae, 29—34 were placed in the tomb in pairs; so no doubt were 35 and 36, but the find spot of 36 is uncertain.
*29. Fibula with characteristics of arched and Attico-Boeotian types (B.II.12/B.VII.5). L. 14.4. H. 7.8 (not including spread of pin). Widest section of bow 2 × 1.2. Plate 5.9 high × 3.6 wide. Complete save chips of catch; part of plate broken and re-attached. The fine detail is obscured by crusty surface oxidisation.
   Very sharply divided into pin, spring, stem and large catch-plate. Bow set off from the stem and from the catch by a fillet and bead moulding. The beads appear to be undecorated. The section of the bow is approximately plano-convex, but the underside is slightly convex, rather than flat. On the spine of the bow are three parallel relief ridges, of which the centre is slightly wider than the two outer, but a little lower. On either side of the centre ridge, between it and the outer ones, is a line of close-set incised or impressed elongated 'esses'. The edges of the bow are set off by a fine line of pointillé dots. The stem is of rhomboid section; each of its four faces has a line of fine pointillé dots outlining the edges as far as the spring. The spring is also of rhomboid section, and is set off from the pin by a bead and fillet moulding. The pin itself is of round section, and tapers evenly to the point.
   A very fine fillet separates the catch-plate (FIG. 5) from the adjacent bead-moulding. The plate is very thin (less than 0.05), and was presumably hammered after casting. The incised design is obscured by the crusty patina. By conflating the two sides of the plate it seems that there is an identical linear panel at the head of the plate on each side, framed by a border of close-set pointillé dots. The central element of the panel is composed of three double triangles, the inner ones stippled, set off

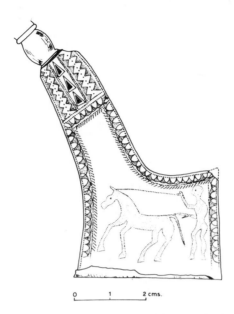

FIG. 5 Catch plate of fibula S 59,29

on each side by double vertical lines of close-cut dots. The two outer panels are made up of opposed stippled dogtooth, the resulting reserved zigzag band between being picked out by a vertical band of heavy pointillé dots. The lower part of the plate is enclosed within an elaborate border. This consists of a line of adjacent semicircles, overridden by a similar line, with the interlocking spaces stippled. This is outlined on either side by a single line of close-set dots, parallel to which, on the inside edge, is a line of cable of incised or impressed 'esses'. Within this border, on the side of the catch, is a driven horse followed by a man; this may represent part of the training of the horse, using the long rein method (see W. Browne's illustrations in *His Fifty Years* (1924), reproduced in *History Today*, Nov. 1970, p. 777, and for a discussion of early equitation, Snodgrass *DAG* 414 and fig. 126). Their out-lines are drawn in heavy pointillé dots, while their inner surfaces are stippled with a very light pointillé. In the equivalent space on the reverse side is a compass-drawn pointillé six-petal rosette enclosed within a triple concentric pointillé border, also compass-drawn. The whole workmanship is extremely fine.

   Spring (one turn) and catch to left. FGI no. 1524. PLATE 240e—g.
30. Fibula, the fellow of 29. L. 14.6. Pres. H. 8.2. Widest section of bow 2.1 × 1.2. Plate 6.1 high × 3.8 wide. L. of pin (from moulding) 12.6. Complete, though pin broken at spring and again near tip. Plate broken in several places and re-attached; small parts missing. Apparently an exact pair to 29. Oxidisation prevents certainty for the design on the front of the plate, but from slight traces it could be the same as on 29. Spring (one turn) and catch to right. FGI no. 1525. PLATES 240a, 249, 4.
*31. Attico-Boeotian fibula (Akin to B.VIII.2?). L. 3.6. H. 2. Max. th. of bow 0.6. Pin lost, catch-plate chipped. Clearly separated into stem, bow and catch-plate by bead and fillet mouldings. The stem is of rhomboidal section, the bow elliptical. The forearm spreads into a broad, square catch-plate, too oxydized for any decoration to show. Spring (two turns) and catch to left. FGI no. 633. PLATE 240c.
*32. Arched fibula with symmetric swollen bow (B.II.12/14). L. 3.2. H. 1.9. W. of swollen bow 1.0. Pin lost, catch-plate chipped. Clearly articulated into stem, bow, forearm and catch-plate by the bead and fillet mouldings that separate bow from stem and forearm. Stem of rhomboidal section. Section of bow a steep plano-convex. Relatively large rectangular catch-plate expanding from a short forearm. Undecorated. Spring (probably one turn) and catch to right. PLATE 249, 2.
*33. Arched fibula with symmetric swollen bow (B.II.12/14). L. 0.3. H. c. 2.2. W. of swollen bow 1.1.

Much of spring, all pin, part of catch-plate lost. The fellow of 32, though the moulding of the swollen bow is sharper. Undecorated. Catch to left. *FGI* no. 1048.

*34. Arched fibula with symmetric swollen bow. (B.II.12/14). Pres, L. 3.2. Pres. h. 2. W. of swollen bow 1.05. Pin, most of spring lost, catch-plate chipped. The fellow of 32 and 33 — closer perhaps to 33. Catch to left. *FGI* no. 1047.

*35. Small arched fibula with central boss (B.II.14). Pres. l. 1.5. H. 1. D. of boss 0.8. Catch-plate and pin lost, spring broken. The short stem and forearm are set off from the boss by finely executed bead and fillet mouldings. The stem is of rectangular section, the boss spherical, flattened on the underside. Spring (one turn) to right.

36. Small arched fibula with central boss (B.II.14). Pres. l. 1.8. Pres. h. 1.3. D. of boss 1.0. Spring and pin lost. The fellow of 35. Catch to left.

*37. Plate from scale cuirass. L. 3.7. Top W. 1.9. Th. less than 0.1. Rib 1.5 × 0.4. Complete and intact. Three straight sides, the fourth curved, strengthened by a central vertical rib (created, presumably, by hammering into a matrix); seven stitch holes, punched, two above and two below the rib, three more at the side. PLATE 239l.

## Lead

*38. Decorated plaque. L. 5.2. Max. w. 2.7. Th. 0.1. (th. at largest boss 0.5). Complete in two pieces. Cast, in the form of two circlets either side of a lozenge with concave sides, each element picked out with concentric lines in relief; at the centre of each element is a large encircled boss, each enclosed by four equally spaced smaller bosses. In the case of the circlets these smaller bosses were joined by curved lines tangential from the outer edge of one boss to the inner edge of its neighbour. The effect recalls a running spiral band. PLATE 239 m.

## Faience

39. Jar, rim and neck fragment. D. (rim) 4.5. H. (pres.) 4.9. Green surface, dark and glossy where well-preserved, inside and out. Decoration of dots in black on the rim and upper surface of the handle. The black areas have a glossy surface, and the colouring material penetrates as far as 0.5 mm into the fabric.

**S Tomb 60** (PLATE 89; Contents, PLATE 111). Cist. 58 × 22. Rectangular side slabs and three cover slabs of limestone, schist, and conglomerate. Pebble floor.

**Pottery.** Three vases, intact except for no. 1, which has small fragments restored. Locally made. Surface decayed in some places.
1. Deep bowl. H. 7.6. Decorated as shown. PLATE 256d.
2. Cup. H. 4.4. Monochrome except reserved foot.
3. Lekythos. H. 7.5. Airhole. Three sets of hand-drawn semicircles with half-moon filling. Otherwise decorated as shown.

## Bronze

*4. Arched fibula (B.II.3). L. 4.7. H. 3.8. Th. 0.3. Complete except catch and tip of pin. Slim rod of rhomboidal section, even thickness, one end hammered flat and rolled into catch-plate. Arch symmetrical, except for slight angularity at its crown. Spring (one turn) and catch to left. *FGI* no. 159. PLATES 238c, 247, 7.

**S Tomb 61.** Cist. 42 × 24, depth 20. Sides of small uncut stones, and a single cover slab of oolite. Pebble floor. Intact, no contents. Probably a child's grave.

**S Tomb 62** (PLATE 87; Contents, PLATE 111). Covered pit grave. c. 155 × 45, depth 20. A long narrow pit, cut into the rock and covered with five limestone slabs. Lining of small stones along part of one side only. Pebble floor. The pit was dug after S Tomb 52: a side slab at the SW corner of 52 was removed during the encroachment of 62. The floor of 52 was c. 10 cm deeper than that of 62, but the cover slabs were at exactly the same level; one large slab was reset to cover both the N end of 52 and the W end of 62. The cover slabs of both later formed a level paved floor for Tomb 51.

At the S end of the grave were found a lekythos, and two pins at the 'shoulder' position. With each pin was found a fragment of burnt bone, brittle, white and calcined by burning in the pyre; the larger measures 3 × 1.2.

### Pottery
1. Lekythos. H. 12.7. Local ware; two or three white grits in the fabric have caused large pock marks. Airhole to right of handle. Decorated as shown. Vertical paint-stroke on handle.

### Bronze
*2. Dress pin. Pres. l. 14.5. D. of head 0.5. D. of bulb 0.6. L. of bulb c. 1.5. Tip lost, otherwise complete. Small domed button head, slim oval bulb, not set off from the shaft. Undecorated. PLATES 242a, 250, 2.
3. Dress pin. Pres. l. 14.3. D. of head 0.4. D. of bulb 0.45. L. of bulb 2. D. of shaft c. 0.2. Tip lost, what remains broken between head and bulb. Though the head is poorly formed, this is the fellow to 2.

**S Tomb 63** (PLATE 89; contents, PLATE 111). Cist. 165 × 45, depth 120. Five heavy limestone cover slabs, dressed rectangular side slabs of white magnesite and softer limestone. Pebble floor. At the S end one fibula was found above, and the other below, a small pile of burnt bone fragments. The pins were also set amongst a number of small bone fragments.

### Bronze
*1. Dress pin. L. 13.5. D. of head 0.6 × 0.5. D. of bulb 0.7. L. of bulb 2. Complete, repaired. Flat button head, slim oval bulb, not set off from the shaft. PLATES 242b, 250, 3.
2. Dress pin fragments. L. 10 and 7.6. D of both 0.2. Both broken at each end. Probably shafts of pins such as 1. Not illustrated.
3. Arched fibula (B.II.7). Pres. l. 5. Pres. h. 3.5. Th. 1.5. Shattered — bow, spring and part of pin remain. Slim rod of round section and even thickness, twisted (at c. 0.2. intervals) probably from spring to catch-plate. What remains of the arch is symmetric. Spring of one turn.
4. Arched fibula fragments. (?B.II.7). L. of pin 4.5. Consists of pin, part of spring, scrap of bow. The bow fragment is a twisted rod of round section. This may have been the fellow to 3. Not illustrated.

**S Pyre 1** (Contents, PLATE 112). Rectangular, tending to a spool shape, with rounded ends and narrowing in the centre. 120 × 34—40, depth 70. The bulldozer had cut slightly into the NW corner. Carbon fill, with fragments of charred wood. One section of the multiple vase no. 1 was found 45 above the floor on the E side, the other 20 deeper at the W side.

### Pottery. All fragmentary, the clay burnt to grey, few traces of paint surviving.
1. Quadruple vase. H. 10. Two belly-handled amphoriskoi, joining; made up from fragments and complete except for handles and rim fragments. Each section has the join for a further section, including in one case part of the wall; the missing sections were on the same side, and the vase originally formed a rectangular group of four, with high basket handle, of which only the start now remains on one side, in the centre. Traces of paint on the outside, and inside the lip; decoration uncertain.
2. Stirrup vase fragments. H. c. 17. About one half preserved, including the spout. Surface badly damaged; traces of paint, but decoration uncertain.
3. The burnt fragments of at least three other small closed vessels. They include a fragment of a trefoil oinochoe, grooved on the outside, a sherd with hand-drawn semicircles, and one with triple zigzag lines. Not illustrated.

(S Pyre 1A. See p. 110 and S Tomb 4).

**S Pyre 2** (PLATE 90; Contents, PLATE 112). Rectangular at the top, rounded below. D. 90—100, depth 40. One side had been bulldozed away. Carbon fill with charred wood fragments. At the bottom, a layer of small stones and pebbles, over which were found some sixty small scraps of burnt bone, white, brittle and calcined, none over 5 cm long.

There were also a gold ring and fragments of two gilt iron pins at the bottom. No pottery found.

**Gold**
1. Finger ring. D. 14—16 mm. Carinated section. Broken and bent out of shape.

**Iron with gold**
2. Dress pin, head and part of shaft. Pres. l. 1.7. D. 0.9. Disk head; pin of round section, corroded away, leaving the gold foil covering hollow.
3. Dress pin, head and part of shaft. Pres. l. 5. D. (head) 1.0. Plain disk head; shaft of round section, heavily corroded. Possibly originally gilt as 2. Not illustrated.

**S Pyre 3** (PLATE 90; Contents, PLATE 112). Rectangular. Contiguous with S Pyre 2 but deeper; about one half destroyed by bulldozer. Carbon fill with charred wood (one fragment 20 × 8), and a large boulder at the bottom.

**Pottery.** Found in surface level, probably to be associated with S Pyre 3.
1. Amphora fragments. Some of the fragments join, others do not. Pinkish buff clay, pale buff slip, orange-brown paint: i.e. local. The colour of the joining fragments varies considerably, from grey to orange-red, due to burning after the vase was broken. This makes it harder to assign the non-joining fragments with certainty to the same vase. A restoration has been attempted on the assumption that all the sherds belong, thus probably making it a four-handled amphora. H. (rest.) 68. Photo of sherds, PLATE 282, A.
   (a) Base and lower body, three main fragments not joining. D. of base c. 16. Broad ring foot, wall suggesting a broad ovoid shape; band at foot, and 14 cm higher a wide band between two narrow ones.
   (b) Body and handle fragment. Note on the shoulder the groups of hand-drawn semicircles, with half-moon filling and dot-fringed, in one case interlocking.
   (c) Shoulder and shoulder-handle fragment. Handle triple, with two rolls added to the flat central strap handle; the central section is decorated with a double row of cut triangles, cut out with the knife but not going through, thus resembling the impressed-triangle kalathoi. Note the start of a second group of hand-drawn semicircles to the left of the handle (not in restored drawing).
   (d) Rim and neck fragment. D. (rim) c. 21. On the lower neck a reserved band enclosing two rows of zigzags. Flattened rim with groups of transverse strokes.

**S Pyre 4 (upper)** (PLATES 91, 196d; Contents, PLATES 112–3, 222). Rock-cut pit similar in shape and dimensions to S Pyre 2; partly destroyed by the bulldozer. Carbon fill with small stones and bone fragments. At the surface of the fill were found the amphora fragments no. 3; the majority of the other objects were in the carbon at a depth of c. 15. The two pins 9 and 10 lay parallel and c. 40 apart, perhaps associated with the iron fibulae 15 and 16, and worn on the burial garment. Two of the gold rings, 6 and 7, were melted out of shape, and the bronze fibulae 11 and 12 had also suffered in the pyre. The two vases, 1 and 2, were blackened by the fire, as were all six clay buttons, 19—24.

**Pottery**
1. Cup. H. 7.5. Intact. Burnt; grey clay with fine micaceous flecks; black paint. Opposite the handle and below the rim are two warts, 9.5 apart, and fully painted over. Decorated as shown. Reserved band inside lip. Attic EG II import.
2. Skyphos. H. 5.3. D. (rim) 7.5—8.3. Made up complete. Burnt: grey clay, black paint. The rim was pushed out of the round at one side, for a drinking spout. Decorated as shown. Thin reserved band inside rim.
3. Amphora fragments. From at least three vases. Local fabric.
   (a) Neck and shoulder fragments. D. (neck) c. 21. Rays on neck, two tiers of semicircles on shoulder. See under (c). PLATE 281B.
   (b) Rim and neck fragments. D. (rim) c. 31. Not from same vase as (a). Rays below rim. Flattened rim with bars. PLATE 281B.

(c) Assorted fragments, not illustrated. A large fragment with concentric circles and reserved cross filling is from the belly of 3(a); another has 'open' circles and a wart; two others show circles, one with hourglass filling; the fifth has a rectilinear decoration. All are from massive amphorae.

## Gold

4. Finger ring. D. 2–2.1. Wt. 1.0 gr. Two rings of identical form, the one fitting loosely inside the other to form a double thickness. Slightly damaged on one side. The section has a double carination. Closed hoop.
5. Finger ring. D. 2–2.1. Wt. 0.8 gr. As 4, but single. Damaged on one edge.
6. Finger ring. D. c. 1.5. Wt. 0.3 gr. Similar to 5. Melted out of shape, broken and damaged at edges.
7. Finger ring. Wt. 0.4 gr. Form and condition as 6. Not drawn.
8. Earring pendant. Two disks joined by a single coil of wire. D. (disk) 8 mm; (wire) 1 mm. Wt. 0.5 gr. The disks are curved to the shape of a very shallow hollow cone, and have a small sleeve attached in the centre, into which the wire was inserted.

## Gold with iron

9. Dress pin, gilt iron. D. (head) 12 mm; (shaft) 3–4 mm. Pres. l. 12.5. Broken, point missing. Button head, probably with a shank attached into which the shaft fitted, as with 10. Plain shaft with round section. Gold foil well preserved over most of the surviving length. PLATE 231f.
10. Dress pin, gilt iron. D. (head) 12–14 mm; (shaft) 3 mm. Pres. l. 9. Broken, point missing. Oxydisation has left a hollow centre and a hard crust outside most of the gold foil. The head has a shank attached, into which the shaft fits. Not drawn.

## Bronze

*11. Arched fibula with central boss. Pres. l. 6.2. Pres. h. 4.5. D. of boss 3.9. Catch-plate, part of spring, and pin lost. The short stem and forearm are set off from the boss by two fine fillets each side; stem and forearm of square section. The boss is considerably broader than the part of the bow it occupies. Spring to right.
12. Arched fibula with central boss. Largest fragment 5.5 × 4.5. Th. 2.7. Bow, spring and pin fragments. Probably the fellow of 11, but ruined. Not drawn.
*13. Leaf-bow fibula (B.I.8). Pres. l. 5.5. Pres. h. 2.4. W. of bow 1.3. Spring, part of stem and pin lost; what remains bent out of shape. The slightly curved elliptical flat bow is clearly set off from the stem and forearm. Apparently undecorated. Made from a rod thickened at the centre and hammered flat to form the bow. Catch to right. *FGI* no. 16D.
14. Arched fibula. (?B.II.1). Pres. l. 3.7. H. 3.4. Th. less than 0.4. Catch-plate, forearm and much of pin lost; in two pieces. Rod of round section, possibly rather thicker at the centre; symmetric arch as preserved. Spring (two turns) to right.

## Iron

15. Fibula with crescent bow. (B.IX.1). L. c. 11.5. H. 8. W. of crescent 3.3. Complete, but broken. Stem apparently of rhomboid section, bow flat, rectangular forearm. Asymmetric since stem appreciably higher than forearm. Traces of bead and fillet mouldings above spring and catch. Spring (one turn) and catch to right. PLATE 241d.
16. Fibula with crescent bow. (B.IX.1). Pres. l. 10.3. Pres. h. c. 8. W. (vertical) of bow 3.5. Part of bow, stem, spring and most of pin lost. Probably the fellow to 15. Traced line visible following edge of crescent top and bottom.
17. Pin. Pres. l. 4.5. Th. c. 0.25. Two joining fragments of the shaft of a dress pin, or of the pin of a fibula. Not drawn.
18. Dress pin? fragments. Pres. l. 18. D. c. 0.8. Three joining fragments. Shaft of ?pin, of which head and tip are lost. Six or eight facets, set off by very fine relief ridges. The shaft may taper slightly, but its condition is too ruined to be sure.

## Terracotta

19–24. Six buttons or spindle whorls, of conical or concave–conical shape; they could have come from one garment. 22–4 were found fairly close together. All are burnt and have a grey fabric, 20 rather whiter than the others, 24 with many white grits. H. 2–2.8.

**Objects found in disturbed ashy earth above Pyre 4,** probably to be associated with it.

25. Pyxis lid fragments. H. 3.5. D. 7.8. Less than one half of lid with cylindrical knob, and rim fragment of another. Fabric burnt to grey, streaky dark brown to black paint. Each has one string hole preserved.
26. Flat dish. H. 1.4. D. (rim) 13.7. About one half preserved. Trace of two handles applied outside the rim. Fabric burnt to grey, paint blackened. Reserved band on rim and central dot on floor. Fully painted outside, except for a reserved band at the resting place, and a larger central dot beneath.

**S Pyre 4 (lower)** (PLATE 91). Rectangular. 170 × 65, depth 80. Carbon fill. The carbon deposit of S Pyre 4 (upper) rested on a bed of yellow gravel; that of S Pyre 4 (lower) was beneath this, and stratigraphically separate. The fill contained small burnt fragments of bone of bone and charred wood, over a bed of large blackened stones.

**S Pyre 5.** Unexcavated. This pyre appears to lie on the W side of the bulldozed trench.

**S Pyre 6** (PLATE 90; Contents, PLATE 114). Rectangular. c. 125 × 70, depth 60. A small area of black carbon survived on each side of the bulldozed trench at the N end of the field. Here were found a few burnt sherds, including the jug neck no. 1, and twenty-six small calcined fragments of burnt bone.

**Pottery**
1. Jug, fragmentary. D. (mouth) 7.3. Top half to shoulder preserved, including handle. Two ridges with incised rope-pattern at the collar. Local pink to buff clay, mostly burnt to grey; orange-brown paint. Compass-drawn semicircles on shoulder.
2. Amphora fragments. About twelve sherds, the majority burnt to grey. One has compass-drawn semicircles on the shoulder, another a close wavy line. Not illustrated.

**S Pyre 7** (PLATE 90). Rectangular. c. 130 × 70, depth 85. Close to Pyre 6 and same orientation. Mostly demolished by bulldozer. Carbon fill, large stones at bottom; a few burnt sherds and about twenty scraps of burnt bone, including two hard and thick skull fragments.

**S Pyre 8** (PLATE 196c; Contents, PLATE 114). Rectangular. c. 160 × 65, depth 62. Carbon fill with charred wood, scraps of burnt bone and sherds. Fragments of two pins in the fill. Two large pieces of burnt wood (l. 45 and 25) found at the bottom of the pit.

**Pottery**. Not illustrated. About twenty sherds, half of them burnt, including the fragments below.
1. Jug, rim and body fragments. Linear decoration, a series of alternating thick and thin horizontal bands (see S 5,2). Flat strap handle, attached to rim.

**Bronze**
2a. Pin fragment. Pres. l. 9.6. Head d. 0.8. Bulb d. 0.8. D. of shaft 0.5. Two fragments, doubtfully joining. Traces of a button head and a slim bulb on the shaft in the manner of, e.g., S 62,3.
2b. Pin fragment. Pres. l. 5. Th. up to 0.7. Broken both ends. Possibly part of the shaft of a dress pin, though pin of a large fibula conceivable.

**S Pyre 9.** Irregular area of black carbonised earth and grey ash, found over the N end of tomb 14. c. 60 × 55. No contents other than four burnt sherds, featureless, and about twenty burnt bone fragments. This may represent the cleanings from a nearby pyre prior to re-use.

**S Pyre 10** (PLATE 90; Contents, PLATE 114). A roughly circular rock cutting close to S Pyre 7. c. 80 × 52 (extending irregularly on one side), cut away at one edge by the bulldozer; depth 40. Carbon fill. Kalathos at bottom in central position. In the earth above the pyre a few burnt sherds (not illustrated) — a fragment of a large closed vessel with compass-drawn circles (?), and another of a cup with high offset rim with close zigzag motive.

### Pottery

1. Kalathos. H. 6.5. D. (rim) 13.7. Complete. Burnt, except for one rim fragment which has been broken off and escaped the fire, showing the original clay as pinkish, with red-brown paint; elsewhere grey clay, near black paint. Two string holes 1 cm apart. Four rows of impressed triangles (the first and third inverted) and a multiple wavy line in the combed technique, done before the pot was painted. Painted inside and out except for the underside. PLATE 261c.

**S Pyre 11** (PLATE 90). Only a small part excavated, at the extreme edge of the trench. Carbon fill, no contents.

**S Pyre 12** (PLATE 91). Rectangular. 170 × 75, narrowing to 60 at centre, depth 50. At the bottom a carbon deposit c. 35 deep, containing stones and small fragments of burnt bone. Above this an earth and rock fill, consisting of the fragments of conglomerate originally dug out, and partially rehardened.

**Pottery**. In the upper fill two sherds, probably from a large jug, the one decorated with wavy lines, the other with a plastic wart, concentric circles or semicircles and a fringe of languettes. Not illustrated. In the surface earth near the pyre, a few amphora fragments (not illustrated), including two body sherds with compass-drawn circles, possibly associated with this pyre.

**S Pyre 13** (PLATE 91; Contents, PLATE 114). Rectangular. 175 × 80, narrowing at centre to c. 70. Depth 25. Carbon fill, containing a few burnt bone fragments, highly calcined, and two poorly preserved iron objects.

### Iron

1. Knife. L. 12. W. at butt 3.5. Th. of metal at back 0.5. Probably complete. The blade curves up to a point; the back of the knife is concave. Traces of one rivet in the butt.
2. Blade, fragment. Pres. l. 2. W. 1.7. Th. 0.15. Broken both sides. Fragment of a knife blade? (The possibility cannot be excluded that this is part of the bow of a B.IX.1 fibula).

**S Pyre 14** (PLATE 91; Contents, PLATE 114). Rectangular. 130 × 50, depth 20. Carbon fill. Overlying S Pyre 13 at the N end, but less deep. In the fill, a number of small calcined bone fragments; in the centre of the pyre, a jug, and amphora fragments.

### Pottery

1. Jug. H. 9.6. Red Slip ware (light red clay, pink slip). Unpainted.
2. Amphora fragments (from at least two amphorae). Not illustrated.
    (a) Fragment from lower body. D. 42. Burnt. Three narrow reserved bands on dark ground.
    (b) Fragments from upper body. D. c. 45. Unburnt. Broad and narrow encircling bands on clay ground, semicircles above these, circles below. A rim fragment with thickened lip may belong.

### Iron

3. Pin fragments. Pres. l. 8.3. Th. c. 0.15. Four fragments, probably joining. Probably part of a dress pin with shaft of round section.

**S Pyre 15** (PLATE 91; Contents, PLATE 114). Rectangular, 150 × 70, narrowing to c. 50 at S end, depth 60. In the carbon fill, which was deeper at the two ends of the pyre, were found vases 1–3; the amphora and other fragments (4) were at the top of the fill, and were mostly unburnt.

**Pottery.** 1–3 burnt to grey, with traces of black paint. 1 complete except for one handle and a rim fragment, 2 about three quarters preserved, 3 about one half. For the amphora and other sherds see under 4 below.

1. Amphoriskos, vertical-handled. H. 9.6. A heavy and irregular pot. Two large string holes above the handles (d. 3–5 mm, conical) suggest that there was originally a lid. Reserved band beneath handles. Panels between handles on each side have a vertical line of dots at left and right, and hand-drawn PSC in the centre (groups of five and six). Rim reserved, with oblique strokes near handles; top and inside of rim painted.
2. Lekythos. H. 15.2. No airhole. Three groups of four compass-drawn circles on the shoulder. Reserved band on neck.
3. Lekythos. H. (pres.) 11. Mouth, handle missing. Cross-hatched triangles on shoulder.
4. Not illustrated.
    (a) Belly-handled amphora: substantial fragments of lower neck, shoulder, belly and lower body. D. (max) 53. Local. Two tiers of semicircles on shoulder, circles on belly. Similar to S Pyre 41,1 (PLATE 156). Note that four burnt fragments join unburnt ones.
    (b) Cup: fragments of lip and wall, with handle. D. (rim) 10.5. Unburnt. Bell-shaped. Reserved band inside lip, and small area of lower body above foot; otherwise brown paint inside and out.
    (c) Skyphos: fragment of rim. D. c. 15. Unburnt. High offset lip. PSC on body.
    (d) Jug(s): fragments. Three fragments burnt, including ring base (d.6.5), painted on outside; body sherd with semicircles; two neck fragments showing collar with incised rope decoration.

**S Pyre 16** (PLATE 91). Rectangular. 130 × 50, depth 100. Filled with earth and stones to a depth of c. 40. Carbon fill below, with large blackened stones at depth c. 60. A higher deposit of ash at the S side of S Pyre 16 appears to derive from the later S Pyre 17. No sherds or other contents.

**S Pyre 17** (PLATE 91; Contents, PLATE 114). Rectangular. 165 × 65, depth 50. On the floor a carbon fill, only c. 20 deep at the S end, but rising to c. 60 at the N, and spilling out beyond the rock cutting. Two boulders at the surface of the pyre; beneath and beside one, sherds from two lekythoi. A number of small calcined bone fragments were found in the fill.

**Pottery.** The handle and almost one half the body preserved in each case. Thoroughly burnt fragments joint unburnt ones which retain traces of the painted decoration.

1. Lekythos. D. (max.) c. 10. Note the shoulder decoration of compass-drawn semicircles supported by a band, with a wavy line below this. One group of three semicircles is preserved, and it has a very small half-moon filling.
2. Lekythos. D. (max.) 9.5. Groups of double chevrons on the shoulder.

**S Pyre 18** (PLATE 91). Irregular 150 × 50–100, depth 30. Large boulders at one side, rising higher than the surface of the pit. Carbon fill. No contents.

**S Pyre 19.** Rectangular. 135 × 60. Carbon fill. A few burnt bone fragments; no other contents.

## Surface finds associated with the Cemetery

The abbreviated reference to the objects found on or near the surface is S (Skoubris) followed by the letters SF (surface find) and the serial number of the object.

**Pottery** (PLATE 111). Unless otherwise indicated, all the vases are of local fabric. Almost all will be from disturbed tombs.

*1–5, 7 and 8* were found in the spoil heap beside the water pipe trench, and are probably from tombs destroyed by the bulldozer. They were recovered by G. Christou of the Chalkis Museum, by S. Boules of the Eretria Museum, or by the excavators.

1. Jug. H. 10.7. About two thirds preserved. Decorated as shown.
2. Jug. H. 12.7. About two thirds preserved. Decorated as shown.
3. Jug. H. 12.5. About half preserved. Handle missing. Monochrome, reserved areas.
4. Cup. H. 5.8. About half preserved. Shape as 6. Not illustrated.
5. Cup. H. 5.4. About half preserved. Shape as 6. Foot unpainted. Reserved band below handle, and another inside the lip. Not illustrated.
6. Cup. H. 6.7. Given by A. Skoubris in June 1964. Complete except for chips. Monochrome, reserved foot. Reserved band inside lip.
7. Hydria. H. 13.6. Rim fragment missing. Three groups of five hand-drawn semicircles with half-moon filling. Neck handle barred.
8. Cup. H. 6.1. About half preserved. Flaky orange-red paint inside and out (local). Monochrome. Reserved band inside the lip as well as outside.

   *9 and 10* were found in the surface (or sub-surface) soil in Trench *Rho.*
9. Kalathos. H. 5.5. Reserved band inside the rim.
10. Lekythos fragment. H. (restored) 7.6. Neck and handle missing. Biconical body as S 46,2; conical ring foot; rather heavily made. Foot and lower body reserved; reserved band at base of neck. Not illustrated.

    *11 and 12* come from the surface of Trench *Xi.*
11. Skyphos. H. c. 7. About two thirds preserved in three non-joining fragments. Low conical foot. Reserved are the foot, two bands below the handles, one band inside the lip, and central dot on floor. Not illustrated.
12. Clay ball. D. 3.1. About half preserved. Handmade. Fine pink clay, with uneven surface; spherical. Painted with narrow rings in light orange-brown paint.

    *13 and 14* come from the surface of Trench *Sigma.*
13. Mug, fragmentary. D. (base) 4; (rim) 7. H. c. 9. Rim, base and body fragments, not joining. Handmade coarse ware; red gritty fabric with black smoothed surface.
14. Cup fragment. Wall fragment; glossy black paint inside; dark brown paint on buff slip outside, with decoration of cross-hatched lozenge, zigzag, and meander. May not be local; on the other hand, the cross-hatched meander is not an Attic feature. Photo on PLATE 273.

    *15* is from the subsurface soil of Trench *Omicron.*
15. Lekythos, fragmentary. D. (max.) 9.5. About one quarter preserved. Biconical body, trumpet lip, sloping handle. Three groups of five chevrons on the shoulder; horizontal bands on the neck, handle barred. Not illustrated.

    *16 and 17* come from the Gully Fill (Trench *Pi*).
16. Cup. H. 5.5. D. 6.7. Intact. Local light buff clay, streaky brown to black-brown paint, roughly applied. Poorly made ring foot. Monochrome except lowest part of body and foot, which are unpainted. Submycenaean. Photo on PLATE 273.
17. Stone mould. Pres. h. 14. Greatest th. 5.7; least th. 3. Incomplete on two sides; what remains somewhat battered. Open mould of micaceous schist. One corner preserved, where very carefully cut square, as a right angle. Double faced, but no matrices in the surviving parts of the narrow faces.
    (a) Parts of three roughly pointed billets, of which:
        1 = pres. l. 12.5, w. at bottom 1, estimated depth 2.
        2 = pres. l. 12, w. at bottom 1.2, estimated depth 2.
        3 = pres. l. 8.3, w. at bottom 0.8, estimated depth 2, w. at top 1.8.
    (b) ?Axe-blade. Greatest w. 6; greatest restored w. 7.5; greatest th. 1.3. This matrix widens rapidly.
    Both matrices show heavy signs of use. Trace of pouring funnel on long narrow face, feeding into the axe-matrix. Restored d. of funnel top 2.0. PLATE 284.

## TOMBS IN THE FIELD OF A. KHALIOTIS

After the chance find of two vases and two pins (see below), two cist tombs were investigated, the one at E edge of the village road, the other c. 10 m further SE, in the field; these two are c. 50 m from the main area of cists in the Skoubris field. The cemetery may extend further E on the hill slope immediately opposite the settlement site of Xeropolis.

**KT Tomb 1. Cist.** About one half preserved, running into the band under the road, the other half destroyed during levelling work in the field. One cover slab of white magnesite remained. Pebble floor. KT, 2—4 below are said to have come from this cist: if so, it is probably the earliest datable cist yet found at Lefkandi (see the lekythos no. 2).

**KT Tomb 2. Cist.** 170 × 33, depth 40. Partly destroyed by the plough. The construction is of long conglomerate slabs; the SE corner was destroyed and only one cover slab remained at the W end. Pebble floor. No contents.

**Objects from the Khaliotis field.** Given by A. Khaliotis (PLATE 114).

**Pottery**
1. Lekythos. Said to be from a cist in the field. H. 15:2. Two-thirds complete, made up from fragments. Airhole to right of handle. Fabric fired (burnt?) to a uniform light grey, with smooth surface very similar to grey Minyan.
2. Lekythos. Said to be from KT Tomb 1. H. 12.4. Complete except for chips at rim and part of the handle. Airhole to right of handle. White fabric with small grits, creamy white slip, dark brown paint. White ware, as characteristic of the latest LH IIIC of the Xeropolis settlement. Decorated as shown. PLATE 255a.

**Bronze.** Both objects said to be from KT Tomb 1.
3. Dress pin. Pres. l. 13.6. Th. of shaft 0.3. Tip and head broken away. Shaft undecorated, apparently hammered from a rough billet, not perfectly.
4. Dress pin. Pres. l. 12.7. D. of shaft 0.25. Tip and head lost. A slimmer fellow to 3.

# PALIA PERIVOLIA AND EAST CEMETERIES (PLATES 76a, 77—8, 115—56)

**P Tomb 1.** Rock depression. No tomb.

**P Tomb 2** (Contents, PLATE 125). Shaft grave. c. 195 × 40, depth 75—90. Rectangular, rock ledge at depth c. 60, partly bedded with stones. Pebble floor. Fragment of large skyphos on floor at S end, upright.

**Pottery**
1. Skyphos. H. 15.6. About two-thirds preserved. Standard local fabric. Two sets of PSC on each side. Central reserved dot on floor.

**P Tomb 3** (PLATE 115; Contents, PLATES 125—8, 213, 214a). Shaft grave. 240 × 60—75, depth 150. Six rough and unworked cover slabs of limestone originally rested on a rock ledge at depth c. 90, now partly collapsed. Fill of earth, stones and large boulders in the shaft above the cover slabs silt below. Four pots on the slabs: a skyphos (14) at the N (head) end, the others at the S. On the tomb floor the pottery was clustered at the S end, except for an amphoriskos (12) at the N with beads, pins and fibulae.

**Pottery**
Twenty-four vases, 2, 8, 11, 14 above the cover slabs, the rest inside, but all were deposited at the same time (2 and 3 perhaps from the same firing). The kalathos 16 is in a fragmentary and decayed condition; the rest are intact or have only chips missing, except where otherwise noted.

All except three (7, 12, 20) are of the standard local fabric, with the usual range of variations of slip and paint; 10 differs in that the paint is matt, with a rough, almost gritty, surface, and it is fired unusually hard. One potter, to judge from the quality, may have been responsible for groups 2, 3 and 9; 4, 5 and 14; and 17—23 (kalathoi). 7, 12 and 20 have a grey fabric: 7 is hand-made, black burnished; 12 is wheel-made Black Slip ware; for 20, a standard impressed-triangle kalathos, fabric and colour presumably resulted from exposure to the pyre.

1. Trefoil oinochoe. H. 18.7. Decorated as shown. Six cross-hatched triangles on the shoulder.

1a. A small conical foot found near 1; it may have been used as a stopper for it or for 3.

2. Trefoil oinochoe. H. 15.2. Decorated as shown. Four sets of semicircles.

3. Jug. H. 13.3. Decorated as shown. Three sets of semicircles.

4. Lekythos. H. 17. Decorated as shown. Three sets of semicircles.

5. Lekythos. H. 14.2. As 4; same potter (and same firing?), but a different multiple brush.

6. Lekythos. H. 13.3. Decorated as shown. The cross-hatched motive on the opposite side lacks the curious butterfly appendage. PLATE 264d.

7. Juglet, cutaway neck. H. 6.6. Handle and part of rim missing. Handmade.

8. Trefoil lentoid flask. H. 19.5. One side is as 9 below, the other is broken away at the centre. PLATE 261f.

9. Pilgrim flask. H. 20.5. Decorated as shown. Part of one handle, rim and body fragment missing, restored. PLATE 261g.

10. Small amphora, handles shoulder to lip, with lid. H. 16.1. H. of lip 2.8. Mint condition. Decorated as shown. There is a string hole at the junction of each handle with the lip, corresponding to another on the lip. PLATE 264e.

11. Amphoriskos. H. 13.1. Heavy and clumsy. Decorated as shown. Two cross-hatched triangles on each side.

12. Amphoriskos. H. 13.3. Black Slip ware. Decoration of combed wavy lines done with a multiple tool with eight points; the horizontal grooves above and below could have been done with the same tool (there are three to five grooves depending on the pressure applied). The incised decoration continues beneath the handles which were attached later. PLATE 268f.

13. Amphoriskos. H. 9.8. One handle restored. Heavy and clumsy. Monochrome except for a reserved line with dots on the handle.

14. Skyphos. H. 9.5. About one quarter restored. Two sets of PSC, with hourglass filling, on each side. PLATE 259e.

15. Bowl. H. 14.4, with handles 18.2. Decorated as shown. The two metopes at the right have the same cross-hatching and chequer design on each side of the bowl. PLATE 262c—d.

16. Spouted bowl. H. 4.6. L. 28.2. Decorated as shown. The handle is in the form of a bucranium without representation of detail; it has chevrons above. PLATE 262a—b.

17. Kalathos H. 8.3. A single large string hole beneath the rim. Reserved dot on the floor. The underside is reserved with five incised concentric circles. Two double rows of impressed triangles between horizontal guide-line incisions. A fifth incised line was inserted, presumably in error, as only five triangular impressions were completed.

18. Kalathos. H. 6.4. Fragmentary and decayed. Single string hole. Impressed triangles and guide lines as shown.

19. Kalathos. H. 6.2. Two string holes. Impressed triangles and guide lines as shown.

20. Kalathos. H. 8.7. Two string holes. Impressed triangles as shown.

21. Kalathos. H. 7.2. One string hole. Impressed decoration done with a round-ended tool, no incised guide lines. Underside reserved.

22. Kalathos. H. 5.8. Two string holes. Impressed triangles and guide lines as shown. Reserved dot on floor.

23. Kalathos. H. 5.7. One string hole. Reserved dot on floor. Impressed triangles and guide lines as shown.

24. Kalathos. H. 8.7. One string hole. Monochrome. Underside reserved.

**Bronze**

*25. Asymmetric arched fibula with swollen bow. (B.II.19). L. 5. H. 3.5. Th. of bow 1.2. Part of pin and catch lost. Clearly articulated into stem, bow and forearm by the bead and fillet mouldings that separate bow from stem and forearm. Stem of square section, forearm rectangular, bow circular apart from flattened face on underside. Spring (one turn) and catch to right. PLATES 239c, 248,9.

**Bronze with iron**

*26. Leaf-bow fibula with loop. (?Variant of B.I.8) L. 7.4. Estimated h. 3.2. Max. w. of bow 1.5. Almost complete, but shattered. Bronze bow and catch-plate; pin and spring of iron. The iron is perhaps a replacement for bronze parts broken and lost, though there is no proof that the use of two metals was not an original feature of the design. Bow hammered from a basic thick wire casting of which the centre has been pinched into a vertical open loop, possibly to hold some wire attachment of the type of S 15B, 6a. Apparently undecorated. Spring (two turns) to right. *FGI* no. 16B. PLATES 239h, 249,6.

**Iron**
27. Pin, fragments. L. 3.3 and 3.8. Th. not recoverable. Both fragments broken at each end. Non-joining sections of dress pin shafts. Cloth remains.
28. Pin, fragments. L. 3.5, 3.4 and 2. Th. not recoverable. Non-joining fragments, all broken either end. Probably parts of the shafts of one or more dress pins.
29. ?Identity. L. 2. Very doubtful, but perhaps tips of two pins, or parts of tips, lying across each other, adhering through oxydization.

**Clay.** Twelve beads: seven (a—c) incised, five (d) plain conical. All are of a warm red-brown clay with few grits, unbaked and crumbling; good brown burnished surfaces the same as those of the birds and dolly P 22, 28—30. See p. 83 for further discussion.
30. (a)  Five beads, flattened spherical. D. 3—3.4. H. 2.4—2.6. Each has six to eight double incised concentric circles on the side, with a row of vertical incisions above and below.
    (b)  One bead, biconical and pentagonal. D. (from point to flat edge) 3.3. H. (rest.) 3.1. Double incised concentric circle at each of the five protrusions; fringe of vertical incisions above and below.
    (c)  One bead, biconical and quadrilateral. 2.7 × 2.7. H. 2.4. Single incised circle at centre of each of the four protrusions; fringe of vertical incisions.
    (d)  Five beads, conical. Two fragmentary. H. 1.5—2.5. D. 2—2.9.

**P Tomb 4** (PLATE 115; Contents, PLATE 128). Rectangular shaft grave. 165 × 55, depth c. 125. No cover slabs; rock shelf at depth c. 100, 10—15 wide, presumably for wooden covers. Earth and stone fill. Pebble floor. Two vases at S end, four at N.

**Pottery.** Intact except for 4 and 5. 1, 2, 5 and 6 of standard local fabric and wheel-made. 3 has light red clay with glossy pink to buff slip (Red Slip ware); 4 is handmade, yellow to grey fabric, burnished grey.
1. Neck-handled amphora. H. 20.9. Paint inside the lip, carelessly applied as elsewhere on the vase. Vertical strokes on the shoulder on both sides. The horizontal neck bands run beneath the handles, leaving splodges on the side of the handles as the brush went through. Body below handles monochrome.
2. Jug. H. 10.9. Monochrome, reserved bands on belly.
3. Jug. H. 10.4. Red Slip.
*4. Trefoil oinochoe. H. (with handle) 10.1. Handmade; poorly fired, surface flaking. Rim, neck and handle fragments missing, restored.
*5. Cup H. 6.1. Monochrome, zigzag on outer lip, reserved dot on floor.
6. Kalathos. H. 5.3. Two string holes, close together. Monochrome, reserved bands.
7. Pierced clay disc. D. 5.5. Cut from a body fragment of a large vase. Not illustrated.

**P Tomb 5.** Shallow rock depression, depth 20, to E of olive tree in Square J. Not a Tomb.

**P Tomb 6** (PLATE 115; Contents, PLATE 129). Rectangular pit grave. 155 × 75, depth 40. No covers or rock ledge surviving. Earth and carbon fill, the latter from P Pyre 25, which was cut by P Tomb 6. A first attempt at this tomb hit directly on P Pyre 25, and was abandoned for a second attempt a little further to the S. Pebble floor, on which a cup rested. See under P Tomb 9 for the later stratigraphy.

**Pottery**
1. Cup. H. 10.1. Broken, but complete. Local fabric. Monochrome. The paint continues under the handle; it does not reach the base at all points.

**P Tomb 7** (PLATE 115; Contents, PLATE 129). Rectangular shaft grave. 170 × 80, depth 57. Rock ledge, with bedding of stones 15—25 wide, at depth 30; no cover slabs. Earth and rock fill. Pebble floor. The lower compartment is a rectangle, 135 × 45.

**Pottery**. Six vases of local fabric.
1. Amphoriskos. H. 13.7. Decorated as shown. Two sets of semicircles on each side.
2. Trefoil oinochoe. H. 11. Decorated as shown. The handle has a rough vertical band.
3. Kalathos. H. 8.2. Two string holes. Impressed triangles. No guide lines.
4. Kalathos. H. 7.2. Two string holes. Impressed triangles. Incised guide lines, including one for a fourth tier of triangles of which only two impressions were completed.
5. Kalathos. H. 7.2. One string hole. Impressed triangles. This vase contained the ten white marbles (no. 7 below).
6. Kalathos. H. 5. Two string holes. Reserved dot on the floor. Impressed triangles, guide lines.

**Stone**
7. Marbles. Ten spherical stones of limestone, coated with white lime over most of their surface. Five are small well-shaped spheres, average d. 2.1—2.2, wt. 10—12 gr. Five are larger and less regular, average d. 2.5—3.0, wt. 30—32 gr. PLATE 237e.

**P Tomb 8** (PLATE 116; Contents, PLATE 129). Shaft grave. 145 × 60, depth 110. Rock ledge at depth 45. Pebble floor. Stone and earth fill. One vase, on the floor.

**Pottery**
1. Kalathos. H. 7.6. Intact. Local fabric. One string hole. Four incised guide lines, in spite of which the tiers of impressed triangles have slipped badly at one point.

**P Tomb 9** (PLATE 116; Contents, PLATE 129). Shaft grave. 125 × 65, narrowing at each end; depth 165. Broad rock shelf at depth c. 120. The top of the shaft is rectangular, the lower chamber a narrow and irregular oval, w. 35. Compact earth and stone fill in the upper shaft, loose silt at the bottom. Pebble floor; cluster of vases at the centre. At its N end the shaft of P Tomb 9 cut through the floor of the earlier P Tomb 6; it therefore also post-dates P Pyre 25 (see under P Tomb 6).

**Pottery**. Five vases, intact or only chipped. 1, 4 and 5 are of the standard local fabric. 2 and 3 are Red Slip ware, of identical quality and probably made together.
1. Jug. H. 12.4. Decorated as shown. Note that the handle is barred. In the mouth was found a conical cup foot (not illustrated), used as a stopper.
2. Jug. H. 9.7. Red Slip ware
3. Jug. H. 9.9. Red Slip ware.
4. Miniature lekythos. H. 7.3. Monochrome.
5. Cup. H. 9.1. Monochrome, but lower body and foot unpainted.

**P Tomb 10** (PLATES 116, 199e; Contents, PLATES 130—1, 214b). Rectangular shaft grave. 135 × 50, depth c. 50. Narrow rock ledge at depth c. 20. Compact earth and stone fill. Pebble floor.

**Pottery**. Twenty vases, chiefly remarkable for the number and varying types of kalathoi. All are intact, except as otherwise noted in the catalogue. All of local fabric.
1. Amphoriskos. H. 14.8. Chip at rim, restored. Handles painted, otherwise monochrome.
2. Jug, high handle. H. 16. Note rouletting at belly. Monochrome, reserved bands.
3. Trefoil oinochoe. H. c. 14.7. Handle, and most of neck, and lip except at tip of trefoil, missing. Three sets of semicircles.
4. Cup. H. 5.7. Small fragments missing, restored. Thin walled. Monochrome, reserved bands as shown.
5. Openwork kalathos. H. 10.1. Two string holes. Ten crudely cut alternating triangles in the upper tier, eight in the lower, including the only one which does not reach the incised guide lines. Reserved central dot on the floor.
6. Openwork kalathos. H. 6. No string hole. A thick incised guide line below the tier of cut triangles seems to be superfluous.

7. Kalathos. H. 6.3. Two string holes. Impressed triangles. No guide lines.
8. Kalathos. H. 5.9. Two string holes. Impressed triangles. None of the four incised guide lines goes the full circle round the vase. Reserved dot on the floor.
9. Kalathos. H. 6.7. Rim fragments missing, restored. No string hole. All impressed triangles inverted. Transverse strokes on the lip. Reserved dot on the floor.
10. Kalathos. H. 5.6. One string hole. Monochrome.
11. Kalathos. H. 4.5. Two string holes. Reserved dot on the floor. Monochrome, reserved band.
*12. Kalathos. H. 5.9. Two string holes. The clay is a dark buff with a few micaceous particles, and is soft-fired with buff slip and glossy orange-red paint, appled thickly and distinctly darker than the normal Lefkandian range. Monochrome.
13. Kalathos. H. 7.2. Broken, small fragments missing, restored. Two string holes. Flattened lip. Underside unpainted. Body monochrome, reserved bands.
14. Kalathos. H. 5.3. Two string holes. Monochrome, reserved bands.
15. Kalathos. H. 6.9. Two string holes. Underside fully painted. Body monochrome, reserved bands.
16. Kalathos. H. 6.1. Two string holes. Monochrome.
17. Kalathos. H. c.6. Conical, with flaring rim. Unbaked, and disintegrated into powder on lifting. Probably monochrome inside and out. Not illustrated.
18. Miniature hydria. H. (rest.) 6.7. Lip and belly handles restored. Concave underside. On each side of the vertical handle interlocking triangles, carelessly drawn. Opposite this handle, vertical solid diamond chain between triple vertical bars.
19. Miniature plate. D. 10. H. (with handles) 3. One handle missing, restored. Transverse strokes on the rim and handles. Carelessly painted spiral on floor. Underside monochrome.
20. Miniature plate. D. 10. H. (with handles) 3. Two of the three handles missing. Small reserved cross with central fill on the underside.

**Bronze**
*21. Open ring. D. 0.8 × 0.95. W. 0.3 Th. 0.05. One terminal lost; what remains intact. Plain flat strip rolled into an irregular hoop.

**Iron**
22. Pin, fragments. Pres. L. 4. D. less than 0.4. Two scraps, probably non-joining, of the shaft of a dress pin. Some cloth remains. Not illustrated.

**P Tomb 11 (PLATE 116).** Shaft grave. 145 × 80, depth 91. The upper shaft is a broad rectangle with wide rock ledges at depth c. 60, w. of lower compartment 37. Pebble floor. Earth and rock fill in the shaft, dark earth and silt over the floor. Sole contents one iron pin fragment. At its N end Tomb 11 cut through the floor of Tomb 14, which is earlier. Pyre 24 cut the upper shaft of both tombs, and so is later.

**Iron**
1. Pin, fragment. Pres. L. 2.1. Th. not recoverable. Broken both ends. Scrap of shaft of dress pin? Cloth remains. Not illustrated.

**P Tomb 12 (PLATES 116, 124; Contents, PLATE 131).** Shaft grave. 195 × 100, depth 130. Rock ledge at depth 75. Pebble floor. The ledge is very narrow, and the lower compartment appears to have been lined and covered with a combination of wood and mud brick, to form a rectangle c. 195 × 65. Fill of earth and stones in the upper shaft, but of looser red earth in the lower part, representing the collapse of a timber and mud brick roof. Two of the three pyxides must have been placed above this covering, as they were found in the mud brick fill 30 cm above the floor; the third rested directly on the floor in the centre of the tomb. Around the sides of the lower chamber, and partly collapsed over the floor, was a lining of darker brown earth or clay c. 20 wide, but broader and rounded at the corners — possibly upright logs were set here as props. See PLATE 124 for a hypothetical reconstruction. In the SE corner Tomb 12 intersects with the N end of P Tomb 19, and a stone blocking wall divides the two chambers. The truncated shape of 19, and the fact that the blocking wall was constructed on its floor, shows that P Tomb 12 was the later of the two.

**Pottery.** Three globular pyxides, no. 2 intact, 1 and 3 broken, the latter with much of the surface missing. Local fabric. Each pyxis has one string hole on each side beneath the lip, matching others on the lid.
1. Pyxis with lid. H. (without lid) 16.2. Rim painted. Knob of lid lost. Decorated as shown.
2. Pyxis with lid. H. 14. H. of lid 3.5. A flaw in the firing has left a depression on one side. There are fourteen groups of opposed diagonals on the belly. Rim unpainted.
3. Pyxis with lid. H. (without lid) 11.2. Rim painted. Knob of lid lost. Monochrome, reserved bands.

**Lead**
4. Attachment. Pres. l. 6.8. W. 4. Th. 0.5. In three fragments, part missing. General resemblance to similar objects of gold (e.g. T 36, 6—15). Pointillé decoration — border of dots, with added dogtooth at the top, and three parallel lines down the centre.

**P Tomb 13** (PLATE 117; Contents, PLATES 132—3, 215). Shaft grave. 240 × 80, depth 150. Broad rock shelf at depth 100, supporting a full series of large cover slabs of unworked limestone, collapsed at the N end. Two similar slabs and several smaller ones were thrown in with the fill in the upper shaft. Rectangular lower compartment, 215 × 60. Pebble floor.

**Pottery.** Twenty vases, found in two groups, except for the pyxis 20, which was placed in the centre. Ten were intact, the rest had breaks or had lost minor fragments which have been restored. 1—12, 17—20 are of standard local fabric; 13—16 are Red Slip ware.
1. Amphoriskos. H. 10. The paint goes just over the inside of the lip; otherwise as shown.
2. Amphoriskos. H. 11.9. One handle restored. See 21 for its possible use as a stopper for this vase. Decorated as shown. PLATE 266c.
3. Jug, high handle. H. (without handle) 13.1. Monochrome, reserved bands, barred handle.
4. Jug, high handle. H. (without handle) 14.5. Monochrome, reserved band, barred handle. PLATE 266b.
5. Jug, H. 11.4. Irregular base. Three vertical lines on the handle. Three sets of semicircles. PLATE 266d.
6. Jug, cutaway neck, H. 12.9. Most of paint flaked off. Triple horizontal grooves on neck and below lip; incised rope decoration at collar. Monochrome, reserved bands. Note that the handle is barred.
7. Lekythos. H. 13.8. Monochrome, reserved band.
8. Lekythos. H. 16.6. The upper half of the neck was pushed off centre when the handle was attached. Decorated as shown.
9. Lekythos. H. 12.5. Trumpet lip pushed down opposite handle to form a spout. Monochrome, reserved bands, barred handle.
10. Lekythos. H. 14.5. Most of rim missing, restored. Angular biconical body with ridge where the upper half was joined on. Decorated as shown. The outlined cross-hatched triangle is repeated on the other side.
11. Lekythos. H. 16.2. Four sets of semicircles; otherwise as shown.
12. Amphoriskos. H. 11.2. Four sets of cross-hatched triangles. Both handles are barred, with long bars below them. One handle also has vertical lines crossing at the top. Otherwise decorated as shown.

*13—16.* Four kantharoi of Red Slip ware, all found at the S end of the tomb. Light red, well levigated clay with no mica. Well finished inside and out with a thickly applied and polished light red slip, partly peeled off on 13 and 14. Probable imitation of metalwork. See p. 347.
*13. Kantharos. H. 12.6. Broken, small fragments missing, restored.
14. Kantharos. H. 12.1.
15. Kantharos. H. 11.3. PLATE 264a—b.
16. Kantharos. H. 10.3. Broken, small fragments missing, restored. Clay and surface lighter in colour than the others, and lacks their glossy finish.
17. Pyxis with lid. H. 14.2. H. of lid 3. Two pairs of diametrically opposed string holes below the lip, matching others on the lid. Seven sets of semicircles, with solid triangular fill in the interstices above; one set, the last to be painted, intersects with the two adjacent sets.
18. Pyxis with lid. H. 12.2. H. of lid 3.4. Note the five transverse grooves beneath the foot. Two string

holes diametrically opposed, matching those on the lid only when the latter is off centre. Eight sets of semicircles, intersecting slightly in two cases.

19. Pyxis with lid. H. 10.6. H. of lid 3.2. Two string holes diametrically opposed. The knob of the lid has a star formed by two crosses. Monochrome, reserved bands.

*20. Pyxis with lid. H. 10.1. H. of lid 3.4. Hard fired. Two lug handles with vertical string hole through each lug, corresponding to holes on the lid. The decoration on the unillustrated side differs only in the broad central panel, which has a chequer motive. The handles are laddered, the ladder continuing down the full length of the metopal frieze. PLATE 263b.

This vase's central position in the tomb suggests a place of honour.

21. Conical foot. D. 7.3. Perhaps a stopper for amphoriskos No. 2.

**Iron**
22. Axe. L. 14.7. W. at cutting edge 4.3. W. at butt 3.5. Th. c. 1.3. Complete. Straight butt, lunate cutting edge, widening slightly from butt to edge. No evident sign of hafting method. PLATE 244F.

**P Tomb 14** (PLATE 116; Contents, PLATE 134). Rectangular shaft grave. c. 125 × 70, depth 79. Broad rock shelf at depth c. 55. The lower compartment is a roundended slit trench, l. (preserved) 80, w. 28. The S end is cut by Tomb 11; Pyre 24 cut into the SW corner of the shaft at a higher level.

**Pottery.** Four vases. 2 and 4 intact, 1 chipped at rim, 3 shattered and restored from badly damaged fragments. 1 and 2 of standard local fabric; 3 Red Slip, 4 Black Slip.

1. Hydria. H. 16.8. Three groups of languettes on the shoulder, one of four and two of five. Doubly intersecting vertical lines on the neck handle. Otherwise as shown.
2. Cup. H. 9. Central reserved dot on the floor. Monochrome, reserved lower body and upper foot.
3. Miniature jug. H. 7. Red Slip ware.
4. Cup H. 6.3. Black Slip ware. Combed and incised decoration.

**Bronze**
*5. Bracelet. D. 4.1 × 4.2. W. 0.9. Th. 0.05. Extended l. 15.6. Complete and intact; dark green patina. Strip hammered flat, rather irregular rounded terminals, tapering evenly from centre to terminals. Decorated with a continuous zigzag from terminal to terminal. PLATE 241j.

**P Tomb 15** (PLATES 117, 124; Contents, PLATE 134). Rectangular shaft grave. 110 × 66. Five limestone slabs (3—9 thick) resting on a rock ledge at depth c. 100, and covering a small oval trench 80 × 30. Pebble floor at depth 152. Earth and stone fill above the cover slabs, silt and decayed rock below. One vase only a feeder.

**Pottery**
1. Feeder (jug) H. 11. Tip of spout restored. Local fabric. Decorated as shown. There are three groups of the chevron motive, separated by cross-hatched diamonds.

**P Tomb 16** (PLATES 117, 199c; Contents, PLATE 134). Rectangular shaft grave. 187 × 100, narrowing to 80 at the S end. A lining of mud brick forms a shelf 16—38 wide at depth c. 50; the bricks were laid in at least two layers and have clear horizontal divisions at the S end, which give a width for individual bricks varying from 25 to 45. The lower brick-built compartment thus formed resembles a slit trench, 145 × 35, and 30 deep. Pebble floor. The vases and metal objects were placed on the floor, except for the trefoil oinochoe (1) set on the shelf at the S end (see PLATE 199, taken after the removal of the mud bricks), presumably after the covering over of the lower compartment.

**Pottery.** 2 was intact, the others broken but complete except for small fragments of 1 and 3. Surface decayed, especially on 3—5. 2 is Black Slip ware, the rest of standard local fabric (3 and 4 could be from the same firing).

1. Trefoil oinochoe. H. 15.8. The trefoil lip is asymmetrical. Decorated as shown. Four sets of semicircles.
*2. Jug. H. 12. Black Slip — grey fabric, streaky black paint remaining brown in the area of the handle. The combed wavy lines were done with a four-pointed instrument.
3. Jug. H. 14. The seven groups of chevrons have their apices intersecting. Otherwise as shown.
4. Lekythos. H. 11.4. Three groups of four chevrons on the shoulder. Otherwise as shown.
5. Cup. H. 9.8. Reserved dot on the floor. Monochrome, reserved bands, lower body and foot unpainted. PLATE 258 f.

**Bronze**
6. Fragment. L. 0.8. D. 0.15. Part of fibula spring and pin? Featureless. Not illustrated.

**Iron**
7. Knife. Pres. l. 12.9 Max. w. 2.5. L. of haft 4.5. Tip lost. With convex back, haft and blade a continuous profile. Limit of haft clear from difference in oxydization pattern. No trace of flanges or rivets on the haft. Cutting edge may have been much whetted. PLATE 246h.

**P Tomb 17** (PLATE 116; Contents, PLATE 134). Pit grave. 72 × 50, depth 25. A shallow rectangular pit, intersecting with the SW corner of Tomb 12. Earth fill; pebble floor. One vase.

**Pottery**
1. Kalathos. H. 6. Local fabric. Paint inside and out except for a reserved dot on the floor, and the underside. Two string holes.

**P Tomb 18** (PLATE 118; Contents, PLATE 135). Shaft grave 225 × 85—100. Broad rock shelf c. 30 wide, at depth 65. The lower compartment, 207 × 55, has a partial lining of mud bricks on the W side, apparently not continuous since vases 4 and 6 intrude into its line. Decayed mud brick in the fill derives from the lining of the other side (cf. Tomb 16) and from roofing material. Pebble floor, at depth 115, with six vases on it.

**Pottery.** 2 and 4 intact; handle missing on 1 and 3, restored; upper neck and mouth of 6 missing, restored; 5 shattered, badly decayed. All standard local fabric except 5, which is Red Slip.
1. Amphoriskos. H. 13. Rouletting on lower belly. Monochrome.
2. Amphoriskos. H. 14.1. Monochrome, reserved band with zigzag on belly.
3. Amphoriskos. H. 10.2. Zigzag on belly less neat than on drawing.
4. Jug. H. 13. Monochrome, reserved bands, handle barred.
*5. Jug. H. (without handle) 12.8. Red Slip ware.
6. Jug, cutaway neck. H. (rest.) 11. Three horizontal grooves preserved on the lower neck; incised rope decoration on collar. Monochrome, reserved bands.

**P Tomb 19** (PLATE 117; Contents, PLATE 135). Rectangular shaft grave. L. (pres.) 145. W. 95. Broad rock shelf at depth 80. The lower compartment is a shallow slit trench, c. 135 × 40, depth 15. Pebble floor. Built over this floor at the N end is a blocking wall of rough stones, inserted by the diggers of the later Tomb 12, which cuts Tomb 19.

**Pottery.** Three vases, intact except for a break at rim of 3. 1 and 3 of local fabric, probably from the same firing. 2 is Red Slip.
1. Trefoil oinochoe. H. 21.1 Groove at the collar. Three sets of semicircles, the arcs coming over the supporting band. Otherwise as shown.
2. Jug. H. 14.3. Red Slip ware.
3. Cup. H. 5.8. Reserved dot on the floor; otherwise as shown.

**P Tomb 20.** No tomb

**P Tomb 21** (PLATES 118, 198c—d; Contents, PLATES 136, 223). Shaft grave. 195 × 130.

Wide rock ledge at depth c. 50, supporting five unworked cover slabs, partially collapsed. Upper fill of earth, and large stones which were heaped up over the covers, especially at the N, E and S sides; pyxis (1) on the covers at the W end. Lower compartment rectangular, 175 × 75. Pebble floor at depth 115 with deposit of grave offerings. In the NE corner P Tomb 21 intersects slightly with the upper level of the earlier Tomb 24, the stones in this corner forming a rough blocking wall against the loose fill in the shaft of P Tomb 24.

**Pottery.** Ten vases, the Attic pyxis (2) being placed in the centre of the tomb. All complete except for small fragments missing in some cases. All of standard local fabric except the Attic pyxis; it is notable that the clay of the Attic vase is indistinguishable from that of 3, 4, 9 and 10, but the quality of the paint, a glossy black, and the technique of the painting are superior to those of the local vases. The other pyxides are probably all from the same workshop.

*1. Pyxis with lid. H. 23.2, with lid 26. Two string holes diametrically opposed, matching two on the lid. The knob of the lid has a cross painted on the top. Decorated as shown.
 2. Pyxis with lid. H. 12.1. String holes as for 1. Missing knob of lid restored as for S 59,4, a near parallel. Decorated as shown. Attic EGII import.
 3. Pyxis with lid. H. 14.9, with lid 18.4. String holes as on 1. Decorated as shown. Top of rim unpainted. PLATE 267c.
 4. Pyxis with lid. H. 12.4, with lid 16.3. String holes as on 1. Top of rim unpainted. Groups of twelve opposed diagonals done with a multiple brush, except for one group which has thirty-three, where the painter came full circle. Reserved dot on top of the knob of the lid.
 5. Pyxis with lid. H. 12.2, with lid 16.2. The twin of 4 (same multiple brush), except that the rim and the top of the lid knob are fully painted.
 6. Pyxis with lid. H. 11.9, with lid 14.1. String holes as on 1. Top of rim painted. Reserved dot on top of the lid knob. Monochrome body, reserved bands.
 7. Pyxis. H. 9. String holes as on 1. Top of rim unpainted. Thirteen groups of nine opposed diagonals, done with a multiple brush.
 8. Pyxis. H. 10.4. String holes as on 1. Top of rim unpainted. Otherwise as shown.
 9. Pyxis. H. 8.2. String holes as on 1. Thin band of paint on top of rim. Otherwise as shown.
10. Skyphos H. 5.7. On the one side the PSC do not intersect; on the other they intersect as to two arcs only.

**Bronze**
*11. Dress Pin. Pres. l. 13.7. D. 0.48. Tip missing. Broken. Shaft of round section, one end worked to a point, the other beaten flat and rolled into a round loop to form the head. PLATE 242F.

**Faience**
12. Necklace. 68 disk beads, d. 6–11 mm, th. 2.5–4 mm, and fragments of perhaps 40 others. Two cylindrical beads, d. 6 mm, th. 6 mm. Three smaller disk beads, d. 5–6 mm, th. 1–2 mm. Very friable, white at the core, with green surface; for the most part decayed.

**P Tomb 22** (PLATES 119, 198a–b; Contents, PLATES 137–140, 212a–c). Shaft grave 205 × 80 at top of shaft, 205 × 53 at bottom. Rock ledge with bedding of large stones at depth 60–85. Earth and stone fill in the upper shaft, including a large stone slab in the centre of the tomb. Below this a set of coarse conglomerate cover slabs, collapsed and much disintegrated (only the larger fragments shown on the plan). Pebble floor at depth c. 160. In the SE corner, where the tomb intersected with Tomb 23, there was a blocking wall of rough stones at depth c. 100. On the floor thirty-five grave offerings in two groups at the E and W ends respectively. The gold rings and hair spirals were laid out at the E end, which may be considered the 'head' of the tomb.

**Pottery.** Twenty-nine vases, either complete or with small fragments missing, and a 'dolly' figurine (30), badly fragmented. Twelve vases are of standard local fabric: 6, 8, 10–16, 22, 26, 27. 17 and 18 are Black Slip. There are twelve Attic or probably Attic LPG imports: 1–5, 7, 9, 20, 21, 23–25. 19, the Cypriot flask, has a fairly coarse buff clay with pink core, a cream slip, and bichrome decoration. 28 and 29, the birds, and the 'dolly' 30, are imports of unknown origin; all three have a soft grey-brown clay, pink at the core; the birds have a brown burnished finish, on the 'dolly' much of the surface crust has peeled off.

  1. Small amphora, handles shoulder to lip. H. 16.2. No string holes. Decorated as shown. Six sets of outlined cross-hatched triangles. Attic.
  2. Small amphora, handles shoulder to lip, with lid. H. 16.4, with lid 18.8. Two string holes with matching ones on the lid. Decoration as 1. Attic.
 *3. Small amphora, handles shoulder to lip. H. 18.8. Two string holes, but no lid found. Decorated as shown. Attic. PLATE 271b.
  4. Chest with lid. H. (with lid) 11.2. L. 15.9. L. of lid 16.4. Cut from a single block of clay. Two projecting lug handles are covered by corresponding projections at each end of the lid; string holes pierce these. Decorated as shown. Attic. PLATE 271d.
 *5. Jug. H. 16.2. Handle barred; otherwise monochrome, with reserved bands. Probably Attic (see p. 350).
  6. Trefoil oinochoe. H. 18.5. Four sets of semicircles.
 *7. Trefoil oinochoe. H. 17.2. Monochrome, reserved bands, handle barred. Probably Attic (see p. 350).
  8. Trefoil oinochoe. H. 10.5. Handle barred; otherwise as shown.
  9. Trefoil oinochoe, high handle H. 17.2, with handle 20.1. Decorated as shown. Attic. PLATE 271c.
 10. Jug, high handle. H. 13.6, with handle 17.2. Triple grooves at collar and below lip. Decorated as shown.
 11. Jug, high handle. H. (with handle) 18.9. Grooves and decoration as on 10.
 12. Jug, high handle, H. (with handle) 16.5. Grooves as on 10; decoration similar, but no horizontal scribble.
 13. Jug with cutaway neck. H. 10.5. Lip painted inside; decoration otherwise as shown.
 14. Jug with cutaway neck. H. 11. Decorated as shown. Similar chequer design on the other side.
 15. Jug with cutaway neck. H. 9.2. Lip painted inside; otherwise decorated as shown.
 16. Globular jug. H. 12.4. The three sets of semicircles have an hourglass fill not drawn. On each side of the handle there is an unusual motive, a triangle with parallel lines to its sides drawn internally, thus forming a small central triangle, which is painted over.
 17. Lekythos. H. 9.4. Black Slip ware. Combed decoration done with a six-pointed tool. PLATE 268c.
 *18. Lekythos. H. 11.8. Black Slip ware, soft fired and friable. Paint to well inside lip. PLATE 268b.
 *19. Flask. H. 14. Narrow band of paint inside lip. Encircling bands. Cypriot Bichrome II(?). PLATE 270a.
 20. Pyxis with lid. H. 10.7, with lid 14.4. Two string holes, with matching ones on the lid. Top of rim painted. Decorated as shown. The number of diagonals in each of the fourteen groups varies from nine to thirteen. Attic, but note that the fabric and paint closely resemble that of the local vase 13. PLATE 271a.
 *21. Pyxis. H. 10.7. Two string holes. Top of rim painted. Decorated as shown. Fourteen groups of opposed diagonals, either seven or eight in each. Attic.
 22. Pyxis with lid. H. 9, with lid 12.1. Two string holes, matching ones on the lid. Top of rim painted. Body decoration as shown. For the lid, two bands half way between the edge and the knob, and bands on the knob.
 23. Spherical vase. D. 9.6. W. 7.2. Slight protrusion on one side, central airhole on the other (d. 8 mm). Decorated as shown. Purpose unclear. Attic.
 24. Kalathos, one-handled. H. 9. D. 15. Decorated as shown. Small reserved central dot on underside. Attic.
 25. Kalathos, one-handled. H. 9. D. 19.6. Decorated as shown. Reserved cross with central filling on underside. Attic.
 26. Openwork kalathos. H. 10.1. Two string holes, 2.2 apart. Sixteen cut-out triangles in the upper tier, fourteen in the lower. Incised guide lines above and below each tier. Reserved dot on floor.
 27. Openwork kalathos. H. 11. Two string holes. Twenty cut-out triangles in the upper tier, twelve in the lower. Reserved dot on floor.
 28. Bird vase. H. 10.7. Hollow body with solid legs and neck. Eyes not represented. Hole at front of junction of neck and body. Handmade. Import.
 *29. Bird vase. H. 11.9. As 28, but with large hole (d. 13–15 mm) between handle and neck. Handmade. Import. PLATE 254d.
 *30. Dolly, bell-shaped with movable legs. Pres. h. 8.4. L. of legs 5.4. Hollow body. Neck and head pierced by a vertical string hole, d.2 mm, emerging at the slightly concave top surface of the head. Slight ridge at the nose, small horizontal incision for the mouth. Incised circles mark the breasts, and also

ridge at the nose, small horizontal incision for the mouth. Incised circles mark the breasts, and also appear between the breasts and arms at the neck, and at the back between the arms. Patterns of incised horizontal and vertical lines, and dots. One suspension hole half-way between arms and base, another close to the base; these are for the legs, which were made separately, and pierced near the top. The central suspension string through the head would have allowed manipulation of the legs. Import. See p. 344 for parallels. PLATE 269f.

**Gold**
31. Finger ring. D. 1.7. W. 0.5. Wt. 0.5 gr. Plain, slightly rounded section. Closed hoop.
32. Finger ring. The twin of 31.

**Gilt lead.** Two hair rings. 33 is carefully gilt, giving a good impression of solid gold. 34 is badly bent, revealing the lead core — perhaps a deliberate act of investigation before committing such a potentially valuable object to the grave?
33. Hair ring. D. 11—13 mm. Th. 3 mm. Wt 3.5 gr. Open coil of thick wire, terminating at each end in a low conical head. The twist of the coil gives an opening of c. 3 mm. to grip the hair or, possibly, the lobe of the ear. PLATE 230 l.
34. Hair ring. Wt. 4 gr. The twin of 33.

**Iron**
35. Pin fragment. Pres. l. 4.2. D. less than 0.4. Two joining fragments. Small section of pin-shaft. Cloth remains.

**P Tomb 23** (PLATES 120, 124, 199d; Contents, PLATES 140—1, 212d—e). Rectangular shaft grave. 155 × 80. Broad rock ledge at depth 70. Lower compartment a narrow trench c. 165 × 35; pebble floor at depth c. 100. Earth and stone fill in upper shaft; silt, decomposed rock, and mud brick in lower shaft, the latter probably from a collapsed lining and cover of wood and clay. Eight vases found on the rock shelf, and five in the lower chamber with the pins and fibula. All these were at the S end; the double-spouted vase (1) was alone in a position of honour at the N end. Tomb 23 intersected with the shaft of Tomb 22 (*q.v.*) at the extreme NW corner; there was evidence of a blocking wall of rough stones, which was built up to the height of the rock shelf.

**Pottery.** Fourteen vases, intact except for: 10, much lost; 11, a few crumbling fragments only surviving; 7 and 8, rim breaks. Most of the vases are of standard local fabric; no. 1 may be — it is of superior workmanship, hard-fired with pale grey-brown slip, and glossy black paint (almost entirely decayed on one side); one cannot tell for 10 and 11.
*1. Double-spouted jug, cutaway necks. H. (with handle) 20.4. Six cross-hatched triangles and four cross-hatched diamond chains. Beneath each 'spout', reserved bands with grooves (three on the one, four on the other). PLATE 263a.
  2. Small amphora, handles shoulder to lip. H. 16.5. Two vertical string holes at the top of the handles. Top of rim painted (as shown on 3). Decoration as shown, the same on both sides.
  3. Amphoriskos, vertical-handled. H. 16.8. Decoration as shown, the same on both sides.
  4. Small neck-handled amphora. H. 17.5. Four sets of semicircles.
  5. Amphoriskos, vertical-handled. H. 13.7. Six cross-hatched triangles.
  6. Amphoriskos, vertical-handled. H. 12.7. Five groups of four opposed diagonals on one side, seven on the other.
  7. Amphoriskos, vertical-handled. H. 12.7. Almost the twin of 6. Body rather more slender, foot not quite so high. Six sets of opposed diagonals on each side: of these, four sets have four diagonals, seven have five, and one has six. Not drawn.
  8. Jug, cutaway neck. H. 13.1. Nine horizontal grooves beneath the lip. Three groups of chevrons, taken down over the supporting band.
  9. Jug. H. 12. Three cross-hatched triangles.
 10. Lekythos fragments. H. (rest.) 10.3. Four fragments, in a very decayed and friable state. Poorly fired and soft purple-brown to red clay. No trace of surface decoration survives.

11. Lekythos (?) fragments. Shape probably as 10. Only fragments of lower body and flat base (max d. c. 6) survive. Not illustrated.
12. Pyxis with lid. H. 5.9. H. of lid 2.1. Two string holes were made obliquely with a single stroke through the lid and the flat upper surface of the lip. Three reserved bands on the lid; otherwise decorated as shown. PLATE 264c.
13. Kalathos. H. 7.2. Two string holes. The impressed triangles are inverted, each row between two guide lines.
14. Kalathos. H. 5.1. Two very small string holes. Impressed triangles and incised guide lines.

### Bronze
*15. Arched fibula with symmetric swollen bow. (B.II.14). L. 5.1. H. 3.4. Max. d. of bow 1.5. Complete and intact. Articulated into stem, bow and forearm by bead and fillet mouldings that separate bow from the other elements. The bow section is round, but flattened underneath. Forearm and stem of square section. Spring (two turns) and catch to left. PLATES 239d, 248, 10.

### Iron
16. Dress pin. Pres L. 6.7. D. of head 0.8 of bulb 1.0. D. of shaft 0.5. Two joining fragments. Lower shaft and point lost. Small disk head; oval bulb, set off from the shaft. Cloth remains. PLATE 250, 8.
17. Dress pin. Pres. l. 4.8. D. of head 0.9 × 0.7. D. of bulb 1. D. of shaft 0.5. Most of shaft and tip lost. The fellow to 16.

### Ivory
18. Fragments, the largest being a flat piece 12 × 7 mm, th. c. 1.0 mm. Smoothed on one side, perhaps from an inlay. Not illustrated.

**P Tomb 24** (PLATE 119; Contents, PLATE 142) Shaft grave. 175 × 92. Rock ledge at depth 80; narrow lower compartment (w. 50–55); pebble floor at depth 125. The amphora (1) was found lying on its side, broken, at the surface of the shaft; the other vases were on the floor in two groups, 3–5 with the pins and necklace at the N end, the remainder in a cluster at the S end.

This tomb was cut by Tomb 21 at the upper level at the S end.

**Pottery.** Eleven vases, intact or only small fragments missing. All except 4 and 5 are of the standard local fabric. 4 is Red Slip ware; 5 is Black Slip ware.
1. Neck-handled amphora. H. 21.6. Monochrome, one reserved band, handles barred.
2. Amphoriskos, vertical-handled. H. 17.1. Decorated as shown. Four sets of semicircles, the arcs of which continue through the supporting bands.
3. Amphoriskos, vertical-handled. H. 17.2. Decorated as shown, the same on both sides.
4. Jug. H. 12.7. Red Slip ware.
5. Jug. H. 10.4. Black Slip ware. Combed decoration of six wavy lines between incised grooves (four above and four below). PLATE 268e.
6. Shallow bowl, tab handles. H. 6. D. 18.7. Cross-hatched triangles beneath the lip, except for one instance of chevrons. Seven sets of PSC on the lower body, one of which is only half complete where the design comes full circle. The white marbles (15) were found inside this bowl. PLATE 261a–b.
7. Kalathos. H. 7.2. One string hole. Inverted impressed triangles, and guide lines. Reserved dot on floor.
8. Kalathos. H. 5.5. As 7, but one additional guide line at the base. Reserved dot on floor.
*9. Kalathos. H. 6.2. Fired grey. Two string holes. Impressed triangles, guide lines. Underside monochrome.
10. Kalathos. H. 6. Two string holes. No guide lines. Inside lumpy where the impressed decoration has penetrated deeply.
11. Kalathos. H. 4.6. Two string holes. No guide lines. Two upper rows of triangles inverted. Inside lumpy, as on 10.

### Iron
12. Dress Pin. Pres. l. 8.3. D. of head 1.2. D. of bulb 1.0 D. of shaft c. 0.4. Broken, point and part of shaft lost, plain disk head above an oval bulb. Cloth remains.
13. Dress pin, fragment. Pres. l. 3.7. D. of bulb 1.2. Head, tip and most of shaft lost. Oval bulb, with part of shaft above and below. Cloth remains. Not illustrated.

**Faience**

14. Necklace (or wristlet) of small beads. Strung length 22.5. Preserved are 56 disk beads (d. 2–3 mm, w. 1–2 mm), two quadruple, eight triple and twelve double beads of about the same diameter, and two larger cylindrical beads (d. 3.5 mm, w. 4 mm). About ten broken beads were also found, making a total of 122 disk segments. A few have traces of a whitish glaze, most have a pink or buff clay-like surface; the core is bright red, soft, and slightly porous.

**Stone**

15. Five white marbles. D. 2–2.3. Wt. 12–14 gr. Roughly shaped from a white calcinous limestone, they could form a set for the knucklebones game. See p. 82 for discussion. Found inside 6. Not illustrated.

**P Tomb 25A.** Rock depression, no tomb surviving.

**P Tomb 25B** (PLATES 120, 195e; Contents, PLATE 143). Cist tomb. 80 × 20, depth 25. Cover slabs and two uprights of dressed magnesite. Pebble floor. The S end, and probably the N, were built of rough stones and lined with mud brick. The cist was set in a rock-cut pit, depth c. 100.

**Pottery.** Four vases, intact, local fabric; paint decayed from much of surface of 2 and 4.

1. Trefoil oinochoe. H. 13.8. Note ridge at belly where the upper part, made separately, was poorly joined to the lower. Decorated as shown. PLATE 258c.
2. Trefoil oinochoe. H. 12.3. The shoulder decoration is restored on the lines of 1, but is quite uncertain.
3. Trefoil oinochoe. H. 9.9. Four cross-hatched triangles, one later filled solid over the cross-hatching.
4. Cup. H. 6.4. Monochrome, lower body and foot unpainted.

**Faience etc.**

5. Necklace. 36 beads of varied shape and colour, as below. PLATE 233a. 13 elongated hexagonal beads, swelling at the centre. L. 18 mm. D. 7 mm. at centre, 3 mm at ends. Clear bright blue frit, compact, hard, and well made with clean cut angles at the facets.

   2 elongated conical beads. L. 11 mm. D. 2.5–5 mm. Frit similar to those above, but a brighter blue, and a softer, more friable, substance. One quadruple spacer bead. L. 10 mm. W. 15 mm. Rectangular, grooved on either side to form four linked cylinders, each with a string hole pierced through. Material as conical beads.

   16 small disk beads. D. 7–8 mm. Th. 2–3 mm. Faience: white at the core, rather worn, a few traces of light green glaze.

   3 flattened globular beads. D. 13 mm. Th. 6.5. mm. Glass paste, black with white mottling.

   One globular bead, slightly flattened. D. 8 mm. H. 6 mm. Amethyst: highly polished and of attractive appearance.

**P Tomb 26** (PLATE 124). Pit grave. Shallow rock depression. 50 × 25, depth c. 35. Earth fill with some carbon. Pebble floor, no contents. Possibly an infant burial.

**P Tomb 27** (PLATE 120; Contents, PLATE 143). Shaft grave. 140 × 60, depth 120. Several large boulders at surface of shaft; rock ledge, much decayed, at depth c. 85, with traces of mud brick surviving to a height of 13 cm. Narrow lower compartment; pebble floor. In the upper earth fill, at depth 30–90, a sherd deposit (see below) was found at the N end; disintegrated mud brick at the S. Decayed mud brick and rock fill in the lower compartment, no other contents.

**Pottery.** Deposit of sherds apparently thrown in with the fill. In addition to 1 and 2 below there were a barred handle, probably of a neck-handled amphora; fragments of two skyphoi, one with PSC, one plain; a cup sherd; a sherd with circles or semicircles, from a closed vase; and a handful of grey Minyan sherds.

1. Trefoil oinochoe. H. 31.5. About three-quarters preserved; restored. Local fabric. Four sets of

semicircles. On the handle two slight vertical grooves, each with a painted line linking a circular band around the top of the handle with another at the root.
2. Large skyphos. D. c. 27. One fragment only. Local fabric. PSC.

**P Tomb 28** (PLATES 120, 124; Contents, PLATE 144). Pit grave. 87 × 48 as preserved, depth c. 15. Two large mud bricks at the S and E sides, presumably to support a cover (of wood?) and protect the grave offering. A child's grave to judge from the miniature vases.

This tomb overlay Pyre 32 on the W side.

Pottery. Eleven vases. Handle and rim of 6, and handle of 10, missing; otherwise intact or nearly so. Local fabric for all. Most have worn or flaking surfaces. 3 and 4 could have been fired together. Of the miniature vases, 6–9 are soft fired with lustrous orange-brown paint; 7–11 are monochrome with only the flat underside reserved.
1. Jug. H. 10.8. Handle painted. Monochrome, reserved bands.
2. Kantharos. H. 8. Bands on light ground body.
3. Cup. H. 5.7. Monochrome. Uneven reserved area at the base.
4. Shallow bowl, lug handles. H. 4. D. 11.9. Two string holes. Monochrome.
5. Kalathos. H. 4.2. One string hole. Monochrome, very narrow reserved area at base. Underside painted.
6. Miniature neck-handled amphora. H. (rest.) 11.7. Max. d. 6.5. Monochrome, reserved bands, handles barred.
7. Miniature jug. H. 7.3. Monochrome.
8. Miniature jug. H. 5.3. Made so badly that it leans over. Monochrome.
9. Miniature cup. H. 3.2. Monochrome.
10. Miniature cup. H. 3.6. Monochrome.
11. Miniature shallow bowl. H. 2.5. Hand-made and irregular. Monochrome.

**P Tomb 29** (PLATES 124, 200a). Shaft grave. 150 × 65, depth 110. No rock ledge (the conglomerate here is formed of very loosely knit pebbles); broad mud brick lining at depth 95. Pebble floor. Earth and stone fill in the upper shaft; mud brick and silt in the lower compartment, which is a trough 15 deep and 15 wide, running the length of the shaft cutting. Sole contents the fragment of an iron pin.

Iron
1. Pin, fragment. Pres. l. 2.6. D. c. 0.2. Broken both ends. Part of dress pin shaft or fibula pin. Section round. Not illustrated.

**P Tomb 30.** Shaft grave. 190 × 70, depth 150. Rock shelf, mostly disintegrated, at 90–105. Earth and stone fill in the upper shaft, pebble and disintegrated rock below. No other contents.

**P Tomb 31** (PLATE 120; Contents, PLATES 144–5). Shaft grave. 185 × 80–95, depth 145. Rock ledge at depth 67, built up with stones (to three courses on the E side). Pebble floor. Earth and stone fill in the upper shaft, including two large boulders. Decomposed mud brick from depth 115, from the inner lining of the rock sides and perhaps also from covering material. Vases 2–4 and 6 were in the centre of the floor; 1 and 5 were at the N end, shattered, and were perhaps originally set above the cover.

Pottery. Six vases, complete or nearly so. All of standard local fabric.
1. Amphoriskos, vertical-handled. H. 16.4. The groove at the junction of neck and body gives the shape a metallic appearance. Very thin walled at the centre of the base. Monochrome.
2. Amphoriskos, vertical-handled. H. 12.2. Decorated as shown.
3. Amphoriskos, vertical-handled. H. 15.2. Very thick walled at the base. Decorated as shown.

3A. Conical foot (of a jug?). Found beside 3, probably serving as a stopper.
4. Lekythos. H. 15.9. The upper neck band runs upward to meet the handle where it joins the neck. Decorated as shown: there are three triangular motives. In mint condition, perhaps by the same potter as 3. PLATE 263c.
5. Lekythos. H. 20.1. Decorated as shown. The three lower neck bands continue beneath the handle. Three sets of semicircles.
6. Lentoid flask with trefoil lip. H. 17.4. Decorated as shown.

**Iron**
7. Knife. Pres. l. 7. W. 1.8. Th. c. 0.6. Probably consists of butt and start of blade. Traces of wood or ivory plates on the butt; no detectable rivet; wedge-shaped section.

**P Tomb 32.** No tomb.

**P Tomb 33** (PLATE 120; Contents, PLATE 145). Shaft grave. 125 × c. 75, depth 82. Rock ledge at depth 48. Pebble floor. Cut at the W by the later Pyre 33, at the upper level only.

**Pottery**
1. Lekythos. H. 11. Intact; of local fabric. Decorated as shown. The triangles are undifferentiated from the remaining fully painted area of the upper body.

**P Tomb 34** (PLATE 121). Shaft grave. 175 × 90, depth 168. Rock ledge, at depth 85, supporting six limestone cover slabs, thickness c. 10 — a seventh lay beneath these, across the centre of the tomb. Fill of earth and pebbles in the upper shaft; a layer of dark reddish earth on the slabs suggests a mud brick sealing above the slabs. Similar fill below the slabs probably from disintegrated lining at the sides. Pebble floor at depth 120; sole contents two badly decayed bone fragments. Beneath floor level a deep *strosis* of pebbles (20–50 deep), including water-worn sherds, placed over the bedrock.

This tomb was cut at the E, at the upper level only, by the later Pyre 33.

**P Tomb 35** (PLATES 121, 124; Contents, PLATE 145). Shaft grave. 100 × 70, depth 40. Rock ledge at depth 25. The lower compartment is a small rectangle, only 75 × 32, containing mud brick fill perhaps from a wood and mud brick cover. Pebble floor. Probably a child's grave.

**Pottery.** Two vases, complete except for small fragments. Local fabric.
1. Juglet. H. 8. Possibly a feeder: a small hole (d. 3 mm) on the belly, to the left of the handle, could mark the spot where a spout has broken away. One hatched, two cross-hatched, triangles.
2. Cup H. 8.7. The top band enclosing the zigzag fails, for most of its length, to reach the rim. Reserved central dot on the floor.

**P Tomb 36** (PLATES 122, 124; Contents, PLATE 145). Shaft grave. 145 × 80, depth 70. Rock shelf, at depth c. 57, with a thick mud brick lining, forming a small rectangular compartment 95 × 30. Pebble floor. Child's grave.

**Pottery.** Five vases, intact or nearly so, and a pierced sherd; local fabric.
1. Feeder (jug). H. (without handle) 8.4. Monochrome, reserved band, barred handle.
2. Small trefoil oinochoe. H. 8. Monochrome: even the underside is painted over.
3. Juglet. H. 7.4. Unpainted.
4. Juglet. H. 7.5. Crudely made. Monochrome.
5. Cup. H. 5.4. Monochrome, reserved bands on lip and at base of body.
6. Pierced sherd. D. 5.5. From an amphora.

**P Tomb 37** (PLATE 121). Pit grave. 65 × 37, depth 10. Earth fill. Pebble floor. Cut at N end by Pyre 20.

**Pottery**
1. Kalathos. H. 7.2. Conical. Two string holes, d. 4 mm. Reserved dot on floor. Reserved band inside rim, and two outside on lower body. Chequerboard underside. Not illustrated.

**P Tomb 38.** Shaft grave. 115 N 52, depth 108. Rock shelf at depth 68. Lower compartment 70 × 30. Pebble floor. No contents. Cut at N end by Pyre 36.

**P Tomb 39** (PLATE 121; Contents, PLATE 146). Shaft grave. 180 × 85, depth c. 100. Rock ledge at depth c. 60, broader on the W side (where this tomb intersected with Tomb 39A). Pebble floor, on which lay several large bone fragments, five vases and two fibulae. At c. 30 from the N end there was a low cross-wall of rough stones, evidently built to give better support to the covering at this point, and to receive a secondary deposit of pottery above, catalogued as Tomb 39B. Pots 2 and 4 were found in the small area N of the cross-wall, on the pebble floor, and are taken with the Tomb 39 group (i.e. the floor deposit), but these and others may have fallen from above when the covering collapsed. In any case the entire deposit, 39 and 39B, surely belongs to the one burial (cf. S59 and 59A, p. 129); this is borne out by the fact that the lids of the pyxides 39,2 and 3 were found in the 'secondary' deposit 39B.

**Pottery.** Four wheel-made vases, intact or nearly so, and of local fabric; one fragmentary hand made pyxis (3 — see below).
1. Amphoriskos. H. 10.5. Decorated as shown. Four sets of semicircles; the compass points are well up in the reserved zone, and marked with a painted dot (not shown on drawing).
2. Pyxis with lid. H. 7.5, with lid 9.6. Two string holes matching two on the lid — a fine needle was thrust through both in one movement, and penetrated the outside of the pyxis wall. Monochrome, reserved bands.
*3. Pyxis with lid. D. of lid 6.5. Hand-made. The lid is complete except for the knob, which has crumbled away; it has two string holes. The pyxis itself has crumbled to dust; profile not recoverable; one fragment preserves the rim profile, which is straight and rather thick, (3—4 mm), with one string hole below. Unbaked purplish clay, very friable, with grey burnished surface. No trace of incised or other decoration.
4. Kalathos. H. 4.5. Of the five rows of impressed triangles the second and fourth are inverted. At least two incised guide lines, but these have been almost entirely smoothed over.
5. Kalathos. H. 4.4. Centre row of impressed triangles inverted. Underside unpainted.

**Iron**
6. Arched fibula with central boss (B.II.14). L. 3.5. H. 3. Shattered — catch and pin lost. Short stem and forearm, large boss occupies centre of bow, but fibula too ruined by oxydisation to see detail of shape. Cloth remains.
7. Arched fibula with central boss (B.II.14). L. 3.8. Pres. h. 3.3. The fellow to 6, similarly preserved.

**P Tomb 39A** (PLATE 121; Contents, PLATE 146). Pit grave. c. 117 × 58, depth 45. Intersects over much of its area with Tomb 39. A rectangular pit without rock shelf. Pebble floor. Only content a small feeder. Child's grave.

**Pottery**
1. Feeder (jug), H. 5.8. Hand-made. Intact except for rim chip. Local fabric. Monochrome except handle.

**P Tomb 39B** (PLATE 121; Contents, PLATES 146—7). An unusual deposit of pottery placed on a specially constructed shelf at the N end of Tomb 39 (see above), at depth 70. The pottery was found in a fragmentary condition, as though thrown in as part of the fill, and should belong with Tomb 39.

**Pottery.** Seventeen vases (and the lids of 39, 2–3, see above). Poor condition. All made up from sherds, and restored complete except for 2 and 14–17, which are fragmentary. There is one hand-made bowl (16 – for fabric, etc. see catalogue entry); the remainder are of standard local fabric.

1. Jug. H. 11. Decorated as shown: three sets of semicircles.
2. Lekythos fragment. D. (rim) 5.7. Neck and handle only. Fabric burnt to grey throughout, from the pyre; traces of brown paint over entire outer surface.
3. Amphoriskos, vertical-handled. H. 11.2. Decorated as shown, same on both sides.
4. Pyxis and lid. H. 9.4, (with lid) 14.8. Decoration of pyxis as shown, the same on both sides. Four sets of semicircles on the lid.
5. Skyphos. H. 7.2. The PSC intersect on both sides of the vase.

6–15. Ten kalathoi. The lips of 8–14 are flattened and decorated with bars (usually in four groups of 15–20). All but one have two string holes (d. 2–4 mm) set close together beneath the lip. The exception, 7, has one string hole (d. 5–6 mm) and has a deeper shape than the others. 6–14 have impressed triangles, 6 having additional reserved bands; 15 has reserved bands only. The decorations of the undersides are as illustrated.

6. Kalathos. H. 6.5.
7. Kalathos. H. 5.5.
8. Kalathos. H. 6.7.
9. Kalathos. H. 7.1. The potter began a fourth tier of triangles below, but only completed two. Rows of lumpy protrusions in the interior, caused by the instrument used for impressing.
10. Kalathos. H. 7.4. Similar to 9.
11. Kalathos. H. 8. Similar to 9.
12. Kalathos. H. 8.2. Similar to 9.
13. Kalathos. H. 6.6. Reserved cross on underside, not shown.
14. Kalathos. H. 6.3. About one quarter preserved. No incised guide lines.
15. Kalathos. H. 4.8. About one half preserved. Central reserved dot on the floor.
16. Bowl fragment. H. 5. D. c. 14. About one half preserved, including two handles and full profile. Hand-made. Red fabric with large schist bits and white grits; smooth red-burnished surface. One of the lug handles has two string holes (d. 2 mm).
17. Bowl fragment. D. 15. About one quarter preserved. Brown-buff clay and slip with black paint: unusual for Lefkandi, but could be local. Combed decoration of wavy lines, and four to five horizontal incised grooves, all done with the same instrument. Another fragment, non-joining, was found in Pyre 41.

**P Tomb 40.** Shaft grave. 175 × 65, depth 140. The lower compartment is built of mud brick and forms a trough, 150 × 30, depth 30. Pebble floor. No contents.

**P Tomb 41** (PLATE 122; Contents, PLATE 147). Shaft grave. 150 × 70, depth 115. Broad rock shelf at depth 85. The lower compartment is comparatively small, 107 × 25; pebble floor. This tomb was cut in the NW corner by the later Pyre 37.

**Pottery**

1. Lekythos. H. (rest.) 13. Max. d. 8.8. Rim missing. Local fabric. Two sets of semicircles (done with a multiple brush whose points were arranged in pairs) flanking three vertical lines.
2. Trefoil oinochoe. H. 11. Intact. Probably local: buff clay with purplish brown slip, and dark brown paint which has decayed over most of the surface. Decorated as shown: three sets of semicircles.

**P Tomb 42** (PLATE 123; Contents, PLATE 147). East Cemetery. Shaft grave. 150 × 90, depth 120. Cut into the rock in a natural gully. Broad ledge formed by a layer of natural clay which occurs beneath the upper conglomerate rock, at depth 70. The lower compartment, cut into the soft clay, is a regular rectangle, 125 × 60. Pebble floor.

**Pottery.** Two vases. Intact; both clumsily made. Local fabric.

1. Kalathos. H. 6.4. One large string hole. Inverted impressed triangles; the incised guide lines have been smoothed out; lumpy protrusions on the interior.

2. Kalathos. H. 4.5. Two string holes. Two rows of rectangular impressions on the lower body, clumsily applied. Monochrome inside and out.

**Faience**
3. Necklace of disk beads. White friable faience, traces of green glaze on surface. 387 were collected, complete but in a very decayed state, and there were perhaps as many again which had disintegrated into fragments or dust. Two only are cylindrical (d. 8 mm, th. 7 mm), all the rest are flat disks (d. 5–9 mm, th. 3–4 mm).

**P Tomb 43** (PLATE 123; Contents, PLATE 148). East Cemetery. Pit grave? A rectangular rock cutting only c. 25 below the surface, with no surviving rock shelf, 125 × 55, depth c. 60. Earth and stone fill. Pebble floor.

**Pottery.** Six vases, intact except for small breaks. Local fabric.
1. Trefoil oinochoe. H. 18.5. Ring foot set off by a groove. Monochrome, reserved band.
2. Kalathos. H. 5.3. Two string holes. Monochrome, reserved band. Underside reserved.
3. Kalathos. H. 3.5. Two string holes. Monochrome, reserved bands.
4. Kalathos. H. 3.3. Two string holes. Monochrome, reserved bands. Underside reserved.
5. Kalathos. H. 3.5. Two string holes. Monochrome, including the underside, but a reserved band below the lip outside was perhaps intended.
6. Cup. H. 4.1. Monochrome inside and out.

**Bronze**
*7. Arched fibula with central boss. Pres. 1. 2.5. Pres. h. 1.7. Th. of boss 1.0. Part of stem, spring, pin, and part of catch lost. Separated into stem, bow and forearm by a pair of fillet mouldings either side of bow. Bow section plano-convex, steep sided. *FGI* no. 1048.
*8. Bracelet. D. 3.9 × 3.7. D. of rod 0.4. Extended l. 15.5. Overlap 4.5. Complete and intact. Rod of round section rolled into shape, with wide overlap; plain terminals. PLATE 241i.
9. Bracelet. D. 4 × 3.8. D. of rod 0.3. Extended l. 15.5. Complete, but in three pieces. The fellow to 8.

**Glass**
10. Bead. D. 1.3. H. 1.3. Spherical, with three horizontal grooves, and large vertical string hole (d. 4 mm). In good condition, with a hard black crust over most of the surface.

**P Tomb 44** (PLATE 122, 124; Contents, PLATE 148). Shaft grave. 165 × 80, depth 110. Rock shelf at depth 65, on the W side; supports of mud bricks on the E side, partly collapsed, and at the S. Upper fill of earth and stones, silt and decayed mud brick below, covering eight vases and a dress pin on a pebble floor. A trefoil oinochoe (7) was found in the upper fill, depth 60, at a point where the tomb shaft seems to have been cut by an unexcavated pyre in square H, and so may not belong with the other offerings. A child's grave, to judge by the miniature vases.

**Pottery.** 4, 7A and 8 fragmentary; 1 and 6 intact; the rest made up complete. All of standard local fabric except for 8, which is Red Slip ware.
1. Amphoriskos. H. 15.9. The vase was squeezed before firing, so that the mouth has become oval (9 × 8). Monochrome with reserved bands, handles barred.
2. Cup. H. 6.1. Decorated as shown (zigzag between bands on outer lip). Reserved central dot on floor.
3. Kalathos. H. 5.2. Two string holes. Four rows of impressed triangles, the first and third inverted; one guide line below the bottom row. Reserved central dot on floor.
4. Triple vase, belly-handled amphoriskos type. Pres. h. 7.5. Max. d. 7.1. Fragmentary and in poor condition, evidently old and battered before being placed in the tomb. One segment preserved, badly chipped at rim and base, belly handle missing. Remains of two attachments to the side walls show that it was a triangular triple vase as S 38,2. Monochrome, but double chevron beneath the handle.
5. Miniature vertical-handled amphoriskos. H. 7.3. Decorated as shown, zigzag at belly.
6. Miniature jug. H. 5.6. Decorated as shown: six cross-hatched triangles.

7. Trefoil oinochoe. H. 22. Decorated as shown, with another group of languettes on the unillustrated side; there are five sets of semicircles, whose arcs continue over the supporting band.

7A. Miniature jug fragment. Pres. h. 7.3. Max. d. 7. Base missing. As 6, but larger and with longer neck. Three groups of three chevrons on the shoulder, otherwise monochrome. Band of paint 0.8 wide inside the mouth. Not illustrated, nor on plan.

8. Jug fragments. Max. d. 10.4. About one quarter preserved, rim, neck and handle missing. Ovoid body, flat base. Red Slip ware, see P 19,2 for probable shape. Soft fired. Not illustrated, nor on plan.

**Iron with bronze**

9. Dress pin. Pres. l. 8. D. of head 0.7. D of bulb 0.7. L. of bulb 1.0. D. of shaft 0.3. Six fragments, ?joining. Apparently has a small disk head. A small oval bronze bead slipped on to shaft serves as bulb.

**P Tomb 45** (PLATES 123, 200b; Contents, PLATE 149). East Cemetery. Shaft grave containing double inhumation. 170 × 115, depth 85. A broad rectangular pit, rounded at the corners, and cut into the loose stony fill of a rock gully, using (and cutting straight) the vertical rock edge at the W (head) side and on the S. The floor of the tomb was cut no more than 10 cm into the rock surface at the bottom of the gully. Two skeletons in extended position, the hands crossed over the midriff; the bones poorly preserved, the skulls very fragmentary (see Appendix C). At the shoulder of one, two bronze fibulae, close together; at the upper arms of the other, two iron ?fibulae.

**Pottery.** No vases were placed in the tomb. The sherds found in the tomb fill, and those in the fill which accumulated over the tomb cutting afterwards, are dealt with on pp. 273—5.

*Bronze*

*1. Fibula with crescentine bow (B.IX.1). L. 8.4. H. 6.6. Complete, cleaned and in good condition. Broken in antiquity at the spring and repaired with a lead rivet. Clearly articulated into stem, bow and forearm. The stem is enlivened by close-set encircling traced lines, over which is fitted a separately made star-shaped ('Paddle-wheel') bead. The stem is separated from the bow by a moulding outlined by very fine fillets. The forearm is picked out with a bead and fillet moulding; on the bead are vertical traced lines. The bow is decorated on both sides in pointillé technique with an identical design; it is outlined by close-set dots; the main ornament is an encircled equal-armed cross (Maltese cross) whose arms are stippled. This design is tangential to a widening chevron band drawn from the centre of the bottom edge of the bow out to its perimeter. The catch-plate is broad but shallow; four traced lines on its outer surface suggest a feline paw. Spring (two turns) and catch to right. PLATES 241a, 249,5.

*2. Fibula with crescentine bow (B.IX.1). L. 8.4. H. 6.6. In two pieces, but complete apart from extreme tip of pin. Cleaned, and in good condition. The fellow to 1. *FGI* no. 1527. PLATE 241b.

**Iron.** Not illustrated

3. ?Fibula. L. 11. Max. w. 6.5. W. of metal up to 1.0. Completely ruined by oxydization; raised in wax, in which it is still embedded. Possibly originally an arched fibula of which part of bow — perhaps of swollen asymmetric type — survives.

4. ?Fibula. L. c. 9. W. 5. W. of metal c. 0.8. In the same ruined condition as 3. Possibly bow and forearm of arched fibula; traces of a boss or bulb on the bow.

**P Tomb 46** (PLATES 122, 124; Contents, PLATE 149). Shaft grave. 185 × 95, depth 170. Six heavy limestone cover slabs on a rock shelf at depth 105—120. Rock and earth fill above, fine silt and heavy gravel from the decomposed conglomerate rock wall below. Pebble floor in narrow central trough, 175 × 40. On the floor two pins and five bone fragments — two, much decayed, found at the E side of the tomb, three smaller, including two teeth, at the N end. The sherd of a conical foot with rouletting (not illustrated) was also found in the tomb. Stratified beneath Pyres 34 and 35.

**Bronze**

*1. Dress pin. L. 18.4. L. of decorated head 3.0 D. of largest boss 0.7, D. of shaft 0.2. Complete, but

assembled from fragments. The head takes the form of a poppy-head resting on a disk, below which is a spherical bulb set off by disk-mouldings above and below; the modelling is very fine. PLATE 250, 5.
*2. Dress pin. L. 18.4. Complete, but assembled from fragments. The fellow to 2. PLATE 242E.

**P Tomb 47** (PLATES 123, 202a; Contents, PLATES 149—51, 219b—d). East Cemetery. Shaft grave with inhumation. Upper shaft 245 × 110, max. depth 170. Lower shaft 245 × 60, depth c. 50. Cut into the side of the rock gully in the same way as Tomb 45. Broad shelves for covers on each of the long sides, cut into the rock and lined with stones on the W side, built up with clay on the E; no trace of the covers survived. On the floor, the skeleton of a warrior in extended position, head to N, very poorly preserved except for the skull and the long bones. Three vases at the head, the others at the feet and beside the legs. One lekythos (11) may originally have been placed on the tomb lid, and have slipped later to the position where it was found, at 28 cm above the tomb floor in the earth of the disintegrated clay shelf. The other objects found were a sword placed at the right side, spearhead (not marked on plan) at the feet, gold attachment on the upper left thigh bone, at the groin, and faience beads scattered beside the pyxis (13) and between the shins. Note that the tomb fill contained nearly 150 sherds, (see pp. 273—5), and a selection illustrated on PLATE 278D and E.

**Pottery.** Sixteen vases, monotonous in shape but with some simple variations in decoration. All but three are intact or nearly so. The exceptions are 3, missing most of one side and one handle; 9, lacking its rim; and 10, badly shattered. All appear to be of standard local fabric.
1. Small neck-handled amphora. H. 22.3. Decorated as shown.
2. Small amphora, handles shoulder to lip. H. 10.2. The three reserved bands on the belly are carelessly drawn, and not continuous round the vase. Otherwise monochrome.
3. Small amphora, handles shoulder to lip. H. 13.5. Small string hole (d. 4 mm) through the top of each handle. Monochrome, reserved bands belly and neck.
4. Trefoil oinochoe. H. 15. Handle painted. Note ridge at join of neck and body. Monochrome, reserved band.
5. Lekythos. H. 15.8. Handle painted. Monochrome.
6. Lekythos. H. 13.9. Monochrome, barred handle.
7. Lekythos. H. 10.7. Monochrome.
8. Lekythos. H. 13.3. Decorated as shown: three cross-hatched triangles.
9. Lekythos. H. (rest.) c. 15. Max. d. 10.5. Decorated as shown: three sets of semicircles — the compass point is placed unusually high in the reserved zone and marked by a small dot.

*10—16.* Seven pyxides. Note that all have two string holes at diametrically opposite points beneath the rim, matching others on the lids where these have been preserved; except in the case of 16 their diameter is 4—5 mm.
10. Pyxis with lid. H. 11.7, of lid 3.9. Monochrome. Paint on rim and slightly inside. Top of the lid knob reserved.
11. Pyxis. H. 13.6. Monochrome, reserved band. Paint on rim and slightly inside. No lid preserved.
12. Pyxis. H. 12. Paint on rim. Decorated as shown. Sixteen groups of opposed diagonals, the number of diagonals in each group varying from five to eleven. No lid preserved.
13. Pyxis with lid. H. 10. H. of lid 1.7. Paint half over rim. Decorated as shown. Solid diamonds/triangles on the belly in groups of three or four, separated by two or (once only) three vertical lines. Top of lid knob reserved.
14. Pyxis with lid. H. 13.7. H. of lid 2.4. Decorated as shown. No paint on rim. The paint on the lid is red, as opposed to black-brown on the pyxis.
15. Pyxis with lid. H. 13. H. of lid 2.3. Paint on rim. Decorated as shown. Five sets of cross-hatched swastikas; for a sixth was substituted two vertical dogtooth motives placed back to back between vertical lines. Reserved dot on the lid knob.
16. Pyxis with lid. H. 20.5. H. of lid 3.5. D. of string holes 7—8 mm. Paint on rim. Decorated as shown. Six groups of either six or seven chevrons on the shoulder. The reserved band on the lid is just above one string hole, but cuts through the other.

**Gold**

*17. Attachment with strap. L. 7.8. L. of strap 8.1. Wt. 1 gr. Broken, part of the strap missing. Border of dots, pointillé, and a line down the central rib, with herringbone pattern. four small holes (two at the top, two at the bottom) for straps. The strap is a straight band of foil with slightly wavy edges at each end, and terminating in a small wire hook. PLATE 232f.

**Iron**

18. Sword. L. 71.5. W. of hilt 4.8. L. of hilt 9.5. W. of blade 3.8. Th. of blade 1.1. W. of hilt flange 0.9. L. of handguard rivets, 1.2, 1.0. Complete; broken and repaired. Hilt has prominent 'ears' at the pommel, grip of sinuous outline, pinched below pommel and above handguard. Outline of handguard straight. Remains of ivory(?) hilt plates, secured by two rivets in grip and two in guard. The rivets appear to be of bronze. Outline of hilt-plates clearly preserved in the corrosion pattern. The blade widens slightly below the guard, whereafter the edges are parallel until the blade narrows to the tip. Traces of wood seen on the blade may represent remains of the scabbard. PLATE 245A.

19. Spearhead. Pres. L. 18.7. Estimated l. of socket 8. Estimated max. w. 4. Part of tip lost; socket damaged. Too damaged for form to be clear. Section probably elliptical, no detectable midrib. A bronze ring 1.4 wide at the base of the socket, evidently to hold socket tight. Trace of wood in the socket.

**Faience**

20. Disk beads. D. 7—11 mm. Th. 2—4 mm. 98 beads of greenish-white faience, and fragments of about ten others. If strung these form a small necklace, d.c. 16. Perhaps the gift of a female relative?

**P Pyre 1** (Contents, PLATE 152). Rectangular. 142 × 80, depth c. 40. Fill of sandy earth and gravel at the surface, with collapsed lumps of bard baked earth crust on the W side. Black carbon fill below, rising higher at the S end, and containing a few small fragments of burnt bone, charred wood, and a spearhead.

**Iron**

1. Spearhead. Pres. l. 23.3. L. of socket c. 11. Max. w. of blade 3.6. Th. of midrib 1.5. Part of socket lost, blade much damaged. Prominent midrib; socket hollow for at least 6.4. A number of (altered) fragments of wood adhere to the socket.

**P Pyre 2.** Rectangular? Only the N half excavated. W. 60, d. 40. Carbon fill; no contents except two plain amphora sherds, one burnt, from the pyre surface.

**P Pyre 3.** Shallow rectangular pit. 150 × 82, depth c. 10. Carbon fill. No contents except two bone fragments and one burnt amphora sherd. Only the bottom of the pyre is preserved.

**P Pyre 4.** Shallow rectangular depression. 105 × 55, depth c. 15. Carbon fill. No contents.

**P Pyre 5.** Shallow rectangular depression. 120 × 70, depth 10. Carbon fill. No contents.

**P Pyre 6.** Shallow rectangular pit. 110 × 60, depth 25. Carbon fill with many pebbles. No contents.

**P Pyre 7.** Rectangular. 135 × 55, depth 10. Carbon fill. No contents.

**P Pyre 8.** Rectangular. 175 × 75, depth 15. Earth and stones at surface. Carbon fill below.

**Pottery.** From the surface, amphora fragments (1), and the lip fragment of a skyphos with a high offset rim — sherd too small to show if PSC, but a thin line of paint below rim suggests not.

1. Amphora fragments. Less than one quarter preserved, about 70% burnt. Ring foot (d.c. 16); narrow reserved bands on the body; semicircles and warts (one preserved) on the shoulder. Not illustrated. See T 7,1 for a vase of comparable type.

**P Pyre 9.** Rectangular. 140 × 65, depth 15. Carbon fill, with amphora fragments at the surface. This pyre cuts Pyre 21 on the E side, and is cut by Pyre 39 at the S.

**Pottery**
1. Amphora fragments. D. of rim 21. Much of the neck preserved with some rim and shoulder fragments. Only two or three sherds burnt. Lip turned out and flattened; neck fully painted; semicircles on the shoulder. Local fabric. Not illustrated.

**Iron**
2. Pin fragment. Pres. l. 3. D. 0.2. Featureless oxidised fragment of pin shaft that could be either dress pin or fibula. Not illustrated.

**P Pyre 10.** Rectangular. 130 × 68, depth 15. Carbon fill; no contents.

**P Pyre 11** (Contents, PLATE 152). Rectangular. 138 × 80, depth 18. Carbon fill. Deposit of broken and burnt pottery at the S end of the pyre. Also bone fragments.

**Pottery.** All made up from sherds, some of which are badly burnt, though most retain their colour. 1 and 3 fragmentary; 2, 4, 7–9 complete except for small fragments; 5–6, 10, 11 sherds only. Local fabric: pale buff clay and slip with brown paint (streaky and worn on 7–9).
1. Neck-handled amphora. Pres. h. 13.8. D. of rim 8.8. Surviving fragment from shoulder to rim, including one handle. Decorated as shown. Four sets of semicircles.
2. Trefoil oinochoe. H. 16.7. Decoration as shown. Two sets of semicircles, with a group of six languettes at either side of them.
3. Trefoil oinochoe. H. (rest.) 22. Max. d. 13.1. Lower body and foot missing. Decorated as shown. Three sets of semicircles.
4. Lekythos. H. 14.1. Decorated as shown. One group of four chevrons, one of five, two cross-hatched triangles.
5. Jug/lekythos fragments. Rims of two, d. 9.5, 6.0. A shoulder fragment with double rough zigzag between horizontal bands is probably from the larger of these. Not illustrated.
6. Lekythos, fragment of neck. D. at narrowest point 1.9. Broken away at rim and shoulder. Seven narrow horizontal bands, running beneath the handle. Not illustrated.
7. Skyphos. H. 12. Decorated as shown. Reserved dot on the floor.
8. Skyphos. H. 10.8. Lip set off by a slight groove. Decorated as shown.
9. Cup. H. 10.5. Decorated as shown, but the motive on the outer lip is a double zigzag, not (as in the drawing) a lattice.
10. Skyphos/cup fragments. Several sherds, including four conical feet. Not illustrated.
11. Pyxis fragment. D. of rim c. 9. Rim and upper body fragment only. Decorated as shown.
12. Clay stopper (?). D. c. 4.5. A roughly spherical lump of clay, baked in the pyre, probably serving as a stopper for one of the lekythoi/jugs. Not illustrated.

**P Pyre 12.** Rectangular. 125 × 63, depth 68. Earth fill at the surface, carbon deposit with wood fragments below. A few body sherds from a light ground amphora with horizontal bands were found, and one very small and calcined bone fragment.

**P Pyre 13.** Not excavated.

**P Pyre 14A** (Contents, PLATE 153). Rectangular 135 × 49, depth 26. Dark earth and stones at surface; below this, a fill of black carbon. Bone fragments and sherds in the lower level. This pyre cut into the earlier and deeper Pyre 14B, and overlay Tomb 16, which was earlier than either.

**Pottery.** Sherds include two amphora body fragments (one with concentric circles), and the upper part of a Black Slip jug.

*1. Jug fragment. H. (rest.) 11.5. D. of rim 4.7. Lower body and base missing. On the shoulder, the incised decoration was done with a three-pointed instrument; this design continues beneath the handle, which was attached afterwards.

**P Pyre 14B** (PLATE 117; Contents, PLATE 153). Rectangular. 127 × 53, depth 53. Carbon fill with bone fragments and pottery. Cut by the later Pyre 14A, but overlay Tomb 16.

**Pottery.** Three vases, intact except for the handle of 3; Unburnt except at the rim of 3, and slight discoloration on 2. Local fabric.
1. Lekythos. H. 11.2. Globular; flat bottom — the original ring foot probably separated. Decorated as shown. Underside reserved.
2. Amphoriskos. H. 15. Decorated as shown; six groups of chevrons, each cut by a vertical line at the centre. With this vase was found a large conical foot, d. 8.4, which served as a stopper.
3. Jug. H. 15. Upper part of handle missing. Monochrome, reserved shoulder and bands below, handle barred.

**P Pyre 15** (Contents, PLATE 153). Rectangular. 140 × 75, depth 30. Carbon fill. Amphora sherds on the surface.

**Pottery**
1. Belly-handled amphora fragments. Max. d. c. 48. Large fragment of belly (with double-loop handle) and lower body, smaller fragment from base of neck. Surviving part of neck monochrome, light ground body, broad horizontal band between two narrow bands on the belly, supporting concentric circles in the handle zone; bull's head double handle as Pyre 41, 1, but here the handle is not fully painted. Not illustrated.
2. Clay button. H. 2.2. D. 2.4. Conical, with concave sides. Burnt.

**P Pyre 16** (Contents, PLATE 153). Rectangular 120 × 60, depth 20. Carbon fill, with stones, spearhead and knife.

**Iron**
1. Spearhead. L. 33. L. of socket 15. D. of socket 3.2. W. of blade 3.8. Th. of midrib c. 1.5. Complete and intact, though much altered by oxydization. The divided socket is hollow for at least 10; a pair of opposite rivets, obscured by oxydization. The rounded shoulders asymmetric. The rounded midrib is prominent. PLATE 244c.
2. Knife. Pres L. 11. L. of tang 2.2. W. of blade 1.5. Th. of blade 0.2. Tip and part of blade lost. Short triangular butt to a blade with convex profile. No trace to be seen of flanges or rivets in the butt.

**Stone**
3. Whetstone. 4.1. × 4.1. Th. 1.4. Rectangular stone slab cut square. A hard white stone, discoloured and cracked by fire. Small fragment of a second, identical, stone found. PLATE 237g.

**P Pyre 17** (Contents, PLATE 153). Rectangular. 120 × 60, depth c. 10. Carbon fill. Three burnt bone fragments, and a small piece of a sword.

**Iron**
1. Sword fragment. Pres. l. 9. W. of blade 3. Th. of blade 0.8. Much distorted. Probably, but not certainly, a mid-section of a sword blade. Flattened oval section. Many (altered) fragments of wood adhere to it.

**P Pyre 18.** Rectangular to oval. 135 × 55, depth 45. Carbon fill. Three bone fragments; no other contents.

**P Pyre 19** (Contents, PLATE 153). Rectangular (to reel shaped). 120 × 55, depth 35. Carbon fill, with two bone fragments and burnt sherds.

**Pottery**
1. Cup, rim fragment. D. 9.5. Burnt. One reserved band on inner lip, two on outer lip.

**P Pyre 20** (PLATE 121). Rectangular. 125 × 54, depth 57. Carbon fill with a few burnt bone fragments. This pyre cut Tomb 37 at the S end.

**P Pyre 21.** Rectangular. 150 × 64, depth 30. In the floor at the N end was a circular depression in the rock, depth c. 75 (from a previous amphora burial?). Carbon fill, no contents.

**P Pyre 22.** Rectangular. 110 × 60, depth 35. Earth fill to depth c. 20. Carbon fill below, with some large stones.

**P Pyre 23.** Rectangular. 182 × 79, depth 31. Carbon fill, and bone fragments.

**P Pyre 24.** Rectangular. 140 × 70, depth 25. Carbon fill; no contents. This pyre overlay Tombs 11 and 14.

**P Pyre 25.** Rectangular. 130 × 70, depth 40. Carbon fill; no contents. This pyre was cut by Tomb 6 at the S end.

**P Pyre 26.** Rectangular. 155 × 60, depth 60. Earth fill at the top, carbon below. A few bone fragments. Ring foot fragments of two amphorae.

**P Pyre 27.** Rectangular. 120 × 55, depth 75. Earth fill to depth 40; carbon below. Eight small burnt bone fragments; no other contents. This pyre was cut at the S end by Pyre 31.

**P Pyre 28** (Contents, PLATE 154). Rectangular. 155 × 90, depth 65. Carbon fill, with some bone fragments and pottery.

**Pottery.** The four kalathoi were made up complete from burnt fragments which are much blackened and have a greasy surface. The amphora fragment was slightly burnt with grey to purple-buff clay and brown paint.
*1. Kalathos. H. 5.5. One string hole. d. 4–5 mm. Monochrome inside and out.
*2. Kalathos. H. 5.3. Two string holes. Three rows of deeply impressed triangles on the lower body.
*3. Kalathos. H. 5.9. One string hole, d. 5 mm. Five incised guide lines, below three of which a row of inverted impressed triangles. Underside monochrome.
*4. Kalathos. H. 4. Two string holes, d. 2 mm. Three rows of impressed triangles.
5. Neck-handled amphora fragments. Pres. h. 30. Max. d. c. 50. One side of the body survives, from shoulder to below belly. Circles on shoulder; three bands below shoulder, two below belly; two intersecting curves below handle stump; otherwise light ground. Not illustrated, but for the type see PLATE 281C, from the surface of Palia Perivolia.

**P Pyre 29** (Contents, PLATE 154). Rectangular to oval. 100 × 45–70, depth 20. Carbon fill. Two pins, bead and loom weight at surface of pyre fill, which was much eroded by the plough.

**Iron**
1. Dress pin. Pres. l. c. 23. D. of head 2.5. D. of shaft 0.5 Tip lost; broken. Plain disk head, shaft apparently undecorated. PLATE 250, 6.

2. Dress pin. Pres. l. 20.5. D. of shaft 0.5. Head and tip lost; what remains, two joining fragments. Probably originally the fellow to 1.

**Clay**
3. Incised bead. D. 2.7. String hole. d. 5 mm. Spherical, slightly flattened. Clay burnt to grey and black. Neatly incised with patterns as shown. PLATE 236K.
4. Loom weight. D. 6.8. String hole, d. 14 mm. H. 3.2. Pierced disk. Clay as 3.

**P Pyre 30.** Not a pyre.

**P Pyre 31** (Contents, PLATE 154). Rectangular. 110 × 58, depth 30. Carbon fill. A few bone fragments and sherds. At the N end this pyre cut into Pyre 27.

**Pottery**
1. Skyphos fragments. D. of rim 16. Two fragments, not joining, with rim and one handle. Clay and paint burnt to grey. High rim. PSC, intersecting.

**P Pyre 32.** (PLATES 120, 124; Contents, PLATE 154, and PLATE 277, 1000–22). Rectangular. 140 × 70–80, depth 50. Earth fill in the centre, including hard-fired lumps of earth crust fallen from the pyre edges (which originally rose higher); black carbon at the edges, and over the whole area from depth c. 40. Large fragments of charred wood (up to l. 20 × d. 20). Many sherds from the top of the carbon fill. Tomb 28 overlay this pyre.

**Pottery**
1. *Amphorae.* Most of the sherds were from amphorae; those illustrated, 1004–19, are a small selection only. Neck-handled amphorae predominated, to judge from the rims; the main system of decoration was for the most part light ground, and banded. The principal motive on the shoulder is semicircles (thirty not illustrated), and a very few have hourglass or triangle filling; in one or two cases there are full circles on the shoulder, and four sherds (two from the same vase) have languettes. The belly, where decorated, has circles, and there is one sherd with opposed diagonals with filled interstices. Some six or seven amphorae are represented, most of large dimensions; insufficient sherds were recovered, however, to allow for even one to be reconstructed. They appear to be of the type common in pyres.
   The period of these amphora sherds seems to be LPG, neither earlier nor later; and this would be a a reasonable date for the few sherds of other shapes.
2. *Kalathoi.* Fragments of three, two with impressed triangles (1000–1, and PLATE 154, 32,2b–c), one of Black Slip ware with combed and incised decoration (1002, and PLATE 154, 32,2a).
3. *Jugs.* One sherd with the combed and incised motive (1003, and PLATE 154, 32,3) from the shoulder of a jug of Black Slip ware (perhaps like P 24,5), but with polished red-brown paint. Three sherds, 1020–2, from shoulders of jugs with cross-hatched triangle motive, the triangles on two outlined.
   It is possible that this material is the result of a tidying up process from the surrounding area, especially from pyres where amphorae stuck out above the ground.

**Clay**
4. Button. H. 2.5. D. 2.8. Conical, with slightly concave sides, rounded beneath. Burnt to grey. Not illustrated.

**P Pyre 33** (PLATE 120). Rectangular. 155 × 70, depth 30. Earth fill at the surface, in the centre only; carbon fill below, and a few burnt bone fragments; no other contents. This pyre overlay the earlier Tombs 33 and 34.

**P Pyre 34** (Contents, PLATE 155). Rectangular. 125 × 80, depth 25. Earth and stone fill at the surface, with ash below. Sherds at the surface of the pyre made up into a small amphora and four pyxides, all thoroughly burnt, except for 2, whose more lightly burnt fragments have brown paint. Presumed to be of local fabric.

This pyre cut into Pyre 35, and overlay Tomb 46.

**Pottery**

1. Small amphora, handles belly to lip. Pres. h. 12.7. D. of rim 10.3. About two-thirds preserved: base lost, and most of handles missing. Decorated as shown: the sets of diagonals are arranged in groups of eleven.
2. Pyxis. Pres. h. 10.5. D. of rim 9.3. Base and lower body lost. Decorated as shown.
3. Pyxis and lid. Pres. h. 8.3. D. of rim 8. Base missing, lid fragmentary. Monochrome, reserved bands. Lid light ground, with one band.
4. Pyxis and lid. H. 14.7. H. of lid 3.8. Though fragmentary, the profile is complete. Decorated as shown.
5. Pyxis and lid. Pres. h. 7.4. of D. of rim 10.5. About one quarter preserved. Monochrome, reserved bands on belly and lid.

**P Pyre 35.** Rectangular 135 × 70, depth 50. Earth fill at the surface, in the centre only; carbon fill below, with stones and the collapsed crust (hard fired) of the earth wall. One burnt bone fragment (l. 2.5); no other contents.

**P Pyre 36.** Rectangular. 150 × 60, depth 40. Earth fill at the surface, carbon below, with stones. At the N side the pyre was cut by Tomb 36, at the S it cut Tomb 38.

**Pottery.** A few sherds, most from the body of a large burnt amphora, light ground with sets of concentric semicircles with hourglass filling. Not illustrated.

**P Pyre 37.** Rectangular 140 × 65, depth 30. Earth and stone fill at the surface, carbon below. A few burnt bone fragments; no other contents. At the N the pyre cut Pyre 39, at the S it cut Tomb 41.

**P Pyre 38.** Rectangular. 145 × 80, depth 45. Earth and stone fill at the surface, to depth 20 at the centre; carbon at the sides and below. Bone fragments in the NE corner at depth 30; no other contents.

**P Pyre 39.** Contents, PLATE 155. Rectangular. 157 × 62, depth 70. Earth fill to depth 40; rock and earth edges baked to a hard crust by the heat of the pyre; carbon fill below. Fragments of burnt bone, and sherds. The pyre was cut by Pyre 37 on the S side, and by Pyre 9 in the NW corner.

**Pottery**

1. Amphora (?). A few much damaged fragments of an amphora (or jug), unburnt. Not illustrated.
2. Lekythos fragments. Lower body fragment with ring foot, d. 5.2; shoulder fragment, with groups of three chevrons. Local fabric, partly burnt.
3. Clay spindle whorl. H. 2.2. D. 2.8. Biconical, with concave sides. Buff clay, mostly burnt to grey; traces of a brown glaze on the surface, almost all blackened by fire. Incised concentric circles with a filling of white paste — three groups of three on the upper concave face, three further groups below. A carefully made and well finished piece. PLATE 236j.

**P Pyre 40** (PLATE 196e; Contents, PLATE 155). Rectangular. 145 × 70, depth 35. Three large boulders at the surface of the pyre, below these a few fragments of a coarse clay bin (?); carbon fill. Few sherds.

**Pottery**

1. Bowl fragment. D. of rim 11.5. Base and handles missing. Slightly burnt; brown paint inside and out, except for narrow reserved bands inside and outside the lip.

**P Pyre 41** (PLATES 121, 199a; Contents, PLATE 156). Rectangular. 145 × 80, depth 65. Earth fill at the surface; carbon from depth c. 40, with amphora fragments concentrated mainly at the N end. The pyre was closely adjacent to Tomb 39, but did not intersect it.

Pottery. In addition to the illustrated amphora and jug fragments 1–3 (of local fabric), there was also a substantial fragment of the shallow bowl P 39B,17.
1. Amphora with two belly handles and two vertical shoulder handles. Pres. h. 54.5. Max. d. 40. About three quarters preserved; the rim is missing. Decorated as shown. PLATE 282, E.
2. Neck-handled amphora. Pres. h. 63. Max. d. c. 50. About one quarter preserved; the rim and base are missing. Note the concentric circles on the shoulder — thirteen circles, radius 9.2. See also for this type P Surface (p. 268), and P Pyre 28,5.
3. Jug fragment. Pres. h. 9.5. D. of rim 10.1. Rim, neck and part of shoulder and handle. Decorated as shown.

**P Pyre 42** (Contents, PLATE 156). Rectangular. 170 × 65, depth 25. Carbon fill; burnt bone fragments, and sherds. This pyre overlay Pyres 28 and 43.

Pottery
1. Cup. H. 6.4. About one half preserved; profile remains, but handle missing. Local. Decorated as shown.

**P Pyre 43.** Rectangular. 145 × 65, depth 80. The edges were fired to a hard red cement-like crust; earth fill to depth 60, carbon below. Small burnt bone fragments; no other contents. The southern half of the pyre was cut, at the upper level only, by Pyre 42.

**P Pyre 44** (Contents, PLATE 156). Rectangular. Width 70; not fully excavated. The pyre runs N–S across the extension trench (LL) to the E. Carbon fill; at the surface of the pyre, amphora and other sherds, mostly unburnt.

Pottery. Fragments of four vases, including large sherds of two amphorae, one belly-handled (1), the other neck-handled (2); both are light ground, with pink clay and slip, and glossy orange-brown paint. Nos 3 and 4 are burnt.
1. Belly-handled amphora. D. of rim 29.5. Max. d. 55. Fragments preserved from rim to belly. Flattened rim, bars on the top; neck monochrome. Two warts on shoulder, which has sets of circles or (probably) semicircles, eighteen to each set, radius 11.4. Two groups of holes for repair. Not illustrated.
2. Neck-handled amphora. Max. d.c. 55. Body fragments from shoulder to lower body. Circles on shoulder, radius 11. Not illustrated; type as P Pyre 41,2.
3. Lekythos. Restored h. 15.5. Max. d. 10.3. Lip missing. Dark buff clay and slip, black paint; partly burnt, and worn. Monochrome, shoulder unpainted, reserved bands on neck and below shoulder, handle barred.
4. Globular pyxis. H. 10. Max. d. 11.3. About one half preserved; burnt. Monochrome, reserved band on belly.

**P Pyre 45.** Rectangular. W. 70. Carbon patch in trench LL. Not excavated.

**P Pyre 46.** Carbon patch in trench LL. Not excavated.

**P Pyre 47** (Contents, PLATE 156). Carbon patch at N of trench MM. Not excavated.

Clay. From the surface of the pyre.
1. Loom weight. D. 7.1. Disk, slightly rounded above and below. Vertical string hole, d. 7 mm. Burnt.

**P Pyres 48–50.** East Cemetery. Carbon patches in trench OO. Not excavated.

## TOUMBA CEMETERY (PLATES 76b, 79, 157–192)

**T Tomb 1** (PLATE 157; Contents, PLATES 167, 216). Shaft grave. 140 × 90, depth 150. Cover slabs of magnesite, conglomerate and limestone at depth 80 in the shaft, resting on a rock-cut shelf. Lower compartment 105 × 50. Pebble floor. Thirteen grave offerings: at one end the handmade pots (2, 3), the large oinochoe (1) and the centaur's head; at the other end a juglet (4); in the centre the rings, fibulae, bracelets and necklace. Five small scraps of bone found in the grave, the largest c. 2 cm long.

The upper shaft of Tomb 1 was cut in the SW corner by Tomb 5, and overlain at the surface by Tomb 11; both are, then, later than this tomb.

**Pottery.** Four vases, three of which are unusual. All intact except for chips. 1 and 4 are wheel-made, and of local fabric. For the two hand-made vases, 2 and 3, see below.
  1. Trefoil oinochoe with high handle. H. 31; (with handle) 35.5. Note slight ridges marking off the body from the neck and from the base, and the projecting lug at the root of the handle. Decorated as shown. There are five groups of eight semicircles on the shoulder, each with a fringe of dots; there are only four dividing lines of vertical dots.
 *2. Bowl. H. 5.5. Handmade. Fine light red clay with lustrous black burnished surface, tending to peel off. Two opposed string holes below rim. There are three creduly incised swastikas, and one stroke of an uncompleted fourth. PLATE 268a.
  3. Dipper. H. 2.8; (with handle) 4.3. Hand-made. Coarse dark red to black clay with fairly rough black surface, smoothed but unpainted. PLATE 269a.
  4. Lekythos. H. 8.5. Decorated as shown. Three groups of triple chevrons intersecting at the apex. Note that the paint does not everywhere reach the base.

**Terracotta**
 *5. Head of centaur. H. c. 1.4. This is the severed head of the centaur of Tomb 3 (s.v. T 3,3). Solid core. Found face up beside the oinochoe (1). PLATES 251, 252e-g.

**Gold**
  6. Earring. D. 1.0. Wt. 0.5 gr. Cast (?) wire, tapering c. 1.25–0.5 mm. The thin end is pointed, the thick end flattened. Overlap c. 7 mm. PLATE 230k.
  7. Earring. D. 1.0. Wt. 0.5 gr. The fellow to 6, but coiled in the opposite direction.

**Bronze**
 *8. Bracelet. D. 5 × 5.1. Uncoiled l. c. 22. D. of metal 0.8. Overlap 5.8. Complete, cleaned. Probably made from an only slightly altered billet casting; section, plano-convex. Undecorated, plain terminals. PLATE 241g.
 *9. Bracelet. D. 5.1 × 5.2. Uncoiled l. 23.3. D. of metal 0.75 × 1. Overlap 6. Complete. The fellow to 8.
 *10. Arched fibula with asymmetric swollen bow (B.II.19). L. 5.3. H. 3.5. D. of bow 0.8. Part of pin and catch lost. Stem and forearm are set off from the bow by bead and fillet mouldings. The forearm is of rectangular section, the spring square. The section of the bow is round, slightly flattened underneath. Spring (two turns) and catch to left. PLATES 239a, 248,5.
  11. Arched fibula with asymmetric swollen bow. (B.II.19). Pres. l. 0.7. Most of spring, much of pin lost. Forearm broken, but probably joins. Stem and forearm are set off from the bow by rather indistinct swellings, defined by fine traced lines in place of the more usual fillets. Bow round section, flattened underneath. *FGI* no. 601.

**Faience**
  12. Necklace. 293 disk beads, d. 2–3 mm. Most are single disks, l.c. 1–1.5 mm. Twenty-eight are double (segmented but unsevered), l. c. 4 mm; five are triple, l. 5 mm; and one is cylindrical, l. 3.5 mm. The fabric of about one third of these is white and friable; most of the rest are dark red with a good and even lustrous surface; a few, including the triple beads, are of a coarser hard black substance. When strung, the surviving beads make up a necklace of length 46.5.

There is also one larger, melon, bead; d. 12 mm, th. 9 mm, d. of string hole 2–3 mm. It is of white faience. If strung with the small beads, two buffer beads must have been placed on either side, since the string hole is larger in diameter than many of the small beads. On PLATE 233 two small faience

disks are placed here, but do not belong. It is possible that the glass beads (13) served this function.
PLATE 233b.

**Glass**
13. Bead fragments. Several small fragments, brown at the core, hard white patina outside and at the string
hole. Probably from at least two spherical beads.


**T Tomb 2** (PLATE 157; Contents, PLATE 168). Shallow shaft grave. 135 × 37. Cut partly
into the rock and partly into earth, including the earth fill of the earlier Tomb 11. Pebble
floor. The central part of the tomb was cut away by Trial II.

A mud brick division separated this tomb at its W end from the contiguous Tomb 6;
chronological relation uncertain.

**Pottery.** Seven vases. 1, 3 and 7 are broken, the rest intact. 7 was removed in digging the surface level of
Trial II, before Tomb 2 was recognised, but probably belongs. 1–3 are of local fabric, and so probably
is the jug (5), which is hard fired to grey, with dull black paint. For the hand-made vases 4, 6 and 7, see
below.
1. Cup. H. 5.9. Monochrome except reserved bands outer and inner lip, and dot on floor.
2. Kalathos. H. 4.5. Two string holes (d. 1–2 mm) 5 mm apart. Unpainted.
3. Kalathos. H. 5.2. One string hole, d. 6 mm. Monochrome, reserved bands.
*4. Cooking pot. H. 18.2. Gritty coarse ware, hand-made. Vertical burnishing marks on neck. Base and
lower body blackened by fire; elsewhere reddish brown. PLATE 269d.
5. Jug, high handle. H. 14.3, with handle 17.2. Monochrome, but paint fails to reach the base at all points.
6. Trefoil juglet. H. 9. Hand-made. The clay is a mottled grey and brown, with lustrous surface; vertical
burnishing marks on neck and upper body, horizontal marks on belly. PLATE 269b.
7. Trefoil juglet. H. 6.5. Hand-made. Shape, fabric and surface as 6.


**T Tomb 3** (PLATES 157, 201b and d; Contents, PLATES 168–70, 217). Shaft grave.
200 × 115, depth 170. Rock-cut ledge at depth 75–95 in the shaft, supporting a set of
limestone cover slabs, one of which had collapsed. Pebble floor. Cut near the surface by the
later Tomb 15.

Most of the offerings, the pottery, the animal vase and the centaur body (1–7) and
the shell (12) were laid above the cover slabs at a depth 60–70, in the shaft; the metal
objects (8–11) were found on the pebble floor along with four bone fragments. These
latter were found below the fibula; l. of largest fragment 6.4 (left clavicle).

**Pottery and figurines.** Of the two terracotta figurines (2 and 3) the ?donkey was found cracked but unbroken, the centaur in fragments, its head having already been found separately in Tomb 1. Neither is
complete (see below). Both are of local fabric, but the clay of the centaur tends more in places to pink or
light red, with cream-buff slip and reddish-brown paint, while the ?donkey has buff clay, pinkish buff slip,
and streaky chestnut brown to black paint.
As to the five vases (1, 4–7), no. 1 is broken, and the rest are intact except for rim chips. All are local,
the paint thinly applied and with a matt surface.
1. Lekythos. H. 13.3. Decorated as shown. Three cross-hatched triangles, carelessly painted, on the
shoulder.
2. Terracotta rhyton of ?donkey (or mule). H. (pres.) 14. L. (pres.) 21. Missing: loop handle on top,
ears, end of nose, end of legs; all are old breaks, and three of the leg stumps had been smoothed flat.
Scratches on underside of belly where it scraped the ground in subsequent use. Body a hollow wheel-
made cylinder. Spout pierced through mouth, communicating through neck with the hollow body.
Square cut-out from top of body, done when clay was moist – paint has partly run into cut. Eye-
circles stamped when clay moist, but centres not extracted. Holes pierced through back of neck (mane)
and through tail. Body slightly cracked in firing. Crude painted decoration, as shown. PLATE 253.
*3. Centaur. H. 36. L. 26. Broken, now mended. Missing: end of tail, and left arm from just below
shoulder, together with object carried on shoulder. Legs and human torso solid. Animal body a hollow

wheel-made cylinder; an oval hole, d. 12 mm, in front, and a circular hole, d. 8 mm on back, about a third of way along body. Groove down back of human torso. Two light incisions down back of hair. No genitals. Five incisions on surviving right hand, the centaur being thus provided with six fingers. Attachment at left shoulder, probably part of what was being carried rather than the missing left hand. Eyes punched out while clay still moist. Groove across forehead, perhaps marking edge of hair (and also eyebrows?). Mouth indicated by groove; nostrils pierced; ears pierced. Knobbly front knees, with deep incision below left knee-cap. Underneath of animal body unpainted, otherwise decorated as shown. PLATES 251–2.

4. Lekythos. H. 13.7. Decorated as shown. The three lower neck bands run beneath the handle. Five languettes on each side, seven opposite the handle. Vertical line down the handle, ending below in a circle round the root of the handle, with tassel.
5. Lekythos. H. 8.6. Decorated as shown. Three cross-hatched triangles.
6. Lekythos. H. 8. Decorated as shown. Two groups of three chevrons, and one of four, the smallest being added rather as an afterthought.
7. Lekythos. H. 8.6. Decorated as shown. Three groups of four chevrons.

**Gold.** Two objects in thin sheet gold, intact, slightly bent but otherwise in good condition.
8. Attachment. H. 5.2, with straps 9.4. Wt. 3.8 gr. Elongated strip of sheet gold broadening towards the lower end, then narrowing to a rounded point; forked at the top where it extends to form two straps. Tiny holes for attachment on each strap and at lower centre; dot-repoussé decoration of triangles. See pp. 219–220.
9. Attachment. H. 4.6, with straps 8.2. Wt. 2 gr. Shape as 8; zigzag on each side of central vertical line. PLATE 232e.

**Bronze**
*10. Arched fibula with asymmetric swollen bow. (B.II.19). Complete apart from catch. Stem, bow and forearm distinctly articulated by the bead and fillet mouldings dividing bow from stem and forearm. Section of bow rounded on top, flat underneath. Lozenge-sectioned stem, forearm rectangular. Spring (two turns) and catch to right. *FGI* no. 662. PLATES 239b, 248, 7.

**Iron, Bronze and Ivory**
*11. Knife. L. 27.6. L. of hilt 7.7. Max. w. of blade 2.5. Th. of blade not measurable. L. of rivets 2. Complete save tip and part of ivory hilt plates. Convex profile from tip to start of butt. Butt flanged to hold the ivory hilt plates, firmly secured by three bronze rivets. These plates extend at least 1.5 beyond the metal butt; their section is plano-convex. Iron stud(?) on hilt plate close to junction of butt and blade: function uncertain. PLATE 245f.

**Miscellaneous**
12. Sea shell. Not illustrated in group, but see PLATE 201d, view of tomb above covering slabs.

**T Tomb 4** (PLATE 157; Contents, PLATE 170). Probably a small earth-cut grave with mud brick surround. No edge was noted, the objects catalogued being found as a surface deposit on the rock.

**Pottery.** Six vases, all of local fabric. All intact except for rim chips, and breaks at the rim and neck of 1 and 2.
1. Jug. H. 9.3. Monochrome, reserved bands, barred handle.
2. Small neck-handled amphora. H. 17.4. Slight ridges mark off the body from the neck and from the foot; pronounced groove at rim. Sharply angled close zigzag in reserved band on belly (drawing inaccurate).
3. Kalathos. H. 4.8. Two string holes, d. 1–2 mm. Monochrome.
4. Kalathos. H. 5.5. One string hole, d. 3 mm. Monochrome. Underside reserved.
5. Kalathos. H. 4.1. Two string holes, d. 2 mm. Monochrome. Underside reserved. Crude and irregular.
6. Shallow bowl with lug handles. H. 4.5. One of the protruding lug handles is pierced by a string hole, d. 2–3 mm, for suspension. Monochrome.

**T Tomb 5** (PLATE 158; Contents, PLATES 171, 220a-e, 234a-b). Shaft grave. Length uncertain; width 45–60; pebble floor at depth c. 50. Cut by Trench II, in which a collapsed slab was removed, as well as the small objects 23–6. Two other cover slabs found *in situ*, one on each side of the test trench. The tomb cutting extended beyond the cover slabs to the W, for a total length of c. 180, cutting the rock at the N side, and the earth fill of the earlier Tomb 14 at the S. No cover slabs or grave offerings were found at the W end of the tomb, except a fibula fragment (18). The W part of the cutting may belong to another tomb (12A?), but no dividing line was observed. It may be concluded that the offerings listed below, all (except 18) found beneath the cover slabs, form a single and probably complete grave group. For the bone fragments see no. 26 below. Further remarks on stratigraphy will be found under Tomb 11.

**Pottery.** A group of nine. 1–4, 6–9 intact, except for rim breaks, and for the surface of 3, much of which has flaked off due to soft firing. All are of standard local fabric. The condition of the oinochoe (1) suggests that it was placed in the tomb new. 5 is fragmentary, of a coarse red ware (see below).
1. Trefoil oinochoe. H. 26.5. Articulated with grooves at the foot and ridges on shoulder, neck and rim. Decorated as shown. PLATE 266g.
2. Trefoil oinochoe. H. 10.4. Poorly made. Monochrome except reserved lower foot, and barred handle.
3. Lekythos. H. 11.8. Monochrome, reserved base of body.
4. Jug. H. 8.2. Monochrome except reserved bands and base of body, and barred handle.
5. Bowl with lug handles, rim fragments. Pres. h. 2.8. D. 11.2. Rim about three quarters preserved, including one lug handle and part of the other. Lower body and base missing. Coarse friable red fabric with grits, smoothed surface. Much of the bowl has disintegrated into powder. Vertical string hole, d. 2 mm., through the fully preserved handle. The bowl probably had a flat base, as has the parallel bowl P39B, 16, which is of the same fabric, and differs only in the lip.

    *6–9.* Four kalathoi, each with two string holes 1–2 cm apart, at the lip.
6. Kalathos. H. 4.3. Reserved dot on the floor. Faint rouletting. Monochrome, reserved bands.
7. Kalathos. H. 4.9. Rouletting. Monochrome.
8. Kalathos. H. 5.2. As 7, but no rouletting. Not drawn.
9. Kalathos. H. 5.1. Monochrome. Reserved underside and central dot on floor.

**Gold.** All in good or excellent condition, except for 14, which is bent. The yellow gold of the earrings (10, 11) differs from the redder gold of the other objects. The rings (12–14) are of thin sheet gold, too fine to have been intended for regular use in the owner's lifetime.
10. Earring. H. 16 mm. D. 10 mm. Wt 1.5 gr. Coil of cast (?) wire, tapering to a point at both ends, overlapping c. 7 mm. Attached below are three mulberries (or grape clusters?) in granulation technique; the grains are coarse and have fused into each other. PLATE 231d.
11. Earring. H. 16 mm. The fellow to 10. PLATE 231d.
12. Finger ring. D. 14 mm. W. 8 mm. Wt. c. 0.5 gr. Plain hoop of sheet gold, hammered surface; convex outside, concave inside.
13. Finger ring. D. 14 mm. The fellow to 12. Not drawn.
14. Finger ring. D. 14 mm. W. 2 mm. Wt. c. 0.25 gr. Carinated hoop of sheet gold.

**Gold with bronze.** Two bracelets in fair condition.
15a. Bracelet D. 3.7–4. Th. 4 mm. Bronze wire coil with gold covering. Wide open hoop, forming a horseshoe.
15b. Bracelet. D. 3.7–4. The fellow to 15a.

**Gold with rock crystal**
16. Two rock crystal beads with gold sleeve. D. 8 mm. D. of string hole 2.5 mm. Spherical, with gold lining held in place at each end by a fine wire collar. Excellent condition.

**Bronze**
*17. Arched fibula with swelling bow (B.II.1/II.6). L. 7. H. 5. Th. 0.8. Complete, but pin broken. Symmetric arch, swelling slightly to the centre, section round. Large catch-plate, spring (two turns) and catch to left.
18. Fibula, fragments. L. of pin 5.7. L. of catch 1.4. Pin, catch and spring fragments. Type not recognisable. Not drawn.

19. Asymmetric arched fibula (B.II.15). Estimated l. 4.8. Pres. h. 3.2. Th. 0.5. Broken: four pieces preserve most of bow, part of spring and pin. Slim rod of round section, thickening slightly at the centre of the bow. Spring (probably one turn) and catch to right.
*20. Arched fibula with central boss. (B.II.14). Pres. l. 3.8. Pres. h. 2.5 Th. of boss 1.8. Catch plate and part of pin lost; what remains broken at spring. Articulated into forearm, bow and stem. The bow is entirely occupied by the boss (large depressed globe), set off either side by two fine fillets. Stem and forearm of square section. Spring (two turns) to right.
21. Fibula, fragment. L. 4.1. Spring and pin only. Spring (two turns) to left.

**Faience.** All white, with pale green surface, in many cases worn off.
22. Small necklace and pendant. One biconical bead, d. 12—13 mm, d. of string hole 1—5 mm. 550 small disk beads, d. 5—6 mm, d. of string hole 1—2 mm, and fragments of about 50 others.
22a. Large beads. 324 large disk beads, d. 8—12 mm, d. of string hole 2—5 mm. A few may be from Tomb 12A (*q.v.*). Roughly made and irregular; the string hole is sometimes off centre and so large that the bead has the form of a ring. No evidence is available from the find positions to enable the necklaces to be strung in their original form. The small and the large disks are strung separately, the biconical bead being allotted to the smaller beads as a central pendant. The length of the small beads, with the biconical beads, as strung, 154 cm; of the large beads, 105 cm. PLATE 234a.

To be associated with Tomb 5: removed in digging Trial II, before Tomb 5 was recognised.

**Gold**
23. Finger ring. D. 15 mm. W. 5 mm. Wt. 0.25 gr. Plain hoop of thin sheet gold, hammered; convex outside, concave inside.
24. Finger ring. D. 16 mm. The fellow to 23.

**Iron**
*25. ?Fibula, fragment. 4.7 × 2.0. Th. 0.9. Part of bow? Thickest at the centre, where section is rhomboidal.

**Bone**
26. Two milk teeth, and three other bone fragments. See Appendix C. Not illustrated.

**T Tomb 6.** Shaft grave (?). 108 × c. 65. Only the S and E edges remain, the rest being cut away by Tomb 14. It intersected Tomb 2 at its E end, and was probably partly overlain by Tomb 4. Earth fill, no surviving contents.

**T Tomb 7** (PLATE 158; Contents, PLATE 172). Shaft grave 243 × 55—75. Depth 60. Earth fill, including red clay (mud brick?); pebble floor. Trench I cut across the centre of Tomb 7 before it was recognised; no objects were found in this cutting nor in the apparent long extension of the tomb on the E side of the trench. Perhaps an inhumation grave, as Tomb 12, unless this long cutting originally contained two shaft graves of average length, that at the E having no contents. At the W end of the tomb were three pots, several skull fragments, and teeth. See p. 277 for the sherds from the fill, which may affect the date of the tomb.

At its W end Tomb 7 cut down through Tomb 8 and partially destroyed it; a dividing wall was built at the S side of Tomb 7, presumably as a support for its cover.

**Pottery.** Three vases of local fabric, the cup no. 2 found in the mouth of the jug no. 1. 1 and 2 lack rim fragments, and 2 was broken, 3 was unbroken, but much of the shoulder and neck has a cracked and flaking surface.
1. Jug. H. 44.6. Two plastic nipples on the shoulder, and a broad neck handle of four separately rolled segments. Decorated as shown. Four groups of semicircles on the shoulder, with three dividing rectilinear panels; in many cases the semicircles run over the first reserved band below, in one case over both. PLATE 260d.

2. Cup. H. 9.3. Decorated as shown; small reserved dot on floor. PLATE 259c.
3. Jug. H. 29.6. Decorated as shown. Four groups of semicircles on the shoulder, with three dividing cross-hatched triangles. Note small painted dots at the compass point; the semicircles run over the reserved bands as on 1. Originally two plastic nipples, one now missing. PLATE 260c.

**T Tomb 8.** Shaft grave (?). L. c. 110. Trace of rock shelf at S and W. About half of the grave was destroyed by the later, but deeper, Tomb 7. No surviving contents. See, however, p. 277 for the sherds from the fill, and their probable date.

**T Tomb 9** (PLATE 158; Contents, PLATE 173). Shaft grave. 130 × 70. Depth 120. Cover slabs at depth c. 60 in the shaft, resting on earth or rock ledges, and held in position by the weight of a second layer of small stones round the edges. The lower compartment was a regular rectangle, 80 × 45, lined with mud brick at each end, and a thin stone slab on one side. Pebble floor. Sole contents, fragments of two fibulae.

**Bronze**
*1. Arched fibula with asymmetrically swollen bow. (B.II.19). Restored l. 4.2. Restored h. 2.8. Th. 0.5. Non-joining fragments of bow, catch, spring and pin. Clearly articulated into stem, bow and forearm; bow set off from the other members by bead and broad fillet mouldings. Swollen bow of round section. PLATE 248,8.
2. Arched fibula, fragments (B.II.1?) Largest piece l. 2.5. Th. 0.15. Non-joining fragments of bow and pin. Apparently parts of symmetric arch, possibly with straightened forearm; slim rod of rectangular section. Not illustrated.

**T Tomb 10.** No tomb.

**T Tomb 11.** Shaft grave (?). c. 100 × 75. Depth c. 20. Shallow rock cutting with pebble floor. Trace of earth and stone ledge at each side. Most of the grave was removed in Trial I. No objects were found, but it was noted that Tombs 1 and perhaps also 2 lay partly beneath it, and so are earlier; the cover slabs of Tomb 5 lay in part over Tomb 11, so 5 is the later. The cutting of Tomb 11 also intersects with the upper shafts of Tombs 6 and 14, which are probably earlier.
      Consequently Tomb 5 is stratigraphically later than Tombs 1, 2 and 11, and probably also later than Tombs 6 and 14.

**T Tomb 12A** (PLATE 159; Contents, PLATE 173). Pit grave with mud brick lining in the upper rock shaft of Tomb 12B, forming a 'double decker'. A mud brick division, th. 12, ran across the upper shaft, at 125 from the S end, and continued along the E side of the tomb as a lining; this forms a rectangular grave, c. 125 × 48. Pebble floor at depth 30. Two jugs were found at this level. The pebble floor appeared to continue beyond the mud brick division to the N, in an area c. 45 × 55, so that possibly two tombs or a double tomb had been placed here. No objects were found at the N end of Tomb 12A, which also lay partly over the earlier shaft cutting for Tomb 8.

**Pottery.** Two vases, 1 intact except for rim breaks, 2 soft fired with crumbling surface, part of lower body and base missing. Local fabric: crudely made.
1. Jug. H. 12.3 Shoulder crudely painted with cross-hatched triangles and vertical lozenge chains (one solid, one cross-hatched, one reserved with solid outline).
2. Jug. H. 8.5. Monochrome.
**Faience**
3. Beads. Several disk beads found inside 2, similar in type to those of Tomb 5. Not illustrated. Found in the surface level at the W edge of Tomb 12A, and possibly to be associated with this tomb.

**Bronze**

*4. Arched fibula with central boss. (B.II.4). L. 4. H. 2.7. Th. of boss 1.2. Complete and intact. Clearly articulated into stem, bow and forearm. The boss set off each side by bead and fillet mouldings; each inner fillet has fine oblique traced lines, suggesting a rope twist. Stem and forearm of rectangular section. Boss of round section, flattened beneath. Spring (two turns) and catch to right. PLATES 239e, 248, 11.

**Faience**

5. Beads. Three disk beads, white with pale green surface. D. 5—8 mm. D. of string hole c. 2 mm.

## T Tomb 12B (PLATES 159, 202d; Contents, PLATE 173). Shaft grave with inhumation. c. 180 × 55, depth 50. Pebble floor. Skeleton in extended position, head to SW; poor condition. On the left shoulder a small oinochoe; on (or beside?) the nose and jaw the fragments of a dress pin. Two glass seals were found in cleaning the tomb.

**Pottery**

1. Trefoil oinochoe. H. 11.5. Standard local fabric. Decorated as shown. PLATE 258a.

**Iron and Bronze**

2. Dress Pin. Pres. l. 6.5. D. of head 1.2 × 0.9 D. of bulb 0.7 D. of shaft 0.3. In three pieces — tip lost. Small oval bronze bead slipped on to shaft 1.5 below the flat disk head. PLATE 250,10.

**Glass.** Two lentoid seals. Both are of yellow-green glass paste with mottled brown and black surface.

3. Lentoid seal. D. 1.5 × 1.7. Th. 0.6. D. of string hole 0.1. Reverse slightly conoid. Surface extremely abraded, Lion right with head down between the forelegs, seen *en face*, mane dotted. PLATE 235b.
4. Lentoid seal. D. 1.6 × 1.8. Th. 0.7 D. of string hole 0.1. Reverse conoid. Broken across string hole, and surface badly abraded. Two calves couchant, regardant in radial symmetry, belly to belly. PLATE 235b.

## T Tomb 13 (PLATES 159, 201b; Contents, PLATES 173—4, 221). Rectangular earth-cut grave, mud brick construction. 160 × 85. Mud brick lining wall 12—16 thick, best preserved at the N end, where it rose 15 above the rock surface, and was originally in an earth-cut pit. At the S end it overlay the upper shaft fill of the earlier Tomb 15. Both on the E and W sides the outline of the tomb was preserved by a shallow cutting in the rock.

**Pottery.** Fourteen vases. Nos. 3, 10—12 broken, and fragments missing from 3 and 10; the rest intact. Most were in a new condition, and probably made for the burial, including specifically nos. 1, 2, 4, 6—9. Nos. 9—11 seem to have been disturbed by the plough. Standard local fabric for all.

1. Trefoil oinochoe. H. 20.5. Note double groove below the rim. PLATE 266f.
2. Miniature jug. H. 9.3. Monochrome.
3. Miniature jug. H. 7.1. Monochrome, lower body and foot reserved.
4. Cup. H. 6.2. Reserved dot on the floor.

*5—14.* Kalathoi. All have two string holes c. 1 cm. apart at the rim, except 8, which has a single larger hole d. 5 mm. All have a small reserved dot on the floor. 5, 7, 11—14 have reserved undersides, 10 is fully painted, 8 and 9 have a reserved cross, and 6 has a cross-hatched underside.

5. Kalathos. H. 6.1. Decorated as shown.
6. Kalathos. H. 3.9. Monochrome, reserved band.
7. Kalathos. H. 4. Reserved band as on 6. Not drawn.
8. Kalathos. H. 5.9. Monochrome.
9. Kalathos. H. 6.7. Monochrome, three reserved boards on the body. Not drawn.
*10. Kalathos. H. 4.8. Monochrome, reserved band at rim.
11. Kalathos. H. 2.7. Monochrome.
12. Kalathos. H. 4.4. Monochrome.
13. Kalathos. H. 4.6. Monochrome. Not drawn.
14. Kalathos. H. 3.5. Crudely made. Monochrome.

**Gold.** Intact, undamaged except 20, which is bent. 15—17 of yellow gold, in excellent condition; the rest have a reddish tarnish.

15. Fibula. L. 5.3. H. 1.2. Wt. 1.25 gr. Bow of sheet gold in the form of a double leaf, with hoop at the top, between the leaves. Catch, with small rectangular catch-plate, to the right. Made from a single piece of gold. PLATE 231c.
16. Earring. L. 1.5. H. 0.9, with wire attachment 2. Wt. 0.75 gr. Spectacle — spiral pendant. Two coils of fine wire linked by a loop; the wire attachment from which it hangs is slightly thicker, has a loop to hold the pendant, and tapers to a point at both ends, which originally overlapped. PLATE 231b.
17. Earring. L. 1.6. The fellow to 16. PLATE 231b.
18. Finger ring. D. 1.4. W. 6 mm. Wt. 0.5 gr. Sheet gold, hammered; convex outside, concave inside.
19. Finger ring. D. 1.3—1.4. W. 3 mm. Wt. 0.5 gr. Sheet gold; profile in form of double ridge.
20. Finger ring. D. 1.4. As 19.
21. Finger ring. D. 1.5. W. 7 mm. Wt. 1 gr. As 18.

**Bronze**
*22. Arched fibula with swollen bow. (B.II.12d) L. 5.6. H. 3.8. Th. of bow 0.8. Complete apart from catch and tip of pin. Clearly articulated into stem, bow and forearm by the two bead and fillet mouldings that set off the bow. Stem of rhomboidal section, forearm rectangular. Section of bow rhomboidal — each facet set off by two fine traced lines; similar traced lines enliven both stem and forearm. Spring (one turn) to left. A particularly fine piece. PLATES 240d, 249, 1.
*23. Bracelet with overlapping ends. D. 4.6 × 4.5. Th. 0.4. W. of terminal 0.5. Complete. Rod of round section, slightly wider, domed terminals. Lightly traced herringbone pattern on the outside near the terminals. Analysis shows an exceptionally high iron content. PLATE 241h.
*24. Bracelet with overlapping ends. D. 4.5 × 4.5. Th. 0.4. W. of terminal 0.55. Complete. The fellow to 23.

**Iron**
25. Fragment. L. 3.3. W. 0.6. Broken at both ends. Rod of rectangular section, a right-angled bend at one end — ?staple. Not drawn, see PLATE 221c.

**Faience**
26. Disk beads. D. 4—5 mm, d. of string hole c. 1 mm. White, with few remaining traces of green glaze. Ten beads found below kalathos no. 10. A further 160 (c. 20 in fragments) found in the soil at the top of the shaft of Tomb 15 which lay below. These very probably belong to Tomb 13, and are strung together on PLATE 221. Included are two cylindrical beads (d. 5 mm, l. 4 mm), one triple segmented bead (d. 4 mm, l. 5 mm), and one double. They form a necklace of length c. 32.
27. Beads found at N end of tomb near nos 1, 11, 12. 68 disk beads, d. 5 mm, d. of string hole c. 1 mm; two short cylindrical beads, d. 5 mm, l. 4 mm, and one larger, d. 4 mm, l. 8 mm; white, surface very worn. Also two smaller cylinders with four segments, d. 2 mm, l. 5 mm, of a blue compound. Strung together these form a small necklace c. 16.5 long. PLATE 221 b, the inner string.

**Bone**
28. Small rectangular plaque. 24 × 10 mm. Th. 3—4 mm. Central hole, d. 5 mm. Surface very worn and irregular.

**T Tomb 14** (PLATES 159, 202d—f; Contents, PLATES 174—5). Shaft grave with cremation urns. Upper shaft 110—130 × 90, trapezoidal shape; cover slabs resting on a broad rock shelf at depth 90. Beneath these a single rectangular stone slab, 65 × 52, resting on a further rock shelf at depth 102. Lower shaft a regular rectangle in plan, 52 × 42, containing two amphorae with cremated ashes. Pebble floor at depth c. 150. On the floor in the NE corner, beside the neck-handled amphora, a 'killed' iron sword and an iron spearhead with bronze ring.

The later Tomb 5 cut into the upper shaft of Tomb 14 in the NE corner; at the S Tomb 14 cut through and destroyed the earlier Tomb 6.

**Pottery.** Two amphorae. No. 1 has pale yellow clay and slip with a rather matt brown paint, thinly applied and much worn — the slip has a tendency to flake off. It is an import. No. 2 is of local fabric. Both intact except for rim breaks on 1.

*1. Belly-handled amphora. H. 43. Decorated as shown. Seven groups of semicircles on the shoulder. Import. PLATE 260a.

2. Neck-handled amphora. H. 38. Decorated as shown. Three groups of semicircles with triangular central filling on the other side; two of the groups intersect. PLATE 260b.

### Iron with bronze

*3. Spearhead. L. 22.8. L. of socket 9.5. D. of socket 2.8. Greatest w. of blade 3.4. Th. of midrib 1. Complete and intact. Divided socket, with opposite rivet holes. End of socket rolled back to hold a bronze crimping ring (0.7 wide) in place. Socket hollow for at least 6 cm. Flattened midrib. PLATE 244a.

### Iron

4. Sword. L. c. 74. L. of hilt 10.5. W. at hilt 4.7. W. of blade 3. Th. of blade 0.9. W. of hilt flange 1.2. L. of rivets from pommel downwards 2.2, 1.6, 1.6. Complete, but bent double at burial; broken in four pieces. Hilt has prominent ears at the pommel; the grip is pinched above the guard, but not below the pommel. Outline of hand-guard straight. The flanges are unusually broad. Two rivets in the grip, two in the guard (iron). No trace of hilt plates to be seen in oxydization pattern. Blade straight-edged, elliptical section. The lower part (below the fold) is covered in cloth remains — woven cover to wooden scabbard? PLATES 237a, 245d.

*5. Fragment. 3 × 1.5. Th. less than 0.1. Scrap of sheet metal broken all round; well preserved. Identity? Not illustrated.

### Faience

6. Bead. One disk bead, d. 5 mm, w. 2 mm, string hole 2.5 mm. White with pale green surface. Not illustrated.


**T Tomb 15** (PLATES 159, 201b−c; Contents, PLATE 176) Rectangular shaft grave. 38−45. Depth c. 35. The grave was cut into the rock except at the S end, where it cut the shaft of Tomb 3, and was provided with a small stone blocking wall. Pebble floor. The later Tomb 13 was constructed with a mud brick lining wall directly above 15; the tomb floors were no more than 30 apart vertically, but disturbance to the contents of Tomb 15 seems to have been limited to the removal of the rim and neck of hydria no. 1.

**Pottery.** No. 1 broken and rim and neck lost, 2−8 intact except for rim chips on 6 and 7 and small breaks on 8. Standard local fabric; note that 7 was burnt to grey throughout.

1. Hydria. Pres. h. 22. Decorated as shown. Five sets of semicircles with triangular central filling on the shoulder; the three sets opposite the neck handle intersect.

2. Lekythos. H. 11.5. Decorated as shown. Three groups of chevrons, the two side ones with three chevrons, the central one with four.

3. Lekythos. H. 10.2. Heavily made; thick wall and handle. Decorated as shown. Four groups of four chevrons.

4. Trefoil oinochoe. H. 9.8. Monochrome, barred handle.

5. Small jug with cutaway neck. H. 6.8. Monochrome.

6. Cup. H. 5.3. Decorated as shown. Reserved dot on floor.

7. Miniature cup. H. 3.7. Monochrome.

8. Openwork kalathos. H. 6.9. Monochrome except for underside and dot on floor. Four incised guidelines on body, marking off two tiers of interlocking cut-out triangles, to form an open zigzag line. In both tiers the standing triangles are smaller than the inverted ones. Careless work: triangle points are often left uncut — too ambitious for the size of the vase?

**Gold.** Four finger rings, no. 9 slightly damaged. Of sheet gold, and unsuitable for normal use in their present form.

9. Finger ring. D. 10−12 mm. W. 6 mm. Wt. 0.25 gr. Hoop of sheet gold, hammered; convex outside, concave inside.

10. Finger ring. D. 12 mm. W. 6 mm. Wt. 0.25 gr. As 9.

11. Finger ring. D. 12 mm. W. 6 mm. Wt. 0.25 gr. As 9.
12. Finger ring. D. 12–13 mm. W. 5.5 mm. Wt. 0.25 gr. As 9.

**Bronze**
13. Dress pin? (fragment). Pres l. 1.4. Th. 0.4. Broken both sides. Slim oval bulb with fillets either side; could come from either a dress pin or the bow of an arched fibula.
14. Rivet. L. 1.5. Th. 0.4. Section round, roughly formed heads; probably from a knife or small weapon. (No trace of iron oxide).

**Iron**
15. Dress pin. Pres. l. 7.4. D. of head 1.0. D. of bulb 1.2. Adhering to 16. Tip lost. Round head, oval bulb defined by fillets. PLATE 250, 11.
16. Dress pin. Pres. l. 8.2. D. of head 1.0. D. of bulb 0.8. Tip lost; in three pieces. Flat disk head, slim oval bulb. PLATE 250, 9.
17. Dress pin. Pres. l. 7.3. D. of head 1.2. In four pieces — joins uncertain. Disk head, shaft apparently plain (an oval bulb might have been expected).

**Faience.** White, surface very worn; slight trace of original green glaze on one or two beads.
18. Disk beads. D. 5–8 mm. D. of string hole 1–2 mm. Ten beads and the fragments of three others.
19. Pendant. Pres. h. 2.6. Broken at upper end. Shape of elongated droplet. A second worn fragment, preserving trace of string hole (h. 9 mm) may belong.

## T. Tomb 16. No tomb.

## T Tomb 17 (PLATE 160; Contents, PLATE 176). Shaft grave. 100 × 45. Rock shelf without cover slabs. Pebble floor. Intersection with Pyre 1 at W end of Tomb 17; the pyre is probably the earlier since no line of burnt earth was noted running across the tomb.

**Pottery.** Local fabric. Intact except for rim chips on 1 and 2.
1. Miniature cup. H. 4.7. Monochrome except reserved foot, band inside lip, dot on floor.
2. Cup. H. 6.8. Decorated as shown. PLATE 259b.
3. Cup. H. 6.7. Decorated as shown. Reserved dot on floor.

**Bronze**
4. Arched fibula with asymmetric swollen bow. (B.II.19). L. c. 6.7. H. 3.8. Th. of bow 1.1. Shattered, but almost complete; catch lost. Clearly articulated into stem, bow and forearm by the bead and fillet mouldings at either end of the bow. Bow of round section. Stem section round, forearm rectangular. Spring (two turns), probably to right. PLATE 248, 6.

**Clay**
5. Pierced clay disk. D. 5. Made by cutting a sherd. Not illustrated.

## T Tomb 18 (PLATE 160; Contents, PLATE 177). 'Trench and hole' shaft grave. 180 × 85. Depth 60, with hole 130. Fill of earth and gravel, with a quantity of ash and sherd at the lower level. In the centre of the floor a stone slab (c. 60 × 60) was found, partially collapsed, covering a circular hole (d. c. 45, depth 70). In this, resting on a floor of conglomerate rock, an amphora containing cremated remains.

**Pottery**
1. Neck-handled amphora. H. 38.7. Intact, excellent condition, placed in grave new. Local fabric. Decorated as shown. Four sets of semicircles; the compass points are c. 8 mm above the supporting band, and covered with a dot (not shown on drawing).

## T Tomb 19 (PLATE 160; Contents, PLATE 177). Shaft grave. 140 × 80. Depth 115. A single large cover slab (c. 125 × 65) rested on a rock ledge at depth 80 in the shaft. Deposit of vases and gold band fragments on floor of natural conglomerate.

**Pottery.** Intact and in good condition, except for handle break on 3. 1 and 2 are Attic imports, and 3 is also an import, but not Attic (see below). 4, with warm pink clay and slip, and dark brown paint, is local.

1. Trefoil oinochoe. H. 12.8. Pale buff clay and slip with black paint. Squat body with slight carination, where two pieces of clay were joined. Decorated as shown. Three cross-hatched triangles on the shoulder. Attic.
2. Feeder (trefoil oinochoe). H. 7.5. Pale buff clay, cream slip, streaky black paint. Monochrome. Attic.
*3. Kantharos, high-handled. H. (with handles) 8.6. Pale buff clay and slip, black paint. Decorated as shown. Neither local nor Attic. PLATE 270c.
4. Pyxis. H. 6.7. Local fabric. Slightly everted lip with opposed string holes, d. 4 mm. Decorated as shown.

**Gold**

5. Diadem. L. 36. W. 1.2. Wt. 2.25 gr. Broken, two small fragments missing. Gold foil. Ends rounded and pierced. Decoration lengthwise in repoussé with a zigzag between double parallel lines, and alongside this a more open double zigzag. PLATE 232d.

**T Tomb 20.** Shaft grave. 115 × 70. Cover slabs resting on a rock ledge at depth c. 80, collapsed in the centre; small lower compartment c. 65 × 55. Rock floor at depth 135. Fill of earth and many stones in upper shaft, yellowish silt and some stones below. The grave was apparently intact, but had no contents.

**T Tomb 21.** Shaft grave 125 × 80. Cover slabs of white magnesite (the largest 65 × 60 × 10), resting on a rock shelf at depth 75 in the shaft. Upper fill of earth and stones, dark silt below. Rock floor at depth 110. Grave intact; no contents.

**T Tomb 22.** (PLATE 160; Contents, PLATES 178–9, 218, 219a). Shaft grave. 160 × 110. Rock ledge at depth 120–145 in the shaft, supporting a set of limestone cover slabs. These were in some places double: at the E end a thinner slab (th. 8) overlay a thicker (th. 15); large central slab, 100 × 60 × 25; heavy stone packing all round the slabs and above them at the W end. Narrow lower compartment, 150 × 55; rock floor at depth 190. The lowest 30 cm were cut into a soft stratum of yellow marl intrusive in the conglomerate. Upper fill of earth and stones, including a large dressed rectangular slab (c. 50 × 40 × 15) at depth 40–60 in the centre of the shaft, perhaps a grave marker. Fine yellow silt below the cover slabs, becoming dark at depth 185, over the floor.

On the floor were five pots together at the E end, and one cup (4) separate, towards the W; also a large number of smaller objects grouped in some order – see PLATE 160 and separate discussion of gold and of bronze objects below. The faience and glass beads were clustered in several groups, and there was a wide scatter of the plain faience disks (29) at W end of grave.

The former presence of another object or objects now perished is suggested by the finding of a number of clay impressions, probably sealing fragments, since at least two preserve a double string hole where two strings unite, and may have covered a knot.

The occurrence of a feeder suggests that this was a child grave.

**Pottery.** Six vases of standard local fabric. The feeder (2) broken, and its spout has been restored; the rest intact and in good condition. 1, 3 and 4 perhaps from the same firing. 5 has an unusually large number of white grits in the fabric.

1. Trefoil oinochoe. H. 19.4. Slight ridge and groove at base of neck. Monochrome, reserved bands.
2. Feeder (trefoil oinochoe). H. 11. Decorated as shown. Three cross-hatched triangles.
3. Jug. H. 12.4. Monochrome, reserved band.
4. Cup. H. 5. Monochrome, reserved bands outside and inside lip, dot on floor.
5. Kalathos. H. 4.5. One string hole. Monochrome, reserved bands.

6. Kalathos. H. 5.2. Two string holes. Monochrome, reserve band.

**Gold.** The objects were placed in a logical position for the head to have been at the W end: rings 7–10 on the left hand, 11–13 on the right hand; bracelet 15 at the left wrist, 14 at the right wrist. All of thin sheet gold.

7. Finger ring. D. 17 mm. W. 6 mm. Wt. c. 0.4 gr. Hoop of sheet gold, hammered; carinated profile. PLATE 230e.
8. Finger ring. D. 15 mm. W. 7 mm. Wt. 0.9 gr. Closed hoop; rounded with slight carination.
9. Finger ring. D. 12 mm. W. 4 mm. Wt. 0.25 gr. Shape as 8.
10. Finger ring. D. 11 mm. W. 6 mm. Wt. 0.5 gr. Shape as 8.
11. Finger ring. D. 15 mm. W. 7 mm. Wt. 0.75 gr. Shape as 8.
12. Finger ring. D. 15 mm. W. 7 mm. Wt. 0.4 gr. Shape as 8.
13. Finger ring. D. 11 mm. W. 6 mm. Wt. 0.5 gr. Shape as 8.
14. Bracelet. D. 4.2–4.6. Th. c. 4 mm. Wt. 1.75 gr. Sheet-gold covering only preserved; no trace of bronze or iron has survived, so perhaps the core was of a perishable material. Plain with flat disk terminals; grooves in three rings at each terminal.
15. Bracelet. D. c. 4.8. Wt. 1.75 gr. The fellow to 14.
16. Bead. D. c. 16 mm. H. c. 7 mm. D. of string hole 3.5 mm. Only gold foil covering preserved, broken and crushed out of shape; originally biconical. Possible trace of glass core.
17. Bead. D. 9 mm. H. 8 mm. D. of string hole 4.5 mm. Sheet gold. Damaged on one side. Decayed fragments of original tin core remain. Biconical.

**Bronze.** A bowl and nine fibulae. The fibulae were found grouped as follows: 20–2 and 27 together to NE of the centre of the tomb, 25 and 26 paired at the centre, 23 and 24 paired slightly to the W. of the centre, 19 separate, between the first two groups.

*18. Carinated bowl. D. at rim 9.7–10. H. 4.7. D of base 3.5. Recomposed from fragments; part of base and wall lost. Raised from a disk casting; undecorated. Slightly carinated at the rim, raised foot. PLATE 243d.
*19. Arched fibula. (B.II.1, variant). L. 6.8. H. 5.3. Th. of bow 0.5. Complete. Symmetric arch, swelling slightly to the centre, section round. Wide catch-plate. Spring (two turns) and catch to right. PLATES 238 m, 248, 3.
20. Arched fibula (B.II.1, variant). L. 4.3. H. 2.5. D. of bow 0.35. Broken but complete. Symmetric arch, swelling slightly at the centre, section round. Relatively wide catch-plate. Spring (two turns) and catch to right.
*21. Arched fibula. (B.II.1, variant). L. 3. H. 1.9. Th. of bow 0.2. Complete; cleaned. Symmetric arch, swelling slightly, section round. Relatively wide catch-plate. Spring (one turn) and catch to right. *FGI* no. 74D.
22. Arched fibula. (B.II.1, variant). L. 3.2. H. 1.9. Th. of bow 0.3. Complete save small part of pin. Symmetric arch, very slightly swelling, section round. Spring (two turns) and catch to right.
23. Arched fibula (B.II.1, variant). L. 3.3. H. 2. Th. of bow 0.2. Catch, part of spring, and all pin lost. Symmetric arch, rhomboidal section rod of even thickness. Spring (two turns) to right.
24. Arched fibula, fragments. (Probably B.II.1). Two fragments, l. 2.8 and 1.9. Part of bow and pin. Probably from a fibula with symmetric arch. Catch to right.
*25. Arched fibula. (B.II.1, variant). L. 3. Pres. h. 1.9. Th. of bow 0.25. Catch-plate and spring lost. Symmetric arch, very slightly swollen at centre, section rounded rhomboidal. *FGI* no. 158.
*26. Arched fibula with central boss. (B.II.14). L. 2.4. H. 1.5. Th. of boss 1.4. Pin and catch lost. Clearly articulated into stem, bow and forearm; boss set off each side by two fine fillets. Stem and forearm square in section by the boss. Spring (two turns) to left. *FGI* no. 1188.
*27. Arched fibula with central boss. (B.II.14). L. 2.5. H. 1.8. Th. of bow 1.2. Complete, pin broken. Strengthened by addition of *iron* rivet through the spring. The fellow to 26. *FGI* no. 1187.

**Faience.** See also under 31(a).
28. Beads and pendant in the form of seated figurines. Beads. H. 19–31 mm. Th. 5 mm. D. of string hole 1–2 mm. 53 beads, pierced laterally at the back of the head: 42 complete, 11 broken and lacking the lower part. Good condition; white core with green glaze well preserved over almost the entire surface.

The beads represent a lion-headed goddess seated in an upright position, with hands resting on the knees; high pointed crown, feline features with prominent nose and protruding jaw; aegis cut in rectangular form hanging from the neck. The throne is flat and trapezoidal with high back; it is marked off from back and thighs by a groove, from lower legs by a narrow slit. In some cases the lower legs are also separated by a slit at the front.

Pendant. H. 15 mm. Th. 3—6 mm. D. of string hole 1—5 mm. Same fabric as beads. It represents Isis nursing the infant Horus, and differs from the rest in several details: high square crown, smaller and more human features, hands clasped over the child on the lap, throne (and consequently the angle of the legs) more rectangular. PLATES 218c, 233d—e.

29.  Small disk beads. D. 3—6 mm. W. 1—2 mm. D. of string hole 1—2 mm. White core, green glazed surface mostly worn off. About 550 beads, strung together on PLATE 219a (third from left); a few others broken. Included are ten double beads, two with three segments, and one with five.

30.  Large disk beads. D. 8—10 mm. W. 2—4 mm. D. of string hole 2—4 mm. Fabric as 29. About 1800 beads strung in six necklaces on PLATE 219a (top, two at left, three at right); about 15 others broken.

### Glass

31.  Necklace. 107 beads strung together. Most were near the bronze bowl (18), but some of the small ones were found separately towards the E end of the tomb. Black vitreous core with pale green or yellow-brown surface patina, slightly lustrous, flaking off in places. Where flaking, the surface of some shows bright purple or turquoise. PLATES 219a (centre), 233c.

(a)  Small beads. 101 complete, about 40 in fragments. Most are oval to barrel-shaped (d. 4—6 mm, th. 5—6 mm, d. of string hole 2 mm); seven are spherical (d. 4—5 mm); eighteen are flattened or disk shaped (d. 6 mm, th. 2—3 mm); one is a rough spiral (two disks not cut through?, d 6 mm, th. 2—3 mm). Seven of the oval beads have a pattern of black and white rings, formed by the addition of a creamy white inlay. One of white faience with pale green glaze was included.

(b)  Large beads. Six altogether: four spherical and two flattened, d. 10—11 mm, th. 7—10 mm, d. of string hole 3—5 mm. Three are plain with slightly lustrous brown and black surface. One has a central groove where an original band of inlay has been lost. Two have the inlay preserved: of these one (d. 13 mm, d. of string hole 4 mm), has a caramel brown patina with central band of inlay in creamy yellow, with oblique division lines showing black; the other (d. 16 mm, th. 12 mm) has an olive green patina and central band of inlay with white border and leaf-shaped pattern in creamy yellow.

**Clay.** Clay impressions, cylindrical or amorphous. Dark red clay, unfired, with hard lime-encrusted surface, soft core disintegrating to powder on exposure. Finger-marks, impressions of wood, reed or basket-work, and string holes show that these were sealings for some perishable object now lost. 32 and 34 (part) were found at the NE of the tomb, 33 and 35 of the SW. PLATE 236 a—g.

32.  Cylinder. D. c. 25 mm. L. c. 32 mm. Broken and disintegrating. A string impression on one side runs up obliquely to meet a string hole (d. 3 mm) on the other, so that the cylinder may have sealed a knot.

33.  Cylinder fragments. D. c. 23 mm. Impression of basketry on one. Not drawn.

34.  Cylinder fragments. One small, d. 15 mm. Two larger, d. 25 mm trace of string hole (d. 3—4 mm) on one, finger-impression on the other. One fragment was beneath the feeder (2), the others were removed with the earth. Not drawn.

35.  Two amorphous fragments. The larger, l. 50 mm, preserves two string holes (d. c. 5 mm) uniting at one side, and impressions of wood or basketry. The smaller, l. 22 mm, has a finger-print.


**T Tomb 23** (PLATE 161; Contents, PLATES 179—80, 220f). Shaft grave. 175 × 85, pebble floor at depth 40. No cover slabs or rock shelf surviving, but fragments of white stone slabs were found in the fill both of this and adjacent tombs. The surface earth in this area (Square VII) was only c. 15—25 deep, and the upper shafts of the tombs have probably been eroded or ploughed away. Tomb vases appeared at the level of the rock surface (Tomb 23) or higher (Tomb 28).

Tomb 23 cuts Tomb 23A at the S, Tomb 24 at the SE, and Tomb 28 at the N. 23A is earlier than 23, since in the area common to both tombs three pyxides (8, 11, 12) lay on the slightly higher floor level of 23, to which they belong, 24 is probably later than 23; its area does not form a complete rectangle, but is cut off at the line of 23, and a blocking wall was put in. 28 is shallower than 23, and the earth line dividing the tomb fills was difficult to identify. It appeared that the cutting for 28 was the earlier; 28 itself, however, was probably disturbed, and its contents not the original ones (see below).

**Pottery.** Thirteen vases: twelve pyxides and the lower part of a jug or oinochoe (no. 1). The pyxides are all complete, but 2 and 11 were broken; no lids were found for 5, 10 and 13, and that of 12 is about three-quarters complete. All are of standard local fabric. 4, 8 and 12 (note same multiple brush for groups of diagonals) probably from same firing; perhaps 3 and 13 also belong to this group. The pyxides are homogeneous, all with slightly everted flattened lip, two string holes (one on each side), and monochrome except for the belly zone, but there are numerous minor variations both in shape and in decoration.

1. Jug or trefoil oinochoe. Pres. h. 13.5. Upper part missing. Probably similar to T 22,1. Monochrome, reserved band.
2. Pyxis with lid. H. 18. H. of lid 3. Decorated as shown. Carefully drawn panelled motives. PLATE 267d.
3. Pyxis with lid. H. 11.4. H. of lid 3. Shape and decoration as 4, with the addition of a narrow reserved band above and below the belly zone. Ten groups of ten alternating diagonals in the belly zone, crudely done and running together. Not drawn.
4. Pyxis with lid. H. 11.7. H. of lid 2.3. Nine groups of nine alternating diagonals; same multiple brush as on 8 and 12.
5. Pyxis. H. 8.5. No lid. Zigzag on belly.
6. Pyxis with lid. H. 10.8. H. of lid 4.4. Reserved bands on belly.
7. Pyxis with lid. H. 10.1. H. of lid 3.1. On belly six double-axe (butterfly) panels alternating with groups of eight vertical lines.
8. Pyxis with lid. H. 11.2. H. of lid 2.4. Shape and decoration as 4, with same multiple brush. Not drawn.
9. Pyxis with lid. H. 12.3. H. of lid 2.2. Double-axe motive alternating with groups of nine vertical lines.
10. Pyxis. H. 7.5. No lid. Shape and decoration as 5. Not drawn.
11. Pyxis with lid. H. 15. H. of lid 2.6. Varied but crude sequence of panels, including meander, multiple rectangles, chequerboard, diamond pattern. PLATE 267b.
12. Pyxis with lid. H. 11.3. H. of lid 3. Shape and decoration as 4, but only eight groups of alternating diagonals; same multiple brush. Not drawn.
13. Pyxis. H. 11.5. Shape as 9, but with underside almost flat. Decoration as 3, but eleven groups of ten alternating diagonals. Not drawn.

**T Tomb 23A** (PLATE 161; Contents, PLATE 181). Shaft grave. 135 × 45—50. Depth 45, pebble floor. Boulder in upper fill at S end. Earlier than Tomb 23 (see above).

**Pottery.** Four local vases, probably made and fired together. All have a reserved zone on rim (1, 2) or body (3, 4) with two crudely painted horizontal zigzags, in all cases done with a double brush.

1. Mug H. 7.7. Decorated as shown.
2. Cup. H. 6.2. Decorated as shown.
3. Pyxis with lid. H. 7.5. H. of lid 2. The lid had no knob. Decorated as shown.
4. Skyphos. H. 5.9. Decorated as shown.

**T Tomb 24** (PLATE 161; Contents, PLATE 181). Shaft grave. 180 × 60; pebble floor at depth 30. In making the first cutting for the tomb the diggers seem to have hit the SE corner of Tomb 23, and then placed a rough division of mud brick to protect 23 and inserted a second blocking of large stones c. 50 from the N end, thus reducing the effective length of the tomb to c. 110.

**Pottery**
*1. Spouted bowl. H. 15.4. Intact except for breaks at the base. Pink to buff clay, purple at the core, with small white grits and micaceous flecks; cream buff slip, thin brown to near black paint inside, pale orange outside. Both slip and paint flaking. Not local. Groups of from seven to eleven oblique strokes on the rim, at handles, spout, and opposite the spout.

**T Tomb 25** (PLATE 161; Contents, PLATE 181). Shaft grave. 215 × 75; rock floor at depth 50. No covers or ledge survive.

**Pottery.** Three vases, of standard local fabric.
1. Trefoil oinochoe. H. 15. Monochrome, reserved band on belly, upper handle barred.
2. Kalathos. H. 8. One string hole, d. 5 mm. Monochrome.
3. Kalathos. H. 8. One string hole. Monochrome; impressed triangles as shown.

**T Tomb 26** (PLATES 162, 202 b–c; Contents, PLATES 182–3, 211). Shaft grave, containing the inhumation burial of a warrior. Rectangular upper shaft, 220 × 110, into which Pyre 4 was dug; ledge at depth 155–160 at a point where the conglomerate rock is interrupted by a band of soft yellow marl. The lower shaft is a regular rectangle, 205 × 65, cut cleanly into the marl. The tool marks are clearly preserved in the sides of the cutting; blade of tool c. 9 wide, with slightly oblique edge; marks mainly horizontal. Rock floor at depth 210.

A little below the rock shelf, lying on earth c. 30 above the floor, thirteen vases (2–6, 8, 9, 11–14, 16, 17) were found at the S and W edges of the graves, and one skyphos (1) at the N end. Beneath 12 and 13, in the SE corner, were stacked two others (7, 10); these had slipped slightly, but could have originally been supported by a wooden cover to the grave, or a coffin whose upright sides would have supported the vases even after the collapse of the lid.

On the floor, skeleton in extended position, head to the S; condition poor. At the left pelvis the corroded remains of ten arrowheads (19); along the left leg an iron sword (18) with the hilt towards the feet; and between the thighs an amphoriskos (15). The position of the sword, and the manner of its break (the hilt higher in the earth than the blade), suggest that it fell from above the covers or the coffin lid, on which it was perhaps placed without regard to the position of the body beneath.

**Pottery.** Seventeen vases. Rim fragments missing from 4 and 5; 9, 12, 16 broken but complete; the rest intact. 1, 2, 7–9, 12, 14, 15, 17 are in an unused condition. The surface of 4, 5, 10, 13 and 16 is worn, 10 and 13 have much surface flaking; 16 burnt to grey (over-firing?) and most of paint lost. Most are of the standard local fabric, including no doubt 16 (see above) and 3, fired grey with streaky black paint. There remain three: 1, 10 and 11. No. 1 is of fine quality, with pale pinkish buff clay and slip, and lustrous black paint; analysis has shown that it is not Attic, and is in fact likely to be Lefkandian. No. 11 is an example of Black Slip ware, and so probably of local origin); no. 10 has the typical combed and incised decoration of Black Slip ware, but is soft fired and flaky, with thick lustrous orange-brown paint where surviving. Most, therefore, are certainly local; all may be.
*1. Skyphos. H. 10.3. Decorated as shown. The side opposite that illustrated has five vertical zigzags between double or triple bars, with no fringe of dots. PLATE 259a.
2. Cup. H. 6. Decorated as shown. The wavy lines on teh outer lip were done with a double brush. PLATE 259d.
3. Lekythos. H. 19.3. Slight ridge at the collar. Monochrome.
4. Lekythos. H. 19.7. Decorated as shown. Four sets of semicircles.
5. Lekythos. H. 13.6. Decorated as shown. Three sets of semicircles.
6. Lekythos. H. 15.5. Decorated as shown. Two sets of semicircles flanking a cross-hatched triangle. This vase contained the iron ?needle (20).
7. Lekythos. H. 15.1. Decorated as shown. Four sets of semicircles. The compass points are well above the supporting band, and the arcs continue below this band (as also on 8, 9 and 16).
8. Lekythos. H. 16.5. Decorated as shown. Three sets of semicircles. As 7 for the arcs.
9. Jug. H. 14.2. Decorated as shown. Three sets of semicircles. As 7 for the arcs.
*10. Jug. H. 14.2. See introductory note for colour and firing. Combed decoration done with a fine six-pointed tool.

11. Trefoil oinochoe. H. 13.4. Black Slip ware. Combed decoration with deep grooves, done with a four-pointed tool. PLATE 268d.
12. Trefoil oinochoe. H. 21.8. Decoration as shown. Four sets of semicircles; cross-hatched triangle opposite handle. PLATE 261e.
13. Trefoil oinochoe. H. 16.5. Surface very worn; decoration probably as PLATE 183.
14. Trefoil oinochoe. H. 15.4. Decoration as shown. Three sets of semicircles. PLATE 261e.
15. Vertical-handled amphoriskos. H. 15. Decorated as shown on both sides. PLATE 261d.
16. Vertical-handled amphoriskos. H. 15.9. Decorated as shown, on both sides.
17. Vertical-handled amphoriskos. H. 16.3. Decorated as shown, on both sides.

**Iron**

18. Sword. L. 56.2. L. of hilt 9.7. W. at hilt 5.2. W. of blade 3.5. Th. not measurable. L. of rivets from pommel 2.1, 2.0 — guard rivets not measurable, but smaller than those in grip. Complete save one pommel ear. Pommel ears barely distinguishable; grip slightly pinched above guard. Outline of hand-guard convex. W. of flange 1.5. The hilt plates seem to have been of ivory, traces of which extend from pommel to end of handguard. Two rivets in the grip, two in the guard (iron). Blade (with elliptical section) straight-sided from below guard until narrows to the paint. Copious remains of wooden scabbard from top to bottom of blade. It seems the top of the scabbard ended in a point which fitted into the V-shaped gap at the bottom of the hilt-plates. Traces of horizontal binding 3 cm below hand-guard line. PLATE 245c.
19. a—j. 'Quiverful' of arrowheads. PLATE 244G.
    (a) L. 3.7. Rest. W. 1.8. Tang th. 0.15. Almost complete; one barb missing. Shaft matrix quite clear both sides.
    (b) Pres. l. 2.7. Pres. W. 1.6. Th. not measurable. Tips of barbs and tang lost. Shaft matrix visible both sides.
    (c) Pres. l. 2.2. Pres. W. 1.5. Th. not measurable. Tang and barbs lost. Shaft matrix visible both sides.
    (d) Pres. l. 3. Pres. w. 1.7. Th. not measurable. Tang and barbs lost. Shaft matrix visible both sides.
    (e) Pres. l. 3.2. Pres. w. 2. Trace of shaft matrix on one face. Fragment of tang embedded in oxydized mass, surrounded by a 'ring' of oxydisation covering the completely decayed split shaft. To this mass should be attributed two tips:
    (f) L. 2. W. 1.3. Not drawn.
    (g) L. 2.5. W. 1.5. Not drawn.
    (h) Pres. l. 2. Pres. w. 1.1. A tang and barb fragment. Not drawn.
    (i) Pres. l. 2.7. Pres. w. 1.6. Point and one barb preserved. Shaft matrix on both sides.
    (j) Pres. l. 2.2. Pres. w. 1.5. Point and barb fragment. Trace of matrix on one side. Not drawn.
    There are in addition two larger and four smaller shapeless scraps of iron from the group.
    These were all flat arrow plates of a type recalling the standard Mycenaean bronze arrow plates. They were evidently slotted into a split shaft tip and probably bound in place by thread or gut. There are no remains of wood as such on the tangs, but the traces of wood replaced by iron oxide, give this impression and show the size and shape of the original shaft, whose diameter was 0.5.
20. Needle? Pres. l. 4.1. Th. of shaft 0.2. Two joining pieces, tip lost. Flattened round head, with round eyelet.

**T Tomb 27** (PLATES 162, 199b; Contents, PLATE 184). Shaft grave. 140 × 65. Narrow shelf at depth 45, thick *strosis* of pebbles on rock floor at depth 112. Large fragments of mud brick in the upper fill, depth 50—80, possibly from collapsed cover. The two vases were found at the E side, high up in the fill (depth 40) and may have been placed over the tomb after covering — the kalathos lay at the edge of the tomb where it cut Pyre 5, but was not associated with the ash fill of the pyre. The other finds were placed on the pebble floor in a logical position for head at N — fibulae at the upper end; below these, strings of beads and two bracelets, each with two finger rings nearby. Further beads were scattered over much of the centre and E side of the grave. Position of three fibulae (12—14) and seal (15) not recorded.

Tomb 27 cut through Pyres 5 and 7, and also cut the S end of Tomb 29, and so was later than all these.

**Pottery.** Two local vases.
1. Cup. H. 5.9. Monochrome, except reserved lower body, and bands outside and inside rim. PLATE 265c.
2. Kalathos. H. 4.5. Two string holes. Monochrome.

**Gold.** Four finger rings, intact and in good condition, of fine sheet gold too fragile for normal wear.
3. Finger ring. D. 1.3–1.5. W. 4–5 mm. Wt. 0.4 gr. Thin sheet gold, hammered, profile rounded like 4–6, but with slight carination.
4. Finger ring. D. 1.3. W. 8 mm. Wt. 0.5 gr. Thin sheet gold, hammered; profile convex outside, concave inside.
5. Finger ring. D. 1.3. W. 4.5. mm. Wt. c. 0.4 gr. As 3.
6. Finger ring. D. 1.3. W. 8.5 mm. Wt. 0.5 gr. As 4. Not illustrated.

**Gold with bronze**
7. Bracelet. D. c. 3.5–4. Th. 4 mm. Open hoop; bronze wire with gold covering. Slightly rounded ends. PLATE 231g.
8. Bracelet. D. 3.5–4. Th. 4 mm. As 7. Not illustrated.

**Bronze**
*9. Arched fibula. (B.II.1, variant). L. 4.7. H. 3.6. Th. of bow 0.3. Complete save tip of pin. Symmetric arch, swelling slightly at the centre, section round. Three groups of fine traced encircling bands — above spring, near centre of arch, above catch-plate. Spring (one turn) and catch to right. PLATE 248, 2.
*10. Arched fibula. (B.II.1, variant). L. 5.2. H. c. 2.8. Th. of bow 0.4. Pin broken, tip lost, catch lost. Symmetric arch, swelling slightly at the centre, section round. Three groups of fine traced encircling bands — above spring (seven), at centre of arch (five), above catch-plate (five). Spring (three turns) and catch to right.
*11. Arched fibula. (B.II.1, variant). L. 4.1. H. 2.6. Th. of bow 0.25. Almost all pin lost. Symmetric arch, swelling slightly at the centre, section round. Three groups of fine traced encircling bands — above spring, on bow much off centre, and above catch-plate. Spring (one turn) and catch to left.
*12. Arched fibula. (B.II.1, variant). L. 3.4. H. 2.3. Th. of bow 0.2. Part of catch-plate and pin lost. Symmetric arch, swelling slightly at the centre, section round. Undecorated. Spring (two turns) to left.
13. Fibula, fragment. Spring d. 0.5. Pres. l. of pin 1.3. Pin tip and part of shaft; spring. Spring of two turns. Not illustrated.

**Iron**
14. Fibula, fragments. 2.2 × 0.7 and 1.9 × 0.5. Both broken at each end. Featureless, but probably from a fibula bow; section probably round. Not illustrated.

**Steatite**
15. Seal. H. 11 mm. L. 19 mm. Soft greyish white fabric; intact and in good condition. Couchant lion: anatomical divisions, features and mane represented with incisions; longitudinal string hole (d. 1.5 mm). Hieroglyphs in three registers engraved on base. See p. 224 for discussion. PLATE 235c.

**Faience**
16. Beads. White, with green glazed surface surviving in places. Larger disk beads. D. 8–10 mm. Th. 2–4 mm. D. of string hole 1–3 mm. About 1095 beads, rather crudely made. One or two are cylindrical, th. up to 7 mm.
    Smaller disk beads. D. 4–5 mm. Th. 2–3 mm. D. of string hole 1–2 mm. About 900. Fragments of about 100 others were collected.

**Glass**
17. (a) Beads, rounded or flattened spherical. D. 9–10 mm. Th. 6–8 mm. D. of string hole 2–3 mm. Pale green core with darker patina, black in places; very friable. Crudely made and irregular. Ten, and fragments of four others.
    (b) Beads, cylindrical or barrel shaped. D. 5 mm. L. 7–9 mm. D. of string hole 2 mm. Black vitreous core with brown or green patina, and an inlay of white bands. Five, and fragments of two others.

**Amber**
18. Beads. Four fragments, surface patinated, cracked and friable. Two are illustrated. The smaller is from

an approximately oval bead, d. c. 8—9 mm, th. 7 mm, d. of string hole 3—4 mm, about one half preserved. The larger is from a bead or pendant, d. c. 14 mm, pres. l. 18 mm, d. of string hole 7 mm. Two other fragments, l. 18 and 19 mm, from this or a similar bead.

**T Tomb 28** (PLATE 161; Contents, PLATE 184). Shaft grave. 120 × 55, depth 30. No ledge surviving. Many stone slab fragments (white magnesite) in the fill, evidently disturbed rather than fallen. Two vases at the N end of the grave, no. 1 upright, no. 2 upside down; both were found above the surviving rock surface, and may represent a later or secondary group of offerings placed there after the disturbance had taken place.

Tomb 23 cuts the S end of Tomb 28 and is later, but not necessarily later than vases 1 and 2.

**Pottery**
1. Miniature neck-handled amphora. H. 17.1. Local fabric. Intact except for break on rim. Slight ridge at the collar. Monochrome, reserved band, barred handles.
2. Cooking pot. H. 11.4. Intact. Hand-made. Coarse red clay with grits, burnished surface, blackened on side opposite handle. An unusually strong and thick-walled example of this shape.

**T Tomb 29** (PLATES 162, 199b, Contents, PLATE 184). Shaft grave, c. 105 × 60. Broad rock shelf on the E side, at depth 30, corresponding to the floor of the earlier Pyre 7, as this survives on the W side. Pebble floor at depth 60. In the fill, a boulder at the N end, mud brick fragments and stones at the centre are probably partly collapsed covering material, and partly a blocking against the loose fill of Pyre 7. On the floor a cup.

**Pottery**
1. Cup. H. 6.7. Broken, but complete except rim chips. Local fabric. Decorated as shown. Zigzags done with double brush.

**T Tomb 30.** Shaft grave. 100 × 50. Mud brick lining on long sides at depth 20, leaving a central slit with rock floor at depth 40. Above the floor, a layer of dark earth 10 cm deep; no other contents. From the size, probably a child's grave.

This grave was the farthest north of those so far dug, set apart from the others, and cut into the flat rock platform at the apparent edge of the cemetery.

**T Tomb 31** (PLATES 163, 200d; Contents, PLATES 185—6, 226). Shaft grave. 140 × c. 85. Cover slabs at depth 30—55, resting on a rock shelf at the N side, and a mud brick support at the S side, which ran across the fill of Tomb 35 beneath. On the cover slabs lay a cooking pot (9), whose top was level with the rock surface. Pebble floor at depth 75, on which rested a rich group of pottery, gold and bronze objects. Dimensions of individual mud bricks 45 × 20 × 35. Tomb 35 lay beneath at the S side.

**Pottery.** Nine vases. 7—9 have fragments missing, 2 is broken but complete, the others are intact. 1—4 are Attic, with pale buff clay and slip, and lustrous black paint on the broad areas and bands, but lighter brown on narrow bands and for the panel decoration. 7, a miniature vase, is also Attic. 5, 6 and 8 are local, the clay being a similar pale buff to that of the Attic, the slip cream buff, and the paint varying from orange-brown on 5, to brown on 6, and streaky black on 8. For the hand-made pot 9 see the catalogue entry.
*1. Trefoil oinochoe. H. 26. The underside has concentric circular ridges. There are two plastic nipples on the shoulder. Decorated as shown. Attic. PLATE 272a.
2. Feeder (cup with high handle). H. 7.7, with handle 9.3. Decorated as shown. Attic.
3. Trefoil oinochoe. H. 11.7. Decorated as shown. Attic.

4. Trefoil oinochoe. H. 17.3. Decorated as shown. Attic.
5. Skyphos. H. 4.7. Decorated as shown, both sides identical. Local atticising.
6. Kalathos. H. 5.1. Two string holes. Monochrome, reserved bands.
*7. Miniature trefoil oinochoe. H. 7.9. Monochrome, reserved bands. Attic.
*8. Miniature cup. H. 3.8. Very thin walls. Monochrome, reserved bands.
9. Cooking pot. H. 20.1. Hand-made. Coarse ware with white grits, burnished surface. Blackened beneath and on side opposite handle.

**Gold.** Six finger rings, all intact and in good condition; 10–13 were found clustered together, 14 inside the bronze bowl (20) with its finger-bone, 15 on its own at the S side of the tomb. Also three rectangles of foil.

10. Finger ring. D. 17 mm. W. 5.5. mm. Wt. c. 0.4 gr. Hoop of sheet gold. Five ridges. PLATE 230h.
11. Finger ring. D. 14 mm. W. 9 mm. Wt. 0.4 gr. Hoop of sheet gold. Profile carinated between double ridges. Not drawn. PLATE 230c.
12. Finger ring. D. 11 mm. W. 9 mm. Wt. 0.25 gr. Plain hoop of gold foil. PLATE 230a.
13. Finger ring. D. 10 mm. W. 8.5 mm. Wt. 0.25 gr. Like 12, but slightly ridged at the edges. One edge has two ridges, the other, one. PLATE 230b.
14. Finger ring. D. 15–16 mm. W. 9 mm. Wt c. 0.4 gr. As 11.
15. Finger ring. D. 12 mm. W. 8 mm. Wt. 0.25 gr. Hoop convex outside, concave inside.
16–18. Foil, three cut rectangles. 16 × 17 mm. One intact, the other two broken or frayed. The covering for perishable objects now lost.

**Gold with rock crystal**
19. Pendant. H. 19 mm. Max d. 11 mm. Globular pendant of rock crystal, with cylindrical extension at upper end, over which a gold sleeve is fitted; upper suspension loop now lost. (cf. the surface find, PLATE 243e, which is complete). The pendant is pierced and has a gold lining. The crystal element is broken at the shaft, but otherwise intact and in excellent condition.

**Bronze**
*20. Phiale mesomphalos. D. at rim 11. H. 4. Complete, but cracked. Raised from a disk casting. The omphalos is very small, with only a slight indent on the underfoot. Plain lip; undecorated. PLATE 243e.
21. Arched fibula (B.II.4). L. c. 4.8. H. c. 2.3. W. of bow 0.7. In several fragments; part of pin lost. Bow a flat crescent; pin and spring, round section. Spring (one turn) and catch to right.
22. a, b. Leaf-bow fibula with loop, two fragments. (?Variant of B.I.8). Pres. l. c. 4. W. 0.5. All that remains is parts of the bow and pin. Bow probably hammered from a basic wire rod of which the centre was pinched into a vertical open loop (nearly all lost). Cf. P3,26, and the gold version T 13,15. But restored in drawing as *two* tiny fibulae with leaf bow (l. c. 2.8 and 3.0), PLATE 186.
*23. Arched fibula with swollen bow. (B.II.12c). Pres. l. 2.4. Pres. h. 1.8. Forearm, catch-plate, and part of pin lost. Small and delicate brooch, clearly articulated into stem, bow and forearm by a pair of fine fillets either side of the bow. Bow section plano-convex. Stem section round. Spring of at least one turn.

**T Tomb 32** (PLATES 164, 201a; Contents, PLATES 186, 280). Large shaft grave, 280 × 130. Rock shelf at depth c. 100, forming a lower compartment c. 240 × 80; traces of mud brick or mud plaster lining on the N side. Rock floor at depth 160. Blocking wall at the W end where the shaft cut the earlier Tomb 35 and Pyre 9. Running across the centre of the tomb at depth 80–90 is a dividing or blocking wall, c. 35 wide, two courses high and resting on earth fill, presumably later, purpose unclear. At the SW corner Tomb 32 apparently cut another shaft grave (Tomb 37), not yet fully excavated. The character of the fill to the E of the central wall is unusual. The presence of mud brick fragments and large stones at depth 90–140 is not surprising; but as well as these there were numerous sherds (discussed separately, pp. 278–279), most of which belonged to amphorae, and of these the majority to massive amphorae (at least five) of the type closely associated with pyres; and there was also a considerable amount of black ash. A likely interpretation is that some of the sherds, and the ash, represent the disturbed fill of a pyre (10) which was entirely cut away and destroyed in the construction of Tomb 32, and this is reinforced by the presence, around the E end of the tomb shaft, of a thick crust of red fire-baked earth, explicable as the side wall of the destroyed pyre. The massive sherds represent, however, more amphorae than would be placed in one pyre, and it may consequently be hazarded that the fill contained material from other disturbed or destroyed pyres as well.

In contrast to this, the offerings associated with the tomb were all found on the floor, at the E end. The plan shows an arrangement of objects suitable to a body with head to the E — a hair spiral at the head, groups of dress pins and fibulae by the right and left shoulders respectively, five rings by the left hand, one ring (and two small fibulae) by the right. Only the Ptah figurine, furthest to the W, is not connected. No trace of bone was found, so the arrangement would be symbolic. No vase was found that could be attributed to this tomb.

**Gold.** Unless otherwise stated, intact and in good condition.
 1. Hair spiral. L. 2.7. D. of finials 9 mm. Wt. 2.8 gr. Plain wire, thickening at the ends, where attached to two disk finials which are conical above and flat beneath. Bent out of shape from the original spiral (see S 33,14).
 2. Finger ring. D. 20—21 mm. W. 3 mm. Wt. 0.5 gr. Hoop of sheet gold; profile with double carination. PLATE 230f.
 3. Finger ring. D. 20—21 mm. W. 3 mm. Wt. 0.5 gr. As 2.
 4. Finger ring. D. 17—20 mm. W. 5 mm. Wt. 0.5 gr. Broken. Plain hoop of sheet gold, with ridge at upper and lower edge.
 5. Finger ring. D. 19 mm. W. 4 mm. Wt. 0.5 gr. As 2.
 6. Finger ring. D. 16—17 mm. W. 4 mm. Wt. 1.0 gr. Like 2, but with three ridges. PLATE 230g.
 7. Finger ring. D. 16—17 mm. W. 4 mm. Wt. 1.0 gr. As 6.
 8. Foil. Three fragments of twisted foil. L. 8.6, 3.5, and 2. Wt. 0.9 gr. Probably the covering for the gilt iron pin 9. Found laid separately, and near 9 on the tomb floor.

**Gold with iron and amber**
 9. Gilt iron pin. Pres. l. 22.5. D. of head 1.4. D. of bead 1.3. D. of reel 0.5. Disk head, long pin of round section; at 3.3 from the head a gilt reel, l. 1.5, with amber head. The next section of the pin, which is very encrusted, was made separately; details probably as for 10 below. PLATE 231e.
 10. Gilt iron pin. Pres. l. 19.3. D. of head 1.4. Fragmentary. Gilt surface preserved on the head, and on a separate section, l. 4, which will have come below the reel with amber bead (now missing); at each end of this section is a ring of fine gold wire, d. c. 4 mm., with granulation — this latter preserved only at the lower end.

**Bronze**
*11. Arched fibula. (B.II., but of a type not represented). L. 7.5. H. 4.5. In three pieces, but complete apart from chipped catch-plate. Symmetric arch of even thickness, round section. The bow is decorated with three oval bosses (th. 0.7), each set off by fillets either side. Catch-plate short but wide. Spring (two turns) and catch to left. *FGI* no. 1559A. PLATE 238n.
*12. Arched fibula. (B.II.?). L. 7.5. H. 4.5. Complete. The fellow of 11. Spring (two turns) and catch to right. *FGI* no. 1559B. PLATE 248, 4.
*13. Arched fibula with central boss. (B.II.14). L. 5. H. 3. Th. of boss 2.6. Complete. Clearly articulated into stem, bow and forearm; the boss is set off both sides by two fine fillets with fine oblique traced lines, suggesting a rope twist. Stem and forearm of square section close to the boss. Spring (two turns) and catch to left.
*14. Arched fibula with central boss. (B.II.14). L. 5.2. H. 3. Th. of boss 2.6. Complete. The fellow of 13. Spring (two turns) and catch to right. PLATES 239f, 248, 12.
*15. Arched fibula. (B.II.1, variant). L. 3.7. H. 2.3. Th. of bow 0.3. Complete. Symmetric arch, slightly swollen at the centre, section round. Three groups of fine traced encircling bands — above catchplate and at two points off-centre of bow. Spring (two turns) and catch to left, PLATE 248, 1.

*16. Arched fibula. (B.II.1, variant). L. 3.6. H. 2.1. Th. of bow 0.3. Nearly complete; pin broken, tip missing and catch chipped. The fellow of 15. Spring (two turns) and catch to right.

**Faience**

17. Amulet, in the form of a Ptah figurine. H. 2.8. D. of string hole 1.5 mm. White with patches of pale green where surface less worn. Flat at the back and beneath; string hole beneath ears. Features entirely worn. Large head with protruding ears and bulging forehead; hands on pot belly; stumpy legs. Crudely made. For discussion see p. 224 below. PLATE 235a.

**T Tomb 33** (PLATES 163, 200c, 201a; Contents, PLATES 187–8, 227, 228a–b). Shaft grave. 160 × 110; heavy stone slabs (20–30 thick) resting on a rock ledge; pebble floor at depth 140. A large boulder (25 × 40, h. 40) was found in the fill at the E end of the tomb, projecting above rock surface: perhaps a grave marker. On the floor a rich group of offerings, pottery, bronze vessels and jewellery. The objects (note the absence of dress pins and fibulae) may be laid out as though the head was at the W: a diadem at the 'head', then bracelet, beads and pendants, and below, centrally, a gold leaf attachment.

Tomb 33 slightly cuts the shaft of Tomb 35, and is later.

**Pottery.** Five vases. Rim chips missing from 1, handle and spout tip from 3, rim and neck from 4; 2 and 5 broken but complete. 1–4 are Attic imports. is hand-made, local, with pink clay, buff slip and pale orange-brown paint.

1. Trefoil oinochoe, high handle. H. 17.7, with handle 20. Decorated as shown. Attic.
2. Feeder (high-handled jug). H. 8.5, with handle 10.5. Decorated as shown, add as follows: four zigzags along the flat surface of the spout; opposite the spout the meander panel has a fill of chevrons, then two vertical bands with chevrons and zigzag, between bars. Attic. PLATE 272b.
3. Feeder (trefoil oinochoe). H. 7.7. Decorated as shown. Attic. PLATE 272c.
4. Trefoil oinochoe. H. 9.7. Decorated as shown. Attic.
*5. Miniature trefoil oinochoe. H. 6.3. Hand-made. Monochrome, one reserved area.

**Gold**

6. Diadem. L. 17.4. W. 9–10 mm. Strip of gold foil, rounded at the ends, and pierced for attachment. Decoration in repoussé: border of raised dots, impressed zigzag down centre. PLATE 232b.
7. Diadem fragments. Two fragments. L. 5.1 and 2.1. W. 0.75. Wt. 0.5 gr. Gold foil band, turned over at the ends (l. of fold 2 mm). Both ends preserved, decayed at the centre, original length uncertain. Slight traces of decoration in dot-repoussé: at the right a stag (?) running to right, with hound at its neck; next to this a large animal (lion couchant?) to left. At the left end traces of a bovine (head and one leg) facing left. PLATES 187, 232c.
8. Band. L. 19 mm. W. 7.5 mm. Plain rectangular band of gold foil turned over at one end (l. of fold 3 mm); seven tiny gashes at the other end. Not drawn.

   *9–12.* Foil coverings for beads etc.
9. (a) L. 3. D. 8–12 mm. Shape approximately cylindrical, with central swelling. Repoussé decoration of fine lines: about 28 rings with light horizontal hatching between.
   (b) Three other bead coverings. L. 3.5, 2.5, 2.5. As 9a.
10. (a) L. 3.3. Poor condition; plain, probably cylindrical.
    (b) Five other beads. L. 2.1, 1.9, 2.8, 3.7, 1.7. As 10a. Possible traces of repoussé on one.
11. Foil covering. L. 2.8. Rectangular. Traces of dot-repoussé decoration.
12. Three beads (?). L. 10, 19, and 20 mm. W. 4–5 mm. Plain; simple strip of sheet gold, with a slight fold at one edge.
13. Strap (?). Pres. L. 2.7. W. 4 mm. Gold foil, folded over at one end, rounded at the other; edges slightly undulating (as the attachment straps).
14. Attachment with straps. H. 5.3. L. of straps 4 and 7. Wt. c. 1.0 gr. Concave sides, flat at the top, triangular at the tip. Repoussé decoration of zigzag lines within a border. The straps are of gold foil, w. c. 5 mm; they attach with tiny hooks to holes at each side of the top and bottom; the lower one forms a circle c. 16 mm. diameter, the upper one c. 3 cm.

**Bronze**

*15. Squat oinochoe. H. 8.6. Max. d. 11. D. of mouth 7.2. D. of base 9. D. of rivet head 1.3. Complete, though badly cracked. Body in one piece, with separately attached cast handle. The body may be hammered. Slightly flaring round mouth and neck set on shoulders broad in relation to height. Handle attached through its rotelles below lip and through the lower attachment on to the shoulder. The strap and upper attachment are in the form of a lotus spray, with a bud between two leaves; the three stems are 'tied' at two points. The lower attachment has light relief ornament suggesting either a palmette or a scallop. Traces of cloth remains on the shoulder. PLATE 243a—c.
16. Hemispherical bowl. D. 13.7—14.4. H. 7. W. of lip 0.35. Complete. Raised from a disk casting. Plain rim, flat top, internal lip. In raising the vessel, the smith left a zone 1.5 wide inside immediately below the lip of double thickness, evidently to strengthen the rim. Undecorated. PLATE 243f.
17. Bracelet. D. 5. W. at terminal 0.7. Th. c. 0.1. Broken in three places, chips lost. Flat strip, wider at the squarish terminals, which apparently overlapped. Very finely traced decoration of double zigzag follows edge, apparently all the way round.

**Rock Crystal**

18. Pendant. H. 3. D. of string hole 3.5 mm. Slightly chipped. Droplet shape, but flat at back. Decorated with a vertical groove at the centre, both above and below the string hole. PLATE 234d.
19. Bead. D. 1.4. D. of string hole 4—5 mm. Flattened globular. PLATE 234d.

**Amber**

20. Pendant. H. 2.4. W. 1.4—1.8. D. of string hole 4—5 mm. Broken but complete. Dark red at surface and core, of resinous appearance with waxy lustre. Trapezoidal, surfaces slightly curving, edges rounded. An attractive deep red jewel. PLATE 234c.
21. Bead(s), three fragments. L. 2.3, 2 and 2. Condition inferior, cracked and friable surface; clear deep red core with orange-brown surface; patinated. Outside surface slightly rounded. Trace of string hole on long axis. Possibly from two elongated oval beads.

**Glass**

22. Bead (or pendant). L. 1.9. D. of string hole 3 mm. Oval, flattened on one side. Orange-brown core, surface decoration in white and brown.
23. Bead. D. 1.1. D. of string hole 3 mm. Flattened globular yellow-brown core, black surface with central band in white.
24. Bead(s). Three fragments. D. 1.0—1.1. From bead or beads in same techniques as 21. Pale greenish brown to fawn core; surface decoration in white streaks.
25. Bead fragments. D. c. 7 mm. Flattened globular.

**T Tomb 34** (PLATES 165—6). Shaft grave. 180 × 95. Five cover slabs of limestone and white magnesite in position on broad mud brick shelves at depth c. 110. The slabs well cut and only c. 10 thick; double layer at the S end. In the upper fill, almost level with the rock surface two slabs (L. c. 50), perhaps displaced grave markers. The fill contained black ash from the two pyres overlying the tomb. Trough-like lower compartment 180 × 40, depth 27, containing sections of fallen mud brick (dimensions 17 × 6 × 8). The shelves on the long sides were constructed of regular layers of mud brick (or pisé) 8 cm. high, separated by a thin layer of yellow clay, c. 3 thick. Pebble floor at depth 135; no contents.

Pyres 8 and 9 lay over Tomb 34 and were later.

**T Tomb 35** (PLATE 201a). Shaft grave. 225 × 110. Cover slabs resting on rock cut ledges at depth 125: one missing, the rest *in situ*. The lower compartment, 195 × 57, forms a regular rectangle, cut into a layer of soft yellow marl which underlies the conglomerate from a depth of c. 90. Shape of cutting, technique and tool marks very similar to those of Tomb 26. Rock floor at depth 180. No contents.

Tomb 35 was cut by Tombs 31, 32 and 33, and is earlier than all three. The absence of one cover slab, which lay in the line of both Tombs 31 and 32, and the close similarity of this tomb to Tomb 26, suggests that it was robbed during the period of the cemetery's use.

**T Tomb 36** (PLATE 164; Contents, PLATES 188–9, 228c–d, 229). Disturbed surface tomb of mud brick construction found only 15 below the surface (within reach of the plough blade), when Trench VII was extended to include the whole of Tomb 28. It was not possible to define the area of the tomb; there were slight traces of mud brick at N and W, but nothing survived at S or E. It was perhaps a rectangle c. 100 × 125 (cf. Tomb 5).

The very rich objects found, though disturbed both before and in the first minutes of excavation, appear to form a coherent and contemporaneous group. The position of most is noted on the plan.

**Pottery**
1. Kalathos. Pres. h. 2.8. D. at rim 12. Rim and upper body fragments only. Local fabric. Conical, with flaring lip. Two reserved bands preserved on outer body.

**Gold.** Sheet gold for the two rings (4, 5) and two larger attachments (6, 7), foil for the other objects.
2. Diadem. L. 37. W. 1. Broken, but complete and in good condition. Rounded at the ends, and pierced. Decoration in dot-repoussé, border of dots with central zigzag. PLATE 232a.
3. Band fragments. L. 38 mm and 33 mm. W. 5–6 mm. Rectangular strips of plain gold foil, folded over at the ends (fold of 1–2 mm).
4. Finger ring. D. 12 mm. Wt. 0.5 gr. Plain hoop of sheet gold. Profile convex, with very slight carination. Clear marks of hammering on outside surface.
5. Finger ring. D. 12 mm. As 4.

*6–15.* Attachments. 8 broken (fragments of two? see below), 12 fragmentary, 10 frayed at one corner; the rest intact and in good condition. All have repoussé or dot-repoussé decoration. Two (6, 7) are larger and stouter than the others, and are somewhat rounded in profile, so as to fit closely over a cylindrical object. The rest are flat, and of these two (14, 15) are smaller than the others. Most are triangular or slightly rounded at the lower end; 8 tapers to a fine rounded point. All except 15 are pierced, with two holes at the top, and two at the broadest point towards the lower end, so as to hold straps. Straps or strap fragments are preserved in place on 8 and 11–15; the lower straps of 8 and 12–14 form a circle of diameter c. 15 mm and 12 mm respectively. The strap of 14 is threaded through two slits in the attachment, and pierced at each end for a string or wire, while the others taper to form a fine wire hook which fastens to the attachments. The straps at the upper end are the longer — 14.0 (8), and 8.5 (11); see also no. 16 below. The strap of 15 differs in that it extends at the top to form a band in one piece with the body, l. 5.2. (cf. Tomb 3, 8–9, which however are split, and do not have the same flat top).
6. Attachment. L. 7. W. 20–25 mm. Wt. 3.3 gr. Ridge at the borders; vertical at the centre with zigzag on either side; narrow band across the widest point. PLATE 232g.
7. Attachment. L. 5.8. W. 19–31 mm. Wt. c. 1.9 gr. As 6 but without cross-band at the bulge. On this example only the sheet metal is folded over at the edges (fold of 1–2 mm.) as a strengthening. PLATE 232h.
8. Attachment. L. 7. W. 10–16 mm. Straps in position at top and bottom. The decoration of the upper fragment differs from that of the lower, and (unless we are dealing with the fragments of two with identical break, thus making a total of eleven, and not ten, attachments) this suggests that an ancient mend was made, joining parts of two separate attachments. Border and central vertical line of dots; zigzag on the lower fragment, cross-hatching on the upper — but if the suggestion of a mend is correct, the fragment was used in reverse, with original face back up.
9. Attachment. L. 5.6. W. 13–20 mm. Wt. 1.0 gr. Border and central vertical line of dots; cross-hatching on either side. Associated are a strap l. 3.9, tapering to a fine pointed hook, and the fragment of another, l. 5. PLATE 232g.
10. Attachment. L. 5.5. W. 10–15 mm. As 9.
11. Attachment. L. 5. W. 8–11 mm. Border and double central line of dots. Upper strap in position (l. 8.5, w. c. 0.8 mm). PLATE 232h.

12. Attachment. Pres. l. 2.4. W. 8—11 mm. Lower end fragment only, with circling strap intact (d. 12 mm, w. 1 mm). The fellow to 11.
13. Attachment. L. 4.7. W. 9—13 mm. Decoration as 9. Lower strap in position but broken (l. 27 mm, w. 3 mm). A small fragment of the upper strap is also attached.
14. Attachment. L. 4.2. W. 8—16 mm. Wt. c. 0.6 gr. Herringbone decoration with border of dots.
15. Attachment. L. 3.2. W. c. 7—15 mm. For shape see introductory note. Finely decorated with a border of hatching between parallel lines; the central area has a border of dots, central vertical line of dots, and a cross line at the widest point.
16. Straps. Associated with the attachments 10—15.
    (a) L. 13.4. W. 4 mm. Tapering to a fine wire hook. Also the fragment of a second similar strap, and of a narrower one, w. 3 mm.
    (b) L. 5.3. Max. w. 4 mm., with hooks as 16a. L. without hooks c. 4.5.
17. Disk(s). D. 3.2. Broken and frayed. Plain disk of gold foil with central hole for attachment, folded over at the edges — the cover for an object of perishable material. Two fragments, the second probably from another similar example.

### Gold with Rock Crystal
18. Bead. D. 17 mm. W. 13 mm. D. of string hole 5 mm. Flattened sphere of rock crystal, with gold sleeve inside the string hole. PLATE 234f.

### Rock Crystal
19. Bead. D. 17 mm. As 18, but no gold sleeve surviving.

### Gold with Faience
20. Scarab. L. 16 mm. H. 8 mm. D. of string hole c. 1 mm. The gold fitting covers the lower part of the beetle, and there is a wire ring, th. 0.7—0.8 mm, round the base and round the string holes. Scarab of white faience; slight trace of green glaze in the upper hieroglyph; the wings and horns represented by light incisions. Hieroglyphs in three registers. See p. 224. PLATE 235d.

### Steatite
21. Cuboid amulet. L. 12.5 mm. H. 22 mm. W. 11—12 mm. A small fracture in the upper surface shows a grey-blue core; hard white surface, well preserved, but covered with small cracks. Traces of dark green colouring matter in the incisions and between the crenellations on the upper barrel 'roof'. See commentary, p. 224. PLATE 235a,e.

### Faience
22. Disk beads. D. 4—6 mm. W. 1—2 mm. White, with pale green surface in many cases. 40 beads, which form a string l. 6.5, and the fragments of about eight others.

### Bronze
*23. Fibula with crescentine bow (B.IX.1). L. 10.8. H. c. 9.2. Complete but broken. Clearly articulated into stem, bow and forearm. The stem is enlivened by close-set fine encircling lines, over which is fitted a separately made star-shaped bead ('paddle-wheel'). The stem is separated from the bow proper by two fine fillets enclosing a small panel decorated with two fine traced zigzag bands. The forearm is picked out by a bead and fillet moulding; the bead is decorated with traced crossed lines. The bow is decorated on both sides in pointillé technique, apparently with an identical design. It is outlined by close-set dots. The main ornament is an encircled equal-arm Maltese cross, whose arms are stippled. This design is tangential to a widening chevron band drawn from the centre of the bottom edge of the bow out to its perimeter. Spring (two turns) and catch to left. PLATES 241c, 249, 7.
*24. Arched fibula (B.II.12). Pres. l. 13.1. H. 7.5. Th. of bow 1.7 × 1.0. Nearly complete — tip of pin and scraps of catch-plate lost. Clearly articulated into stem, bow and forearm by the bead and fillet mouldings which set off the swollen bow. Groups of fine traced crossed lines on the forearm. Bow elliptical section, with fine relief ridges on both upper and lower surfaces. The spring was anciently broken, and clumsily repaired with a crude bronze rivet. Spring (two turns) and catch to right. PLATES 240b, 249, 3.
*25. Arched fibula. (B.II.12). L. 8.9. Pres. h. 3.7. Bow, part of stem and forearm only. Similar to 24, but smaller, and lacking its refinement. The bow is set off by bead and fillet mouldings; its section is an angular ellipse. The stem is rhomboidal, the forearm rectangular. No relief ridges on the bow.

26. Child's bracelet. D. 3.5 × 3.5. Th. 0.25. Broken; one terminal lost. Slim rod, slightly swollen at the centre, bent into open hoop. Tapers to rounded terminal.

**Amber.** Two beads and a pendant, all partly decayed and incomplete, though the original shape is clear. Dark red glassy core, brittle surface with deep cracks.

27. Pendant. H. 1.1. D. 1.2. D. of string hole 5 mm. Rounded cone with flat underside. Surface plain and worn.
28. Bead. L. 2.7. D. 1.1–1.7. D. of string hole 4–5 mm. Broken and much worn. Amygdaloid, with oval section. The fragments Tomb 33,21 are of the same bead type.
29. Bead. D. 15 mm. W. 10 mm. D. of string hole 3 mm. Flattened spherical.

**Ivory**
30. Pin fragments. Four fragments, not joining; combined l. c. 12.5. Badly decayed, surface cracked and pitted. Flat head, section slightly oval, d. 10–11 mm.
31. Flakes of ivory, with flat surface, from a separate object, form now lost. Not illustrated.

**Clay**
32. Pierced disk. D. 4.5. Counter formed by cutting a plain sherd.

**Bone**
33. Four human teeth, immature. See Appendix C.

**Shell**
34. Two large pecten shells. H. 9.6. PLATE 237c.

**T Tomb 37** (Contents, PLATE 189). Shaft grave, partially excavated, apparently cut into by Tomb 32. Pebble floor at depth c. 90. It is presumed that the pottery below is from this tomb.

**Pottery**
1. Lekythos. H. 10.2. Reddish brown clay, buff slip, black paint. Decorated as shown. Five cross-hatched triangles.
2. Trefoil juglet fragments. Rim, neck and handle, and some body fragments, preserved. Soft friable brown clay with black burnished surface. Not illustrated. For two similar vases see Tomb 2, 6 and 7.

**T Pyre 1** (Contents, PLATE 190). Rectangular rock cutting c. 180 × 100, depth 160. Black carbon deposit c. 20 thick on the pyre floor, higher at the sides. Above this a fill of earth and stones, with some grey ash. The spearhead (2) was found in the grey ash, the other objects in the carbon layer on the floor.

Pyre 1 intersects with Tomb 17 in the SW corner and is probably earlier.

**Bronze**
1. Arched fibula. (B.II.19). with asymmetric swollen bow. Pres l. 11. Estimated h. 8.2. Th. too distorted to measure. Forearm, catch-plate, and much of pin lost. Severity of oxydisation makes it difficult to recover the original appearance. Clearly articulated into stem, bow and forearm by bosses either side of bow. Bow of swollen asymmetric form; stilted forearm. Spring (at least one turn) to right.

**Iron**
2. Spearhead. L. 28.2. L. of socket 8.6. D. of socket 2.8. W. of blade 4.2. Th. of midrib c. 1.2. Complete, though broken and repaired. Socket too obscured by oxydization to see if divided; no detectable rivet holes; prominent collar (w. c. 1) at base of socket. Socket hollow for at least 5.5. Prominent rounded midrib. PLATE 244d.
3. Axe/Adze. L. 23.5. W. of blade 6.8. W. of butt 5.4. Th. in oxydised state 3. Shattered and heavily split. Will have been a very heavy tool or weapon. May have been hafted in a sleeve, which would account for the slightly better state of preservation just below the butt for 9.5. If an adze, could only have had a knee-joint haft. PLATE 244e.

**Iron with ?faience**
*4. Decorated dress pin. Pres. l. 7. D. of head 1.0. D. of beads 1.0, 0.8, 0.7. D. of shaft 0.5. Lower shaft

and point missing. Flat disk head on shaft of round section, on which are mounted a series of disk beads, probably of faience — analysis reveals a considerable iron content, probably the result of absorption during the oxydization of the pin. PLATE 242h.

**Antler.** The use of these objects is discussed on p. 226. 6 is well preserved, black and hardened from exposure to the pyre; 5 more brittle.

5. Implement, fragment. L. 6.6. D. 1.7—2.0. Broken at one end, chipped at the other. Pierced laterally at the thicker end near the break (d. of hole c. 6 mm), notched at the other end. Two grooves run long-itudinally along the concave side, the inner edge of each undulating. Signs of abrasion below the notch on the convex side. PLATE 236h—i.

Several other non-joining fragments are preserved; two of smaller diameter and tapering (d. 1.2—0.8) have the same grooves with undulating edge, in this case only 5—6 mm apart. On these and one other fragment there are traces of at least four small pierced holes, d. 4—6 mm.

In addition there are other substantial horn or antler fragments, apparently unworked. All are burnt.

6. Peg. L. 4.5. Max d. 1.5. Flat at the top, tapering to a point. Knife paring marks are clear. Pierced laterally near the top (d. of hole 4—5 mm). PLATE 236i.

**T Pyre 2** (PLATE 166; Contents, PLATE 190). Rectangular. 165 × 75, depth 40—50, deeper at the N end. Black carbon deposit c. 10—15 thick in the centre, up to 35 round the edges; upper fill of reddish earth. Pottery fragments occurred in both layers, the principal deposit being at the surface of the black carbon at the N end of the pyre. The bronze fibulae and burnt bone fragments were found on the pyre floor.

**Pottery.** There are fragments of at least two locally made amphorae, one of which was burnt (2). A sherd belonging to the unburnt no. 1 was found in the fill of Tomb 22 adjacent. There are also four pyxides and a kantharos, all shattered but made up almost complete, and partly burnt; of these the kantharos (3) and the pyxis (4) are Attic imports, the pyxides 5—7 are local. Finally, there were a few sherds from small closed vases, and one from a PSC skyphos: these have not been catalogued.

1. Belly-handled amphora, fragments. D. at belly c. 46. Broad belly zone with sets of 'empty' concentric circles, two narrow and one broad encircling bands below, two narrow bands above; the shoulder has two tiers of 'empty' concentric semicircles, with a single broad band between. See P Pyre 41,1 for a similar general scheme. Not illustrated.
2. Amphora fragments. D. at belly c. 26. Fragments of lower body are fully painted; reserved bands on the belly. Belly-handle with four mending holes. Two rim fragments (d. 24) with flattened lip, one also with a mending hole, may belong. All are burnt. Not illustrated.
*3. Kantharos. H. 9. Reserved band inside and outside lip, barred handles; otherwise monochrome. Attic LPG import.
*4. Pyxis with lid. H. 12. H. of lid 2.1. Decorated as shown. Attic LPG import.
5. Pyxis with lid. H. 9.8. H. of lid 3. Decorated as shown.
6. Pyxis with lid. H. 9.5. H. of lid 2. Monochrome, reserved band at belly and on lid.
7. Pyxis fragment, with lid. D. of lid 9. Fragment of rim and upper body of globular pyxis. Paint on top of lip; monochrome except for scribble between bands on belly. Lid has two diametrically opposed string holes. Not illustrated.

**Bronze**
*8. Arched fibula with central boss (B.II.14). L. 4.5. H. 3. Th. of boss 2.2. Complete. Clearly articulated into stem, bow and forearm; the boss that forms the bow set off from the other elements by two fine fillets either side. Stem and forearm of square section. Boss round with flatter under-surface. Spring (two turns) and catch to right. PLATE 248, 13.
*9. Arched fibula with central boss (B.II.14). L. 2.9. H. 2.1. Th. of boss 1.5. Complete. Clearly articulated into stem, bow and forearm; the boss that forms the bow set off from the other elements by two fillets with traced fine oblique lines, suggesting a rope twist; the effect recalls milling. Section of stem and forearm square. Spring (one turn) and catch to left. PLATE 248, 14.
10. Arched fibula with central boss (B.II.14). Pres. l. 2.6. Pres. h. 2. Th. of boss 1.6. Pin and catch-plate broken. The fellow to 9, but the spring is of two turns (to right).
11. *a—d*. Fibula fragments (?). A collection of scraps of uncertain identity.

(a)  Pres. l. 4.4, w. 0.57, th. 0.2.
(b)  Pres. l. 3.5, w. 0.6, th. 0.2.
(c)  Pres. l. 2.5, w. 0.6, th. 0.2.
Fragments of what may have been the bows of leaf-shaped fibulae. Eleven smaller scraps of pin and spring.
(d)  Four scraps: 0.8 × 0.12, 1.1 × 1.0, 1.0 × 1.2, 0.8 × 1.0.
Shapeless pieces. ?Remains of traced ornament; impossible to determine what type of object these composed.

**T Pyre 3** (Contents, PLATE 191). Rectangular. 150 × 65, depth 60. Black carbon deposit 30 thick at the centre, rising to the surface at the edges; upper fill of reddish earth.

**Pottery.** Two fragmentary local vases, 1 burnt, some fragments of 2 burnt after breaking. The fill also contained rim fragments of a PSC skyphos with high offset lip, of a trefoil oinochoe, of an amphora handle, and of other amphora fragments with circles, and with cross-hatched rectangle: these are neither catalogued nor illustrated.
1. Trefoil oinochoe. Rest. l. 18.5. Max. d. 11.5. Base and lower body fragments, not joining those from upper body, rim and neck. Monochrome, reserved band on belly.
2. Cup. H. 6. About three-quarters preserved. Monochrome, reserved bands inside and outside the lip.

**T Pyre 4** (Contents, PLATE 191). Rectangular. 155 × 90. Depth 40—60 at the ends, sloping down to 90 at the centre. Pyre 4 was a later cutting in the shaft of Tomb 26; its edges and sloping floor were defined by a line of red hard-baked earth crust. It contained a black carbon deposit (with some large stones), c. 35 max. thickness, rising to the surface at the edges and spilling out over the upper shaft of Tomb 26. Upper fill of reddish earth and stones, in which were the fragments of four amphorae (1—4), and one krater fragment, uncatalogued. The lower fill contained a clay button (5) and burnt bone fragments.

**Pottery.** Standard local fabric.
1. Belly-handled amphora. Estimated h. 78. D. of rim 32.5. D. of belly c. 52. D. of base 19.5. About one quarter preserved, including upper body to rim, base (not joining), and other non-joining sherds. High funnel neck with flattened rim, double belly handles (note the ancient mending holes, clearly visible on PLATE 282), and low conical foot. The whole upper part was cut off and re-used, presumably as a stand. The neck and lower body are monochrome. The elaborate decoration of shoulder and belly is as shown, but does not give the full variety: an unillustrated belly sherd shows a panel with the filled semicircle motive in the lower register, above it four horizontal scribbles in the MPG manner, and above these a pendent dogtooth design — furthermore, the adjoining panel shows the start of a kind of diagonal tongue, a motive not otherwise encountered in this period. PLATE 282, D.
2. Belly-handled amphora. Estimated h. 68. D. of belly c. 52. Rim, neck and base missing. Decorated as shown, with semicircles on shoulder and circles on belly.
3. Belly-handled amphora. Pres. h. 36. D. of belly 54. Upper body, neck and rim missing. Decoration of horizontal bands and concentric circles, as 2. Not illustrated.
4. Neck-handled amphora. Estimated h. 48. D. of belly 34. base and body fragments only, not joining. Monochrome, one reserved band on lower body, five on belly.

**Clay**
5. Button. H. 2.1. Conical, with concave sides. Yellow clay, yellow and grey burnished surface. Not illustrated.

**T Pyre 5** (PLATE 162; Contents, PLATE 191). Rectangular. W. 60, depth 45. Cut at the E end by the later Tomb 27. Carbon deposit 20—30 thick, rising higher at the S side. Upper fill of earth and stones. Two small lead earrings and a quantity of burnt bone, including skull fragments, found in the carbon layer.

**Lead**

1. Small earring. D. 2.3 × 1.9. Th. 0.15. Probably complete. Short length of wire roughly bent into irregular open circle. Terminals do not overlap. Roughly finished.
*2. Small earring. D. 1.6 × 1.5. Th. 0.15. One terminal lost. Probably the fellow to 1.

**T Pyre 6.** W. 60, depth c. 25. Shallow carbon deposit. The only contents were fragments of burnt bone. Pyre 6 overlay the earlier Tomb 21, and its N end was lost when this tomb was excavated.

**T Pyre 7** (PLATES 162, 199b). Mostly lost when cut through first by Tomb 29 and later by Tomb 27. Probably rectangular, c. 145 × 65, depth 45. The depth of the rock cutting was only c. 25, but a red-fired earth crust survived c. 20 higher at the N, showing that the earth cover was at least as great here at the time of the use of the cemetery as it is today. In the carbon deposit were found burnt bone fragments, and sherds in the fill and in the earth above the pyre.

**Pottery.** Amphora fragments with concentric circles and semicircles, several jug or amphora sherds with dogtooth or ray fringe at the neck, two fragments with battlement motive, and the burnt fragments of a small globular pyxis. Not illustrated.

**T Pyre 8** (PLATES 166, 201a; Contents, PLATE 192). Rectangular. 165 × 70–90, max. depth 70. Sloping floor. Black carbon deposit 20–30 thick, rising to the surface at the edges; central fill of earth and stones containing krater and amphora fragments (1, 2). In the carbon deposit c. 10–15 above the floor were found the shattered pieces of an amphoroid pithos (3), badly burnt and contorted. The broken sword and spearhead (4, 5) were found above the pithos fragments, and were perhaps originally placed inside it.

Pyre 8 cut into the shaft of Tomb 34 and is later.

**Pottery**

1. Krater fragments. High conical base, d. 20, h. 8; unburnt. Light red clay and slip, red-brown paint inside and on a broad and narrow band at the foot. Ancient mending holes at the upper break. A single body fragment has concentric circles in a panel. Not illustrated.
2. Amphora fragments. One burnt fragment preserves concentric circles on the belly, with semicircles in the zone above. Not illustrated.
3. Amphoroid pithos. H. 61. Hand-made. About three-quarters preserved; burnt. Coarse fabric with large white grits, light red where unburnt. Large funnel neck, oval at the mouth. (d. 21.5–17.0); piriform body with small flat bottom. Many fragments badly distorted. PLATE 269e.

**Iron**

4. Sword. L. 65.5. L. of hilt 11. W. of hilt 5.6. W. of blade 3.8. W. of hilt flange 0.9. Th. of blade 0.9. Rivets not measurable. Complete, but broken and repaired; guard broken. In unusually good condition for a Lefkandian iron object.

   Convex outline to the pommel top eliminates pommel ears. Grip pinched below pommel and above guard; outline of grip convex, of guard straight. One rivet in the grip, two in the guard. The outline of the blade swells from hilt to near the point, where it narrows to the tip. Elliptical section, with distinct but narrow midrib which extends the full length of the blade to the top of the handguard. Blade bent, but not properly 'killed'. PLATE 245b, 246d.
5. Spearhead. L. 33.4. L. of socket 13. D. of socket 3. W. of blade 4.5. Th. of midrib 1.4. Complete; broken and repaired. Divided socket; one rivet hole visible. Prominent collar (w. 1.3) with two traced encircling bands. The end of the socket folded over the collar to keep it in place. Socket hollow for at least 11.6. Prominent rounded midrib runs whole length of blade. PLATES 244b.

**Stone**

6. Whetstone. L. 7.5. Th. 1.3. Fragmentary and burnt; one side split away. Pierced at one end; d. of string hole 6 mm. PLATE 237f.

**T Pyre 9** (PLATES 165, 201a). Rectangular. c. 170 × 65. Lower deposit of black carbon; upper fill of earth and stones. Cut by the later Tomb 32 at the S side; overlying the earlier Tomb 34. No contents except the handle of a large coarse vessel such as T Pyre 8,3.

**T Pyre 10.** Destroyed by the cutting of Tomb 32. Dimensions unknown.

### Surface finds

**Gold with rock crystal**
1. Pendant. H. 4. Max. d. 2.8. Description as for T 31,19 (see p. 186) but larger, and this pendant has preserved its upper suspension loop. From Square VIII. PLATES 189, 234e.

**Bronze**
2. Vessel handle. L. 7.2. Max. w. 3. Th. of handle plate near centre 0.3. W. of left terminal 2.7. W. of right terminal 2.5. D. of vessel restored 10.8. Horizontal handle with ring attached in the centre; broken. The inner d. of the ring 1.5; attached by three large rivets, with large heads inside (1.2, 1.1, 0.9). Rivets barely visible on the outside. The vertical ring is offset from the centre by c. 0.2. The terminals are asymmetric. Not a well-made piece. From Square VII. PLATE 246g.

# Section 8

# Tomb Types and Pyres

## L. H. SACKETT

## THE TOMBS

There were two main types of tomb: the cist grave, which occurred principally in the Skoubris cemetery, with two examples in Khaliotis' field and one in Palia Perivolia;[1] and the basically later shaft grave which occurred in each of the four main cemeteries. Other variations, which are less frequent, are the pit grave, the built grave of mud brick and the urn cremation (these last two in shaft or pit).

**Cist graves** (fifty-nine graves) PLATES 193–6
The cist graves were set in rectangular cuttings in the earth or rock, and lined and covered with stone slabs. The average internal length was 75–100 cm, the width c. 30 and the depth 20–30; but there was a great variation in size: some were little more than small boxes (e.g. S 61, length 42) very small even for an infant, others larger than a human body (e.g. S 38, length 200). The vertical slabs were in most cases cut to a rectangular shape, sometimes well finished and even jointed (S 10, S 34), others left in a rougher condition, and including irregular round stones (S 8, S 50, S 63). The construction of S 10 and S 34 is particularly interesting in that sophisticated techniques suitable for wood jointing were used and the lids were sunk, suggesting a knowledge of wooden chests or perhaps coffins (PLATES 81, 83, 195a, 196a). The cists were usually packed with small stones on the outside, and levelled up with others to receive flat cover slabs; the cover slabs were often tool faced and from one to three in number, occasionally as many as five. The better

constructed cists had paved floors (S 10, 11, 16, 34, 35), but the normal flooring was a bed of pebbles or gravel up to c. 5 cm thick. S 51 was superimposed on and used the covers of S 52 and 62 as paving.

The material used in the best cists was a soft and easily worked sedimentary rock, oolite[2] or laminated mudstone of yellow or greenish colour; this was easily split into large slabs as thin as 4–6 cm (S 16) and given a smooth finish (the toolmarks are clearly preserved on S 10 and 34). Also characteristic is the local white magnesite[3] a soft chalk-like stone easily cut and dressed (e.g. S 20, S 52); it was a favourite material and was used in at least thirty-four of the cists. Slabs were also cut from a coarse and gritty or pebbly conglomerate, generally dark grey (e.g. S 4, S 23, S 39), green or grey schist, a hard bluish limestone, and occasionally grey marble (S 11, and cf the shaft grave S 59).

**Shaft graves** (seventy-two graves) PLATES 124, 197–201
The commonest grave form at Palia Perivolia and Toumba was the shaft grave; three were also found in the Skoubris cemetery (S 45, 46, 59), and three in the East cemetery (P 42, 45, 47). This type of grave consisted typically of a rock cutting of approximately rectangular shape, with a ledge about two thirds down to receive a cover, and a narrow lower compartment sometimes no more than a slit trench (e.g. P 29, PLATE 200a). The shafts were cut into the soft conglomerate, and were refilled with the same material; occasionally large boulders were thrown in over the tomb cover or in the upper fill (P 13, 27, 31). In Toumba the upper shafts and the rock shelves were broader on average than those in the Palia Perivolia cemetery, but the lower compartment was of a closely parallel size.[4] The average depth of the shaft was 1.35 m, but some were cut unusually deep and lay in a stratum of soft marl or mudstone, which runs beneath the conglomerate at a depth of about 1.60 m (T 22, 26, 32). A number of Toumba graves had no shelf surviving; in the case of some shallow graves this was probably due to the erosion of the rock surface (e.g. T 23–5, and 28).[5]

There is considerable variety of detail in the form of the shaft graves, and we may distinguish three general types (PLATE 124a-c), based principally on the amount of effort and hence expense given to preparing a particular grave.

(a) *Shaft graves with stone cover slabs* (PLATE 124a).
Twenty-one graves (out of a total seventy-two) had stone cover slabs resting on a rock shelf in the shaft (PLATE 124a).[6] The slabs, often large and heavy with a minimum of dressing were of friable conglomerate (P 22), magnesite (T 1 partly, T 21), limestone (P 3, 13, 15, 21, 34, 46, T 3, 22) or even marble (S 59). In most cases they had fallen partially or wholly into the lower compartment, usually due to the collapse of the ledge. In one case (P 34) the covers were fully in position and a layer of reddish earth found above them suggests a deliberate sealing of clay or mud brick; the sides of this tomb may also have been lined with mud brick, as with T 9. Grave offerings were sometimes placed on top of the covers after these were in position.[7]

The tombs of this type are not a contemporary group, but included some of the largest and richest in the cemeteries during successive periods.[8]

(b) *Shaft graves without cover slabs* (PLATE 124b).
Most shaft graves had rock cut shelves but no trace of the original cover for which these were cut (sixteen in Palia Perivolia, sixteen in Toumba with three others probable, one in

Skoubris, three in the East cemetery).[9] One may assume that a wooden cover was used in these cases, whether of planks or of logs and branches.

(c) *Subsidiary use of mud brick* (PLATE 124c).
The use of mud brick, not found in the Skoubris cemetery, was quite common both in Palia Perivolia and Toumba. In Palia Perivolia it occurs in the cist (P 25B), and in eight shaft or pit graves (P 16, 18, 27–9, 31, 40, 44); it was used structurally to support the cover, either fully – on all four sides (e.g. P 16) – or partially (e.g. P 44). The principal reason for this will have been the great difficulty in cutting stable ledges in the coarse and loose conglomerate rock. No superimposed courses of mud bricks were observed; where vertical division lines could be distinguished, the bricks had lengths of c. 60 and 80 (P 16); one measured 60 × 30 (P 28).[10]

In Toumba mud brick was used as a subsidiary material (for tomb lining or blocking wall) in several tombs (T 7, 9, 24?, 29?, 30, 31, 34), and also in the 'perimeter' wall.

Graves of mud brick build were also probably roofed with wood, and in some cases there had been a further layer of clay above this (P 23, 31, 35). In P 16 an offering was placed on top of the mud brick structure after the cover had been placed in position, as frequently on the stone slabs of other tombs.

(d) *Possible use of wood*
A possible variation, though unique, is P 12, where the evidence suggests that the grave was at least partially lined with timber, and then roofed with a combination of wood and clay (PLATE 124d). No surviving mud bricks were found, but red clay in the fill appeared to be collapsed roofing material. A dark colouration of the soil was observed at the edges of the tomb, continuing down through several spits of digging (PLATE 124d, left and centre); it formed a narrow lining of rather pure dark earth along the sides of the tomb, and spread in each of the corners to form approximately circular features. Possibly these preserve the hollow left by decayed timber uprights with props in each corner (PLATE 124d, right).[11] Alternative interpretations could be a strongly built wood coffin – but no inhumation was found – or even an oddly shaped lining wall to the compartment.

**Built graves of mud brick** (four graves) PLATE 201b
In Toumba two graves constructed of mud brick were found and two others are possible. Two were shallow graves based directly on the rock surface (T 13, T 36), but may originally have been set in a shallow cutting in an earth level which covered the rock. A third, T 4, which was excavated as an isolated deposit of pottery on the rock surface with no trace of a surround, may have been of the same type. T 12A re-used the upper shaft of T 12B on which it was directly superimposed and lined it with mud brick. Where measurements are available (T 12A, T 13), the inner dimensions of the tomb are 110–120 cm in length, and 45–55 in width; the mud brick surround is 12–15 broad and preserved up to 15 high.

**Pit graves** (twelve graves) PLATE 124e
Pit graves are simple rock cuttings, shallow and without rock shelf, often rather irregular in shape; many of them are smaller graves, but some larger ones are included (e.g. S 33). The distinction between pit grave and shaft grave is sometimes difficult to draw, and the classification has not been applied with full consistency: some shallow graves of rectangular type have been included (P 6, P 43); others in parts of the Toumba Cemetery where erosion

was thought to have taken place are classified as probable shaft graves (T 2, 7, 23–5, 28), or mud brick graves (T 4). On the other hand the pit grave S 62 might properly have been included with the cists.

In the Skoubris cemetery five are classified as pit graves (S 5, 33, 54, 56, 62). Two of these (S 33, and probably S 56) were shallow oval pits with no surviving trace of ledge or cover, in which the offerings may have been simply covered in with earth and stones; or possibly there was a cover of wood or branches. S 56 contained an amphora at the upper level, which may have been set up over it as a marker. S 54 was a small pit bordered by an elliptical line of small stones and covered with a single slab, possibly a child grave. S 62 was a shallow rectangular pit with cover slabs resting on the rock sides, similar to a cist grave but having a line of stones in place of side slabs. S 5, an amphora cremation set in a pit, is considered separately below.

In Palia Perivolia six graves had offerings laid in a shallow rock-cut pit, usually quite small, oval or rectangular in shape (P 6, 17, 26, 28, 37, 39A). The average depth of the cuttings as they now survive is less than 30 cm. With the possible exception of P 6, all appear to be child graves. The pits were filled in with earth and stones, originally perhaps over a cover. Mud bricks placed in P 28 may have supported such a cover (see PLATE 124f for reconstructed section).

One shallow grave in the East cemetery (P 43) is classified as a pit grave.[12]

In Toumba none is classified as a pit grave. Several shallow graves are of uncertain types (T 2, 4, 7, 28); one (T 4) may have had a mud brick surround, while the others, in an area of heavy erosion, may originally have had rock shelves, and so have been included with the shaft graves.

### Urn cremations (PLATE 202d-f)

One urn cremation (S 5) was found in the Skoubris cemetery. The amphora S 5,1 containing cremated bones was set in a pit and was surrounded by a circle of small stones. It was found close beneath the surface, the upper part having been destroyed by the plough. Others could have been removed by cultivation, leaving only the amphora sherds which were found in the surface levels.

In Toumba two shaft graves (T 14, T 18) had urns containing the cremated ashes; these are comparable to the common Attic 'trench and hole' type. T 14 had a short rectangular shaft, inside which a smaller shaft of the same proportions had been cut to receive two amphorae; this was covered by a regular, squared stone slab. T 18 had a shaft of normal proportions in which a lower cutting had been made, roughly circular in shape, to contain a single amphora; this was covered with a single slab.

### THE PYRES (PLATES 196c-e, 199a) Eighty pyres.

The pyres were built over large rectangular or spool shaped pits whose dimensions were close to those of the human body, and which were cut often quite deeply into the rock.

The rock cuttings varied in length from 100 to 180 cm, and in width from 50 to 100; their preserved but not always original depth ranged from 10 to 180.[13] A total of eighty were found, and of these seventy one were excavated.[14]

The fill consisted of a thick layer of black ash lying compact on the bottom of the pyre; this ash was sometimes covered at the centre with a layer of earth and stones and compressed,[15] but it remained at full depth around the edges where it could be traced at the top (see T Pyre 8 section, PLATE 166). On the floor of some of the pyre cuttings were found large boulders, blackened and calcined by fire, possibly placed there to produce a good draught and a higher temperature,[16] PLATE 196e. In several instances there also remained large pieces of charred wood,[17] PLATE 196c. Bone fragments were found in many of the pyres — most were small scraps of about 5 cm and less in length, in a highly brittle and calcined condition[18] (see Appendix). The heat of the pyres, and the quantity of the wood burnt is shown both by the depth of the ash deposit and by the thick hard-fired crust of earth or rock at the edge of the pyres (e.g. P Pyres 39 and 43; T Pyres 4 and 7).

Three pyres in the Skoubris cemetery, S Pyre 2, Pyre 4 (the upper of the two super-imposed pyres) and Pyre 10, survived as shallow, roughly circular pits (d. 80—100, depth c. 40); all were partially destroyed by the mechanical excavator in 1968, and their original dimensions are not certain.

ANALYSIS OF TOMB AND PYRE CONTENTS (see table of contents in Appendix A, TABLES I—III)

### Cists

Seventeen of the cists contained nothing except a fill of fine silt; ten of these were disturbed but seven were found intact and appeared to be cenotaphs (S 1, 11, 35, 48, 50, 57, 61); no trace of ash or bone was observed in these. The remainder contained offerings varying in number from 1 to 31 — pottery, metal and other objects, unburnt and usually covered in a fine, light silt. Cloth impressions were found in three. In some cases objects were arranged on the tomb floor in a manner appropriate for an inhumation (especially S 10, 38, 62, 63), see discussion on p. 212 below. In one case (S 17) a cup had been placed outside the cist and two finger rings inside; in another (S 4) unburnt pottery was found in the cist, and a deposit of burnt pottery and ash, presumably from a pyre, was on top of the covers (S Pyre 1A). In one case a cist was re-used, apparently twice (S 25A and B), in another a cooking pot had later been placed near a cist (S 21). This re-use comes at a much later date, however, and seems to have no connection with the *construction* of the cists. Bone fragments, usually very small, were found in a few cists; see Appendix for details; their significance is discussed below in the section on inhumation.

### Shaft and pit graves

In Palia Perivolia five graves were found empty; the others contained from 1 to 34 offerings, usually covered with a layer of silt, crumbled rock or mud brick from the tomb sides and fill collapsed from above. In Toumba there were eight empty tombs, of which three had been destroyed by later tombs (T 6, 8, 11), and one had probably been robbed (T 35); the rest were found intact as cenotaphs (T 20, 21, 30, 34). Offerings in the others varied in number from 1 to 35.[19] Graves of this type in Skoubris and the East cemetery were similarly furnished (three in Skoubris with from 3 to 51 offerings; four in the East Cemetery with from 4 to 20 offerings).

In most cases the offerings were placed on the gravel floor of the tomb, sometimes with rings, pins and other jewellery in a position of some logical order (see especially S 59, P 3, 22, 24, 46; T 1?, 13, 21, 22?, 27?, 32, 33?, 36?). Sometimes the pottery was placed in two distinct groups at either end (P 3, 4, 22, 24), occasionally with a third central group (P 7, and P 10). In several cases a vase of quality was placed separately, possibly a special offering (P 13, 20; P 21, 2; P 23, 1). Sometimes objects were found both above the tomb cover and below: S 59/59A, P 3, 12?, 16, 21, 23, 31?, 36, 39 and 39B, T 3, 27?, 31. Tomb P 39B differs in having a mass of broken pottery, with some bone fragments, placed apart in a separate walled-off compartment.

### Urn cremations

For the ash contents of cremation urns, and other bones found, see discussion on cremation below, and Appendix C on the human remains. One urn (S 5,1) contained the fragments of a bronze macehead, recovered from the pyre. In one tomb (T 14), metal objects were placed on the tomb floor beneath the urns. The other (T 19) had no offering beyond the urn itself.

### Pyres

The pyres did not contain grave goods to the same degree as the tombs. Thirty-four pyres contained no objects. Burnt bone fragments were found in thirty-eight. Thirty-six pyres did contain offerings and some of these seem to have acted as the place of burial as well as of cremation.

Nine of the Skoubris pyres contained burnt pottery and other objects, most having from 2 to 6 offerings; one, S Pyre 4 (SPG I), exceptionally contained 25 objects. Not included in these figures are the fragments of large amphorae, some unburnt, some partly burnt *after* being broken (see S Pyres 3, 6, 14, 15), found at the surface of seven pyres (S Pyres 3, 4, 6, 10, 12, 14, 18).

About half the Palia Perivolia pyres (23) contained no pottery or other objects. Fourteen (P Pyres 8, 11, 14A, 14B, 19, 28, 31–2, 39–42, 44) did contain pottery, seven of these in a substantial quantity (P Pyres 11, 14B, 28, 32, 34, 44).[20] It was noted that this was usually badly shattered and burnt; but some was unburnt and may have been thrown on to the ashes after the cremation. Other objects found were spearheads, whetstone, knife fragment, clay weights (P Pyres 1, 16, 17, 29, 47), and small objects probably to be associated with dress: pins and beads or buttons (P Pyres 9, 15, 29, 32, 39). Amphora fragments were found at the surface of fourteen pyres (P Pyres 2–3, 8–9, 11–12, 14A–15, 26, 32, 36, 39?, 41, 44); in several cases these showed signs of burning (P Pyres 2–3, 8–9, 11, 28).

Only two of the pyres excavated in Toumba were empty. The others contained objects similar to those found in the tombs, from two to ten in number: pottery (T Pyres 1–4, 7, 8), weapons and tools (T Pyres 1 and 8), fibulae, pin, earrings (T Pyres 1, 2 and 5) and objects in clay, stone and antler (T Pyres 1, 4 and 8). Amphora fragments, burnt and unburnt, were found in or above four (T Pyres 2, 4, 7 and 8) and an unusual coarse pithos in one (8). The latter was badly burnt and had apparently been placed on the pyre with the grave goods of a warrior inside it.

### POPULATION OF THE CEMETERIES, AGE AND SEX IDENTIFICATION

It is not possible to establish with accuracy the total population even of the excavated parts of cemeteries. We have a total of 147 tombs and 80 pyres, but it is uncertain how many of these pyres were the cremation places of the *same* remains later placed in one of the tombs.[21] Thus the total figure of 227 (147 + 80) is not a safe one. Furthermore there was an occasional re-use or multiple use of pyres (e.g. S. Pyres 6 and 17, see Appendix) and of tombs (e.g. the double graves P 45 and T 14), but in general evidence on the point is lacking. The statistically conservative method which has been adopted in our historical conclusions (Section 14), is to take account only of those tombs and pyres which contain datable objects and which therefore provide hard archaeological evidence. Thus we have 138 dated burials (tombs or pyres), 23 Submycenaean, 24 EPG–MPG, 34 LPG, and 57 SPG I–III. However, since no account is taken of many known but undated cenotaphs, these figures are low even for the excavated tombs and pyres, and are likely to fall far short of the total original population of the cemeteries, none of which has yet been fully excavated. Only in the case of Palia Perivolia, is an estimate possible and we can say that nearly 75% of the total cemetery has been excavated, which would suggest that it originally contained about 60 tombs and the same number of pyres (population not less than 60, and probably greater). In the following discussion of age and sex identification only the tombs are considered, and the conservative round figure of 150 is used.

The paucity of human remains makes the attribution of graves to adult or child, and their distribution between the sexes very difficult, and in many cases impossible. Dr Musgrave has examined the remains of 71 individuals (Appendix C), a tentative figure in itself, and he has identified 4 adult males, 4 adult females, 10 other adults and 7 children.[22] This is a reasonable proportion of the scanty remains available to him for examination, but only some 16% of the total. However, a few additions and adjustments may be made by taking account of the nature of the grave offerings, and some other, tentative, suggestions derive from the size of the graves. Discussion of this problem starts best with the Palia Perivolia cemetery[23] since this forms a comparatively full group to which the other cemeteries may then be related.

### Child graves

In the Palia Perivolia and East cemeteries four graves contained feeding bottles (15, 35, 36, 39A) and six contained miniature vases (9, 10, 14, 28, 44, 25B), both likely concomitants of child burials. It is worth examining this group in terms of their other contents and of their size, to attempt to isolate the common features of child graves in this cemetery. All the tombs in this group except Tomb 44 are well below the average in size, and the fairly natural supposition that child graves are in general small and adult graves large is borne out by the histogram (FIG. 6), on which the area of individual tombs is plotted: the tombs cluster into two groups, all identified child graves, with the exception of 46 fall into one group, and the identified adult graves into the other.[24]

This result makes it worth while comparing the grave offerings of the probable child graves with those of the other small graves, on the hypothesis that *all* the small graves were dug for children and that an adult, even after cremation, would get a larger one.[25]

In examining the offerings of our group of ten probable child burials, we find that three graves are rich (P 10, 28, 44), while the rest are comparatively poor, containing only from one to five vases. The feeding bottles and miniature vases account for 19 out of 61 vases; the others comprise 15 kalathoi, 15 closed vases (juglets, hydria), 7 cups, 4 amphoriskoi, 1 bowl. Most tombs have, in addition to miniatures, from one to three closed vessels and a single open shape (cup or kalathos); pins occur singly in two graves, and the only other objects are one faience necklace and one bracelet.

Turning to the sixteen small tombs which can be grouped with these by size (P 2, 4, 6, 8, 11, 17, 23, 26, 27, 29, 33, 37, 38, 40, 41, 43) we find that the range and number of grave offerings is closely comparable. Three are empty, eight have only a single object and those with more include at least one closed vessel (total 16) and one open, whether cup or

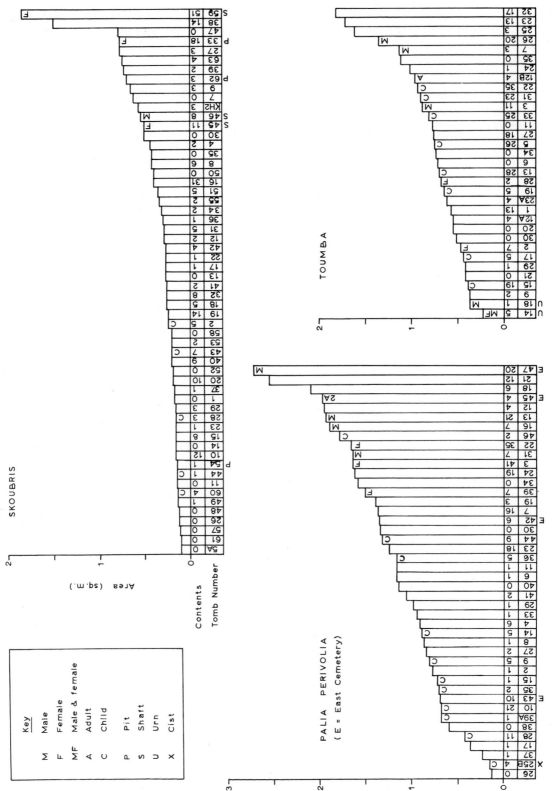

FIG. 6. Histogram showing suggested age/sex identifications in relation to tomb size and the number of offerings

kalathos (total 17); two are comparatively rich (P 23, 43). Where only a single object is found, this is a kalathos, cup, pin or fibula; pins occur singly, except in P 23 which has two pins. Two (child's) bracelets occur in one tomb (P 43, East cemetery), and other objects are very rare (P 23, P 43).

The incidence of finds in the two groups, then, is closely comparable and the analysis above may be an acceptable description of the average offering given to a child's burial in the Palia Perivolia cemetery.

This group could be extended to include the six next largest tombs (P 30, 7, 19, 39, 34, 24 and 42 of the East cemetery), without altering the picture substantially.[26] The smaller group of 25 is 62% of the total, the larger group of 31 is 77% — reasonable upper and lower estimates for the pre-adult population of a cemetery at this period.[27]

In the Skoubris cemetery five tombs contained a total of ten feeding bottles and miniature vases. Three are Submycenaean (S 43, 44, 60) whose other contents consisted of two closed, two open and one other vase, and four fibulae. Two are EPG (S 2, S 28), which contained in addition two cups. There are twenty tombs which can be grouped with these on grounds of their small dimensions, and again the range and number of their grave offerings are quite comparable, see FIG. 6 and TABLE I. The group taken consists of S 5A, 61, 57, 26, 48–9, 11, 54, 10, 14, 15, 23, 29, 1, 37, 20, 52, 40, 53, 58. Of these, ten are empty, four contained a single object (cup, bowl or fibula) while four (S 10, 15, 20, 40) are comparatively rich, having from 8 to 12 objects.

In most cases, then, these graves were provided with few offerings; closed and open shapes occur in about equal numbers, and of the metal objects which occur, both singly and in small groups, the fibula is far the most common.

The Toumba cemetery is more difficult to analyse, both in terms of the offerings and the size of the graves.[28] The three graves where the remains of children have been identified anthropologically (T 5, T 22, T 36) are large and rich. Feeding bottles and miniature vases are found in tombs which on other grounds might seem to belong to adults, or at least not to young children (T 3 with knife, T 1 with coarse dipper; cf. also T 31 with coarse jug found outside the tomb, and T 15 with open-work kalathos).

Leaving T 3 and T 1 out of consideration, if we examine the other possible child graves on the same principle as the other cemeteries, the results are rather different. Accompanying 10 miniature vases and 4 feeding bottles in 7 tombs (T 13, 15, 17, 19, 22, 31, 33) are 14 closed, 20 open (including 14 kalathoi) and 2 other vases; also 4 pins, 2 earrings, 21 finger-rings, 15 fibulae and 49 other objects. These tombs are comparatively rich: two contain only 5 objects each, but the others run from 19 to 35; gold is found in all except one.

As regards size these graves do include some of the smallest (T 15, 17, 19), but there are also several larger ones (T 33, 31, 22), FIG. 5. Child graves and adult graves do not divide into two clear groups so far as dimensions are concerned. None is as large as the inhumations of T 12B and T 26 — but the difference between T 22 and T 12B is not significant; furthermore one of the smallest (T 2) contained a coarse jug, one of the criteria for female graves. Possibly many of the smallest tombs were those of children, as the largest would surely be for adults, but there seems to be no direct correlation between these factors in this cemetery. There may have been cases of the joint burial of adult and child.

## Male burials

The surest indication of a male burial is the presence of weapons or tools.

In the Palia Perivolia cemetery three graves contained objects of this kind, comprising one axe (P 13) and two knives (P 16, P 31). The associated pottery is rather homogeneous: in each grave is one or more lekythoi, from three to six closed vessels (amphoriskoi, juglets, oinochoai) and one drinking vessel (kantharos, cup, flask); in addition there were four pyxides in P 13, and one fibula in P 16. A comparison with the objects placed in the warrior inhumation grave (P 47, East cemetery), certainly male, gives the same picture since these are reasonably parallel with those of P 13 (5 lekythoi, 2 amphoriskoi, 1 oinochoe, 1 kantharos, and again 7 pyxides).

Tools or fragmentary weapons also occur in three pyres (P Pyres 1, 16, 17) but without associated objects.

In the Skoubris cemetery no Submycenaean tomb contained a characteristic male object; one EPG tomb (46) contained a dagger, and the only other objects were two fragmentary knives with no associated finds (S Pyre 13). The armour scale (S 59,37) is evidently a token gift in an otherwise female context. With the dagger in S 46 occur one lekythos, one cup, a juglet and four fibulae, categories which are also found in the male graves in Palia Perivolia.

In the Toumba cemetery weapons occur in two tombs (T 14, urn cremation; T 26, inhumation) and in two pyres (T Pyres 1 and 8); there is also a knife in T 3 (with miniature vases). But an analysis of the other objects in these graves is not helpful for establishing common features — indeed five objects are unique.[29]

### Female burials

For female burials the surest indications agreed on elsewhere are coarse pots, spindle whorls and buttons, loom-weights and open-work kalathoi.[30] Likely concomitants are belly-handled amphorae, dress pins, and perhaps a preponderance of jewellery.

In the Palia Perivolia cemetery there are no coarse cooking pots, though a coarse ware bowl occurs in P 39B, identified anthropologically as probably female; there are incised buttons or beads with small hand-made jug in P 3, and open-work kalathoi in P 22, and in P 10 (with miniatures). The analysis of other objects is not very helpful; each of these three (P 39/39B, P 3 and P 22) have from one to three lekythoi, with a variety of other closed shapes, kalathoi are common in all, pyxides occur in two, and each has at least one pair of jewellery items. None of these characteristics would mark these graves off from others tentatively identified as male or as child burials; lekythoi and pyxides are common to male, kalathoi to child burials, and jewellery to both. Clay weights, buttons or spindle whorls occur in six pyres (P Pyres 15, 29, 32, 39, 47); the accompanying objects — belly-handled amphorae (P Pyres 15, 32), neck-handled amphora, jug and kalathoi (P Pyre 32), lekythos (P Pyre 34) and two pins (P Pyre 29) provide some confirmation for the criteria suggested but do not add anything new. We are left with three suggested female burials, but insufficient criteria to apply to other unidentified graves.

In the Skoubris cemetery there are coarse jugs in S 33 and 45, also outside S 21 but with no associated objects; a coarse hand-made cup occurs in S 59. Clay buttons or whorls occur in S Pyre 4 with other objects, and an open-work kalathos in S 59. All these tombs belong in the late, SPG phase. An analysis of the associated objects does not reveal any distinctive common features; all have one or more small closed vases, kalathoi occur in two, pyxides in two, dress pins in three, and jewellery is common in three of the four. This gives much the same picture as that at Palia Perivolia. However, we might tentatively add the earlier tombs S 10, S 16, S 38, on the evidence of pins, fibulae and jewellery.

In the Toumba cemetery coarse jugs occur in T 2, T 28 and outside T 31 (which has miniatures inside); there is other coarse ware in T 5 and T 1 (with miniature); an open-work kalathos is found in T 15 (with miniatures); there are no clay buttons or whorls. Leaving aside the main deposit of T 31 and T 15 as possible child graves, the remaining four tombs (T 1, 2, 5, 28) contain ten closed vases, one cup, six kalathoi and one other (hand-made bowl in 1). There are no dress pins. Jewellery is present in two graves (T 1 and T 5) but absent from the other two. So again no consistent common features appear. A number of graves might be added on the evidence of jewellery alone; T 32 is perhaps the most likely.

This discussion leads to the conclusion that at Lefkandi, where reliable anthropological information is so scanty, it is extremely difficult to make definite attribution of graves to child, adult male or female. The evidence from Toumba cemetery is particularly difficult to interpret. For the Skoubris and Palia Perivolia cemeteries the evidence of feeders and miniature vases, and more tentatively a consideration of tomb size allows one to attribute a fair proportion of the graves to children; weapons or tools occur in only four graves (and two others in Toumba), coarse pottery, spindle whorls/buttons and open-work kalathoi in eight graves and six pyres. These sometimes tentative attributions are included on the charts of dated groups TABLES I—III in Appendix A.

# Section 9

# Burial Customs

## P. G. THEMELIS

## THE CHRONOLOGICAL DISTRIBUTION OF TOMB TYPES

The chronology of tomb groups is fully discussed in Section 13, but before turning to the methods of burial used, it will be useful to give here a brief résumé of the numbers and types of grave assigned to each period and, with a strong *caveat* as to its limitations, to give a list of dated pyres also.

The cists are assigned to the following periods: 21 SM, 11 EPG, 5 MPG, 22 undated; the suggested date range is c. 1100–950. The distribution of shaft graves is: 1 EPG, 4 MPG, 15 LPG, 6 LPG/SPG I, 13 SPG I, 4 SPG I/II, 6 SPG II, 2 SPG II/III, 6 SPG III, 15 undated; suggested date range c. 1025–825. Pit graves occur sporadically in most periods (2 SM, 1 MPG, 1 SPG I, 2 SPG II, 6 undated). Four graves with mud brick build are; 1 LPG/SPG I, 2 SPG II, 1 SPG III; urn cremations: 3 LPG and 1 SPG I.

For pyres a breakdown into periods is difficult since so many pyres are undatable. Those dated are as follows: 1 SM, 1 SM/EPG, 1 MPG or later, 3 LPG, 4 LPG or later, 9 LPG/SPG I, 7 SPG I, 2 SPG I/II, 2 SPG II, and 1 other SPG. Before attempting to derive any generalisation from this evidence, for instance as to frequency of cremation in different periods, it must be emphasised that most pyres are undatable, and that except in the case of Palia Perivolia, an unknown proportion of the cemeteries has been dug. In Skoubris, for instance, while the paucity of pyres in the main area of SM tombs at the south is notable, there does seem to have been a tendency to build pyres at the north end of the field (at least in the later period). Thus the ratio of 2 Submycenean pyres to 20 tombs seems unlikely to be representative. For the other periods, too, we have only those few pyres which contained objects to go on.

## CREMATION AND INHUMATION

### Cremation

That the practice of cremation at Lefkandi was general is attested to by the finding of pyres in every burial ground investigated. In addition to the three main cemeteries, their presence in Khaliotis' field is indicated by surface traces; three pyres observed though not excavated in the East Cemetery are counted among the total of 80 found. We should first consider the nature of the pyres and their contents, including the human remains.

Ten Skoubris pyres contained, in their fill of ash, charred wood and boulders and a small number of bone fragments remaining from the cremation. These were very small, brittle and calcined and although all fragments were collected, the total weight recovered was surprisingly small, see discussion in Appendix C below. Grave goods (including amphora fragments) associated with eleven Skoubris pyres make it possible to assign them dates, which range from Submycenaean to SPG II. There was one urn cremation (S 5), partly destroyed, but containing a small collection of cremated bones. And in one case a deposit of burnt pottery and ash had been placed over a cist (S Pyre 1A and S 4).

In Palia Perivolia bone fragments in a similar condition were found in about half the pyres (20 out of 47). No deposit of bones or other trace of bone fragments or ashes (except for those in the tombs P 34 and 39) has been found anywhere in the quite fully excavated cemetery area, so that it seems probable that these small amounts are the total survival from the cremations. Twenty of the pyres contained pottery (P Pyres 8, 11, 14A, 14B, 19, 28, 31–2, 39–42, 44), other grave goods (P Pyres 1, 8, 15–17, 29, 32, 39, 47) or had amphorae at their surface level (P Pyres 2–3, 8–9, 11–12, 14A, 15, 26, 32, 36, 39?, 41, 44); in eight cases a pyre was stratified above a tomb (P Pyres 14A, 14B, 24, 28, 33–7, 41) or cut into one (P Pyre 20); thus it has been possible to assign dates to 17 pyres, and these range from LPG to SPG II — the main period of the cemetery's use.

In Toumba ten pyres were found, all except two (T Pyres 9 and 10, the latter destroyed) containing small bone fragments. These pyres generally contained pottery (T Pyres 1–4, 7–8) or other objects (T Pyres 1, 2, 4, 8), lying burnt in the ash on the pyre floor, or unburnt pottery principally amphorae, at their surface (T Pyres 2, 4, 7, 8). Dates have been suggested for six of these pyres, and the chronological range is LPG–SPG II.

To summarise the evidence from the pyres: 80 pyres were found, and of these 71 were excavated and the contents examined. All had a fill of black ash and were the actual place of cremation. Bone fragments were found in 38, burnt pottery and other objects in 36, fragments of amphorae, often burnt, at the surface of 25.

The remarkable paucity of bone fragments surviving in pyres raises the question as to whether the bones were normally collected after cremation. We know that they were in four cases, when they were placed in cremation urns (S 5, T 14,1, T 14,2, T 19); these were protected from further decay, and were found well preserved and in reasonable quantities. But these were unusual burials, and the Toumba graves so closely reflect the Attic 'Trench and Hole' system as to suggest actual immigrants from that region. It seems probable that the collecting of bones was a more general practice, but before considering this possibility it is best to review the evidence for inhumation.

One further point may be made first: the fact that some pyres contained only ash, but that in others grave goods were deposited and allowed to burn, while amphorae were placed on the surface of some either before or after cremation, suggests some variety in the burial practices. Behind the latter activities seems to be the attitude that the pyre is sometimes the burial place of the dead and performs the function of a grave.

## Inhumation

The practice of inhumation is equally well attested, though only five certain examples were found. These were: T 12B, T 26, P 47, and P 45 (double). In considering whether there were others, we must examine carefully the nature of all the human remains surviving in each cemetery.

No cist was found to contain a skeleton, or the trace of a skeleton surviving in the form of discoloration in the soil. The most that existed in the Skoubris Cemetery were tiny fragments measurable in millimetres and often found in close association with metal objects (cists S 10, 16, 17, 19, 36, 51, 53, 62; also shaft grave S 59, pit grave S 63). The cist S 36, exceptionally, had two long bones and a number of others; these are described as unburnt by Dr. Musgrave, who was unable to be certain about the fragments from the other cists. Finger bones were found with their rings in several cists (S 16, 17, 19, 53).[1]

Again no skeleton was found in the Palia Perivolia graves, nor the impression of a skeleton. Small, white and brittle bone fragments were found in Tombs P 11, 34, 39/39B, 44 and 46. Those examined by Dr. Musgrave (P 34, 39, 46) are considered to be unburnt fragments.

The East Cemetery contained three skeletons in two graves (P 45, P 47). The bodies, poorly preserved, lay supine in an extended position, and one (the warrior of P 47) had been furnished with a wooden coffin, to judge from the disposition of the grave goods.

Two inhumations occurred in the Toumba Cemetery (T 12B, T 26). These were also in a poor state of preservation, and for the warrior of T 26 there was again evidence for a coffin. Eight other tombs contained small bone fragments (T 3, 5, 7, 22, 31, 32, 26), most considered by Dr. Musgrave to be unburnt. A finger bone was found inside a bronze bowl in T 31.

To summarise the evidence for inhumation: first, there are five burials (in four graves) with skeletons preserved; then, in two tombs, S 36 and P 39, is a number of larger limb fragments, probably unburnt, which could be the sole surviving remains of a skeleton.[2] Apart from these there are very small scraps of bone, often found beside a metal object, surviving in 21 graves (including cists and shafts).

These fragments are in some cases considered to be unburnt; in others no certainty was possible. For these fragments there are perhaps two possibilities — either they too are the sole surviving fragments of a full inhumation, or they are survivors only of a token burial after cremation, in effect the interment in a grave of the unburnt bones from a pyre.

We are left with some 117 tombs in which no trace of bone was found. In these cases we must suppose either that decay has removed all trace of full inhumations (though this did not happen to others); or, secondly, that it may have destroyed a token amount of burnt or unburnt bones collected from a cremation pyre; or else that these were cenotaphs in the proper sense (the symbolical burial in home ground of a totally absent body). Against the third suggestion are the sheer numbers involved — we are dealing with 80% of all tombs found. The first suggestion, involving a random or very complex pattern in the process of decay, is perhaps possible, but hard to evaluate. Firmly against it is the series of soil analyses made in the Fitch Laboratory, Athens, and discussed in the following section. To accept it would certainly have important implications on our view of the total population of the cemeteries, and on the ratio of inhumation to cremation burials. But the second possibility, which seemed very real at the time of excavation, is worth considering at greater length.

## A combined cremation and inhumation rite?

The combination of cremation and the burial of a token collection of more or less well cremated bones in a grave (but without the urn usual elsewhere) may find support from several considerations.

Numerous pyres have been found, containing a surprisingly small number of bone fragments; so that a general practice of collecting bones is quite probable. Decay of bones in both pyres and tombs must be assumed, but the degree to which this went in a particular case is difficult to assess; chemical analysis shows that the soil is neither excessively acid nor excessively alkaline.[3] The inhumations found, though poorly preserved, were clearly observable on the ground (see photographs PLATES 200b, 202a, c, d, tomb plans PLATES 123, 159, 162); laborious care was taken while excavating other tombs, to search for possible traces of discoloration in the soil left by an inhumation, but none was found. The total disappearance of 117 bodies, a large number of them carefully protected in built and sealed cists is difficult to accept in these conditions. The conclusion that total decay did not take place is further confirmed by the negative results of a phosphate test on soil samples taken from tomb fills.[4] One might expect a strongly positive reaction to indicate the presence of a completely decayed skeleton in a small and comparatively well sealed area.

In the cemetery most fully excavated the ratio of pyres to tombs is about one to one: there are 47 pyres to 40 tombs in the excavated part of Palia Perivolia. Thus a general practice here of combining the use of pyre and grave is statistically quite possible, at least for the main period of this cemetery (MPG–SPG II).

Finally there is a particular case where the combination of the rites seems highly probable in the placing of a deposit of burnt pottery and ash over the covers of a contemporary cist (S Pyre 1A and S 4).

There is, however, another factor which must be taken into consideration, and this is the regular disposition of grave goods in a number of cists and shaft graves. The EPG cist S 10 is one of the best examples: it was well built, paved, sealed with fitted lid and was found intact. In it the grave goods were set out in an order appropriate for an inhumation, with head to the west; the occurrence of two (possibly three) different types of cloth suggests that the clothed form of a child (cist length less than 62 cm) was laid here. Yet the only human remains were three token fragments, bronze stained and the largest 7 mm in length. If prior cremation had taken place in this instance, we would have to assume that some kind of simulacrum was later placed in the grave with the possessions of the dead. Other tombs where the arrangement of pairs of earrings, pins, fibulae or bracelets points to the same conclusion are: S 38, S 59, S 62, S 63; P 46; T 1?, T 13, T 22?, T 27, T 32, T 33?, most of which are unlikely to have been child burials. The list includes Sub-mycenaean and SPG I–III tombs. Evidence exists for the placing of clothing in fifteen tombs, Section 10, p. 227f. below; here all periods are represented, and three of the tombs listed above are included (S 59, T 13, T 33). Again, if the body had already been cremated, the clothing might have been laid over a substitute of some kind.[5]

Although this suggestion has not been made in connection with other cemeteries of Dark Age Greece, it is worth briefly re-examining the evidence provided by two cemeteries, at Assarlik and Vergina, for possible parallels to the practice suggested here for Lefkandi.

### Assarlik

At the end of the 19th century large cemeteries were excavated on the Carian Peninsula between the cities of Myndus and Halicarnassus, as well as around the acropolis of Assarlik, which may be identified with the ancient Sauagela or Termera.[6] We can distinguish three categories of grave construction during the Submycenaean to Geometric period: (1) chamber tombs in Mycenaean form that go on to the end of antiquity, (2) tumuli called by the excavators 'circular enclosures', (3) 'rectangular enclosures' or 'bone enclosures'.

In the 'double enclosure' N. of Assarlik[7] there were five small cist graves, described by the excavators as 'ostothecae' or 'Tombe a pozzo'. They contained burnt bones and ashes. Their form and small size — few were as much as a metre in length — may be compared with some of the cist graves of the Skoubris cemetery. It is worth mentioning here that one cist grave at Assarlik was lined not with stone slabs, but with clay slabs,[8] thus giving the impression of a clay larnax. This unique example may help us to interpret also the small cists of four slabs set on edge and covered by a cap-stone, both at Assarlik and Lefkandi (Skoubris) as imitations of clay larnakes. On the other hand the construction of some cist graves (S 10 and S 34, p. 197 above) suggests knowledge of wooden chests or coffins.

Another type of cist grave also appears at Assarlik, the large cist, lined like the small ones with slabs of stone, but covered by long slabs laid transversely; these are called by the excavators 'full length graves'.[9] In these no clear traces of burning, but also no skeleton was found. It seems that we have here a possible parallel to Lefkandi,[10] but unfortunately the excavators left no exact description of how the grave goods were arranged inside these cists, and so we cannot tell if pins and fibulae were found in their normal position, as if a clothed simulacrum of the dead was placed in the tomb, as we have assumed for some of the Lefkandi graves.

## Vergina

The cemetery at Vergina provides another possible parallel to the case of 'inhumation' without traces of bone. Here 32 burial mounds (tumuli) with a total of 220 burials were excavated by Professor Andronicos.[11] Another 75 burial mounds were investigated by Professor Ph. Petsas in the same area.[12] In contrast to Lefkandi, inhumation was the normal practice at the Vergina cemetery, according to Andronicos.[13] Only two cases of cremation were noted by him in Tomb Delta (inside the vase D10) and in Tomb E (child cremation inside the vase E5). Two more cremations are mentioned by Petsas in Tomb LXIV (Burials A and H).[14] We must note, however, that no tomb in the Vergina cemetery was found to contain a complete skeleton. Sometimes a few unburnt teeth were the only remains (*cf.* the Lefkandi grave P 46). Despite this, inhumation is considered certain by Andronicos not only because the grave goods (personal objects of the dead) were set out in an order appropriate for an inhumated body. Normally men were buried with their weapons and women with all metal ornaments on their garments.

It seems likely that we have here at Vergina the same phenomenon as at Lefkandi. Would it be possible to suggest that a simulacrum was placed in the Vergina graves with the possessions of the dead in their right position, while the body was previously cremated somewhere else? In any case, the absence of skeletons in the Vergina cemetery remains problematic. The explanation that Andronicos gives, that the bones decayed without leaving any trace[15] is not very convincing, because the soil of Vergina, as the example of the complete skeleton of Tomb P suggests,[16] like that at Lefkandi (where five skeletons were preserved) is not so acid as to account for the total disappearance of the skeletons.

## Summary

In summary then, the Lefkandi Iron Age cemeteries present us with a complex pattern of burial customs. Cremation occurs throughout the life of the cemetery, in a variety of forms; inhumation is certain in only five instances, which include two warrior burials, but there may have been others. In the great majority of cases however, there seems to have been an unusual combination of cremation and the subsequent furnishing of a grave for token human remains and grave goods. One result of this practice is that we have rather little secure evidence for the size of the human population, or for the sex, age and life expectancy of the people buried here.[17]

Given that cremation was the normal practice in the cemeteries at Lefkandi, the continued co-existence of certain rites associated with inhumation is of particular interest. The burial custom of inhumation practised by the last Bronze Age inhabitants of the area (Phase II of LH IIIC at Xeropolis) seems to have been gradually absorbed by cremation, and it is perhaps this transitional period in burial customs that is represented in these cemeteries.

Again, it is interesting that two of the five certain examples of inhumation are warrior graves (P 47 and T 26, in both of which there was evidence for a wooden coffin), and that a third inhumation (T 12B) contained an adult who was buried with two rare glass seals of Late Mycenaean date (T 12B,3 and 4). This may imply that the leaders of the Protogeometric community continued to be buried in the old custom (inhumation) of the Mycenaean heroic age. Such an interpretation presupposes that the warriors of the Protogeometric community who were buried in the 'Mycenaean' manner, were conscious of their Mycenaean descent or that they believed that they were descendants of Mycenaean families. However, this is something which is not subject to proof, and which on archaeological grounds does not seem very likely for Lefkandi.

## FUNERAL RITUAL AND THE CULT OF THE DEAD

There are a few pieces of factual evidence which may shed some light on a subject which is inevitably of a largely hypothetical nature. Many of them have been touched on before, but it may be well to bring them together here, and to make some suggestions as to their possible significance.

### Funeral preparations
In Toumba Cemetery there is a carefully flattened area of rock, at least 7.5 × 3.0 m, bordered by a wall (whether enclosure wall or building is not known), and containing three rock cuttings, evidently for the feet of a very large tripod. They measure 14 × 18 cm, and the distance diametrically between them is c. 60—70 cm, giving the probable diameter for a cauldron as 1.00—1.20 m. This would be a natural area for preparations for the funeral and for ritual activities associated with the funeral.

### The funeral ceremony
As indicated above, there was some variety in the nature of the burial rite. In cremation the body was, at least in some cases, laid supine on the pyre (see Musgrave, Appendix C), as it was when laid in a coffin and buried in a grave (P 45, P 47; T 12B, T 26). Where offerings were found burnt in the pyre, they will have been set there before or during the cremation, and this may sometimes have been the end of the ceremony, the pyre being regarded as the grave. In a few cases the bones were gathered, pounded, placed in an urn and buried in a pit or shaft grave. In others, as suggested above, there may have been a more

complicated secondary rite, including the placing of token bones with offerings and personal belongings, possibly even a simulacrum, in cist or shaft grave. Sometimes the final activities may have been the throwing of a second lot of offerings down over the grave, covering it with earth, perhaps a mound (for which no evidence remains), and the setting up of amphora or slab as a marker.

### Funeral libation and funeral feast

The occurrence in the cemetery deposits of krater, plates and other pottery fragments not found in tombs or pyres, suggest that a ritual libation and perhaps feast took place in the cemetery area at the funeral. This may be supported by the finding of 115 sea shells in the excavated part of the Palia Perivolia north boundary ditch. Most of these were certainly edible, and all may have been (see pp. 229—30).

### The cult of the dead

A large number of amphora fragments were found in all the cemeteries; some of these may have been used in connection with the funeral libations, others seem to have been set up over a pyre or grave, either as a marker, as surely was the case with a number of stone slabs,[18] or possibly as receptacles for liquid offerings poured over the grave in a cult of the dead. Similar interpretations could be given to the setting of a bowl (S 17,1) or cooking pots (S 21, 1 and 2; T 31,9) beside or above a grave.

### A chthonian rite; the centaur

The Toumba grave T 1 contained four vases, two bronze bracelets, two gold earrings, two bronze fibulae and beads. A terracotta human head that must have belonged to a terracotta statuette and had been broken away at the neck was found lying beside those grave offerings. The problem of the broken head was solved when grave T 3 was dug 3 m away to the SW of grave T 1. Five vases, a shell, a barrel-shaped animal figurine and finally a centaur without a head were found on top of the cover slabs of that grave. When the finds had been cleaned and put together, it became apparent that the head of grave T 1 belonged to the centaur of grave T 3. Neither of the two graves had been disturbed, so that the head of the centaur must have been deliberately separated from its trunk before the burial; the terracotta statuette, here in the form of a centaur, a counterpart of which is the Minotaur and other chthonian daemons, was symbolically beheaded at the grave shortly before burial. The act of beheading a statuette could be interpreted as a cult ritual performed in a necropolis.

The open area at the west of the Toumba Cemetery, where the colossal tripod stood, fits the hypothesis that a ritual of chthonian character took place around that tripod.[19]

An iron knife was also found in the Toumba grave T 3; it was perhaps a sacrificial knife, as the ivory hilt and possible goldplate attachment suggest. Placing the sacrificial knife into the grave is clearly of the same symbolic significance as the sickle-shaped knives of the Rheneia graves or the votive sickles in the sanctuary of Ortheia.[20] Such archaeological material — beheaded terracotta centaur and sacrificial knife — thus seems to point to the myth of the slaying of a chthonian daemon.

That the man-horse or centaur may represent a death daemon has been fully argued elsewhere.[21] Chthonian features are observed in the various centaur legends. And there is no difference in significance or iconography between those man-horses and the centaurs in the Heracles legends.[22]

Although we have departed some way from strict archaeological fact into the realm of hypothesis in this excursus on the centaur, it seemed worth while to attempt some reconstruction of ritual here, and it may be fitting to end with what is perhaps the most interesting and outstanding find from these cemeteries, and one marked by the unusual circumstances of its burial.

# Section 10

# Jewellery, Seals and Other Finds

THE JEWELLERY[1]

The jewellery from the tombs at Lefkandi falls chronologically into three groups: Sub-mycenaean, from c. 1100 to 1050 BC; Protogeometric, (stopping just before the end) from c. 1050 to 925 BC; and Late Protogeometric and Early Geometric, extending just into Middle Geometric, from c. 925 to 825 BC. Throughout this dark period of nearly three centuries the quality and quantity of the jewellery is surprisingly high.

    The Submycenaean period, a blank in most places as far as jewellery is concerned, has at Lefkandi a certain amount of (admittedly primitive) gold jewellery to offer.

    For the bulk of the Protogeometric period no gold is recorded, and this seems to be the rule throughout Greece. But, exceptionally, the Lefkandi tombs are full of faience and glass ornaments of high quality. Imported they must be, but the source (Cyprus or the Levant, surely) is yet to be determined.

Then, near the end of this period, about 925 BC, the use of gold starts again and continues unabated for the remaining century during which the cemeteries were in use. Much of the gold, which is amazingly plentiful, is flimsy in appearance, but from about 860 BC certain articles of considerable complexity begin to appear, probably under Phoenician inspiration. Granulation is seen again, for the first time for some three centuries; sheet gold is laid over objects of bronze, iron, lead and tin; and amber is incorporated in the shanks of pins — one of a number of indications of a northern connection. In addition, seals of soft stone and faience were imported from the Levant.

### Submycenaean, 1100 to 1050 BC

Three graves in the Skoubris cemetery (which constitute one in seven of those excavated) contained gold jewellery; a very high proportion for a poor period. It is restricted to tiny hoops of thin block-twisted wire, PLATE 204e.[2] In two tombs the hoops were found in pairs, and were presumably used as earrings;[3] in the third only one was found, and probably served to decorate the hair.[4]

There is no stylistic connection with Mycenaean jewellery (whether from Euboea or elsewhere). More surprisingly, there is no resemblance to the Submycenaean jewellery of Athens, the only other plentiful and well authenticated Greek source for this period.[5]

Such a poverty-stricken style need have no antecedents, and may have been the result of local enterprise; or perhaps we should look to the north. The raw material, which cannot have been easy to come by in the virtual absence of foreign contacts, was possibly obtained by robbing Mycenaean tombs.[6]

### Protogeometric, 1050 to 925 BC

Gold jewellery is extremely scarce in Greek tombs in the Protogeometric period, until just before the end. However, two tombs, one in the Skoubris and one in the Palia Perivolia cemetery, contained beads of less precious materials.

One tomb at Palia Perivolia, P 25B, of Middle Protogeometric date, contained a set of beads originally forming a necklace, PLATE 233a.[7] They comprise:

(1) Small disc beads of white faience with a green glaze. Such beads are common in Egypt at all periods, and in Cyprus and the Levant about the date of this tomb.[8] They also recur in Protogeometric contexts at Knossos and on Kos and Rhodes,[9] in a mid-ninth-century context in Athens,[10] and are found again at Lefkandi in the ninth century.[11]

(2) Beads of blue compound, hexagonal in section and tapering at the ends. This material, also known as blue frit, is similar to faience, but differs in being homogeneous in colour and substance. It lacks a glaze, being finer in texture than the body of faience, but coarser than its glaze, and friable throughout. It is extremely rare in Egypt, but common in Cyprus and the Levant in the Late Bronze Age and the Early Iron Age.[12] This shape is also a rare one.[13]

(3) Conical beads of blue compound. The shape is rare.

(4) A quadruple spacer bead of blue compound. Beads of this shape are particularly common in Egypt, but the material of this specimen points rather to Cyprus, where the shape is also represented.[14]

(5) Flattened globular beads of speckled glass. At this date one thinks of Cyprus or Phoenicia for glass beads.[15]

(6) A globular amethyst bead. One would be tempted to see this bead as a Mycenaean survival. A similar one from a contemporary tomb at Knossos should probably be explained in the same way.[16]

Another tomb, also in Palia Perivolia, (P 24) of Late Protogeometric date contained disc beads of red faience with a whitish glaze, PLATE 142, P 24,14. Most were of the usual form, but some were double, some triple and some quadruple.

There is no doubt that all these beads from the Protogeometric tombs are exotic, and little doubt that they all originated in Cyprus or possibly the Levant coast.

## Largely Geometric (late LPG and SPG I into III) about 925 to 825 BC

Jewellery was found in all three main cemeteries, but Toumba is the richest. All in all, in this period, one tomb in two of all those excavated contained jewellery — a surprisingly high proportion.

The earliest jewellery, of perhaps 925 to 860 BC, is very flimsy, consisting principally of gold diadems, wire spirals, and finger rings which could well have been made specifically for funerary use, and which have many parallels in contemporary Athenian burials. The inspiration for these objects seems to have come from Cyprus. There are also the mysterious 'attachments' which are otherwise attested only on Skyros. Then there are also beads in faience, blue compound and glass, whose origin, as with their Protogeometric predecessors, is evidently also in Cyprus, or the Levant coast.

Later, perhaps about 860 BC, more substantial gold jewellery appears. The origin of, or inspiration for, most of it would appear to be Phoenicia or North Syria, although there are also connections with Thessaly and the Balkans. A little amber also points to the north, while there are also a few imports from the Levant in the form of seals of soft stone and faience.

## 1. Gold

### (a) *Diadems*

Diadems of gold foil with patterns of zigzags, etc. impressed on them are occasionally found from SPG I (EG I) to SPG III (MG I), PLATE 232a, b and d.[17] They are so flimsy that to have been worn in life they would have needed a backing of felt or leather; in all probability, however, they were purely funerary in purpose. Such diadems were very common in Cyprus in the Late Bronze Age and are also found there in the Early Iron Age.[18] Very similar ones have been found in Athenian tombs of the ninth century.[19]

Two fragments of a more elaborately decorated example were found in a tomb of SPG III (MG I), PLATE 232c.[20] On them are embossed figures of animals in an exuberant style which must surely be of oriental origin. It is further developed in an eighth-century gold diadem from Tomb 14 at Eretria.[21]

### (b) *Attachments*

The most puzzling of all the jewellery are a number of objects, most of them made of gold foil but some of thin sheet gold[22] PLATE 232e-h. They are found in tombs from SPG I (EG I) to SPG III (MG I), sometimes one to a tomb, sometimes two to a tomb and in one instance ten (perhaps eleven) in one tomb, PLATE 229.

Averaging 7 to 8 cm in height, some look like an elongated pen-nib; others are similar, but with a splayed base. All originally had thin gold ribbons threaded through them at top and bottom or attached to them, presumably to fasten them to some other object.

To judge from their flimsy construction, their purpose must have been purely funerary, but their precise function is a mystery. The only comparable objects so far recorded are two from a Late Geometric tomb on Skyros, now in the Dolly Goulandris Collection in Athens.[23] These pieces have human figures embossed on them in such a way as to establish that the pointed end is at the top, but throw little light on the vexed question of their function.

They might be a form of headdress, as suggested by Miss Lila Marangou in connection with the Goulandris pieces. A fragmentary diadem(?) from Eretria has the rudiments of such a crest incorporated in it,[24] and it also contains embossed decoration similar in kind to that on the Goulandris diadems. A later form of such a hypothetical crest can probably be seen in the ubiquitous Tarantine terracottas of the sixth to fourth centuries BC depicting a reclining banqueter.[25] They might have decorated a lady's back hair, or they could have decorated the hilts of real or (more probably) imitation swords.[26]

## (c) *Spirals*

A simple spiral of $2\frac{3}{4}$ turns of block-twisted gold wire was found in a Skoubris tomb of SPG II (EG II), PLATE 230j, S 45,11. Wire spirals, in gold or bronze, seem to have been used throughout the Submycenaean, Protogeometric and Geometric periods as hair rings, earrings and finger rings.[27] This, from its size and shape, was probably a decoration for the hair. A similar object comes from a tomb of c. 900 BC at Homolion in Thessaly.[28]

A pair of spirals of $1\frac{1}{4}$ turns from a Palia Perivolia tomb of LPG date, evidently earrings, has a very different appearance,[29] PLATE 230l. They are made of lead, plated with sheet gold, and the ends are expanded to form very shallow cones. No close parallels are known for this period. A number of somewhat similar objects are recorded from Curium in Cyprus, but are apparently dated in the fifth century BC, and their resemblance may well be coincidental. In the present state of our knowledge, the origin of these spirals remains enigmatic, though a northern origin is possible.[30]

Small spirals of block-twisted wire come from an SPG III (MG I) tomb (a pair)[31] and an SPG II (EG II) tomb (a singleton).[32] The ends of the wire fit into collars set on the undersides of shallow cones of sheet gold, PLATE 231a right. The pair were surely earrings, but the singleton may perhaps have been a hair spiral.

A related group of gold spirals is represented by two singletons from SPG II (EG II) tombs.[33] They differ from the previous group in that the cones are solid and the wire is thickened at both ends, PLATE 231a left. They were evidently cast solid in one piece and subsequently bent to shape. They, too, could have served as earrings or hair spirals.

Spirals of this kind have no place in the Cypriot or Levantine repertoire, and may well be a creation of north—central Greece. They are evidently the ninth-century ancestors of a common group of much larger cone-ended spiral earrings in gold, silver and bronze with a very wide circulation in Greece in the eighth century.[34] In a related Corinthian group, the cone is replaced by a disc.[35]

## (d) *Hoop earrings*

Here are grouped a few types of whose function as earrings there seems no doubt.

A pair of small hoops of tapering wire (probably cast), with slightly overlapping ends, comes from an SPG I (EG I) tomb,[36] PLATE 230k. They are like the SM hoops mentioned above, but with such simple objects coincidence rather than continuity seems probable.

A more ornate pair of gold earrings consists of hoops like the foregoing, but with three elongated clusters of granulation attached to them, PLATE 231d. They come from an SPG II (EG II) tomb.[37]

Hoops with one granulated appendage ('mulberry earrings') were common in LM jewellery,[38] and in Cypriot Early Iron Age jewellery,[39] but with three appendages are unknown in Crete and Cyprus. They are, however, attested in Phoenicia at least as early as the ninth century.[40] The inspiration for these examples is certainly Phoenician, but the inferior quality of the granulation makes one wonder whether they were a local product, as the granulated pins (PLATE 231e) perhaps were. If so, we have here the first identified revival by Greeks of the Mycenaean technique of granulation, which was kept alive in Phoenicia through the Dark Ages.

Earrings of this pattern, once established, had a long life in Greece, and are plentiful in sixth-century vase-paintings.[41] They have been identified as the model for the *Hermata triglena moroenta* of Homer.[42]

A more elaborate type of hoop earring is represented by a pair from an SPG II (EG II) tomb, PLATE 231b.[43] The upper part consists of a figure-of-eight of block-twisted wire, the bottom loop being much smaller than the top one. From the bottom loop is suspended a spectacle-spiral pendant of thinner block-twisted wire.

As an ornament, the spectacle-spiral has a long history. In the Late Bronze Age it is plentiful in Western Asia and Central Europe, and occurs sporadically in Mycenaean Greece. But in the Early Iron Age it flourishes principally in Central Europe and the Balkans,[44] and seldom (except in the form of the spectacle fibula) extends into Greece.[45] We may, therefore, conclude that the inspiration for these earrings, if not the earrings themsleves, reached Lefkandi from the north, and probably from Macedonia.

### (e) *Finger rings*

Finger rings were very common. With one exception, they were all comparatively flimsy, but may not, on that account have been exclusively funerary in purpose. Many, too, are so small that they could only be worn by children. Nor need this fact cause surprise, in view of the large number of infant burials in these cemeteries.

The rings, though flimsy, are carefully made. In no instance is there any sign of a join, but we may suppose that a strip was overlapped and pressure-welded by hammering so as to render the joint invisible. Such a process would be quite feasible for a craftsman using almost pure gold.

There are very few different types. The commonest is represented by nineteen examples, from seven tombs, ranging in date from early SPG I (EG I) to SPG III (MG I.)[46] It consists of a band of thin sheet gold, convex outside and correspondingly concave inside, PLATE 230d. The type appears to be of Cypriot origin,[47] and is also found in Athens at this time.[48]

This type also occurs with a slightly carinated outline in ten examples from four tombs of SPG I (EG I) and SPG II (EG II), PLATE 230e.[49]

Other rings occur, but less commonly, with two, three, four, five and six carinations, PLATE 230f-i.[50] These varieties, also represented in Athenian tombs,[51] may well be derived from Cypriot models,[52] or are, less probably, descended from somewhat similar rings from LH IIIC levels at Lefkandi.

The simplest possible type of finger ring, a band of very thin sheet gold (PLATE 230a), is represented by two examples from an SPG III (MG I) tomb.[53] In two other examples, from two other tombs, the edges are slightly flanged, PLATE 230b.[54] This variation is also represented in tombs at Homolion in Thessaly and Fortetsa.[55]

Finally, the most substantial type of ring, of really stout sheet gold, PLATE 230c, is represented by two elegant examples from an SPG III (MG I) tomb.[56] It may well be a local development of the type represented in PLATE 230b. Similar rings are found, not in ninth- but in eighth-century contexts at Athens, Corinth and Perachora,[57] so that we could well suppose a north-Greek origin for this type.

### (f) Bracelets
Pairs of gold-plated bracelets for children occurred in three tombs of SPG I-II (EG I-II) PLATES 231b and 234g.[58] In two instances the bronze core was preserved; in the third no core survived.

### (g) Pins
Gold-plated iron dress-pins, PLATE 231f, occurred in pairs in burials of SPG II (EG II)– SPG III (MG I).[59] Although gold-plated iron pins are well known from Athenian Geometric tombs,[60] the type of pin in use at Lefkandi has not hitherto been found in these materials. In fact, although remarkably simple, it is a very rare form indeed, and could be local in origin.

Another tomb, probably contemporary, has produced a pair of identical pins, with the addition of an amber bead on a gold reel with granulated edges, PLATE 231e.[61] This addition brings the pin more into line with contemporary pins from other sites; but as the basic form is local, we may suggest that the goldwork, with its granulation, is also local. It could then, with the earrings in PLATE 231d, be the earliest example of Greek granulation since the Mycenaean period.

### (h) Fibula
In marked contrast to the bronze fibulae from the Lefkandi tombs, only one of gold came to light, in a tomb of SPG II (EG II), PLATE 231c.[62] It is basically of the Mycenaean violin-bow type, but with a small stilted catch and a double leaf-shaped bow with a loop between the two leaves for a safety-chain. The type, hitherto unknown, also occurs here in bronze in a LPG tomb,[63] and may be presumed to have evolved here or hereabouts in the PG period. The violin-bow type, which gave it birth, is known to have survived very late in this part of the world.[64] Another factor in its evolution is the Cypriot 'a gomito' fibula, which evolved in western Asia in the early first millennium BC.[65]

### (i) Beads
Strangely enough, very few gold beads are recorded from the Lefkandi tombs. A hollow biconical gold-plated tin bead comes from an SPG I (EG I) tomb, PLATE 178,[66] whilst another tomb, of SPG III (MG I), has produced gold foil coverings for other biconical beads, PLATE 187, T 33, 9–12.

## 2. Other materials

### (a) Rock-crystal beads
Two globular beads of rock-crystal were found in an SPG II (EG II) tomb, PLATE 234b,

and another in a SPG III (MG I) tomb, PLATE 234d.[67] Similar beads were found in a rich Athenian tomb of late EG II, with a number of Phoenician or Syrian objects, and in a tomb at Amathus.[68]

The same type, but with a gold lining to the string-hole, occurs in a tomb of uncertain date but probably of SPG II (EG II), PLATE 234f.[69] It is closely paralleled in somewhat later tombs, one at Salamis in Cyprus, of MG II, and another at Khaniale Tekke of the same date.[70]

A further elaboration on this type is provided by two examples, one from a SPG III (MG I) tomb at Toumba, the other a surface find from the same cemetery, PLATE 234e.[71] They comprise a drop-shaped rock crystal pendant with a gold collar and a gold lining.

Finally, an elongated rock-crystal pendant comes from a SPG III (MG I) tomb, PLATE 234d.[72]

There is little doubt that all the objects of rock-crystal are imports. The balance of probability would indicate their source as Cyprus, but their high quality suggests a Phoenician origin at one remove.

(b) *Amber beads and pendants*

Apart from the amber beads on the pins (PLATES 231e, 186), there were a few amber beads and pendants in tombs of SPG II (EG II) and SPG III, (MG I), (PLATES 234c, 228b, d).[73] Amber, whose northern connections need no comment, is found in small amounts in Greece in the ninth century, and becomes commoner in the eighth,[74] and the few examples recorded from Lefkandi need cause no surprise.

(c) *Glass beads*

Glass beads, already in use at Lefkandi as early as MPG, are also found in tombs from SPG I to SPG III (EG I to MG I). Whenever found in Greece in contexts around this period, glass beads are generally regarded as Phoenician, and these need be no exception.

Globular beads with polychrome glass inlays occur in tombs of SPG I to SPG III, (EG I to MG I), PLATES 233c, 228b.[75] Similar beads are recorded from contemporary tombs at Orchomenos and Marmariani.[76]

Secondly, cylindrical or barrel-shaped beads of brown or green glass inlaid with bands of white glass occur in a tomb of SPG II, (EG II), PLATE 184.[77]

Thirdly, small globular beads of blackish glass were found in a tomb of SPG I, (EG I), PLATE 233c.[78] They are paralleled in a rich Athenian tomb of late EG II.[79]

Finally, globular beads of pale green glass with a darker surface were found in a tomb of SPG II (EG II).[80]

(d) *Faience and blue compound beads*

Beads of these related materials were in use at Lefkandi as early as MPG and have been discussed above (see p. 000). Their use continued into SPG II (EG II).

Disk-beads of white faience with a green glaze, like those described on p. 000 were the most popular variety, PLATES 234a, 219a.[81] They were found in eight tombs of SPG I—SPG II (EG I—EG II) date, in some cases to the number of several thousand per tomb. Exactly similar ones were found in a rich Athenian grave of late EG II,[82] and many of the same kind have been discovered in Cypriot tombs.[83]

Others with a red body and a whitish glaze, as in PLATE 142, were also found in a tomb of SPG I, PLATE 233b.[84] And a third variety of disk-bead, of blue compound, was found in a tomb of SPG II (EG II).[85]

A single melon-shaped bead of white faience was found in an SPG I (EG I) tomb, PLATE 233b.[86]

A pendant of green-glazed white faience in the form of a crouching dwarf was found in a tomb of uncertain date, but probably SPG II, (EG II), PLATE 235a.[87] He represents the Egyptian god Ptah-Seker-Osiris, who was known to the Phoenicians (who made this example, and others like it) as Pataikos.[88]

The type is found in faience in tombs at Beth-Pelet in southern Palestine and in Cyprus.[89] It is found in terracotta in Cyprus as late as the sixth century,[90] and was copied in that medium in Eastern Greece.[91]

Another tomb, of SPG I (EG I) date, produced a pendant of white faience with a pale green glaze in the form of the goddess Isis wearing horns and a solar disc and nursing the infant Horus; and no less than 53 pendants of similar faience in the shape of a seated lion-headed goddess wearing the double crown of Egypt PLATE 233d, e.[92] This latter creature, possibly also represented at Beth Pelet,[93] is not a regular Egyptian deity, but is evidently a Phoenician conflation of two different types.[94]

### (e) *Imported seals*

Three seals in particular are clearly imports from Phoenicia or (less probably) north Syria. All bear debased hieroglyphs in intaglio of a type already recognised by T. G. H. James as Phoenician.[95] One comes from a tomb of SPG II (EG II) date, while the other two were found together in another tomb, probably SPG II–III (EG II–MG I).

(i) A gold-mounted faience scarab, PLATE 235d.[96] A somewhat similar scarab was found at Zincirli, and others, mounted in silver, at Perachora.[97]

(ii) A steatite figure of a recumbent lion, PLATE 235c,[98] which is paralleled in a general way by one from Beth Pelet.[99]

(iii) A green-glazed steatite seal in the form of a shrine with intaglio designs on all four sides, PLATE 235e.[100] A somewhat similar object was found in a contemporary tomb at Ialysus in Rhodes.[101]

*Additional note on the above,* by T. C. Mitchell: The scarab and lion seals can be more or less paralleled at Carthage, mostly of seventh– sixth century BC. Scarab – J. Vercoutter, *Les objets égyptiens et égyptisants du mobilier funeraire Carthaginois* (Paris, 1945), nos. 151–234, pls V–VII (no. 208 has a gold mount; and many have garbled hieroglyphs). Lion seal – Vercoutter, nos. 510–19, pl. XIV (these are not exact parallels, and appear to have been cast, not carved); cf also A. Rowe, *Cat. of the Egyptian Scarabs . . . in the Palestine Arch. Museum* (Cairo, 1936), pl. XXXI, p. 275, no. A. 36, not a seal, sixth–fifth century, from Athlit).

These are not earlier than the seventh century at Carthage because relatively few material remains earlier than this have yet been found there, but such things, which could reasonably be called Phoenician in an Egyptianising style, could quite well be eighth, or even ninth century, I should think. Scarabs, of course, abound in Bronze and Iron Age Palestine. Archaeologically speaking there is no major change in Palestine-Phoenicia between the tenth century and the Assyro-Babylonian conquests, so anything from a seventh century Phoenician colony could be taken as typical of the period as a whole, though it is not easy to prove this.

I think the same could apply to the prism seal. Decorated or inscribed prisms (without the pierced lug) occur in late second millennium Palestine (e.g. *Lachish*, IV pls. 37, 38.295, 317), and something vaguely similar from Carthage is illustrated in P. Cintas, *Amulettes puniques* (Tunis, 1946) pl. XIX, 128 (p. 88). The back-to-back animals and the style of the human figures can be paralleled on late Bronze-Early Iron Age scarabs from Palestine (Rowe, nos. 733, 838 (different headdress), respectively).

## SEALS OF GLASS PASTE (PLATES 173, 235b)

The two glass paste seals, T 12B, 3 and 4, though from a MPG burial find parallels only from Mycenaean contexts and therefore must be survivors in this tomb.

For the lion of T 12B, 3, to right with head down between the forelegs and seen *en face*, mane dotted, compare the following, on glass paste seals: (a) with dotted mane: *CMS* V 733 from Mega Monastiri Tomb Delta; (b) without dotted mane: *CMS* V 363/364/385 from Medeon Tombs 29 and 29a (the same mould as that which produced ours?) and VII 137. On sealstones: *CMS* I 106 from Mycenae Tomb 68 and XII 244.

The subject of T 12B, 4 is not paralleled exactly; most radial designs use two animals back to back, not belly to belly. Close in concept, however, are the two glass lentoids *CMS* V 351/352 from one matrix, from Medeon Tomb 29.

These two glass paste seals belong to a large class of seals manufactured on the Mainland of similar material and shape — lentoids of pale grey or yellow glass paste with conoid backs. The iconography is similarly restricted in this class, mostly goats and calves, occasionally lions and a few other animals.

The Lefkandi seals are therefore Mycenaean in type, and on the basis of the preserved almond-eyed heads on their parallels and their rather fullsome modelling they should date early, prior to LH IIIA. A detailed analysis supporting this early date will be published elsewhere, under the working title of 'The New York Mould Master'.

The survival of these seals over four centuries is unusual but not without parallels: early LB seals in the so-called Cut-Style are regular survivors in LH IIIC cemeteries and Minoan–Mycenaean gems have come to light in such Greek sanctuaries as those at Sounion and Perachora. So far as the present author is aware, however, these Lefkandi seals represent the only survivors of prehistoric glass paste gems into Protogeometric times, probably so cherished for their material as well as their venerability.

## OBJECTS OF IVORY, BONE AND ANTLER

Few objects were found in these materials, but any occurrence of ivory in Greece in the early Iron Age is itself significant, though perhaps not surprising in view of the frequency of gold at Lefkandi. Two objects of deer antler, presumably local, have their own particular interest.

The finds number ten in all, but two are uncertain and several are no more than fragments. There may have been others, since conditions were not favourable for their preservation, to judge by the condition of the human skeletons found. Good preservation was sometimes assured by attachment to or the close proximity of a metal object, and the ensuing chemical alteration.

(a) *Ivory* (S 38,14, T 26,18, T 3,12, P 31,7, T 36,30 and 31)
Apart from some scraps from an unidentified object in the Submycenaean tomb S 38, the

first occurrence of ivory (as with gold at Lefkandi, p. 218) is late in the LPG period. It was probably the material used for the hilt plates of an iron sword T 26, 18 (PLATE 246c — LPG), as it was for those of an iron knife T 3,12 (PLATE 246e — SPG I). These were prestigious objects (the former from an important warrior grave, the latter from the Centaur tomb), but are noteworthy at this early date, when Greece was emerging from comparative isolation and poverty, whether the sword was imported as a finished manufactured object or not. An iron knife in the late LPG tomb (P 31,7) may also have had hilt plates of ivory.

One later tomb contained ivory, T 36 (SPG III), a rich group with numerous imports. Here the much decayed fragments of a spindle (or long pin?) were found (T 36,30, PLATE 228d), as well as flakes from an unidentified object (T 36,31). It is tempting to restore T 36,30 as a spindle shaft, on to which a whorl would have been threaded at the thicker end, and perhaps some other attachment at the thinner end, as on an example from Delos.[102] No ivory pin of this heavy form seems to be known in Greece, but similar objects continued over a long period in Egypt[103] and the Near East,[104] and were known in Late Bronze Age Cyprus.[105]

## (b) *Bone/Ivory* (T 13,28, P 23,18) PLATE 221c

One small rectangular plaque, pierced, was found in the SPG II tomb, T 13; function uncertain, attachment or inlay? In addition a few scraps of ivory or bone occurred in the late LPG tomb P 23, no identification possible.

## (c) *Deer antler* (T Pyre 1,5 and 6) PLATE 236h, i

Two objects from an LPG pyre (T Pyre 1,5 and 6) are intriguing. The main fragment of 5 is a curved piece, decorated longitudinally with incised grooves which have one undulating edge. The preserved end has a notch cut out at right angles to the curve of the antler; the other end is broken off but near the break a hole is preserved on one face. 6 is a small pointed peg with flat top, pierced near the head. Interpretation is difficult: suggestions include the tip of a musical instrument such as a horned cithara, with peg for adjusting strings and tuning,[106] or the tip of a composite bow, with peg attached to the string as an aid in stringing the bow.[107] In favour of the latter suggestion are the signs of abrasion behind the notch (PLATE 236h), as though considerable tension had been applied in use, but in neither case is the placing of the notch or groove across the tip and at right angles to the curve well explained. A third, less probable, interpretation is as a fragment of jointed furniture.

A number of other, non-joining fragments of antler or horn were found at a late date with the bones gathered from this pyre; further study of these may help to solve the problem of their original form and use.

## CLAY SEALINGS (T 22,32–5) PLATES 178, 218f, 236a-g.

One tomb of SPG I date, T 22, evidently contained an object or objects of perishable material, which had been closed and sealed with lumps of fine red clay. Some of these preserved the impressions of straw or reed packing (?) on the upper surface, and of a flat and regular lightly grained surface below, almost certainly wood; three had string holes or string impressions; there were a few fingerprints and one possible cloth impression. There were no actual seal impressions.

The clay was never fired or burnt, and where the impressions have kept their form, this is due to a hardening of the surface crust in the tomb; the inner core remains extremely soft and friable, and the smaller fragments were held together only by the application of polyvinyl acetate.

There are two types of sealing:

(I) Cylindrical or conical plugs of clay (32, 33 — fragments of several, 34 — three, 35 — one). Most were of this shape, four with a diameter of 2.5–1.8, two smaller d. 1.5–0.8. No. 32 sealed a string which it pressed against on one side, and covered entirely on the other, PLATES 178, 236 g. A second, smaller, cylindrical fragment bears the impression of a string running across its flat end, PLATE 236 f. The smallest is irregular, somewhat like the leg of a figurine, and perhaps filled some irregularly shaped orifice.

(II) Rectangular (35). PLATES 178, 236a-b. One was larger, approximately rectangular in shape and triangular in section, and had apparently been pressed down against a flat surface (wood?). It also bears the clear impression of straw or reed packing on the two upper surfaces. It completely covered two strings which ran obliquely up, uniting (presumably in a knot) at the apex of the triangle.

It is difficult to see how these sealings were applied, or what shape of container they closed. There is a general similarity in shape with the early clay sealings from Lerna (EH II),[108] whose function is not fully understood, but probably included the closing of a wooden object with pegs (unlike ours), and the mouths of jars. Noteworthy is the contrasting richness of seal impressions in that context, totally lacking in our small group. The surviving objects most likely to have been placed in a container are the imported necklace beads, in the form of Egyptian figurines (T 22,28) and the inlaid glass beads (T 22,31). The find spot of the sealings is not very helpful here. They were found principally in two locations, most at the SE corner close to a group of faience beads (T 22,29–30) and not far from T 22,31, but at least one at the N end of the grave, some distance away with fibulae and pottery.

The sealings may have been used to close a small wooden casket for this jewellery, or for other objects of perishable material now lost.

## CLOTH REMAINS (PLATE 237a, b)

Traces of cloth were preserved on twenty-three metal objects.[109] The remains of cloth surviving in tombs S 10, 33 and 38, P 10–11, 22–23 and T 33 were examined by Dr. Jill Carington Smith, and the following is based on her observations.

These scraps are preserved only on the oxydised surface of iron pins and other metal objects, where they had remained in direct contact with these in a tomb; they are in the form of a positive matrix rather than a negative impression, and it is still possible to see, under magnification, not only the individual threads in the weave, but in some cases the individual fibres in each thread. This enables one to tell in which direction the threads were spun,[110] and this in turn may give an indication of the types of raw materials used.

Two different types of cloth were identified, a weft-faced tabby (= plain) weave (Type A), and an ordinary tabby weave (Type B). Type A has widely spaced threads in one direction, almost entirely hidden by tightly packed threads in the other — a widely spaced warp covered by a loosely spun, tightly packed weft, which bends around the warp threads, producing a weft-faced cloth such as is employed in tapestry weaving. Type B is a plain weave, but with approximately equal numbers of threads in each direction, and with both warp and weft threads showing on the face of the textile.

The quality of the cloth was good and would bear comparison with similar modern materials; for instance under magnification the MPG weave on S 51,5 bears a general resemblance to the coarse but strong white linen of the sherd bags used on the excavation, the fine SPG II weave on T 13,23 is closer to that of the excavator's cotton shirt.

In the list which follows an attempt has been made to give a thread count, for comparative purposes. However, in many cases the remains are too fragmentary for a genuine count per centimetre to be made. An approximate count has then been made by doubling the count for a half centimetre, and this may be taken as a rough guide; in these cases the figure given is preceded by the notation c. (*circa*).

*Submycenaean.* S 38,12 (iron pin fragments). Type A, PLATE 237b.
The probable weft threads are lightly Z-spun, and do not appear to be plied — so this may be a woollen fabric. The cloth is regularly and evenly woven. A piece measuring 2.2 × 1.5, adhering to the bulb of the pin, has 25 × 9 threads per cm; of the two largest sections on the shaft, one has 22 × 10, the other 18 × 6 threads per cm.

S 38,11 (iron pin fragments). Type A. Both halfway down the shaft and at the bottom are remains of cloth very similar to those of S 38,12, very likely from the same garment; Z-spun, c. 10 × 22 threads per cm. Type B. Near the head of the pin is a scrap of a different cloth, showing both warp and weft threads. Both sets of thread appear again to be Z-spun and non-plied (so probably wool), but it is difficult to be certain due to the fineness of the weave and the oxydisation; about 22 × 22 threads per cm.

S 38,13 (iron fragment?); traces of cloth. Type A, Z-spun, c. 10 × 19 threads per cm.

These traces suggest that tomb S 38 may have contained the remains of a thin under garment and a thicker outer garment, both perhaps of wool.

*EPG.* S 10,12 (iron pin fragments). Types A and B. Remains of certainly two, and possibly three different fabrics are preserved. Since some are woven from Z-spun thread and some from S-spun, it is possible that two different materials were in use.[3] Type A: remains of a cloth similar to, but finer than that of S 28,12, well and evenly woven from a Z-spun thread. Type B: a fine weave with both warp and weft showing, S-spun with approximately equal numbers of threads in each direction, c. 18 × 20 threads per cm. Third, there appear to be remains of a coarser cloth of Type B, poorly preserved.

S 10,11 and 13 (iron pin fragments). Type B, traces of the same weave as for S 10,12.

S 46,8 (iron fibula fragment). Traces of a rather coarse cloth on one side. Type B, threads S-spun in both directions, c. 14 × 22 threads per cm.

*MPG.* S 51,5 (iron fibula fragments). Traces of a rather coarse cloth. Type B, S-spun, c. 16 × 20 threads per cm.

*LPG.* P 3,27 (iron pin fragments). Type A, Z-spun(?), c. 10 × 20 threads per cm.

P 22,35 (iron pin fragments). Type B, slight traces of a coarse weave; threads in one direction (probably the warp threads) S-spun, or more probably, plied; c. 12 × 14 threads per cm.

P 23,16 (iron pin fragment). Type B, slight traces.

P 24,12 (iron pin fragment). Type A. Traces perserved on head bulb and shaft; Z-spun, c. 25 × 10 threads per cm. Similar traces on P 24,13 (the fellow of 12).

T 14,4 (iron sword). Type A. Substantial areas of cloth were preserved adhering to the lower blade, Z-spun, c. 12 × 22 threads per cm. PLATE 237a.

*SPG I.* P 10,22 (iron pin fragments). Type B; some traces. Either S-spun or, more probably, S-plied.

P 39,6 and 7 (iron fibulae). Heavy encrustation with much foreign matter adhering, including cloth. Type B, S-spun or plied; a close weave with approximately equal number of threads in each direction, 10 × 12 and 12 × 14 per cm.

*SPG II.* S 33,19 (iron pin). Traces of cloth on both bulb and shaft. Type B, S-spun with an approximately equal number of threads in each direction, c. 18 per cm.

T 13,23 and 24 (bronze bracelets). Type B. Traces of a very fine weave, c. 26 × 40 (−) threads per cm. Probably S-spun.

*SPG III.* S 59,27 (gilt iron pin). Traces of cloth on the shaft. Type A.

T 33,15 (bronze jug). Faint impression of cloth on the shoulder. Type B; a rather loose weave with an approximately equal number of threads in each direction, c. 12 per cm.

*Undated.* P 11,1 (iron pin fragment). Type B, traces of ?charred cloth with bone adhering. Approximately equal number of threads in each direction.

*Summary*
The traces which remain are extremely fragmentary and it is hazardous to attempt to draw any broad conclusions from them. One may say, though, that rather coarse and perhaps strong garments, probably of wool, were used in Submycenaean times; that there was a variety of cloth including finer weave used in EPG, and that by SPG II a very fine linen was known.

All the evidence comes from the graves, and, given the probable nature of burial rites at Lefkandi, it is of interest to note that cloth was often placed in the graves, as clothes or shroud for the human remains and as part of the ritual offerings.

## THE SHELLS

The following shell identifications were made on the basis of photographs.

(I) Shells found in tombs.
*Pectinidae*
Pecten jacobaeus (jacob's Scallop); edible. Three shells, from T 3 and T 36 (two), PLATES 201d, 237c.
*Cardiidae* (Cockle)
One shell, from S 19, PLATE 203b, upper right.
*Veneridae*
Dosinia *cf.* exoleta (Artemis). Two shells.
*cf. Tellinidae* (Tellin). Two shells, from S 19 (PLATE 203b, lower right) and S 27 (PLATE 237d)

(II) Deposit of 115 shells found in the north boundary ditch of Palia Perivolia cemetery (not illustrated).

*Patellidae*
Patella *cf.* vulgata (Limpet). Seven shells.
*Cerithiidae*
Cerithium *cf.* vulgatum. One shell.
*Pinnadae*
Pinna *cf.* nobilis (Pen Shell). Eleven fragments.
*Ostreidae*
Ostrea edulis (Edible Oyster). Two shells; edible.
*Cardiidae*
Cerastoderma edule (Common Cockle). Seventy-nine shells; edible.
*Veneridae*
Venus verrucosa (Warty Venus). Eight-eleven shells; edible.
*cf.* Dosinia sp. One shell.
*cf. Tellinidae* (Tellin). One shell.
*cf. Thraciidae.* Two shells.


See Section 5 for whetstones, loomweights, clay beads and buttons.
See Appendix for the human remains.

# Section 11

# Objects of Bronze, Iron and Lead

H. W. and E. CATLING

## INTRODUCTION

Over 250 base metal objects were found in the three cemeteries, divided between sixty-three tombs and thirteen pyres. The number of tombs in which no metal objects were found comfortably outnumbers those containing such material, while less than one fifth of the total numbers of pyres contained base metal. There was some difference from one cemetery to the other in this respect — overall, 42% of the tombs contained metal objects, 16% of the pyres. In the case of Skoubris, just over 42% of the tombs contained metal objects, 21% of the pyres. For Palia Perivolia, the equivalent figures were 32% for the tombs, 10% for the pyres. In Toumba, the figures were 46% and 40%.

The base metal objects very largely had served as personal decoration — bracelets, finger rings, earrings — or as dress fasteners — fibulae and straight pins. Of the sixty-three tombs in which objects of base metal were found, only seventeen (28.5%) contained other categories of object. The proportion was higher in the case of the thirteen pyres in which metal was found, where six (46%) contained other categories. Nine of the sixty-three tombs (14%) containing base metal had *no* ornaments or dress fasteners; again, the proportion of pyres without such objects was considerably higher — five out of thirteen (just over 38%).

These figures can be further compared according to period. Thirteen SM tombs included metal objects. Every one of these included ornaments or dress-fasteners; none contained objects of other categories. Of the seven EPG groups concerned, all, again, included ornaments or dress fasteners — only one had an object of any other category.

The MPG position is less clear, for only four tombs were involved. Two, certainly, had nothing but ornaments or dress fasteners; a third contained only fragments of iron, possibly part of a fibula. The last had a knife and a fragment, perhaps part of a fibula.

With the ten LPG groups, the position begins to change somewhat; three groups contained no ornaments or dress-fasteners, while in the other seven groups only ornaments and dress-fasteners were found.

Of the eleven relevant tombs dated SPG 1, six consisted exclusively of ornaments or dress-fasteners, two contained only other classes of objects and the remaining three groups included both. In the two tombs assigned to the SPGI/SPG II transition there were no ornaments or dress-fasteners.

A striking reversion occurred in SPG II, where none of the seven relevant groups contained anything except ornaments or dress-fasteners. There are seven groups attributed to SPG III, all of which include ornaments or dress-fasteners. Four of these seven also contain objects of other categories. The figures for the groups which cannot be dated independently are of less interest. Of a total of sixteen groups, ten of which are pyres, only ten include ornaments and dress-fasteners. Nine of these ten include no other class of object.

Pyres and tombs give rather different results. To start with, only three of the thirteen pyres containing metal objects proved independently datable. Of the thirty-three objects recovered from these pyres, only two were ornaments (the lead earrings from Toumba Pyre 5). Twenty-one were dress-fasteners (eight pins, thirteen fibulae). The remaining ten objects are all weapons, or over a third of all the weapons found, if the ten arrowheads from Toumba 26 are counted as individual pieces, nearly half the weapons if the quiver-full is regarded as a single item. The pyres accounted for two thirds of the spears found, two fifths of the swords and half the knives.

There is fluctuation in the relative quantities of bronze, iron and lead in use in the cemetery, of an apparently more capricious nature than might have been anticipated. The table appended below expresses both the totals for each period and the percentage representation of each material. These figures show an initial great preponderance of bronze

|          | Total | Bronze | Iron | Bronze and Iron | Lead |
|----------|-------|--------|------|-----------------|------|
| SM       | 49    | 45     | 4    | —               | —    |
|          |       | 91%    | 9%   | —               | —    |
| EPG      | 38    | 29     | 9    | —               | —    |
|          |       | 76%    | 24%  | —               | —    |
| MPG      | 5     | 2      | 2    | 1               | —    |
|          |       | 40%    | 40%  | 20%             | —    |
| LPG      | 36    | 11     | 23   | 2               | —    |
|          |       | 30%    | 65%  | 5%              | —    |
| SPG I    | 31    | 24     | 5    | 2               | —    |
|          |       | 77%    | 16.5%| 6.5%            | —    |
| SPG I/II | 3     | 1      | 2    | —               | —    |
|          |       | 33%    | 66%  | —               | —    |
| SPG II   | 31    | 20     | 10   | 1               | —    |
|          |       | 65%    | 32%  | 3%              | —    |
| SPG III  | 36    | 32     | 1    | —               | 3    |
|          |       | 86%    | 5%   | —               | 9%   |
| ND       | 28    | 11     | 15   | —               | 2    |
|          |       | 39%    | 53%  | —               | 8%   |
|          | 257   |        |      |                 |      |

to iron in SM which is steadily reduced until in LPG there are more than twice as many iron objects as bronze. The position changed considerably in SPG when, in SPG III, the quantity of bronze objects almost reverts to the SM level. Other fluctuations of chronological interest concern the relative popularity of dress-fasteners. Except in the MPG and SPG I/SPG II phases, where the numbers of groups involved are not large enough to have much statistical value, it may be noted that fibulae never form less than 33% of the total number of metal objects (LPG) and that in SPG III they constitute as much as 72% of the total. Pins fluctuate less dramatically from a highest level of 22% in SM to nil in SPG III. The sharpest contrast between successive phases in the use of pins comes between the 22% of SM and the 13% of EPG. Overall, dress-fasteners greatly outnumber personal ornaments − 176 of the former (nearly 70%), only thirty-two of the latter (12%). The use of rings is almost entirely confined to SM (24.5%) and EPG (21%) with one for SPG I, and another from a group undated by pottery.

Finally, note may be taken of changes of numbers of base metal objects in individual tombs. The contents of pyres are omitted here. One hundred and forty seven tombs were numbered, sixty-five of which contained base metal objects. Half of the sixty-five contained either one or two objects only; another twenty-four (36%) contained between three and six objects. Five more (7%) contained between seven and ten objects. Only two tombs contained more than this − twelve objects (ten of them arrowheads) in the LPG grave T 26, and the quite exceptional S 16 with its eighteen objects. This information may be set out in tabular form (below) to show the changes during the history of the cemetery. The SM period shows the greatest diversity in this respect. LPG and SPG I, out of a total of

NO. OF GROUPS

| Period | 1−2 objects | 3−6 objects | 7−10 objects | Over 10 objects | TOTAL |
|--------|-------------|-------------|--------------|-----------------|-------|
| SM | 5 | 4 | 3 | − | 12 |
| EPG | 2 | 4 | − | 1 | 7 |
| MPG | 4 | − | − | − | 4 |
| LPG | 5 | 3 | − | 1 | 9 |
| SPG I | 7 | 2 | 1 | − | 10 |
| SPG I/II | 2 | − | − | − | 2 |
| SPG II | 1 | 5 | − | − | 6 |
| SPG III | − | 6 | 1 | − | 7 |
| ND | 6 | − | − | − | 6 |

nineteen groups containing base metal objects has twelve with only one or two and this seems to represent the period of least generosity in metal goods. The SPG II and SPG III figures are in marked constrast; thirteen groups contained objects; only one of these had a single object, while twelve contained three or more.

## FIBULAE

Of the base metal objects recovered from the cemeteries, the bronze and iron fibulae form at once the most abundant and the most important category of material. One hundred and twenty-four fibulae (including identifiable fragments) were found, of which eleven are of iron. Of the thirty-nine find complexes in which fibulae were found, only three were pyres. The table below summarises some of the relevant numerical information.

The student of bronze fibulae in Greek lands returns again and again to the work of Chr. Blinkenberg.[1] His classification of this difficult class of object, (hereafter abbreviated to B) though in certain obvious respects overtaken by events, still serves as a most valuable point of departure for the study of any large group of new material such as the Lefkandi finds. Many studies have been made since Blinkenberg wrote in 1926,[2] but none has attempted to be so catholic — perhaps, indeed, it is no longer possible to attempt such a survey. I shall have occasion to refer to much of the post-Blinkenberg literature in what follows,

| | Bronze fibulae | Iron fibulae | No. of grave groups | No. of pyres | Total no. base Metal objects | Fibulae as % of total |
|---|---|---|---|---|---|---|
| SM | 21 | — | 8 | — | 49 | 43% |
| EPG | 21 | 3 | 6 | — | 38 | 63% |
| MPG | — | — | — | — | 5 | 0% |
| LPG | 11 | 1 | 4 | 1 | 36 | $33\frac{1}{3}$% |
| SPG I | 14 | 2 | 4 | — | 31 | 51% |
| SPG I/II | — | — | — | — | 3 | 0% |
| SPG II | 15 | 5 | 5 | 1 | 31 | 64% |
| SPG III | 26 | — | 6 | — | 36 | 72% |
| ND | 5 | — | 3 | 1 | 32 | 15% |
| | 113 | 11 | 36 | 3 | 261 | |

and in particular to a very newly published work by Mrs. Efi Sapouna Sakellarakis, *Die Fibeln der Griechischen Inseln*.[3] Mrs. Sakellarakis' study is a comprehensive one of the material from the islands. Included in her geographical terms of reference are all the islands E, NE and SE of the Greek mainland, including the great islands of Euboea and Crete. Her study of Euboea concentrated on the material from Lefkandi[4] but she did not take account of all the material. Her treatment of the Skoubris cemetery is fuller than Palia Perivolia and Toumba. I begin my discussion of the Lefkandi material by quoting (in translation from the German) part of her account of the fibulae of Euboea, to clarify the classification she has adopted.[5]

'The finds (sc. from Euboea) come mainly from the cemeteries of the settlement at Lefkandi . . . Three cemeteries were excavated, which are of great interest . . . Cremation is normal, inhumation rare.

'A full publication of the fibulae, and of the pottery from these three cemeteries has not yet appeared, so close dating of the material is not possible . . . The greater number of the Lefkandi fibulae are bronze; there are, however, a number of iron, and individuals of gold and of lead. They are of average size, or a little below, suggesting they were actually used and were not simply made for funerary purposes.

'The majority of the types of Lefkandi fibulae may be compared with their SM/PG contemporaries in Attica — particularly in the Kerameikos as well as with Skyros and Lemnos. Of the Lefkandi fibulae known to me the commonest type belongs to my Form II (45 examples, representing several examples, of which II a.c.l. is the most popular). Group I has at least four instances (one of type Ib and four leaf-bow examples, one of which (type Ig) is decorated in *tremolo* technique). Group IV is also represented several times (probably more than ten examples), particularly with a type which is represented in Athens and

Skyros. Boeotian fibulae are represented by eight examples. De Vries puts the Lefkandi Boeotian fibulae in the 9th century, while the comparable silver material from Eretria is assigned to the 8th century. According to De Vries the Euboeans in the west made fibulae without footplates in imitation of the fibulae of other western colonies. There are probably two northern fibula types, including a probable lead spectacle fibula, which is in fact not included in my catalogue.

'So in Lefkandi, there appear both the leaf-bow fibulae and the arched fibulae that are common at the end of the Bronze Age. Of the fibulae belonging to the beginning of the Iron Age, Group IV appears (in which case the method of manufacture is similar to those of Skyros, Lemnos and Attica, a relationship which is also clear from the Lefkandi pottery.)

'The case is the same with Group V fibulae which show a close relationship with the Skyros fibulae. Neighbouring Boeotia is likewise represented with all its varieties, admittedly only with a few examples. Type III, so popular in the islands, is not represented by a single example. It remains to determine whether this really means the type did not reach Euboea at all, or whether its origin post-dates 850 BC. The numerous Lefkandi fibulae were found in three cemeteries which were in use from the SM period until the end of the 9th century BC. Naturally the use of bronze objects — just as in the rest of Greece — during the early Geometric period is not really normal. This first becomes the case in LG. The Lefkandi bronze fibulae allow us to suppose local manufacture, and finds of moulds for casting bronze objects on the nearby settlement have proved the existence of workshops manufacturing bronze objects.'

Mrs. Sakellarakis' classification will be quoted as S-S hereafter.

Before we consider the Lefkandi fibulae in detail, certain generalisations may be made. The SM and EPG brooches are of great simplicity and, though certain variations in their form are obvious, the great majority belong to the same basic type. Between SM and EPG fibulae of this basic pattern, there is surprisingly little variety in essentials — of the twenty SM brooches that can be grouped in this fashion, the smallest is 2.8 long, the largest 7.7. The average length is 4.5. The equivalent figures for the EPG brooches (of which there are seventeen) are 3.6 and 7.1, with an average length of 4.6. They are all relatively flimsy and would have been of limited use for pinning heavy cloth, because of both the small space between bow and pin, and their general fragility. The normal SM and EPG arched fibulae are composed of very slim gauge rods of different section — the chief varieties are round, rectangular, square or rhomboidal. The occurrences of the two former are virtually the same in the SM and EPG periods; four SM fibulae are square in section — only one EPG; four SM brooches have rhomboidal sections — seven EPG have this feature.

The practice of twisting the material (perhaps to increase tensile strength) is confined to SM (four examples) and it seems quite likely, therefore, that the undated S 54, 1 (PLATE 247, 14) should be dated submycenaean.

Only very limited efforts were made to decorate the standard arched fibulae. In the SM brooches S 40, 5, whose material was of square section, carries fine traced lines on the bow. Among the EPG fibulae, S 16, 28 (PLATE 247, 10) has impressed notches on its bow; the material is of rhomboidal section.

Fibulae were not reported from any of the MPG graves. As only four of these contained base metal objects, too much stress need not be placed on this feature. The position in LPG is very different. None of the simple brooches has survived; instead, of the eight identifiable fibulae, seven have heavy bows, where a solid central section of varying size and shape is set off by carefully articulated mouldings. The contrast with what had gone before could hardly be more marked. The position changes again in SPG I, for a more diverse collection of brooches was in circulation. The ornate, heavy pieces which had first appeared in the preceding period continue, as well as a heavily built brooch that is probably an Attic import. Of great interest is the reappearance of arched fibulae, in a version that superficially resembles B type II.1 (= S-S IIa), but in a form that shows an appreciable change. Not only is the form of the bow more carefully shaped into a semi-circle, or more than a semi-circle, but the material thickens appreciably, usually at the centre of the bow, and the bow itself is regularly picked out by up to three groups of traced rings. In SPG II the diversity of fibula type introduced in the previous period continues. The newly revived arched brooches make up one third of the total number, after which the heavy ornate variety is the next most popular. At least three of the remainder seem to be imports (including a mangificent pair of 'Attico-Boeotian' brooches with flattened crescent bows).

Finally, SPG III, which has more fibulae than any other phase in the life of the cemetery. Tendencies already apparent in SPG I and II develop further – both the heavy, ornate brooches and the light arched fibulae, with an even longer number of imported decorated fibulae, including very fine examples of Attico-Boeotian brooches.

Some general conclusions follow this rapid survey of the development of fibula use at Lefkandi. Firstly, there is little or no difference in this respect between SM and EPG. Secondly, the combined periods MPG and LPG generally fairly weak in bronze objects have only a relatively small number of fibulae. A new type appears in LPG, quite unlike anything in the SM–EPG series – it continues, with little change, until the end of the life of the cemetery. It is joined in SPG I by a refreshed version of the arched fibula, possibly indebted to Italian inspiration, which also lasts for the rest of the site's history. At the same time, throughout the whole of SPG, there is a steady enjoyment of exotic fibulae, culminating with the importation of some splendid 'Attico-Boeotian' brooches.

We may now consider the bronze fibulae in greater detail, period by period.

### Submycenaean

Twenty-one fibulae were recovered, of which one (S 63,4) was too damaged to classify. The material may be considered in the light of Blinkenberg's classification, with appropriate reference to Sapouna-Sakellarakis.

B II. 1 + 2 + 7 symmetric arched bows, material round or square in section (includes S-S types IIa, c and f) (PLATES 238a, j; 247, 4, 15–16.) The following: S 15B, 2, 3, 4 and 5, S 19,13, S 38,8 and 9 (round or square in section) S 22,7, S 40,6, S 63,3 (bar twisted – material originally of round section). The small S 40,6 lacks the symmetry of the two other twisted-bow fibulae, but this is less a sign of typological difference than maladroitness on the maker's part. The lack of symmetry on S 19,13 should be explained in the same fashion, not by invoking typology.

B II. 3, symmetric arched bows, material of rhomboid section, PLATES 238c; 247, 8. S 19,11, S 22,8, S 60,4. The first two brooches are clumsily made; the pin of S 22,8 is too long for the bow, and in both cases the springs are badly formed. S 22,8 is the largest of the Lefkandi SM and EPG arched bow fibulae.

Two arched fibulae stand apart from the others. Although they would fall into B class II as a whole, they are not closely matched in any of his subdivisions:

S 19,12, (PLATE 247, 6,) (which S-S classes with her type IIe) has an almost symmetric arched bow. The material is of very shallow rectangular section, with a slight raised rib in the centre.

S 40,5 (S-S Type IIc, no. 165, but not really conforming to her definition) is abnormal among the SM arched fibulae in the manner in which the bow widens from the centre towards the catch plate, and in having two very fine traced lines on the bow from spring to catch. The piece has some of the characteristics of B type II.4 (most of the examples of which come from Crete. The unusual nature of this piece suggests it might be an import.

B II.15 and 16, asymmetric arched fibulae (including examples categorised in S-S classes IIf, k and l), (PLATES 238g, h, i, l; 247, 12–13.) S¯19,10, S 40,4, S 43,7 (material of square or rectangular section), S 43,5 (material twisted - originally square).

S 43,6 (PLATES 238k; 247, 18) is a brooch of considerable interest, and may well be an imported piece. The bow is asymmetric, and angular, dividing the brooch into bow and forearm — the bow is swollen and set off by two elegant mouldings. It corresponds to B type II.17 in shape, though he reserved this category for gold brooches, all found in Cyprus. There is close similarity with a Cypriot bronze version — B XIII.1d. It is not mentioned by Sapouna-Sakellarakis, but she would presumably have classed it with her group IVb. There is a close parallel in the late SM grave 108 in the Kerameikos, where it is one of the twelve fibulae in this remarkable group. Five others of similar type were found in the Kerameikos SM graves — one in SM 33 (Early), three in S.42 (Middle) (one illustrated *Ker* III, 83, fig. 2, left) and one in S.70 (Middle). Fibulae very similar in design have been found in Cyprus. A fragmentary brooch of this type comes from the LC IIIB Tomb 26 at *Kaloriziki*, Episkopi[6] and a complete example from Kouklia, *Kaminia* Tomb 1:1.[7] The general type was probably also represented by the two groups of fibulae from two other LC IIIB groups — Lapithos *Ayia Anastasia* Tomb 2[8] and Episkopi, *Kaloriziki* T. 40.[9] Though the evidence is not conclusive, fibulae of this class may have been developed in Cyprus and moved back to Greece. I say 'moved back', since the fibula owes is presence in Cyprus to Greek (Mycenaean) initiative in the 12th Century BC.

Be that as it may, this type of fibula (in a fashion at present obscure) must have exercised a profound effect on the development of Greek fibula design. I shall try to explain below how I think this happened.

Unclassified: S 63,4 was too damaged to identify.


### EPG fibulae

The most popular brooch is the symmetric arched bow corresponding in minor variations to B II.1 and 2, repeating a type that was also popular in SM, PLATES 238b; 247, 2 and 5. The examples are arranged according to the section of their material. S 8,6, S 10,8, S 16,19, S 20,8 (round section); S 16,21 (square section); S 16,20, 23, 24, 25 and 26 (rectangular section). Not all these brooches were made with the same care, not all are as symmetric as the best: S 8,6 is the only brooch that manages to preserve its curvilinear quality from spring to catch plate. One or two (S 16,26, for example) seem almost determined upon asymmetry — but not to the point where typology must step in and call for fresh categories. Six more symmetric arched fibulae are made of material of rhomboid section and thus conform to B class II.3, PLATES 238f; 247, 9 — S 8,5, S 10,9, S 16,18, 22 27, S 46,4 — double the number of brooches of this class that occurred in SM.

A variant arched bow fibula is S 16,28, (PLATE 247, 10). The material is rhomboid in section but is made remarkable by its decoration of impressed notches on the crest and edges of the bow.

Rare types in the EPG material were:

S 10,10 = B I.7 — a brooch basically of violin-bow type, whose bow has been flattened to leaf shape, without ornament.[10]

S 46,5, (PLATE 247, 1,) = B I.8 = S-S type 1e (no. 31). The leaf bow is decorated with simple pointillé patterns — triangles opposed either side of a medial line. A fibula of much this variety was part of the rich Kerameikos S 108 group (*Ker* I, pl. 28, third row, right hand). A second fibula of the same class was found in the same grave.[11] Kraiker and Kübler have commented on this class of brooch.[12]

### LPG fibulae

There are eight categorisable brooches in this period and a group of fragments from T Pyre 2 (no. 11) which are difficult to assign to types. Symmetric arched fibulae have disappeared; in view of the reappearance of what is probably a cognate form later, in SPG I, the gap in the type series is important for the view we may take of the origin of the reintroduced brooch. The LPG series consists almost entirely of thickened bow types, closely interrelated so that, on the surface at least, it seems as though a full typological development takes place during LPG.

The steps in this development appear to have been as follows:

T 17,4 (PLATE 248, 6). Asymmetric bow, the back part considerably swollen, set off at each end by a group of three relief ridges. Corresponds in most essentials with B type II.19, and falls within the very wide limits of S-S type IVb.

P 3,25 (PLATES 248, 9; 239c). Bow rather less asymmetric, the swelling having moved nearer the centre. The swelling is shorter than in T 17,4 and is thicker in relation to the size of the brooch as a whole. Still within the limits of B type II.19 and S-S. type IVb.

P 23,15 (PLATE 248, 10). Bow almost symmetric, with an even shorter swelling set off by mouldings either side, the swelling almost circular in section, but the underside flattened. The development is carried still further by: T 12A,4 (PLATE 248, 11; 239e) where the articulation of the various elements in the design of the brooch are harmoniously composed — catch, forearm (square in section) central swelling/boss set off either side by neat bead mouldings (with tidy oblique traced lines — almost like milling — on the innermost elements), square stem leading to a spring of two complete turns. This form is not really represented by either Blinkenberg or Sapouna-Sakellarakis, though the nearest approach would be B II.14.

The end product of the development is a brooch-type exemplified by T Pyre 2,8, 9 and 10, (PLATE 248, 14–15), of which the latter two were almost certainly made as a pair. The swelling at the centre of the bow now becomes dominant and unbalances the brooch — it is often wider than it is long, and the resulting clumsiness is not really apparent in photographs or drawings; the brooch needs to be seen and handled for its aesthetic shortcomings to be fully apparent. On the other hand, the brooches are technically extremely competent, and the pair of mouldings either side of the boss are very finely executed, including the emphasis laid on them by milling.

The development of this fibula type stops at this stage; as we shall see, it continued to be popular into SPG, and was imitated in iron. It appears in a variety of sizes, from tiny pieces like S 59,36 (PLATE 110, SPG III) to the clumsy-looking pair from S Pyre 4,11 and 12, PLATE 113.

It is tempting to suggest that this type of fibula, with the heavy swollen element in the bow, grew originally out of an instinct to allow brooches to develop in much the same fashion as dress pins — in fact, to design brooches to look much as they would if they were to be fashioned from an actual dress pin.

This variety of brooch has a very restricted distribution. B II.14b is fairly close; the type corresponds to S-S class Vb, which is composed of ten Lefkandi examples[13] and two (unpublished) from Skyros. Dr. Marangou[14] has recently published an example, said to have been found on Skyros.

The brooch, P 3,26 (PLATE 249, 6), made of a combination of iron and bronze, is unique, though its shape is virtually the same as the gold brooch in T 13 (PLATE 231c). It is uncertain whether the brooch started life as a hybrid, or whether the iron spring and pin replaces original bronze counterparts that broke away and were lost. Typologically it is difficult to place.[15] I suggest that this brooch belongs somewhere in the development of the Cypriot 'broken-backed' variety (B XIII.14) (exemplified, for instance, by a brooch in the Cesnola Collection).[16] As Blinkenberg pointed out, this type leads on to the more common triangular fibula crowned by a knob, the bow embellished in various ways (B XIII.15).

It is possible, but uncertain that the fragments T Pyre 2,11 belong to one or more fibulae of this type.

## SPG I fibulae

There are fourteen identifiable SPG I fibulae, which combine to demonstrate a fresh initiative in fibula design and use, and to suggest that by this date, if no sooner, bronze brooches were used for a variety of purposes, and that designers were taking this into account. The most interesting new development is the reappearance of the symmetric arched bow fibulae, superficially corresponding to B II.1, which, as we have seen, was well represented in the SM and EPG material.

But even slight acquaintance with the SPG I arched bow fibulae shows an important difference in design. The brooch-makers had a much closer control over the symmetry of their bows (for example T 22,19, PLATE 238m); secondly, they had evidently learned from experience that even a slight thickening of the metal at the centre of the bow improved its rigidity very considerably. This, in its turn, suggests that this class of fibulae was by now cast rather than fabricated — a likely consequence of the casting of other, more elaborate types of fibulae.

Two brooches — T 22,20 and T 25A,4 — could perhaps be regarded as prototypes of this new arched-bow class for, though they have the thickening at the centre of the bow, they are not symmetric, for in both cases the forearm has strayed out of the even curve of the bow.

The remainder — T 22,19, 21, 22, 24, 25 — all have symmetric bows — T 22,19 (PLATE 248,3) is the finest, and also the largest, with a length of 6.8. The others are at most half this size. None of these brooches has any sign of decoration. As we shall see, later developments in this type of brooch included a decorated bow — even if only in a very simple fashion.

Two factors in particular suggest that the reappearance of the symmetric arched fibula at Lefkandi is the result of external stimulus. First, it follows a complete hiatus during MPG and LPG, long enough to suggest a real break. Second, in its late version, it exhibits important differences when compared with the old SM—EPG series, seen most obviously in the broad catch-plates and the carefully controlled symmetrically swelling bows. It is not a variety noted either by Blinkenberg or Sapouna-Sakellarakis, which makes either foreign origin or local development very probable. The latter explanation seems to be unlikely, given the long interval without symmetric arched bow brooches. I suggest that the source of inspiration may be Italy, though it is quite possible that none of the series that we have is actually of Italian fabric, particularly since many examples in the Italian series are relatively elaborately decorated.[17] Sundwall dates that series from 900 BC[18] which harmonises satisfactorily with the proposed chronology for the Lefkandi material.

The type of Italian fibula to which I suggest we should relate this class from Lefkandi is well distributed. It is represented in south-east Sicily in the Molino della Badia inhumation cemetery,[19] apparently attributed to Pantalica II, 11th and 10th centuries BC.[20] In central Italy examples are recorded at Terni, with groups of traced lines encircling the bow very much in the manner of T 27, 9, for instance, (PLATE 248, 2).[21] This group seems to be attributed to Terni II, ascribed by Müller-Karpe to the 9th century BC.[22] The same type appears at Tarquinia in Poggio dell'Impiccato grave 29,[23] assigned to Tarquinia I (9th century BC).[24] We may also note its presence in grave 10 at Cumae,[25] which can evidently also be dated to the 9th century BC.

Earlier I suggested a typological succession taking place during LPG leading from the asymmetric arched fibulae with swollen element in the bow to the brooch with heavy boss on an otherwise small bow. If that evolution is sound we have to accept the fact that certain types of brooch which, according to that analysis, were early in the sequence continued in production long after their typological successors were fully developed.

Within this category I include T 1,10 and 11, T 3,10 (PLATE 248, 5 and 7). The former pair stand extremely close to T 17,4 (PLATE 248, 6), which I placed at the head of the typological development described above for LPG. Very close to them must be T 3,10, whose bow is perhaps more symmetric than T 17,4. This fibula can most closely be compared with a brooch in a child's grave in the Athenian Agora.[26] It is possible that the Lefkandi brooch is an Attic import, and that brooches such as T 1,10 and 11 are Euboean imitations of a Mainland design. In any event, a brooch of this kind illustrates some kind of relationship between Attica and Euboea.

T 22,6 and 27, T 25A,5, (PLATE 248, 15) are examples of the heavily bossed fibulae that first appear in LPG, described above. These brooches exhibit no feature not already encountered in the equivalent LPG series.

### SPG II fibulae

Thirteen SPG II fibulae can be attributed to identifiable types. A proportion of these belong to types familiar from earlier periods. For instance S 33,15 and 16, S Pyre 4,14, T 5,17 and, probably, T 5,19, are associable with the SPG I series of symmetric bow types, which, I have suggested, may well owe something to contact with Italy. Three brooches (S Pyre 4,11 and 12, T 5,20) illustrate the continuance of the heavily bossed variety first introduced in LPG, continuing in SPG I, and, as we shall see, continuing popular into SPG III.

P 43,7 (PLATE 148) is the fragment of a small brooch belonging to the class distinguished by a swollen element in the bow. This resembles, but is not precisely the same as, two of the brooches (P 23,15 and T 12A,4 PLATES 248, 10—11; 239d—e) that have a place in the evolution of the heavily decorated varieties. It is also similar to B II.19b from Vrokastro, Crete.

S Pyre 4,13 — a leaf bow brooch of B I.8 is an anachronism but such anachronisms are familiar — A. M. Snodgrass has called attention to a similar typological displacement at Vitsa Zagoriou.[27] P 43,7, a very small brooch with relatively large central swelling, recalls the fibulae transitional between brooches of B types II.19 and II.4, particularly P 3,25, P 23,15 and T 12A,4, and it is here that the brooch finds its most natural home. On this assumption, it will have been locally made.

T 13,22 (PLATES 249, l; 240d) is closely to be compared with B type II.12e = HM 898, a brooch found at Praisos in Crete. The latter is almost double the size of the Lefkandi fibula, but the elegance of the mouldings in the swollen bow and of the bead and reel that sets it off are exactly matched. It must stand quite close to the SPG III pair form S 59,29 and 30 (for which see below), and it seems quite possible that it comes from the same source as these — Athens, most likely.

The fine pair of flattened crescent bow fibulae from P 45,1 and 2 (PLATES 241a–b; 249, 5) are technical masterpieces, though there may be reservations concerning their aesthetic suitability. Blinkenberg traced the likely typological evolution of this form from certain arched fibulae, the material of whose bows is hammered flat so that the broadened face of the bow is vertical. Such a brooch has been found at Lefkandi (the SM S 40,5). But nothing in the Lefkandi series prepares us for the treatment of the stem, with its finely milled surface, or the fine mouldings which help to mark off the stem from the bow. Nor has anything led us to anticipate the paddle-wheel bead of six points threaded on to the stem. The ornament on the bow each side is also executed with delicacy and skill, though the significance of the design is obscure. The texturing of the arms of the encircled cross by very light, close-set punch marks is remarkably imaginative. The craftsmanship exhibited by this pair of brooches presupposes a long workshop tradition. So many features of these brooches' design are unrelated to their function that we can hardly guess at the factors that brought them into being in this form. If we compare them with another group of fibulae with flattened crescent bows — Kerameikos Geometric grave 41, which contained three pairs of very similar brooches which resemble ours in the form of the bow, but have sail-shaped catch plates instead of the small paw-shaped catch, while the stems are plain and there is no sign of the bead that is so distinctive a feature of our brooches, we do not find strong compulsion to derive our paddle-wheel variety directly from these. Sapouna-Sakellarakis' list of her type IXd(?) fibulae to which she attributes those from P 45, is very brief, including a fragmentary example from the Aphaia temple, Aegina, and two pieces (one only a fragment) from Skyros. To these pieces should be added two or three noticed by Blinkenberg, viz:

(1) Oxford G.336 'Greek Islands'. No moulding either side of the crescent bow. Simple linear patterns in *tremolo* on the bow. (B IX.1c)

(2) Oxford E.337. Similar (B IX.1d)

(3) Copenhagen 752. 'Todi, près de Thèbes'. Bow set off by simple mouldings — traced figured marked off by zig-zags, etc.


## SPG III fibulae

The SPG III series of fibulae at Lefkandi is at once the largest attributed to any period and the most intricate, in some cases raising questions of place of manufacture that can hardly be resolved with available evidence. More obvious pairs of brooches belong in this period than any earlier — there are four pairs and one set of three.

The types continue to include a majority already encountered in the earlier period, including five with thickened symmetric arch-bows, large spreading catch-plates and groups of traced rings on the bar, which, as I have suggested above, recall certain types of Italian fibulae (T 27,10, 11, 12, PLATE 184, and the pair T 32,15 and 16, PLATE 248, 1). Also familiar from earlier groups are the ugly swollen bow fibulae with fine mouldings either side of the boss. These include the pair T 32,13 and 14, (PLATE 248, 12) and five brooches from S 59: 32, 33, 34, 35 and 36, (PLATE 110). There is no obvious development in these brooches when they are compared with the earliest appearance of the type in LPG.

All the remaining SPG III fibulae are unusual in one fashion or another. The pair T 32,11 and 12 (PLATE 248, 4) basically comprise a symmetric arch bow type, rather larger than normal among the Lefkandi arched bow fibulae, enlivened by three evenly spaced prominent bead-mouldings 'threaded' onto the bow — the catch-plates are unusually wide. Mrs. Sapouna-Sakellarakis[28] has grouped with this pair, fragments from Emporio (Chios) and from the Hephaisteia cemetery on Lemnos; I am unconvinced by those attributions for in both cases the fragments are too small to preserve sufficient of the determining features. In view of the lack of convincing parallels elsewhere, and the anomalous composition of the metal (see below) it is at least possible that this pair of brooches was a local aberration on the part of a Lefkandian designer. Mrs. Sapouna-Sakellarakis proposes an Italian northern origin for the type on the strength of the broad catch-plate. This is a seductive suggestion, but needs the support of actual instances of brooches from these regions.

The decorated brooch with flattened crescent bow T 36,23 (PLATE 249, 7) is very close to the pair T 45,1 and 2 already discussed above, though it is appreciably larger than these.

A very simple brooch with flattened crescent bow, undecorated, T 31,21 (PLATE 247, 11) may well belong to the brooch series that leads to the elaborately decorated brooches of B class IX. But, chronologically, it is an anachronism since in this very simple form it finds itself side by side with the most sophisticated versions. A possible explanation for the anomaly would be the fairly obvious one that manufacture of simple versions of a basic type did not come to an end simply because a more sophisticated (and, obviously, expensive) version had been devised.

The small T 31,23 brooch with very swollen element setting off the centre of the bow probably belongs to the developing series of swollen-bow brooches that culminates in the squat heavily bossed variety described above.

The remaining fibulae (S 59,31, T 36,24 and 25, S 59,29 and 30, see PLATE 240) are of exceptional importance for the place they hold in the early stages of the development of the decorated fibulae of Attica and Boeotia which have understandably attracted much attention since they first began to appear in the late 19th century.

In fact, this series shows a second process of evolution from the swollen bow fibulae, one process of which we have already seen culminating in the ugly squat heavy bows that had evolved already in LPG. In that development interest concentrated on the form of the swelling at the centre of the bow, and the mouldings which were introduced to set off the boss. In the second process of development, though interest was shown in the bow, the enlargement and change of form in the catch plate and forearm as a single unit adapted for elaborate decoration was the dominant idea. This was much the more successful line of evolution. The elaborate decoration of the catch-plate may be related to the equally intricate decoration of Italian 'Blattbogenfibeln' which had already developed considerably by the date of the appearance of the parallel Greek phenomenon.

The contribution of Lefkandi to a fuller understanding of this process is best shown by the fine brooch T 36,24 (PLATE 249, 3) which appears typologically to be intermediate between the relatively simple swollen bow as exemplified by T 1,10, T 17,4 or T 3,10. At this stage of development the swollen element of the bow is asymmetric, so that the stem is always shorter than the forearm that culminates in the catch. Two developed brooches show different approaches to the next stage of development. The SPG II brooch T 13,22 (PLATE 249, 1) shifts the swollen element so that it is centred on the bow;

stem and forearm are of equal importance in the design. They are given some life by fine traced lines but the swelling becomes the object of attention, being enlarged and given sharply defined planes set off by very fine mouldings. A different approach is seen in T 36,24 (PLATE 249, 3), where the asymmetry in the location of the swollen arm is kept but attention is shifted from the bow to the forearm and catch. A little very simple traced ornament appears in the stem and the forearm foreshadowing the much richer decoration on the T 59,29 and 30 pair (PLATE 249, 4). If we look back from this pair to T 36,24 we see that the process whereby the unity of the brooch design gives way to a design that subordinates everything to the decorated plate has already begun. The pair S 59,29 and 30 obviously go extremely closely with Kerameikos grave 41, the major differences being that the stem of the Kerameikos brooch is richly decorated with traced patternwork and the main ornament of the catch-plate is different. But these are trifling differences. Both in size, general character and particular detail the Lefkandi brooches are so close to the Kerameikos brooch that they must come from the same workshop and their date of manufacture must be the same. With the revival of contact between Attica and Lefkandi such a relationship is not surprising.

The representation of a man following behind a horse has been suggested as a 'horse-tamer' and should be seen as such. Professor Coldstream has remarked on the lack of precedents for this subject and suggested that, though there is nothing oriental about the style of the figures, the impulse for attempting them may have resulted from familiarity with oriental figure work. The device on an ivory seal[29] from Athens recalls this catch plate, but there is a second man, at the horse's head. Notice a Mycenaen version of the horse-and-man theme on the Varkiza ring.[30]

The abstract patternwork in the upper part of the catch plate, and the border around much of the rest of it recalls embroidery, and I suggest these designs may, *mutatis mutandis*, have been embodied in the garments with which our pins were worn.

The following fibulae, then, compose what we may call the 'Horse-Tamer Group':

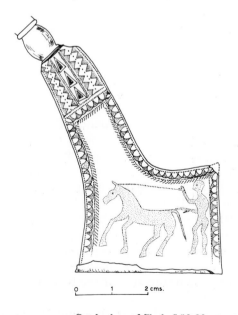

Catch plate of fibula S 59,29

(1) and (2) S 59,29 and 30
(3) and (4) Kerameikos G 41
within the group, but diverging in form, I suggest:
(5) Kerameikos, stray find = *JdI* 77, 106, fig. 24:4
(6) Berlin Pergamum Museum MI. 8064.103. Said to be from Boeotia = De Vries, *Staatliche Museen zu Berlin-Forschungen und Berichte* Band 14, *Archäologische Beiträge* 114 and Taf. 13.1
(7) Copenhagen 723. Said to be from Athens, Dipylon. Blinkenberg 171, VIII 5 i.

### Fibulae from undated contexts

Three fibulae come from contexts lacking independent evidence of date. T 54,1, an arch bow brooch of twisted wire of square or rhomboidal section is probably SM in date. From T 9, no. 1 is a fragmentary arched fibula with asymmetric swollen bow recalling closely brooches encountered in LPG contexts, which is a possible date for this tomb.

### Iron fibulae

Twelve brooches of iron were recovered, in varying states of preservation. Three of these are from EPG groups, two from SPG 1, five from SPG II and only one from SPG III. Three types are identifiable. Symmetric arched fibulae — S 32,8, S 20,10 (both EPG), perhaps T 5,25 (SPG II) and T 27,14 (SPG III). All of these are of moderate size only — similar to their bronze counterparts.

Two poorly preserved brooches (a pair, P 39,6 and 7, SPG I) were probably comparable with the small swollen bow type which first appears in LPG. No trace of detail survived.

Perhaps the most interesting type is the flattened crescent brooch represented by SP 4,15 and 16 (SPG II), PLATE 241d. They are only very slightly larger than the larger bronze version T 36,23 — there is sure sign on SP 4,15 of mouldings on the stem and above the catch; the bow itself was picked out with a traced line that follows its contour just inside the edge — no other ornament can be detected.

The remaining brooches and fragments are not susceptible of attribution to types.

## DRESS PINS (PLATES 242 and 250)

Some forty-seven pins were found in the cemeteries, the commonest category of object after fibula. Fifteen of these were bronze, twenty-eight iron, three a mixture of the two metals, while one was a combination of iron and faience. The sharpest distinction in use of materials comes between the SM and later periods. Nine of the fifteen bronze pins belong to tombs datable to SM. Of the remaining six, four come from undated groups, one from a SPG I group, the last from SPG II. Of the twenty-eight iron pins, on the other hand, only two are datable to SM, five to EPG, none to MPG, seven to LPG, five to SPG I. Their popularity then wanes; four are dated SPG II, nine SPG III. Pins occur in twenty-six find complexes, (five of which are pyres) in ten of which there are also fibulae. In twelve cases, a single pin was found, in fourteen cases two were found together. There was one instance of three pins found together, and a single case of four pins from the same tomb.

Not all the pins were sufficiently well preserved to be of much value in making a typological analysis of their forms. This applies to five of the bronze pins and sixteen of the iron pins.

Early pins have recently been discussed by Desborough[31] and Snodgrass,[32] expanding

Jacobsthal's fundamental analysis.[33] The account of the Lefkandi pins that follows relies heavily on these sources.

The Lefkandi SM bronze pins are undistinguished. The common type is a relatively small pin (PLATE 250, 1–3) with small head, like the head of a nail, usually flat, but occasionally slightly domed. The head is separated by a slim neck from an oval swelling, more pronounced in some cases than others. None of the pins has any kind of decoration though this is a regular feature of SM bronze pins elsewhere, for instance, traced rings often appear on the shaft above and below the swelling. A pin from Kerameikos SM grave 16 (early SM, according to Styrenius[34]) is somewhat similar to our pins, more so than two pins in the Kerameikos middle-SM tomb 42.[35] No examples of the disk-topped pin with strongly marked spherical globe on the upper shaft occur, though they do appear among both the iron pins and the iron-and-bronze pins (for which, see below). The standard SM pin type at Lefkandi may have been a local product, well aware of fashion in contemporary Athens, for example. It could be that the local smiths lacked the ability to produce pins of the refinement of the Attic series. A variant (S 36,1 – PLATE 250, 4) with small, almost spherical head and swelling relatively lower down the shaft seems to be striving after greater elegance. These bronze SM pins are also much smaller than the Attic series, which are all over 20 in length, and in some cases are over 40 long.

It has not been possible to find parallels for the pair of very delicate floral-headed pins, P 46,1 and 2 (PLATE 250, 5), which, unfortunately were the only objects in the grave though it was stratified below SPG I, P Pyre 34. At first sight, the terminal seems either a pomegranate or the seed-head of a poppy. In fact, it is better regarded as a sphere surmounted by a rosette, and resembles in this a much later pin from Ephesus.[36] The sphere (which would represent the body of the poppy-head or the pomegranate) lacks detail. The use of two globes to decorate the pin-head, the first topped by its rosette, the second set off by a ridge moulding top and bottom, has no SM or PG parallel. It is tempting to regard the pins as imports, though I cannot identify their source (which, for instance, seems unlikely to have been Cyprus).

The remaining bronze pin, the roll-top P 21,11 (PLATE 242F), comes from a SPG II group, and may well be an import, though the idea is so simple that it could easily have been imitated in Greece. I have elsewhere commented on their distribution and dating,[37] and Jacobsthal discussed their appearances in the West.[38] Kerameikos SM T 85 contained two bronze pins that lay in the left shoulder of the skeleton of a girl — one (l. 9.6) was a roll-top, the type of the second is not mentioned in the publication (Ker 1, 40). The grave cannot be closely dated since it contained no other objects. Another roll-top pin was found in Kerameikos SM T 104. With a length of 13 it was very close in size to the Lefkandi pin. Two more were found in the Salamis SM cemetery, one of them illustrated.[39] These pins were 16.5 and 12.5 respectively. The origin of this type of pin is oriental; it was current in the Late Bronze Age as well later.[40–42]

Three hybrid iron and bronze pins were found — one MPG (T 12b, 2, PLATE 250, 10) one SPG I (P 44,9), one SPG II (S 33,17, 18, PLATE 242I); none of them is complete. In each case a bronze bead of ellipsoid form had been slipped onto the shaft of an iron pin. Only in one case was the head of the pin preserved well enough to decide its form — a plain disk. This hybrid type of pin is considered particularly characteristic of Athens by Desborough[43] though instances have been reported as far afield as Theotokou in Thessaly, and in Kos, as well as nearer home in the Argolid. Snodgrass[44] points to the great popularity of these pins in PG Athens, particularly in the Kerameikos, where he points to thirteen

MPG and LPG instances; the type continues into EG (in Attic terminology). It is at least possible that these three pins are imports from Athens.

The iron pins, in general were very poorly preserved, and it is doubtful whether more than one or two were found complete. This was particularly unfortunate in the case of the SM pair, S 38,11 and 12. They will have been at least 10 long when complete, and seem to have had a small head and slight swelling below it, resembling closely the shape of the normal SM bronze pins, a pair of which were found in the same tomb — S 38,6 and 7. Iron pins have been found in other SM tombs, though in Attic terms, these seem to be late burials — Kerameikos S 113, PG 22 and PG 23.[45]

Of the remainder preserved with identifiable characteristics, one (S 10,11) is dated EPG, four (P 23,16—17, P 24,12—13) are dated LPG, three (T 15,15—17) to SPG 1, one (S 33,19) to SPG II and a pair (P Pyre 29,1 and 2) have no independent evidence of date. There are three distinguishable varieties, each of which is represented by one example in the T 15 group of SPG I date. One of these resembles fairly closely the main SM type, with smallish flat disk head and a slim oval swelling on the shaft close below the head (PLATE 250, 9). This form is attested in LPG (P 23,16—17) and presumably remained in circulation continuously from SM. The second variety has what seems to have been a rounded head (eg. T 15,15) and a globe-swelling on the shaft close below the head (PLATE 250,11). As has been pointed out, this is no more than a translation into iron of a second common type of SM pin.[46] The third pin type has a relatively broad disk-head and a plain shaft. The small T 15,17 and the undated P Pyre 29,1 illustrate the variety (PLATE 250, 6). This type seems unrecognised elsewhere, but, clearly must have existed in this form as a preliminary stage in making the hybrid pins with iron shafts and bronze globes.

The abnormal object T Pyre 1,4, apparently part of the shaft of an iron pin (though it seems to be hollow) with beads threaded onto it may possibly be related to a remarkable object from Grave 182 at Bologna (S. Vitale) which consists in this case of a bronze shaft with a variety of disks threaded onto it. The context is Bologna I (9th century BC).[47]

Earlier writers concerned with SM and PG pins (particularly Styrenius, *Studies* and Snodgrass, *DAG*) have pointed to the fact that dress pins are usually (though not invariably) the concomitant of the burial of women - presumably therefore, a majority, at least, of those Lefkandi graves containing pins were women's.

Almost half the number of iron pins and fragments of them showed traces of cloth preserved in the oxidisation products by which they were covered. Details of the cloth remains are given on pp. 000—000.

## BRACELETS (PLATE 241g—j)

Nine bracelets were recovered, the earliest (P 14,5) from a MPG group. The remainder are all of SPG date — a pair in the SPG I grave T 1 (nos. 8 and 9), two SPG II pairs (P 43,8 and 9; T 13,23 and 24) and two SPG III singles (T 33,17 and T 36,26).

The earliest piece, P 14,5, is a slim metal strip hammered flat with overlapping terminals, the surface decorated from terminal to terminal with a continuous *tremolo* zig-zag line.[48] Bracelets somewhat of this kind and with similar decoration were found in Marmariani[49] tombs I and II. Heurtley and Skeat compare these Marmariani bracelets with later ones found at Chauchitsa in Central Macedonia,[50] though the comparison seems not very close so far as the Lefkandi bracelet is concerned.

The rather heavy SPG I pair, T 1,8 and 9, though undecorated, offer comparison with a rather larger pair in a late PG grave on Skyros. The Skyros bracelets (d. 8.5) have simple traced or incised patterns at the terminals. It is of some interest that the fibulae in the Skyros group are of very similar type to those in T 1 (nos. 10 and 11).[51] Another pair of heavyish bracelets is among a tomb group said to have come from the 'northern Peloponnese'.[52]

The SPG II pair T 13,23 and 24 stands apart from the other bracelets both in form and decoration, and in having a most unusual metal composition (see Appendix 0). The terminals are somewhat enlarged, slightly domed and carry traced or incised herring-bone ornament.

The two bracelets making up the second SPG II pair (P 43,8 and 9) are of very slim metal, round in section, and undecorated.

In SPG III, T 36,26 is a tiny bracelet, open ended with tapering terminals to metal of round section.

The slim bracelet T 33,17 of flattened but angular section, the terminals slightly flaring, is decorated with considerable delicacy by its very finely traced double zig-zag line that follows the edge all round the loop. It recalls the rather broader LPG bracelet P 14,5, decorated *a tremolo*; it is possibly a Lefkandian copy of that style of bracelet and ornament which is itself unlikely to have been made locally.

As we saw, Lefkandi has no SM bracelets; three are recorded in Athens.[53] Very few PG bracelets are recorded, at least in Athens. Styrenius notes two in Agora XLII — a child's grave;[54] there is also a bracelet in Heidelberg B (transitional SM/PG).[55] Bracelets were evidently little more popular in Athens later in the Dark Ages — Kübler[56] refers to examples in tombs 49 and 87. A. M. Snodgrass, speaking of the prevalence of metal types in the later Geometric period, states that 'Bronze bracelets are now no longer a rarity'.[57] But they seem never to have been particularly popular, and the Lefkandi cemetery, viewed against the Athens/Attica evidence, must be regarded as relatively rich in these ornaments — though, it may be noted, there is a restlessness about the types in use which raises a variety of interesting questions.

## FINGER RINGS

Three types of ring — presumably all intended for use as finger rings, came from the cemeteries
  (1) shield-shaped bezel
  (2) closed ring, fairly solid, usually of plano-convex section
  (3) open ring, overlapping terminals, usually made of flat, hammered strip, coiled into a ring.

One example of the first type, S 38,10 was found in a group which also contained both bronze and iron dress pins, and two bronze fibulae. Unfortunately, it was too shattered to repair, but its two elements, ring and bezel, were held together by a slim rivet, and the bezel may have been decorated *en pointillé*. This type of ring is characteristically Submycenaean, echoing earlier Minoan/Mycenaean types in its shape, hinting at Urnfield relationships in the manner and technique of its decoration.[58] At least nine rings of this type were found in the SM tombs of the Kerameikos — one each in tombs 19$^E$, 27$^E$, 42$^M$, 44, 52$^M$, 60, 70$^M$ and two in tomb 108$^{LA}$. They were thus distributed throughout the chronological succession of these groups set out by Styrenius. Müller-Karpe suggested that there is a consistent association of certain pin and fibula types with the 'Schild-ringer' — certainly the Lefkandi association in S 38 is perfectly consistent with this view.

Twelve closed rings were found, five (S 17,2 and 3, S 22,5, S 40,7 and 8), belonging to SM groups, six (S 16,14a, 15–16, S 20,9, S 31,4, S 32,7) coming from EPG groups. One (S 39,1) is undated. They are fairly uniform in size and appearance — outer diameters varying from 1.8 to 2.3, the plane-convexity varying somewhat in intensity from one ring to another. None shows any sign of decoration. Finger rings later in the use of the cemetery are exclusively of gold, though the form remains close to the earlier bronze version.

There are nine rings with overlapping terminals, six of which (S 15B,6, S 19,14–15, S 22,6, S 40,9 and S 53,2) are datable to SM. In two cases, these rings come from groups that include solid rings. Two rings are datable to EPG, S 16,14b and 17, and a fine piece, P 10,21 (much smaller than any of the others) may be attributable to SPG I. It is unlikely that this last piece should be taken with the rest. The rings are unsophisticated, their material varying in width from below 1.5 to 0.7. Their interest is less intrinsic than that of their distribution, which may usefully be compared with that of the rings of the Kerameikos SM graves.[59]

According to the analysis of the Kerameikos excavations, single rings were found in the graves of men and women indifferently. Women's graves sometimes contained several rings. One or two problems of attribution, however, arise.[60] A more thorough analysis of the occurrence of rings in SM graves is made by Styrenius.[61]

In Athens, at any rate, the use of bronze rings as a grave gift becomes much rarer in PG.[62]

## BRONZE EARRINGS

Only two objects of bronze have been identified as earrings, both from SM contexts — S 19,9 (PLATE 98) and S 22,4 (PLATE 99). They are alike in being an incomplete rod of slim wire of round section, width under 1.5, and wholly undistinguished. No rings of this kind are reported from the Salamis or Athens SM cemeteries, but a small spiral ring from Kerameikos SM 83[63] may have been used as a hair ring, though Styrenius describes it as 'probably an earring'.[64]

An earring may be represented by the two fragments of slim wire curled into tight spirals from a SM tomb, S 15B,6a (PLATE 95) — they might have come from an earring similar to the much later (SPG III) gold pair from T 13, where double spirals of fine wire hang from a simple ring with open ends. The bronze spirals are too fine to have belonged to a finger ring with double spiral terminals.[65]

## BRONZE VESSELS (PLATE 243)

During the earlier part of the Neopalatial period bronze had been used liberally in Crete and on the Greek mainland for the manufacture of a varied series of vessels.[66] The series had dwindled virtually to nothing by the closing phase of the Bronze Age, so that the few examples known from the Dark Ages represent a fresh start and a new tradition in the use of bronze for this purpose. It is very probable that this new start was owed to the importation of metal vases from outside Greece.

At Lefkandi, no vessels earlier than SPG I have been recorded; only one, T 22,18, a slightly carinated handless cup, is as early as this. Three others (T 31,20; T 33,15 and 16) were found in SPG III groups, while the fragment of a fifth found in T sq VIII was a surface find.

There is no very obvious parallel for the carinated cup T 22,18, despite a superficial similarity with the shape of the Early Orientalising bronze skyphos from Fortetsa Tomb P.[67] The Fortetsa vase is larger and (quite apart from its handles) is unlike the Lefkandi piece in having a heavy ring foot with a recess underneath. In view, however, of several possible links with Italian metalwork, suggested above in the case of fibulae, note might be taken of the profile of certain bronze one-handled cups from Tarquinia, many of them with high conical feet attached separately to a vessel with base profile not unlike the Lefkandi piece. This analogy need not be pressed, but, in view of the nature of the remaining metal vases, it is important not to assume that they need all have a common origin.[68]

Of the three SPG III vessels, the most interesting is the small, angular jug with lotus-bud handle, T 33,15.[69] No fewer than seven jugs of this type have been found in Crete, five from the Idaean Cave,[70] and two in Fortetsa Tomb P,[71] a context described by Brock as confused, though he doubted if they could be earlier than Orientalising. Boardman[72] suggests that a find reported by Marinatos from Amnisos[73] may make an eighth lotus-bud jug.

A handle of this kind in New York (no. 690) was originally in the Cesnola Collection, and was presumably found in Cyprus.[74] It was described by J. L. Myres, who dated it 1300–1200, commenting on its likely Egyptian relations.[75] It was republished by Miss Richter[76] who repeated the information concerning its likely Egyptian relationship.

There seems no doubt that both the vessel shape and the handle type in combination are paralleled very much earlier in Egypt. Randall-MacIver and Mace[77] reported complete examples from the Abydos cemetery, 'In bronze the favourite object was the lotus-handled vase . . .'[78] and mention an example from the XVIII Dynasty tomb D 116,[79] the XVIII Dynasty tomb D 115 (re-used in the XX and XXII Dynasties)[80] and the XIX Dynasty tomb 33 (re-used in the XXVI Dynasty).[81] Petrie illustrates the handle of another with the comment that such handles are 'of the XVIII–XIXth dynasties . . .'.[82] Von Bissing[83] adds two more examples, of which the one he illustrates has a less angular body than our vase. There are three more in London[84] but there is no independent evidence of date.

The same type of handle may be attached to other bronze vessel shapes in Egypt. Petrie[85] for example illustrates a jug with very full neck, somewhat recalling a jug reported by Brunton from a group found in a pit at Matmar, dated by him to the XIX–XXI Dynasty.[86] This same Matmar group included a very shallow basin nearly 30 cm in diameter fitted with a lotus-bud handle; a bronze in Cairo,[87] perhaps of the XIX Dynasty, goes closely with this.

The foregoing is sufficient to show the popularity of this type of handle in Egypt and its association there with smallish squat jugs very similar to T 33,15 from the XVIII Dynasty. That is satisfactory so far as it goes. If we were dealing solely with the Lefkandi piece, we might accept that an antique vessel could be buried in a context that is up to 450 years later than its date of manufacture. But it is very difficult to accept this explanation for the seven, perhaps, eight, more examples found in Crete, and it becomes necessary to inquire whether the vase type may not have had a very much longer history than the evidence so far described suggests.

W. Culican[88] has recently published a survey of the question in which his general conclusion seems to be that the manufacture of bronze vessels with lotus-bud handles continues as late as the middle of the first millennium BC. He points to bronzes that he considers of Phoenician origin with handles of somewhat similar type and supposes them made under close Egyptian influence. At the same time, it seems, lotus-bud handle jugs were still being made in Egypt by XXV Dynasty craftsmen.[89] His analysis concentrates attention on a feature of the handle design that suggests the Lefkandi vessel is Egyptian rather than Phoenician — '. . . one peculiarity of the Egyptian metalworker is evident, namely the placing of a third non-functional rivet between the two rivets which fasten the rotelles to the upper rim of the jug. Many of the jugs of this type which I have been able to examine have this third, purely decorative rivet, and it appears to be an attempt to use rivetting decoratively in a manner which the Phoenician metalsmiths did not adopt, or perhaps experimented with briefly and later abandoned.'[90] This account fits T 33,15 very closely. On general grounds of probability, then, the Lefkandi jug is of Egyptian fabric and is more likely to have been made within the lifetime of its Lefkandian owner than to be an antique, but it could have been in Phoenician hands before it reached its final owner and was buried in Euboea. A much closer study of the Egyptian and Phoenician evidence is required before a more satisfactory account of this evidence can be offered.

The jug just discussed was found with a bronze bowl, T 33,16; the two evidently compose a wine service.[91] Our bowl is undecorated, but exhibits an unusual technical feature at the rim zone where, on the inside, the bronzesmith in raising (? or sinking) the vessel has managed to leave a thickness of metal at least double that of the remainder. This feature militates against Cyprus as the place of origin of the bowl. Hemispherical bronze bowls were made in Cyprus in large quantities during the latter part of the Late Cypriot period and, on a lesser scale, during the Cypro-Geometric period.[92] Rim forms are either plain, slightly thickened or stilted in a very distinctive fashion; they do not resemble the Lefkandi bowl, and an alternative source should probably be sought for it. This is not to say that none of the hemispherical bronze bowls found in EG and MG I contexts at Athens, in particular, can be of Cypriot fabric, as Coldstream has, indeed, proposed.[93]

One of the earliest Dark Age occurrences must be the bowl from the SM Arsenal cemetery on Salamis.[94] PG instances are rare, but one was found in PG Tomb 48 in the Kerameikos (d. 16.3) in the mouth of the ash-urn doing duty as a lid.[95] During EG and MG I this practice was relatively common, at least in the Kerameikos where bronze bowls served as covers for ash urns in ten graves. In one case (T 42), the bowl was decorated elaborately in relief,[96] but the remainder were evidently all undecorated hemispherical bowls.[97] A similar use for a bronze vase of uncertain type was described in the case of a Geometric grave at Eleusis.[98] Outside Attica bronze bowls of similar type have been found in 9th and 8th century graves at Argos, though not used in the Athenian fashion.[99]

The contrast between usage in Athens and at Lefkandi is very clear — in the former the bowls were without exception used as covers for cremation urns, suggesting that, in these cases, one of the final acts in the committal of the ash urn was the pouring of a draught for the thirsty dead in the vessel that covered the mouth of the ash urn itself. In the latter, the bronze bowl was one among several laid as offerings within the grave — the hemispherical bowl can be taken as a foil to the wine jug and the two seen as a service. Given this difference of function it is very probably that the source is different; it is tempting to suggest that both bowl and jug in T 33 come from the same source, which was either Egyptian or Levantine.

The phiale mesomphalos T 31,20 is a particularly interesting piece, since it occupies a very early place in the development of a metal vase form that has a long and important history in Greece, *in corpore* and in representational art. It belongs to a small class of spike-omphalos phialai of which the earliest example may be a piece from a group from Athens, dated by C. W. Blegen to c. 900 BC.[100] The possible source from which such a form might have come is suggested by a pottery version from Amathus T 5, no. 37[101] datable to the mid-9th century BC.[102] A phiale with a very prominent spike omphalos from Corinth, datable to c. 750 BC, has been published by Mrs. Weinberg[103] who refers to a similar piece from the Sanctuary of Athena Pronoia at Delphi.[104] Notice, too, two spike-omphalos phialai found at Perachora,[105] one of which (unillustrated) is described as having a shorter spike than the other. In view of slight uncertainty attending the Athens find, the Lefkandi phiale is the earliest securely dated instance of a metal vase form generally agreed to have derived from the Orient.

The handle escutcheon found in surface soil in T Square VII, (PLATE 246g), has a vertical ring attached to it within which there was, presumably, a drop-ring handle. The vessel of which this originally formed part must have been of considerable size; it may have had two handles of this type. I have no suggestion as to the appearance of the complete vessel, whose date of manufacture should, by association be no later than the middle of the 9th century BC.

Two at least of the Lefkandi bronze vases[106] originated in the east — the jug and the phiale. I have suggested reasons for thinking the same may be true of the hemispherical bowl T 33,16. This should not be taken to mean that the local metal industry at Lefkandi was only of the simplest; the evidence of the foundry refuse (qv.) from Xeropolis of c. 900 BC shows this was not so. Interest should focus rather on the effect that such Oriental metal-work may have had on the local industry.


## MISCELLANIA

The scale-plate T 59,37 (SPG III), (PLATE 239l), is an object of exceptional interest, which must have been brought to Lefkandi from the east — be it Cyprus, the Levantine coast or Egypt. It is very likely to have been an antique when it was buried, and, perhaps, to have been picked up as a treasured curio by a Euboean visitor to foreign parts. Recent finds[107] suggest that Cyprus could have been the source from which this scale reached Euboea, though the evidence is not conclusive.

The first plate from a bronze scale corslet identified in the Aegean, at Mycenae, comes from a context datable to the 12th century BC.[108] In Troy three plates were found in a house datable to Troy VIF.[109] Scale-plates have been found in Cyprus at Enkomi[110] (in a level probably datable to the 12th century BC) while three others come from Alaas in a tomb of LC III B (1100–1050 BC).[111] The Cypriot examples are very similar to the Lefkandi piece, though they are all rather larger. Scale armour was current in Cyprus in the post-BA period, though iron had replaced bronze.[112]

A detailed analysis of the origin and distribution of bronze scale armour is not called for here — the reader is referred to V. Karageorghis and E. Masson's recent study.[113] These authorities, in commenting on the two groups of finds from Cyprus, note that each represents only a minute fraction of the whole corslet to which they once belonged. They point out that one find spot was a tomb; as they note, there is evidence from other contexts in the Near East that suggests the plates may sometimes have been offered in a sanctuary.

At the time of the deposition of the Lefkandi plate early in the 9th century BC the manufacture of bronze scale armour had very probably long been over. The context is one of the latest anywhere, and the piece must have been an antique. It is not difficult to imagine that such an object could have had a talismanic quality and that, if its original function was understood by its owner, it was seen as a potent protector.

The macehead, (PLATE 239j—k), from S 5 (a SPG I group) is an object of great interest and rarity; its fragmentary state is a matter for regret, but the restoration on paper (PLATE 93) is reasonably certain. The form is oriental, and the Lefkandi piece is almost certain to have been imported. Jantzen[114] has published six rather similar pieces from the Heraion of Samos. They also each consist of a cylindrical sleeve with central swelling; the form of this swelling varies from ellipsoid to flattened sphere. In three cases one end of the sleeve is decorated with appendages in the round. The swellings were in every case decorated with inlays of iron, and are unlike our piece, which is decorated simply with vertical ribs and no trace of the addition of a second metal. There is one more of this type from Lindos.[115] Mrs. J. Birmingham's suggestion of other examples from Olympia seems unfounded.[116]

Moorey has published two rather similar objects from Persia, now in Oxford, but these have their swellings near the upper end, not centred. Moorey calls attention to the difference and points out that the Persian variety is likely to date to 'late in the third and early in the second millennium BC'.[117]

There is a relatively wide distribution of such maceheads in the Orient and in Cyprus. Jantzen[118] notes that objects somewhat of this kind are to be seen in the hands of warriors on Neo-Hittite reliefs. Moorey[119] observes that a mace-head of this kind was excavated at Zinjirli[120] in a context dated to the reign of Tiglath-Pileser III. Further afield, the type has occurred in Scythia, Urartu and Luristan.

Only one of several maceheads reported from Cyprus seems to be well dated. This is Amathus 5,19.[121] The group was dated CG III by the excavators,[122] which, on the Swedish chronology, would assign the group to the end of the 8th century BC. Note, however, must be taken of Mrs. Birmingham's proposed revision of the Swedish chronology, which involves dating Amathus 5 to c. 850 BC.[123] Further comment on this chronological argument has been contributed by Coldstream.[124] The documentation of the remaining Cypriot maceheads is unsatisfactory. Mrs. Birmingham[125] refers to examples at Tamassos (Politiko) and at Kurion, but the account of these finds[126] leaves much to be desired, especially as they are not illustrated. Three others, better published, are without provenance, *MMA Bronzes* 457 f, no. 1812. Cesnola. *RDAC* 1935, 31, pl. xii.i, left. Purchased in Famagusta. *RDAC* 1935, 31, pl. xii,i, right. Purchased in Gypsos.

It is impossible to identify the source from which the Lefkandi macehead reached Euboea, but obviously Cyprus must be a strong candidate — though another source may have been the place of manufacture. It is, in any case, an important link between Euboea and the East in the early 9th century BC.


## IRON WEAPONS

### Dirk or dagger (PLATE 245E)

The earliest iron weapon is the EPG dagger S 46,7, a mere 22.7 long as preserved and thus no larger than the smallest of the spearheads.[127] This reflects experience elsewhere in Greece where, with the important exception of knives, the earliest iron weapons are daggers or dirks made, like this piece, on the pattern of the Type II sword. One of the best instances is the weapon (length 31) from Tiryns, T XXVIII, in which was also found a bronze shield boss, a spearhead, a stirrup jar, and, it seems, fragments of another iron dagger of the same type.[128] A rather similar group of objects was found at Knossos in 1978 where in Tomb 186 at the University site, a cremation grave provisionally dated Late Minoan IIIC, produced a stirrup jar, a large bronze spearhead, a bronze shield boss, an iron knife and an iron dagger of the type under review. Somewhat later is the Kerameikos Grave PG A with a much smaller iron dagger, its ivory hilt and pommel still remaining.[129] A rather larger dagger, also with an ivory hilt and pommel completely preserved, was found in the late SM Grave B.[130] This weapon (including its pommel) is 21 long, and therefore smaller than the Lefkandi piece, which must have been at least 25 when it was complete with its hilt. Larger than this — dirk, rather than dagger — is a blade whose hilt plates were secured by eleven bronze rivets, from the SM grave 11.[131] Snodgrass has pointed out that the Kerameikos dirk, though within the fairly wide typological limits of the type II weapons, resembles the version found in Cyprus and the Near East, and not any of the canonical stages in the development of the sword type in bronze. It has been suggested, indeed, that Cyprus may have been the immediate source from which working in iron spread to the Aegean, and that this could be reflected in the design of the earliest iron weapons in Greece.[132]

## Swords (PLATES 245–6)

Four complete iron swords and fragment of a fifth came to light in the cemeteries — two came from groups dated to LPG (T 14,4 and T 26,18), one from a group transitional between SPG I and SPG II (P 47,18) and two from context for which there is no independent dating evidence (P Pyre 17,1 and T Pyre 8,4).[133]

With one exception (P Pyre 17,1), the swords were found with other weapons (three with spears — T 14,4, P 47,18 and T Pyre 8,4 — one with arrows — T 26,18). At Lefkandi, at any rate, the Dark Age warrior (or ?huntsman) was skilled in the use of more than one type of weapon.[134] If the SM warrior was a swordsman, he was not at Lefkandi, or elsewhere on the mainland, buried with his sword, though occasionally he might be buried with a dirk.[135]

It is very familiar ground that the dominant Greek sword type of the Early Iron age, to which the four identifiable Lefkandi swords belong, derives from the last major development in sword design to take place in Late Bronze Age Greece which saw the appearance during the later 13th century BC, of the famous 'cut-and-thrust' sword that seems probably to have been introduced to the E. Mediterranean from Central Europe. The class is known variously as 'Naue's Type', 'Sprockhoff's Type IIa', or, simply, the 'Type II sword'. Various attempts, including efforts of my own, have been made to refine the classification of these bronze versions.[136] The suggested internal typology of the bronze weapons does not apply to the evolution of this design as an iron weapon, as A. M. Snodgrass pointed out some time ago.[137] It may be hazardous to look for a typology, particularly in a weapon that was to have so long a renewed lease of life once the translation from bronze to iron had been made. The history and use of the Type II iron swords extends comfortably into the 8th century BC.[138] A further notable instance of the continuing use of the iron Type II sword is given by the series from the West Gate cemetery at Eretria, where at least six swords were found in a cremation grave complex datable to the period 720–680.[139] The chronology of the tumulus cemetery at Vergina in central Macedonia is insufficiently secure to place much reliance on that site as an index of the latest use of iron Type II swords, though it is notable for what is perhaps the largest number from any site yet known.[140]

In general, the sword evidence from Lefkandi harmonises with what is known in Athens, where sword-burial was never common, but was unknown in SM and very rare in the earlier PG period. In at least one case there is very close comparison between Athens and Lefkandi. P 47,18, from a transitional SPG I/II group, at 71.5 long is almost the same length as the nearly contemporary weapon from an Agora tomb[141] 69 long. There is a close similarity in hilt form between the two weapons. In hilt form, T Pyre 8,4 (for which there is no independent evidence of date) is very similar to a sword from Kerameikos G. grave 38,[142] but the similarity is otherwise less marked, for the Athens sword is 80 long compared with 65.5 at Lefkandi. Both weapons have a midrib. Both these swords were found with spears, but there is little similarity between the two spearheads. Two other Athens swords — Kerameikos PG grave 28[143] and Agora Tomb XXVII[144] resemble T Pyre 8,4 in the convex outline of the butt. The Kerameikos grave may be dated to late PG, while Agora Tomb XXVII is transitional PG/EG. Though the evidence is slight, T Pyre 8 may be contemporary with these two Athenian graves. The Lefkandi LPG sword T 26,18 from the 'Archer's Tomb', though preserving traces of its wooden scabbard[145] and of ?ivory plates is not well enough preserved at the hilt for it to stand close comparison with other weapons. The outline of the handgrip is straighter than almost all other swords reviewed here. Kerameikos PG grave E's iron sword has a much less swollen hilt than most,[146] but the proportions are unlike T 26,18, and so is the shape of the blade. T 14,4 is notable for very prominent pommel 'ears' (or, in other terminology its very pronounced 'fish-tail' hilt), a feature that closely recalls the design of the first bronze swords of Type II to appear in Greece.[147] Prominent 'ears' appear on at least one of the iron swords in Tomb 6 of the West Gate cemetery at Eretria[148] but the manner of execution is not the same as our sword; there must be at least 200 years' difference in the date of the contexts in which these weapons were found.

Iron type II swords differ among themselves in a variety of ways, some of which are more variable than others. After variety in length overall perhaps the most capricious feature is the relationship between pommel width and handguard width — in a number of cases the former is only half the latter; in a very few instances the pommel is almost as wide as the guard, the situation with T 14,4. The closest approximation to similar proportions is found on the otherwise very different sword in Agora Tomb XXVII.

The publication of the Lefkandi material is not the right vehicle for an exhaustive reappraisal of iron Type II swords in Greece. We note Bérard's observation[149] 'On voit, que l'on ne peut tirer aucune conclusion chronologique précise de l'observation morphologique.' This is a cry of despair, understandable but unnecessarily pessimistic. The subject, I am sure, must be treated in a different fashion from the approach applied to the bronze swords; other criteria are relevant, one of which should be a rigorous scrutiny of the character of whatever other weapons were found with the swords. An attempt should also be made to relate each iron weapon, at however great a remove, to its nearest bronze ancestor. A sword such as T 14,4, so close to Group I bronze swords of the late 13th and early 12th century BC seems only explicable if we assume that the swordsmith had direct experience of such a prototype, particularly when it is recalled that most contemporary swords stand much further apart from the Bronze Age pattern.

### Spearheads (PLATE 244)

For only two of the six spearheads from Lefkandi is there pottery evidence of date, the LPG weapon T 14,3 and the SPG I/II P 47,19. The remaining four came from pyres (P Pyre 1,1; P Pyre 16,1; T Pyre 1,2; T Pyre 8,5). Only one spear was found alone ( P Pyre 1,1) and it is likely to be LPG on stratigraphic grounds. P 47,19, T 14,3 and P Pyre 8,5 were each in association with a sword; T Pyre 1,2 was found with an axe, while P Pyre 16,1 was found with a fairly substantial knife.

The dimensions of the spears are interesting, and suggestive. An even larger sample would have been of great value to test the validity of the deductions drawn here. Leaving aside the incomplete weapon (P 47,19), the size range was relatively narrow, from the smallest blade of 22.8 to a largest of 33.4 — the average of five amounts to 28.2. There is much more variation in the socket length, from 8 to 15. There is remarkable variation in the ratio of socket length to overall length, from a lowest level of 1:2.11 to a highest of 1:3.27. Other measurements are more stable. For example, the greatest thickness (at the midrib, that is) varies only between 1 and 1.5 — on the whole, the larger the spear, the thicker the midrib. Blade widths vary from a lowest of 3.4 to a maximum of 4.5 — these variations are not closely related to the lengths of the spears — thus, P Pyre 16,1 is 33 long, its width 3.8, while T Pyre 8,5 which is 33.4 long, is 4.5 wide.

If the shape of the blades only is taken into account, and the incomplete blade P 47,19 is ignored, the remaining five weapons are of a single type, even if there is not exact resemblance between them all — the blade is round shouldered, leaving the socket at a clearly defined point, quickly curving round to the blade's widest point, from which it narrows steadily to the point. Four of the spears have a ring collar at the broad end of their sockets — both dated spears (T 14,3 and P 47,19) have bronze collars — the others (T Pyre 1,2 and T Pyre 8,5) are iron. This detail suggests that spear-makers in the Dark Ages were having more trouble with spearheads that would not remain on their shafts than their predecessors working in bronze had experienced. This might partly explain the general tendency for sockets to be proportionately longer in relation to the length of the blade than is normal with bronze weapons.

The iron spearhead gained slow currency in the Dark Ages, if we may judge from its frequency as a grave offering. As A. M. Snodgrass has already noticed, bronze spearheads continued to be used in EPG Athens,[150] and could recur from time to time still later, both in Athens,[151] and Eretria.[152]

The Athenian material known to me is as follows:

**PG**
1. Kevameikos PG tomb 17. Length 23.5 = *Ker* 1, 192 and pl. 76
   *JdI* 77, 99, Fig. 17,15 and p. 124. Snodgrass type A — *EGAW* 118, A.8, where it is suggested this may be the earliest all-iron spearhead in Greece.
2. Kerameikos PG tomb 34. Length 19 = *Ker* IV, 27 and pl. 38
   *JdI* 77, 90, fig. 8,1 and p. 120. Snodgrass type A — *EGAW* 118, A.9, with the suggestion that it may be nearer to Snodgrass type M.
3. Kerameikos PG tomb 32. Incomplete = *Ker* IV, 36. Possibly the same weapon as Snodgrass *EGAW* 122, type 1.
4  Athens, Metropolis tombs. Estimated length 28 = *AE* 1953—4, 92, figs. 6 and 94. Stuck by oxydisation to an iron sword.

**Transitional PG—EG**
5. Agora tomb XXVII Length 37.3 = *Hesperia* 21 (1952) 281, fig. 3,2.
   *JdI* 77, 110, fig. 28,2 and p. 127. Snodgrass type G — *EGAW* 122, G.3.
6. The same. Length 27.5 = *Hesperia* 21, 281, fig. 3,3.
   *JdI* 77, 110, fig. 28,3 and p. 127. Snodgrass type G — *EGAW* 122, G.4.

**EG**
7. Kerameikos G tomb 2. Length 32 = *Ker* V, 212 and pl. 165 (M.63)
   Snodgrass type G — *EGAW* 123, G.6.
8. Kerameikos G tomb 23. Length 25.3 = *Ker* V, 225 and pl. 165 (M.66)
   Snodgrass type M — *EGAW* 127, M.4.
9. Kerameikos G tomb 38 Length 49.5 *Ker* V, 234 and pl. 165 (M.53)
   Snodgrass type D — *EGAW* 121, D.4.

10. Kerameikos G tomb 74. No measurements — damaged *Ker* V, 261.

Papadimitriou's warrior grave — PG — on Skyros contained the fragments of an iron spearhead.[153]

The effect of this summary is to emphasise that Lefkandi seems rather richer in spearheads than the contemporary Athenian cemeteries, though there is no trace of the survival of the use of bronze spears in the earlier PG period, as we have noted was the case in Athens. No Lefkandian spearhead is as massive as the largest Athenian weapons. T Pyre 8,5, the largest of our series, at 33.4 long looks slight by comparison with Kerameikos G.38, which is 49.5 long. But the type of spearhead is essentially the same in both places in so far as the shape of the blade in relation to the socket is concerned. It is not entirely easy to relate our weapons to Snodgrass' typology.[154] He allocates the Athenian PG and EG spearheads to four of his types — A, D, G and M — but the nuances of this division are difficult to apply to the six Lefkandi spearheads. P Pyre 16,1, with its long socket, is rather like his type D, while the others have features of type G, though our shoulders are in all cases more rounded than his definition of type G should permit. In the case of the Lefkandi material it may be simpler to regard all the weapons as basically the same. They are certainly more homogeneous typologically than the iron swords.

### Axes (PLATE 244E and F)

Two iron axes were found in the Lefkandi cemetery of which one (P 13,22) is datable to SPG I. The second (T Pyre 1,3) may be earlier, LPG, on stratigraphical grounds.

A. M. Snodgrass,[155] writing some years ago, comments on the very limited evidence for the use of the axe in the Dark Ages as a weapon. At the end of the period two double axes occur in the LG Panoply Tomb at Argos, and have given rise to the rather frivolous comment that the warrior would have found them useful for hewing logs for his fire. Even in this context which included fire-dogs and spits, it is unlikely that the axes buried with the warrior were anything but weapons. It is, surely, in this light that we should view the earlier finds of iron axes, among them the Lefkandi pieces.

There are at least two companions for the P 13,22 trunnion axe — a weapon in Kerameikos LPG grave 40, 13.4 in length and thus slightly smaller than the Lefkandi axe.[156] The second axe comes from the rich and important LPG/EG 1 grave XXVII from the Agora, the finds from which included several other weapons — a sword, and two spearheads — as well as two iron bits.[157] Of uncertain date is an iron axe in Oxford, said to have come from the Dipylon cemetery together with an iron sword, two small iron spearheads and an iron ?axe–adze.[158] The possibly earlier T Pyre 1,3 axe is a more formidable weapon than the P 13,22 blade. It is less easily closely paralleled, and reference to the group of iron axes in Fortetsa tomb P[159] is doubtless of comparatively little relevance.

### Arrowheads (PLATE 183)

Lefkandi evidence has significantly changed the description of Dark Age archery that could be given by A.M. Snodgrass[160] 'But for a solitary iron arrowhead in . . . Kerameikos grave . . . two examples of obsidian in a probably EG burial at Tiryns, and two iron examples . . . at Corinth, there is no evidence whatever . . . in Greece proper in the eleventh, tenth and ninth centuries BC.' Lefkandi has two, perhaps three contributions to make: the schematic drawing of archers on the MPG hydria S 51,2 (FIG 3), a 'quiverful' of iron arrows from the LPG group T 26 (nos. 19a–j) and possible remains of a composite bow (of horn and antler) from T Pyre 1 (undated).[161] The catalogue description of the arrowheads bears repetition: '. . . flat arrow plates (sc. length of best preserved 3.7, width (restored) 1.8 . . . evidently slotted into a split shaft tip and probably bound in place by thread or gut. There are no remains of wood as such on the tangs, but the traces of wood replaced by iron oxide give this impression (sc. of a hollow wooden shaft) and show the size and shape of the original shaft, whose diameter was 0.5.'

As H. G. Buchholz's study has shown, arrowheads, and, presumably the practice of archery that is implicit in their existence, were abundant throughout the Late Minoan and Mycenaean periods, from the fine flint and obsidian points of LH I to the mass produced bronze arrow plates of the Knossos armoury and other palatial contexts.[162] Their rarity in the subsequent Dark Ages may partly be the result of almost exclusive reliance upon grave evidence, where much of the BA material comes from occupation sites. Yet even allowing for this, the lack of evidence for archery in the Dark Ages is very noticeable.

There are two iron arrowheads from Athens of PG and EG date[163] and another possible example from Corinth.[164]

Notice that there were iron swords in the same tombs as the Lefkandi and Athens (PG T 28) arrowheads and an iron sword in the same pyre as the possible Lefkandi bow. This suggests that archery had not, by this date, become a specialised skill indulged in only by 'certain low fellows of the baser sort'. The roll of honour of archers starts with Apollo and Artemis, passes to Harkles and embraces Philoktetes, Odysseus and Paris.

There is no need to assume that the Lefkandi evidence for archery is a sign of foreign contact — on the contrary, the drawing of archers on the hydria suggests that this skill was very much embedded in local custom. It must be chance that there is so little evidence for archery elsewhere in the contemporary vicinity.

### Iron knives

With one exception, the Lefkandi knives do not impress by their size or design. There are no SM–EPG knives, and only one each in the successive periods MPG (P 16,7), LPG (P 31,7), and SPG I (T 3,11). The remainder, all found with pyres (S Pyre 13,1 and 13,2, P Pyre 16,2) come from undated contexts. One of these (S Pyre 13,2) is too fragmentary for further consideration. Two, P 16,7 (PLATE 246h) and P 31,7 are small knives with stubby butts and short convex-backed blades, ideal general purpose implements that would be equally useful for cutting food, cleaning game, whittling, pruning and — conceivably — shaving. None is quite complete, and their original appearance is probably considerably altered by whetting. Both will have had hafts of wood, ivory or bone; traces survive on P 31,7.

The shape and size of T 3,11 (PLATE 245F), suggests a different function, though it would be possible for the other knives described above once to have been of the same size, but to have snapped after honing down to a slimness too great for their length, and to have been resharpened to their present form. It still has its ivory (?) hilt plates, secured by three bronze rivets, PLATE 246e. It is of interest that the use of the bronze rivets continued as late as this.[165]

S Pyre 13,1 and P Pyre 16,2 differ from the other knives by having an inverted profile — that is to say, the convex edge is the cutting edge, the concave is the back of the knife. The former may be complete at 12.0 but its original size could considerably have been reduced by sharpening during its years of use. The latter lacks its point and may 'have been up to 15.0 when complete.

Only P Pyre 16,2 has an association with weapons, having been found with a spearhead. Other metal objects were found with T 3,11, a bronze fibula, and P 16,7, a bronze fragment, possibly from a fibula. These details suggest no special function for the knives, or role in life for their owners. It is interesting, by contrast, that a large majority of the iron knives found in the Athenian cemeteries are associated with weapon burials — viz. (iron weapons, unless stated otherwise): Ker. PG A, two bronze spearheads, dagger; Ker. PG 28, sword; Ker. PG 17, spearhead; Ker. G 13, sword; Ker. G 38, sword, spearhead; Agora T XXVII, sword, spearheads, axe; Areopagos 1944 T, sword; and Agora cremation, sword. The only Athens knife, I know that was found without weapons is that from Agora T XXVI.[166]

The large knife T 3,11 may perhaps be compared with one of almost equal length (28) in Ker. PG tomb 28[167] bent into a circle around the neck of the ash urn (the sword in the same tomb had been treated in the same fashion).[168]

The two knives S Pyre 13,1 and P Pyre 16,2 with convex cutting edge may be compared with the two knives in the Agora warrior grave tomb XXVII.[169] At 14.3 and 12.2 long respectively these Athens blades are very similar in size to the Lefkandi ones.

Müller-Karpe[170] picks out iron knives as one of the hallmarks of the grave inventories in the third of his three stages in the development of the use of metal objects as grave offerings in the Dark Age — his stage III is, in effect, contemporary with Attic EG. But there are at least three PG instances of knives as grave goods (Ker. PG A, PG 17 and PG 28), while the EG instances are hardly so frequent as to make this a very compelling item in EG = Müller-Karpe stage III. The evidence at Lefkandi, anyway, suggests an altogether different role for the knife.

There is nothing to suggest foreign influence on knife design, unless we see T 3,11 so unusual that a non-Lefkandian origin has to be supposed. It and its Athenian couterpart in Kerameikos PG 28 are obviously unusual, but are not necessarily exotic for that.

## OBJECTS OF LEAD

Six lead objects were found, among which are two pairs — the 'scale-pans' of S 59A and the 'earrings' of T Pyre 5. The earliest find is the ornament P 12,4, of SPG I–II date. The plaque S 59,38 and the 'scale-pans' S 59A,11 and 12 are dated SPG III. The little 'earrings' from T Pyre 5 have no independent evidence of date.

The lead ornament of P 12, (PLATE 131), is directly comparable with the series in gold of identical shape, size and type of decoration, (PLATE 232f–h). Observations on the origin and function of the gold versions (above p.219) may be taken to apply to the lead example.

The 'plaque', which bears a superficial resemblance to the design of ivory 'spectacle fibulae'[171] is probably to be seen as a copy of a piece of gold jewellery. Conceivably it once had a covering of gold foil — it may be noted that scraps of foil were found in the grave, though none of them can be directly connected with the plaque. The plaque must have been cast. It is tempting to connect it in some way with:

The two 'scale-pans' found in S 59A, that is, the fill in the shaft over the cover slabs of the tomb, within which the plaque was discovered. These plano-convex, quite solid discs owe their identification as 'scale-pans' to the four very small 'suspension holes' pierced at equidistant points very close to the edges of the 'pans', (PLATE 246f). The identification also had in view the gold scale pans from Circle A at Mycenae[172] as an example of the funerary use of a miniature version of the object in an entirely inappropriate materials. Account was also taken of the relative frequency with which bronze scale-pans occur with Minoan and Mycenaean burials.[173] It is possible that these objects could have been covered with gold foil and stitched on to a shroud or some other piece of textile that was used during the funeral ceremonies. The traced lines on the inner surface might seem an obstacle to this explanation, but they could be seen as the setting out lines for the location of the stitch (or suspension) holes. They are very lightly traced and, had the objects been sheathed in gold foil, they would certainly not have showed through the foil. Of course, the setting-out lines would have been equally appropriate had the objects been 'simulacra' of scale-pans. No parallel is known to me for either eventuality.

The undated 'earrings' from T Pyre 5, (PLATE 191), are perhaps a copy of gold earrings though they are so tiny that it is surprising that it was thought worth while to copy them in a base metal.

It is interesting to relate this work in lead at Lefkandi from early in SPG to the information that lead was being produced at Thorikos in the 9th century BC.[174]

## UNIDENTIFIED OBJECTS

### Bronze

SPG I T 15,14 (PLATE 176) is perhaps a rivet from a weapon, but, if so, the lack of iron oxide on it suggests it could only have come from a bronze weapon — a sword, in fact. This is improbable.

### Iron

Sm S 38,13 (PLATE 204c). A very puzzling fragment; at least one of the joining fragments has cloth traces on both sides. SM S 15B,7. Shapeless, small and probably only a fragment of oxidisation from a larger object.

LPG T 26,20. A needle-like object only 4.1 long, from the tomb of the Archer. As a unique object in this cemetery it is tempting to relate it to the other unique feature of this burial, the arrowheads, though if so, its function in an archer's daily work is not clear.

LPG T 14,5. Scrap of very thin sheet iron. Could this fragment in any fashion be connected with the process of piling thin laminations of metal, already carbonised, for forging — a process described by A. M. Snodgrass?[175]

SPG II T 13,25 (PLATE 221c). Part of an implement? Impossible to place this piece. Note however the loop or hasp from the Agora Warrior grave XXVII;[176] though our fragment is large to be part of such a hasp, this object is a useful reminder of the occasional capriciousness of tomb offerings, stepping outside the normal canon of their own period. Object no. 7 from the same tomb, 'javelin point or small chisel', is a further illustration of the kind of object from which our fragment might have come.

## BASE METAL OBJECTS: A SUMMARY

Constant reference has been made in the preceding pages to parallels between Lefkandi and the Dark Age cemeteries of Athens. It is natural, then, that we should begin our summary of these results by a general comparison between the two. In the first place, it is clear that there is a close *general* similarity between Athens and Lefkandi throughout the years represented by the use of the Lefkandi cemeteries. We have seen that almost every category of object finds reasonably close parallel in Athens, and that it is only in the case of quite exceptional finds at Lefkandi (the bronze mace-head, and the bronze scale-plate) that there is no Athenian parallel for the find. In the same way, very few of the categories of base metal object familiar from the Athenian cemeteries of Athens are altogether missing from Lefkandi. A notable omission is the bronze shield boss, found in a few late SM and PG contexts in Athens[177] and *bronze* spearheads, found in Kerameikos PG graves A and B.[178] Also missing from Lefkandi is the 'horse and vehicle' evidence provided on the one hand by the iron bits from the Agora Warrior burial T XXVII, on the other by the iron and bronze from eg. Kerameikos G 13 and G 58.[179]

There is, further, a distinct tendency for some objects at Lefkandi which have a typological match in Athens to be of different size — usually, to be smaller. This is most noticeable with all classes of pins, where throughout the period of their use on the site they are smaller and simpler than their Athenian equivalents, even though Lefkandian pin design in general keeps step with Athens so that there is no important Athenian type missing at Lefkandi. The same tendency applies, though to a lesser extent, to the fibulae, especially the SM and PG series. Moreover, one particular fibula series — the brooches with heavy bosses on relatively small bows — was developed at Lefkandi starting in LPG, which has no counterpart at all in Athens, although its origin can be traced to a distinctive fibula with asymmetric swollen bow which was current both in Athens and at Lefkandi.

Some years ago H. Müller-Karpe, in a classic paper 'Die Metallbeigaben der Früheisenzeitlichen Kerameikos — Gräber'[180] defined three groups of metal objects from the Dark Age Athenian cemeteries which, in his view, characterised three successive periods. These three periods were, in round terms, Submycenaean, Protogeometric and Early Geometric. The groups of objects concerned were as follows:

The earliest stage.

1,2. Slim, symmetric arched fibulae of bronze with bows of round, square or twisted metal, the majority with springs of only one turn and a small symmetric catch-plate.
3. Asymmetric, stilted arched fibulae of bronze with twisted bars.
4. Asymmetric, stilted arched fibulae of bronze with slim bow, groups of fillets on the bow.
5. Asymmetric, stilted arched fibulae with swollen bow and two bosses.
6. Leaf-bow fibulae of bronze, decorated in *repoussé* or *a tremolo*.
7. Bronze pin with round to oval boss by the head, conical to nail-like head.
8. Bronze pin with swollen, occasionally faceted 'neck' with conical sometimes nail-shaped head.
9. Bronze finger rings of shield type, chiefly decorated *en pointillé*.

The characterizing material for the second stage consists of the following:

1. Thick arched fibulae of bronze with two three-part bosses on the bow, spring of two turns, symmetric catch-plate.
2. Thick arched fibula of iron with double spring and symmetric catch-plate.
3. Iron pins fitted with bronze bosses on the shaft, with disk-heads.
4. Iron axe.
5. Iron 'Griffzungenschwert' with arched shoulder.
6. Iron spearheads.

The third stage is characterised by:

1. Bronze arched fibulae with swollen angular elements at the centre of the bow, set off by three-part bosses, rhomboid stems, and asymmetric catch-plates, often decorated.
2. Bronze arched fibulae with flattened, decorated bows, three-part bosses and large, asymmetric catch-plate.
3. Iron arched fibula with swollen and large asymmetric catch-plate.

4. Iron pin with bone or bronze boss, head disk-and-vase shaped.
5. Bronze pin, the boss sometimes set off by fillets, the head of disk-and-vase-type.
6. Iron 'Griffzungschwert', sometimes with angular handguard.
7. Iron spearheads, sometimes long, the midrib extending to the point.
8. Iron knife with grip or grip plate.

Obviously there is a variety of other objects found with the graves of each of these stages but, in Müller-Karpe's view, they do not epitomise the phase so directly. It is of some interest to compare his findings for Athens with Lefkandi.

For phase I (SM) the results are as follows:

| Müller-Karpe's Athenian characteristic | | Lefkandi representation |
|---|---|---|
| I | 1,2 | Abundantly represented SM and EPG |
| | 3 | Present, but not common |
| | 4 | Not represented |
| | 5 | One example only (much smaller than the Athenian example) |
| | 6 | Two examples, both EPG. One plain, one decorated *pointillé* |
| | 7 | Present only in a version with slight oval swellings. The large pins with spherical bosses are missing |
| | 8 | Not represented |
| | 9 | One example only (SM) |

For the second phase (equivalent to PG in Athenian terms)

| Athenian characteristic | | Lefkandi representation |
|---|---|---|
| II | 1 | Present, though not very common — LPG and SPG I |
| | 2 | Not represented |
| | 3 | A rare type, one example in each of MPG, SPG I and SPG II |
| | 4 | One example, smaller than the Athenian weapon |
| | 5 | Two weapons dated LPG |
| | 6 | Rare — one dated LPG |

For the third phase (equivalent to EG, in Athenian terms)

| Athenian characteristic | | Lefkandi representation |
|---|---|---|
| III | 1 | Present, in several minor stages of development |
| | 2 | Not present in this form, though occurs in an allied (paddle-wheel) form |
| | 3 | Not represented (Lefkandi iron fibulae exist, but are of different types) |
| | 4 | No pins of this type — pins, in general, become less common |
| | 5 | Not represented |
| | 6 | One sword, early in the period |
| | 7 | One spear, early in the period. (Nb. two thirds of Lefkandi spears are undated) |
| | 8 | Though there is one SPG knife, this type of object occurs at Lefkandi from MPG onwards. |

Lefkandi thus harmonises reasonably well with Athenian usage, though the correspondence between the two is not complete. Particular to Lefkandi in the SM/EPG periods may be noted the use of two types of earring and a particular type of iron pin. For the PG period (= Müller-Karpe's phase II) Lefkandi develops its own fibula series out of the swollen arched bow variety which, doubtless was first developed in Athens — this culminates in the huge boss type which, as we have already seen is an independent Euboean development (evidently shared by Skyros). For the same period, Lefkandi develops its own iron pin type; the hybrid type — iron shaft with bronze bosses — are perhaps to be regarded as imports.

The evidence from the third period at Lefkandi is equivocal. At once we are dealing with material that has diverged considerably from Athenian practice — seen particularly clearly in the wide currency of the fibulae with heavy swollen boss at the centre of the bow and the symmetric arched fibulae with slightly swollen bows. Occasional exotic fibula types appear which are quite unknown in Athens. The representation of vessels is diverse, and again types occur unknown in Athens, e.g. the lotus-handled jug. On the other hand, a number of objects, including the most elaborately decorated fibulae, are so closely paralleled in Athens that I have suggested the work of the same fibula maker is present in both places.

To what extent do the base-metal objects found in the Lefkandi cemeteries point to links between Euboea and regions either remote in Greece, or still further afield? For the SM period there is little or no sign of such contact, with the doubtful exception of the asymmetric arch fibula with swollen bow, S 43,6, which recalls approximately contemporary fibulae in Cyprus. Kerameikos SM tomb 108[181] contains another example of the type — larger than the Lefkandi piece — but no others are known to me in Greece as early as this, though there must be a connection with this form and the typologically very important asymmetric swollen arch bow fibulae which was standard in PG.

The position shows little change in EPG, when (apart from the temporary disappearance of bronze dress pins) the type of base-metal offerings remains very similar to the preceding period. The only innovation is the iron dagger in S 46, but there is no need to look further afield than Athens for its source.

Unfortunately the MPG sample is too small to decide whether the pointers it shares are of true application. Bracelets appeared for the first time — as we argued above this ornament is rare in the Athenian cemeteries, and one might look elsewhere not so much for the custom of making and using, but for this detail in the practice of decking the dead.

The most noticeable development concerning the outside world observable in LPG is the changed balance between objects of bronze and objects of iron, and, with it, the appearance of a diverse and developed (though not abundant) weapon series. Again, the immediate origin for these innovations need not necessarily be further afield than Athens. Depending on our interpretation of Euboea's role in the early development of iron technology one might even suppose that these innovations were self generated. Though important developments took place during the period in fibula design they seem quite natural changes in the light of what had gone before, even though it is clear that the Lefkandians were no longer looking so closely towards Athenian practice.

A probable import in SPG I is the carinated bronze bowl T 22,18; no particular location positively suggests itself, though possible links with Italy should not be ignored. The most obvious overseas link is provided by the mace head in S 5; this is probably the earliest example in Greek lands of an oriental metal type best represented, as was seen above, in the sanctuary of Hera on Samos. The Lefkandi piece recalls Cypriot finds more closely than any other, and this could easily be the source from which it reached Euboea.

It should be noticed that the change in balance in the use of iron and bronze noted in LPG reverses itself in SPG I, when once more bronze objects are in a majority. This may or may not reflect economic facts concerning the availability of imported copper and its alloys.

It is very likely, though not certain, that the new style symmetric arch fibula with slightly swollen bow was influenced by developments in Italian fibula design. It might be argued that this design is, in fact, no more than an evolved version of the fibula type that had been very popular in SM and EPG, the symmetric arched bow fibula. But this type disappeared completely during MPG and LPG, and we must be dealing with an innovation, from whatever quarter.

SPG II is not remarkable for signs of foreign contacts, unless we should look overseas for the origin of the decorated fibulae with flattened crescent bow and paddlewheel bead on the stem.

SPG III contains more obviously imported base-metal objects than any other period. The little scale plate from a bronze scale corslet must come from an oriental source. It is presumably an antique curio bought by a travelling Lefkandian in a Levantine port, or given by a visiting oriental on a trading trip to Lefkandi. A less convincing import is the small decorated bracelet in T 33. It is tempting to suppose that all three of the bronze vessels were imports too — this seems certain in the case of the jug, likely in the case of the phiale and quite possible for the hemispherical bowl. We note, nevertheless, that there are parallels for all three of these shapes in other Greek Dark Age contexts. In particular, several lotus-flower jugs are known from Crete. Such diversity of provenience for the vessel series (Athens, Lefkandi, Crete) means that oriental contacts may have been direct in each case, but the alternative explanation of one receiving centre redistributing to others must not be ignored. A case could be argued for casting Athens in this rôle.

We have so far reviewed the evidence for Lefkandi's contacts furthest afield. Some account should now be given of relationships nearer home, particularly with Athens. First, however, it must be noted that when the evidence from Skyros has been fully published there will almost certainly be need of revision on what is now being said concerning Lefkandi's relationships with her close neighbours. (Note, for instance, that for six of the eight base-metal objects in the Goulandris collection said to be from Skyros[182] there are close Lefkandian parallels.)

In essentials, SM and EPG Lefkandi go very closely with Athens and Salamis. We have already seen that certain pin-types are rare or missing at Lefkandi, certain others are much smaller than their mainland equivalents. A fibula type present but rare in Athens[183] is missing at Lefkandi. There are no shield bosses, and weaponry is represented by a single iron dagger. But the fibula types most popular in Athens are the most popular types in Euboea, where there is the same concentration upon closed and open-ended finger rings.

Circumstances began to change in LPG, when it becomes clear that fashion in dress pin and fibula design at Lefkandi are no longer keeping in close accord with developments in Athens. It is not so much a break with the area or a change of allegiance as a drifting away from the closeness of the ties that seem to have existed between the two areas in the earlier periods. A salient fact is the period of bronze shortage at Lefkandi (if that is the correct way to interpret the change of balance in bronze and iron objects in LPG) comes later than its supposed occurrence in Athens. In fact, at least until SPG II, bronze was always used rather sparingly at Lefkandi and if bronze objects appear numerically abundant, particularly in SM and EPG, it must be remembered that they are all small and their total weight is relatively trivial.

The separation from the mainland is seen in the development of iron pins, which remain relatively small, and, during LPG at least, are never of the iron pin—bronze boss type popular in Athens. Also remarkable is the (relatively) rapid local development of a fibula type (the heavily bossed arched brooch) out of the asymmetric arched fibula with swollen bow, which was itself common to Attica and Euboea. The bossed brooch is missing in Athens. Its development makes it almost certain there was a bronze workshop active at Lefkandi from early in PG onwards — if no earlier. Independent evidence as we have seen has established that sophisticated bronze work was produced at Xeropolis by 900 BC at latest. It is presumably not coincidence that there is only one LPG fibula (T 17,4) of a type that would be in place in Athens. It may also be suggestive that one of the earliest iron swords from Lefkandi (T 14,4) appears to be following a model that is most unlikely to have come from Athens. Either it was brought to Lefkandi from a non-Athenian source, or it was the work of a Lefkandian blacksmith following an unusually antique pattern, perhaps copied directly from a bronze Nenzingen sword. The 'Tomb of the Archer', too has a non-Athenian look — who knows but that his grave may once have contained his bow as well as his quiver full of arrows.

In matters of dress, SPG I carried a stage further the divergence of Lefkandi from Athenian practice, for the period sees the introduction, perhaps from a source ultimately Italian, of a second brooch design that has nothing to do with Athenian brooches. Though not plentiful, this type was to remain in use to the end of the life of the cemetery — so, too, was the bossed fibula, apparently without developing any further from the stage already achieved in LPG. It is noteworthy that a pair of bossed fibulae was made in iron in SPG I — almost certainly these brooches must have been made at Lefkandi. Iron brooches and pins at Lefkandi, in general, are at all times further removed from the Athenian canon than the bronze series. We may probably suppose blacksmiths established at Lefkandi from EPG onwards.

From SPG II until the end of the life of the site, although the non-Athenian fashions in dress accessories remained dominant, there is a reversion of interest in what was taking place there. Lefkandians, obviously, were pleased with the Athenian development of the asymmetric arched brooch with swollen bow that culminates, as far as we are concerned, in the S 59,29 and 30 pair. It is a matter for keen regret that the cemeteries did not last any longer to allow us to see what effect the introduction of these magnificent decorated brooches had on Lefkandian taste. But it must be re-emphasised that by SPG Lefkandi existed in its own right as a designer and manufacturer of base metal objects, and its enjoyment of imported products such as the decorated fibulae from Athens was simply a bonus.

# Section 12

# Fragmentary Pottery and a Stone Mould

*The Pottery*    V. R. d'A. DESBOROUGH

## THE POTTERY

**Skoubris cemetery: surface, pits, and fills (PLATES 273–4, 283, 284, no. 11).**
Two sets of material are discussed. First, there are the sherds from a small pit in the NW extension of Trench A, lying above S 3 and S 4. Second, there is the deposit from the Gully Fill.[1] Apart from these, there is little or nothing of note.[2] All the pottery appears to be in the local fabric.

1. *Trench A, pit*: The contents comprised fifteen sherds only; the most significant are shown on PLATE 273, and are as follows.

819    Handle of a multiple vase.
820    Shoulder of a closed vase. The semicircles are compass-drawn.
821    Handle of jug or oinochoe, with hatched diamond decoration running vertically.
822    From shoulder and body of jug or oinochoe. Dark ground, hatched diamonds on shoulder. Probably from the same vase as 821.
823    From shoulder of jug or oinochoe. Dogtooth motive, multiple triangles below.
824–5  Two sherds one showing two, the other four, rows of dogtooth, dark ground below. Probably from the same vase as 823.

Of the unillustrated sherds one, from a small closed vase, seems to have a decoration of a set of multiple triangles with filled inverted triangles in between. Another has a wavy line motive; the rest are indeterminate.

The fact that many of the sherds were burnt suggests that they may have come from a pyre. But did they all come from the same original context? One cannot know. This is unfortunate, because it appears that some of the sherds reflect the Attic EPG phase,[3] and if this were a homogeneous group we would have the earliest known example at Lefkandi of compass-drawn semicircles, a motive which does not otherwise appear in the local repertory till appreciably later. But at least we may have a possible link with the Athenian 'wild' type of decoration that is found in the earliest stage of the Protogeometric style in that community.[4]

2. *The Gully Fill* (PLATES 273–4, 283, 284, no. 11).

*Open vases.* PLATE 273, 826–876. No sherd of a kalathos, with or without impressed triangles, was identified.

*Cup.*[5] 826. Very common. The rims nearly all belonged to the usual flat-based SPG type, with reserved band on the outer surface, or monochrome; rims with zigzag extremely rare. All fragments were discarded save for the one handle illustrated.

*PSC skyphos.* 827–834. See PLATE 283, 8 (= 828). Common. Lips vary from high to medium. Note the unusual, probably early, hourglass filling of 834.

*Circles skyphos.* ?835, 836–9, ?840, 841–2. See PLATE 283, 7 and 9 (= 835, 838). Reasonably common, and of interest in view of its absence so far from tombs. 835 is not certainly of this type; 840 could be a panelled example, but not enough has survived to tell whether it had circles.

*Small conical feet* (cups or skyphoi). 943 (= PLATE 283, 21). Not more than five.

*Shallow bowl with strap handles.* 844–7, ?848. See PLATE 283, 11, (profile shown too deep) and 12 (= 846, 845). Several, mostly with everted lip. A shape not yet found in tombs.

*Miscellaneous skyphoi and bowls.* 850–1, and PLATE 283, 10. A very few. Those not illustrated include monochrome skyphoi (two with sharply everted lip) and a shallow bowl with slightly everted lip and circles on the body.

*Plate.* 852–3. See PLATE 283, 13 (= 853). From the same vase. No other sherds found.

*Flat dish.* 854 = PLATE 283, 24. Monochrome. An exceedingly rare shape.

*?Kantharos.* 855. The handle suggests this shape, a very unusual one for Lefkandi.

*Krater.*[6] 856–76, and PLATE 283, 14–23 (where 14, 17, 18, 23 = 863, 862, 859, 869). A surprisingly large number for a cemetery context. The flat-topped rims occasionally have groups of bars. Body motives are fairly varied, including circles (filled, 868), chevrons, opposed diagonals with unfilled interstices, hatched triangle and diamond, horizontal and vertical dogtooth, and hatched meander (871 and 872 join). At least one large pedestal foot, 869, and perhaps two others, PLATE 283, 20 and 22.

*Closed vases.* PLATE 274, 877–917, and PLATE 283, 1–6 (where 1–5 = 877, 878, 882, 916, 912).

*Amphorae.* This was by far the most common shape, to judge from the number of sherds.[7] Some of the sherds certainly seem to belong to the massive type often placed in pyres; conversely, it is not always clear whether one is dealing with an amphora or a smaller closed vase of jug or oinochoe type. Both neck-handled and belly-handled types are represented, and the general system of decoration is as a rule clay ground, with occasional exceptions so far as the neck is concerned.

Almost all the banded or undecorated body fragments were thrown away. A selection of rims is shown, 877–8, 880–2, and 916; there are many unillustrated. Similarly, 887–9 and 895–7 show the variety of decoration on the neck handles.[8] For examples of necks see 883 and 886; they are normally monochrome or clay ground, but 886 illustrates a rare instance of panelling (for the hourglass motive see below on the dark ground type). As for the decoration of the shoulders and body, the main motives are shown on 884–5, 890–4, 898–904 and possibly 906 and 910 (these might be from jugs or oinochoai). They include cross-hatched rectangles and triangles,[9] chevrons, opposed diagonals probably with unfilled interstices, and wavy lines, but the most popular motives are the semicircles for the shoulder and the circles for the belly (note the hourglass and reserved cross fillings). 892 has a wart on the shoulder. No feet are illustrated: they are of the usual ring-base type.

*The dark ground type.* This includes both amphorae and trefoil oinochoai (see the settlement, under the SPG Pit and the Levelling Material), and one of its features is a slender neck with panelled hourglass motive. There were a few of these neck fragments, and most of them are illustrated, see 913–17, of which 914 is clearly from an oinochoe, and 913 and 915–16 (the lip of 916 is not a trefoil) certainly or probably from amphorae. 917 has the start of semicircles or circles on the shoulder. With these I include 912, from a large trefoil oinochoe. It appears to have the start of a meander design on the neck, and if it is locally made, as it seems to be, it is almost the only instance at Lefkandi of an attempt to imitate a popular Attic neck motive.[10]

*Trefoil oinochoai and jugs.* A relatively small number in comparison with the amphorae. 879 is probably the neck of a jug, rather than of an oinochoe. Of the group 905–11 only four are certain; 905 shows semicircles on the shoulder; 907 is from a neck, with most unusual hatched triangle zone; 909 has a zigzag in a reserved band round the belly; and 911 has reserved bands round the belly, with a handle stump above. A few others were kept as samples. The system of decoration, as is conventional for small closed vases, is dark ground.[11]

*Coarse hand-made ware.* A few sherds were kept, but none illustrated. They seem to have been of the usual type.

*The 'ship' sherd.* 918 = PLATE 284, 11. Buff clay, black-brown paint: all the appearance of being locally made. From the body of a krater. To the right, part of a cross-hatched rectangle flanked by a vertical line, this motive supported by an area of paint which must have extended right across the body. The central motive, drawn with extreme care, is a ship, of which what remains is the bow part. For the detailed description below I am indebted to Mr. R. T. Williams, formerly of Durham University.

Ship's bow to right. The thickest piece of vertical painting on the right represents the bow compartment, from which project, above, the extension of the horizontal rail and, at the level of the hull, the ram,[12] above the compartment is a back-curving stem-post. Above the hull are two verticals which are the supports for the rails and which divide the ship up into rowers' 'rooms'. The second 'room' from the right contains some unexplained object.

According to Professor Coldstream, the date of this sherd falls within the ninth century, which would be in accordance with that of the rest of the material. We thus have one of the earliest representations of a post-Bronze Age ship.

*The chronological range*

An SM cup, SF 16, can be set aside as the product of a disturbed tomb (p. 139f); apart from this there is only the sherd of a flat dish, 854, which might belong within the main period of the cemetery as so far excavated, i.e. SM to MPG, but this is no more than a possibility.[13]

There is little doubt that the material as a whole does not precede LPG. Many of the sherds could belong to LPG, but none inescapably so, the nearest being 834, on the basis of the hourglass filling to the PSC. Some weight may here be allowed the negative evidence, in particular the almost complete absence of the cup with zigzag on the outer lip, characteristic of LPG and continuing into SPG I, well attested both in the settlement and in the tombs.[14]

The remarkable conservatism of the Lefkandian potter makes any precise judgment rather perilous, but it is extremely likely that many, if not most, of the sherds should be assigned to the SPG I and SPG II phases. To SPG I could belong the closer approximations to LPG, as for example the conical feet, and perhaps the circles skyphoi; on the other hand, the hourglass panels on amphora and oinochoe necks, and the shallow bowls with strap handles, are characteristic of SPG II (and later) and absent from SPG I.

It is also likely that at least some of the pottery should be classed as SPG III. This may be based on the close similarity in style of SPG II and SPG III, on the sherd of the atticising trefoil oinochoe 912 (imitation of Attic Geometric is rare before SPG III), perhaps on the curious meander on the joining sherds 871–2, but above all on 852–3, two sherds of a plate, an unusual shape not yet found in a context earlier than SPG III, and elsewhere still current in the second quarter of the eighth century.[15]

The appearance of SPG III sherds in the Gully Fill would not be surprising, as the latest known tomb of the cemetery, S 59, belongs early within this phase. Whether any of them are appreciably later, however, is uncertain and doubtful, if one bears in mind the material from the other two cemeteries and from the Levelling Material in the settlement, where there is a reasonable amount of evidence for Attic MG imports and for local atticising bases. Also, there seem to have been no sherds of PSC skyphoi with low rims, a development probably to be assigned to SPG III.

## Palia Perivolia Cemetery: surface and fills (PLATES 275–7)[16]

As will be clear from the introduction to the main catalogue, there are two distinct areas. There is the cemetery itself, which contains all the tombs and pyres; and there is a rock channel which marked the cemetery's northern boundary, and which produced a considerable number of sherds from surface and fill.

*The cemetery area*

The cemetery area can be dealt with very briefly.[17] No pottery is illustrated except for the fragments which made up into a third of a very large neck-handled amphora with full circles on the shoulder (PLATE 281C), certainly from a disturbed pyre, as there are traces of burning.[18] Between fifty and sixty other sherds were retained; with one important exception, a krater fragment that appears to have fringed hand-drawn arcs and vertical wiggly lines and so should be SM, they fall within the period covered by the tombs and pyres (MPG to SPG II). Most of them came from amphorae, including several burnt pieces of a massive amphora with semicircles on the shoulder and (probably) circles on the belly; a few belonged to jugs or oinochoai, a few also to cups, skyphoi and kraters. The one identified kalathos sherd has impressed triangles; and there were two sherds with combed and incised decoration, one of which makes a join with the fragmentary shallow bowl P 39B, 17 (PLATE 147). Finally, there was a sherd of a massive closed vase with cross-hatched decoration, horizontal ridges below this, and a vertical ridge at its side.

*The North Channel, squares A, C and E*
The North Channel, together with its contents, appeared in three separate squares, A, C, and E, the two intervening squares B and D remaining unexcavated. There is no doubt that we are dealing with one long continuous depression in the rock, but in the analysis I have kept the material from each of the three squares distinct. I take the pottery from square E as a whole; for C, I divide between surface and fill; for A, which contained the bulk of the material, I make a further subdivision, surface, upper fill and lower fill. In all except the lower fill of A the pottery seems to be reasonably homogeneous in style and in chronological range, and I give a brief summary of it before analysing and discussing the lower fill. It may be added that throughout there were more amphora sherds than from any other shape.

*Square E.* About 200 sherds, most from amphorae; cup, skyphos and krater fragments were present in small numbers, and there were seven coarse handmade sherds. None is illustrated; there is nothing unusual, and the material could all lie within the known period of the cemetery's use.

*Square C: surface.* PLATE 277, 1023–30, and PLATE 284, 10 (= 1023). About 250 sherds, with much the same distribution of shapes as in square E. The illustrated selection includes a cup sherd with reserved bands on the outer lip (1024), fragments of a PSC skyphos (1025), of a circles skyphos with filled circles, so perhaps early (1026), of two kraters (1027–8, the motive on the latter otherwise unknown to me), and of two amphorae (1029–30). The most interesting, however is the pyxis rim 1023: it is probably from an Attic pointed pyxis, and the vertical chevron motive places it not earlier than MG,[19] in other words later than the date suggested for any of the tombs or pyres in this cemetery.

*Square C: fill.* PLATE 277, 1031–49. Nearly 600 sherds, including over 200 scraps. The statistics for the rest were similar to elsewhere in the channel for wheelmade, but coarse handmade constituted about 12%. Some ninety sherds were eventually retained.

1031–9 are sherds from open vases. 1031 is from a large circles skyphos, unusual for its high carinated rim; 1032, 1034 and 1039 are from kraters, the many ridges of 1032 also being unusual; 1033 is from a PSC skyphos, with the semicircles intersecting, and the skyphos is notable in having a distinctly low lip, a development which seems characteristic of SPG III. And finally there are four sherds (1035–8) of the rare plate shape, which may not appear before SPG III. Among the unillustrated sherds are PSC and circles skyphoi, a straight skyphos rim with cross-hatching on the body, flat and ring bases, only three conical feet, and the rim of a shallow bowl with strap handles.

1040–9 illustrate closed vases, both large and small. Most have circles or semicircles; of these, 1043 is from a very large amphora, and from a pyre; and note the unusual flanking verticals of 1047. 1040 is one of the few handles with herringbone decoration. Rare motives appear on 1048 and 1049, a diamond lattice and a multiple diamond, witnesses that the local potters could and did get away from the conventional circles. The unillustrated sherds include two ridged trefoil oinochoe lips, and part of the base of what looks like a straight-walled jug.

The material ranges in style from LPG to SPG III.

*Square A: surface.* (PLATE 275, 919–34). There were nearly 800 sherds, with the same ratio of open to closed as in the channel generally, and again, as in the fill of Square C, a relatively large number of coarse hand-made sherds.

The stylistic range, in shape and chronology, is also similar: amphorae in the majority, cups and PSC skyphoi fairly well represented — circles skyphoi rather less so, and kraters and small closed vases relatively scarce. LPG to SPG III.

A few of the illustrated sherds are typical — the jug or oinochoe 927 and the amphora 934 with their semicircles, the krater sherd 928 with part of the handles — but most of them display less usual features. Both the circles skyphos fragments, 920 and 921, have panelled decoration, and could be LPG, especially the 'branch' pattern on 920.[20] The only cup sherd shown, 922, has a low and slightly everted rim and might perhaps be an imitation of Attic EG II, and certainly Attic — and not earlier than MG I[21] — is the skyphos fragment 919. Two atticising krater pieces are shown: 923 with ?meander motive below the rim, probably not earlier than MG I; and 929, the bottom of a tall flaring base, reflecting EG II or MG I. The underside of the kalathos base 930 has several parallels in the tombs, but 931, a fragment of a flat dish with high straight rim and opposed diagonal motive, belongs to a very rare shape. For the amphorae I have illustrated the only three panelled necks (the rest are monochrome or unpainted): 924–6, none earlier than SPG II, and 924 and 926 atticising, probably EG II. Finally, there are two belly sherds from amphorae or large oinochoai, both with opposed diagonals, the one (932) with unfilled, the other (933), with filled interstices.

*Square A: upper fill.* (PLATE 275, 935–63). This area produced about 1100 sherds (including over 150 coarse hand-made), of which rather more than 200 were eventually retained. The same stylistic range was found as in the surface level, and the relative distribution of open and closed shapes was even more heavily weighted in favour of the amphorae, the sherds of which made up some 70% of the whole.

The unillustrated material reveals that, for the open vases, the few cups and skyphoi were of the usual types current from LPG onwards; shallow bowls with strap handles were poorly represented, and krater sherds were rare, though they include a number of rims with ridges below, and one with the start of PSC on the body; one fragment may belong to the rim of a kalathos. For the closed vases, the amphorae were of the usual local type: where there was decoration apart from bands it is normally semicircles and circles, though there is one instance of vertical filled diamonds, and at least one of opposed diagonals. Small closed vases were extremely scarce, and provided nothing unusual.

The illustrated selection follows the principles adopted for the surface, and is not, therefore, to be thought of as representative of the whole.

Of the locally made open vases I show only two cup rims with zigzag(s) (937–8), two sherds of PSC skyphoi (939, 947), an unusual skyphos fragment with high carinated rim and the start of a panel on the body (940), and a krater sherd with ?opposed diagonals (941). But there were also krater sherds imported from Attica: 935, with meander below the rim, is probably MG; the fine piece 944 (note the butterfly ornament on the rim) is certainly MG, and so are the joining sherds 950 and 957, showing a stirrup handle.[22]

As to the locally made closed vases, almost all amphorae, I illustrate two rims with opposed diagonals on the outer surface (951–2), and six fragments of bellies, mostly from massive vases (948, open circles; 955, circles flanking a 'branch' pattern; 958, circles (?) on belly and semicircles on shoulder; and 956, 962 and 963, showing panels of cross-hatched rectangles and cross-hatched diamonds in conjunction or alone). There are also several interesting sherds from panelled amphora or oinochoe necks: 954, with its elongated rays, probably reflects a local tradition,[23] the multiple zigzags of 949, 953 and 961 are atticising EG or MG I, and so is the meander of 943; the dogtooth and hatching of 959 and 960 — joining, and note the start of some shoulder decoration — could be atticising MG I.[24]

In addition to these there were a few Attic sherds from closed shapes. 942 is an amphora or oinochoe neck with meander in a panel;[25] 936 may be from a pointed pyxis of EG II—MG I type; 945 is also from a pyxis, of MG I style — and 946 may go with it.

Taking an overall view of the material so far discussed from the North Channel, it is evident that the pottery covers the periods from LPG to SPG III. The presence of the LPG element cannot be substantiated with absolute certainty, in view of the conservative attitude of the Lefkandian potter, but (as has been seen) certain shapes and motives seem more likely to belong to this phase — a phase in any case well represented in the cemetery. At the other end, the Attic and atticising MG sherds make it clear that pottery continued to be deposited into the SPG III period. This presumably means that some of the sherds of local fabric and style are to be classed as SPG III: but which? We may reasonably accept the plate sherds 1035—8 and (I think) the PSC skyphos fragment 1033, but we cannot say more with any certainty, a fact which emphasises the serious problem of distinguishing between SPG II and SPG III. A small but curious point is that although there were a fair number of panelled amphora/oinochoe necks, no example was found of the hourglass panel which was reasonably common in the settlement deposits.

What connection has this material with the cemetery? The very large number of amphorae shows that most of it did not come from tombs; the sherds of massive amphorae probably came from pyres, but these are not all that numerous in comparison with those of normal size, and there is very little evidence of burning. Also, if we were dealing with disturbed tombs, we would expect many sherds of small closed vases; these are in fact extremely scarce. Then the krater sherds, though relatively few, provide evidence of a shape found neither in tomb nor in pyre so far; and the surprisingly large number of coarse hand-made fragments does not reflect a tomb context. If, as seems the case, we are not dealing with settlement material (where cups and skyphoi would be much more common), we may perhaps conclude that much of the pottery was used in connection with the rites of burial, but not deposited in tombs or pyres.

*Square A: lower fill.* (PLATES 276, 964—99; 282 C and F; 284, 7 (= 966)). About a thousand sherds, all kept except those with no feature (about 50%). Cups and skyphoi were the two main open shapes, amphorae the main closed one.

For the cups, those with zigzag(s) on the outer lip seem to be in the majority (965—8, 974);[26] there were, however, a number of monochrome (973) or ?unpainted lips — but none with reserved bands. All appear to have had monochrome bodies and handles, with bases either flat (967) or high conical or flaring (964).

As to the skyphoi, it is remarkable that only one sherd with PSC was found (969) — and even this is unusual, if not unique, as its lip is very sharply outcurved, with no carination. For the rest, wherever verifiable, the circles skyphos (970—2) was the type used. There are at least twenty-four sherds of such skyphoi, including two instances of central fillings to the circles, the reserved cross of 971, and an hourglass on an unillustrated fragment.

Other open vases of small size are rare. 976—7 (joining) belong to a shallow bowl with incurved rim, and a handle which is not of the usual SPG II strap type, but rolled and very probably rising above the rim; whatever the decoration may have been, it starts with a crossed diagonal (see PLATE 18, 328). There is also an unillustrated sherd from a shallow bowl with everted rim, but the handle element is missing. 975, finally, with a thick zigzag below the rim, is from some unascertainable shape.

There were twelve krater sherds, one a high foot, nine body sherds, monochrome or banded, and two with decoration (979, some panelled motive, 978, circles).[27] One complete profile of an impressed-triangle kalathos was found (982 — the underbase has simply one large circle painted on it); and 981, a small fragment of Red Slip ware, with incised horizontal and wavy lines, could be from a kalathos.

Closed vases provided nearly 60% of the total.[28] Omitting the two main amphorae, made up of many joining sherds, which will be discussed below, about 250 amphora sherds were retained, and some twenty from jugs or oinochoai. The amphora material included fragments of seventeen bases, forty-four handles (24 neck, 20 belly), fourteen rims (chiefly of neck-handled amphorae), and about a hundred body sherds, unpainted or with banded decoration only, with only a handful dark ground, thus showing the predominance of the light ground system. None of these is illustrated. For the rest, those which have individual motives, the almost invariable decoration is semicircles or circles (983–6, 988, 991–3). The semicircles were used for the shoulder on all verifiable instances except the major piece described below, and in several cases were accompanied by languettes (see 983 – and 987, on the assumption that there were semicircles as well); the belly usually had circles, e.g. 992, and 993 where the circles have a Maltese cross filling and flank a 'branch' motive (see above), but in two instances, 994–5, there are rectilinear designs, diamonds between verticals, and cross-hatching. Decoration is then simple, and no example was found of opposed diagonals on the belly, or of any motive on the neck.

The most distinctive oinochoe piece is 989–90, made up of seven joining fragments and two joining fragments which do not join the main group but belong to the same vase. They show the shoulder (note the wart) and belly of a fairly large oinochoe, over 20 cm high; the shoulder has semicircles, the rest of the body is dark ground except for four reserved bands on the upper belly. The paint is a distinctive red-brown.

Four other oinochoe sherds are shown: 996, trefoil lip; 997, semicircles on shoulder, dark ground body; 'branch' motive on shoulder; 999, barred handle.

Two fragmentary vases remain to be described in greater detail.

(i) Neck-handled amphora (PLATE 282C). The whole lower part is lost. Pres. h. 28. H. from shoulder to lip 175. Outer d. of mouth c. 18. Clay brick-red, paint dull black. Lip thick and grooved; the outer part is painted over, but one cannot tell whether the paint continued inside, as the surface was much worn and broken away. The neck curves inwards sharply below the lip, thence descending almost vertically to the shoulder; a poorly executed band encircles the neck where the handle curves over to join it, and there are two further bands at the base — the effect is light ground. The surviving handle has a decoration of two doubly intersecting vertical curves. The junction of neck and shoulder is marked by a striated ridge, and the shoulder decoration consists of two sets of compass-drawn circles on each side. Below the shoulder, two bands: the rest is lost. LPG suggested: it is quite different from the SPG amphorae.

(ii) Four (?) handled amphora (PLATE 282F). Pres. h. c. 55. Max. d. c. 36. Outer d. of lip c. 24. Very fragmentary, but the profile is certain except for the base, which was not recovered. Soft light brown clay with a mauve core; pale brown slip, matt dark brown paint. Short thick neck coming up to a sharply flaring lip. The lip is flat on the top, and decorated with bars. Beneath it, inside, a broad band is supported by a narrower one.[29] Outside, paint covers the outer lip and underlip and the flaring part of the neck; the neck itself has four encircling bands. The body is heavy and rather globular. The top of the shoulder has a narrow striated ridge at the junction with the neck. A vertical loop handle made up of three strips was attached to the shoulder, and there seems little doubt that there was a second one. The shoulder decoration consists of sets of hand-drawn semicircles with an outer fringe, below which are two bands enclosing two horizontal scribble zigzags. The belly was also provided with two handles (assuming the existence of one lost) of the horizontal loop type, painted on the upper surface. The decoration of the belly is simple: one broad band, two narrow ones, a very broad painted area covering the central and lower part, and then a further narrow band. What remains of the lower body is unpainted, though no doubt a band of paint will have marked out the junction between the body and the missing base. SM.

The very existence of this vase is important, as one of the rare examples of an amphora in the SM style.[30] Its presence in this fill is also important; little is known of the development of amphorae before LPG, but such a shape and decoration seem hardly likely to have survived EPG, and in that case it supports the rather dubious sherd from the main cemetery (see above) in providing evidence of earlier use of the cemetery than can be established from the tombs and pyres.

Over what period was pottery deposited in the lower fill? One factor may be stressed, that there were more joining sherds, and more nearly complete vases, than in any other deposit except Area SL. One thing at least is certain, that there is no trace of SPG III in the shape of Attic or atticising MG, or any local feature. Further, there is no certain example of a shallow bowl with strap handles, no cups with reserved bands on the outer lip, no opposed diagonals, no panelled necks of amphorae or oinochoai, no unindented kalathoi; in fact, there is nothing that is demonstrably SPG II. Then, there are no PSC skyphoi except for one which is atypical: in view of the popularity of this type throughout SPG, does this absence suggest nothing later than LPG? Here one must be cautious; there are indeed PSC skyphoi in the upper fills and surface of the North Channel, but one must remember that they are so far almost non-existent in the Toumba cemetery. Also, the number of flat bases of cups and of monochrome cup lips would suggest an SPG I element, though even here the flat-based cup was already known in LPG.

There is a certain amount, in my opinion, that is very probably LPG, in particular those cups with zigzags on the lip, and flaring or conical feet, and the numerous circles skyphos sherds, including those with central filling to the circles; also the 'branch' pattern on two of the closed sherds. The impressed-triangle kalathos and the Red Slip ware sherd could, of course, be LPG (though continuing into SPG I), and the languettes could be of the same period. In fact, there is nothing in the decoration that need be later. My strong impression is that it is a predominantly early deposit, certainly earlier than SPG II, quite possible not later than LPG.

That there is material even earlier than LPG is proved by the amphora of SM style; unfortunately, no sherds can be attributed with certainty either to EPG or to MPG.


## East Cemetery: surface and fill (PLATE 278)

This section examines the pottery deposited in the fill of a natural gully or depression in the rock surface, and its relation to three of the tombs which with unexcavated pyres constitute the East Cemetery, inasmuch as tombs 45 and 47 were dug into the gully subsequent to the fill, and tomb 42 could have been but its stratigraphical relation is uncertain.[31] A brief discussion of the sherds from the surface of the fill as a whole is followed by remarks on the material from the northern part of the fill and the relationship of tomb 45 to this; the sherds from the southern part of the fill, connected with tombs 42 and 47, are then similarly discussed, and this discussion is linked to an analysis of the sherds (not illustrated) found immediately above tomb 42 and to the contents of the tomb, with a corresponding analysis of the material found in the fill of tomb 47, also in relation to the tomb's contents.

The six sherds on PLATE 278A will suffice to give an idea of the surface material, which is stratigraphically later than the tombs mentioned. The bowl with double zigzag on the outer lip has a sharply angled body; the circles skyphos is unusual only in the small number of its circles; the two sherds in the middle row are from necks, that to the right from an amphora with elaborate panels, that to the left probably from an atticising EG II oinochoe with multiple zigzag; the ribbed fragment is from the pedestal foot of a krater, and could be atticising MG I.[32] The sixth, with combed decoration, is from a jug neck; its fabric is soft-fired and brick-red, and there are traces of red-brown paint on the outside.

The unillustrated sherds include one from an impressed-triangle kalathos, and a cup lip with zigzag. So there is probably SPG I, or even LPG; but the latest, as illustrated, should be placed in SPG III.

The North fill produced about 250 sherds, of which seven are illustrated on PLATE 272B. The open vases, on the top row, include a PSC fragment, a sherd of a bowl with unusual type of zigzag, and one from a shallow bowl with rough zigzag. The other four are from amphorae or oinochoai with semicircles on the shoulder — one has vertical lines (?languettes) flanked by wiggly lines pendent from the neck. One of the unillustrated amphora sherds had opposed diagonals with unfilled interstices. There is nothing that need be later than SPG II, and many could be earlier.

It was this area within which tomb 45 was later inserted. The thirteen sherds from the tomb's fill, and the forty from the wash above the tomb cutting, are all of types common in SPG I and SPG II, and need no illustration. The tomb itself produced no vases, but it had two extraordinarily fine fibulae which cannot be earlier than the end of SPG II (PLATE 241a, b).

Thus we have a clear chronological sequence here: the filling of the rock gully in SPG I–II was followed by the use of the ground for tomb 45 (late SPG II); surface fill above this included at least one SPG III (MG I) sherd, along with earlier material.

The South fill contained about 140 sherds and is less easily explained. Nine sherds are shown on PLATE 278C, four from small open vases (top row), three from kraters, centre and left, and two from amphorae on the right. Most, like those from the North fill, could be SPG I or SPG II. The panelled amphora neck, however, is more likely to be SPG II; and the skyphos sherd on the top left, with multiple zigzag motive, is definitely atticising EG II, so not earlier than SPG II.[33]

It is in relation to this material that the fills and contents of tombs 42 and 47 have to be discussed. Tomb 42 can be dealt with briefly. The small group of sherds found immediately above it is of too indeterminate a character to affect the LPG or fairly early SPG I date indicated by the two kalathoi with impressed triangles that were the only vases deposited in the tomb. So if the tomb was dug after the use of the gully as a deposit for discarded pottery, there is a problem, and my analysis of the development of kalathoi would have to be amended. If it was dug before, the problem ceases to exist.

Whatever may have happened in the case of tomb 42, tomb 47 was definitely dug through the deposit above, and one would expect its pottery to be stylistically SPG II or later. There are in fact vases which seem to me to belong to SPG I (e.g. the lekythoi with cross-hatched triangles and semicircles), and none that I would assign inescapably to SPG II, though some certainly could be. The dividing line between the two phases is not easy to determine (see pp. 288–90), and it may be that the group as a whole should be considered SPG II.[34]

The question is not solved by the sherds found in the fill of the tomb. There were nearly 150, of which thirty-five are illustrated on PLATE 278D and E — a fully representative selection. The open vase sherds fill the three top rows of PLATE 278D, flat bases, conical feet, cup handles,[35] cup lips with zigzag, sherds of PSC skyphoi, one from a circles skyphos with Maltese cross filling, and a leg of what may have been a tripod dish (see the restoration on PLATE 284, 9). None of these need be later than SPG I, three or four could be LPG. Much the same picture is provided by the closed vase sherds. The bottom row of PLATE 278D shows jug fragments and one sherd of a pyxis (see the restoration on PLATE 284, 8). PLATE 278E illustrates the amphora sherds,[36] both neck-handled and belly-handled; it is notable that the only decoration, apart from sets of bands and the handle motives, is semicircles and circles — this applies equally to the unillustrated sherds. As for the open vases, there is nothing that need be later than SPG I.[37]

There are three possible answers: my stylistic analysis is incorrect; it is in broad outline correct but does not allow for overlaps and survivals; or the gully continued to be used for depositing sherds after tomb 47 had been constructed. These answers need not be mutually exclusive.

### Toumba Cemetery: surface and fills (PLATES 279, 280, 281A)

The excavated area was divided into nine squares (p. 105). I deal first with the surface sherds from all squares except V and VI, and then with these last two separately.[38] To finish, I give a brief account of such material from tomb fills as is relevant for chronology or of intrinsic interest.

### 1. *All squares except V and VI* (PLATE 279, 1050–74)

About a thousand sherds were recovered, some two hundred were kept, and twenty-five are illustrated. The proportion of open vases as opposed to closed is much greater than is found in tombs and pyres. A number of sherds were burnt.

*Cups and skyphoi* were numerous. Cups are either of the type with zigzag(s) on the outer lip (1050–3) or monochrome (1055), the latter of a shape which differs from that of the normal SPG type, and appears sporadically in other contexts.[39] There were several sherds of circles skyphoi (1054), but no identifiable example of a PSC skyphos was found.[40] Other open vase sherds include one of Black Slip ware (1056), and one of what is probably a shallow bowl with strap handles (1057). Several kalathos sherds were found, both with impressed triangles and without.

*Kraters* were reasonably well represented (several were burnt): eight are illustrated, and these show an interesting variety of motives. 1058 with hand-drawn semicircles and half-moon filling is in the SM style; the two rows of zigzags on 1062 recall MPG; the circles with Maltese cross filling of 1059 could be LPG;[41] the battlement motives of 1060 and 1063 take us into SPG. Note also the use of the dot technique on 1063-5 — 1065 appears to have a 'branch' motive. The continuation of the design on 1061 is quite unclear, but the idea of placing chevrons sideways seems unique. An unillustrated fragment has opposed diagonals.

*Amphorae* were, as always, numerous, but provide little worth special comment. Apart from the usual circles and semicircles,[42] there are rare examples of languettes and vertical wiggly lines pendent from the neck. I illustrate one sherd only, 1069, with opposed diagonals with unfilled interstices.

The *smaller closed vases* were relatively few, but included some interesting fragments. 1066, with bands and dogtooth on the lower neck, could perhaps come from a lekythos;[43] 1067 is from a jug with cutaway neck; the internally barred double arc of 1068 recalls S 8,2 (PLATE 93) of EPG date; 1070 shows a jug rim with panelled decoration on the neck; and 1071 has an unusual panelled motive of hatched triangle, verticals, and fringed ?circles. In addition, there are sherds of a large jug with latticed belly decoration, others of which were found in the fill of tombs 27 and 29 (see below and PLATE 281, 1151). And there were five probable pyxis sherds (unillustrated), three with zigzag on the belly, two with butterfly motive.

All these appear to be of local fabric: there are, however, three Attic sherds. 1072, of EG II date, is from a skyphos with multiple zigzag. 1073–4, both burnt, are not earlier than MG I; they are from small kraters or large skyphoi, and have a meander (?) motive and subsidiary zones of decoration.

Handmade sherds were extremely scarce, not more than about twenty-five.

2. *Squares V and VI* (PLATE 279, 1075–111).
Square VI (1075–80) may be dealt with first, and briefly. Just over forty sherds were retained, of which fourteen (not illustrated), all burnt, belonged to two or three small closed vases, one a pyxis. Only one sherd from an open vase is illustrated, 1075, from a cup with double zigzag on the outer lip. Seven other cup and skyphos fragments were kept, and eight krater sherds with conventional motives (circles, cross-hatched rectangle, dogtooth). The rest are from amphorae, and five are shown: 1076–7, from a shoulder, have the same multiple brush for the circles as on 1059 above; 1078, circles on the belly, shows signs of burning; 1079 is a shoulder fragment, and 1080 has a dogtooth motive. The only unusual one not illustrated has groups of vertical lines on the body.

*Square V* (1081–111, and PLATE 284, 1–6) yielded about 650 sherds, open fragments providing at least half, closed rather less than half, and coarse hand-made ware about 5%. Most of this collection was thrown out, virtually insignificant scraps, plain, monochrome or banded. About a quarter of the material was kept, many more sherds from open vases than from closed; only these are discussed below. No clear evidence was found for kalathoi or pyxides.

*Cups and skyphoi.* The most common type of cup is monochrome, or mostly so, with gently outcurving rim: there were twenty-seven sherds of this type (for six, see PLATE 284, 1–6). Two, also monochrome, have a high and slightly offset rim; and there were six lips with zigzag(s) on the outer surface (see 1081–3). Seven cup, and eight skyphos, handles were kept, and of the eight retained bases, cup or skyphos, seven are conical and one is ring — no example of a flat base was identified. The thirteen body sherds with decoration certainly or most probably belong to skyphoi; eleven have circles[44] (see 1085–7), in one case (1085) with a Maltese cross filling; 1088 shows a panelled cross-hatched rectangle; and 1084 has what seems to be part of a lip with dogtooth band below.

Thirty of the retained *krater* fragments were monochrome body sherds, conical feet, handles and rims — two of the last had a grooved ridge below the lip (see 1089). Of the decorated sherds three have circles (see 1093), and the rest can best be described as assorted. Five are shown: 1090 is unintelligible, 1091 has hand-drawn arcs, 1092 a battlement, 1094 a zone of cross-hatched diamonds, and 1095 dot-fringed vertical lines flanking ?diamonds.

Two sherds of other open vases may be noted, both from shallow bowls, one monochrome, the other (1096) with everted lip and, beneath it, pendent cross-hatched triangles and a wart.

*Amphorae.* None of the seven retained rims or handles is illustrated; one rim has bars on its upper surface. The motives on the seventeen body sherds are usually circles or semicircles (see 1099–1103). There were four examples of languettes (see 1097–9), combined on 1097 with fringed hand-drawn arcs, on 1098 apparently with some other hand-drawn design, and on 1099 with compass-drawn semicircles. For other motives, note the triple wavy line of 1104, and the double rough zigzag of 1105.

*Jugs and oinochoai.* Three of the retained sherds are not illustrated: two trefoil lips and a sherd of light brown fabric, with combed and incised decoration. The six decorated pieces are shown: 1106, full circles on the shoulder; 1107, semicircles with zigzag beneath, and an unclear motive below this; 1108, semicircles; 1109–10, multiple triangles, and 1111, multiple zigzags (atticising EG II?)

To sum up on squares V and VI, this is a thoroughly early-looking collection of sherds. If it were not for three of them, 1111 with its zigzags, 1092 with its battlement, and probably the bars on the unillustrated amphora rim, one could claim that there was no trace of SPG — no PSC skyphoi, no cups of the characteristic SPG type, no flat cup bases, no panelled necks, no opposed diagonals with unfilled interstices. Furthermore, a few sherds are clearly SM in style (1091, 1097, ?1098). Is it possible that the numerous monochrome cups with gently outcurving lip should be classed as MPG or earlier (see p. 296)? At the very least, we have evidence of earlier use of the cemetery than known from the tombs and pyres.

*3. Sherds from the inside or fill of tombs* (PLATES 280, 281A).
I divide this section into three parts: a small selection of sherds of intrinsic interest; the material from the fill of tomb 7, insofar as it may affect the date of the tomb; and the material recovered from the fill of tomb 32.

*A. 1151–60.* Two substantial pieces come from tomb 29: 1151 is from a large jug with lattice design on the belly;[45] 1152 belongs to a neck-handled amphora, and shows an unusually-placed triple rough zigzag just below the lip. Of the remaining eight, 1153–4 are from skyphoi;[46] 1155, cut from an amphora, is one of the pierced circular sherds of which there are several examples at Lefkandi; 1156 is the base of a kalathos, and 1157 the rim of a krater; 1158, delicately drawn, may come from a pyxis; 1159 is part of the bull's head handle of a krater; and 1160, an amphora sherd, provides the only example known to me from Lefkandi of circles joined tangentially.

These sherds have no effect on the date of the tombs to which they belong.

*B.*[47] *1161–3.* Tomb 7 contained a cup with high flaring foot, stylistically LPG; its two other vases, large jugs or lekythoi, could still be LPG, but would not be out of place in SPGI. There were about fifty sherds in the fill, which should be contemporaneous or earlier. All are or could be, including 1161, a cup lip with double zigzag. There is however a question mark against the two others illustrated, the PSC skyphos sherd 1162,[48] and the amphora sherd 1163, whose decoration seems unusual for LPG.

*C.* 1112–50. The unusual nature of the deposit in tomb 32, probably a collection of sherds from disturbed or destroyed pyres, is described and discussed in the main catalogue, and it seems best to deal with it in this section.

The total of sherds collected was a little over 120, of which twenty-six small and indeterminate scraps were thrown away.

Of those retained remarkably few, not more than twenty-five including joining ones, came from open vases. Three sherds, all burnt, are Attic imports: 112, a krater piece, may be compared to an Athenian vase of early MG I style;[49] 1113 is from a rather smaller krater, and 1114 perhaps from a skyphos, both of much the same date as the first. With these may be taken a fourth Attic sherd, 1115, also burnt, a handle or lug from a vase of unknown shape.[50] Of the sherds in the local fabric, 1116–18 are from the same vase, a circles skyphos, 1119 is probably from a circles skyphos with vertical flanking the circles, 1120–1 are from kalathoi (1121 is a complete profile), and 1122 is the only identifiable krater rim, heavily ridged. Apart from these illustrated pieces, one flat base may be from a cup, another from a large bowl; there were no other bases, nor rims or handles, of cups or skyphoi. Two other kalathos sherds were found, and three krater fragments. And that is all.

Before coming to the closed vases, mention may be made of three massive cut-out sherds (see 1123–4), whose purpose is not clear. They are unpainted on the inside, and the apices of the 'teeth' do not have any lower attachment, nor are they painted. The outer surface is monochrome, but the upper surface of the 'rim' is unpainted.[51]

Smaller closed vases are even scarcer than the open ones: two ring bases, one monochrome body sherd, and the fine fragment 1150 with decoration of multiple zigzag based on dogtooth.

The remainder, over seventy sherds, are from amphorae,[52] and at least half of these from very large ones indeed. The illustrated fragments 1125–49 (some made up of two or more joining sherds) give a fair idea of the remarkable nature of the material. A massive amphora needs a massive lip, and gets it – see 1125 and 1126 (note the start of a neck panel on 1126). The body has to be made in more than one stage, and the Lefkandians felt it desirable to add strengthening ridges on the body: see 1131, 1133, 1140, 1144. The main body decoration is circles and semicircles, filled or unfilled (1127–35, 1138), including an example of two tiers of semicircles (1128) and an otherwise unparalleled instance (1129) of a set of circles standing immediately above what must be another set. Other motives are found as well: the panelled cross-hatching of 1137–9 and 1144 might belong to the same vase; hatched rectangular and diamond panels also occur (1140–1, 1143, 1147, 1149); a hatched meander (with a second similar zone below?) may reflect Attic EG II or MG I (1142); and there are instances of chequers (1146), solid diamonds (1143), zigzag (1145), and a curious vertical panel with wavy line enclosing horizontal line filling (1148). Of those not illustrated nearly thirty were plain, banded, or monochrome, and the rest have circles or semicircles.[53]

It is by any standard an impressive body of material, and an interesting point that emerges is the variety of motives other than the conventional circles and semicircles that is used, especially on the outsize amphorae. This is indeed observable elsewhere, but can be seen to its best advantage in this fill.

It was noted at the begining that the pottery probably came from disturbed or destroyed pyres. This is confirmed by the fact that at least five amphorae of the type found in pyres were represented, while not even a quarter of any one could be made up. A pyre source would also be supported by the four burnt Attic sherds, though it is noticeable that not many other sherds showed signs of burning.

As to the chronology, the lower limit is determined, insofar as this is possible, by the latest Attic piece, which is probably early MG I. But my impression is that the rest of the material could cover both SPG I and SPG II.

## A STONE MOULD — ADDITIONAL EVIDENCE FOR METAL-WORKING

A stone mould (S SF 17) from the Gully Fill of the Skoubris Cemetery may be added to the Xeropolis foundry refuse as evidence for early metallurgical activity at Lefkandi. Unfortunately this fill (SPG I–III) does not provide adequate evidence for close dating, see p. 266 above.

Fragment of open mould of micaceous schist. Extant L. 14.0. Extant W. 9.3. Greatest Th. 5.7. Least Th. 3.0. One corner of the original mould preserved, where very carefully cut as a right angle. Double faced mould; no trace of matrices on what survives of the narrow faces, PLATES 237h–i and 284.

Side (a) Matrices for casting three roughly pointed billets of which: (I) = preserved L. 12.5. W. at bottom 1.0. Depth restored 2.0. (II) = preserved L. 12.0. W. at bottom 1.2. Depth restored 2.0. (III) = preserved L. 8.3. W. at bottom 0.8. Depth restored 2.0.

Side (b) Matrix for an ? axe-blade. Greatest W. 6.0. Greatest restored W. 7.5. Greatest Th. 1.3. This matrix widens rapidly.

Both sides show signs of heavy use. There are traces of a pouring funnel on the long narrow face, feeding into the axe-matrix. Restored D. of funnel 2.0.

# Section 13

# The Dark Age Pottery (SM–SPG III) from
# Settlement and Cemeteries

## V. R. d' A. DESBOROUGH

## INTRODUCTION

The pottery to be discussed in the major section that follows is divided into Submycenaean, Early, Middle, and Late Protogeometric and Sub-Protogeometric I, II, and III. The divisions, which are those of the current conventional terminology, are based on stylistic development whose general lines are reasonably clear overall, but wherein, as between one phase and another, the process can be so gradual (and for certain types of vase impossible to recognise) that definite attributions cannot always be made with any assurance. There is in any case an element of subjective arbitrariness in stylistic analysis, and it is essential that in the first place the relative chronology should be based on stratigraphical evidence.[1]

This evidence, from both settlement and cemeteries, has been set out in detail elsewhere (pp. 16f. and 105f.). For the cemeteries, of the 147 tombs and 80 pyres, 34 of those containing pottery were in stratified sequence, and the relevant information is tabulated on in Table IV.[2] There is no case of a tomb or a pyre with SM pottery being stratigraphically later than a tomb with any other kind of pottery, with one possible exception at the time of transition between SM and EPG; on the other hand there are two instances of EPG tombs, and one of an MPG tomb, being stratified above those of the SM phase. No similar evidence, unfortunately, was forthcoming for the sequence EPG to MPG, MPG to LPG, or LPG to SPG I; but there are examples of burials with SPG II pottery being later than those with EPG (one), MPG (one), LPG (three), and SPG I (four). There are also instances of sequence within individual phases, EPG[3] and SPG I. For SPG III, all we have at present is one instance of a tomb of this phase cutting into another, and that is of the SM period.

The most important evidence from the settlement is that of Area 2: earliest is the deposit in which the fragments of moulds were found, probably of very short duration, and characterised by LPG pottery; above this is the SPG Pit, most of the sherds from which can be assigned to SPG I–II; and above this, not so clearly separated as for the Moulds and SPG Pit Deposit, came the Levelling Material, which included a reasonable amount of pottery which can be classed as SPG III. This upper deposit constituted a levelling operation in preparation for the constructions of the Late Geometric period, whose floors seal the whole. Another area in which the stratification is of value is that of Area 3 South, the sherds from beneath the yard floor, which are (with one or two possible exceptions) of LPG type.[4]

Although nearly all the suggested stylistic phases receive at least some support from the stratigraphy, the value of this is lessened in that several of the tombs involved had only a few vases, and most of the settlement deposits contained pottery earlier than the time of their depositing. Other evidence may then be called in to assist, and this may be set out under four headings.

1. Two large collections of fragmentary vases and sherds which, on the criteria adopted, seem to be stylistically homogeneous. One is the surface material (including many complete or nearly complete vases) gathered from the SL area, just north of the Xeropolis mound, of settlement type: this is of SPG II–III date (see pp. 49–52). The other is the contents of the lower fill in the North Channel of Palia Perivolia, mostly LPG, not later, but there is at least one substantially earlier vase (pp. 271–3).

2. The several large tomb groups, which provide useful nuclei of representative local shapes for certain phases;[5] one each for EPG, SPG I–II, and early SPG III, and six equally divided between LPG and SPG I.[6]

3. The presence of imported pottery from areas (particularly Attica) where the sequence is already well established, to which may be added the local vases which imitated or adopted features from outside Lefkandi, and which are likely to be more or less contemporary with their models. These are to be found mainly in the LPG and SPG III periods, and their appearance in the latter in the Levelling Material is of great importance.

4. The distribution of the two main types of tomb, the cist and the shaft grave. The figures are as follows. 59 cist tombs: 2 from Khaliotis' field (probably the earliest), 56 from Skoubris, 1 from Palia Perivolia, none from Toumba. 72 shaft graves: 3 from Skoubris, 33 from Palia Perivolia, 3 from the East Cemetery, 33 from Toumba. The evidence as a whole indicates a change from one to the other during the course of MPG: no burial

(i.e. cenotaph) in a cist tomb has been identified in LPG or later; only one shaft grave is earlier than MPG.[7] The conclusions drawn depend on stylistic considerations as supported by the stratigraphy, and if valid are of value in filling the stratigraphical gap in MPG.

Several factors, then, combine to support the stylistic divisions proposed.

## Submycenaean, Early and Middle Protogeometric

These phases can be taken together for two reasons. First, the local style exhibits a fairly logical and consistent development throughout, and a number of shapes are common to the whole period: cup, deep bowl, trefoil oinochoe, jug, hydria, amphoriskos with vertical handles, and almost certainly the lekythos.[8] Second, the material from these phases comes exclusively from tombs, pyres, or deposits connected with them: no trace of occupation between LH IIIC and LPG having been identified, our knowledge of the pottery is one-sided.[9]

### A. *Submycenaean*

In addition to the shapes mentioned above, of which the most common are the cup, the deep bowl, and the lekythos, there are four which appear to die out at the beginning of PG, the stirrup jar, the alabastron, the feeding bottle with basket handle, and the askoid vase; and three which link SM with EPG but go no further, the amphoriskos with belly handles, the multiple vase, and the bird vase.[10]

The open vases are often top heavy, and their feet are either ring-base or low conical, sometimes poorly moulded. The closed vases normally have globular, biconical, or slightly sagging bodies, with the same rather heavy look; note the poor moulding of the lip and mouth element on the lekythos. The general system of decoration tends towards the dark ground, but there are instances of light ground vases. Subsidiary decoration is mostly restricted to wavy lines, zigzags, vertical wiggly lines, triangles, and hand-drawn semicircles with occasional half-moon filling, and fringed in the case of the large amphorae. One unusual feature is that there is as a rule no reserved band on the interior of the cup and bowl rims. The general effect is one of lack of sharpness both in the fashioning of the vase and in its decoration. It represents the dying stage of the Mycenaean tradition, with little or nothing in the way of innovation.

### B. *Early Protogeometric*

The following guide-lines may be of use in distinguishing EPG from SM. There is an improvement in the modelling of the current vase types. On the open vases the lip blends more easily with the body; the body becomes gradually deeper; the low conical foot has now ousted the ring base, and it usually looks better proportioned in relation to the vase as a whole than its SM predecessor. On closed vases greater care is taken in the modelling of the lip and handle, and the body tends to have an ovoid profile, terminated by a low conical foot. The general effect is to produce a vase whose constituent elements blended more harmoniously than earlier.

The decoration also underwent certain changes. The dark ground system, now more consistently used, is sometimes relieved by one or two well-placed reserved bands to lighten the appearance of the vase; and it is not uncommon to find the lower part of the body and the foot left free of paint, with the same result. As opposed to the practice in SM, the inner rims of cups and bowls usually have a reserved band. Perhaps most important, a new policy was adopted in the use of subsidiary motives. Most of the rather carelessly drawn designs found in the SM phase were discarded, and all that was retained, with rare exceptions, was a wavy line, open or very close, encased between two horizontal bands. It was a style in which proportion and severe simplicity played the major roles.[11]

It may sound from the above that the change in style was a simple and logical affair. This is not, however, the case, to judge by the number of tomb groups in which vases of SM style are found with those which should be classed as EPG, and by the number of instances where a single vase – if we use the criteria suggested, which are of course subjective – may combine features of both phases. In other words, what we have is a gradual and tentative evolution.

So far as concerns the types of vase, we have seen that four dropped out at the end of SM, and that three more continued into EPG but no further. Only one vase type, a shallow bowl with high conical foot, was introduced into the regular repertoire, but the EPG phase is remarkable for the appearance of a number of unique or unusual types of vase – a tall pyxis with straight sides, a four handled bowl with high conical foot, a bottle, a lentoid flask, and a tripod dish – all of which may be classified as experimental.

## C. Middle Protogeometric

As this phase exhibits in many of its vases the stylistic features which typify the preceding one, one could reasonably argue that it should be viewed as the logical culmination of EPG, and not as something separate.

It is nevertheless preferable to make a distinction between the two. None of the MPG tomb groups contains any vase of SM style – not a cogent reason for distinction, of course. There are no more experimental vases; and two earlier types, the belly-handled amphoriskos and the multiple vase, are no longer found.[12]

There are positive factors as well. The conical foot of open vases is appreciably higher,[13] and the inner rims of such vases seldom have a reserved band. In the later stage of MPG the light ground technique is applied to a number of trefoil oinochoai; rectilinear motives and languettes appear on the shoulder – and also the earliest datable example of the local use of compass-drawn semicircles. And it is during this stage that we encounter the first examples of Black Slip and Red Slip wares.

At least the latest tomb groups can be distinguished from those assigned to EPG; but it seems better to place the dividing line a little earlier, at the time when the local PG reached its stylistic culmination. It must be admitted, however, that the number of tomb groups assigned to MPG is relatively small, and further evidence could lead to modification.

## D. External influences and links

That the Submycenaean pottery at Lefkandi had a Mycenaean pedigree is self-evident. Not only, however, can no specific regional type of LH IIIC pottery outside Euboea be suggested as its inspiration, but also there is no clear link with the latest material from the nearby Mycenaean settlement on Xeropolis,[14] even allowing for the differences between tomb offerings and settlement pottery. This would be understandable if those who made and used the SM pottery were new settlers (a wider problem, discussed elsewhere, pp. 355 ff.), and it would also mean that we were dealing with a phase whose earlier (i.e. pre-Lefkandian) stages are hidden from us – a supposition that the relatively static nature of Lefkandian SM, and (in my opinion) the scarcity of stirrup jars, would tend to support. However that may be, there is no better evidence for SM than there is for LH IIIC to show that any particular area provided the source for the style as we have it.[15] There is, nevertheless, a strong family resemblance between Lefkandian SM and that from other areas, both in types of vase and in their decoration, and it is reasonable to suppose that the Lefkandians were in touch with their SM neighbours, and that to a certain extent the respective series ran in parallel.

This suggested contemporaneity has an obvious bearing on the question of the time, in relation to other districts or sites, when the Protogeometric style evolved at Lefkandi; and with this may be taken the question whether the local potters were indebted to any other style in the development of PG.

These questions, which are interrelated, are very difficult to answer. Negatively, certain shapes fell into disuse, and subsidiary decorative motives were so far as possible eliminated; positively, the relatively heavy look of SM vases was gradually replaced by sharper and more pleasing profiles, and by a better sense of proportion (possibly due to the use of a faster wheel?); one new shape, with high conical foot, was introduced, and a number of experimental vases, all at the beginning of EPG. For the improvements in the style as such, however, there is no reason why the Lefkandian potter could not have been solely responsible. But as the same sort of thing was happening elsewhere in the construction of the vase (notably Athens, probably the Argolid as well), may there not have been some link, whether deliberate or not?

A clue may be provided by the experimental or unusual vases. One of these, the straight-sided pyxis, was a shape characteristic of Crete in LM IIIC and sub-Minoan (see p. 330). There is, though, no other evidence of contacts with this island, and it is possible that the source should be sought in Cyprus, when a number of these pyxides (themselves of Cretan influence) have been identified. Now it is clear, from the presence of the Syro-Palestinian dipper juglet S 46,3, in an EPG group, that there was contact with the East Mediterranean. And specific links with Cyprus,[16] certain or less certain, may be recognised in the bird vase S 16,1, the only one in mainland Greece at the time of this particular Cypriot type, very likely the lentoid flask, and possibly the shallow tripod dish, if its inspiration is to be found in the bronze cast tripod.[17] It is also possible that the higher conical foot (see S 16,5) derived from a knowledge of Cypriot PG pottery.[18]

As to Athens, whose potters brought the PG style to its state of greatest perfection, and where some contact with Lefkandi might reasonably be expected due to their geographical proximity, provable connexions are minimal, only two or three local sherds from a small and undatable deposit in the Skoubris cemetery (p. 266), which recall strongly the Attic 'Wild' style that is characteristic of the early PG development in Athens.[19]

The fact remains, however, that the Lefkandians adopted none of the main vase types from either Cyprus or Attica, and made no use of the decorative elements current in those areas, either the cross-hatched designs of the former or the compass-drawn circles and semicircles of the latter. We may suspect that the improvements in vase construction, the cleaner outlines, the more ovoid body, the higher conical foot (to be found in Athens as well as in Cyprus), were due to familiarity with one or both districts, but one cannot prove any determining influence in the creation of the style.

It would then seem to follow that we cannot say when Lefkandian PG emerged in relation to other styles. There are, however, two considerations which may help towards establishing this. The first is the presence of Cypriot ceramic features (including the bird vase, assuming a Cypriot source) in Athens at the time of transition from SM to EPG.[20] It was a very short-lived phenomenon, so far as one can tell, and it is tempting to equate it in time with the Cypriot features at Lefkandi mentioned above, equally short-lived, and attributed to the beginning of EPG — still a time of transition, indeed, for there are several vases of SM type in the relevant tomb groups. For the second, we may make use of a tomb group from Naxos.[21] This contained three vases: a lekythos, a feeder with basket handle, and a cup. What it provides us with is cross-connexions with both Lefkandi and Athens. The links with Lefkandi are evident in the shape (though not the basket handle, only so far found in SM) of the feeder, and particularly its decoration, which is typical of EPG there; and just as important, in the shape of the cup, again characteristic of Lefkandian EPG. For the link with Athens, it is the decoration of the cup, the compass-drawn circles: this is a motive surely derivable from Athens, where the technique used was perhaps the most startling single innovation of the nascent Attic PG style. So we can say that these two vases are sufficiently close to Lefkandian EPG to be contemporary with it, and that the cup must be placed after the start of Attic PG. The third vase, the lekythos, is also of interest, for it is in the SM style, globular and with hand-drawn semicircles; this survival of the SM type of lekythos in PG tomb groups is found not only at Lefkandi but at Athens as well (pp. 314), which may or may not be coincidental.

Taking the evidence as a whole (and much more could be wished for) it would seem a reasonable provisional conclusion that PG at Lefkandi started at about the same time as in Athens, and is roughly contemporaneous with the beginning of Cypro-Geometric I.

The Lefkandian PG style appears then as an independent creation: it owes little to other styles, so far as one can yet tell, but we have sufficient evidence from the pottery found in EPG tombs to be sure that there was at least contact with Cyprus and the East Mediterranean, with Naxos, without much doubt with Athens, possibly with Crete. To these may be added Chalcis,[22] not unnaturally, perhaps Theotokou[23] in Thessaly, and the district which produced the bird vase S 16,10.

The transition from EPG to MPG is so gradual that no outside explanation is needed. During the later course of MPG the evidence seems to point to a growing interest in the Attic style,[24] and one can reasonably assume that there was contact. The presence at Argos[25] of a pedestal bowl of the type found at Lefkandi may suggest some link. There is no trace of contact with Crete, and connexions with Cyprus and the East Mediterranean seem to be at a low ebb.[26]

This is disappointing, but it is not the whole picture. Vases of closely similar shape and decoration to those in Lefkandian MPG tomb groups have been found in Chalcis, Thebes, Delphi, Iolkos, Skyros, and Naxos.[27] Further information will be found in the sections on individual shapes; when the material is viewed as a whole it is very impressive, in spite of the small quantity: virtually all the types of vase found at Lefkandi (including the Black Slip) are represented, and types of vase different from those of Lefkandi are very few.[28] The evidence is sufficient, in my opinion, to allow the conclusion that at least by MPG[29] a cultural (or at any rate a ceramic) *koine* had become established, stretching along the sea lanes from coastal Thessaly in the north, through Euboea and Skyros, to Naxos in the south.[30] Whether the mainland districts of Phocis and Boeotia should also be regarded as belonging to this *koine* is not altogether clear. The importance of this *koine*, especially as it will be found to continue to operate for some considerable time, needs no stressing.

### Late Protogeometric

The appearance of Late Protogeometric pottery provides one of only two clear-cut stylistic breaks in post-Mycenaean Lefkandi;[31] it happened at about the same time as Xeropolis was reoccupied, an event which may not be unconnected with the change in style (see pp. 358–62),[32] and which is of value for us, as we can now add the testimony of the settlement to that of the burials.

Up to and including MPG progress was sedate and gradual, the local potter eventually achieving a simple and severe style, with a strictly limited range of vase types, and decoration reduced to a minimum; he depended chiefly on his own resources, and borrowed little from outside styles, except perhaps during the later stage of MPG, when there are a few intimations that Attic PG was beginning to exercise some attraction. In principle, however, the style had been inward-looking.

The LPG style is radically different from its predecessor, and the changes are sudden and profound. The reluctance to apply subsidiary decoration disappears completely, and the range of vase shapes is considerably widened, though still preserving some continuity with what had gone before. The reason for this is that the potters now looked outwards, beyond their own community (whose attitude they reflected) and beyond the regional *koine* discussed above; and they were ready to accept, adopt, and adapt ideas from other styles. Chief among these was the Attic LPG style, to such an extent that I have defined the limits of the phase at Lefkandi by reference to the appearance and disappearance of its influence (which coincides with the transition from LPG to Early Geometric).[33]

Attic LPG types of vase, normally with their appropriate decorative apparatus, are represented as follows: the cup with carinated lip and high conical foot, the circles skyphos (two sets, not three as in Athens) and the panelled skyphos, the trefoil oinochoe, the lekythos, the globular pyxis (a new shape at Lefkandi), and three varieties of amphora — neck-handled, belly-handled, and with handles from shoulder to lip. The openwork kalathos should possibly be added to these (but see below). The decorative motives, not always applied in the Attic manner but close enough, include the compass-drawn semicircles and circles, the cross-hatched triangles and other rectilinear designs, and the zigzag on the outer lip of cups.[34]

Other vase types as well can be shown to have been introduced to Lefkandi from outside: Thessaly is responsible for one, Cyprus certainly or possibly for three. From Thessaly came the jug with cutaway neck, perhaps also including its shoulder decoration.[35] Cyprus certainly provided the model for the shallow long-spouted bowl P 3,16,[36] and for the three lentoid flasks from P 3 and P 31, though the trefoil lips of two of them are at this time paralleled only in Attica.[37] These are confined to the closing stages of LPG, and not known later at Lefkandi. It is possible that Cyprus was also the source of the openwork kalathos, a type still in use in the cemeteries in early SPG III (p. 305).[38]

Influence, especially from Attica, is also to be traced in the vases of local style, whether of the type already known in the MPG phase, or introduced in LPG. As to the survivals from MPG, the Black Slip and Red Slip wares are in a class of their own so far as decoration is concerned, and may be disregarded; there remain[39] the vertical-handled amphoriskos, the relatively globular trefoil oinochoe, and the small traditional jug; and all three, especially the amphoriskos, are given decorative motives derived from Attica.

Of the newly introduced local types the most distinctive is the low-footed skyphos with high overhanging and carinated lip, and pendent semicircles — only the concept of the compass-drawn semicircles is Attic. The flat-based cup, with similar lip to that of the PSC skyphos, and with zigzag on the outer surface of the lip, is a development of the type with conical foot — a parallel development is found in Athens in respect of the flat base, and there may be a link.[40] Other types of skyphoi and cups are known from the settlement, perhaps reflecting a brief experimental phase. The kalathos with tiers of impressed triangles is a new shape, purely Lefkandian or regional.[41] There are also very tall jugs (rare), with Attic type of decoration, a new type of jug with straight walls, uncompromisingly monochrome, perhaps a harbinger of SPG I (see p. 324), and (from the settlement) the krater, admittedly not a new shape, but absent from tombs.[42] Of the experimental vases mention may be made of the large bowl P 3,15, with elaborate decoration, the motives including two of probable Thessalian inspiration, the butterfly and the multiple squares.

There are too many influences at work for Lefkandian LPG to be described as uniform or simple. It is, on the whole, experimental and eclectic, and the stylistic features borrowed from outside combined at times a little uneasily with the potter's ingrained habits; the result was certainly lively, with a welcome variety in shape and decoration, the product of a fresh outlook that marked a turning-point in the history of the community.

Discussion of the reasons for this change of, or development in, outlook belong to the concluding chapter (p. 358 f.). Two attendant aspects may, however, be mentioned here, insofar as they are based on the pottery: an increase in prosperity is suggested by the fact the average number of vases in each tomb is greater in this phase than previously — one group has as many as thirty, several have more than ten; and the presence of numerous imported vases may imply that such prosperity was bound up with contacts outside the region.[43]

Comparison of the Lefkandian LPG vases with those found on other sites in the region shows that the uniformity visible in MPG persisted during this phase; not only were the Attic elements similarly absorbed (no sign yet of any Cypriot), but the general development runs roughly parallel to that at Lefkandi.[44] In spite of a few differences in distribution and in the types of vase used, the region remained a cultural whole, and it is possibly in the sense of a co-ordinated activity that one should infer an outward movement — as opposed to the passive reception of ceramic imports and influences from outside the region — as shown by certain vases carried to, or imitated in Boeotia,[45] Macedonia[46] and Cyprus.[47]

Finally, the time of duration of the LPG phase at Lefkandi: this cannot be estimated with any precision, not even in Attic terms, as we do not know at what stage of Attic LPG the local potters decided wholeheartedly to imitate the style (nor indeed do we know how long the latter lasted). The number of LPG tombs at Lefkandi is about the same as those of EPG and MPG combined, but we cannot tell whether or not the population increased. It is as well to realise that this problem exists when we try to speculate, as is almost inevitable, about absolute chronology in a period where there are no fixed points whatever.

### Sub-Protogeometric I and II

These two stages constitute, in essence, a period during which the Lefkandian potter modified the innovations introduced in LPG, and for the most part resisted any external influence during the major part of its course. SPG I and II are closely connected: rather as with SM, EPG and MPG, the changes are usually quite clear when one compares the earliest group with the latest, but the process is a very gradual one, and by no means uniform; it may well be that my attributions of certain groups to a particular phase will be found to be incorrect.

### A. *SPG I*

The only evidence for new shapes is two trays or *kanouns* with three loop handles rising from the rim,[48] and a shallow bowl with rolled handles at the rim.[49]

All the more common types of vase continued in use, including the Black Slip and Red Slip wares; such changes in structure as occurred were in the nature of modifications, as a rule not very substantial. The one deliberate change was the tendency, on the smaller closed vases, to dispense with the low conical or ring foot and to substitute a flat base. And for the open vases, the conical foot of cups and skyphoi may either have disappeared completely or been gradually phased out.[50] Otherwise, it is a matter of relaxation in uniformity of structure. Not so much care was taken: sometimes, for jugs, lekythoi and oinochoai, the body will be ovoid, sometimes more squat and biconical; pyxides may retain the globular profile, but there are variations, and some are more flattened, and the everted rim less prominent; the rims of cups and PSC skyphoi, still sharply out-turned and carinated, may vary appreciably in height. In other words, it is impossible to perceive any orderly stylistic progress. The large amphorae may have continued with no modification at all; so perhaps may the kraters, but for these we have insufficient evidence to be at all sure.

The most striking factor in the SPG I decorative system, when compared with that current in LPG, is the simplification adopted on certain of the smaller types of vase. What happened was that the subsidiary decoration introduced in LPG fought a progressively losing battle against the old habit of covering most of the surface with paint, barring the occasional reserved band (which might enclose a zigzag). This new, or revived, monochrome trend is particularly noticeable on the trefoil oinochoai, lekythoi, and jugs, which previously had decoration on the shoulder, but in this phase have it in the minority of instances only, to judge from the cemetery evidence.[51] Even the zigzag on the outer lip of the cup gradually gave way to a monochrome treatment or to reserved bands.[52] It may be, too, that one should regard the decline in popularity of the impressed-triangle technique on kalathoi, as against the unindented monochrome or reserved-band type, as a further instance of simplification.

On other shapes the subsidiary decoration of LPG type is retained: on the amphorae and kraters,[53] on the vertical-handled amphoriskoi,[54] and on the PSC and circles skyphoi, where the motives had become too firmly established for any change to be desirable. In these the legacy of LPG is perpetuated, but one important shape, the pyxis, provides an exception. During LPG the belly decoration of the local atticising pyxis seems to have been very simple, and one might expect in SPG I a fundamentally monochrome system, with one or more reserved bands on the belly. Examples of such are found, but more often the belly zones are wider than in LPG, and these are variously ornamented, with such motives as the butterfly design and opposed diagonals, and even more elaborate ones.

To summarise on SPG I, almost all the Attic and local (or regional) vase types were retained with only minor modifications, chief among which was the frequent use of the flat base for small closed vases; in terms of decoration, the return on several shapes to a system which is almost unrelievedly monochrome style marks it out from LPG — but there are notable exceptions to this. The picture is as yet incomplete, but it is clear that for the potter the time of experiment had passed, and that an era of conservatism, almost of stagnation, had set in.

External relations during this phase will be summarised later, after the analysis of the SPG II phase, combining both phases.

## B. *SPG II*

During this phase the elements which distinguish it from its predecessor are far more in the shape than in the decoration: new or modified vase types are introduced, and several types characteristic of SPG I are no longer found.[55]

First, though, many types went through from SPG I to SPG II: the flat-based cup with monochrome or reserved-band lip, the PSC skyphos, the unindented kalathos, the pyxis, the small jug with fairly globular body, the straight-walled jug, the massive amphorae, the krater, and most probably the circles skyphos, to judge from the settlement material (pp. 32, 43).

As against these, the following have not yet been recorded in SPG II: the lekythos, the traditional amphoriskos with vertical handles, the jug with cutaway neck, and the trefoil oinochoe with ovoid body of Attic LPG type. To these may be added, on the basis of decoration, the cup with zigzag on the outer lip, and perhaps the kalathos with impressed triangles.[56] Furthermore, no Black Slip or Red Slip vase has been confirmed in any context that can be shown to be later than SPG I, and these wares probably disappeared during its course.

There is one important new shape, probably introduced at the beginning of, or at least during, SPG II: this is the shallow bowl with flat base and horizontal handles, with rim either incurved or everted.[57] And there is one important development which covers two vase types, a medium-sized neck-handled amphora and a trefoil oinochoe: both shapes have high and fairly slender necks, a very slender ovoid body, and both are or may be distinguished as regards decoration by an hourglass panel on the neck and a belly design of zigzag between bands or, more often, opposed diagonals with unfilled interstices, the rest of the body surface being usually monochrome.[58] It may be noted that hand-made cooking pots of jug type are first used as tomb offerings in SPG II.[59]

There is virtually no significant change, as between SPG I and SPG II, in the system of decoration or, for the most part, in the specific motives used. For small and medium closed vases, the tendency in SPG I to eliminate the shoulder decoration on some types becomes more pronounced in SPG II, to judge from the tomb groups (but see above, n. 51); it is the belly zone, if any, which is chosen for subsidiary motives, as can be seen in the new development of the dark ground oinochoai and medium neck-handled amphorai; the pyxides and pouring vases simply reflect the trends of the preceding phase. For the smaller open vases there are no innovations in the decoration of cups, skyphoi or kalathoi; as for the new shallow bowl with strap handles, the simplicity of the design, usually a narrow reserved area, sometimes a rough zigzag, seems to indicate some lack of imagination. The larger vases whether open or closed, i.e. the amphorae and the kraters, are indeed treated rather differently: amphorae are light ground, as a rule, and subsidiary decoration is freely used on them and on the kraters, but this is also a continuation of SPG I practice, though a few new motives may have been introduced (see above, n. 53).

## C. *External influences and connexions*

In this section I combine the evidence for SPG I and SPG II, deal first with links outside the regional *koine*, and then review the situation inside it.

In view of the developments in LPG, it is remarkable that the Lefkandian potter borrowed almost nothing from outside the region. This is above all to be observed in relation to the Attic EG style. The SPG I style cannot be shown to owe anything to Attic EG I, nor have any Attic imports been identified, apart from one or two possible vases from P 22 (pp. 349–50). Whatever in the local style is obviously of Attic inspiration — and there is much — represents a continuation of features adopted in LPG; even the new fashion of applying reserved bands to the outer lip of cups, a known Attic practice,[60] cannot be proved to have originated in Attica. During SPG, however, Attic imports reappear, now of EG II date,[61] forerunners of a more substantial flow in the next period. Awareness of, and borrowing from, Attica may be recognised in the occasional use of the battlement, meander and swastika motives, difficult to date in their Lefkandian contexts and perhaps even SPG I, but the examples of true atticising SPG II are very rare indeed.[62] It is possible that the Lefkandians borrowed both the shape and system of decoration of the dark ground slender amphorae and oinochoai from the Athenians,[63] but even here the motive almost without exception used for the neck panel, the hourglass, is not Attic. Taking SPG I and II as a whole, it seems fair to conclude that the Attic style had no more than a minimal effect on the Lefkandian.

Nothing can be traced to Cyprus, nor indeed to anywhere else, with the possible exception, at the very beginning of SPG I, of the dot fringes of the large trefoil oinochoe T 1,1, which could have been borrowed from East Greece,[64] but this may be a hangover from the euphoria of LPG.

It should be stressed that this lack of interest in external pottery styles did not mean that Lefkandi (and its region) was isolated — other finds show very clearly that it was not, expecially as far as the East Mediterranean was concerned. All one can say is that the potters themselves were evidently perfectly satisfied with what they were producing on their own, and that there seems to have been no desire, until near the end of EG II, to import pottery from elsewhere.[65]

The situation in the regional *koine* merits discussion from the point of view of the pottery, in particular the question whether the Lefkandians maintained links with the other communities.[66] It is difficult to assess, because the quantity of material is very uneven as between district and district; also, apart from Lefkandi itself, we are dealing almost exclusively with the contents of tombs.[67] Furthermore, the distribution of vase types, as favoured for tombs, may differ from one community to another, and it may therefore be unsafe to draw conclusions from the absence of one or more types.[68]

I shall discuss the Lefkandian pottery in relation to each main district of the region. And it may first be made clear that there are two features common to all: the presence of the PSC skyphos, and the apparent resistance to influence from Attica until near the end of SPG II.

*Euboea.* Only two other productive sites, Chalcis and Theologos, and few vases, in the same style as those of Lefkandi.[69]

*South Thessaly.* Halos tomb 6. Similar types of vase, but variations in shape and decoration.[70]

*North Thessaly.* A reasonable amount of material, chiefly from Kapakli (Iolkos), Marmariani, and Theotokou; a few minor sites as well. Several vase types are common to this district and Lefkandi: the PSC and circles skyphos, the flat-based cup, the small jug and trefoil oinochoe, the globular pyxis, the *kanoun*, the krater, the shallow bowl with strap handles, the large neck-handled amphora with circles on the shoulder and the medium type with hourglass on the neck. A few Lefkandian types are missing (as they are from LPG contexts): the vertical-handled amphoriskos, the lekythos, the kalathos, and the belly-handled amphora — the first three are significant absentees. And two types of vases well known on north Thessalian sites, the high-handled kantharos and the cup with handle wholly below the rim, have not been found at Lefkandi. Other differences are that the jug with cutaway neck probably survived longer in North Thessaly, that the rectilinear decoration there was far more common than at Lefkandi, and that there are only rare examples of a flat base ousting the low foot on small closed vases — in contrast to Lefkandi. So there are some notable differences, but I believe they are outweighed by the similarities, especially in the PSC skyphoi, the neck-handled amphorae, and probably the krater.[71]

*Skyros.* Despite the lack of full publication of the relevant material from Skyros one can confidently say that the stylistic links with Lefkandi were very close indeed, probably closer than with any other district except Euboea itself.[72]

*North Cyclades.* On Andros there is nothing till after SPG II, unless the five (or six) vases from Zagora are SPG I rather than LPG — to whichever phase they belong, they show development, owing much to the Attic style, similar to that of Lefkandi.[73]

Kambos on Tenos has produced a group similar to the one on Andros (see above), but there is later evidence as well, from Kardiani and Ktikados, and other vases of unknown context and provenance, including the Vatican group.[74] The types represented, and their decoration, are mostly such as would fit comfortably into the Lefkandian series — PSC and circles skyphoi, cups (not quite the same shape), trefoil oinochoai, and especially a neck-handled amphora with panelled hourglass on the neck.[75] Others are somewhat different: the vertical-handled amphoriskoi and a cup with handle wholly below the rim.[76] The only atticising shape is the monochrome low-footed skyphos of EG II date, and this is also found at Lefkandi.[77] So far as our evidence allows, the resemblances are reasonably close between Tenos and Lefkandi.

The conclusion from this survey is that ceramic links were maintained, and it is not only a matter of the LPG tradition, but of specifically SPG developments as well; there is evidence for independent development, and doubtless further material will add to it, but on the whole it still seems correct to speak of a regional *koine*, in the ceramic sense, in SPG I and II. Consequently, as in LPG, when pottery of regional type is found in other districts, it cannot be traced back to any particular part of the region: such districts include Boeotia,[78] Phocis,[79] Macedonia,[80] and the west coast of Asia Minor,[81] and it is likely that there were others.

**Sub-Protogeometric III**
I equate the beginning of SPG III with the emergence of Attic Middle Geometric. Four tombs only, and no pyres, can with certainty be assigned to this phase, and the evidence of their associated vases is startling. In three of them (T 19, T 31, and T 33) Attic MG I imports outnumber the local vases — and two even of these are imitations of Attic originals. The fourth tomb, S 59 + 59 A, has far more local ware, and is then exceptional: it also, however, has the earliest vases stylistically speaking, and must be close to the latest SPG II (e.g. P 21). If we had no more than these tombs, it would be possible to argue that SPG III was a phase dominated by Attic MG, and that it should be called MG.[82]

Once we turn to the settlement, however, it soon becomes clear that such a picture is entirely misleading. The main evidence is based on a single important deposit, the Levelling Material, which is sealed[83] above by an LG floor and constructions, and which contains numerous Attic or atticising MG sherds which are missing from the SPG Pit Deposit below it (see pp. 36—42). The situation is as follows. There are five certain Attic MG sherds, two of which are MG II, and there may be a few more; there are also at least thirty local atticising MG fragments, many of which are MG II.[84] The first conclusion, then, is that the period covered is longer than that so far found in the cemeteries, which contained MG I material only; and a second conclusion is that the tendency to imitate Attic MG seems to be more prominent in MG II than earlier. This is an interesting and significant body of material, but when set against the total number of sherds found in the Levelling (probably at least 1500), the proportion is extremely small. Now it is evident that the nature of the deposit is such that a fair number of sherds of earlier periods appear within it (there are in any case instances of joins with sherds from the SPG Pit), but even allowing for this it is a reasonable conclusion that a considerable number are contemporaneous with the Attic and atticising. These sherds are in the local SPG style, and it is a fair inference that this, based on a long and virtually unchanging tradition, continued to be the characteristic ware during MG, and justifies our calling the phase SPG III.

Whether SPG III, as a style, differed substantially from what was current in SPG II is the then extremely doubtful: for the most part, the same types, decorated in the same manner, are found in the Levelling as in the SPG Pit — this applies to amphorae (including the dark-ground type with panelled neck and belly decoration), oinochoai/jugs, shallow bowls with strap handles, kraters, cups, and circles skyphoi.[85] One new shape may, however, possibly be attributed to this phase — the plate with PSC below the rim — but there are too few examples for certainty.[86] And there is one development in the PSC skyphos that one can with reasonable confidence attribute to SPG III, the far greater tendency towards a low instead of a medium or high lip.[87]

The information provided by other areas of the Xeropolis mound is disappointing when compared with the Levelling Material, though at least it confirms the situation as visible in the Levelling, that the amount of Attic and atticising MG I and II was relatively small.[88] The surface material of settlement type from sector SL, immediately north of the mound, is however of some relevance and help (pp. 49—52). Among the sherds recovered were fine fragments of an Attic MG I krater: if, as has been argued, the material as a whole covers a short space of time, then much of the local ware will fall within SPG III, and we would have confirmation of the continued use of the local vase types most commonly found in this area, the shallow bowls with strap handles, the cups (none, it may be noted, with zigzag on the outer lip), and the amphorae. But the material need not take us far into SPG III.

One question remains unanswered: what happened between the latest SPG III (and the atticising MG II which is a feature of it) and the Late Geometric pottery as exemplified by the pottery found in the settlement (see p. 77)? There is as yet no trace of transition or development from the one to the other.

There is, finally, little of significance to say about external links, except that the region seems to have preserved some ceramic interconnexions, and except for the obvious links with Attica which, though going back to the latter part of SPG II, become so much more marked in this phase. As to the connexions with the East Mediterranean, one must assume that the Lefkandians played their part with others of the region, not only in trade, but also in the setting up of small trading posts in Syria.


THE ONE-HANDLED CUP. FIG. 7

The cup is one of the most common shapes found at Lefkandi, both in the cemeteries and in the settlement, and since successive variations are identifiable its value for relative chronology is great. As the settlement material belongs to the later stages, and is usually fragmentary, I commence with an analysis of the vases deposited in tombs and pyres.

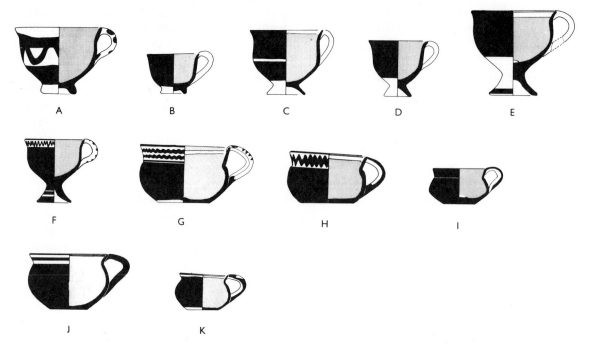

FIG. 7. (A) SM S 49,1 (B) SM S 60,2 (C) EPG S 46,1 (D) MPG S 18,5 (E) MPG P 14,2 (F) LPG T 17,3 (G) LPG T 26,2 (H) SPG I T 15,6 (I) SPG I T 15,7 (J) SPG II T 2,1 (K) SPG III T 31,8. Scale 1:4

## I. The Submycenaean type (FIG. 7, A—B)

The execution of the vase is somewhat careless; the body is fairly shallow, curving up to a slightly flaring lip; there is either a ring base or a very low conical foot, usually disproportionately small for the body; the handles are rounded. The decoration may be monochrome, or only the lip and the junction of body and foot are painted, or there is a reserved area on the body, in which a wavy line or lines have been encased.[89] As a rule there is no reserved band inside the lip.

There are nine, eight from tombs, one from a cemetery deposit and almost certainly from a disturbed tomb.

## II. EPG—MPG, persisting into the beginning of LPG. (FIG. 7, C—E)

In comparison with class I these cups are usually better made, the body is appreciably deeper, the foot is normally low conical[90] (becoming higher in the later stage) and better proportioned in relation to the body. The system of decoration is now predominantly monochrome, with no individual decorative motives at all: either the whole vase was painted except for the lowest part of the body and the foot,[91] or the body was painted except for one reserved band below the belly (a new feature), and the foot wholly or for its lower part unpainted. Inside, a reserved band below the lip is more customary during EPG, but sometimes absent in MPG.

There are 26 cups of this class, 22 from tombs, 1 from a pyre, and 3 from the surface, no doubt from disturbed tombs. Thirteen may be assigned to EPG, 3 may be EPG or MPG, 9 are MPG, and 1 is LPG.[92]

## III. LPG[93] (FIG. 7, F)

There is one important innovation: the lip is now high, markedly offset, and has a rough zigzag decoration along its outer surface. The lower body and foot are much the same as in the latest states of class II. The decoration is monochrome below the lip, except for T 17,2 (FIG. 7, F), which has two reserved bands on the foot.

We have at least five cups of this class,[94] and an overlap with class II in T 17. The new type of lip, with its zigzag, is surely adopted from the Attic PG style.

## IV. LPG and SPG I (FIG. 7, G–H)

The high conical foot of class III is replaced by a flat base. Otherwise the shape and system of decoration are the same, though the zigzag(s) of the outer lip can have one or two supporting bands.

Eight cups can be assigned to this class, two in LPG contexts, the rest certainly or possibly SPG I, but nothing later.

## V. SPG I, SPG II, SPG III (FIG. 7, I–K)

In this class the characteristic zigzag of classes III and IV disappears, giving way to a lip with one or more bands, or which is completely monochrome. The lip itself remains offset, but tends to be lower. The body is fairly shallow, and generally monochrome, though the lowest area is sometimes left free of paint. There seems to be no chronological significance in the occasional variations of decoration or shape.

Of the seventeen cups of this class from the cemeteries three occur in SPG I contexts, eight in SPG II, one is either SPG II or SPG III, and four cannot be placed precisely.

### Unclassifiable

P 6,1 (PLATE 129). An unusually large cup, diameter of mouth 12 cm. The body swells up to a prominent belly, then comes in again to a very low everted lip; the base is flat; the vase is monochrome. Not later than MPG, as the tomb lay below P 9, itself MPG.

S 25 B,1 (PLATE 100). Globular body, flat-based, prominent handle, monochrome. SPG II.

### The Settlement

During the period of later occupation, from LPG through SPG to Late Geometric the cup was one of the most common shapes: hundreds of vases are represented, to judge from the number of handles[95] and bases.

There were no identifiable sherds of cups of classes I and II (but see below). The distinction between class III with conical foot, and class IV with flat base, is difficult to make, due to the fragmentary state of the material, but both types are present. Class III is best exemplified by a cup from Area 3 South (PLATE 24, 69/P 10), and by the large number, especially in the Moulds Deposit, of conical feet of appropriate size;[96] several profiles attest to the presence of class IV.[97] The zigzag rims common to both classes are found almost exclusively in the Moulds Deposit, in some quantity in the SPG Pit, and in smaller numbers in the Levelling Material. Did at least class IV then not persist far longer than the evidence of the cemeteries indicates? Not necessarily, as earlier material is present in the later deposits on Xeropolis. Furthermore, one must take into account the material from the SL Area: this was collected from the surface, and not the product of excavation, but it is remarkably homogeneous, and roughly datable to the end of SPG II and early SPG III, and many nearly complete vases were found,[98] the cup being one of the two commonest shapes; no example of a zigzag rim was found — all were of class V.

As to class V, the flat-based type with monochrome or banded lip, only one example (with high monochrome lip) was found in the Moulds Deposit (PLATE 13, 66/P262), and only one sherd, a banded rim, in the underfloor level of Area 3 South (PLATE 24, 629). In the later deposits it is common. If it did not come in at the beginning of SPG I, it cannot have been introduced much before the end of LPG, on this evidence; on the other hand, there is no reason why it should not have continued in use throughout SPG III, to judge from its popularity in the Levelling Material. It is the characteristic SPG cup. It may be noted that banded rims are more common than monochrome ones on Xeropolis, but that the opposite is the case in the SL Area.

Variations on the conventional types of cup, as analysed above, are for the most part undetectable, but there are instances of decoration on the body.[99] Also, there are sporadic examples both in the settlement and in the cemetery surface material of monochrome cup sherds with gently outcurving lips (not offset) strongly reminiscent of class II; unfortunately, they are very difficult to date.[100]

### Origins and comparative material

The SM cups (class I) are closely related to the latest LH IIIC ones, which are usually light ground with an occasional wavy line. It is noteworthy, however, that on Xeropolis, though this type is found in the earlier IIIC settlement, it is completely absent from the final phase.[101]

There are parallels, mostly light ground, on other SM sites,[102] but nowhere else in Greece was the cup so popular as a tomb offering as at Lefkandi.[103] From sites later to be associated ceramically with Lefkandi (see below), the only cup that can be classed as SM is one from Iolkos[104] — but material from this period is almost entirely lacking.

Class II (EPG and MPG) was in the main, it seems, a local development. It is difficult to attribute the improvement in the construction of the vase[105] (a general feature of EPG) to an outside source without further evidence from individual features — it may be that the greater emphasis given to the conical foot reflects Attic,[106] or even Cypriot, developments, but there is nothing else. It is therefore extremely interesting that cups of this class have been found at Chalcis, in Thessaly, and on the island of Skyros and Naxos[107] — over an area, in fact, in which close correspondences in other shapes will be found during this period and on the basis of which evidence it will be argued that the area constituted a distinctive and interlinked geographical region, of which Lefkandi formed a part, from this time on.

The innovation which distinguishes class III, the high offset lip with zigzag on the outside, is surely a direct imitation of the Attic LPG cup, but the later flat-based class IV (LPG to SPG I) seems to have originated locally. Vases of these two classes have few parallels outside Lefkandi. One of the class III, from Iolkos tomb 12, has already been mentioned (n. 107); there are two from a Skyrian group recently published;[108] and there is a not unsimilar one from Vergina in Macedonia.[109] And this last site, surprisingly, has provided the only parallel to class IV yet published.[110]

Class V, finally, would seem to be a local variation of a type that was fairly widespread from SPG I to SPG III throughout the region from Thessaly to the North Cyclades.[111] The one or two bands on the lip, a feature of many Lefkandian cups, are equally a feature of Attica and the Argolid, but if there was influence it is not clear in which direction it flowed.

To sum up, the popularity of the cup shape, and the fact that it is divisible into several distinct but occasionally overlapping classes, make it one of the most useful criteria for stylistic development.

**List**

*I*

SM                     S 19,1; S 24,1; S 37,1; S 40,2; S 42,1; S 43,4; S 49,1 (FIG. 7, A); S 60,2
                       (FIG. 7, B); S Gully Fill.

*II*

EPG                    S 8,1 and 4; S 10,1–2; S 16,6; S 20,6–7; S 27,1; S 28,1–3; S 46,1 (FIG. 7, C);
                       S Pyre 1A,4.
EPG or MPG S SF 4–6
MPG                    S 12,2; S 18,4 and 5 (FIG. 7, D); S 29,1–2; P 9,5; P 14,2 (FIG. 7, E); P 16,5;
                       P 25B,4. (Nb. P 14,4 – Black Slip)
LPG                    T 17,1

*III*

LPG                    P 35,2; P Pyre 11,9–10; P Channel, Lower Fill (?); T 7,2; T 17,2 and 3 (FIG.
                       7, F).

*IV*

LPG                    P 19,3; T 26,2 (FIG. 7, G).
LPG or SPG I P Pyre 42,1; T 29,1.
SPG I                  P 4,5; P 44,2; T 15,6 (FIG. 7, H); T 23A,2.

*V*

SPG I                  P 10,4; T 15,7 (FIG. 7, I); T 22,4.
SPG I or II   S SF 8; P 36,5; P Pyre 19,1; T Pyre 3,2.
SPG II                 S 33,7; S 45,4; P 28,3 and 9–10; P 43,6; T 2,1 (FIG. 7, J); T 13,4.
SPG II or III T 27,1
SPG III                T 31,8 (FIG. 7, K)

*Miscellaneous*
MPG                    P 6,1
SPG II                 S 25B,1

*Import*
SPG II                 S Pyre 4,1. Attic EG II.


THE TWO-HANDLED BOWL (SKYPHOS).[112] FIG. 8

This section is divided into three main parts: SM to the end of MPG; LPG on its own; and
SPG.

**I. SM to the end of MPG**
Seven bowls, matching the cup and lekythos in popularity, can be attributed to the SM
period (FIG. 8, A–B). The foot is usually very low conical, disproportionately small for the
body, which curves upwards and outwards to a flaring lip. The handles are rounded, and
placed horizontally. The main system of decoration is dark ground. The body can be wholly
or for its upper part monochrome, or have a reserved panel containing a rough zigzag; the
foot is unpainted, and so also, in three cases, is the lower body. Four of the seven have no
reserved band inside the lip.[113]
      The bowl, in complete contrast to the cup, is found much less frequently in tombs of

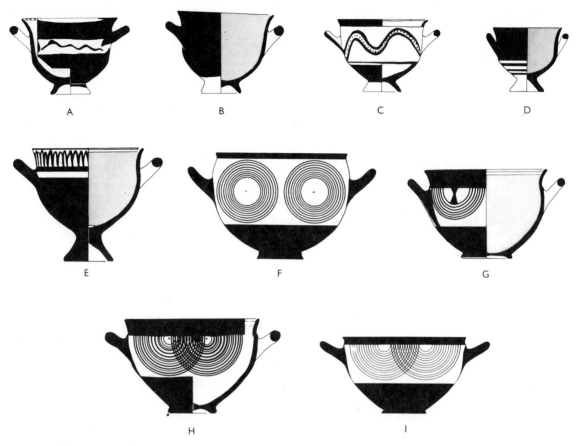

FIG. 8. (A) SM S 3,2 (B) SM S 41,2 (C) EPG S 32,6 (D) MPG S 18,2 (E) LPG P Pyre 11,7 (F) Xeropolis, reconstruction (G) LPG P 3,14 (H) SPG III S 59 A,4 (I) Xeropolis, reconstruction. Scale 1:4

the EPG and MPG phases. In EPG there are only two on which one can base any deductions as to stylistic change: the shape does not differ greatly, but the bodies are slightly shallower and the feet more neatly formed; for the decoration, one is monochrome, the other has an unusual motive between the handles (FIG. 8, C); both have a reserved band inside the lip.[114] Two others, of unusual type, belong to this phase. S 20,4 (PLATE 99) is unique, having four handles, two horizontal and two vertical — a curious blend of bowl and cup; it also has a higher conical foot than any other EPG vase. The second, S 2,2, is a fragment of a multiple vase, and the only instance at Lefkandi of such a vase being fashioned from bowls; the decoration is monochrome.

A distinct development is observable in the two bowls assigned to the MPG phase (see FIG. 8, D). They are deeper, have high conical feet, and have a monochrome upper body with three narrow bands below; they have no reserved band inside the lip. They are probably contemporaneous, not only because they are so like each other, but also because they are associated with similar types of vase. Both belong to the earlier part of MPG; none has yet been recorded for the later stage.

This concludes[115] the account of the bowls in use from SM to MPG. For their antecedents one inevitably goes back to LH IIIC in general, and to the IIIC settlement of Xeropolis in particular, where the bowl was prominent from phase 1 until the end.[116] In the SM tombs the shape is in principle the same as those of the settlement, but the lip flares out rather more sharply, the body curves inwards at a more pronounced angle below the belly, and the foot tends to be low conical rather than ring base. The dark ground system is common to both, and there are already instances, in Xeropolis phases 2 and 3, of the lower body and the foot being left unpainted; on the other hand the tendency in the SM bowls to omit a reserved band inside the lip is a reversal of the previous trend, and there are no examples from the settlement of the wavy line in a reserved panel on the body.[117] The evidence cannot be used to prove or to disprove continuity between the IIIC settlement and the earliest SM tombs at Lefkandi.

As to contemporaneous comparative material, the bowl is characteristic of most sites which contain SM pottery though, Athens excepted, it was not often used as a grave offering.[118] The development in EPG, such as it is, appears to have been a purely internal matter. So perhaps was the advance visible in MPG, though it is possible that the influence of the Attic style is to be recognised in the high conical foot; there are, however, two vases[119] from other sites that are close in shape and decoration to the two from Lefkandi. The one is from Skyros,[120] and affords useful confirmation of the ceramic homogeneity of the region. The other was found in a tomb at Asine with a shallow hemispherical bowl and a trefoil oinochoe of LPG date.[121]

## II. Late Protogeometric

At Lefkandi this phase saw many innovations, and a fresh approach which can be observed more clearly in the two-handled bowl — from now onwards called the skyphos — than in any other shape. There is no further evidence of the preceding MPG type; there are, on the other hand, several new types (new by shape or decoration or both together) which appear, so far as we can tell, for the first time in LPG. They come not only from certain tombs and pyres, but also from two settlement deposits, the Moulds in Area 2 and the underfloor material from Area 3 South, and from the lower fill of the North Channel of the Palia Perivolia cemetery.[122]

The two most commonly used types were the circles skyphos and the pendent semicircles (PSC) skyphos. The circles skyphos (FIG. 8, F) has been found in the three deposits mentioned,[123] but neither now nor later in any tomb or pyre. For the upper part of the vase,[124] the body usually comes up to a gently outcurving lip; the lip is painted; there is a reserved band inside, and there may be a supporting band below the lip outside; the body decoration is two sets of circles between the handles, with bands or solid paint below. There are several examples of circles with central filling,[125] and in three instances there is a variation in the design, a central panel dividing the two sets of circles.[126] This latter feature, taken with the characteristic body and lip profile, strongly suggests that one should look to Attic LPG for the source.[127]

The PSC skyphos (FIG. 8, G) can be attested in LPG both in tomb and settlement contexts. The body is normally surmounted by an everted and carinated lip,[128] and there is no evidence so far of a foot other than base ring, though the same cautionary remarks apply as for the circles skyphos. The lip is monochrome outside, and has a reserved band inside; the pendent semicircles are the invariable feature of the handle zone, and the lower body and foot are painted over. The lips vary from high to medium (see below). The semicircles often intersect, but in several cases do not; there are two instances of a central filling, and one unique case of a dividing central panel.[129] This type of skyphos was developed locally, at Lefkandi and in the region around it. It seems from the evidence at Lefkandi that it emerged in LPG, but towards the end of it,[130] perhaps later than the first appearance of the circles skyphos.

Four other types of skyphos have been identified in LPG contexts.

(a) T 26,1 (PLATE 182). Gently outcurved lip, high conical foot, panelled rectilinear motives between the handles. Fairly small and close to a similarly small Attic type.[131]

(b) P Pyre 11,7 (FIG. 8, E) and 8 (PLATE 152); PLATE 13, 28 and 31–2. High everted and carinated lip with zigzag(s); conical foot where preserved; body monochrome except for no. 28 from the Moulds Deposit, which has circles. A local development, with the lip and its decoration no doubt taken from the Attic PG cup. These are the only known instances.

(c) PLATE 24, 634. Out-turned lip, zigzags between bands in handle zone, base-ring foot. The only one from an LPG context, but sherds of similar type, with single zigzag between two bands, have been found in other contexts.[132]

(d) PLATE 14, 45. High carinated rim, banded, two reserved bands below handles; body otherwise monochrome; foot not preserved. The only certain example.[133]

On this evidence, then, the LPG phase was a time of innovation and experiment for skyphoi, a conclusion confirmed by what we know of other vase shapes.

## III. Sub-Protogeometric

The two main types of the LPG period, the circles and PSC skyphoi, continue to be the preferred ones in SPG, the PSC type being by a long way the more common.

The chief evidence for the circles skyphos comes from the settlement, particularly the SPG Pit and the Levelling Material. In comparing SPG and LPG there is little useful to say about the shape of the vase, since the number of LPG upper body profiles is relatively so small, and in any case no judgment is possible on the type of base. For the main body decoration, however, it is a fair deduction that the central panel inserted between the two sets of circles is mainly if not wholly an LPG feature.[134] It is also likely that the custom of adding a central filling to the circles was rare after LPG.[135]

It is not possible to trace any stylistic progress during that part of SPG when circles skyphoi continued to be made. No alternative to the ring base has been detected. The lip element can vary considerably: in most cases, as in LPG, the body continues without interruption to a gently outcurving lip, but there are examples both of a straight lip, and of a fairly sharply everted one.[136] What it is possible to do, on the evidence of the SPG Pit, is to make a distinction between a smaller and a larger type, each with its own features: the larger (lip diameter 18–20 +) has one or two bands beneath the lip, and the circles well down on the body; the smaller (lip diameter 13–14) has no such bands, and the circles come up fairly close to the lip area, and can even touch it.[137]

For the PSC skyphos (FIG. 8, H for SPG) we have a number of examples from the tombs in addition to the settlement material. In this instance it is best to discuss the stylistic development for the whole known series.

So far as concerns the shape, there is no known variation from the use of the ring base, and the relative shallowness or deepness of the body cannot yet, I feel, be shown to be a stylistic criterion. It is the lip that is the most informative. The very great majority of lips are straight (or with a very slight inward curve only), everted and carinated, but there can be appreciable differences in their heights. Arbitrarily dividing into high (1.5 cm or over), medium (1–1.4 cm) and low (under 1 cm), we can use the Area 2 deposits to indicate a gradual change. In the Moulds Deposit (LPG), all lips, except one medium, are high; in the SPG Pit (SPG I–II) most of the lips are still high, but there were also a fair number of medium ones, and just a very few which were low; in the Levelling Material (SPG III) the proportion of high lips decreases sharply to about 15%, medium lips remain fairly constant, but there are far more low ones (FIG. 8, I). There is, in other words, a development from high to low, with lips of medium height probably used throughout SPG.

In addition, different types of lips are very occasionally found: of these the most note-worthy, apart from the two uncarinated ones of the LPG period, are three which are incurved and slightly swept back, and almost certainly belong to the end of the series.[138]

The decorative system, apart from the PSC, yields no helpful results – the lower body was normally monochrome, though there can be exceptions, and the outer lip is always painted over. The PSC are an inescapable feature,[139] but it can be stated with some confidence that the use of a panel to divide the two sets of semicircles, and the use of a central filling, were LPG features – rare enough in that period, no later example has been identified among the hundreds found. It is possible that the practice of interlocking the two sets became much more common in SPG.

As to the relative popularity of the circles and PSC skyphoi, a comparison between the minimum[140] figures from the Area 2 deposits provided a helpful pointer: Moulds, 4 circles, 19 PSC; SPG Pit, 45 circles, 85 PSC; Levelling, 20 circles, 170 PSC. The PSC skyphos, once it became established, was always the more popular – a conclusion borne out by other deposits. As well as this, though, the figures given above for the SPG Pit and the Levelling strongly suggest (a) that the PSC skyphos retained its popularity till the end of SPG III, and (b) that the circles skyphos went out of fashion by early SPG III at the latest.

The comparative material for these two types confirms that the PSC skyphos was more popular and survived longer, and shows that the home of both (notwithstanding the Attic inspiration of the circles skyphos) lay in the region of which Lefkandi formed one community.

Only about a score of circles skyphoi have been found outside Lefkandi, but they cover a fairly wide area: inside the region, Andros, Kardiani on Tenos, Skyros, Phthiotic Thebes in Thessaly; outside, Rheneia, Thebes, Vergina in Macedonia, Old Smyrna, and Cyprus.[141] All have low ring bases except for the two from Andros, and the one from Kambos on Tenos, which have high pedestal or flaring feet. In all cases but one where the context allows, the date is probably within the first half of the ninth century, i.e. SPG I and II;[142] the added white used for the vase from Cyprus (without context) suggests that this one could be much later.

The PSC skyphoi, with their vast distribution, both inside and outside the region, and in favour down to the middle of the eighth century, are too well known to need discussion:[143] even their previous absence from central Italy and Sicily is now beginning to be remedied;[144] only the Peloponnese and north-west Greece have so far produced no specimens. The great merit of the Lefkandian series is that it establishes this site and its surrounding region as the homeland of the type (not that there was much doubt before), and puts its origin back into LPG. It raises one problem, however – the nature of the relationship of the type with fairly straight overhanging lip, so characteristic of Lefkandi, to that with incurved and slightly swept-back lip. Is the distinction chronological or geographical, or a mixture of both?

Though the SPG period is not renowned for innovation and experiment, it need not be doubted that other types of skyphoi accompanied the two discussed. That this is so is clear from two vases from tombs, T 23A,4 (PLATE 181), a shallow flat-based skyphos with high everted lip and double zigzag on the belly, of SPG I date, and the deep skyphos S Pyre 4,2 (PLATE 112), with cross-hatching on the body, SPG II.[145] And the settlement has others, among them a monochrome type with high everted lip[146] which probably continued to be made during SPG, but are too few for one to be certain.

Finally, there is a class of skyphoi belonging to the later stages only, the local imitations of Attic. These may have a monochrome body,[147] or have a panel with multiple zigzag, meander, or vertical chevron decoration.[148] In Attic terms the range is EG II–MG II, the vertical chevrons being MG II;[149] at Lefkandi the imitations are mostly of MG I and MG II, to judge from the scarcity of identifiable EG II pieces, whether imports or imitations.[150] I have equated SPG III with Attic MG I and MG II; the atticising skyphoi will then be a major feature of SPG III, though making a tentative appearance during SPG II.

List (cemeteries only)
SM        S 3,2 (FIG. 8, A); S 17,1; S 22,1; S 41,2 (FIG. 8, B); S 43,3; S 55,2; S 60,1.
EPG       S 32,6 (FIG. 8, C), S 34,1. Possibly S SF 11. Note S 2,2, a multiple vase, and S 20,4, which has four handles.
MPG       S 18,2 (FIG. 8, D); S 51,3. Possibly P Pyre 40,1.
LPG       P 3,14 (FIG. 8, G); P Pyre 11,7 (FIG. 8, E) and 8; T 26,1.
SPG I     S 56,3; S Pyre 15,4; P 27,2 (outsize); P 39B,5; T 23A,4.
SPG II    S 33,1–2; S 45,3; S Pyre 4,2; P 21,10.
SPG III   S 59,2; S 59A,3 and 4 (FIG. 8, H); T 31,5.
Undated   P 2,1 (PSC); P Pyre 8,1; P Pyre 31,1 (PSC).
Nb.FIG. 8, F is a restored circles skyphos from the SPG Pit. FIG. 8, I is a restored PSC from the Levelling Material.

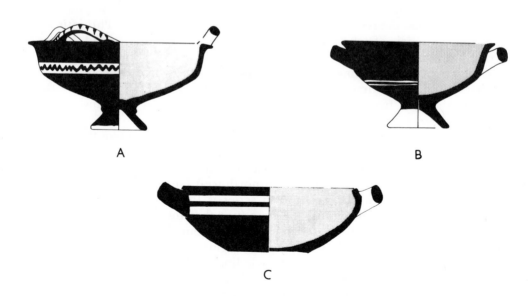

FIG. 9. (A) EPG S 16,5 (B) MPG S 51,4 (C) Xeropolis 65/P77. Scale 1:4

## THE SHALLOW BOWL. FIG. 9

### A. With high foot (pedestalled bowl)

There are five, all EPG or MPG. The earliest is from S 16 (FIG. 9, A), a tomb that contains several vases of SM type.[151] The foot is conical with an upper rib, and the upper body comes up almost vertically to a sharply everted wide flat rim with three ribbon handles on it. The decoration is monochrome except for barred rim and handles, unpainted lower foot, and a rough zigzag in a reserved band on the body. The two from S 2 (PLATE 92) are also EPG, differing from the first in that the feet have no rib and are wholly unpainted, and that the bodies are either altogether monochrome (S 2,1) or have two reserved bands on the lower part (S 2,5).

These are followed by two from S 18 (PLATE 97) and S 51 (FIG. 9, B), of MPG date; these have two handles placed horizontally below the rim, and not on it, with the result that the body is relatively deeper, and the rim less wide. The decorative system, however, is much the same as on those from S 2.

This is a fairly close-knit group, with no antecedents either in LH IIIC or in SM. It was probably a local shape.[152] Outside the region, two are known, both of the type with handles set vertically on the rim — the one from Argos,[153] the other most likely from Athens, to judge from the circumstances of its acquisition.[154]

### B. Flat-based, with horizontal strap handles

This is a simple but quite distinctive type. The diameter varies between 12 and 15 cm, the height between 5 and 6; it has two broad horizontal (occasionally slightly angled) strap handles just below the rim, which is either out-turned (the more common) or incurved; the body curves in fairly sharply to a flat base. The system of decoration is monochrome except for the area between the handles; in the great majority of cases this consists of two reserved bands (FIG. 9, C), but the type with everted rim may have a rough zigzag in a reserved panel. A third motive, vertical bars, is extremely rare.[155]

The type is almost exclusively confined to the settlement.[156] Though never as popular as the PSC or circles skyphos, it is fairly frequent both in the SPG Pit and in the Levelling Material, and in other areas,[157] but no fragment was found in the LPG deposits, either of the Moulds in Area 2 or of the fill under the yard in Area 3 South. The present evidence suggests that it may not have developed fully until some time in SPG,[158] a conclusion which would be supported by its remarkable popularity (eleven complete profiles, and fragments of very many more) in group B of the SL area, whose pottery, with the exception of an impressed-triangle kalathos sherd, seems to be uniformly SPG II or early SPG III.[159] There is indeed no proof of the existence of this type before SPG II.

As with the pedestalled bowl, it could have evolved locally, either at Lefkandi or within the region. The only parallels known to me come from the region, Marmariani[160] and Skyros,[161] from tombs in all cases, but not datable more closely than within the broad range LPG to SPG II.

### C. Lug or similar handles

This is a small group of five, all from tombs, not particularly uniform. All are shallow in varying degrees, and S 45,6 (PLATE 105) is almost a dish (it is very poorly made); two have a low foot, two are flat-based, and the base of the fifth, P 39B,17 (PLATE 147), was not found. The handles are some form of lug, considerable variation being shown. P 39B,17 is in a SPG I context,[162] and has combed and incised decoration; it is either Black Slip or an imitation of it.[163] The rest are monochrome and certainly or probably SPG II.

Similar vases are known at Marmariani,[164] and at Athens in EG contexts.[165] The evidence is too slight on the one hand, and of too diverse a nature on the other, to allow origin or interconnexion to be established.

### D. Unusual bowls

(i) S 4,1 (PLATE 92). Bowl with tripod base. EPG. The bowl element is fairly similar to the pedestalled bowls above, but note the four tab handles. The tripod undercarriage may imitate a metal prototype,[166] and in any case shows excellent workmanship. No close parallel in Greece and the Aegean.[167]

(ii) P 24,6 (PLATE 142). LPG. In shape very like S 4,1 without its tripod base; even the tab handles are there. The base is flat. Individual decoration: cross-hatched triangles surmounting sets of PSC, and concentric circles adorning the underbase. No parallel known.

(iii) P 3,15 (PLATE 127). End of LPG. Unique in shape, and unusual in decoration; very large, nearly 15 cm high. The curved base suggests that it originally had a stand, and also that it may imitate a metal cauldron, which could also explain the handles being taken up above the rim.[168] The decoration combines three sources of inspiration, the local tradition (the rough zigzags, perhaps the multiple triangles), Attica (chequerboard and cross-hatched panels),[169] and Thessaly (the multiple enclosed rectangles and perhaps the double-axe motive).[170] Altogether it is a good example of an experimental vase, as are several others of this period.

### List
A. *Pedestalled bowl*

EPG        S 2,1 and 5; S 156,5 (FIG. 9, A)
MPG        S 18,1; S 51,4 (FIG. 9, B)

B. *Flat base, horizontal strap handles*
Cemeteries
SPG II        P 28,11 (handmade). No wheel-made example.
Undated. S Gully Fill, 844–7; T Surface, 1057.

Settlement
SPG Pit,  137–8, 141–2, 147–8; Levelling, 323–7; various areas, 65/P77 (FIG. 9, C),
          690–4; Area SL, 70/P3–4 and many others.

C. *Lug or similar handles*
SPG I        P 39B,17.
SPG II        S 45,6; P 28,4; T 4,6; T 5,5.

D. *Unusual bowls*
EPG        S 4,1.
LPG        P 3,15; P 24,6.

### THE KALATHOS. FIG. 10

Since, as will be seen, kalathoi were rare in the settlement, I shall deal first with those from the cemeteries: indeed, more kalathoi were deposited with the dead at Lefkandi than any

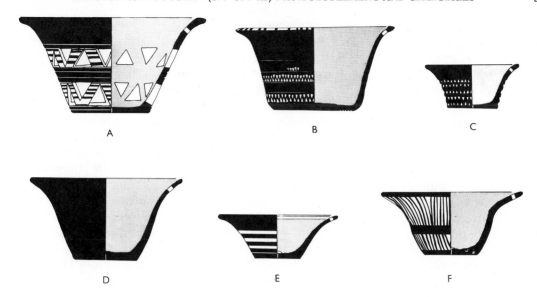

FIG. 10. (A) LPG P 22,26 (B) LPG P 3,17 (C) SPG I P 39,4 (D) LPG P 3,24 (E) SPG I P 39B,15 (F) SPG II T 13,5. Scale 1:4

other kind of vase,[171] even though they have not yet been found before LPG. There are three main types: the openwork kalathos, with triangular sections cut out of the body, larger than the other two; the kalathos with rows of small impressed triangles; and the unindented kalathos, either monochrome or banded.

There are only seven openwork kalathoi, two in a LPG context (FIG. 10, A), three of the SPG I phase, and two belonging to SPG III. There are some differences between individual pieces – the number of tiers, the standard of cutting out, the designs on the underbases – but none is valid as a stylistic criterion.

The kalathoi with impressed triangles numbered forty-four,[172] and were found only in LPG and SPG I tomb and pyre groups, so far as can be ascertained (FIG. 10, B–C). The shape is simple: conical, of varying depth. The base is always flat, and the lower body rises from it in a straight outward slant;[173] the upper body usually curves outwards to finish in a sharply offset horizontal lip with string holes, but there are instances where the line of the body continues straight up from the base, with the rim hardly distinguished from the body. The way in which the impressed triangles were arranged seems to have been quite haphazard, and the number of tiers varies (three is the most popular); incised guide lines were usually, but not invariably, provided. With one exception,[174] the body is monochrome; for the underbase the motive is usually a Maltese or a reserved cross. No stylistic development can be recognised – note particularly the variations in shape that can occur within a single tomb.

There are sixty-five unindented kalathoi (i.e. lacking the impressed triangles), and they range in date from LPG to SPG III (FIG. 10, D–F). They are similar to the impressed-triangle examples in their shape and variations of depth, and generally in their underbase motives. In many cases the outer body is monochrome, but some have one or more reserved bands. The later groups provide certain exceptions: T 13 (PLATE 174 – SPG II) has one with a slightly convex profile, one with a body decoration of two sets of vertical lines divided by a horizontal band, and one with cross-hatched underbase; S 45 (PLATE 105 – SPG II) has one with convex profile, three bands on the body, and sixteen rays under the base, while another has eight rays under the base, as also have the only kalathos from T 31 (PLATE 185 — SPG III) and a surface find S SF 9 (PLATE 111). Three of the specimens from S 59 + 59A (PLATES 108–9 — SPG III) have elaborately decorated underbases, and two of these have the body entirely covered by horizontal bands.[175] This evidence is perhaps sufficient for one to suggest that there was a tendency towards greater variety, at least in decoration, in the closing stages. Apart from this, no internal stylistic development can be seen.

Although stylistic development is generally lacking within each of the last two classes (both popular), one can say with reasonable confidence that the type with impressed triangles was the first to be used, and that the unindented type, for a while concurrent with the former, eventually replaced it altogether. The figures are: LPG, twenty-one with impressed triangles, one unindented; SPG I, seventeen with impressed triangles, fourteen unindented; SPG II and III, none with impressed triangles, forty unindented.[176]

The settlement, as stated, has yielded very few identifiable fragments of kalathoi. The openwork kalathos is altogether missing. Sherds of the impressed-triangle type appear in the Moulds Deposit, the SPG Pit, the Levelling Material (one sherd only), in Trial W, in SL group B (one only), and there are a few from other sectors — there are not more than about fifteen altogether. The unindented kalathos is represented by one sherd in the Moulds Deposit, and by eight sherds in the SPG Pit; and that is all.

The chronological range does not, on the whole, conflict with that suggested by the cemetery groups. The appearance of a sherd of the impressed-triangle type in the Levelling Material is not significant, nor necessarily so is the sherd of the same type in SL.[177] The complete absence, however, of the unindented type from the Levelling, when compared with the number found in the SPG Pit, may possibly indicate that the kalathos fell into disuse early in SPG III.

The scarcity of identifiable sherds in settlement contexts deserves to be stressed. The rim is distinctive, and so is the characteristic decorated underbase; and sherds with impressed triangles are immediately recognisable. The answer must surely be that the two main types of kalathos were rarely used for everyday life — and the openwork type not at all.

It seems then that the kalathos was chiefly made to serve as an offering, or as a receptacle for offerings, at a burial — a situation paralleled in Athens, and Attica.[178]

The mention of kalathoi from elsewhere than Lefkandi leads to the question whether the Lefkandian examples were locally inspired. As to openwork kalathoi, they are not very common at Lefkandi, the technique[179] is not used for any other shape, and they have not been found anywhere else in the region. Nor, for that matter, are such kalathoi at all common outside the region. As things stand, the chronology and the known links would permit the introduction of the shape to Lefkandi either from Attica or from Cyprus.[180] Other find spots are Crete, Samos, and Kos.[181]

As to the two main types encountered at Lefkandi, the impressed-triangle and the unindented, the only parallels are within the region — for both on Skyros (probable date from the context SPG I),[182] for the impressed-triangle type one example of MPG date from Iolkos.[183] The context of this last vase reinforces the hypothesis of the chronological precedence of this type over the unindented, but there is no need to conclude, because no MPG instances have yet been found at Lefkandi, that its origin must be sought elsewhere. For both types, either Lefkandi or (just possibly) the region around it will have provided the origin.

**List**
*Openwork*
LPG              P 22,26 (FIG. 10, A) and 27
SPG I            P 10,5—6
SPG III          S 59,8; S 59A,2.

*Impressed triangles*
LPG              S Pyre 10,1; P 3,17 (FIG. 10, B)—23; P 7,3—6; P 23,13—14; P 24,7—11; P Pyre 32,2b—c.
LPG or SPG I     P 8,1; P 42,1—2; P Pyre 28,2—4.
SPG I            S 25A,1; P 10,7—9; P 39,4 (FIG. 10, C) and 5; P 39B,6—14; P 44,3; T 25,3.

*Unindented*
LPG              P 3,24 (FIG. 10, D)
SPG I            S 25A,2—3; S 56,5; P 4;6; P 10,10—17; P 39B,15 (FIG. 10, E); P Pyre 28,1; T 22,5—6; T 25,2.
SPG I or later   S SF 9; P 17,1; P 39,1.
SPG II           S 25B,2; S 45,7—10; P 28,5; P 43,2—5; T 2,2—3; T 4,3—5; T 5,6—9; T 13,5 (FIG. 10, F) — 14.
SPG III          S 59,9—16; S 59A,6—9; T 27,2; T 31,6; T 36,1.

*Black Slip*
                 P Pyre 32, 2a.

*Attic*
                 P 22,24—5

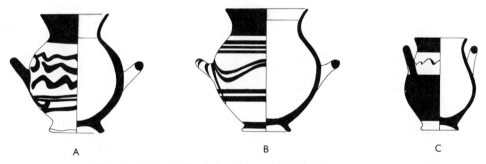

FIG. 11. (A) SM S 53,1 (B) EPG S 32,3 (C) EPG S 16,2. Scale 1:4

## THE BELLY—HANDLED AMPHORISKOS. FIG. 11

There are only four single, not multiple, examples of this shape,[184] and they are confined to SM and EPG tomb groups. Three of them have the same shape, a globular body with low conical foot, handles at an angle of about 45°, a short wide neck and a sharply out-swung rim;[185] there are also similarities in the decoration, monochrome neck and lip, subsidiary motives on the upper body,[186] with bands above or below, or both; but while two have the lower body unpainted, that of S 16,7 is monochrome. The fourth, S 16,2 (FIG. 11, C) has a much deeper, rather sagging body; the lip is much less prominent, and the handles rise almost vertically; it is monochrome except for the lower body and foot, and a relatively narrow unpainted band on the shoulder with a single rough wavy line.

This type of amphoriskos had its origin in LH IIIC;[187] in the IIIC settlement of Xeropolis it is well represented in the first two phases, but it is not certain whether it continued into the third.[188] It was also a familiar shape on other sites with SM pottery, notably in the Salamis and Kerameikos cemeteries, but it disappears at the beginning of the PG style.[189] Here at Lefkandi it may be regarded as characteristically Submycenaean, and one of the types which survived into EPG.

**List**
SM    S 53,1 (FIG 11, A)
EPG  S 32,3 (FIG. 11, B); S 16,2 (FIG. 11, C) and 7

## THE VERTICAL-HANDLED AMPHORISKOS. FIG. 12

The main interest of this shape is that it was localised at Lefkandi and (at least in the later stages) in its related region. Significant stylistic changes are few: basically, the SM amphoriskoi, of fairly globular body and with handles from belly to neck, are the origin of the subsequent type whose body becomes more ovoid, and whose handles loop vertically up from the belly, then over and down to the shoulder instead of joining the neck, features which with occasional variation, and with a gap at present in the MPG phase, continue from EPG to SPG I, the date of the latest examples. During this time dating is only helped where the decoration on these mainly dark ground vases clearly reflects that used on other vases which lend themselves to closer classification. The evidence comes almost wholly from cemeteries.

There are only two SM amphoriskoi, quite unlike each other. S 38,3 (PLATE 103) has a globular body and a short thick neck, and is monochrome except for a careless reserved area on the shoulder. S 19,3 (FIG. 12, A) is more advanced, with its body already tending to the ovoid, and a wide flaring neck and flat lip; but it is still top heavy compared with later examples. The central body is light ground, with two bands and a prominent zigzag.

The transition from SM to EPG is clearly visible in the profiles of the amphoriskoi from S 16 (PLATE 96) and S 10 (PLATE 94). 16,3 is almost globular and has a ring base; 16,4 has an ovoid body and a well-proportioned low conical foot (reasonably close, in fact, to the series from LPG onwards). 10,5 is poorly proportioned, and light ground, in contrast to the otherwise predominantly dark ground system; 10,3, a triple vase, is better proportioned and entirely monochrome. The three succeeding EPG amphoriskoi (FIG. 12, C for S 31,2) follow, with minor variations, the shape as shown by S 16,4, and in decoration conform to the simplicity observed in other vases of this period.[190]

No vase of this type has yet been found in an MPG context, but as the shape when found in LPG is fundamentally the same this absence must be fortuitous.

The series that follows is confined to LPG and SPG I, and consists of twenty-seven amphoriskoi[191] from twelve tombs and one pyre, sixteen of them from five tombs only.

The shape, as already noted, provides the basic link with the earlier stage, but it is by no means uniform. The body is often a good ovoid, but it can be squat, baggy or biconical. The foot is usually of high or low conical type, but can also be base-ring; no example, however, is known of a flat base. The chief variation is in the neck and lip element; some vases have a high neck, others a low and relatively thicker one — on occasions no neck at all. Such variations do not necessarily have any chronological relevance, as they can occur within a single tomb.[192]

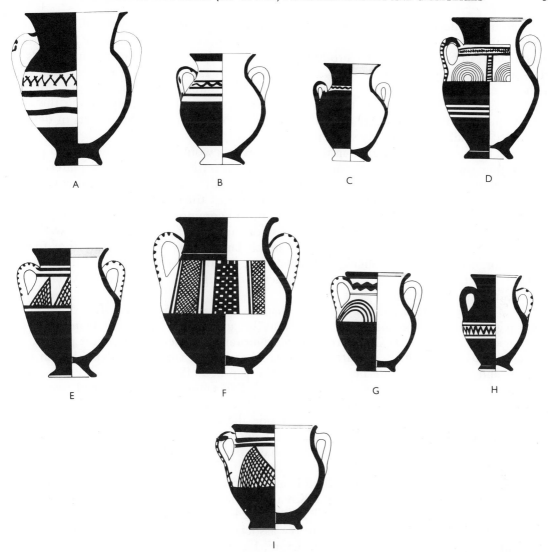

FIG. 12. (A) SM S 19,3 (B) EPG S 16,4 (C) EPG S 31,2 (D) EPG T 26,15 (E) LPG P 23,5 (F) LPG P 23,3 (G) SPG I P 39,1 (H) SPG I P 18,3 (I) SPG I P 13,12. Scale 1:4

In decoration, while the dark ground system was maintained, a division may be made between the vases where the whole area is left free for subsidiary motives, and those which are monochrome or whose decoration is limited to a narrow relieving zone. For the former, seven amphoriskoi have compass-drawn semicircles.[193] Sets of triangles, mostly cross-hatched, are also popular, with seven examples.[194] Finally, P 23 (PLATE 141) has two amphoriskoi, 6 and 7, with opposed diagonals with unfilled interstices on the shoulder, and one (no. 3, FIG. 12, F), with panels judged to be by the same potter who produced P 23,2. As to the second group, there are four amphoriskoi which are totally monochrome, and one with reserved bands on the belly;[195] four have a zigzag on the belly, and one a zigzag on the neck.[196]

No stratigraphical information is available to help us in establishing the priority of any of the groups concerned over any other of them. Even the associated vases do not always suggest a precise stylistic answer. It is worth noting, however, that T 26 and P 24, the most unmistakably LPG in style, each produced an amphoriskos with a feature that recalls the earlier series. I would suggest that the amphoriskoi with rather atypical profiles, and those which are monochrome or whose decoration lacks the compass-drawn semicircles, are later. In most cases this is clear from the associated vases, but not invariably so. On the other hand, it appears to me that there are sufficient interconnecting links in matters of detail to suggest that all fall within a fairly short period of time.

On the basis of this material from the cemeteries one would have to conclude on present evidence that the vertical-handled amphoriskos did not outlast SPG I.[197] The material from the settlement is most disappointing, due in part to the difficulty in distinguishing one small type of closed vase from another, though the absence of the characteristic shoulder handle suggests that the shape, as for the lekythos, was not in common use. One fragment only can with certainty be said to have come from a vase of this type.[198] It differs in two ways from the vases discussed above: it comes from a much larger vase, an amphora rather than an amphoriskos, with short thick neck, out-turned lip, and opposed diagonals on the shoulder; and its context, the Levelling Material, suggests that it may be appreciably later than anything from the cemeteries.

It was stated at the beginning that this shape was characteristic of Lefkandi and of its related region. This is generally true, and it may be added that its absence from other sites of the region in SM and EPG simply reflects our ignorance of them during these phases.

Chalcis, to start with, is of particular interest in having two amphoriskoi which could be MPG, and would therefore help to bridge the gap at Lefkandi between EPG and LPG; their main motive is rough horizontal zigzags.[199] The same site has produced two others, of LPG or SPG I date.[200]

The next site, Paralimni in Boeotia, is outside the region as defined, but has produced an LPG amphoriskos which both in shape and decoration would not be out of place at Lefkandi.[201] It is by no means impossible that at least certain parts of Boeotia will be found to be part of the cultural *koine* that forms the region.

Eight amphoriskoi have been recorded from various sites in Thessaly;[202] disappointingly, none from the Iolkos cist tombs or the Kapakli tholos tomb. Of these eight, the example from Theotokou is similar to those of T 26 and P 24 and, like them, has an LPG context — perhaps early in the phase, to judge from the associated cup. Six of the remaining seven are also of similar type to those found at Lefkandi, but none is in a securely dated context.[203] The last, from Halos, and not earlier than SPG I, is of a different type, as it has a low collar neck; nor have the PSC that adorn its shoulder been found on any Lefkandian amphoriskos.

Skyros may be passed over quickly: there are at least three examples, of probable SPG I–II date,[204] but details are lacking, and one must await the full publication.

The evidence from the North Cyclades is confined to Tenos and Rheneia. Two of the amphoriskoi, both from Tenos, have a prominent and sharply everted lip, and no neck,[205] much in the manner of the Halos vase; they are datable to SPG I or SPG II. The remainder[206] usually have a short thick neck and slightly everted rim, in which feature a comparison may perhaps be made with P 3,11 and P 13,2, but most of them are much taller than is the norm for our vases, and their context suggests a date in SPG II and early SPG III. Only the fragment from the Levelling Material is really comparable to these larger ones[207] (which may serve to support its suggested dating), and they seem to constitute a separate development, confined to the Cyclades.

Outside the region, variations of the shape are encountered at Iasos[208] and at Kavousi Kisamou[209] in Crete, but these seem to have no links with the Lefkandian series.

**List**
SM    S 19,3 (FIG. 12, A); S 38,3.
EPG   S 10,3 (triple) and 5; S 16,3 and 4 (FIG. 12, B); S 20,3; S 31,2 (FIG. 12, C); S 32,4.
LPG   P 3,11 and 13; P 7,1; P 23,3 (FIG. 12, F), 5 (FIG. 12, E) and 6–7; P 24,2–3; P 31,1–3; P Pyre 14B,2; T 26,15 (FIG. 12, D) and 16–17.
SPG I S Pyre 15,1 (probable); P 10,1; P 13,1–2, and 12 (FIG. 12, I); P 18,1–2 and 3 (FIG. 12, H); P 39,1 (FIG. 12, G); P 39B,3; P 44,1 and 5.

*Black Slip*
LPG   P 3,12.


## THE SMALL AMPHORA WITH HANDLES FROM SHOULDER TO LIP

There are only six vases that answer to this description, and they do not form a single stylistic group.

P 3,10 (PLATE 128) stands on its own, as being an imitation of the Attic LPG shape, of which three imported examples were found in P 22.[210] Bearing in mind its context, that it is the only one known of its type, and the short-lived vogue for the shape in Attica, I have assigned this vase to LPG.

The next four seem to form a group of their own, a variation on the vertical-handled amphoriskos. P 23,2 (PLATE 141),[211] thick-necked and globular-bodied, is particularly closely linked with amphoriskos P 23,3, the resemblances being so striking that one may conclude that they were the work of the same potter. The context suggests an LPG date. P Pyre 34,1 (PLATE 155) is very similar in shape to P 23,2, and has a shoulder decoration of opposed diagonals with unfilled interstices; it is probably SPG I.[212] The other two, P 47,2 and 3 (PLATE 150), come from a tomb which I have assigned to the transition from SPG I–II. 3 is noteworthy for its surprisingly high conical foot, string holes in the handles, and banded neck and belly; 2 is much smaller, with short and rather narrow neck, and reserved bands on the belly.

Finally, there is P 28,2 (PLATE 144) of SPG II date, a small vase with virtually non-existent neck, perhaps unconnected with the others, and not properly classifiable as an amphora. In contrast to the rest, it is light ground, and has three bands on the body.

There are no identifiable fragments of this shape from the settlement nor, to my knowledge, any useful comparative material for the SPG period.


**List**
LPG       P 3,10; P 23,2.
SPG I     P Pyre 34,1.
SPG I–II  P 47,2–3
SPG II    P 28,2


## THE MULTIPLE VASE. FIG. 13

Eight multiple vases were found in tombs and pyres, all except one[213] in SM and EPG contexts. Three types of vase were used in assembling the known examples. S 2,2 (PLATE 92)

FIG. 13. (A) EPG S 16,8 (B) EPG S 10,3, Scale 1:4

was made up of deep bowls; S 10,3 (FIG. 13, B) was composed of vertical-handled amphoriskoi. Both are triple vases (S 2,2 probably) either in line or in triangular form; both have high basket handles and are monochrome; and both come from EPG tomb groups.

The remaining six, a significant group of their own, were made up of belly-handled amphoriskoi, the shape discussed in the preceding section, and can be viewed as a continuation and elaboration of the analysis therein contained. Three are from SM contexts, one double (S 19,2 – PLATE 98), one triple and hand-made (S 38,2 – PLATE 103), one fragmentary but quadruple (S Pyre 1,1 – PLATE 112);[214] P 44,4 is probably SM; the other two (S Pyre 1A,3 – PLATE 92; S 16,8 – FIG. 13, A) belong to EPG groups, but seem to be SM in style; they are both triple. S Pyre 1A,3 has no basket handle, the rest (where known) have; P 44,4 is almost entirely monochrome, S Pyre 1,1 is too badly preserved to tell, the others have a variety of motives on the shoulder area,[215] but are otherwise monochrome. All have the traditional belly-handled amphoriskos shape, even the hand-made one.

It is this group that reveals the closest links with the Mycenaean style: the multiple vase as such had for long been one of its characteristic shapes, and the amphoriskos type was one of the two commonly in use in LH IIIC.[216] But what is of considerable interest is that, although the multiple vase was a reasonably well-known type in LH IIIC,[217] the Lefkandians were idiosyncratic in continuing to use it in the Submycenean period. The only other one known to me in such a context is from Chalcis.[218]

**List**
SM     S 19,2; S 38,2; S Pyre 1,1.
EPG    S 2,2; S 10,3; S 16,8; S Pyre 1A,3.
(SPG I) P 44,4.

## THE STIRRUP JAR

There are only three of these, S 19,6 (PLATE 98), S 38,1 (PLATE 103), and fragmentary S Pyre 1,2 (PLATE 112). Each is individual in shape and decoration; and each is accompanied by a multiple vase of the belly-handled amphoriskos type, of which there are but six altogether.

The LH IIIC ancestry of the shape is clear, but no connexion can yet be made with the IIIC Xeropolis settlement, as sherds of stirrup jars are so rare. There is no close resemblance between these three vases and stirrup jars with SM material; nevertheless, there seems no doubt that they should be classed as SM — it was only in Crete, and very marginally in Cyprus and Athens, that the shape survived the SM period. The stirrup jars of Lefkandi do not only look SM, but so also do the vases which accompany them. As in Athens, it appears that the function of the stirrup jar was usurped by the lekythos.

## THE LEKYTHOS. FIG. 14

This section may be introduced by two chance-found lekythoi from an as yet uninvestigated cemetery, KT 1 and 2 (PLATES 114, 255A, FIG. 16, A for KT 2). KT 1) was incomplete, of undecorated grey ware; the profile could be SM. KT 2 has a squat globular body, small mouth, and ring base; its shoulder decoration, mainly multiple and outwardly fringed triangles with the central one solid, is not paralleled at Lefkandi, though not unknown in SM contexts elsewhere.[219] So far, there is nothing to prevent its being SM; but it is in the White Ware fabric, typical of the latest LH IIIC settlement on Xeropolis,[220] and not yet found in any of the excavated tombs. It should perhaps be classed as LH IIIC, but the question is better left open until this area has been properly investigated.

We can now come on to a major group, which spans the SM and EPG phases; twelve or thirteen[221] lekythoi belong to it, and all are of SM type or exhibit certain SM features. These features are a rather heavy biconical or oval body, a small mouth, a rather crudely attached handle, and shoulder decoration of hand-drawn semicircles with occasional half-moon filling.

Those listed as belonging to the SM phase, omitting KT 1–2 and excepting S 9,1–3 (see below), are clearly such by context as well as in style. Those assigned to EPG, except S 8,2 (FIG. 14, D) which is in a different category,[222] have SM features, notably the hand-drawn semicircles, but the vases associated with them include one or more which I would define as EPG. There remain the three lekythoi, the sole vases of S 9 (PLATE 94), and they present a problem. This tomb is by stratification earlier than S 10, whose single lekythos (FIG. 14, C) has every one of the SM features noted above. Of the three from S 9, two have trumpet mouths, fairly neatly attached handles, low conical feet, and cross-hatched triangles on the shoulder; one of them (FIG. 14, B) has a biconical body, the other more oval; stylistically, both could be transitional SM–EPG. The third is a mixture of both styles: the handle and fringed hand-drawn semicircles are purely SM: the conical foot is EPG. I have arbitrarily, and perhaps incorrectly, assigned the tomb group to SM. But this and the later tomb S 10 provide a good example of the danger of dating purely from style.

The presence of the surprisingly large number of lekythoi of SM style, or at least displaying some SM feature, in EPG groups shows that the borderline between SM and EPG at Lefkandi was far from clear-cut, which is not surprising; but this does not justify the creation of an intermediate category, transitional SM–EPG, for the lekythos seems to have been a special case. Comparison with lekythoi from other sites in the general neighbourhood produces similar evidence. At Athens, the only other site well provided with lekythoi, there are two tomb groups whose lekythoi exhibit both SM and EPG features.[223] And a tomb on Naxos provides another instance of lekythos of SM style associated with an EPG vase.[224]

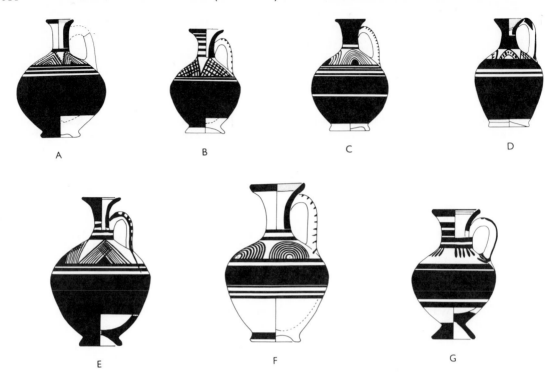

FIG. 14. (S) LH IIIC/SM KT,2 (B) SM S 9,1 (C) EPG S 10,4 (D) EPG S 8,2 (E) LPG P 31,4 (F) SPG I P 13,11 (G) SPG I T 3,4. Scale 1:4

The next major group seems to start effectively in LPG, but one must first consider the evidence for MPG. This phase is moderately well represented in the cemeteries, but only two lekythoi can with confidence be attributed to it, the miserable and monochrome miniature P 9,4 (PLATE 129 – note its high conical foot), and P 16,4 (PLATE 134) which has an ovoid body and very low conical foot, and groups of four chevrons on the shoulder. It is not easy to decide whether they should be linked with the earlier group or with the later.

However scarce the lekythos was in MPG, it was popular as a tomb offering during LPG and SPG I, by which time the SM features had disappeared, and new influences were at work. About forty vases of differing shapes and sizes are involved, and they are found both in tombs and in pyres.[225] I leave those from the pyres to the end, as there are problems of dating.

The most common features are an ovoid body, a low foot, a slender neck which the handle came up and over to join below the trumpet mouth, and a shoulder decoration of semicircles, now compass-drawn instead of hand-drawn, or cross-hatched triangles, or some combination or variation of these, the rest of the body usually being monochrome.[226] These features can be observed in LPG on five from T 26 (PLATE 182),[227] three from P 3 (PLATE 126), two from P 31 (PLATES 144–5, FIG. 14, E for P 31,4) and one each from P 41 (PLATE 147) and T 7 an outsize one with warts[228] (PLATE 260); in SPG I on four from T 3 (PLATE 168), two each from P 13 (PLATE 132 and FIG. 14, F for P 13,11) and T 15 (PLATE 176), and one from T 1 (PLATE 167); in SPG I–II on two from P 47

(PLATE 150); and in undatable contexts, one each from P 33 (PLATE 145, note the solid triangles on the shoulder) and T 37 (PLATE 189). In addition to these, four — all of SPG I date — have the same shape, but decoration other than that mentioned: T 3,4 (FIG. 14, G) had languettes — and an unusually high foot; the other three are from P 13 (PLATE 132), two with reserved band only, one with a rough zigzag round both belly and neck.[229] Finally, there is one completely monochrome example, of LPG date, the tall and very slender T 36,3.

There is one major comment, and two minor ones, on these lekythoi. The combination of the ovoid body and the shoulder motives of semicircles and cross-hatched triangles indicates an origin in the Attic LPG style;[230] the triangle motive is usually, but not invariably,[231] related to the size of the vase, in other words applied to pots too small for semicircles; and the four small lekythoi from T 1 and T 3, probably close to one another in time,[232] have the peculiarity that the handle was attached to the lip and not to the neck.

A rather different tradition is shown by a few lekythoi whose chief characteristic is a broad flat base. This feature is about the only recognisable one in two extremely fragmentary vases from P 23 (PLATE 140) of LPG date. The main group comprises four: three monochrome, biconical and flat-based vases from P 47 (PLATE 150), stylistically SPG I–II, and a very similar one from T 5 (PLATE 171), which probably falls early in the SPG III series. The same tendency towards the flat-based and monochrome is visible in other closed vases during SPG (see under the jug and oinochoe).

This virtually completes the evidence from the tombs. P 39B, 2 (PLATE 146) is too fragmentary for classification, but comes from an SPG I context. Then there are two miniatures, both monochrome and flat-based: P 28,7 (PLATE 144) is I think better classified as a jug, and has been included among those; S 59,7 (PLATE 108), squat and crudely made, if correctly classed as a lekythos, would prolong the life span of the shape just into SPG III; otherwise we must return to early SPG II for the last recorded one.

There are also nine lekythoi, whole or fragmentary, from pyres, all belonging certainly or probably to the later series. Two of them, P Pyre 11,4 (PLATE 152) and P Pyre 14B,1 (PLATE 153), with designs of cross-hatched and intersecting triangles and chevrons, can from their associated vases be assigned to LPG. Four, all fragmentary, cannot be given any precise date: S Pyre 6,1 (PLATE 114) with semicircles; P Pyre 39,2 (PLATE 155) with chevrons; and the two from S Pyre 17 (PLATE 114), the one with chevrons, the other with semicircles and a wavy line beneath.[233]

Two of the remaining three are from S Pyre 15 (PLATE 114); no. 3 has cross-hatched triangles and a relatively globular body, and no. 2, uniquely for a Lefkandian lekythos, has full circles on the shoulder. These are not necessarily criteria for earliness. The associated vertical-handled amphoriskos, in spite of its hand-drawn PSC, looks in other respects to be LPG or later, and this is confirmed by sherds found in the pyre, assuming that they are contemporaneous or earlier.[234] It is likely that these two lekythoi should be dated SPG I rather than LPG, and I think that the same date can be given to P Pyre 44,3 (PLATE 156), with ovoid body and undecorated shoulder, on the basis of the other contents of the pyre.[235]

None of these need be earlier than MPG, nor later than SPG I, which would accord well enough with the material from the tombs. No sherd of a lekythos has with certainty been identified in the settlement; the shape must have been very rare in occupation deposits, or there would have been some trace of the characteristic trumpet mouth, or of the narrow neck with handle attached.

To sum up briefly, the lekythos was a familiar shape in the Lefkandian cemeteries from SM to early SPG II, but possibly no later. Continuity throughout is possible, in spite of a scarcity in the MPG phase, for there are two features (the leaving of the lower body and foot unpainted, and the chevron motive) which appear – mostly on shapes other than lekythoi – in the period from SM to MPG and are still to be found in LPG and later lekythoi, and which at the same time are unfamiliar to the Attic style which so strongly influenced the Lefkandian lekythoi from LPG onwards.

Attic influence did not mean a slavish imitation, but it evidently renewed an interest that may have flagged in MPG, and the shape – whether the 'Attic' type or the relatively globular and sometimes flat-based variety –thereafter persisted into SPG II, in contrast to Athens where it dropped out of use at the end of LPG.

The lekythos is known in the region to which Lefkandi belonged, but the examples are relatively few. In addition to the two early ones from Naxos and Theotokou in Thessaly, mentioned above, only five have been published. Two come from Chalcis:[236] one, surely LPG, is closer to the Attic lekythos than any from Lefkandi; the other, with a biconical body and full circles on the shoulder, and probably associated with a jug with rough zigzags on the shoulder, should be MPG, or even LPG.[237] In Thessaly, Iolkos has produced one,[238] probably LPG, and Marmariani a second,[239] not unsimilar to T 7,3. Skyros, finally, has only one illustrated example – and that by a drawing: the tomb group to which it belongs is MPG.[240] On the whole, the style of these lekythoi is the same as that of the Lefkandian ones, but none can be placed later than LPG.

List

SM or LH IIIC KT 2 (FIG. 14, A)
SM          KT 1; S 9,1 (FIG. 14, B), 2–3; S 55,1; S 60,3; S 62,1; S Pyre 1,3 (possible)
SM or EPG   S SF10
EPG         S 8,2 (FIG. 14, D); S 10,4 (FIG. 14, C); S 20,5; S 31,3; S 32,1; S 46,2.
MPG         P 9,4; P 16,4.
LPG         P 3,4–6; P 23,10–11; P 31,4 (FIG. 14, E) and 5; P 41,1; P Pyre 11,4; P Pyre
            14B,1; T 7,3; T 26,3–8.
SPG I       S Pyre 15,2–3; P 13,7–11 (FIG. 14, F); P 39B,2; P Pyre 44,3; T 1,4; T 3,1,4
            (FIG. 14, G), 5–7; T 15,2–3.
SPG I–II    P 47,5–9
SPG II      T 5,3.
SPG III     ? S 59,7 (miniature)
Uncertain date S Pyre 6,1; S Pyre 17,1–2; S SF 15; P 33,1; P Pyre 39,2; T 37,1.

*Black Slip or allied*
LPG         P 22,17–18.

THE TREFOIL OINOCHOE. FIG. 15

This useful pouring vase, usually between 10 and 25 cm high, remained in the Lefkandian potter's repertoire throughout the period of use of the cemeteries, the evidence from which will be discussed first, but there are many variations in shape and decoration, and no type ever established itself for long. It has a Mycenaean III C ancestry, but has not so far been found in the final phase of the Xeropolis settlement. There was then perhaps no local

FIG. 15. (A) SM S 40,1 (B) EPG S 34,2 (C) MPG P 25B,3 (D) LPG T 26,12 (E) SPG II P 22,8 (F) LPG P (44),7 (G) SPG I T 22,1 (H) SPG I P 27,1 (I) SPG II T 13,1. Scale 1:4

tradition for the later potter to draw on; the associations are presumably with the Sub-mycenaean area of central Greece, but there are no particularly close parallels.[241]

## Cemeteries

Only two oinochoai can be assigned to the SM phase. Both are small, and have a globular body and low foot, but differ in the modelling of neck, lip and handle. The decorative system is much the same for both, monochrome except for the lower foot and the shoulder (and lower neck on S 41,1, PLATE 104), these areas being left unpainted except for the narrow band on the shoulder of S 40,1 (FIG. 14, A). The latter has a barred handle, the other a monochrome one.[242]

The succeeding EPG oinochoai probably developed locally. The earliest, S 16,9 (PLATE 96), is under 10 cm, but better proportioned than the two of SM date, and the only one of the early group to have a decorative motive,[243] sets of multiple triangles. S 32,2 (PLATE 101) and S 34,2 (FIG. 14, B) have prominent trefoils, and the point of maximum diameter set a little higher than earlier. S 8,2 (PLATE 93) has a short thick neck, a broad base, and a poorly marked trefoil. The shape may vary, but these last three have the typical EPG (and early MPG) decorative treatment, monochrome except for reserved bands and/or lower body unpainted.

S 12,1 (PLATE 95) belongs to early MPG. It has the same decorative system as the three above, but the height of the neck and the more ovoid body indicate some stylistic advance.

A further development takes place later in MPG. This is not a matter of shape, though the foot becomes more markedly conical, but rather of decoration, wherein the previous monochrome system gives way to an unpainted neck and shoulder, the latter now the basis for individual motives, languettes, cross-hatched triangles, and the first datable example of compass-drawn semicircles. Four oinochoai illustrate this breakaway, three from P 25B (FIG. 15, C and PLATE 143) and one from P 16 (PLATE 134).[244]

The new trend was carried over into LPG, as can be seen on the two from P Pyre 11 (PLATE 152); even the lower body is left unpainted. But this was temporary: from now on no further oinochoai with unpainted neck, far less light ground overall, are encountered at Lefkandi. Whether it was a local development or not one cannot say, but if there was out-side influence (note the semicircles) it could have come from Athens, where light ground oinochoai are known, in the early rather than the later stages of PG.[245]

Be this as it may, the usual design for the Attic oinochoe, especially in the LPG phase, is to coat the outer surface completely except for the shoulder area, left free for such motives as semicircles or cross-hatched triangles. And it is this type, with its elegant ovoid shape and low conical foot, that provides the inspiration for many of the local Lefkandian oinochoai of the LPG phase. The clearest examples are T 26,12–14 (FIG. 15, D and PLATE 183).[246] Others of the same type are P 22,6 (PLATE 140) and P 3,1 and 2 (PLATE 126).[247]

Not all the locally made LPG oinochoai copied an Attic model. A rather different type is represented by three vases. All have semicircles on the shoulder: P 19,1 (PLATE 135) and P 44,7 (FIG. 15, F)[248] have squat biconal bodies and a high thick neck; P 41,2 (PLATE 147) is more sharply angled at the belly, perhaps because of its small size. This squat oinochoe can perhaps be traced back through MPG to S 8,2 (see above); if so, it typifies the local style as unaffected by the Attic shape.

Although, then, LPG was a time of radical innovation, the traditional local style was not entirely superseded, as is shown by the trefoil oinochoe and a few other shapes. The end of this phase and the beginning of the next, SPG I, were also characterised by certain fairly short-lived experiments, outside the main stream of the local style: three trefoil oinochoai qualify as such, and may conveniently be discussed at this point.

The first, P 22,8 (FIG. 15, E) is small, and has a very squat biconical body, slender neck and flat base, and a shoulder decoration of rough zigzag between bands; the group from which it comes is, in my opinion, LPG, but the closest comparable vases are to be found in Athens in EG graves, and could have been its inspiration.[249] The second, P 7,2 (PLATE 129), has no connexions with Attica or anywhere else: squat-bodied and flat-based, it has a crude design of thick criss-crossing bands eminently suited to its shape. The associated vases suggest the end of LPG. The third, T 1,1 (PLATE 167) is a splendid example of an experimental vase, and the largest oinochoe from the tombs.[250] For the shape, the high handle with connecting bar is unusual, and the overlarge pedestal foot is paralleled, as far as I know, only at Marmariani.[251] As to the decoration, the semicircles on the shoulder are conventional, but the assorted fringes and rows of dots are characteristic of the East Aegean,[252] and the conception and certain motives of the neck decoration take us northwards to Thessaly again.[253] The context seems to be early SPG I.

We can now return to the further development of the two main types observable in LPG, those imitating the Attic oinochoai, and those which seem to perpetuate, in their shape, the local tradition. These persist into SPG, though it must be stressed that the lines of distinction are not so sharp, and that there are vases which conform neither to the one nor to the other.

No oinochoe found in an SPG group reproduces the Attic model as faithfully as in LPG. The nearest is P 10,3 (PLATE 131, SPG I), with semicircles on the shoulder and an ovoid body; but its base is flat — a common feature of the small closed vases of SPG I and SPG II. Two fairly large oinochoai, P 27,1 (FIG. 15, H) and T 5,1 (PLATE 171) seem to combine the local and Attic traditions. Both have a fairly heavy ovoid body, high thick neck with centre rib, and moulded lip. P 27,1 has semicircles on the shoulder and a reserved band on the belly, and its context is SPG I; T 5,1, early SPG II, is monochrome except for a rough horizontal zigzag between bands on the belly.[254]

Apart from these three, the emphasis is on the local squat globular type. This tradition is to be seen in T 22,1 (FIG. 15, G) and T 25,1 (PLATE 181), both from SPG I groups, T Pyre 3,1 (PLATE 191, SPG I or II) and probably P 47,4 (PLATE 150, transitional SPG I—II). All are monochrome with a single reserved band at the belly. Two other small examples, T 22,2[255] (PLATE 179) and T 5,2 (PLATE 171) also seem to reflect the same tradition.

All these six have low ring bases; there are also two of squat globular body, and monochrome, but with flat bases — T 15,4 (PLATE 176, SPG I), and P 36,2 (PLATE 145, either SPG I or SPG II).[256]

We can now come to an extremely interesting group, reasonably well represented both in the cemeteries and in the settlement (see below). To judge from the tomb contexts the chief period of popularity was SPG II, or at least not before: five can be dated to this phase, S 25B,3 (PLATE 100), S 45,1—2 (PLATE 105), P 43,1 (PLATE 148), and T 13,1 (FIG. 15,I) and one only to early SPG III, S 59,1 (PLATE 108). The characteristic features are: for shape, a slender ovoid body and a tall slender neck; for decoration, a zone of rough zigzags between horizontal bands (SPG II groups) or opposing diagonals with unfilled interstices (S 59) on the belly, and a panelled hourglass on the neck. There is one exception, P 43,1, which is entirely monochrome except for a reserved band on the belly.

Their date makes it unlikely that they reflect any borrowing from Attic LPG. Instead, we may perhaps look to certain Attic EG oinochoai,[257] which are slender, and have a neck panel — but not the hourglass so typical of Lefkandi. In this context, it may be relevant to note that it was during SPG II that Attic imports reappeared at Lefkandi.

To summarise on SPG I and SPG II, those in the local tradition, fairly squat, with ring foot or flat base, appear to be the most popular. There is little development or change: all one can reasonably say, and on the basis of the tomb material, is that the decorative motives carried over from LPG into early SPG I seem later to give way to an almost unrelieved monotony. As opposed to these, oinochoai showing the influence of the Attic LPG ovoid body and characteristic decoration are scarce, and confined to SPG I. In SPG II a new type of trefoil oinochoe with slender body and neck, monochrome except for a neck panel and decoration in the belly zone, established itself alongside a similar development in the medium-sized neck-handled amphora.

We know that this last type of oinochoe continued to be used early in SPG III. We also have a small amount of evidence that the Lefkandians were, during this phase, copying the current Attic MG I oinochoai, as well as importing them, but that is as far as the cemetery material allows us to go.[258]

### Settlement

The results are disappointing, mainly because it is often impossible to distinguish sherds of oinochoai from those of other small or medium-sized closed vases; at the same time, it must be admitted that the one readily identifiable feature, the trefoil lip, is not found at all commonly.

Omitting the Late Geometric material, the range of the settlement is from LPG to SPG III, at the latter end continuing beyond the period of use of the cemeteries. On the whole, the course of development for the oinochoai appears to accord with that of the cemeteries, and the particular innovation of the slender type with hourglass on the neck and decorated belly zone is reasonably well represented — so far as Area 2 is concerned, sherds of this type were found in the SPG Pit and the Levelling, but not in the Moulds Deposit, thus helping to support the date suggested by the tombs. Evidence for atticising MG oinochoai is unfortunately as rare as in the cemeteries.[259]

There is one feature, however, which may indicate that the picture provided by the tomb material is misleading: the apparent persistence throughout the settlement of semi-circles (occasionally with languettes as well) on the shoulders of what are likely to be oinochoai. It may be that the movement towards the elimination of subsidiary decoration from SPG I onwards was not as wholehearted as the cemetery evidence would lead us to believe.

### Comparative material[260]

The most productive area is Thessaly, with about sixty oinochoai covering a wide period of time. No parallel to the Lefkandian series is observable before MPG;[261] to this phase, however, there are assignable at least two from Iolkos,[262] similar in shape to those of P 25B, though in their monochrome necks closer to T 12B,1. As with other shapes, they illustrate the ceramic links between coastal Thessaly and Lefkandi at this time.

The vast majority of oinochoai belong to the LPG and SPG periods. They come from several sites,[263] and so far as one can tell exhibit much the same trends as those from Lefkandi, either the Attic LPG-influenced variety with ovoid body, or the rather squat globular-bodied type. There is a general family likeness between the Thessalian and Lefkandian vases, and one may note the custom, common to both, of inserting one or more reserved bands on a monochrome background: on the other hand, the flat base is very rare in Thessaly,[264] but not uncommon at Lefkandi. Both have oinochoai of Black Slip ware.[265] So far, no oinochoe of the type with slender body and neck with hourglass panel has been found in Thessaly, but this may be accidental, as the closely related type of neck-handled amphora is known at Kapakli. It seems likely that the two series retained similar stylistic features at least to the end of SPG II, though this need not mean specially close links.

Only one oinochoe from Skyros has been published in detail and illustrated, and this is very similar to the later MPG vases from Lefkandi.[266] There is also a record of five oinochoai with ovoid body (one with semicircles on the shoulder) from tombs of probable SPG I date.[267]

For the rest of the region the evidence is poor. There is just one from Euboea, from a tomb at Chalcis;[268] except for a similarity in shape, it differs from those at Lefkandi. And from the North Cyclades, where our knowledge is peculiarly sparse before SPG, there are only two which are relevant,[269] from the Kardiani tombs on Tenos.[270] The one, from tomb 1, is identical in decoration to the probable Attic LPG import P 22,7, and very similar to the local oinochoe T 26,13; its body profile is different, however, with the belly set higher, and the shoulder more flat, then on the Lefkandian examples. Its context seems clearly within SPG. The other, from tomb 2, is stylistically and by context later; it has a relatively slender body, and is monochrome except for a zone of zigzags between bands on the upper belly. It could be related to the similar type at Lefkandi, and its date could be either SPG I or SPG II.

**List**

| | |
|---|---|
| SM | S 40,1 (FIG. 15, A); S 41,1. |
| EPG | S 8,2; S 16,9; S 32,2; S 34,2 (FIG. 15, B). |
| MPG | S 12,1; P 16,1; P 25B,1–3 (FIG. 15, C); T 12B,1. |
| LPG | P 3,1–2; P 7,2; P 19,1; P 22,6,8 (FIG. 15, E): P 41,2; P 44,7 (FIG. 15, F); P Pyre 11,2–3; T 26,12 (FIG. 15, D)–14. |
| SPG I | P 10,3; P 27,1 (FIG. 15, H); T 1,1; T 15,4; T 22,1 (FIG. 15, G)–2; T 25,1. |
| SPG I–II | P 47,4. |
| SPG I or II | P 36,2; T Pyre 3,1. |
| SPG II | S 25B,3; S 45,1–2; P 43,1; T 5,1–2 T 13,1 (FIG. 15, I). |
| SPG III | S 59,1. |

*Black Slip ware*

| | |
|---|---|
| LPG | T 26,11. |
| SPG I | S 56,2. |

*Attic imports*

| | |
|---|---|
| LPG | P 22,7 (probable) and 9 |
| SPG III | T 19,1–2; T 31,1,3,4,7; T 33,1,3,4. All MG I |

*Handmade*

| | |
|---|---|
| SPG I | P 4,4 |
| SPG II | T 2,6–7 |
| SPG III | T 33,5 (local atticising) |

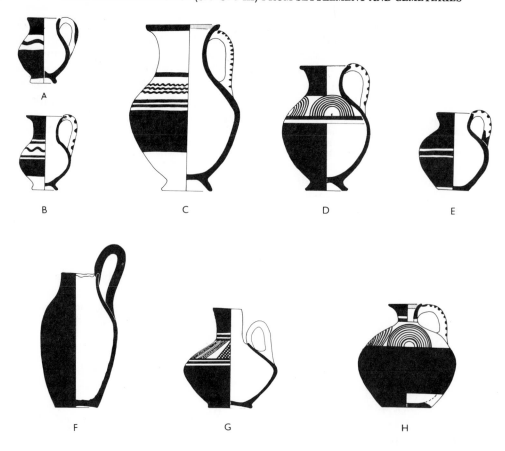

Fig. 16. (A) SM S 40,2 (B) EPG S 27,2 (C) MPG S 51,1 (D) LPG P 3,3 (E) SPG II T 5,4 (F) SPG II T 2,5 (G) LPG P 22,13
(H) SPG I P 39B,1 Scale 1:4

## THE ONE-HANDLED JUG. FIG. 16

This is a common shape in both cemetery and settlement, through in the latter case not always possible to distinguish from other small or medium sized closed vases. There are three main types: the traditional jug; the tall cylindrical jug; and the jug with cutaway neck. These I shall discuss in that order, and shall leave to the end three jugs which are unusual because of their shape or their size.

### The traditional jug

This type, which probably persisted throughout, has its origins in LH IIIC.[271] It is a small vase (some under 10, rarely over 15) with body developing from globular to ovoid, a low foot in the early stages, a fairly broad neck with gently outcurving lip, and a vertical handle from belly to lip or, exceptionally, to neck. Four stages are distinguishable, on the basis of shape of decoration or both.

The first stage (FIG. 16,A—B) includes the only jug assignable to an SM tomb, S 40,2 (FIG. 16, A). Its lip flares out far less than that of the other three, of EPG date, from the same group, but its globular body and wavy line on the shoulder link it, for one or both features, with these. All are predominantly monochrome, but the lower body and foot of S 4,2 (PLATE 92) and S 27,2 (FIG. 16, B) are unpainted.

During the second stage (FIG. 16, C) the body becomes distinctly more ovoid. The technique of leaving the lower body and foot unpainted is found on seven jugs; necks and lips are usually painted, but one neck is plain and another banded; and on five jugs the shoulder has a motive commonly encountered in EPG and MPG, a closely waved line best described as a scribble. There are ten altogether, covering EPG and MPG, with one survival into LPG, P Pyre 14B,3 (PLATE 153).

The jugs of the third stage (FIG. 16, D), still with ovoid body and low foot, have a different type of decoration on the shoulder, and new motives appear. The earliest, P 16,3 (PLATE 134) of MPG date, is unusual in being light ground; it has multiple triangles on the shoulder, and eight bands on the lower body; it also has a relatively high conical foot. The rest belong to LPG: their shoulder motives include semicircles, languettes, cross-hatched and hatched triangles, and vertical filled diamonds.[272]

Sofar, over twenty vases have been reviewed, from SM to the end of LPG. The development in shape is from the globular to the ovoid, in decoration from the simple to the rather more ornate — much as happens in other types of vase. And the one common feature to all is that they have a foot, nearly always low.

If this last feature is taken as a criterion, we have to add two further jugs, in SPG II contexts, T 4,1 (PLATE 170) and T 13,3 (PLATE 174), and I have tentatively attached them to the third group, although they are basically monochrome with reserved bands or areas.[273]

The low-footed traditional jug may well therefore have persisted through SPG I; but, apart from the two mentioned above, all known examples have a flat base, and these I have placed in the fourth stage (FIG. 16, E). There is one LPG precursor, the entirely monochrome T 12A,2 (PLATE 173), but the others fall within SPG I or SPG II. All that need be said about them is that those with decorated shoulders (semicircles, cross-hatched triangles), the earliest, tend to give way to those which are predominantly monochrome.[274]

These four groups or stages cover all the known traditional jugs of typical local fabric. It is important to realise, however, that there are fourteen others of probable local origin, the Black Slip and Red Slip jugs. These are discussed separately, but a summary is given here. One Black Slip jug and three Red Slip can be assigned to MPG: three Black Slip and two Red Slip to LPG; three Red Slip to SPG I; and one of each in an uncertain context, possibly LPG. So far as one can tell,[275] all, except two Red Slip jugs which have a baggy profile (one is MPG), have the shape of the traditional jug. Two of the three complete Black Slip jugs have low feet, one (from an LPG tomb) has a flat base; all the seven complete Red Slip jugs are flat-based. As compared with those discussed above, the stylistic range is restricted, but the links are very close, and it may have been these jugs which inspired the use of the flat base.

The evidence from the settlement is of little value. As will be seen from the relevant sections, there were rims of jugs which are most probably of the traditional type, but it would be difficult to prove from these even whether the type is likely to have continued into SPG III, for which continuation there is as yet no evidence in the cemeteries. As to decoration, it is the usual uncertainty as to whether a sherd is from a jug or some other small closed vase.

Outside Lefkandi, we find good evidence throughout its region for the popularity of the traditional jug; Coldstream makes it clear that the shape was characteristic of the whole area.[276] To the examples given may be added the jugs from two sites probably closely connected with the region at least in the PG period, Thebes[277] and Delphi.[278] All these are MPG or LPG in date, and all have the low foot; they provide further evidence for the ceramic uniformity of the region at this time.

Subsequent to LPG, evidence is very slight; the only published jugs are three from Halos in Thessaly, sharply biconical and not ovoid — one of them has a flat base; they should be dated to SPG I.[279] None has been recorded from the Kapakli tholos tomb, nor from Stavropoullos' tombs on Skyros, so they may in these districts have gone out of fashion at least as tomb offerings. The closest to the jugs current at Lefkandi are in fact two feeders from Vergina in Macedonia.[280]

## The tall cylindrical jug

This type is virtually restricted to Lefkandi, where it is found in both cemetery and settlement. The shape is distinctive: the base is flat, and from it the wall of the fairly slender body rises nearly vertically to the belly, thence returning inwards and upwards to an almost straight neck with very slightly outcurved lip; the handle, springing from the belly, follows the course of the neck and then, in the earlier examples, rises above the rim, curving over sharply to meet it; later it becomes lower.

From the cemeteries, the earliest are LPG, the three from P 22 (PLATE 138). Monochrome with reserved bands on the shoulder, two have an additional rough zigzag between bands; a feature of these is the grooves on the outer rim. Next, in SPG I, come two from P 13 (PLATE 132) and one from P 10 (PLATE 131): the former are the closer in shape to the earlier three. On all, the handle though rising above the lip has lost some of its pristine curvaceous flourish, and all are monochrome except for a single reserved band on the belly. Finally, there are three from SPG II groups, one each from T 2 (FIG. 15, F), T 13 (PLATE 174), and P 28 (PLATE 144). They are entirely monochrome; the last two are miniatures, and the handle of P 28,7 does not rise above the lip.

The evidence from the settlement does little more than show that this jug was in use. Area 3 South has the base and lower body of what surely must be one;[281] a small sherd from the SPG Pit may be part of the base of one,[282] and the same deposit contained six sherds of rims with grooves on the outer lip,[283] though this feature can apply equally to jugs with cutaway necks. The most substantial piece, lacking only the lip and handle, is recorded with the Late Geometric material;[284] assuming that the attribution is correct, we should conclude that the shape was also current in SPG III, a phase for which we have as yet nothing.

There is at present no reason for seeking the origin of the tall cylindrical jug outside Lefkandi.

## The jug with cutaway neck

Eight were found in the cemeteries, and they span a fairly short period, the latter part of LPG and SPG I.

Three are from P 22 (PLATE 138, and FIG. 16, G for P 22,13). The bodies range from globular to sharply biconical; all have a ring base, bands on the lower neck, a more or less elaborate set of rectilinear motives on the shoulder (note the alternating groups of diagonals set vertically on no. 13), and a monochrome lower body. Two from P 23 are most probably LPG. No. 8 (PLATE 140) has an angular biconical body, a flat base, and grooves on the top of the neck; it is monochrome except for multiple triangles on the shoulder. No. 1, the finest of the group, is unique for Lefkandi in having two cutaway necks joined by a basket handle; the rounded biconical body has a very low foot; the shoulder is fully ornamented with cross-hatched motives, and the lower body is monochrome but for four reserved bands; the necks have reserved bands, and are grooved close to the rim.

Two jugs, P 13,6 (PLATE 132) and P 18,6 (PLATE 135), are early in SPG I from their associated vases, and similar enough to be taken together. Both have a flat base, raised rope ridge at the base of the neck, grooves at the top of the neck, reserved bands on the belly, and are otherwise monochrome. T 15,5 (PLATE 176), finally, is small, biconical, flat-based and monochrome; the tomb group also belongs to SPG I.[285]

The settlement[286] is as unrewarding as for the tall cylindrical jug. The only satisfactory criterion in a context of sherds is the neck, and there is just one, from the Moulds Deposit (PLATE 14,78); it has grooves below the rim, and mention may again be made of the six grooved neck sherds from the SPG Pit, which will belong to one or other of the two types.

The origin of this type of jug is to be found in the hand-made vase so common in northern Greece, above all in Macedonia. It is unlikely, however, that the Lefkandians borrowed the shape from this region, for the hand-made tradition persisted over a long period.[287] It is more reasonable to suppose that the source was central northern Thessaly, in view of the material from Marmariani, where both hand-made and wheel-made jugs with cutaway necks are known.[288] From there the shape was adopted by the coastal Thessalians in LPG,[289] and thus entered the region in which Lefkandi is located. It has not so far been found south of Lefkandi in LPG or SPG I.[290]

Finally, chronological range and continuity. The jugs from the tombs are confined to LPG and SPG I, and there is nothing from the settlement to contradict this. On the other hand, there are jugs with cutaway neck from Late Geometric contexts at Lefkandi, and there are also examples from the other main Euboean sites, Eretria and Chalcis.[291] These, however, differ from the earlier ones in both shape and decoration; it seems unlikely that there was a stylistic development at Lefkandi during SPG II and SPG III leading up to the LG jugs, as opposed to an independent re-introduction.

### Miscellaneous

A brief mention may be made of four vases of unusual type which seem to qualify as jugs. Two, P 22,16 (PLATE 138) and P 39B,1 (FIG. 16, H), have only their relatively globular shape and semicircles on the shoulder in common. One is LPG, the other SPG I. The other two are outsize. Of P Pyre 41,3 (PLATE 156) only the neck and lip, and part of the handle, remain; the neck has an odd design of crossed diagonals; it is probably SPG I. The last, T 7,1 (PLATE 172) is 44 cm high, and would have been classed among the amphorae if it had had two handles. It has several unusual features, in structure the handle and the warts on the shoulder, in decoration the dogtooth motive on neck and handle-base, and the elaborate panels separating the sets of semicircles on the shoulder. From the associated cup, the date appears to be LPG. All except the fragmentary one may be added to the experimental pieces of LPG and early SPG I.

### List

*Traditional jug*
*I*
SM            S 40,2 (FIG. 16, A).
EPG          S 4,2; S 20,1; S 27,2 (FIG. 16, B).

*II*
| | |
|---|---|
| EPG | S 2,3; S 32,5. |
| EPG or MPG | S SF 1–3. |
| MPG | S 18,3; S 29,3; S 51,1 (FIG. 16, C); P 9,1. |
| LPG | P Pyre 14B,3. |

*III*
| | |
|---|---|
| MPG | P 16,3. |
| LPG | P 3,3 (FIG. 16, D); P 15,1; P 23,9; P 35,1; P Pyre 11,5 (fragment); P Pyre 32 (three shoulder fragments); T 12A,1; T 26,9. |
| (SPG II | T 4,1; T 13,3). |

*IV*
| | |
|---|---|
| LPG | T 12A,2. |
| SPG I | P 4,2; P 13,5; P 18,4; P 44,6–7; T 22,3. |
| SPG I or II | P 36,1,3–4; P 39A,1 (hand-made). |
| SPG II | P 28,1 and 8; T 5,4 (FIG. 16, E). |

*Black Slip and Red Slip*
| | |
|---|---|
| MPG | B.S.: P 16,2. R.S.: P 9,2–3; P 14,3. |
| LPG | B.S.: P 24,5; P Pyre 32 (sherd); T 26,10. R.S.: P 19,2; P 24,4. |
| SPG I | B.S.: none. R.S.: P 4,3; P 18,5; P 44,8 (fragmentary). |
| Uncertain, LPG? | B.S.: P Pyre 14A,1 (top half). R.S.: S Pyre 14,1. |

*Tall cylindrical jug*
| | |
|---|---|
| LPG | P 22,10–12. |
| SPG I | P 10,2; P 13,3–4. |
| SPG II | P 28,7; T 2,5 (FIG. 16, F); T 13,2. |

*Jug with cutaway neck*
| | |
|---|---|
| LPG | P 22,13 (FIG. 16, G), 14–15; P 23,1 and 8. |
| SPG I | P 13,6; P 18,6; T 15,5. |

*Miscellaneous*
| | |
|---|---|
| LPG | P 22,16; T 7,1. |
| SPG I | P 39B,1 (FIG. 16, H); P Pyre 41,3. |

## THE FEEDER

Eleven feeders were found in the tombs, and of these the four latest are Attic MG I imports and are discussed as such later. None was identified in a settlement context.

The earliest, S 44,1 (PLATE 105), is SM, as is clear from the heavy shape and the careless thick zigzags and bands. It is the only feeder to have a basket handle, thus revealing its Mycenaean ancestry, though differing from most Mycenaean feeders in having the spout set at 90° to the handle.[292] The closest relatively contemporaneous parallel is from Naxos,[293] in a group of EPG date.

The remaining six locally made feeders, including a hand-made one (P 39A, 1 – PLATE 146), range from EPG at least to SPG I. All have the spout at 90° to the handle. Five are adaptations of the traditional local jug,[294] and one (T 22,2 – PLATE 179) was similarly adapted for use as a feeder from the trefoil oinochoe. These six will also be found incorporated under their appropriate sections.

Comparable vases from elsewhere are found sporadically in the region[295] and around the Aegean.[296]

**List**

| | |
|---|---|
| SM | S 44,1. |
| EPG | S 2,3. |
| LPG | P 35,1 (spout lost). |
| LPG or SPG I | P 15,1. |
| SPG I | P 39A,1 (handmade); T 22,2. |
| SPG I or II | P 36,1. |
| SPG III | T 19,2; T 31,2; T 33,2–3. All Attic MG I. |

## THE PYXIS. FIG. 17

Several types of pyxis have been found at Lefkandi, but only one main one, and this will be discussed first, the evidence from the cemeteries taking precedence over that from the settlement.

### The globular pyxis

This type was in use from LPG to SPG III. There are fifty-three examples from the cemeteries,[297] found in twelve tombs and three pyres. Most of the contexts are fairly securely dated within the stylistic sequence on other grounds than the presence of the pyxides, and it is of particular interest that in four cases the local shape was associated with an Attic pyxis or pyxides, one LPG, one on the border between LPG and EG I, one late EG II, and one early MG I. The association is specially important for the first two, as they are themselves globular pyxides, and it may be said straight away that they provide the inspiration for the Lefkandian type;[298] the two later Attic ones are of an entirely different type, which the local potter hardly ever tried to imitate.

The fundamental features are: a globular body, with low foot, and with sharply everted rim pierced by suspension holes corresponding to two similar ones in the rim of a slightly sloping and knobbed lid; and an overall monochrome system of decoration, relieved by one or more reserved bands on or above the belly, which may often enclose a subsidiary motive. These are in principle the features of the Attic LPG pyxis, though it should be noted that the use of a subsidiary motive is an invariable practice in Athens; and that while the Attic potter kept strictly to his set rules for shape, and to the chosen limits of this decoration, the Lefkandian potter felt no need for such uniformity, especially in the shape,[299] as will be seen in the following analysis.

First the construction of the vase. The point of maximum diameter is sometimes, as normally in Athens, slightly above the centre of the body, but more often it is at the centre. The definition of globular, as applied to the body, has to be interpreted with a great deal of latitude; there is a tendency towards a flattened shape, certainly visible in SPG II and SPG III (T 19,4, FIG. 17, G), but the most pronounced example of which is the LPG pyxis P 23,12 (PLATE 140). In the great majority of cases the pyxis is given a low foot, but there are four examples of flat bases, all LPG or early in SPG I.[300] The rim is usually sharply everted (though seldom as much as the Attic ones), but there are several instances where it is hardly everted at all, or even comes up practically straight, as in the two examples from T Pyre 2 (PLATE 190), of LPG date, where the result was that the suspension holes had

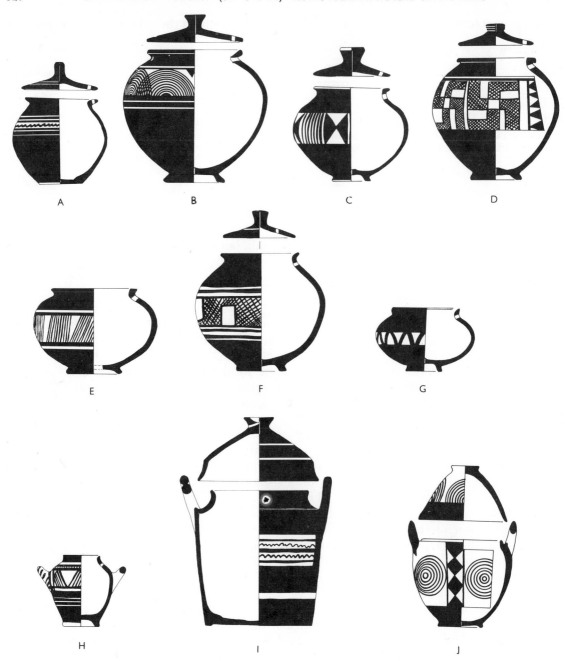

FIG. 17. (A) LPG P 22,22 (B) SPG I P 13,17 (C) SPG I T 23,7 (D) SPG I–II P 47,15 (E) SPG II P 21,7 (F) SPG III S 59A,5 (G) SPG III T 19,4 (H) SM S 19,4 (I) EPG S Pyre 1a,1 (J) SPG I P 39B,4. Scale 1:4

to be pierced below the rim. As to the lids, the angle of slope varies, the knob at the top is by no means always conical (as it is in Attica), and there are one or two cases where the lid does not fit plumb on to the rim of the pyxis. There are then numerous variations: they may occur at all stages, and are observable within individual tomb or pyre groups. It would be unsafe, in fact, to assign a pyxis to any phase from LPG to SPG III purely on its shape.

Second, the decoration. The monochrome system, with a single reserved area, is maintained throughout, with one exception, P 47,10 (PLATE 151), which is completely painted over. The analysis therefore centres on the positioning and make-up of the reserved zone. As to the positioning, this was often just above the belly, but it is equally possible to find it on the belly, and there are instances, mostly in the earlier pyxides, of its being on the shoulder. The make-up of the reserved area is a more complex matter. First, whereas in Attica it was the rule to include a subsidiary motive (zigzag, opposed filled diagonals, dogtooth) between bands, the Lefkandians felt free from the outset to disregard the subsidiary motive and to confine themselves to a reserved band or bands, and this persisted into SPG III.[301] Second, where a subsidiary motive was used, the local potters did not always provide supporting bands. They do not seem at the beginning to have gone beyond the limited Attic repertoire:[302] there is one instance of the use of the dogtooth, and several of the zigzag (though not of the neat Attic type); and these are confined with narrow zones. After the initial stages subsidiary motives become more varied (the zigzag persists to the end), break away from the Attic repertoire, and are enclosed in a wider zone. The most popular seem to be the sets of opposed diagonals with unfilled interstices,[303] and the verticals enclosing a butterfly motive,[304] but note a horizontal herringbone patter (P 12,1, PLATE 131), chevrons in a shoulder zone (P 47,16, PLATE 151), two battlements[305] (S 59 A,5, FIG. 17, F; and P 21,1, PLATE 136), and three pyxides with a panelled zone exhibiting a variety of motives (T 23,2 and 11, PLATE 180; P 47,15, FIG. 17, D), reminiscent of the earlier experimental ideas.[306] To sum up, there is some change in SPG, but new developments did not oust the old.

So we have a pyxis based on an Attic model, probably adopted late in LPG, thereafter current till the beginning of SPG III, showing no regular development in shape, but to some extent in decoration – and it is one of the very few types of vase to display a variety of subsidiary motives in SPG. It was commonly deposited with the dead, and several could accompany a single burial;[307] in this it may be compared to the kalathos, but the two shapes were not mutually exclusive (see P 22 and S 59 + 59A), and it cannot have been a criterion for the sex of the dead person if the kalathos, used in more tombs, signifies a female burial, as it is found in the warrior burial P 47.

The evidence from the settlement is as disappointing as for other fairly small closed vases. The best source is the SPG Pit, which contained the only example of a restorable globular pyxis, two sherds with everted rims, three lid knobs and two lid rim fragments.[308] Area 3 South has two sherds, which might belong to a large globular pyxis; the Levelling Material has a lid rim fragment; and among the miscellaneous a belly sherd with a swastika could well be from a pyxis.[309] Very little is added to our knowledge.

There is a certain amount of comparative material. Within the region, none has yet been found in the North Cyclades; in Euboea, there were four in a group from Theologos, a hill village to the Norther of Eretria;[310] two were among the offerings in Stavropoullos' tombs on Skyros;[311] and from Thessaly there is one from Marmariani, very close to P 47,15 both in shape and in the main decorative motive, the cross-hatched swastika,[312] All these can be dated (mostly by reference to the Lefkandian material) to SPG I or SPG II.

The globular pyxis was also used in other parts of the Greek world. Those from Athens excepted (see above), there is one example from Kos, no fewer than nine from Crete (five with flat bases), and two sites apiece in the Argolid and Corinthia have each produced one pyxis.[313] Though the majority simply have reserved bands, there are three instances of zigzags (two from Crete, one from Tiryns), one of vertical chevrons (Knossos), and one of a windmill design (Arkhanes). In the light of the Lefkandian series it would be rash to suggest any precise date for those whose context is uncertain.[314]

## Other pyxides

### Submycenaean

S 19,4 (FIG. 17, H). No lid found, though there are two string holes at the base of the neck. No parallel known for the shape. For the decoration, the horizontal row of dots is an unusual feature, but not unknown in SM.[315]

### Early Protogeometric

S Pyre 1A,1 (FIG. 17, I). A wide-based straight-sided pyxis, with loop handles rising vertically from the body to above the height of the rim, this sharply incurved to receive the conical knobbed lid.[316] The reserved scribbles are typical of the period. The inspiration for the shape (not the lid, nor the decoration) comes either from Crete,[317] or perhaps from Cyprus, to which this Cretan shape made its way.[318]

### Late Protogeometric

P Pyre 11,11 (PLATE 152). A sherd only, showing an incurving painted rim continuing from a convex body ornamented with semicircles or — conceivably — circles. The profile as we have it is not unsimilar to that of P 13,20 (see below).

### Sub-Protogeometric I[319]

P 13,20 (PLATE 133). Globular body, incurved rim, vertically pierced suspension lugs, conical foot, rectilinear panels on upper body. Shape similar to that of Argive pyxides which first appear in EG.[320] One motive, the lambda ornament, is considered by Coldstream as native to the Argolid,[321] but the panelled complex is not a feature of Argive pyxides, whereas there are other instances of it both at Lefkandi and in Thessaly.[322]

P 39B,4 (FIG. 17, J). Deep truncated oval body, handles rising above rim, rim very low, just sufficiently incurved to allow the curious bowl-shaped lid to fit on to it. Semicircles on lid, circles flanking vertical diamond chain on body. No comparable vase known.

### Sub-Protogeometric III

S 59,6 (PLATE 108). The body curves in almost to a point at the base, flat rim with string holes for the lid. The horizontal row of dots below the rim is an odd echo of S 19,4; the the rest of the body is banded. Nothing comparable, so far as I know.

### Settlement

Area 3 South, 530–1 (PLATE 23). Sherds of a very large straight-sided pyxis with vertical loop handles. Cross-hatched ?meander the main motive. The shape may have been similar to that of an Attic LPG pyxis.[323] SPG.

Miscellaneous, 773 (PLATE 26). Rim of a local atticising MG pyxis.[324] SPG III.

Miscellaneous, 809 (PLATE 27). Sherd of a straight-sided pyxis, monochrome, reserved bands. No comparable piece known. SPG?

**List**

*Globular*
LPG        P 22,22 (FIG. 17, A); P 23,12; T Pyre 2,5,6, and 7 (lid only).
SPG I      P 13,17 (FIG. 17, B), 18–19; P 39,2; P Pyre 44,4; T 23,2–13 (no. 7, FIG. 17, C); T 23A,3.
SPG I–II   P 47,10–16 (no. 15, FIG. 17, D).
SPG I or II  P 12,1–3; P Pyre 34,2–5. Note SPG Pit, 69/P 44.
SPG II     S 33, 8–12; P 21,1,3–9 (no. 7, FIG. 17, E).
SPG III    S 59,5; S 59A,5 (FIG. 17, F); T 19,4 (FIG. 17, G).

*Other*
SM         S 19,4 (FIG. 17, H).
EPG        S Pyre 1A,1 (FIG. 17, I)
LPG        P Pyre 11,11.
SPG I      P 39,3 (disintegrated, hand-made); P 39B,4 (FIG. 17, J).
SPG III    S 59,6.
A few sherds from the settlement.

*Attic imports*
LPG        P 22,20–1; T Pyre 2,4.
SPG II     P 21,2.
SPG III    S 59,4.
Also Attic MG sherds in the settlement and in the cemetery deposits.

## THE LENTOID FLASK

There are four of these, one from an EPG group, the other three in contexts probably assignable to LPG; all are from the cemeteries.

The EPG flask, S Pyre 1A,2 (PLATE 92), is fragmentary: neck and mouth have been lost, there is evidence for one handle only (also missing), and what remains of the body is fairly flat. The body decoration of encircling bands is relieved by three bands of rough zigzag, typical of Lefkandian EPG. It is possible, but not provable, that the vase represents the survival of a Mycenaean shape.[325] If, on the other hand, it was an innovation, one should look either to Crete[326] or to Cyprus[327] (the more likely) as the source.

Of the three LPG flasks, P 3,8 (PLATE 126), the only one with a flattened base, and P 31,6 (PLATE 145) have a single handle, short neck, and trefoil lip; P 3,9 (PLATE 126) has two handles joining the neck beneath a trumpet mouth. All are more globular than the EPG flask. P 31,6, with central nipples, has an unusual decoration of three sets of semicircles on each side of the body, while the other two have the conventional circular bands, except for a rough zigzag round the outer rim of P 3,9.[328]

It is tempting to suggest a Cypriot derivation again, especially in view of the Cypriot import from the nearly contemporaneous P 22, and the clear derivation from Cyprus of P 3,16. This could be true of P 3,9, close to Cypriot models in shape and decoration;[329] the trefoil lip of the two others, and the flattened base of one of them, however, are features not found in Cyprus at this time, but are paralleled in Athens.[330]

Elsewhere in the region only one has been recorded, from Stavropoullos' tombs on Skyros; it differs from the Lefkandian vases in combining a single handle with a trumpet mouth.[331]

Mention may finally be made of four from outside the region; two from Ialysos,[332] one from Mycenae,[333] and one from the Agrinion area.[334] All could belong to about the same period as the later trio from Lefkandi; but if there were any interconnexions, they remain obscure.

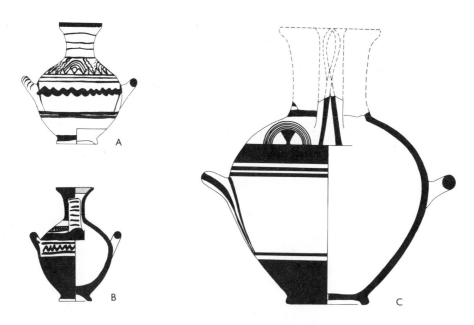

FIG. 18. (A) SM S 19,7 (B) EPG S 31,1 (C) SPG I T 15,1. Scale 1:4.

## THE HYDRIA. FIG. 18

There are only eight local hydriai, seven small and one large, and all were found in, or originally came from, tombs.[335] The shape was handed down from LH IIIC, the two main features transmitted being the light ground system of decoration, and the attachment of the top of the vertical handle to the lip.[336]

### A. The small hydria

None has a height of more than 17 cm. The two earliest, from S 15B (PLATE 95) and S 19 (FIG. 18, A), have the two features mentioned above, and are Submycenaean; both have a fairly globular body, and decoration of SM character.[337] S SF 7 (PLATE 111), of similar shape to these, has a more sharply moulded foot, and the lower body is monochrome; it is still SM in style (note the hand-drawn semicircles), as also is the hydria from S 16, very like a belly-handled amphoriskos in shape, and entirely monochrome except for a double wavy line on the belly. On both, the handle is attached to the lip.

S 31 (FIG. 18, B) is certainly EPG, and probably not far from MPG. It has an ovoid body, a relatively slender neck, a low conical foot, and now for the first time the vertical handle is attached to the neck and not to the lip. The decoration is dark ground, with zigzags on belly and shoulder.[338]

A further, but short-lived, development characterises the hydria from one of the later MPG tomb groups, P 14 (PLATE 134) — the reappearance of the light ground system of decoration.[339] Its ovoid body is relieved by bands on the belly and languettes on the shoulder.

Finally, there is the miniature P 10,18 (PLATE 130), ovoid, with monochrome lower body and cross-hatched triangles on the shoulder. It comes from an SPG I context. We have thus no knowledge at present of any hydria of LPG date.

## B. The large hydria

The fragmentary T 15,1 (FIG. 18, C) is the only example; its original height must have been about 30 cm. It conforms very closely to the Attic LPG type of belly-handled amphora in its broad body and semicircles on the shoulder, but it lacks the wavy lines on the belly. The date, both from the stratigraphy and the associated vases, is SPG I.

The known Lefkandian range extends, then, from SM to SPG I, with a gap for LPG; so far, no hydria later than SPG I has been found, nor has the shape been recorded in any Late Geometric context. Comparative material from other sites is scarce. For SM there is only a mention of three hydriai from Athens.[340] None can certainly be ascribed to most of EPG, but the latter part of EPG, MPG, and early(?) LPG have produced interesting parallels from the region or close to it. The hydria from a tomb at Delphi is close in shape to S 31,1, and some of its associated vases are very like Lefkandian late EPG and MPG ones;[341] one of a rather different shape (closer to a jug) was found in an MPG tomb at Iolkos;[342] and one of Dawkins' tombs on Skyros, perhaps early LPG from its associated jugs, has produced a hydria which resembles P 14,1 in shape, except for the higher neck and lip, and is very close indeed in its decoration.[343] These three vases are small, and illustrate the uniformity of the regional style. From other areas there is practically nothing.[344]

Most later hydriai (LPG, EG, MG), such as there are, are of the larger variety, but it is noteworthy that five of the small ones have been found in LPG tombs on Kos.[345] For the rest, examples are few and far between except in Crete.[346]

Mention may finally be made of a small hydria from Chalcis. It is very difficult to date, but in spite of the high conical foot, the slender body and the decoration on the neck may suggest that it is not earlier than SPG III, and if this is so, it would be evidence for the continued use of the hydria in Euboea much later than at Lefkandi.[347]

**List**

SM     S 19,7 (FIG. 18, A); S 15B,1; S 16,11; S SF 7.
EPG   S 31,1 (FIG. 18, B).
MPG  P 14,1.
LPG   —
SPG I  P 10,18; T 15,1 (FIG. 18, C).
Import S 51,2 (MPG).

FIG. 19. (A) SM S 43,2 (B) LPG T 18,1 (C) SPGI—II P 47,1 (D) SPG III S 59A,1. Scale 1:4

## THE AMPHORA.[348] FIG. 19.

### A. Early amphorae

In this section I discuss the amphorae which precede LPG, irrespective of type or size; they are few, and resist classification.

There are three neck-handled amphorae. Two are small, under 14 cm, and from tombs of SM date, S 3,1 (PLATE 92) and S 43,2 (FIG. 19, A). The third, the fragmentary S 38,15 (PLATE 282B), whose original height was about 40 cm, was found in the upper shaft of an SM tomb. S 43,2 and S 38,15 are similar in shape, thick neck and globular body (probably for the latter), and in decoration, dark ground below the shoulder, vertical wiggly lines on the shoulder. S 3,1 has a rather more ovoid body, is light ground, and has a wavy line on the shoulder. All fit comfortably into their SM context.[349]

The other two vases are in principle belly-handled amphorae, but each has an additional pair of vertical handles, in the one case on the shoulder, in the other from shoulder to neck.[350] Very nearly the complete profile of the amphora from P Channel, lower fill (PLATE 282F, ht. 50 + cm) was able to be assembled. Note the short thick neck, the heavy globular body, the dot-fringed hand-drawn semicircles on the shoulder, and the two scribble zigzags below. The style is SM.[351]

The fragmentary nature of S Pyre 3,1 (PLATE 282A and PLATE 112 for a reconstruction, ht. c. 67 cm) makes stylistic assessment difficult. The relatively oval body would suit PG better, and so might the horizontal scribbles flanking the triple wavy line on the belly; on the other hand, the dot-fringed hand-drawn semicircles (both standing and pendent) belong to the SM style.[352] It could be, as for certain lekythoi an SM survival into the EPG period.

To these five vases may be added one sherd, with fringed hand-drawn semicircles, from the surface of the Toumba cemetery.[353] The group as a whole is valuable as giving some idea of the early stages, but is insufficient to provide any clear link with the later amphorae.

### B. Late Protogeometric

I confine myself to amphorae which can with certainty or great probability be ascribed to LPG, from their context or by clear external parallels. Some were found in tombs and pyres, others from the three deposits considered to be probably not later than LPG, i.e. the Moulds Deposit, Area 3 South, under floor of yard and P Channel, lower fill.

P Channel, lower fill produced the fragmentary top half of a neck-handled amphora (PLATE 282C), probably at least 60 cm high originally. The lip is the usual one for amphorae of this type, and the neck is relatively short and thick, with a rope ridge at the base (as has the four-handled vase from this deposit); the angle of the shoulder suggests that the body may have been fairly globular. The main decorative feature is the compass-drawn 'empty' circles (eleven arcs) on the shoulder. The shape may suggest a relatively early date, which might help to fill the gap after the first group, but the circles would fit better into LPG.[354]

The tombs and pyres provide evidence mainly for neck-handled amphorae. For these, the basic elements are an everted and rounded lip, a high neck, an ovoid body and a ring base; the handles rise vertically from the shoulder and curve over elegantly to join the neck just below the lip.

The two small amphorae are dark ground. P 23,4 (PLATE 141) has semicircles with two supporting bands, P 24,1 (PLATE 142) is monochrome except for a reserved band on the belly. There are three medium-sized neck-handled amphorae, T 14,2 (PLATE 175), T 18,1

(FIG. 19, B) and P Pyre 11,1 (PLATE 152, top half only preserved). They tend to be light ground, but the belly area of T 14,2 is dark ground with reserved bands. All have sets of semicircles on the shoulder.

The two locally made[355] belly-handled amphorae are both from T Pyre 2,[356] and are not illustrated. No. 2, of which the lower part only was found, is of medium size, dark ground with reserved bands on the belly. No. 1 is extremely large and very fragmentary, but the decorative scheme is similar to that of P Pyre 41,1 (PLATE 156), with two tiers of semi-circles on the shoulder and circles on the belly, all 'empty', as though left free for a central filling.[357] It is the earliest known example at Lefkandi of a type that was still current in SPG II.

The two settlement deposits of the Moulds and Area 3 South under yard floor, and the material from the lower fill of P Channel may be taken together.[358] The evidence is from fragments only, and belongs to medium or large amphorae;[359] no complete profile was recovered. Few inferences can be made on the basis of shape, except that neck handles are more common than belly handles, and that the kind of lip associated with the neck-handled type is also more common.

The main decorative features are as follows. The system of decoration for the body was overwhelmingly light ground, with occasional encircling bands; necks were either mono-chrome or unpainted;[360] rims were monochrome;[361] belly handles were usually painted on the outside, but neck handles revealed a variety of motives — bars, intersecting diagonals between bars, intersecting or parallel verticals, and one example of a herringbone pattern.[362] The chief shoulder motive is sets of semicircles, with occasional central filling (standing or pendent triangles, hourglass), and there are several instances of languettes; the usual motive for the belly, probably confined to belly-handled amphorae, is circles, also occasionally with central filling. Less usual ornaments include two sherds (65, 85) with dogtooth on the neck, a double horizontal scribble on the shoulder (63), the 'branch' motive (993),[363] a panelled design (994), and a remarkable 'close' decoration (651) in two zones — filled zigzag and cheque board in panels supported by a zone of diagonals.

The material from these deposits confirms, and adds to, the picture we have from the tombs and pyres. Whatever the situation may have been earlier, there is sufficient from this period to illustrate the influence of the contemporaneous Attic style in both shape and decoration.

## C. Sub-Protogeometric[364]

### 1. *Neck-handled amphorae, light ground body*

*Small* None.

*Medium*. None from tombs or pyres.
The settlement. This is the most common type both in the SPG Pit (SPG I–II) and in the Levelling Material (SPG II–III), but is less well represented than the dark ground in the SL Area (SPG II–III).[365] Shape not fully recoverable due to the fragmentary nature of the material, but note that some lips are grooved. Decoration: lips usually monochrome, but may have bars on the outside; necks perhaps normally unpainted, but statistics suggest that some were monochrome; handles as for LPG, but more examples of the herringbone motive; shoulder, semicircles with or without central filling, occasional languettes,[366] and one or two instances of rectilinear motives of uncertain type; belly, probably left undecorated.

The conclusions are that the system and detail of decoration remained substantially as in LPG, that this type of amphora continued to be used into SPG III, and was still apparently the most popular except in the SL Area (which may perhaps be explained by the selective nature of the pottery types found in the groups belonging to it).[367] SPG innovations may be recognised in the grooving or alternatively the vertical bars on the outer lip, and perhaps also the herringbone motive on the handles (see n. 362). No contemporaneous outside influence demonstrable, and no comparative material.

*Large.* None from tombs and none identifiable from the settlement. *No finial,*

Pyres: P Pyre 28,5 (not illustrated); P Pyre 41,2 (PLATE 156); P Pyre 44,2 (not illustrated); P Surface (PLATE 281C — in the same area as the pyres mentioned).

In no case were the lip and base recovered; in only one instance the neck, light ground, and one of the handles, with crossing verticals. Body ovoid, band or bands at base of neck, below shoulder and belly, and on lower body; sets of full circles on shoulder; in three cases the handle decoration is continued on to the body in two diverging sweeping curves.          *Finials*

P Pyre 28,5 could be LPG:[368] those from P Pyres 41 and 44 are certainly or probably SPG I;[369] the specimen from the surface has no context, but its closeness to the other three suggests a similar chronological range.

This is a small and homogeneous group; whether there are any other varieties of large light ground neck-handled amphorae is uncertain (see below). Both for shape and decoration, the source is traceable to Attic PG.[370] The closest comparable vases are, however, two from Kapakli,[371] in other words in the region of which Lefkandi formed a unit.

## 2. Neck-handled amphorae, dark ground

(a) *LPG survivals.* No large ones.

*Small.* S 5,2 (PLATE 93). Dumpy ovoid body, series of reserved bands. Probably SPG I, but no obvious parallel. Nothing identifiable in settlement.

*Medium.* P 4,1 (PLATE 128). Ovoid body, monochrome from below shoulder, careless splash on shoulder, bands on neck. SPG I. Probably some in settlement, see e.g. PLATE 22, E (Trial W) and PLATE 27, 782, 784–5 (various areas), all with semicircles on the shoulder — but could they be LPG?

(b) *SPG type.* These have a high slender neck and a slim tapering body (less so in SPG I), with a tendency in the later stages towards a high and sharply angled shoulder; lips are occasionally grooved. No large ones.

*Small.* P 28,6 (PLATE 144 — miniature). T 4,2 (PLATE 170); T 28,1 (PLATE 184). Nothing identifiable in settlement.

*Medium.* S 33,4–6 (PLATE 101); S 59A,1 (FIG. 19, D); P 47,1 (FIG. 19, C); T Pyre 4,4 (PLATE 191). A few from cemetery surface deposits, e.g. PLATES 274, 913–7; 275, 932. From the settlement the most noteworthy is the almost complete 70/P2 (PLATES 28 and 35) from SL, from which area there are several others (e.g. PLATE 29). The type is also well represented in the SPG Pit and in the Levelling Material.[372]

The shape has been described above. For decoration, the small amphorae are monochrome with reserved bands on the body, T 4,2 having a zigzag on the belly as well. The medium amphorae, also monochrome, have a zigzag or opposed diagonals with unfilled interstices on the belly, except for T Pyre 4,4, which has reserved bands only. The shoulder is normally monochrome, but S 33,4 and a sherd from SL (see PLATE 29) have semicircles. The neck may be monochrome, or have a design of an hourglass in a panel: from the tombs only S 59A,1 has the hourglass, but the many examples found in the settlement show how much more common this motive is than would be suspected on the cemetery evidence. It is also clear from the settlement that for the belly opposed diagonals were more frequently used than the zigzag; either the zigzag may have been confined to relatively small amphorae (but see n. 375), or the opposed diagonals may have been a later development.

These amphorae, so far as is ascertainable, all fall within SPG. All three phases are represented in the tombs; in the settlement the type was in use during SPG II and surely during at least part of SPG III, but whether any of the sherds should be assigned to SPG I is uncertain.

The development of the type could be a purely local affair. The predominantly dark ground system is a feature of early SPG for many closed shapes, and in the case of amphorae it is already foreshadowed in LPG, in P 24,1. The slimmer profile, and the restriction of subsidiary motives, with rare exceptions, to the belly and the neck, are indeed features to be observed in the Attic EG series, and the Lefkandians may have either consciously or unconsciously imitated these, especially if it could be shown that such imitation took place in SPG II, as that was when links with Attica reappeared. But the Attic vases lack the sharply angled shoulders occasionally found, and (more important) the hourglass panel on the neck and the opposed diagonals with unfilled interstices.

Comparative material comes from the region: two from Kapakli,[373] one from Marmariani[374] of similar shape but quite different decoration, and one from Tenos.[375]

### 3. Belly-handled amphorae

*Small.* None.

*Medium.* S 56,1 (PLATE 107). Sharply everted flat lip, high neck with ridge half way down, broad ovoid body, ring base; dark ground except for bars on top of rim, semicircles on shoulder, and unpainted belly zone. SPG I.

Settlement unhelpful on the whole, but note instances of bars on the rim top, and a ridge below the lip, both so far missing from the local LPG. It is reasonable to suppose that the shoulder often had semicircles, and the belly circles. Which of the very occasional rectilinear motives belong to belly-handled amphorae is quite uncertain. No doubt the LPG type survived with little modification.

*Large.* Divisible into two categories, of which (a) is a homogeneous class of its own.

(a) S Pyre 4,3a–b (PLATE 281B); S Pyre 14,2; S Pyre 15,4; P Pyre 15,1;[376] P Pyre 36,1; P Pyre 41,1 (PLATES 156 and 282E); P Pyre 44,1; T Pyre 4,2 (PLATE 191) and 3; T Pyre 7; Pyre 8,2; T Surface. Other possible instances from pyres were too fragmentary for certainty; and there were a few sherds, probably originally from pyre amphorae, from other contexts.[377]

From the settlement there was just a handful of sherds with circles on the belly that could belong to this class.[378]

These amphorae, as will be evident, were commonly deposited in pyres. In no instance was there a complete pot, nor even a complete profile, as no lip was able to be associated with any of the restored vases.[379] Below the mouth, the shape is very much the same as for the LPG amphora T Pyre 2,1, a fairly high neck, a broad ovoid body, and a ring base; the belly handles are either single or double-loop, and P Pyre 41,1 has two additional vertical handles on the shoulder. For the decoration, the neck, where recovered, is monochrome, except for S Pyre 4,3a (and 3b if it belongs to this type) which has a reserved zone of rays; the body is light ground, and has the customary encircling bands, sometimes very thick; the belly zone has two sets of circles, filled or unfilled; the shoulder has semicircles, filled or unfilled, and the usual practice is for there to be two tiers, due to the size of the amphora — there are five clear instances of this, and only one of a single tier (T Pyre 4,3); for the rest one cannot be sure. In general, the shape and decoration are such as first appeared in LPG.

These amphorae cannot always be attributed to any particular phase of SPG, but most of the main pieces cannot be later than SPG I.[380] It is certain, however, that they were still current in SPG II, for S Pyre 4,3 was associated with an Attic EG II cup.[381]

(b) T Pyre 4,1 (PLATES 191 and 282D); S 5,1 (PLATE 93). Both highly individual.

T Pyre 4,1 has a high flaring neck and mouth.[382] The body is of similar profile to those of category (a), and the shoulder decoration, semicircles, is the same; the belly, however, has semicircles instead of circles, and there are several other unusual motives (see p. 194 and the illustration). Among these latter are a 'branch' pattern and a triple scribble; if these are valid criteria for dating, the vase could have been made in LPG[383] — but this need not apply to the other amphorae from the pyre.

S 5,1 (only the lower half recovered) was used as a cremation amphora. The most notable feature is the fairly high conical base, not paralleled elsewhere on amphorae. The decoration is dark ground below the belly, with three zones of reserved bands; the belly itself has an elaborate pattern of rectilinear motives. On the basis of the use to which it was put, and of the conical foot, I would put this amphora early in SPG I (PLATE 167e).

*4. Neck- or belly-handled amphorae*

This is a small but noteworthy class, whose two main characteristics are massiveness and the use of rectilinear squares, often cross-hatched panels alternating with unpainted ones in a chequerboard pattern. The meander is also probably represented. The material is known from sherds only, infrequent in the settlement deposits, more prominent in the cemetery surface and fill material.[384] Some belong to larger amphorae than any yet discussed: note the strengthening ridges not only below the lip but even on the body, where the vase may have had to be built up in separate sections.[385] They seem to be assignable to SPG.

It will be evident, in conclusion, that Lefkandi is of the greatest importance for the study of amphorae during these centuries, and that there is much more yet to be learnt about them from the site itself.

## THE KRATER

No kraters were placed in tombs or pyres, and the main evidence therefore comes from the settlement, not established before LPG.[386]

The settlement material is reasonable in quantity, but suffers from being fragmentary (the nearest to a complete profile is PLATE 28, 70/P1, from the SL Area), and the specifically, or at least predominantly LPG groups have little to offer.[387] It is not yet possible to discern any clear stylistic progress on the basis of shape, and the system of decoration varies little; it will be simplest to give a straightforward description, noting such chronological pointers as may seem valid.

The lip usually projects horizontally from the body, square or rounded at the outer edge, with a flat upper surface; it may however have a distinct outward and downward slope. Beneath the lip, usually depending on the size of the vase, there may be one or more strengthening ridges, which are occasionally of the rope type or some variant of this. The body comes down more or less straight, then curves inwards gradually to the foot. The foot may be high conical, or of the flaring pedestal variety, but such evidence as we have suggests that a heavy ring base was the most common. There are two handles of the loop type, attached horizontally to the upper part of the body above the belly; there is no known example of a vertically placed handle.

In the matter of decoration, it may first be noted that the flat upper lip surface is either unpainted (very rare), or painted over, or decorated with groups of bars or solid triangles.[388] Apart from this, the system is that the inside of the vase (though there may be a reserved band below the lip), the outer lip and usually an area beneath it, the lower body and foot are monochrome, and only the upper part of the body between the handles is left free for decoration.[389]

The main decorative design is almost invariably, as far as one can tell, symmetrical. The most favoured appears to be two sets of circles flanking a central rectilinear panel;[390] a less common variation is three sets of circles separated by vertical lines;[391] or the circles may form the central feature.[392] There may also be a succession of rectilinear panels, with no contrasting set or sets of circles.[393] Alternatively, there are instances of a single motive repeated horizontally across the whole area between the handles, for example alternating diagonals with unfilled interstices,[394] or (only one example) alternating upright and pendent semicircles.[395] All these are circular or rectilinear designs, most probably symmetrically arranged: there is just one exception, the sherd which portrays part of a ship.[396]

As to the individual motives, the circles need little comment: they often have central fillings such as reserved cross, Maltese cross, wheel-spoke (unusual[397]), and there were a few instances of dot-fringes.[398] For the rest, there are diamonds and triangles, hatched, cross-hatched or solid; cross-hatched rectangles, chequers, and vertical zigzags: all these are familiar from other shapes, and from the evidence of the Area 2 deposits it seems likely that they continued in use from LPG into SPG III. Among the less common motives there is the battlement,[399] the *lambda* ornament,[400] and a curious sort of step meander,[401] not earlier than SPG.[402]

The origin of the krater goes back to Mycenanean times, but lack of evidence prevents us from being able to trace any continuity between the latest Mycenaean on Xeropolis and the material of the later settlement from LPG onwards.

More rewarding is the study of the relationship between Lefkandi and other contemporaneous sites. The closest links are to be found in Thessaly, in the well-known series of kraters from Marmariani and Kapakli;[403] the principles of shape (to judge from 70/P1) and decoration are very much the same, but at Lefkandi the motives are more varied. No doubt other sites in the region will produce similar material, but so far there is only one krater, from Skyros.[404]

Outside the region the evidence is very patchy. Our fullest knowledge comes from Knossos,[405] but here and on other sites in Crete the normal shape is the deep bell-krater. There is an interesting group of sherds from Aetos[406] in Ithaca, but no complete profile;

and even in Attica the material is scarce, and for the most part fragmentary.[407] There is nothing to suggest that the shape of the krater at Lefkandi, from what we know of it, owed anything (except perhaps the very high foot) to outside influence. Many of the decorative motives and ways of combining them, on the other hand, can be paralleled on kraters or other types of vase from a number of sites over a wide area, suggesting frequent intercommunication and, in certain instances, the widespread influence of Attic LPG.[408]

## THE PLATE

This is a rare, but very distinctive, shape. It is very shallow, and has a diameter of c. 15–18 cm. The lip is either slightly offset and separated by carination from the body, or incurved. In the one known example of a handle it is of the double-loop type, and below the lip — evidence from elsewhere shows that there were almost always two such handles; it can also be assumed from comparative material that the foot was normally base-ring. The only decoration known is sets of semicircles pendent from the lip.

Sherds have been found in small numbers in the settlement and in the cemetery fills, but none in tomb or pyre.[409] The quantity from the Levelling Material of Area 2, and the lack of any fragment from the SPG Pit from the same Area (see n. 409) or from any early context suggests that the shape was probably not introduced until some time during SPG III.

This would agree well with the only datable specimens outside Lefkandi, the ten from the 'Royal' tomb 1 at Salamis in Cyprus, which can be assigned to the second quarter of the eighth century, or towards the end of MG II.[410] Since the fabric of these indicates that they came, if not from Euboea, perhaps from the North Cyclades,[411] there is a distinct possibility that the plate as a shape was invented in the region to which Lefkandi belonged.[412]

## MISCELLANEOUS

1. *Alabastron*. S 43,1 (PLATE 104). SM. A very squat globular body with three strut legs, the lower parts cut off, and three ribbon handles on the shoulder; rim and handles barred, sets of chevrons between handles, Looks back to the Mycenaean tradition.[413]

2. *Bottle*. S 20,2 (PLATE 99). EPG. Broad body and foot, almost flat shoulder, trumpet neck and mouth. Hand-drawn semicircles on shoulder, sets of bands on body, barred handles. An SM vase from Athens[414] is reasonably close, but here the context is EPG.

3. *Shallow hemispherical bowls*. S 2,4 (PLATE 92); S 23,1 (PLATE 99). Alike in shape, their function may have been different, as S 2,4 has two string holes. This one is EPG from its context, but the other is the only vase in its tomb, and it would be unsafe to conclude that it must belong to the same period.[415]

4. *Shallow bowl with long tapering spout*. P 3,16 (PLATES 127, 262). LPG. Interior monochrome; flame pattern on outer body and along underspout; chevrons for centre underspout and beneath handle; reserved cross for underbase. The shape, unknown elsewhere in Greece and the Aegean, must have come from Cyprus, where it appeared in Cypro-Protogeometric and continued throughout Cypro-Geometric.[416] The long spout is not known in Cyprus (though when seen in profile it is uncommonly like the Cypriot shaft handles), and there is nothing there quite like the trigger handle.

5. *Miniature plates.* P 10,19–20 (PLATE 131). SPG I. Three handles on the rim, in the manner of the pedestal bowls S 2,1 and 5 (PLATE 92). The closest parallels are from Athens and Marmariani: though not miniatures, they have much the same shape.[417]

6. *Mug.* T 23A,1 (PLATE 181). SPG I. The monochrome rounded body with flat base is too deep for a cup; the high slightly outcurving lip has a double zigzag. One of an odd-looking group. No parallel known.

## HAND-MADE WARES

Hand-made ware was found both in the settlement and in the cemeteries. Most of it was of coarse fabric, the dominating shape being the cooking pot; this I leave to the end, and shall first mention or discuss other groups.

First, there are four vases of the ordinary local fabric, which imitate current wheel-made shapes. These are the multiple vase S 38,2, the miniature shallow bowl with strap handles P 28,11,[418] the feeder P 39A,1 and the miniature trefoil oinochoe T 33,5, which imitates the Attic MG import of the time. These are mentioned in the relevant sectional analyses on shapes.

Next, there are five vases which also imitate wheel-made shapes, but whose fabric differs from that of the normal Lefkandian: it is grey, verging on yellow or brown, in one instance purplish when unbaked, and the surface is black or black-grey and burnished. They are the miniature flat-based jug with cutaway neck P 3,7, the three small trefoil oinochoai P 4,4 and T 2,6–7, (PLATE 269b),[419] and the fragmentary and crumbling pyxis P 39,3. These, with the exception of P 3,7, are also referred to in the shape analyses.

Then we come to the vases which do not imitate the wheel-made. Two of these are of well-prepared clay, or relatively so.

*Fragmentary shallow bowl* P 39B,16. Red clay with grits, red burnished. No parallel known.

*Globular bowl* T 1,2, Fine red clay, lustrous black burnish.[420] Handleless; flat base. string holes; incised swastikas. A similar vase has been found on Naxos.[421]

The rest are of a coarse red gritty fabric similar to that of the cooking pots. Clay analysis indicates that the fabric is not local.

*Shallow bowl, oval-shaped* S 56,4 (PLATE 269c). One string hole below rim. No parallel known.

*Large bowl* with ledge rim D. 42; flat base; coarse fabric with red burnished slip, PLATE 42 no. 51 mistakenly included with LG. No parallel known.

*Mug* S SF 13. Deep, with slightly outcurved lip and flat base. Profile not unlike T 23A,1.

*Dipper* T 1,3 (PLATE 269a). Hemispherical, with curved base; large circular handle rising above the rim. No precise parallel.[422]

*Amphoroid pithos* T Pyre 8,3 (PLATE 269e). Tall body, narrow neck, flat base.[423]

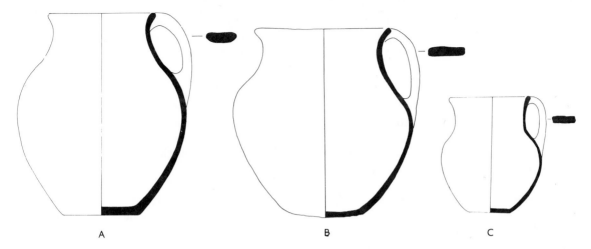

FIG. 20. (A) Xeropolis 65/P11 (B) SPG III T 31,9 (C) SPG II S 33,13. Scale 1:4

## Cooking pots (FIG. 20)

### (a) *Cemeteries*

There are seven, differing in size from 12 to 24 cm, but all of much the same shape, a wide-mouthed oval or globular-bodied jug with flat base and strap handle from belly to rim. The clay is coarse red or red-brown with grits, and some or all of the outer surface is stroke burnished. They are S 33,13 (FIG. 20, C), S 45,5, T 2,4 (PLATE 269d), and T 28,2, all SPG II; S 21,1–2, SPG II or SPG III7 T 31,9 (FIG. 20, B), SPG III.

### (b) *Settlement*[424]

The same type is well represented in the settlement and is dominant among the cooking pot wares in the Moulds Deposit, which carries its earliest attested occurrence at Lefkandi back to LPG. The example at FIG. 20, A from Area 2 was part of a small pottery group which could be as early. Fragments of other larger vessels in the same ware occur but none were sufficiently complete to allow reconstruction of their shapes.

The ovoid, hand-made and burnished jug with strap handle is an Iron Age innovation, since, with few exceptions, the Mycenaean equivalent was wheel-made, different in fabric and shape and had a roll handle.

Best attested, in publication, in the tombs in Athens, it occurs there first in SM and continues practically unchanged through PG when it is a mark of female burials, a criterion thought to extend back to SM.[425] If it began at Lefkandi too in SM, which seems likely, we do not have the evidence since there is no settlement material prior to LPG and the practice of placing them in burials begins on present knowledge in SPG II.

This change in kitchen ware, with its different tradition of skilled manufacture, could be claimed as a strong indication of the arrival of newcomers at the end of the Bronze Age. The marked similarity between the Lefkandian and Attic examples may point to a common manufacturing centre, possibly in neither area.[426]

## BIRD, ANIMAL, AND HUMAN VASES AND FIGURINES

This section cuts across divisions otherwise the subject of separate discussion: hand-made and wheel-made, local and imported; it also combines objects used as vases, and figurines. The common factor is the representation of real or mythical humans, animals and birds, together with one (the askoid vase) which is akin to the bird vases.

## SM and EPG

*Askoid vase.* S 19,5 (PLATES 98, 254). Hand-made. With its three strut legs, basket handle, and slit opening at one end of the body, it may be the intermediate stage between the Mycenaean askos and the vase with the bird head.[427] For the decoration the chief interest lies in the rudimentary animal, and perhaps also bird, motives, the only parallel to which appears on a bird vase from Achaea.[428] SM.

*Bird vases.*[429] S 16,1 and 10 (PLATES 97, 254). Hand-made. Both are pouring vessels, 1 with a perforated beak, 10 with a trumpet mouth; and both have the lekythos-type spout and neck, with attached handle, a feature of the bird vases of the Greek mainland at this time.[430] But there are differences as well as similarities: 1 has a conical foot,[431] and a scribble zigzag motive;[432] 10 has three struts, and an alternating hatched triangle system of decoration;[433] the main difference, however, is that while 1 is local, 10 is an import.[434] These two vases are a useful addition to a small body of evidence from Greece.[435] No. 1, EPG; no. 10, SM.

## LPG and early SPG I

*Birds.* P 22, 28–9 (PLATES 137, 254). Hand-made, black burnished; imported, but not Attic. A rather gawky pair, of whom regrettably little can be said. Their heads are solid, they have no spout, and they are therefore not pouring vases;[436] the two feet endeavour to give an impression of realism,[437] but the semicircular handle on the back of each suggests that they were meant to be suspended or carried. I know of no similar figurines. LPG.

*Doll.* P 22, 30 (PLATES 137, 269). Hand-made, black burnished and imported; but the fabric is similar neither to Attic nor to that of the two birds. A full description is given in the catalogue, and it is clear that both in its structure and in its incised decoration this is a highly individual piece. There are, however, other such figurines, of what appears to be the same fabric, and they are at present confined to the LPG period and to Athens or close to it.[438] It seems likely, therefore, that there is a connexion with Attica, especially since the tomb in which the doll was found contained several Attic imports,[439] but we still do not know where this figurine was originally made. LPG.

*The Centaur.*[440] T 1,5 + T 3,3 (PLATES 169, 251–2). Fully described in the tomb catalogue. The animal body is a hollow wheel-made cylinder,[441] to which have been added the solid and hand-made legs, and human torso and head. It is, to all appearances, locally made. The associated vases can be dated within the SPG I phase, but the curious archaeological history of the centaur itself suggests, as the excavator has stressed,[442] that it was a valued object before its head and body were placed in tombs T 1 and T 3 respectively: it could be LPG from its decoration, but not, I would think, earlier.

   This figurine is unique to Lefkandi. Its origin and background, both in the way it was made and in its representation of a centaur, have been discussed at length by Mr. Nicholls,[443] and I summarise his conclusions here. He shows first that the idea of wheel-made terracotta animals (as votive offerings) goes back to LH IIIB on the Mycenaean mainland, whence it was introduced to Crete and to Cyprus, and that there was then a continuous sequence into the Dark Ages in the two islands mentioned, and probably also in mainland Greece, though for this area the evidence is so slight that continuity is difficult to establish. Second, he considers the particular form here represented, the centaur, and discusses in this context a number of twelfth- and eleventh-century figurines from Crete and Cyprus which, in whatever way they are interpreted,[444] illustrate the technique used for the Lefkandian centaur. Third, he notes the appearance in Cyprus of undoubted centaurs in the tenth and ninth centuries, but concludes that the case for Cypriot influence, as opposed to that of Crete, or of some quite independent mainland development, is not proved, and that all three solutions remain possible.[445]

This brief summary on the question of possible outside influence needs to be qualified in two ways. First it is necessary to bear in mind a factor not yet mentioned, the aesthetic quality of our centaur when compared with that of other similar statuettes. Here it is quite clear that the Lefkandian one is far superior as a work of art (as, indeed, Mr. Nicholls under-lines), and that it stands head and shoulders above anything else of this period yet known, and in this sense is in advance of its time. Professor Schefold[446] has compared the head to the finest early eighth-century bronzes at Olympia,[447] and emphasises 'die stolze feste innere Fügung, die aller späteren griechischen kunst zugrundeliegt'.

Second, the appearance of a centaur, as opposed to some other mythological creature: it is surely not necessary to suppose that the idea came from outside, since the homeland of centaurs was Mt. Pelion, in other words within the region to which Lefkandi belonged. This is where we would expect to find a centaur.

It may indeed be that a particular centaur is meant to be personified. Schefold quotes D. Heilmeyer for the suggestion that the deep incision in the left knee-cap represents a wound;[448] and it is tempting to link this with Apollodorus' story that such a wound on the knee was inflicted on the centaur Cheiron by an arrow shot by Herakles.[449] Cheiron would indeed be a suitable candidate, as of divine origin, teacher of Achilles among others, and renowned for his wisdom.[450]

Whether this hypothesis is true or not, we have in the centaur statuette one of the great artistic achievements of the Dark Ages, a true forerunner of Archaic and Classical Art; and we are also provided with a rare hint as to the religious beliefs of the time.

*Animal-vase.*[451] T 3,2 (PLATES 169, 253). Fully described in the tomb catalogue. The technique — wheel-made cylindrical body, hand-made appendages — is the same as for the centaur, with which it was found, but in this instance the mouth was pierced, and the spout communicates with the hollow body, and so it is a pouring vase. It was locally made. SPG I or earlier.

As with the centaur, it is unique to Lefkandi, but there is less that can be said about it, and I summarise Mr. Nicholls' commentary.[452] He shows that it probably had two stages of use. The original shape is a matter for conjecture: we cannot be sure what animal it was intended to represent, whether a donkey, mule, or even a horse, and we can only guess at the nature of the superstructure on the back; the two attachments flanking the square cut out area probably indicate the earlier existence of a high handle, and it is possible that, as in the Bomford horse-and-rider (of Cypriot provenance),[453] a human figure was set above the square orifice; and if the hole in the neck is original it may have carried a rein-throng. The crude simplicity of the decoration contrasts sharply with that of the centaur and with that of the Bomford piece, and no stylistic conclusions can be based on it. We can say with certainty that this vase was earlier than the tomb it was placed in, but that is all; in its re-used form it may simply have been a toy. In spite of its poor condition, it is, as Dr. Catling has emphasized,[454] an important object, continuing the same tradition noted for the centaur, and the rarity of similar objects on the Greek mainland and in the west Aegean at this time increases its value.

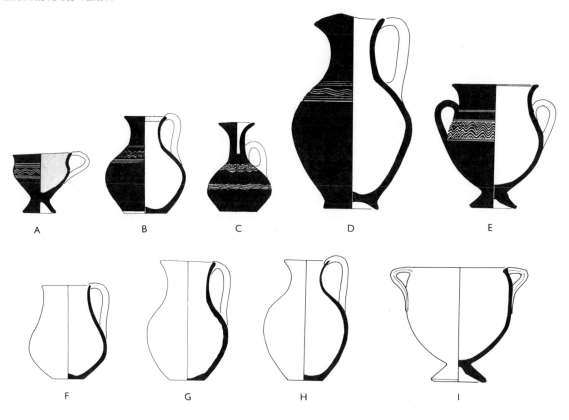

FIG. 21. (A) MPG P 14,4 (B) LPG P 24,5 (C) LPG P 22,17 (D) SPG I S 56,2 (E) LPG P 3,12 (F) MPG P 9,3 (G) LPG P 24,4 (H) SPG I P 18,5 (I) SPG I P 13,14. Scale 1:4

## BLACK SLIP AND RED SLIP WARES. FIG. 21

Each ware is distinctive, but they share a common fabric; spectrographic analysis of a selection of both wares has shown that it is not that normally used by the Lefkandian potter, though close enough to allow the conclusion that the vases were probably made at Lefkandi, and I shall assume that they are local.

### Black Slip
Vases of this ware normally have grey clay,[455] and a black slip over the entire surface.[456] All but one[457] of the examples found at Lefkandi were provided, before firing, with two sets of incised horizontal lines enclosing incised combed wavy lines made by a sharp-pronged instrument.

There are twelve whole or fragmentary vases from the tombs and pyres, and it will be seen from the contexts that none was found in any group preceding MPG, nor in any that is later than SPG I.[458] The main concentration is in LPG. There are also a very few fragments from the settlement, but it is not possible to date these with any accuracy.[459] The types of vase represented are: the cup (FIG. 21, A), the kalathos, a shallow bowl with lug handles, the jug (FIG. 21, B), the lekythos (FIG. 21, C) the trefoil oinochoe (FIG. 21, D), and the vertical-handled amphoriskos (FIG. 21, E). In most cases[460] the shape is very close to that of current and common Lefkandian vases; this and the fairly wide range would support the hypothesis of a local origin.

Outside Lefkandi, vases of this ware have been found only within the region, on Skyros,[461] in Thessaly,[462] and possibly on Tenos.[463]

## Red slip

The vases have a red or pinkish slip, and are undecorated. All come from the cemeteries;[464] only two shapes are represented, the jug and the kantharos; they cover precisely the same chronological range as the Black Slip vases, evenly distributed in MPG, LPG, and SPG I.

There are nine jugs: one is too fragmentary for its shape to be known; six (see FIG. 21, G–H) are similar to the current local ones, with the significant difference[465] that all, including the MPG and LPG examples, are flat-based; the two remaining ones (see FIG. 21, F), also flat-based, have a sagging profile quite unfamiliar to the local tradition. The four kantharoi, all from P 13 (FIG. 21, I and PLATE 264), introduce a shape not otherwise found at Lefkandi; they have sharply angled strip handles which may be thought to copy some metal original, and (in contrast to the jugs) they have low conical feet.

The comparative material is confined to one kantharos from Marmariani.[466]

## List

*Black Slip*
| | |
|---|---|
| MPG | P 14,4 (FIG. 21, A); P 16,2. |
| LPG | P 3,12 (FIG. 21, E); P 22,17 (FIG. 21, C) and 18; P 24,5 (FIG. 21, B); P Pyre 32,2a and 3 (fragments); T 26,10–11. |
| LPG or SPG I | P Pyre 14A,1. |
| SPG I | S 56,2 (FIG. 21, D); P 39B,17. |

*Red slip*
| | |
|---|---|
| MPG | P 9,2 and 3 (FIG. 21, F); P 14,3. |
| LPG | P 19,2; P 24,4 (FIG. 21, G). |
| SPG I | P 4,3; P 13,13–16 (14, FIG. 21, I); P 18,5 (FIG. 21, H); P 44,8 (fragmentary). |
| Uncertain | S Pyre 14,1. |

## IMPORTS OF THE PROTOGEOMETRIC PERIOD.[467]

### A. *Early Protogeometric*

*Dipper juglet.* S 46,3 (PLATE 270).
The fabric, both to the naked eye and to spectrographic analysis, is unlike anything found at Lefkandi, and the shape is characteristic of the Syro-Palestinian area, from which it must surely have come.

The type was so common and so long-lived in its area of origin that one cannot suggest even an approximate locality or date for the Lefkandian juglet. Its distinguishing features are the trefoil lip, the short neck, and the slightly baggy body with curved base; there is no exact counterpart, to my knowledge, but there are several that resemble it. Some of the juglets from the Bronze Age[468] levels at Lachish are close, in fact closer than those from the Iron Age.[469] Megiddo provides similar jugs from both Bronze and Early Iron Ages.[470] Good examples are known from Philistine contexts,[471] and at Ashdod the type is found in bronze;[472] and a reasonably close specimen came from level III at Tell Abu Hawam.[473] Lebanon has also produced similar juglets, as for example from Tell Sukas,[474] Khirbet Silm,[475] and Khalde.[476]

There is then plenty of choice, and the date of the Lefkandian tomb with which our juglet was associated is well within the time range. The remarkable fact is that it should have reached Lefkandi at all at this time.

## B. Middle Protogeometric

*Hydria.* S 51,2 (FIG. 4; PLATES 210 and 270).
Analysis of the fabric has shown that it differs from the typical Lefkandian clay. It is true that the elaborate designs on the shoulder, the multple zigzag and the confronted archers, are quite alien to the local potter's attitude towards decoration at this time; on the other hand, the shape is characteristic both of Lefkandi and of its associated region in EPG and MPG. If it was an import,[477] as is here assumed, it was probably made not far from Lefkandi.

As will be seen in FIG. 4, the drawing of the archers and their weapons is elementary;[478] bearing in mind, however, that the archers are no more than 2 cm high, the draughtsmanship is excellent. There is nothing comparable to these figures either in Late Mycenaean or in Geometric.[479]

There is, so far as I know, no other instance of a multiple zigzag in PG, a motive which in Attica appears first in EG II.[480]

## C. Late Protogeometric

### 1. *Attic*[481]

*Amphorae with handles from shoulder to lip.* P 22,1–3 (PLATES 212, 271). For a general review of this shape in Attica, see my *Protogeometric Pottery*, 40 ff.; apart from one EPG forerunner from Kerameikos tomb A, the few examples are confined to LPG, and have not yet been found in any Geometric context. This conclusion still stands. Of the vases from Lefkandi nos. 1 and 2 find a close parallel in Agora P 3949, whose decoration matches these.[482] No. 3 has no precise counterpart for its decorative system, but is obviously not far from Kerameikos tomb 40, 2012–3.[483]

*Chest.* P 22,4 (PLATE 271). This unusual type of vase is discussed by Professor Smithson in her account of the Nea Ionia cemetery, and brought up to date in her publication of the Rich Athenian Lady's tomb.[484] As with the amphora with handles from shoulder to lip, the LPG shape has a precursor in EPG, but in a different technique. In Athens the chest was still in use in EG II.

The Lefkandian chest is very similar to the one from Nea Ionia, of LPG date, the main difference being in the construction of the lower half, the diagonal struts at Nea Ionia contrasting with the square cut-outs of this one – but even so the motive on the struts is repeated on the Lefkandian vase, and the selection of motives is virtually the same on both. Equally striking is the similarity of the designs of our chest to those of the shoulder-handled amphora 2131 from Kerameikos tomb 39,[485] one of the latest LPG groups. These vases must be contemporaneous, could very well have come from the same workshop, and could take P 22,3 (above) with them.

It is also of importance to realise that for this shape the link may not have been with the EPG Attic example, but with chests from Cyprus, of which two are known.[486] Neither has a precise provenience, but both are assigned to the Cypro-Geometric I phase (conventionally 1050–950 BC), so they are probably earlier than the Attic ones, and suggest possible influence from Cyprus.

*Pyxides.* P 22,20–1 (PLATES 212, 271); T Pyre 2,4 (PLATE 190). All are of the shape invented in Attica in PG, mostly concentrated in the late phase,[487] and extending into EG I,[488] with globular body, prominently everted lip, string holes and lids (that of no. 21 is missing). For decoration, a distinction must be made between P 22,21 and T Pyre 2,4, with one zone, and P 22,20, with three, the latter stated to have been an EG innovation.[489] As to individual motives, the alternating diagonals design (P 22) is the one almost always found on the LPG pyxides from Attica, the dogtooth is known once, on a pyxis from Nea Ionia, and the formal zigzag has so far been found only on a small unpublished pyxis from an Agora LPG group[490] and on the two EG pyxides.

*Trefoil oinochoe, high-handled.* P 22,9 (PLATES 212, 271). This, too, has been analysed. There is no securely attested parallel for the shape in Attica during PG, in the sense of having a handle which curves to well above the lip and is provided with a connecting bar. Reference may however be made to two vases which are probably, but not certainly, Attic, as having no known provenience.[491]

*Kalathoi.* P 22,24–5 (PLATES 139 and 212). Possibly by the same potter. The nearest parallels are those from Kerameikos tombs 16 and 20,[492] the latter the closer on the basis of the handle and the decoration. Both tombs belong to the LPG phase, to which indeed most of the Attic kalathoi of this type can be assigned, though there is a brief survival into EG I.[493]

This type of handled kalathos was not imitated by the Lefkandians, so far as we know.

*Kantharos.* T Pyre 2,3 (PLATE 190). In Attica the shape belongs almost exclusively to LPG and EG I.[494] Since our kantharos has a ring base one should perhaps seek parallels in EG I, where the feet tend to be lower than in LPG. EG I kantharoi, however, are deeper than our vase, and usually have a 'window' panel below the lip. It may be better to make a comparison with an LPG specimen from Kerameikos tomb 26.[495] This would agree with the date attributed to the Attic pyxis found in the same pyre (see above).

There is no evidence that the kantharos was taken into the Lefkandian potter's repertory.

*Spherical vase.* P 22,23 (PLATES 137 and 212). This is a unique vase, and one cannot be sure what it was used for.[496]

## 2. Probably Attic[497]

*Jug.* P 22,5 (PLATE 140). The shape is that of an Attic trefoil oinochoe, with the important exception of the lip itself, which has no trefoil, and as such has no parallel in Attica. The restriction of body decoration to reserved bands on the belly is also very unusual; when such bands are found on Athenian oinochoai or lekythoi they always contain an inserted scribble motive.

The jug differs from the local Lefkandian ones. The only close parallel comes from Asine, and even this has the scribble zigzag on the belly.[498]

*Trefoil oinochoe.* P 22,7 (PLATE 140). A typical and common Attic LPG shape,[499] but the decoration is the same as that on the jug above. Note that the locally made oinochoe P 22,6 has the conventional Attic concentric semicircles on the shoulder.

There are then twelve Attic (or Athenian) vases, ten from P 22 and two from T Pyre 2, and two probably Attic vases from P 22. Some are certainly LPG in style: the three amphorae, two of the pyxides, and the chest. The kantharos and the two kalathoi are more likely to be LPG than EG I; the unique spherical vase and the atypical jug and oinochoe could perhaps belong to either phase. The slender body of the high-handled oinochoe might suggest an EG I date. Only the pyxis, because of its triple zone of decoration, can be accepted as more likely to be EG I than LPG, though the absence of the meander motive indicates that it could be earlier than any of the EG I examples known. Taking these imports by their Lefkandian contexts, those from T Pyre 2 are most likely to be pure LPG, while the twelve from P 22 seem to reflect the stage in Attica when the LPG style was still predominant, but also when the first signs of the EG style were beginning to appear.[500]

## 3. Cypriot

*Bichrome jug.* P 22,19 (PLATE 270). This shape was not only common in Cyprus, but also long-lived.[501] Stylistic development was fairly gradual; expert opinions have differed somewhat on the phase to which this jug should be assigned,[502] and it is clearly the relatively static nature of the type itself which prevents precision, which is regrettable in view of its context at Lefkandi. It is in any case the earliest known vase imported from Cyprus to Greece since the end of the Mycenaean era, and its importance is therefore self-evident.

## 4. Unknown origin

*Belly-handled amphora.* T 14,1 (PLATE 260). The pale yellow clay indicates that it was of neither local nor Attic manufacture, and this has been confirmed by analysis. No positive source can, however, be suggested. It must surely have been made somewhere within the Attic sphere of influence, for in both shape and decoration it follows the Attic LPG style closely.[503] It may also be noted that it was used at Lefkandi as a cremation urn, in the Athenian manner.

## GEOMETRIC IMPORTS

### A. Attic

Out of the fifteen Geometric imports, fourteen are of Attic origin. Some are of intrinsic interest, in that they add to our knowledge of rare Attic shapes. Others, belonging to common types already well known, supply valuable dating evidence for the latest and richest tombs.

### The pyxides (PLATES 136 and 272)

P 21,2, with its depressed globular body and its flange inset for the lid, conforms to a type which in Attica is confined to EG. Within Attic EG I it evolved from, and eventually displaced,[504] the standard LPG pyxis with everted lip. In size and shape, the closest counterpart to P 21,2 is from tomb 2 at Marathon,[505] a group to be dated well down in EG II. The decoration, normal for this shape, consists of a large hatched meander (not found earlier than EG II) between two ancillary zones; this scheme recurs on a fragmentary globular pyxis from the tomb of the Rich Athenian Lady,[506] except that the ancillary dogtooth motif is there replaced by the single zigzag.

At the transition from EG II to MG I the diameter is drastically increased in relation to the height; thus emerges the flat pyxis, which was to remain the standard form in Attica for over a century. If shape is a reliable criterion for dating, S 59,4 will be the earliest known specimen of the new type, made at the very beginning of MG I, and intermediate between the globular version of EG and the extremely flat pyxides first seen later in MG I.[507] This vase thus confirms the affiliation of the flat pyxis to its globular predecessor,[508] and the knob handle on its lid preserves in miniature the memory of an even older form – the PG globular pyxis with everted lip. The three-zone scheme of decoration, another legacy from the globular type, is exactly paralleled on a slightly flatter pyxis[509] from an early MG I group, tomb I 18:2 on the Areopagus.

### The trefoil oinochoai

The broad-based trefoil oinochoe, one of the commonest among Attic Geometric shapes, became established in EG II when it gradually replaced the PG ovoid form. The earliest examples have a dumpy appearance and a low centre of gravity.[510] T 31,1 belongs rather to the beginning of MG I when the base is still very broad, but the shape has now grown taller and the widest diameter is relatively higher. At a more mature stage of MG I the lower profile has begun to curve inwards more gracefully towards a somewhat narrower base.[511]

The decoration is usually limited to a panel on the neck (meander or multiple zigzag, often with ancillaries), and two or three triple reserved bands round the body. T 31,1, PLATE 272a, is abnormally ornate for its time in possessing a second meander panel on the shoulder and no less than eight triple bands. There is, however, an excellent parallel to the shape from Kerameikos tomb 41,[512] also early in MG I, which might have been made by the same potter. Unlike our oinochoe it has a rope handle, a shorter panel of multiple zigzag on the shoulder, and only seven triple bands; both vases, however, share three unusual features – the bars round the lip, the two warts on the shoulder, and the concentric furrows under the base. On our oinochoe, the placing of the meander so as to mask the warts recalls a MG I lekythos-oinochoe from tomb I 18:1 on the Areopagus.[513]

T 31,4 and T 33,1 are small versions of this shape; smaller still are T 33,4 and the baggy miniature T 31,7 (all on PLATES 226–7). All should be contemporary with T 31,1 whether through context or through resemblance of style. A rare feature is the rising handle of T 33,1, reinforced by a strut. High handles are occasionally found on small Attic oinochoai towards the end of PG, one example occurring among the earlier exports to Lefkandi.[514] Two more are known from contexts nearer in time;[515] but these still follow the LPG fashion with their ovoid bodies and their ornament only on the belly, whereas our piece is fully Geometric in shape and decoration. For the next use of the high strutted handle we have to wait until the tankards and pitchers of Attic LG.[516]

### The lekythoi-oinochoai

After the disappearance of the Attic lekythos at the end of PG, the chief slow-pouring vessel was the lekythos-oinochoe – a squat and broad-based vase with a tall, narrow neck. It is represented here by two examples.

T 19,1 (PLATE 177) is still decorated in the PG manner with cross-hatched triangles on the shoulder, a fashion which persisted even into LG on this form.[517] It is not easy to see any consistent development in the profile; yet comparable examples, with shorter necks but similarly proportioned bodies, occur in the tomb of the Rich Athenian Lady (late EG II) and in Kerameikos tomb 11 (late MG I).[518]

T 31,3 (PLATE 226e), decorated in a fully Geometric manner with a zigzag panel on the neck, has its nearest counterpart in a tomb of the same date in the Piraeus area.[519]

### The feeding vessels (PLATES 226–7)

Four small vessels, of various shapes, have this feature in common: a tubular spout emerging from the belly, set at a right angle to a vertical handle. T 19,2 and T 33,3 take the form of a squat oinochoe; T 33,2, an aryballos; and T 31,2, a high-lipped cup. Except for T 33,3 the handles always rise above the rim. T 19,2 is fully coated in paint; the remainder bear the sort of decoration that one would expect in the middle of the ninth century.

These miniatures served the purpose of feeding infants with liquid nourishment. The class with vertical handle and side-spout began in Attic PG in the form of a small round-mouthed jug.[520] The finds from Lefkandi add greatly to our knowledge of these unusual little vessels, which are otherwise unknown in the ninth century. In later Geometric times, Attic feeding vases in painted ware take the form of buckets or drinking vessels with strainer holes across the top, more suitable perhaps for adult invalids than for infants; but miniature spouted jugs and oinochoai still persist in hand-made ware.[521]

The shape of the aryballos, T 33,2, is extremely rare in Attica at this time,[522] and exceptional care has been taken over its decoration. The variety of fillings within the meander recall the elaborate clay chest of the Rich Athenian Lady;[523] the unusual squares above the spout reappear on the belly of an amphora from Kerameikos tomb 13[524] (early MG I); and the dots round the neck would be surprising before MG I.

The shape of the cup, T 31,2, is without parallel – a compromise between the normal Geometric cup (see below) and the newly invented mug.[525] The vertical chevrons round the lip are more often seen in MG II, yet nevertheless occur on other MG I vases,[526] as here, in an ancillary role.

### The cup (PLATE 222)

Most Attic cups of the ninth century are small and undecorated, their bodies being fully coated with paint. S Pyre 4,1 belongs to a class of larger and more ornate cups, bearing a rectangular panel between two warts; the motif is usually a hatched meander. In Attica this class is confined to EG II and MG I, and there is a fairly consistent development in the shape from deep to shallow.[527] In this respect our cup occupies an intermediate place in the series; it could be late EG II or early MG I.

## B. Uncertain origin

### *The kantharos* (PLATE 270c)

The clay of T 19,3 is neither local nor Attic. Furthermore, its occurrence in a mid-ninth-century tomb virtually rules out a southern Greek origin, since the high-handled kantharos is unknown before MG II in Attica, the Cyclades, and the Peloponnese. In Thessaly, on the other hand, the shape is established by the ninth century in a wheel-made form, based on a hand-made prototype of Macedonian origin.[528] Even so, the Thessalian kantharoi do not offer any close parallels, since the prevailing type there[529] is broader, lower, more bellied, with more steeply rising handles and a lip less tall in relation to the body; nor do any Thessalian potters mark off the decorated zone with horizontal grooves, as on our vase. Another possible source is Macedonia, where the wheel-made ware of this period is rare and little known. There, too, the wheel-made kantharoi tend to be broader; but a hand-made kantharos from Vergina,[530] with a single zigzag painted round its tall lip, might perhaps have been the prototype for the form of our vessel, and the horizontal grooving also has precedents at Vergina.[531]

The precise origin of T 19,3 remains a mystery; but in our present state of ignorance 'North Greek' is a convenient blanket title.

### *The one-handled lentoid flask* (PLATE 101)

S 33,3 is a shape of Levantine origin,[532] sporadically imitated in the Aegean at different periods during the Early Iron Age, apparently without any continuous development at any one centre.[533] The pale powdery clay, alien to Euboea, recalls some Geometric pottery of eastern Crete where there was also some knowledge of the shape;[534] yet the export of Cretan pottery is otherwise unknown in the period of our flask (i.e. the early ninth century), and remains extremely rare even in LG times.[535] The origin of this flask, then, remains in doubt; all one can safely say is that it comes from a place which, like Lefkandi, enjoyed some communication with the eastern Mediterranean.

### *The pedestalled bowl* (PLATE 181)

T 24,1 has been found on analysis to have a fabric typical neither of Lefkandi nor of Attica. The profile of body and foot is not at all unlike that of the MPG bowls from S 18 and S 51, but this is a larger vase, its two horizontal ribbon handles are placed along the rim, it has a small spout, and from the stratification it is very likely that its tomb is within the SPG II period. I know of no similar vase.

### General observations on the Attic Geometric imports

The fourteen imports form an extremely homogeneous group. The earliest is probably the late EG II globular pyxis P 21,2; the latest, to judge from the flat pyxis S 59,4 and the large oinochoe T 31,1, are to be placed in the early years of MG I. Thus the whole group belongs to a single generation, which is also thought to be the last generation of the three cemeteries. Among the latest are T 31 and T 33, which are datable through their imports to the middle or third quarter of the ninth century.

These vases do not follow immediately after the Attic Protogeometric imports; in between lies an interval of at least a generation, corresponding to EG I and much of EG II, when there is no sign of contact in the pottery between Attica and Lefkandi. The arrival of the Attic Geometric imports signifies a vigorous renewal of these contacts; indeed, this group comprises the largest known accumulation of Attic ninth-century pottery found anywhere outside Attica.

Until the clay is analysed, we cannot be certain which of these vases were made in Athens, and which in the Athenian countryside. The two pyxides and the large oinochoe, however, have an authentically Athenian look, well up to date in their shapes, and decorated with the fastidious care characteristic of the best Athenian work in the middle of the ninth century. The globular pyxis may be contrasted with a possibly provincial example from Marathon (n. 505), which is underfired, and bears a somewhat awkward meander unaccompanied by the usual ancillary zones. The oinochoe, as we have seen has a very close counterpart — perhaps by the same hand — made for the Athenian aristocratic lady buried in Kerameikos tomb 41.

# Section 14

# Historical Conclusions[1]

## M. R. POPHAM and L. H. SACKETT

## I  SUBMYCENAEAN, THE FIRST HALF OF THE 11TH CENTURY

In considering Submycenaean Lefkandi, the first and perhaps most important question concerns continuity of occupation from the past. Were its inhabitants survivors from the Late Bronze Age settlement, or were they newcomers from elsewhere?

We have only burials, and no settlement evidence for this stage, whereas the reverse is true for the previous occupation at the end of LH IIIC: this leaves us pottery as the single common factor which we can compare. Differences are considerable in both fabric and shapes; for instance the light-coloured fabrics characteristic of the latest Mycenaean are virtually absent in the earliest Iron Age burials, while the standard drinking vessel has changed completely from the earlier small conical bowl to the later globular cup.[2] These and other innovations at Lefkandi suggest a break in occupation and a new beginning in the early Iron Age, albeit one which continues the latest Mycenaean tradition found in areas outside Euboea. To pottery changes may be added indications that the latest LH IIC building on Xeropolis was abandoned and this particular site may not have been re-settled for well over a century.[3] That the earliest burials in the known cemeteries start in Submycenaean may be thought to be another, and perhaps decisive, factor in favour of discontinuity. Some caution, however, would be wise: one vase, a chance acquisition said to have come from cist burials outside the limits of the excavated cemeteries, is of the LH IIIC light fabric and looks IIIC in decoration.[4] A trial dig at the reported find spot of this vase confirmed the presence there of robbed cists. It must, then, remain a possibility that a cist cemetery exists which was in use before the end of the LH IIIC settlement and which might continue into the Iron Age.

These speculations are the more important in that from Submycenaean onwards there is clearly unbroken continuity, so we are talking of the origins of the Iron Age Lefkandians as a people and community.

Present indications, then, combine in pointing firmly to the conclusion that our Submycenaeans are newcomers with a different pottery and burial tradition, who chose a different location at Lefkandi to live in. The alternative, a mixed community consisting basically of new comers but who absorbed a few Mycenaean survivors, cannot, however, be ruled out: such survivors might well leave little trace of their existence and remain undetectable.

We may now concentrate on the newcomers themselves and the question of their origin. Submycenaean Lefkandi clearly shares many of the salient features present at several other contemporary sites, features which in combination are thought to characterise a Submycenaean culture with local variations — a debased Mycenaean pottery tradition, single burials in cist graves, long dress pins, arched fibulae, the introduction of iron for utilitarian purposes, finger rings, most in bronze with a distinctive type with spiral attachment.[5] Nearly all these features are present at Lefkandi.

To the specific question, however, of the place of origin of the newcomers to Lefkandi, no answer can yet be given. It could only be based on a striking similarity of special features; and on this score, while the metalwork is closely paralleled at Athens, in the case of the pottery Desborough considers its characteristics would exclude Athens (with Salamis) and the Argolid as areas of origin.[6] Elsewhere on the mainland information is thin, and especially so in Boeotia and Thessaly, vital regions to any consideration and ones with which Lefkandi is known to have close connections later; the possibility of earlier interrelationship can by no means be excluded. When more is known from these and other areas, it may be that the Lefkandian fondness for triple linked vases and the curious combination of cremation with symbolic cist burial may prove useful pointers.

Parallel features with other communities suggest intercommunication but as yet we cannot determine priority in any particular region. Catling's suggestion that one type of fibula might be an import from Crete and another have been influenced by developments in Cyprus, would be decisive for interrelationship, if correct.[7] These possible Cretan and Cypriot connections could then be the prelude to further influence from these islands at the beginning of the next phase.

Estimates of the size of the settlement or the number of its inhabitants are hazardous, with too many unknown factors. The number of burials for the conventional 50 years ascribed to this stage is comparable with that for the later settlement.[8] So it would not be unreasonable to surmise that the community was large in contemporary terms from its beginning. We are left wondering where the settlement was located at this time.

## II   EARLY AND MIDDLE PROTOGEOMETRIC, THE SECOND HALF OF THE 11TH CENTURY

Two stages can be distinguished within the next 50 or so years but distinctions are often fine between what basically constitutes one phase of development, in terms of pottery at least. Indeed, such is the continuity from Submycenaean until the real change, in Late Protogeometric, and so considerable the uncertainties about chronological divisions within this span, that there would be much to be said in favour of treating it as one whole.

Apart from a burst of initiative at, or soon after, the transition from Submycenaean, change is slow and uneventful, accompanied by a possible decline in prosperity. It must again be stressed that we have no settlement evidence to assist in interpretation.

The beginning of the phase is startling in its indications of long-distance contact. The evidence is small but, taken together, is decisive. It comprises imports and influences; the former, two perhaps three objects — a necklace of faience beads and a Syro-Palestinian juglet — are certain;[9] the latter, local imitations of a specific type of duck-vase and of two other alien shapes in pottery — a flask and a pyxis.[10] Desborough has suggested a Cypriot origin for the duck-vase while the pyxis and flask may have been borrowed from the same source or from Crete. Cyprus, too, could have served as intermediary for the two Near Eastern imports, the necklace and juglet, while another likely import, an iron dirk, found in the same tomb as the juglet, might have originated in the same region.

The arrival of these objects and influences by direct contact, rather than through an intermediary such as Athens, seems more likely on present evidence. At Athens, also, Cypriot influences have been suggested in its early Protogeometric pottery, but they are different from those at Lefkandi; it, too, has produced an iron dirk similar to ours, but no other obvious Near Eastern imports. Who, then, were the carriers of this trade — the Lefkandians themselves, Cypriots or Phoenicians?[11]

Some scholars prefer Near Eastern initiative, now and later, but this may underestimate Euboean potential. Intercommunication nearer at home indicates considerable seaborne traffic, and it is tempting to extend this and see in these imports the first establishment of links with the East Mediterranean by Euboean merchants, ancestors of those who were to be actively involved in the trading centre at Al Mina some 150 years later. It must, however, be acknowledged that, after this initial contact, whatever its explanation, the only evidence at Lefkandi for its continuation for some time to come is a further necklace of faience beads in a Middle Protogeometric burial — little enough, but surprising, even so, for its period.[12] Some continuity of knowledge of the route, at least, seems possible and this would help account for the definite indications of renewed contact with Cyprus in the succeeding Late Protogeometric stage.

Not only trade but innovations in pottery, too, are concentrated at the beginning of the period: the more exotic experiments in imitation of foreign shapes, described above, had no immediate successors. Less spectacular changes, however, did continue, the formation of a neat wavy-line style of decoration, the adoption of the conical foot for open vessels, the introduction of reserved lines to lighten the appearance of monochrome vases and some decline in the popularity of the deep bowl with the appearance of a more open version on a low pedestal. An unexciting and conservative style was the outcome but it was in essentials a local, internal development and one which sufficiently pleased the inhabitants to make them long impervious to the changes taking place in nearby Attica, especially to one of its main features, the use of the multiple compass. Self reliance and conservatism, too, may be reflected in the metalwork.

It would be good to claim as an exception to this general picture, the 'archer vase', unique at this early stage (MPG) for its pictorial representation, but it seems it must be an import, though its source remains an enigma.[13]

During the latter part, there are signs of some decline in prosperity, a condition by no means limited to Euboea. Grave offerings are much fewer, both in pottery and metal objects, while gold is completely absent. The population, however, may have remained fairly constant, provided the total twenty-four or so burials are truly representative and should cover the 50 years or less, which Desborough tentatively allots to these Early and Middle phases. It is far from clear why at this stage two further cemeteries were inaugurated while the old one continued in use.

On the positive side, Desborough has drawn attention to the uniformity of pottery between Boeotia, Thessaly, Skyros and Euboea, and has suggested that some form of cultural unity, if nothing more, already linked these regions.[14] Two Euboean type MPG vases on Naxos, moreover, show at least contact with the Central Cyclades and could mean more in view of later developments. There is little, however, to prepare us for the sudden, massive change in mentality and perhaps fortune that is apparent in the following Late Protogeometric stage.

## III   LATE PROTOGEOMETRIC, THE 10TH CENTURY

The rather stagnant course of the end of the previous phase with its conservative and mostly independent development, changes so thoroughly, and apparently abruptly, that something momentous appears to have happened in the history of the settlement. Traditonalism is cast off, independence is temporarily laid aside, new ideas flood in and are eagerly absorbed: there is a marked move to an international outlook which is accompanied by initiative, a much wider expansionism and a new prosperity. Such interpretations are bound to be partly, even largely, subjective and to depend a great deal on pottery, but, in this instance, the change is so marked and the influences so clear, and sufficiently backed up with concrete evidence in the form of imports and material finds, that we may have less doubts than usual about the validity of such general conclusions. To the evidence from burials we can now add that from the settlement since Xeropolis, the old site, by now has been definitely reoccupied.

The most pervasive aspect of this change is the impact from close contact with Attica which had so far had no obviously great and direct influence on Lefkandi. There are at least twelve vases imported from Attica in the cemeteries, some of outstanding quality, but even without them the connection would have been obvious from the radical change in the local pottery. Many of the basic household vessels are either a close copy of an Attic original or have been profoundly modified by Attic features, in shape, decoration, or both, from large amphoras to the ordinary cup. This is not to say that local individualism is submerged: some important Euboean aspects survive or quickly emerge, and to them we shall return later.[15]

Apart from Attic imports and obvious influences, there are a few objects and aspects, alien to both regions, which might have reached Lefkandi, either indirectly through Attica, or independently — the impressed beads and the incised, hand-made doll, for instance.[16]

More surprising is the presence of three urn burials in the cemeteries, a practice hitherto unknown at Lefkandi but characteristic in general and in detail of Attic custom: one of these burials was provided with a sword and spear.[17]

But Attic influence, however strong, is only one side of developments. Thessaly, too, played a part. This is most clearly seen in imitations of the northern type jug with its characteristic cut-away neck while decorative motives, too, may have been borrowed and adapted from the same region. It is possible that we should look northwards too for the origin of a pair of gilt spiral earrings.[18]

Several imported objects have no known origin, two duck-vases in a burnished dark fabric which is similar to that of a further alien vase which cannot be given a home.[19] So other contacts should be kept in mind, and they continue later.

So far we have been considering influences and imports from regions of mainland Greece, but contacts reached much wider afield, to Cyprus, and perhaps Crete. A flask of Cypriot manufacture provides certainty but there are other indications, clear influences manifested in local imitations of vases of this and other foreign types.[20]

Enthusiasm for new ideas is quite apparent in such eclecticism. It spilt over, though more superficially, into burial customs, a more conservative area. Mention has already been made of urn burials of Attic type: another apparent innovation is inhumation in a wooden coffin, and this, too, of a warrior provided with sword and arrows.[21] These are, however, exceptional: in general there is continuity of practice and, presumably, of population.[22] Some continuity, too, is to be seen in the persistence of the unusual black and red slip wares, the former with a characteristic combed decoration; and other traditional types of pottery continue as well. One of these, a local liking for a particular type of bowl, may have been responsible for an independent creation which was to remain for nearly two centuries a hallmark of Euboean presence, the pendent semicircle skyphos.[23]

Amid, and perhaps because of, this surge of change, the settlement shows sign of a new prosperity and a growth in extent.[24] Grave offerings are noticeably more numerous and contain prized possessions: gold reappears after a long absence – a little only but its mere presence is important. The some twenty burials in this phase do not on their own signify an increase in population but to them we may add the spread of buildings not only to Xeropolis, now clearly reoccupied, but probably to the surrounding ground as well. And it is on the old site that we find evidence for sophisticated metalworking, the casting of bronze tripods. Evidently by now the Lefkandians were expert metalsmiths who, during this phase, evolved a distinctive type of fibula which may be as much a mark of Euboean presence as their characteristic skyphos.[25]

Before attempting to account for these developments, some notice should be taken of what followed. The period we have been outlining is in some aspects transitory, and then there is a reversion to conservatism with a marked resistance to outside influences. This at least in the pottery and burial habits, and it is likely to reflect a more general change of attitude. Foreign contacts continue as before, and are ultimately to intensify, but the period of evident 'internationalism' is over.

How should we account for this sudden transitory episode, characterised by innovation, a readiness to receive and absorb ideas from outside, an international outlook, expert knowledge of metallurgy and a marked rise in prosperity and, possibly, numbers. Details are lost, as too the contribution of any outstanding personality: we can only talk in generalities, and even then with considerable surmise.

One feature in particular might well account for the new extrovert spirit, trade; contact, that is, with different peoples on a much wider scale than before, which widened the range of Euboean ideas. This, of course, presupposes the prior existence of a spirit of initiative which led them to undertake the risk of these voyages and to appreciate the potentialities of a certain item or items for trading purposes: a pressing need for a particular commodity at home (and one naturally thinks of metals) could obviously provide a stimulus, even the main one.[26] This should be viewed against the potential economy of Lefkandi.

Provided the inhabitants owned and controlled the whole or a large part of the Lelantine Plain, one would expect the settlement to be basically an agricultural community and, if true, this might help account for one characteristic of the Lefkandians, an ingrained conservatism. Two developments in particular could disturb this situation, loss of the Plain (or a part of it) or its possession by a few, powerful persons in the community – potentially, a very restricted landed aristocracy. A possible third disturbing feature could be the growth of the population to a stage where the agricultural land was no longer sufficient, either to maintain all the inhabitants or to allow further subdividion for inheritance.

On the other hand, the first newcomers could well have been mainly seafarers: their choice of a harbour site suggests this, and they might well have retained this aspect long after settling. The early development of common features between Lefkandi, coastal Thessaly, and Skyros proves frequent sea communications, facilitated by the sheltered channel between Euboea and the Mainland and the proximity of the N. Sporades to Thessaly, and even to the N.E. coast of Euboea in favourable weather. Granted such a background of travel and experience by water, the voyage south from the tip of Euboea at Karystos, to Keos, Andros and the N. Cyclades presents no great problem.

So, it is possible, perhaps probable, that the Lefkandians early on comprised two basic groups, the sailors (in the broadest sense) and the farmers, which, when in harmony, would contribute to the common welfare.

Though in part hypothetical, some such background is worth reconstructing at this point, since in general outline it would apply throughout the early Iron Age history of the site as well as to the particular stage we are now considering.

Potential points of danger or friction could remain essentially the same throughout — aggression from outside to take the rich hinterland or part of it, internal oppression by a small landed aristocracy, and a conflict of interests, or power, within the community itself between the seafaring and the agricultural sections of it, not that such black and white division may have existed at all times in practice. A considerable growth of population could cause, or aggravate, problems. On the other hand, against nature's hazards, prolonged drought or stormy weather, they were protected more than most communities. We cannot know which, if any, of these factors might have been most at work at this particular stage though there might be slight indications.

We may now return to one such indication, the great change of mentality at this stage, and trade as a possible cause. Evidence for imports and outside influences have already been discussed but it remains to be established who were the carriers of them — adventurous Euboeans, foreign traders in Euboean waters or an intermediary (and here Athens is the only real candidate). This is the same problem we met earlier at the beginning of the PG stage when the evidence was much slighter and more hypothetical. If the Euboeans were then the traders, they could have been the ancestors of the present move, but this is uncertain.

In considering Near Eastern contacts, we again meet the complication of potential Phoenician or Cypriot enterprise: this does not apply in the same way to relations with the North, so there are advantages in examining this aspect first of all.

Close intercommunication with Thessaly (and Boeotia en route) persists from earlier times, while Skyros remains within the Euboean orbit. We have seen that Thessaly contributed one vase shape (and possibly some forms of decoration) to the new Lefkandian repertoire: in that same region, 'not only were the Attic elements similarly absorbed . . . but the general development runs roughly parallel to that at Lefkandi.'[27] In some respects, however, the most important evidence comes from Vergina, a site much further north, in S. Macedonia, where amid a long-lived conservative culture, the arrival of the earliest imports of Euboean character are most conspicuous. Trade with this Macedonian community continues after the period under discussion, and it can hardly be accidental that near 200 years later we are told of the establishment of a colony of Euboeans (perhaps the first in the north) in the immediate vicinity.[28]

If Euboean enterprise could penetrate thus far to the north, it was capable of doing so in other directions. Andros and Tenos, among the nearest islands of the Cyclades, have produced evidence that it did, along a route already established earlier on, where similarities of culture may indicate a community of interests, and perhaps more.

Cyprus is much further off and we have no other links yet attested on the way but the Euboeans seem to have been experienced mariners and sufficiently enterprising to make the voyage. Two vases, Euboean in character, reached that Island and, so far, they are the earliest Greek vases known in the E. Mediterranean.[29] It seems likely that it was the Euboeans (or traders from a region closely related) who carried them there, forerunners of the much closer Euboean interest to come, both to that Island and to the neighbouring Syrian coast as well. The Cypriot vase imported by Lefkandi and the appearance of Cypriot influences in the locally made pottery are followed in later times by a series of imports from the same general region, which imply unbroken relations from now on.

If this picture is correct, even in outline — and much hypothesis and, perhaps, considerable Euboean prejudice have entered into its reconstruction — a reasonable background has been set to account for the revolutionary change in Lefkandian outlook, its outward looking attitude, its eager acceptance of new ideas and the signs of growing prosperity.

We must now turn to the contribution of Attica which supplied not only a large number of the imports and much of the basis for the new developments in pottery but even temporarily intruded into burial customs. Was this due to more Euboean enterprise, or Attic expansionism, or merely a late recognition of superior pottery? If it were time for a change, where better to look, it may be argued, than to Attica whose refined pottery had already received recognition in many parts of Greece, south of Euboea? But a change of style at Lefkandi rather than development along traditional lines, however dull, was by no means inevitable. And there remains a more basic aspect, the burials, admittedly few, in the Attic manner and in Attic-type amphoras. Attic, rather than Euboean, initiative might seem more convincing an explanation, especially since nothing obviously Euboean, not even the Euboean hallmark of the pendent semicircle skyphos, seems to have affected Athens. We might go even further and deduce Attic initiative which proved unwelcome after a while, so accounting for the subsequent reversion at Lefkandi to native tendencies and, in the context of the day, not only a resistance to future pottery developments in Attica but also remarkably few imports from that nearby region for some time thereafter. 'It is even possible that there were some Athenian settlers' is Desborough's suggestion, based on these burials and the number of imports.[30] If true, they made no impact on dress fashions and weapons since fibulae and pins (and perhaps weapons as well), do not reflect current Athenian practice but develop their own local characteristics at this time.

Nevertheless, it is curious that two of the three warrior burials of this stage, and one immediately afterwards, are not Lefkandian in type. In addition to the Attic one already mentioned, the others were interred in wooden coffins, another innovation and not Attic. A further, and normal, cremation contained spear and iron axe.[31] Gentlemen with weapons need not imply warfare, though the possibility is there and foreign assistance not excluded.

Finally, we may ask, provided the psychological change was due to trade, why the subsequent reversion, since trade continues with no obvious decrease in prosperity? Familiarity over a period with alien ways may have blunted the initial impetus they had given. Or, again, if the change reflects the activities of a progressive maritime element, may that element not have gained an ascendency in more concrete terms, one which proved temporary and was followed by a reversion to the more sober, conservative and inward-looking attitude, reflecting the agrarian element and its dominance?

Far-reaching hypotheses of this kind can be little more than imaginative at this stage of Greek history, and much more factual evidence is required to support, or modify them or, indeed, suggest that they should be rejected. Whatever the true interpretation of the momentous change at this time, one reasonably certain fact remains, perhaps the most important for the history of later Greece. At this stage, if not earlier, Euboean enterprise really begins and has already extended far to the north and into the Near East. Its continuation and intensification is one aspect of the periods yet to be considered.

## IV SUB-PROTOGEOMETRIC I, II and III, THE 9TH CENTURY UNTIL ABOUT 750 BC

### (A) c. 900 to 825 BC

The next phase in the history of the site, perhaps the most crucial, embraces the periods SPG I and II with the early part of III; these will be considered as one since they are somewhat arbitrary pottery divisions rather than eventful stages, though there are discernible developments within the whole span of some 150 years to be considered.

Some salient features of this phase have been referred to earlier — a reversion to conservatism and continuing overseas trade. At the beginning this conservatism is manifested in the pottery not by any sudden rejection of previous innovations nor by a return to earlier fashions, which in any case were by now virtually obsolete. Rather, the vases show a slow return to a sober style with a more restricted range of motives and shapes, and this tendency is progressive throughout. Resistance (or indifference) to Geometric developments elsewhere and particularly at Athens, with a basic continuation of earlier fashions, is the reason why we have to adopt the cumbersome term Sub-Protogeometric to describe the pottery of Euboea and of its associated states. In metalwork, too, developments are along traditional lines with an especial fondness for the locally evolved brooch with its heavy boss.[32]

Initially there is considerable hangover from the previous LPG phase which blurs the division; this not only in pottery and metalwork but in burials too. There is a further warrior burial in a wooden coffin, while another was cremated in regular fashion to which may be added a third, a similar cremation, if the iron axe with it is an offensive weapon.[33] A distinctive difference, however, is the indifference to outside developments at Athens and elsewhere until the final years. For some time to come Attic imports are very rare and in the pottery 'taking SPG I and II as a whole, it seems fair to conclude that the Attic style had no more than a minimum effect on the Lefkandian'[34] while the few decorative borrowings that are made, are executed with an apparent indifference or incompetence. This Euboean reluctance to adopt new ideas and fashions may, however, be only one side of the picture. Attica, too, may in part be responsible since it appears to have been passing through a phase of parochialism and a pre-occupation with internal affairs.[35] Parochialism and recession might have been the interpretation of Euboean developments, also, were it not for the offerings contained in the tombs at Lefkandi.

We may start with the centaur figurine, so important for the history of Greek myth and art, which attests not only the skill of its local maker but possible connections with Cyprus for the method of its manufacture and with Thessaly, the traditional homeland of centaurs, for its subject.[36] Continuing relations with Thessaly and with the other states, seemingly associated with Euboea, are amply attested by parallel developments and finds at the other centres; so there was no recession or disintegration in this sphere.

But it is the objects imported by Lefkandi that so vividly demonstrate that its enterprise was not on the wane but expanding, and in no mean manner. The very beginning of this stage sees the Lefkandians placing in their tombs gold rings, necklaces of both faience and glass, and a bronze bowl.[37] The gold, if of uncertain origin, at least shows wealth, while there is no doubt about the Near Eastern origin of the necklaces especially that with its mass of Egyptianising figurines. The bronze bowl could well have come from the same region, while Cyprus is suggested as the probable source for the bronze mace-head, which may be as early as the other depositions. More imports arrive soon afterwards (in SPG II) — gold earrings of a probable Macedonian type, others of Phoenician origin, a seal from the same area, and imported crystal and amber beads.[38] Clearly Lefkandi was prospering through trade, much of which was with the E. Mediterranean and this, too, when no other state on the mainland has, to date, shown evidence of equal initiative or wealth.

The closing quarter century, up to about 825 BC., sees no falling off. Near Eastern imports of much the same kind continue and are joined by vessels of faience and bronze, a scarab and a cuboid seal.[39] An impressive quantity of gold was placed in some of the tombs of this stage — rings, bands or frontlets, and the strange decorative attachments which seem a Lefkandian fashion.[40] The number of burials datable to this stage is insufficient to assess whether this not inconsiderable wealth was concentrated in a few hands only or was more generally distributed but on present evidence some Lefkandians, at least, must have been among the most prosperous in Greece.

Evidence from the receiving end of the Euboean trading routes will be considered later, in the discussion of the next period, for it is not easy to date these exports precisely due to the conservative nature of the Island's pottery and especially the pendent semicircle cup or skyphos which is the vase found most commonly abroad. It is, however, highly probable that some of the considerable number of Euboean exports found in the Levant, Cyprus and Crete were carried there before 825 BC.

In the closing years before this, a new aspect reappears at Lefkandi, after an absence of well over a century, clear signs of contact with Attica, expressed this time not in any revolutionary change or absorption of new ideas but in imports of both vases and fibulae.[41] Two tombs even contain a great preponderance of Attic pots though the evidence from the settlement suggests not only that this picture is unusual but that renewal of close intercommunication with Attica, important as it is, resulted in only occasional imitations.

It is at this point that our evidence from the cemeteries ceases.

We now come to a most crucial and puzzling point in the history of the site. The evidence is by no means as firm as could be desired but appears dependable enough. There are no further burials in any of the three cemeteries extensively explored and there are signs of a destruction on an inhabited area on the slopes opposite Xeropolis, Area SL. Since the issue is of vital importance, the evidence should be set out in some detail.

The stage we are speaking of is early in what Desborough has called SPG III. One of the besetting difficulties is the extreme conservatism of the local pottery. Except for a limited number of changes, and an appreciable difference between the beginning and the end, accurate chronological or stylistic placing of a vase within the whole SPG stage is often very difficult, and especially so between SPG II and III.

There are however other aids. From SPG II onwards Attic imports increase and are occasionally imitated locally. In the Attic series, stylistic changes are more obvious: in fact, it is partly for this reason that Desborough has equated SPG II approximately with Attic EG II (some 75 years) and SPG III with Attic MG I and II (some 100 years). Also, the latest local SPG III can be distinguished by the prevalence of a low-lipped version of the pendent semi-circle skyphos and the absence of some earlier features.

Let us now turn to the cemeteries, where only a few of the tombs will concern us. Applying the criteria set out above, none of the burials is obviously late SPG III: the latest Attic imports are MG I and there are no local imitations of the later MG II style. This absence of post MG I influence is more decisive than might at first appear in that the latest datable tombs are rich in Attic imports and we know from the settlement that the sub- sequent MG II style was not infrequently copied locally. However, three of the richest, and seemingly late, burials have either no pottery or too little to be datable with any cer- tainty: moreover a few of those allotted to SPG II have vases which could go well into SPG III.[42] But, even if we include these in the latest phase there are still no more than eight or ten burials at the most, and these are quite inadequate to be spread over the hundred years assigned to SPG III. It therefore seems reasonably certain that at some stage during SPG III burials ceased in the cemeteries we have explored. This being so, there is no compelling reason why we should not accept what evidence we have, namely that no burials appear to have been made after the Attic MG I stage, the latest attested imports, which gives us a date about 825 BC.

There are uncertainties, too, about the settlement evidence, which comes from Trial SL outside the confines of Xeropolis.[43] This was not an excavation but a collection of sherds brought to light in one field by deep ploughing. The circumstances of finding are clearly unsatisfactory. There are, however, features more reliable than might be expected. The pottery appears to be basically contemporary and unusually it contained large sherds from the same vases. Several, including a large krater and amphora, could be restored from this material, a factor which, together with clear evidence of burning on the pottery in- dicates a destruction deposit. The pottery spread over a considerable area is homogeneous in style and is comparable with the latest datable burial in the cemeteries S 59. This tomb, like the settlement deposit, contains an Attic vase of MG I style.

There are clearly hazards in basing conclusions on less than satisfactory evidence of this kind, especially as the limited area of the excavation on Xeropolis produced no signs of a contemporary destruction. However, provided the nature of the evidence is fully appreci- ated, we believe it justifies a provisional conclusion, which only further excavation can test. It seems that three at least of the cemeteries were abandoned at about the same time as one important building in the settlement was destroyed by fire. The possibility of some disaster to the site and the strong probability of some severe dislocation of the population is indicated.

The interpretation of this situation might be easier if we had more evidence for the immediately ensuing period but the only definite information is that from the N.E. edge of the settlement, the sector where the Late Geometric house was subsequently built. Occupation continued in that area at least and its pottery shows little change apart from an increased tendency to imitate Attic models of MG II style.[44] Elsewhere information is very meagre indeed, but since the extent of the settlement is a most important factor in any reconstruction of events, it might be as well to set out what is known and to recognise its limitations.

Our difficulties in initially finding deposits of the Geometric stages on Xeropolis have been described in the introduction, together with an account of the trials we made to find it. The salient results of these are relevant.

The line of trials across the W. sector of the site, PLATE 4, produced no Iron Age deposit but only surface sherds and few at that: no trial is recorded as having produced more than one to two LG fragments. The evidence for LPG to SPG (indistinguishable to us then) is little better although the fabric of these sherds is more durable; only on the N. edge was sufficient found (46 sherds) to suggest occupation (Trials C and G).

The trials across the mid point of the site (I–X) were equally barren of LG but slightly more productive of LPG/SPG, especially in the centre (III–IV) where enough was found to be certain of the existence of some building there.

The series of trials in the E. sector revealed little sign of Iron Age occupation on the S. edge (A, D and F) but they located an LG building and SPG structure on the E. slope (W and Z). The N. edge, which had the deepest accumulation of levels, subsequently became the main area of excavation with its certain evidence for LPG, SPG I–III and LG habitation, with no obvious break.

To this we may add, from surface sherds, indications of SPG (and possibly LPG) occupation of the strip of Xeropolis between the first two series of trials (near J/K 3/4 of the grid) and along the S. edge (near J/K 1).

Outside the hill, and outside the area covered by our excavation permit, we know of SPG III (early) activity in region SL, discussed above, where there were no signs of subsequent inhabitation, and on the E. promontory LPG/SPG occupation, probably commencing in LPG. In addition, the summit of 'Toumba' apparently contains a building constructed in LPG; the test there was too small to recover evidence of later habitation if there was any.[45] Apart from this, the occasional LPG/SPG sherd has been found while walking in the general region but none of the LG stage.

The problem is how to interpret this evidence. On Xeropolis there has clearly been extensive erosion and considerable levelling due to cultivation, and this is most severe at the highest part of the hill where the Bronze Age levels lie just below the surface. On the other hand, on the E. slope, where we anticipated considerable erosion, LG and SPG buildings were found with their floors still preserved, close to the surface, while the LG house in the main area of excavation had accumulated a deep surface cover to protect it.

Clearly the evidence is ambiguous, and much more testing and excavation are required to reach reasonable certainty. We are left with the impression, and some evidence, that by LG there may have existed a much more contracted settlement, concentrated on the slopes facing the E. Bay, and that this shrinkage of the area of occupation may have been a gradual process, which perhaps began in SPG III. If so, we may link this with the other more definite signs of some disturbance at Lefkandi, suggested by the evidence from Area SL and the cemeteries. The latter, however, raises problems of its own. The abandonment of the old burial places indicates that the families which used them had either been wiped out or moved elsewhere. But what of the people who continued to inhabit Xeropolis? Were they members of other families, whose cemeteries are yet unknown? Or newcomers who buried their dead in a different locality? Or was Lefkandi no longer a secure enough region to entrust with their ancestors' bones? At present there can be no answer either to this problem, or to the more general question of what happened at Lefkandi, though the possibilities should be explored.

Attack by an enemy outside Euboea may be considered first. Archaeologically there is nothing to indicate a possible aggressor who must be presumed to have been successful but not to have taken over the site or settled there afterwards — to judge from the absence of alien aspects, apart from some increase in Attic influence. While this possibility cannot be dismissed, it hardly accounts for the salient fact that Euboean enterprise abroad was not halted; indeed, it is from this time onward that we can date much of the evidence at the receiving end, in the Levant and Cyprus. This, in turn, suggests the more convincing alternative of an internal, Euboean, enemy who profited from the war: only neighbouring Chalcis and Eretria are likely candidates. But there are grave difficulties in this. Eretria really only begins as a settlement at about this time and, on present archaeological knowledge, it hardly qualifies as a potential aggressor. And Chalcis may appear a stronger candidate only because we know far less, hardly anything in fact, about it at this stage and for long to come.[46]

If, however, Chalcis was by now a major settlement and was the aggressor, she could have taken by force such of the Plain as she did not already possess, occupied Xeropolis and forced the surviving Lefkandians to move east to the site of Eretria, an action which could hardly but result in prolonged enmity. This would account for the cessation of the old cemeteries, and new ones might not have been required for neighbouring Chalcidians; nor would their culture be noticeably different from that of the Lefkandians. It must, however, be emphasized that there is as yet no archaeological evidence that Chalcis was a major settlement at this time, and there are some slight indications that there was cooperation rather than hostility between Chalcis and Eretria until much later.[47]

There remains the possibility of internal dissension within the community, followed by a dispersal of population. Potential points of internal friction were considered earlier (pp. 360 ff. above) and they remain the same, land hunger and a conflict of interests involving political power. As for the first, though greater prosperity might be expected to lead to an increase in population, the number of burials in the cemeteries does not support this; the population based at Lefkandi would appear to have been surprisingly stable. Severe political dissension, the alternative, may well seem an anachronism at so early a date, but precocity in trade with resultant wealth may have created problems earlier there than elsewhere. We can, at least, be certain on one point, that the traders were bringing increased prosperity to the settlement and were playing an increasingly important role in its economy. The conservative element, on the other hand, if it is permissible to read so much into pottery and perhaps metal products, continued to withstand innovation, the desire for which had to find an outlet in imports, Attic or otherwise.

Is it possible in these circumstances that some internal conflict reached boiling point and that this is the explanation behind the events we have been considering? The result would be that the community at Lefkandi began to break up, with some families moving to Eretria, others to Chalcis and a remnant, how large we cannot tell, remaining on at the old site. If this surmise were correct, later historical traditions perhaps suggest a major section of the landowners and perhaps of the metalsmiths went to Chalcis, while many of the sailors and traders established themselves at Eretria, though the outlines would not be as sharp as this. Greater bonds with Boeotia and Thessaly on the one side and with Attica on the other could also have played a part. Some such outcome would, perhaps, need a Solon to accomplish it, but, if accomplished, immediate hostility between the two new, or strengthened, communities need not have arisen. Dispossession of land need not have been involved at this stage, even though Chalcidian control of the Plain would seem geographically inevitable. Rivalry, rather than cooperation, in trade could then have been an ultimate rather than immediate result, though the choice of acropolis sites at both Eretria and Chalcis suggests at least foresight.

It would be wise to suspend further conjecture until current excavations at Eretria have further clarified the earlier history of that site, and until something is known of the extent and development of Chalcis at the stage we have been considering.

## (B) After c. 825 BC

Whatever happened at Lefkandi around 825 BC, occupation continued there and Euboean trade, far from falling off, appears to be considerably on the increase. The scanty evidence from Lefkandi has been detailed above. No burials are known for this phase, and our knowledge, limited almost entirely to pottery, comes from the deposit in the main area of the excavations which was apparently dumped there to level off part of the site prior to building.[48]

The main aspect of this pottery is that it continues with little change its previous Sub-Protogeometric character. These are rather more Attic imports of MG II but they are still few, accompanied by the occasional imitation. The standard drinking vessel remains the pendent semicircle skyphos which at some stage in this phase is characterised by a much smaller and somewhat incurving lip. A few new features appear, a distinctive shallow plate being, perhaps, the most noteworthy.

Our main source of information for this stage, however, is not Lefkandi or Euboea but the receiving end of Euboean trade, the E. Mediterranean, especially Cyprus and Al Mina in Syria, and for the first time a few instances in Italy and Sicily.[49]

By far the most popular export was the pendent semicircle skyphos but there are examples of the plate and cup as well: here the conservative nature of Euboean pottery makes close dating very difficult, and particularly the division into pre- and post-825 exports. The final deposit on Xeropolis, which shows that Euboean pottery in LG underwent a virtually complete change involving the disappearance of the old type skyphos, enables us to place a large number of the exports before this stylistic dividing line (around 750). Occasionally the date of the Near Eastern context is of assistance; sometimes, too, the chronology of accompanying vases, such as the deposit in the royal tomb at Salamis in Cyprus where its two Euboean skyphoi and ten plates were accompanied by Attic vases of MG II style and so postdate 825 BC.[50] It is clear that the development of the pendent semicircle skyphoi into the version with a low lip, often with a somewhat incurving profile, is also later than this date and many of the exports are of this type. A number of others, however, may well be earlier including, perhaps, the first surviving evidence from Al Mina where an apparently joint Cypriot and Euboean enterprise had founded a trading post by 825 BC and may be even earlier, if the excavator was correct in believing that the remains of the earliest occupation had disappeared through erosion.[51]

Recent works which detail the evidence in the Syro-Palestinian region and in Cyprus make a complete survey of exports here unnecessary, and in any case it is enough for present purposes to summarise that the evidence for Euboean trade in the E. Mediterranean is already great and new excavations are yearly adding to it.[52] No other Greek region is as well represented; only Attica comes at all near to rivalling it in exports and at this stage it is well behind.

In the West there is as yet no rival; the surprise in this case is not the scantiness of the evidence but that it exists at all for this early period. It would seem only a question of time before excavation reveals the Euboean staging post on the W. coast of Greece which must have existed.[53]

Turning back to Euboea, we are faced with the problem of the role of Lefkandi in this trade, which is our immediate subject. At present, there can be no certainty on this point. So far, the excavations at Eretria have not produced much evidence for occupation at this stage, not enough to claim that Eretria was a major production centre for the exported skyphoi; and we have only a few sherds of this type from Chalcis. There is a likelihood that Lefkandi was still playing a considerable, if not the major, part in this trade but the role of Chalcis, Eretria and, indeed, other Euboean centres remains to be determined by further excavation and, perhaps, clay analyses of the vases.

## V   LATE GEOMETRIC, THE SECOND HALF OF THE 8TH CENTURY

The remaining history of the site, no more than a generation and perhaps less, was eventful in several ways. Earlier we spoke of a revolutionary change in the LPG period, largely reflected in the pottery which previously had persisted for a long time in a local, traditional and 'old fashioned' style. The same is true at this stage, though, perhaps, emphasis should be placed not so much on the change as on the tenacious way in which the Euboeans had resisted for so long developments elsewhere, and especially at Athens. Even so, the transformation, which involved an almost complete rejection of the past, was again abrupt. Also much the same influences, as in LPG, seem to be at work.

The Attic style is clearly most influential but Thessaly again plays a part, and probably Cyprus, to which this time must be added Corinth and other regions.[54] There is no slavish copying but an eclecticism which results in a highly individual and characteristic pottery, in general readily recognisable as Euboean. The need for change is easily explained. For long, one Euboean product which had found a ready market abroad was their pottery for its own sake (and not for its contents) but there was by now competition from other centres whose vases may well have been preferred for their novelty. Of course pottery is only one aspect of their trade and daily life. And it may be, that as earlier there was a more general change with part of the explanation being that innovation was prevailing over conservatism in a wider context. It is unfortunate that we do not have the tomb evidence, and a wider range of artefacts from the settlement. Of those we have, some are less readily interpreted; for instance the strange occurrence of primitive stone tools, the apparently new range of hand-made, plain pottery and the replacement of the traditional loomweight by a type perhaps of Near Eastern origin.[55]

Lefkandi can no longer be regarded as the most important site in the region. It is now only part of a triad, lying between Chalcis and Eretria, the latter at least a considerable and expanding city. Indeed, as has been suggested above, the indications are that Xeropolis was by now much contracted in size, probably concentrated around the East Bay, facing towards Eretria. Whether this reflects the direction of its allegiance lies in the realm of surmise, for archaeology helps little since the pottery of the day, our main indicator, is equally at home in both Chalcis and Eretria; culturally there appears to be no dichotomy, unless it be in the alphabetical script now being used in these cities.[56] Keeping for the moment, however, to surmise and following up the hypothetical situation at Xeropolis reconstructed in earlier periods, we may wonder whether our site was not by this time occupied mainly by remnants of that element of its population which had largely moved to Eretria, so retaining a protective presence nearer the Plain, part of which it continued to own and cultivate. This would explain the subsequent history of Xeropolis.

With firm evidence that by now Eretria was fast becoming a major settlement, and presumably Chalcis also, and with no sure criterion to distinguish between the pottery of the whole region, there is no way of assessing the particular role that our site may have been playing in the continuing trade with E. Mediterranean and in the newly established trading post (or colony) on Ischia and in subsequent colonisation in the West. We can, however, be certain that it was among the earliest to receive and use the new alphabetical script (derived from that of the Phoenicians) and that its occupants wore a type of Near Eastern seal which was so popular in the Euboean settlement on Ischia.[57] Some Corinthian and Attic imports show other contact with Greek areas nearer at home.

Moreover, though we have surmised that our settlement had by now contracted in size (and presumably in importance), the one building we have excavated and the pottery from it and elsewhere on the site will bear comparison in quantity and quality with any other known site of the time. Its inhabitants, who were concerned with agriculture, if we accept their structures to be granaries, included men of substance.

Then, around 700 BC, Xeropolis was sacked and virtually abandoned thereafter. The evidence from the one house fully excavated and the other tested may seem little enough to go on, but the first was burnt, the second hastily deserted and subsequent occupation, after a considerable break, is very scantily attested. The cause is fairly obvious; the site was a casualty in a conflict between Chalcis and Eretria, an inevitable result in view of its geographical position. It is even possible that its destruction was an important part of this campaign, if the idea that Xeropolis was by now an Eretrian 'outpost' is correct, a surmise which its subsequent abandonment might seem to support; it was too far from Eretria and too near to Chalcis to be effectively protected.

The outbreak of hostilities has been assumed. Apart from the seeming destruction of Xeropolis, we have the evidence of the earliest warrior burials at the W. Gate in Eretria, which must be more or less contemporary; the subsequent honours paid them strongly indicate they were war heroes.[58] More than this, however, we have the tantalisingly incomplete references in ancient sources to a war between Chalcis and Eretria which involved other states allied to either side.

This is not the place to restate the literary evidence; enough here to note that before excavation at Lefkandi, and the recent discoveries at Eretria, historians were already tending to place the event (or series of events) around the end of the 8th century.[59]

The subsequent history of Chalcis and Eretria, and of Euboea in general, lies outside the scope of this summary. Xeropolis was already well on the way to earning its present name of the deserted city. One or two buildings of the 6th century housed its last occupants; their purpose — religious, military or agricultural — may one day be clarified by further excavation.

# Notes

## 1. INTRODUCTION TO THE EXCAVATIONS

1. One caique during our excavations came from Kea, and we were able through its skipper to send a letter to our colleague, Professor Caskey on that island.

2. Photographs of the Plain are included in our article in *Archaeology* 25, 10—12.

3. The marsh has almost dried up since we first went there. We have been concerned about possible sea changes and their effects on the local geography. A change, similar to that which has submerged much of the EH settlement of Manika, to the N of Chalcis, could imply that our bays were much smaller in antiquity, not allowing for silting from soil erosion of the higher ground around them. A permit was sought and granted for an interested group to make sondages in the valley but was, unfortunately, not taken up.

4. See *Survey*, under Lefkandi, for references.

5. The section on PLATE 4 shows the depth of our trenches and indicates heavily in black where rock was reached and its incline.

6. The unusually large number of hydrias and amphoras (and perhaps pithoi) in the LH IIIC suggest this.

7. *BSA* 47 (1952) 1ff. and 52 (1957) 5ff. and *The Greeks Overseas* (1st ed.) 65.

8. For Amarynthus, see *Survey* under that heading, a most promising site comparable with Xeropolis at least for the prehistoric periods.

9. A number of preliminary reports have already appeared: M.R. Popham and L.H. Sackett, Excavations at Lefkandi 1964—6, A Preliminary Report (1968); Excavations in Euboea at Lefkandi, *ILN* 5/6/1965; Lefkandi, A Euboean Town of the Bronze Age and Early Iron Age, *Archaeology* 25, 8ff.; elsewhere by editors in *AR* 1964—5, 18; 1965—6, 10; 1967—8, 12; 1969—70, 8; 1970—1, 7 and *Current Archaeology* 7 (1968); M.R. Popham, V. Desborough and R. Nichols, A Euboean Centaur, in *BSA* 65, 21ff.; M.R. Popham and E. Millburn, The LH IIIC Pottery from Lefkandi, A Summary, in *BSA* 66, 333 ff.; P.G. Themelis, A Protogeometric Necropolis near Lefkandi, in *AAA* II (1969) 98ff.

10. See Section 14 note 1 for publications of finds and historical conclusions by other authors. We are grateful to D. French and R. Howell for vetting the paragraphs on the EBA and MBA site respectively.

## 3. THE PROTOGEOMETRIC AND SUB-PROTOGEOMETRIC POTTERY

1. *BSA* 31, 28 and pl. 7, no. 118: Marmariani.

2. The inner lip has a reserved band, and the remainder of the inside is monochrome except, usually, for a reserved circle on the floor.

3. I subdivide lip heights into *high*: 1.5 cm or more; *medium*: 1 to 1.4 cm; and *low*: under 1 cm. It may be noted that the one skyphos with lip of medium height (26 = PLATE 30, 10) has the smallest mouth diameter.

4. For a ring base see *Ann*. 8—9, p. 219 and fig. 22: Tenos, Kardiani 2. For a conical foot see *PGP*, pl. 16: Andros; and *GGP*, 149: Tenos, Kambos.

5. Some of the sherds which show arcs only, especially four with thick arcs, could belong to this, rather than to the PSC, type of skyphos.

6. In addition to those illustrated there is one fragment of a monochrome skyphos with high everted rim.

7. See *Hesperia* 30, pl. 24, 4: very late LPG, from Nea Ionia near Athens.

31         8. Spectrographic analysis of a few vases suggests that this hand-made ware might not have
been produced locally.

31         9. Cf. T square V surface, and PLATE 284, 1—6.

32         10. Reminiscent of an LPG type in Attica: *Ker* IV, pl. 22, no. 1072 (tomb 34) and no. 2011
(tomb 40).

33         11. 139 may also be one of these, but the convex curve below the rim is sharper than on the
rest. It has a single rough zigzag on the upper body.

34         12. Note that although the shoulder is almost always monochrome, it can have sets of
semicircles: see S 33,4 (PLATE 101).

34         13. 204 has hatching on the neck. Whether this is related to the class under discussion I do
not know.

35         14. Also perhaps 193, which looks at first sight as though it might be the trumpet mouth of
a lekythos, as it is pierced, but the diameter of hole is surely too small for such a vase.

35         15. The only alternative is a small amphora with handles from shoulder to lip, see PLATE 128,
but this is a most rare shape for the local ware.

36         16. 143 is Attic MG I, but it comes from a disturbed sector dug at a later date, and could
well belong to the Levelling Material and not to the SPG Pit. This same sector produced a plate
with PSC below the rim, 144, a shape not otherwise represented in the SPG Pit, but of which
several examples were found in the Levelling Material.

36         17. As most of the sherds are very small, one cannot always be sure that one is dealing with a
cup and not with a skyphos.

37         18. It should be noted that the lower part of PLATE 33,1 is a hypothetical restoration. The
set of profiles all come from one small area: none is illustrated on PLATE 18.

37         19. PLATE 33,3 and 28 are two of the very rare Lefkandian examples of the elegant and
well-modelled late type of low to medium lip, which is swept back from the body in a concave
curve. See *PGP* 192 and pl. 25.

38         20. See *BSA* 31, p. 32 and pl. 10, no. 140, a krater from Marmariani, which has not only the
diagonals, but also a barred top rim and grooved rings above the handle zone.

38         21. 350 has an approximation to the *lambda* ornament (see the pyxis P 13,20, PLATE 133),
but it is doubtful whether the painter intended to depict this motive.

39         22. 144, mentioned in the analysis of the SPG Pit, should probably be assigned to the
Levelling Material.

39         23. *AA* 1963, 207 f., figs. 43—7.

39         24. In the one identifiable instance the interstice is filled, but not quite in the same manner
as the earlier examples of this technique. The drawing has omitted this fill.

39         25. This sherd has a thickness of 1.3 cm. If the upper motive is a meander, the piece is
atticising.

40         26. Possibly also 375, but the sherd is not dark ground.

40         27. Several sherds (see 380(?), 381, 383) come from the same vase, and at least one of the
sherds from the SPG Pit, 243, seems also to belong to it.

40         28. PLATE 21 shows a selection of these fragments at scale 1:2.

40         29. I owe these identifications to the expert eye of Professor Coldstream. It is very likely
that 143 should be added to the list.

41         30. For the types with multiple zigzag, chevron, and meander, the best comparative material
will be found in *Ker*. V, i, pls 89—94. See also the relevant sections on Attic EG and MG in
*GGP*.

41         31. See Coldstream, *GGP* 50 and *BICS* 18 (1971), p. 7, fig. 3 a—b; also Blakeway in *BSA* 33,
pl. 31,74. The vertical lines may provide an early framework for later subsidiary motives?

44         32. No stylistic difference can be seen between the sherds from the pit and those from the
rest of this level, and indeed joins were found between the one and the other. I therefore
discuss the material as a single whole.

44         33, The local potter was normally more careful. See PLATES 21 and 26.

45         34. See *PGP* pl. 13. The Lefkandian sherds are presumably of later date; they may be
atticising, though the cross-hatching of the ?meander is not an Attic feature.

45         35. The conical foot 582 could be from a cup or skyphos.

45         36. See e.g. *GGP* pl. 2 f. But for the cross-hatching see no. 34 above.

46         37. See pp. 42 ff. Cf. from the cemeteries P 35,2; P Pyre 11,9; T 7,2; T 17,2 and 3.

46      38. See the SPG Pit, p. 32.

46      39. See *Ker.* I, pl. 49, T 25. One cannot of course say whether the Lefkandian motive was similarly asymmetrical.

46      40. Cf. PLATE 112, S Pyre 4,2, and PLATE 26, 759 (classed as LG by Professor Boardman, PLATE 46) for this motive.

46      41. Perhaps recalling Attic LPG. Cf. *Ker.* I, pls. 67 and 69; *Ker.* IV, pl. 22.

46      42. 649 is upside down, and so probably is 652.

46      43. Cf. *Hesperia* 21, pl. 73 (EG I), and 37, pl. 21 (EG II—MG I). The motive does not seem to appear in Attica before EG I.

46      44. *AD* 22, ii, pl. 70. LPG.

46      45. Other examples at Lefkandi: Moulds Deposit, 34; SPG Pit, 107; Levelling Material, 307; Area 3 South, yard floor, 575; Miscellaneous Xeropolis, 670; Palia Perivolia, Channel surface, 920 and 921.

48      46. The pit contained an inscribed sherd, find no. 102, PLATE 69d.

48      47. See *GGP* 169, with n. 13.

48      48. See *GGP* 50. Perhaps a precursor of the skyphos with bird in central panel: cf. *BSA* 33, pl. 31, 74, and *N.d.S.* 1963, 271, fig. 132 f. (Veii). Also, most recently, Andreiomenou in *AE* 1975, pls. 56a and 57a, from Eretria.

49      49. Among the unillustrated sherds were two from PSC skyphoi (one with high lip) and two conical feet; cups were monochrome, some with outswung lip. No fragments of cups with zigzag on the lip.

49      50. Reminiscent of certain SPG II pyxides from the cemeteries, e.g. S 33,8; P 47,13; T 23,7 and 9.

49      51. A large cover slab 1 m wide was found close to C, and there were reports of a disturbed tomb.

49      52. Twenty-two sherds retained, of which eighteen were LPG or SPG, three Middle Helladic, and one Late Helladic.

49      53. Only one of the eight has a reserved band on the lip.

50      54. One ridged rim noted; two had sets of verticals on the outer surface.

50      55. See S 33,4, which however does not have the belly diagonals.

50      56. Excepting the two illustrated pieces, one cup lip, one cup handle, and a few body and base sherds which may belong either to cups or to shallow bowls. There was also one fragment of a conical foot.

50      57. *BSA* 31,32 and pl. 10, nos 141—2.

50      58. Seven rim sherds had, on the outer surface, opposed diagonals or groups of diagonals.

51      59. Cf. PLATE 277, nos 1020—2, from P Pyre 32 fill.

51      60. See *Ker.* V, i, pl. 20, no. 290 (Grave 22) for the most elaborate example, dated MG II by Coldstream, *GGP* 23, 25 and pl. 5 f. The decorative system, in a simpler form, is found on an Argive krater (Courbin, *CGA* pl. 27, C 204) of probable EG II date (see *GGP* 115—16). The krater here discussed is MG I in Coldstream's view.

51      61. See *AD* 28 (1973), pl. 29b. Athens, S of the Acropolis.

51      62. The latter is perhaps preferable: cf. *AD* 28 (1973), pl. 30a.

51      63. Excepting C, for the reason given above.

52      64. The projection on top of 659 is part of an out-turned uncarinated lip.

52      65. I know of no other instance on a PSC skyphos.

52      66. See also PLATE 14, 34 and 44, from the Moulds Deposit.

52      67. *JHS* 77, 214, fig. 4a. Note the high flaring foot; it is unfortunate that the foot of the Lefkandian vase was not found.

52      68. The centre circle is completely filled in. See also PLATE 23, 522.

53      69. This may also be a sign of earliness.

53      70. Similar skyphoi (and cups) are found sporadically in other deposits, and have so far resisted classification.

53      71. It is uncertain whether either 689 or 686 should be classified as a skyphos.

53      72. It is in fact accepted as LG by Professor Boardman, PLATE 46, 109. For earlier cross-hatching see S Pyre 4,2 (PLATE 112) of SPG II date, and PLATE 24, 626 from under the yard floor of Area 3 South, more likely to be LPG.

53      73. See PLATE 16, 156 from the SPG Pit.

53      74. Cf. PLATE 22, 480 from Trial W for another instance.

53      75. See P 13,20 (PLATE 133) and perhaps 350 from the Levelling Material.

53      76. 688, mistakenly placed among the small open vases, has a similar decoration; its yellow-ish surface and red-brown paint suggest a non-local manufacture.

53      77. 704 might be an amphora, and not a krater, sherd, as paint is applied for a short distance only inside; the width of the rim, however, 3.5 cm, seems too great for an amphora.

53      78. The same principle can be seen on a kantharos from Ithaca (*BSA* 33, pl. 3, no. 34) and a krater from Knossos (*BSA* 55, 130, pl. 31).

53      79. For a probably similar one see PLATE 278 A top left, from the East cemetery.

54      80. For rays on the neck see T 7,1 (PLATE 172) and S Pyre 4,3 (PLATE 281 B).

54      81. The curve of the sherd, and its thickness, suggest that the circles are on the shoulder.

54      82. Compare the sherds from the fill of T 32, PLATE 280.

54      83. Almost invisible in the illustration; there are traces of three arcs.

54      84. This sherd might be from a pyxis.

55      85. Compare perhaps the oinochoe P 22,8 and the jug with cutaway neck P 22,13 (PLATE 138).

55      86. The only other is the EPG pyxis S Pyre 1A, 1 (PLATE 92). This sherd looks appreciably later; I have not been able to identify any closely comparable vase outside Lefkandi.

55      87. Verdhelis, *PGRT* pl. 13, no. 145, illustrates a pyxis from Marmariani with elaborate decoration including a cross-hatched swastika.

55      88. *GGP* 24. See *AA* 1963, 201f., fig. 41.

55      89. In vogue from EG II onwards — see *GGP* 15, 19, 24.

55      90. *GGP* 24.

55      91. *GGP* 19 and 24.

55      92. For an LG dating see p. 63 and PLATE 46, 111.

55      93. For the chain of diminishing diamonds see *Ker.* V, i, pl. 20, no. 290 (grave 22) = *GGP* pl. 4d and f. MG II. See also *AD* 28, pl. 29b (south of the Acropolis).

55      94. *GGP* 18 and 50f. Coldstream contrasts the cross-hatched tongue, 'a flattened gadrooning', apparently new in LG Ib, with the earlier, and continuing, of a metallic prototype.

55      95. Cf. the 'Isis' grave, *CVA* Athens I, pls 3, 15 and 4, 2. Alternatively, it may be LG, see p. 54 and PLATE 56, 281.

55      96. See *GGP* pl. 3.


# 4. THE LATE GEOMETRIC POTTERY

58      1. Summarised in *BSA* 68 (1973) 273; and see now W.B. Stern and J.-P. Descoeudres, *Archaeometry* 19 (1977) 73—86.

58      2. On Eretrian clay appearance see *Eretria* v, 16 f.

62      3. P. Courbin, *Céramique géométrique de l'Argolide* (1966) 75, n. 3, apparently sets some store by the recent history of the study of the multiple brush and by his observations in Argos of 1953, the second year of the new excavations there, so I offer the following additional testimonia: In *BSA* 47 (1952, written in 1950) 17 with n. 83, its use in Euboea and the islands was investigated. To resolve his uncertainty about its continued use after the sixth century there is the late fifth-century Attic skyphos from Old Smyrna, *BSA* 53—54 (1958—9) 176 f., no. 166 with a triple brush; and cf. J.N. Coldstream, *Knossos, Sanctuary of Demeter* 40, no. 29, inter alia.

62      4. *BSA* 47 (1952) pl. 1A.12, and compare the kantharos (?) ibid. pl. 1A.11. On a Cycladic skyphos, *Délos* x, pl. 8A.1.

63      5. *Délos* xv, pls 30—2, 39, 40 passim.

63      6. *BSA* 47 (1952) pl. 1A.23.

63      7. *NdS* 1963, 272, fig. 133a.

63      8. *JHS* 60 (1940) 3, fig. 1p.

63      9. *BCH* 95 (1971) 361, fig. 53; *BCH* 94 (1970) 233, fig. 87 (Kouklia); *RDAC* 1975, fig. 60 (Amathus; bird and diamond pattern).

63      10. *BSA* 23 (1933—4) 194, fig. 16.

63    11. *BSA* 47 (1952) pl. 1B.7–9; *AntK* 10 (1967) pl. 38.6, 7; *AntK* 11 (1968) pl. 27.1 (compare our 3); *AAA* 3 (1970) 318, fig. 2.6; *AE* 1975, pls 55β, 56; cf. *AE* 1903, 1, fig. 1 for linked circles on a kantharos rim.

63    12. *ADelt* 26 (1971) Chron. pl. 227.α7. Cf. *Eretria* v, 44, n. 138.

63    13. *JHS* 60 (1940) 5, fig. 2.a, d, e (and cf. c for the linked circles).

63    14. *Dialoghi* 1969, fig. 30b.

63    15. *Délos* xv, pls 39. Bb 51, 40. 53.

63    16. *AA* 1972, 410, fig. 37.73.

63    17. *Samos* v, pl. 49.282–8.

63    18. Kouklia, *AntK* 10 (1967) pl. 37.5 and 133, fig. 1; *AA* 1978, 13, fig. 2.

63    19. *Boll. d'Arte* 1972, 211 ff., fig. 38b. c.

64    20. But cf. the kantharos, *Délos* xv, pl. 41. Bb 59, and krater rim, *AA* 1972, 397, fig. 19.34; both Naxian.

64    21. For the interchange see V. Karageorghis and L. Kahil, *AntK* 10 (1967) 133–5 and *AE* 1975, pl. 53a.

64    22. Dots — *ADelt* 20 (1965) Chron. pl. 336d; *AE* 1975, pls 55a, 58γ (cf. our 106). Dashes — *BSA* 47 (1952) pl. 1A.9, 13; *Eretria* v, pl. 2; cf. *PAE* 1955, pl. 43a.1.

64    23. *JHS* 60 (1940) 7, fig. 3k.

64    24. *Dialoghi* 1967, pl. 14.

64    25. In the Cyclades the pattern is commoner on kantharoi, *Délos* xv, pls 29. Ae 77; 31. Ae 74, 78.

64    26. *BSA* 61 (1966) pl. 16d.

64    27. *AntK* 11 (1968) pl. 27.1 (Eretria, circles on rim); cf. *JHS* 60 (1940) 5, fig. 2r.

64    28. *BSA* 52 (1957) pl. 2a, d (Al Mina).

64    29. *AE* 1975, pl. 59β. The pattern is also here rendered as a zigzag.

64    30. *BSA* 47 (1952) pl. 1A.22, 24; *ADelt* 21 (1964) Chron. pl. 225b.

64    31. *BSA* 52 (1957) pl. 1.19, 21.

65    32. *BSA* 47 (1952) pl. 1B.5, 6; *Eretria* v, pls 1, 2.

65    33. *BSA* 52 (1957) pl. 1.11 (as a kotyle).

65    34. *JHS* 60 (1940) 5, fig. 2.o.

65    35. An example from Eretria, *BSA* 47 (1952) pl. 1A. 17.

65    36. *BSA* (1957) pl. 1.27.

66    37. *BSA* 47 (1952) pl. 1B.10–13, 17–19.

66    38. Ibid. pl. 1B.10, cf. 13. Another example with the ordinary dotted oval, *ADelt* 20 (1965) Chron. pl. 337a; and with diamonds, *ADelt* 17 (1962) Chron. pl. 167e. See also *AE* 1975, pls 58a, b, 59a for a typical assemblage, and *Eretria* v, pl. 3.

66    39. *Eretria* iii, pl. 15.69; *AntK* 10 (1967) pl. 38.9 and p. 135.

66    40. *PAE* 1955, pl. 43β.1 (= *Ergon* 1955, 37, fig. 37).

66    41. *BSA* 52 (1957) pl. 1.26 and cf. 14 for a lattice-patterned lip of this shape.

66    42. *BSA* 52 (1957) pl. 2. a, b, d.

66    43. *GGP* 193, with n. 12, remarks on this. Compare also *Athenian Agora* viii, pl. 8.135, and the unusual double skyphos in Heidelberg (G. 14; *CVA* iii, pl. 110.5; cited in *BSA* 47 (1952) 47, n. 23) with linked blobs on the lip and the handle zones each bearing two dotted ovals and a squashed swastika, which look more than a little Euboean-inspired.

66    44. Eretria, *AE* 1903, 1, fig. 1, has linked concentric circles at the lip; and cf. *BSA* 47 (1952) pl. 1A.11; *AE* 1975, pl. 60.

67    45. The Euboean imitations of PC are studied in *BSA* 52 (1957) 6 f.; Coldstream, *GGP* 193 f. and *Geometric Greece* (1977) 195; and cf. C.W. Neeft, *BABesch* 50 (1975) 109. Coldstream observes that the latest, deep EPC kotylai are not imitated, but it is not surprising that a Euboean potter would not bother to keep up to date, given his earlier record.

67    46. *BSA* 47 (1952) 3, fig. 1.10.

67    47. *BSA* 52 (1957) pl. 1.8.

67    48. *BSA* 47 (1952) 3, fig. 1 and pl. 1A.1–8; *AntK* 11 (1968) pl. 28.2; *ADelt* 23 (1968) Chron. pl. 184b; *AE* 1975, pl. 54γ; *Eretria* v, 46 f.

67    49. For an ordinary pattern, *ADelt* 16 (1961) Chron. pl. 132γ.

67    50. *JHS* 60 (1940) 19, fig. 8b, c; *BSA* 52 (1957) pl. 2b.

67    51. *Atti III Convegno di studi sulla Magna Grecia* (1961) 263 ff., pl. 1.

67     52. At Eretria, *BSA* 47 (1952) 2 with fig. 2.

67     53. *Eretria* iii, pls 15.62, 63, 65; 16.71, 74; *AntK* 11 (1968) 100; cf. *Eretria* v, 49.

67     54. *ADelt* 16 (1961) Chron. pl. 132a.

67     55. Nea Lampsakos — *ADelt* 27 (1972) A. pl. 66δ; and compare the basket, pl. 57δ, from Chalcis.

67     56. P.N. Ure, *Aryballoi and Figurines* (1934) pl. 3 (91.27); *AAA* 7 (1974) 329, fig. 6, from Akraiphnai (with Middle Protocorinthian).

67     57. E.g. *Ker.* V, 1, pl. 87.364; Berlin 31573 (Boeotian).

68     58. Cf. the spouted crater, *Thorikos* iii (1965) 49, fig. 58.

69     59. The Attic and Melian 'sunburst': *GGP* 183 and pl. 39d (Melian); and cf. *Thorikos* iv (1969) 75, fig. 41; and in Boeotian, A. Ruckert, *Frühe Keramik Böotiens* (1976) pl. 30.10.

69     60. 267 is a surface find, before excavation (*BSA* 61 (1966) pl. 16, d.3).

69     61. *Dialoghi* 1974–5, figs 6, 7. On Boeotian, Ruckert, op. cit., pl. 28.9.

69     62. *AntK* 11 (1968) pl. 28.3 (circles and a white wavy line in the lip); *ADelt* 20 (1965) Chron. pl. 336e; *ADelt* 23 (1968) Chron. pl. 184a; *Eretria* v, 42–4.

69     63. Eretria: *BSA* 47 (1952) pl. 2B. 2–5; *Eretria* iii, pl. 14.58 (= *AntK* 11 (1968) pl. 27.3) with body fragments carrying chequer and an added white zigzag; for chequer and linked circles, *ADelt* 20 (1965) Chron. pl. 336b. Chalcis: *ADelt* 26 (1971) Chron. pl. 227.β.3; cf. a body fragment with added white, *ADelt* 16 (1961) Chron. pl. 132b; *AE* 1975, pls 62, 63, 66b, 67, 68. Compare also *Délos* xv, pl. 19. Acl. Chequer, which appears also on oinochoai (as 303–5) is comparatively rare in Boeotian (Ruckert, op. cit., n. 457).

69     64. In Boeotian this feature appears only later, on Euboeanising amphorae and kraters: Ruckert, op. cit., 26.

69     65. *BSA* 47 (1952) pl. 2.B, 6, 7, 14–18 and 8, fig. 9.

69     66. *ADelt* 20 (1965) Chron. pl. 337c.

69     67. *BSA* 52 (1957) 4, fig. 1.43.

69     68. Ibid. fig. 1.41

69     69. It is also to be seen on a crater, *Athenian Agora* viii, pl. 16.282.

69     70. *BSA* 47 (1952) pl. 4.A5, B6; and compare the Cycladic skyphoi, *Délos* xv, pl. 30 Ae 65, 66.

70     71. E.g. *AR* 1970/1, 65, fig. 6.

70     72. *Samos* v, pls 21, 71–4.

70     73. The shape may be the 'kothon'. For examples in Boeotia see Ruckert, op. cit., pl. 28.6 and p. 38, varia 9–13.

70     74. *Eretria* iii, pl. 16.74 and colour pl. C1 (= *AntK* 11 (1968) pl. 27.6); *AE* 1903, 16, fig. 9. Cf. *PAE* 1941, 37, fig. 9b, from Avlonari in Euboea.

71     75. *GGP* 191; *BSA* 47 (1952) pl. 3.B2; *AE* 1975, pl. 65.β1.

71     76. Eretria: *BSA* 47 (1952) 8, fig. 11, pl. 3A.8–14, 15–16 (lip): *ADelt* 20 (1965) Chron. pl. 337b; *Eretria* iii, pl. 15.67 (simple banding).

71     77. *Zagora* i, fig. 56 (as Corinthian); *AE* 1970, pl. 75d (as Cycladic).

71     78. See now *Eretria* v, 39, Beil. 3.

71     79. *BSA* 43 (1948) pl. 27.427.

71     80. *BSA* 47 (1952) 16 ff.; A4 is now mended, *ADelt* 17 (1962) Chron. pl. 167a.

71     81. Ruckert, op. cit., 54 ff.; Group C is strongly Euboeanising.

71     82. Athens 12856; *GGP* pl. 41e; Ruckert, op. cit., n. 137 rightly adds *ADelt* 26 (1971) Chron. pl. 185.2, 3.

71     83. *AR* 1970/1, 63, fig. 1.

72     84. J.-P. Descoeudres, *BCH* 96 (1972) 269 ff.

72     85. Compare the kantharos, *Délos* xv, pl. 32. Ae 87.

72     86. Group Aa: *Délos* xv, pl. 9. Aa 33, 34; 10. Aa 35.

72     87. See *Perachora* ii, ch. 6. At Eretria, *AE* 1903, 11, fig. 6 (NM 11726); *Eretria* iii, pl. 15.66.

73     89. Cf. Anavysos, *PAE* 1911, 124, fig.

73     90. The standed amphora, *Münzen und Medaillen Auktion* 51 (1975) pl. 11, no. 69, is said to be Cretan but this is not a shape or technique of overall decoration known on the island, and I feel the disposition of three major maeander friezes on the body somehow un-Hellenic.

73     91. And cf. Naxos, *PAE* 1937, 119, fig. 5; and island with close ceramic links with Euboea in these years.

74     92. Here, pp. 114 ff. P. Kahane discusses the subject matter. His article, but in English, appears also in N. Robertson, *The Archaeology of Cyprus* (1975) 151 ff.

75     93. Possibly the fragment of a large stand, with a bird panel and rows of circles, found in Rome, should be mentioned here: E. Gjerstad, *Early Rome* iv (1966) 519 and fig. 155.3; *Bull. Comm. Arch. Rom.* lxxvi (1956/8) pl. 1.1; *RM* lxxi (1964) pl. 2.1.

75     94. *BSA* 68 (1973) 270—8 reviews this.

76     95. And cf. *Samos* v pl. 8.42.

76     96. There is an interesting parallel now from Athens, possibly not Attic — flying birds with raised feathered wings with no ground line between them and a linked dot frieze: *ADelt* 28 (1973) pl. 33b. For the possible Cypriot origin of the raised-wing motif see J.L. Benson's article in Robertson, op. cit., 129 ff.

76     97. Best observed in *AntK* 16 (1973) pls. 25, 26.1. Even the Argive LG artists could manage a comparable frieze better (*GGP* pl. 26). For some hand-drawn circles in Naxos see *AA* 1972, 413, fig. 40.56. Our 306 has small hand-drawn concentric circles but on 274 they are neatly compass-drawn.

76     98. I do not see the painter's hand in *PAE* 1961, pl. 155c, *pace Eretria* v, 57, n. 344.

76     99. We may note the recurrence of this pattern in seventh-century Naxos (*PAE* 1960 pl. 197a). In the Geometric of the island note the fill of *PAE* 1971 pl. 208a. The most distinctive wing type in Naxos is the raised triangle, as *PAE* 1972 pl. 148γ; *AM* 54 (1929) 154, fig. 7; *Délos* xv pls 18, 19, Ac2. The added white zigzags of simpler Euboean styles can also be found in Naxian, as ibid., pl. 36, Bb10. Historically Naxian collaboration is with Chalcis rather than Eretria, as in the foundation of Naxos in Sicily in 735.

76     100. The author's views on this will appear in the new edition of *CAH* iii. 1.

76     101. The main sources are *BSA* 52 (1957) 1—14, pl. 1; *BSA* 61 (1966) pl. 14c; *ADelt* 16 (1961) Chron. pl. 132; *ADelt* 26 (1971) Chron. pl. 227; *ADelt* 27 (1972) pls 57, 66; *AAA* 2 (1969) 27—9.

77     102. But if Neeft is right in proposing an early date for Euboean imitations of bird kotylai (*BABesch* 50 (1975) 116) this absence from Lefkandi is even more remarkable.

78     103. *BSA* 52 (1957) 1 ff.; *The Greeks Overseas* (1980) 37 ff.

78     104. G. Buchner and J. Boardman, *JdI* 81 (1966) 1 ff. and p. 62 for the Lefkandi seal.

78     105. A most useful summary and references by D. Ridgway in *Greeks, Celts and Romans* (1973) 5—38. S.C. Bakhuizen has questioned the Eretrian role in *MedNedInstRome* 37 (1975) 1 ff. but our Lefkandi/Eretria wares, if properly defined, are the most influential in Ischia.

78     106. These have been noticed above. J.-P. Descoeudres, *AntK* 16 (1973) 87 f., suggests that the town at Zagora was founded from Eretria but pre-Eretria pottery has since been found there so Lefkandi seems a more probable source.

78     107. Cf. the one-handler from Eretria, *AAA* 9 (1976) 200, figs 2, 3a.

78     108. Discussed by A. Andreiomenou in *AAA* 7 (1974) 241—3 with fig. 12; and see *AntK* 11 (1968) pl. 28.10—11; *Eretria* v, 48, pl. 7.

78     109. A comparable example from Eretria, *ADelt* 20 (1965) Chron. pl. 336 f., is put in the early seventh century, or its third quarter — *Eretria* v, 47, pl. 6.

## 5. THE OTHER FINDS

82     1. *Hesperia* Suppl. vii, 96 and comment there.

82     2. *Lachish* v, pl. 15,7; stratum iii dated to 8th century.

82     3. *JdI* 81, 1—62.

83     4. E.g. *Megiddo* i, pls 93—5 though with a distinct preference for stone.

83     5. *Hesperia* iii, 476 and Suppl. vii, 73, and *Corinth* xii, 148. If the one described in *BSA* xxi, 41 from Marmariani Tomb V is comparable, it is much earlier.

83     6. Davidson, *Corinth* xii, 172.

83     7. *Hesperia* xxx, 170—3.

84     8. *Hesperia* xxx, 342.

84     9. *Ker* v, 127 and discussion by Desborough on p. 46.

84     10. *Hesperia* suppl. vii, 108 and *Délos* xviiii, 341 f. Ours resembles one from Athens but has 7 instead of 8 spokes. Their possible use is discussed by Deonna in the *Délos* publication.

85   11. From the discussion in R. Martin, *Manuel d'Architecture Grecque* I, 65 f., the incised tile (98) appears to be unexpectedly and uniquely early in date.

89   12. L.H. Jeffery, *The Local Scripts of Archaic Greece* (1961) 68, no. 1, pl. 1.

91   13. The five-stroked sigma is consistently used in the dedication on a bronze kouros-statuette in the Museum of Art, Rhode Island School of Design (David Gordon Mitten, *Catalogue of the Classical Collection* (1975) no. 11). The authenticity of this piece has been disputed (see the careful discussion by Mitten, who concludes that it is genuine and datable c. 540 BC), partly because of similarities between its inscription and that of the Mantiklos Apollo. Its provenance was said to be the Ptoion sanctuary.

91   14. Jeffery, op. cit. 183 f.

91   15. Op. cit. 69, n. 10.

92   16. M.Z. Pease, *Hesperia* iv (1935) 242, no. 38, fig. 14.

92   17. Jeffery, *BSA* lix (1964) 40, no. 2, fig. 1.

92   18. Jeffery, op. cit. 45, no. 1, pl. 5*a* (dinos) and 47, no. 1, fig. 2 (greave).

92   19. Pollux ix. 83; Arist., F379 Rose = Heracl. Lemb., *Excerpta Politiarum* ed. Mervyn R. Dilts (1971) p. 26, para. 37.

92   20. Letter of 10 March 1979 from Dr. Keith DeVries, The University Museum, University of Pennsylvania; here referred to by his kind permission.

92   21. R.S. Young, *Hesperia* xxxviii (1969) 252 ff.

92   22. Cf. Desborough, *Euboean Participation* 25 ff.

92   23. E. Walter-Karydi, *Samos* vi (1973) 9, fig. 11 and pl. 22, no. 179.

96   24. See, in particular, Snodgrass, *DAG* 237 ff.

96   25. *CBMW* 190 ff.

96   26. *CBMW* 223.

96   27. *CBMW* 198, no. 19.

97   28. For Olympia, now see Michael Maass, *Die Geometrischen Dreifüsse von Olympia. Olympische Forschungen* X (Berlin 1978) with full reference to earlier literature.

97   29. Maass op. cit., no. 37, pl. 13; no. 81, pl. 27.

97   30. Benton, *BSA* xxxv, 61 f. fig. 17 and pl. 17e.

## 6. THE EXCAVATION AND LAYOUT OF THE CEMETERIES

101   1. The tombs are distributed as follows: 2 in Khaliotis' field, 64 in Skoubris, 40 in Palia Perivolia, 4 in the East Cemetery, 37 in Toumba. The number of pyres in Khaliotis' field is uncertain, there are 20 in Skoubris, 47 in Palia Perivolia, 3 in the East Cemetery, 10 in Toumba; 9 of these 80 pyres were either destroyed or not excavated.

102   2. The use of a vine spray in the initial stages of the digging helped to reveal the cuttings, while in the final stages much of the soft conglomerate was dug away to ensure that no tombs were missed.

102   3. Tomb types are distributed as follows: 59 cists, 2 in Khaliotis' field, 56 in Skoubris, one in Palia Perivolia; 72 shaft graves, 3 in Skoubris, 33 in Palia Perivolia, 3 in the East Cemetery, 33 in Toumba; 12 pit graves, 5 in Skoubris, 6 in Palia Perivolia, one in the East Cemetery; 4 mud brick built tombs, all in Toumba (although mud brick was used more widely to shore up the crumbling sides of shaft graves); 4 urn burials (in pit or shaft), one in Skoubris, 3 in Toumba.

102   4. Only for SPG III can no definite attribution be made, but this probably has no significance. Many pyres, having no grave goods, could not be dated.

103   5. Several of these spots had been suggested by the low readings taken by M. Aitken on a sample resistivity survey with the proton magnetometer. But the suggestions were very tentative, and a full survey of the field was not attempted due to the high tension cables running directly across the centre of the field.

104   6. These are numbered Tombs P 2–4, 6–19, 21–4, 25B–31, 33–9, 39A, 40, 41, 44, 46; P Pyres 1–13, 14A, 14B, 15–29, 31–47.

104   7. P 22 is LPG, P 21 is SPG II late.

104   8. Included are a ring-stemmed pedestal goblet fragment in Grey Minyan Ware, fragments of several large plain jars or amphorae, pithos fragments and a single piece of matt-painted ware. These comments are based on observations made by Roger Howell.

105     9. P 47, most comparable to the warrior grave T 26, was one of the largest graves found; larger and deeper than any in Palia Perivolia, and wider than any except P 21.

105     10. A fragment of wall of PG date was revealed during building operations just west of the summit of Toumba in 1977; only further excavation can show if this was part of a building connected in some way with the cemetery.

105     11. The principle of 'Horizontal Stratigraphy', as applied for instance by C. Styrenius in his re-assessment of the Keramikos Cemetery (*Studies* 24, 55 sq.) does not seem helpful as a tool in placing the Lefkandi graves into chronological groups.

106     12. See discussion p. 268 below (V. Desborough).

108     13. These include a gold and crystal pendant picked up on the surface of Trench VIII (PLATES 189, 234e), a bronze handle attachment (PLATE 246g), and disturbed bones perhaps from an inhumation (see Appendix C).

## 8. TOMB TYPES AND PYRES

197     1. P 25B was a small cist of the type common in the Skoubris Cemetery; it had sides and cover slabs of magnesite, but used mud brick and small stones in place of end slabs — a variation on the norm found in Skoubris. The pottery shows that this is the earliest tomb so far found in this cemetery; but it is likely that other cists existed. Vertical slabs appearing in the E baulk of Square Q immediately to the S of P 25B almost certainly belong to an unexcavated cists.

198     2. Specimens of oolite, mudstone and magnesite were kindly examined and identified by Richard Jones of the Fitch Laboratory, Athens.

198     3. At present quarried some five miles from Lefkandi, in the Lelantine valley at Afrati, where, however, the stone is harder at the quarry face.

198     4. The average length of the Toumba cuttings was 155 cm (range 100—280), that of the lower compartment 140 (range 80—240); average depth 135 (range 60—210). Palia Perivolia graves had average length 167 (range 100—245), with lower compartment where one existed 148 (range 70—245); average depth 120 (range 40—170).

198     5. These, along with several other comparatively shallow graves and the partially un-excavated T 37, have been classified as shaft graves, bringing the total in Toumba to 33. Tombs with shallow cuttings of depth ranging from 30—60 are T 2, 3, 7, 12B, 15, 23, 23A, 24, 25, 28.

198     6. These were S 46, 59; P 3, 13, 15, 21, 22, 34, 46; T 1, 3, 5, 9, 19—22, 31, 33—5.

198     7. The tombs involved are: S 59, P 3, P 21, T 3, T 31. The same practice applied to other grave forms (S 4, S 17, P 16, P 23, P 36, P 39/39B and probably P 12, P 31 and T 27). See discussion of secondary offerings placed out side or above the burial compartment proper, p. 214 below.

198     8. Thirteen out of the total of twenty-one were rich in grave goods: in EPG S 46; in LPG, P 3, P 22; in SPG I, T 1, T 3, T 22; in SPG II, P 21, T 5; in SPG III, S 59, T 19, T 31, T 33. Three had only one or two objects (P 15, P 46, T 9); five were empty (one, T 35, perhaps robbed).

199     9. This gives a total of thirty-nine out of seventy-two. It should be noted that other shaft graves have comparatively shallow cuttings, and no rock shelf survives. See note 5.

199     10. The dimensions of mudbricks recorded in Athens are 0.49 × 0.44 × 0.09 (*Ker.* v, 1, p. 10) and 0.23 × 0.23 × 0.09 (*Hesperia* 37, 80, n. 1); the divisions observed in Tomb P 16 may represent stages in laying a pisé construction, rather than individual mud brick dimensions.

199     11. Cf. an example at Vroulia, J. Boardman and D. Kurtz *Greek Burial Customs* (Oxford 1976), fig. 30.

200     12. P 43, regular in shape, had no rock shelf (though this is suggested by the contour line on the tomb plan).

200     13. Dimensions of pyres were, in the Skoubris Cemetery: length 120—175, width 50—80, depth 20—100; in Palia Perivolia length 100—175, width 50—90, depth 10—80; in Toumba length 145—180, width 60—100, depth 25—160. It is likely in the case of the very shallow pyres that surface erosion has taken place, and that the original depth was greater.

200     14. In Skoubris nineteen pyres were excavated or partly excavated; one other is probable (S Pyre 5). In Palia Perivolia forty-four pyres were excavated, in the East Cemetery three were located but not excavated, in Toumba nine excavated, one other located. Carbon patches

were observed in the area of Khaliotis' field. S Pyre 1A is not properly a pyre, but a deposit of pottery and ash from a pyre, see S 4, and p. 212.

200          15. In Palia Perivolia sixteen pyres contained earth and stones in the upper fill (P Pyres 1, 8, 12–13, 22, 27, 32–9, 41, 43), as did all the pyres found intact in Toumba. Cf. also S Pyres 12 and 16.

201          16. P Pyres 32, 40; S Pyres 3, 4 (lower), 7, 12, 16–18. Most Toumba pyres contained smaller stones.

201          17. Wood samples have been identified as olive by Miss C. Wood of the Ashmolean Museum.

201          18. The very fragmentary, brittle and calcined condition of the bone fragments closely parallels that described in detail by Calvin Wells in *A Study of Cremation* (*Antiquity* xxxiv, 1960, 29). Experiment in a modern crematorium has shown that a temperature of c. $900^\circ$C ($1650^\circ$F) is needed to reduce bones to this condition, and that the process may be complete (under those conditions) in as little as two hours. The most efficient system requires that the body be raised above the ground, a condition which seems to have been the normal one in our cemeteries, to judge by the arrangement of large stones or boulders in many of the pyres. The comparative state of preservation of any particular group of bones will then depend on the way in which the body was laid.

The cremations described by Wells were for 5th–7th century AD Saxon burials at Illingworth; but there is no reason to suppose that fires could not be brought to the same intensity at Lefkandi in the early 1st millennium BC. The inhabitants were expert in the use of the pottery kiln and were familiar with the problems of the metal furnace both in the Mycenaean and the Protogeometric periods. The use of olive is attested for the pyres (n. 16 above), and possibly olive waste was added, as it is today in lime kilns, with good effect. The occurrence of high temperatures in pyres is also attested by the damage suffered by some of the objects: pottery fabric was burnt to grey throughout; some metal objects were damaged, and for instance the gold rings S Pyre 2,1 and 2 were melted out of shape. The lowest actual melting point of native gold is c. $1,000^\circ$C ($1,832^\circ$F); cf. H. Hofman and P.C. Davidson, *Greek Gold* 23.

201          19. The proportion of metal and other objects to pottery was significantly higher in Toumba than in Palia Perivolia: Toumba 4 to 3 (200–137), Palia Perivolia 1 to 4 (76–261). The Skoubris cemetery, with mostly cist graves, had a ratio of about 3 to 4 (134–188).

202          20. The possibility arises that these might be related to the seven tombs which contained *no* pottery. However, we have no way of dating the empty tombs, and there is no especial proximity between these particular pyres and the empty tombs. There is then, no evidence for such a hypothesis.

202          21. Conversely it is not possible to say how many of the pyres were both the place of cremation and the burial. There may have been as many as 36.

203          22. Males P 47, T 14,1, T 18, T Pyre 8; females T 14,2, T Pyre 5, S Pyre 4 (upper), P 39 (?); other adults P Pyres 14A and B, P 45 (two), T Pyre 2, T 7, 12B, T 26, S Pyres 6 and 17; children S Pyres 2, 6 and 17, P 46, T 5, T 22, T 36. The identifications of T 14,1 and T 14,2 may be questioned, since T 14,1 was in a belly-handled amphora, while T 14,2 was in a neck-handled amphora with sword and spearhead associated.

203          23. The neighbouring group of graves of the East Cemetery is considered along with Palia Perivolia.

203          24. The graves of the East Cemetery are included with Palia Perivolia in Fig. 5 but distinguished. They do not form part of the argument, but do serve as an interesting comparison, since they include both a child grave and two adult graves, which contain inhumations yet are of comparable size to the larger graves of Palia Perivolia.

A similar clustering into two size groups is graphically illustrated for the PG cist graves at Asine, see R. Hägg, *Die Gräber der Argolis*, Uppsala 1974, fig. 33a. There, cist graves for children appear to have measured 50–90 in length and 20–40 in width. This would bring their areas within the range of 0.10–0.36 sq. m, which is quite comparable to the range of the smaller cists in the Skoubris cemetery (FIG 5). They are quite distinct in size from the larger cists which were built for adult inhumations.

203          25. It is necessary to anticipate in this discussion, to some degree, the suggestion made in Section 9 below that it was a frequent practice in these cemeteries to provide a tomb (cist, pit or shaft grave), clearly appropriate for inhumations yet here intended for the burial of remains gathered from cremations which took place in the pyres nearby (p. 211 below).

An alternative explanation for the variation of size in tombs where no bodies were to be placed is an economic one — in which case wealth or status might ensure a large grave, and a small one could indicate poverty rather than childhood. But the richness of the offerings is not in fact correlative with the size of the grave in any of the cemeteries, as may be seen from the lists of total grave offerings in FIG. 5.

205     26. It is interesting that these included two with groups of 'marbles'. P 7 contained a kalathos with ten limestone marbles; P 24 contained a fine shallow bowl with five similar stones. If these are connected with some game (such as knucklebones), this might indicate a grown child rather than an infant; the other finds include nothing to contradict this notion.

205     27. We may compare the statistic that in Crete during 1935 one half of all deaths occurring were of children under five years of age, and that the comparable figures for Mexico in 1939–1943 was almost 75% of the total deaths. L.G. Allbaugh *Crete, a Case Study of an Underdeveloped Area*, 139

205     28. Since the shafts of many graves in the Toumba Cemetery had been removed by the plough, all measurements shown in FIG. 5 are those of the inner or lower compartment. For this reason they appear smaller than those of Palia Perivolia, where the full measurements were available. In fact, the size of tombs in the two cemeteries is quite comparable.

206     29. T Pyre 8, krater fr. and pithos; T 3, horse and centaur; T Pyre 1, antler frs, perhaps part of a bow.

    These additional points may be made: faience beads were found in T 14 (double cremation with male and female); a bronze needle was found inside a lekythos in T 26; the gold 'attachments' of T 3 have a parallel in the warrior grave P 47.

206     30. For the Kerameikos cf. Styrenius *Studies* 106–7 and diagrams 9 and 10, where it is suggested that for the PG graves the kalathos occurs in female but not in male burials; coarse jugs are common in female but absent from male burials; pins are very common in female but do not occur in male, spindle whorls and clay beads occur in female but not in male burials. Fibulae, rings and bracelets are found in female and child burials (diagrams 10–11). For the Submycenaean period, pins are about four times as common in female graves as in male, fibulae are more common in female, not uncommon in male, and rings are about three times as common in female graves as in male (diagram 4, p. 45). *Cf.* also Smithson *Hesperia* 37, 100 and 109.

## 9. BURIAL CUSTOMS

211     1. Finger bones have often been found associated with their bronze rings, in both Late Bronze Age and Early Iron Age contexts. It is presumed that in most cases their good preservation is due to the close proximity of a metal object. At Lefkandi it is noteworthy that in some cases these are the only bones to survive in the grave. Thus the possibility ought to be considered that they were taken from the cremation and buried separately, though no close parallels are known for such a practice.

    The interment of fingers severed before cremation has been reported for 13th century BC Palestine and was a Roman custom, cf. Onians *Origins of European Thought* 496. At Gezer vessels were found containing single (or more) bones, and especially finger-bones, Palestine Exploration Fund Quarterly Statement (1905) 32. Festus describes the Roman custom of cutting off the finger *before* cremation, W.M. Lindsay *Sextus Pompeius Festus* (Teubner 1965) 135.

211     2. The possibility remains that these were taken from a pyre after an unusually inefficient cremation, as is suggested below for the many examples where much slighter remains were found.

212     3. Soil samples with the following proveniences were tested by Glynis Jones of the Fitch Laboratory, Athens: S 6, 10, 15B, P Pyre 2, T 22 fill, T 22 floor, T 27 fill. All the samples had a pH reading of 6.5, i.e. close to normal — very slightly acid but not sufficiently so to account for the total disappearance of the skeletons.

212     4. The same soil samples were given a phosphate test with the expectation that the total absorption of skeletons would give a high reading. Reaction was graded on a scale of 0–4; 0 = negative reaction, 1 = very slight positive reaction, 4 = slight positive reaction. Two control

Samples taken from the subsurface soil, one from the Skoubris field, outside the immediate vicinity of the graves, and one from Toumba summit, gave a reading of 2. The result of the tests of tombs and pyres was as follows: S 6 = 2; S 10 = 4; S 15B = 1; P Pyre 2 (charred wood) = 0; T 22 fill = 3; T 22 floor = 2; T 27 fill = 4. None of these reactions was considered sufficient to suggest the presence of decayed bone.

212    5. Burial rites which included the interment of a simulacrum or substitute for part of the body seems to be unparalleled in Greece. But such a rite is suggested elsewhere, as in the burial of masks in the contemporary Villanovan cemeteries, cf. Onians *Origins of European Thought* 135.

212    6. *JHS* 8 (1887) 46 sq.; 16 (1896) 237 sq. *CVA* Brit. Mus. 5 pl. 6B, 295. Cf. Lorimer, Pulvis et Umbra *JHS* 53 (1933) 166. Desborough *PGP* 218, *LMTS* 162. Andronicos *Totenkult*, *Arch. Homerica* W 56, 68, 113. Bouzek *Homerisches Griechenland* 1969, 108 sq.

213    7. *JHS* 8 (1887) 73, fig. 16; 16 (1896) 244 sq.

213    8. *JHS* 8 (1887) 68

213    9. *JHS* 8 (1887) fig. 16; *JHS* 16 (1896) 244 sq.

213    10. *Cf.* also Protogeometric tombs of similar form at the following sites: (a) Iasos: *Annuario* 43—4 (1955—6) 401 sq.; 45—6 (1967—8) 539 sq.; 20 (1970) 14—16. *AR* (1970—1) 46, n. 96. *Annuario* 47—8 (1969—70) 461 sq. P. Themelis *Frühgriechische Grabbauten* (1976) 36. (b) Çomlekçi: Themelis loc. cit. (c) Skyros: Themelis op. cit. 43 sq. (e) Chalkis: A. Andreiomenou *ChO* B, 248 sq.: Themelis op. cit. 51

213    11. M. Andronicos *Vergina I* (1969).

213    12. *ADelt* 17 (1961—2) A' 218—88, pls 92—153; *ADelt* 18 (1963) B'2 217—32, pls 257—62.

213    13. Op. cit. 161, 164 sq.

213    14. *ADelt* 17 (1961—2) 262, 266.

213    15. Op. cit. 163, n. 1 and 2.

213    16. Opt. cit. 46, pl. 15, P (later burial of the 4th century BC?). Well preserved frs. of bones were also found in Pithoi A3, Z2, Z4 and N.

214    17. In the discussion of these topics on pp. 202—207 no account is taken of the pyres statistically, as possible places of burial. Almost all age and sex identifications are dependent on grave offerings, or on the size of the tomb.

215    18. On the origin and survival of stone markers, see M. Andronicos *Ellinika Epitaphia Mnimeia*, *ADelt* 17 (1961—2) A', 161 sq.

215    19. K. Branigan has shown with persuasive arguments that ring dances were performed around the tholos graves of the Mesara in Crete. It is possible that these earliest ring dances of the Middle Minoan period had to do with the killing of the Minotaur and Ariadne's liberation by Theseus. (K. Branigan *The Tombs of the Mesara* (1970) 135, 138; N. Skoufopoulos *AJA* 75, 334) cf. Nilsson, *History of Greek Religion* I² 339 sq. Minoan religion retained its strong influence also during later periods of time.

215    20. Similar sickle-shaped knives were found in graves on Lemnos of the period 1100—1000 BC, in Enkomi in Cyprus and in Graves A and C at Assarlik (cf. K. Rhomaios *ADelt* 12 (1929) 217; Schaeffer *Enkomi-Alasia* (1952) pl. LXV, 34; *JHS* (1887) 68—70, no. 11, where they are described as 'curved knives' or as 'knives curved toward the point'. K. Rhomaios (loc. cit.), after an analysis of the literary sources and the archaeological finds, comes to the conclusion that sickle-knives in graves are mystical symbols of death and rebirth. At the same time these knives were used as weapons in Caria. Rhomaios reminds us of the *mythos* of Kronos, who cut the genitals of Uranos with a sickle-knife as well as of the *harpe* (sickle-knife) of Perseus with which he cut off the head of Medusa. Cf. P. Themelis *Frühgriechische Grabbauten* 58 and 100.

215    21. Klaus Fittschen *Untersuchungen Zum Beginn der Gegendarstellungen bei den Griechen* (1969) 108 sq. and n. 541.

215    22. Fittschen loc. cit. cf. also P. Auberson—K. Schefold *Führer durch Eretria* (1972) 158.


# 10. JEWELLERY, SEALS AND OTHER FINDS

217    1. I am indebted to the following for valuable help and advice: Professor John Boardman, Professor J. N. Coldstream, Mr. T. G. H. James, Mr. T. C. Mitchell, Mr. M. R. Popham, Professor S. Piggott, Mr. L. H. Sackett, Professor A. F. Shore, and the former Keeper of the British Museum Research Laboratory, Dr. A. E. Werner.

| | |
|---|---|
| 218 | 2. See *BMQ* xxxiii (1968–69) pl. XLIX d, for this technique |
| 218 | 3. S 22,2–3. S 38,4–5. |
| 218 | 4. S 10,7 |
| 218 | 5. Higgins, *GRJ* 90 |
| 218 | 6. The 'Tiryns Treasure', *AM* lv (1930) 119, is probably such a tomb-robber's cache. |
| 218 | 7. The restoration of the necklace to its original form is not possible, since probably some of the hexagonal beads and certainly some of the rounded glass beads have disintegrated, leaving an odd number. We owe the arrangement of the beads in PLATE 233a to Miss Ingrid Metzger of the Swiss Archaeological Institute at Eretria. So strung it forms a very small necklace, d. c. 10, but one of variegated colour and attractive appearance. |
| 218 | 8. *SCE* ii, pl. 20, no. 31; pl. 25, nos 49–50. British Museum nos 1869.4–1.72 and 1894.11–1.436 (from Amathus, unpublished). *Beth Pelet* ii, pl. 54. |
| 218 | 9. Desborough *GDA* 175–6. |
| 218 | 10. *Hesperia* xxxvii (1968) 114, no. 78a. |
| 218 | 11. See below, p. 223. |
| 218 | 12. See *Perachora* ii, 467. |
| 218 | 13. But see *Beth Pelet* i, pl. 37, T. 552 (bottom); *Sendschirli* v, pl. 456. |
| 218 | 14. E.g. British Museum 1897.4–1.1242 from Enkomi Tomb 88, Late Bronze Age; *SCE* ii, pl. 8, Amathus Tomb 12, no. 12, Early Iron Age; *Hesperia* xxxvii (1968), pl. 33, no. 78b Athens, mid-eighth century BC. |
| 219 | 15. Smithson, *Hesperia* xxvii (1968) 115, suggests Syria as the origin of the glass beads in a rich ninth-century tomb in the Athenian Agora. |
| 219 | 16. *BSA* lv (1960) 134, no. 32. |
| 219 | 17. T 19,5, T 33,6, T 36,2. |
| 219 | 18. Higgins, *GRJ* 93; *SCE* i, pl. 55; *SCE* ii, pl. 20:3; |
| 219 | 19. *BMQ* xxiii (1961) pl. 43b (Athens?); *Kerameikos*, v, pt. i, pl. 158, M 69; *ADelt* xx (1965); *Chr* pl. 44a (Athens); *BSA* xii (1905–6) 91 (Athens); *AM* lxxxi (1966) Beil. 13, fog; 6 (Athens). |
| 219 | 20. T 33,7. |
| 219 | 21. *Eretria* iii, pl. B. |
| 219 | 22. P 47,17, T 3,8–9, T 33,14, T 36,6–16; P 12,4 is a poor man's version in lead. |
| 220 | 23. I am indebted to Miss Lila Marangou for acquainting me with these objects, which she has now published. *BCH* xcix (1975) 365; *Goulandris* 214–15, nos 76–7 'funerary ornaments'. |
| 220 | 24. D. Ohly, *Griechische Goldbleche des 8 Jahrhunderts v Chr.* (Berlin, 1953) 49, fig. 27. |
| 220 | 25. *BMC Terracottas* i, pls 171 ff. |
| 220 | 26. It has even been suggested that they were used to cover the fingers or the penis of the dead, the former notion based on the possible set of ten in T 36, the latter on the find position in their respective tombs of P 47,17 and T 33,14. |
| 220 | 27. Higgins, *GRJ* 93. |
| 220 | 28. *ADelt* xvii (1961–2); *Chr* pl. 195 B. |
| 220 | 29. P 22,33–34. Lead identified by British Museum Research Laboratory. |
| 220 | 30. *BMC Jewellery* nos. 1635–40. cf. Axel Hartman, *Prähistorische Goldfunde aus Europa* (Berlin, 1970) 120, pl. 51, AU 340. |
| 220 | 31. S 59,17–18. |
| 220 | 32. S Pyre 4,8. |
| 220 | 33. S 33,14, T 32,1. |
| 220 | 34. *Perachora* i, pls 18:18, 83:1, 84:13; *BSA* xlviii (1953) pl. 67, G5 (Ithaca); *BSA* lxiv (1969) pl. 39a (Thebes). Unpublished examples in gold from the Argive Heraeum and Rheneia and in bronze from Amphikleia. |
| 220 | 35. *Perachora* i, pl. 18:4; Higgins, *GRJ* pl. 15 B. |
| 221 | 36. T 1,6–7. |
| 221 | 37. T 5,10–11. |
| 221 | 38. Higgins, *GRJ* pl. 12 F. |
| 221 | 39. A. Pierides, *Jewellery in the Cyprus Museum* pl. XIII:10. |
| 221 | 40. *AJA* lxv (1961) 62 ff. |
| 221 | 41. K. Hadaczek, *Der Ohrschmuck d. Griechen u. Etrusker* (Vienna, 1903) 17. |
| 221 | 42. *AJA* lxv (1961) 62 ff. |
| 221 | 43. T 13,16–17. |

| | |
|---|---|
| 221 | 44. Higgins, *GRJ* 82; Hadaczek, op. cit., 13, fig. 19. |
| 221 | 45. But see *AAA* iv (1971) 40, fig. 3 (Grevena); M. Andronikos *Vergina* (Athens, 1969) pl. 88. |
| 221 | 46. S 59,24—25, P 22,31—32, T 5,12—13, 23—24, T 13,18 and 21, T 15,9—12, T 27,4—6, T 36,4—5. |
| 221 | 47. Cf. *SCE* i, M. 155:16. |
| 221 | 48. *Ker.* v, pt. i, pl. 159, M 44—5 (with dotted borders); *BMQ* xxiii (1961) pl. 44b, nos 6—7. |
| 221 | 49. S Pyre 2,1, T 5,14, T 22,7—13, T 27,3. |
| 221 | 50. Two carinations: S Pyre 4 (upper); 4—7, T 13,19—20, T 32,2—3 and 5. Three carinations: T 32,6—7. Four carinations: S 59,20—23. Five carinations: T 31,10. Six carinations: S 59,19. |
| 221 | 51. *Hesperia* xxxvii (1968) 112, nos 71—73; *Ker.* v, pt. ii pl. 159, M 72—3, M 46; *A Delt* xx (1965), pl. 44:8; *AAA* i (1968) 29, fig. 11. |
| 221 | 52. *SCE* ii, pl. CLV, L 420, 417. |
| 222 | 53. T 31,12 and 15. |
| 222 | 54. T 31,13, T 32,4. |
| 222 | 55. *A Delt* xvii (1961—2); *Chr* pl. 195β; *Fortetsa* pl. 75, nos 1103—4. |
| 222 | 56. T 31,11 and 14 |
| 222 | 57. *AAA* v (1972) 170, fig. 7a; *BMQ* xxiii (1961) pl. XLIV b, 1—2; *Corinth* xii, nos 1803—7; *Perachora* i, pl. 18:10—15. |
| 222 | 58. T 5,15a—b, T 22,14—15, T 27,7—8. |
| 222 | 59. S 59,27—28, (PLATE 225), S Pyre 2,2—3, S Pyre 4,9—10 (PLATE 222). |
| 222 | 60. *AAA* i (1968) 29, fig. 11; *AAA* v (1972) 172, fig. 10. *Ker.* v pt. i, pl. 159, M 42. |
| 222 | 61. T 32,9—10. |
| 222 | 62. T 13,15. |
| 222 | 63. P 3,26. |
| 222 | 64. See *PAE* (1960) pl. 38. |
| 222 | 65. See *PPS* xxii (1956) 126—42 and 213—15; *PEQ* (1963) 80—112. I am indebted to Professor Stuart Piggott for this information. |
| 222 | 66. T 22,17 (identification of tin by British Museum Research Laboratory). |
| 223 | 67. T 5,16; T 33,19. |
| 223 | 68. *Hesperia* xxxvii (1968) 115, no. 78 f.; British Museum no. 1894. 11—1. 435 (unpublished). |
| 223 | 69. T 36,18—19. |
| 223 | 70. V. Karageorghis *Cyprus* (London, 1970) pl. 136. id. *Salamis* (London, 1969) pl. 4. *BSA* lxii (1967) 69, nos. 30—42. |
| 223 | 71. T 31,19; T, Trench VIII SF. |
| 223 | 72. T 33,18. |
| 223 | 73. T 33,20—21, T 36,27—29, T 27,18 (PLATE 184). |
| 223 | 74. *Perachora* ii, 520. |
| 223 | 75. T 22,31, T 33,22—25. |
| 223 | 76. *Orchomenos* i, pl. XXX; *BSA* xxxi (1930—31) 39, fig. 16:32. |
| 223 | 77. T 27,17(b). |
| 223 | 78. T 22,31. |
| 223 | 79. *Hesperia* xxxvii (1968) 115, no. 78d. |
| 223 | 80. T 27,17. |
| 223 | 81. P 21,12, P 47,20, T 5,22. T 13,26—27, T 14,5, T 22,29—30, T 27,16, T 36,22. |
| 223 | 82. *Hesperia* xxxvii (1968) 114, no. 78a. |
| 225 | 83. *SCE* ii, pl. 20, no. 31 and pl. 25, nos 49—50. British Museum 1894. 11—1. 43 and 1969. 4—1. 72 (unpublished, from Amathus). |
| 226 | 84. T 1,12. |
| 226 | 85. T 13,26—27. |
| 226 | 86. T 1,12. |
| 226 | 87. T 32,17. |
| 226 | 88. See *BMC Terracottas* i (1954) 56; *Lindos* i, 559 ff. |
| 226 | 89. *Beth Pelet* i, pl. 33, no. 361 and pl. 35, no. 415; *Beth Pelet* ii, pl. 49 passim; *SCE* ii, pl. 20:2 and 29 and pl. 159:23. |
| 226 | 90. *BMC Terracottas* (1903) A 152. |
| 226 | 91. See n. 88. |

| | |
|---|---|
| 224 | 92. T 22,28. |
| 224 | 93. *Beth Pelet* i, pl. XLIII, no. 505. |
| 224 | 94. I am grateful to T. G. H. James for this information. |
| 224 | 95. *Perachora* ii, 461 ff. A. F. Shore confirms that these characters are 'nonsense hieroglyphs'. |
| 224 | 96. T 36,20. |
| 224 | 97. K. R. Maxwell-Hyslop, *Western Asiatic Jewellery* (London, 1971) 235, fig. 124a; *Perachora* ii, pl. 192, D4 and D455; pl. 193, D626. |
| 224 | 98. T 27,15. |
| 224 | 99. *Beth Pelet* i, pl. XXXIX, no. 436. |
| 224 | 100. T 36,21. |
| 224 | 101. *Clara Rhodos* viii, 164. I am indebted to J. N. Coldstream for this reference. |
| 226 | 102. *BCH* 71—2 (1947—8), 198 and fig. 10, an ivory spindle (shaft with whorl attached) from the Late Bronze and Early Iron Age deposit from the Artemision. |
| 226 | 103. J. Vandier d'Abbadie *Les Objects de toilettes égyptiens au Musée du Louvre*, 149 sq.; cf. nos. 655—6, and the wood examples 670, 673. |
| 226 | 104. *Lachish II* pl. XX, 23—8 (Late Bronze Age); Early Iron Age: R. D. Barnett *The Nimrud Ivories in the British Museum* pl. CVIII, S 370a—r (similar work but the objects are semicircular in section, and identified as possible harness ornaments); *Beth-Pelet* ii, pl. LVII, nos. 361, 367, ivory spoons, but with handles now lost; pl. LXXIV, 112, 117, pins, but of bone. |
| 226 | 105. *SCE* iv, I, D, fig. 74, 14—17. |
| 226 | 106. Cf. *Hesperia* supp. x (1956), 49, no. 213 and the references there for archaic and later examples. |
| 226 | 107. Suggested by H. W. and E. Catling. |
| 227 | 108. *Hesperia* xxviii (1958) pl. 19. |
| 227 | 109. S 10,11—13, S 38,11—13, S 33,19, S 46,8, S 51,5, S 59,27; P 3,27, P 10,22, P 11,1, P 22,35, P 23,16, P 24,12 and 13, P 39,6 and 7; T 14,4, T 13,23 and 24 and T 33,15. |
| 227 | 110. Fibres may be z-spun (where the twist in the yarn is clockwise, following the direction of the main stroke of the letter Z) or S-spun (with the twist in the opposite direction, anti-clockwise). |

## 11. OBJECTS OF BRONZE, IRON AND LEAD

| | |
|---|---|
| 234 | 1. *Fibules grecques et orientales* (Copenhagen, 1926). |
| 234 | 2. One of the most important recent works on fibulae from Greece is K. Kilian's *Fibeln in Thessalien von der mykenischen bis zur archaischen Zeit*, Prähistorische Bronzefunde XIV. 2 (Munich, 1975). See also A. M. Snodgrass' review, *Antiquity* 50 (1976) 75 f. The new principles of classification proposed by Dr. Kilian for the Thessalian fibulae have not been followed here. |
| 234 | 3. Abteilung XIV, Band 4 of *Prähistorische Bronzefunde*, Munich 1978, hereafter *FGI*. |
| 234 | 4. Some of the material is illustrated in *FGI*; in a few cases, not every detail is quite accurate. |
| 234 | 5. *FGI*, 14 f. |
| 237 | 6. *CBMW*, pl. 42, *m*. |
| 237 | 7. *CBMW*, pl. 42, *n*. |
| 237 | 8. *CBMW* 243 f. |
| 237 | 9. *AJA* 58, 139 and pl. 24:28. |
| 238 | 10. Sight ought not to be lost of the fact that there is more than one fibula-type to which, in theory, such a fragment *could* belong, particularly in the light of the probable Italian connections of other Lefkandi fibulae. See, e.g. *Chronologie* pl. 43 A,2. |
| 238 | 11. *Ker.* I, pl. 28, second row, second brooch from left. |
| 238 | 12. *Ker.* I, 84. |
| 239 | 13. One is illustrated *FGI* pl. 34:1184. |
| 239 | 14. *Goulandris* no. 49. |
| 239 | 15. Dr. Sapouna-Sakellarakis, *FGI* 37, 16c, is incorrect in placing it in her class 1e, equivalent to B type. I.7—9. |
| 239 | 16. *MMA Bronzes* 931 = *SCE* IV.2, fig. 25.42. |
| 240 | 17. See J. Sundwall, *Die alteren Italischen Fibeln* (Berlin, 1943) 'Die Bogenfibeln', pp. 78—119, |

especially his class BII, a, b — 'Fibeln glatt, mit Einritzungen oder Ringrillen, ohne knoten; Fuss klein' — pp. 90—6.

240  18. Op. cit. 269—70.

240  19. Müller-Karpe, *Chronologie* 21 and pl. 5.

240  20. *Chronologie* 23—5 and fig. 64.

240  21. Terri, Grave 135, *Chronologie* pl. 45, B.8.

240  22. *Chronologie*, fig. 64.

240  23. *NdS* 1907, 75; *Chronologie* pl. 30. A.3 and 4

240  24. *Chronologie* 53 ff. and fig. 64.

240  25. *Mon. Ant.* 22 (1913) 100 f.; *Chronologie* pl. 21, D.5, 6, 8 and 9.

240  26. Shear, *Hesperia* vi (1957) 364 ff., fig. 30; Müller-Karpe *JdI* 77 (1962) 126 and fig. 26:3.

240  27. *DAG* 260.

241  28. *FGI* 115 f., type XBd and plate 48, 1557, 1558 and 1559A.

243  29. *Bert* 92 (1968) fig. 9 c.

243  30. *AAA* 7 (1974) 422 ff.; *Bert* 99, 599 and fig. 37.

244  31. *GDA* 294—300.

244  32. *DAG* 225—8.

245  33. *Greek Pins* 1 ff.

245  34. *Studies*, 42.

245  35. *Studies*, 43.

245  36. *Greek Pins* 37, fig. 14.

245  37. *CBMW* 238.

245  38. *Greek Pins* 122 f. and references cited.

245  39. *AM* 35 (1910).

245  40. *EA* 1888, pl. 9, 25.

245  41. Dikaios, *Enkomi*, pl. 163.

245  42. *CBMW* 238, n. 9.

245  43. *GDA* 299.

245  44. *DAG* 232.

245  45. *Studies*, 70, and cf. *DAG* 221.

246  46. *DAG* 226.

246  47. Randall-Maciver, *Villanovans and Early Etruscans* (Oxford, 1924) pl. 2, 13; *Chronologie*, pl. 00.

246  48. For this technique see *Greek Pins* 209 ff., with references to earlier literature.

246  49. *BSA* 31 (1933) 1 ff. For the bracelets, ibid. 35, 9 and 10, and fig. 14.

246  50. S. Casson in *BSA* 24, 14, fig. 10, 16, fig. 16.

247  51. For the Skyros bracelets see *AA* 1936, 230 ff., fig. 1 and cf. others probably from Skyros, in the Goulandris Collection — *Goulandris*, 200, nos 54 and 57.

247  52. *CVA* Mainz 1, 12 f.; *LMS* 265; *GGP* 221; *DAG* 244 f.

247  53. *Ker* I, 18, grave 27, found with fibulae, pins and rings; op. cit. 48, grave 108, found with a similar complex of bronze jewellery. *SMS* 22 and 48, referring to a bracelet from one of the eight SM graves dug by M. Mitsos SW of the Olympeion in 1939—40.

247  54. *Studies*, 108.

247  55. *Studies*, 83.

247  56. *Ker* V, 196 f.

247  57. *DAG* 270.

247  58. See, e.g. *GDA* 304, with reference to examples in gold from Crete — Mouliana and Vrokastro — and *DAG* 317—20.

248  59. *Ker* I, 85 and fig. 3.

248  60. *Ker* I, 85 and ibid. notes 2 and 3.

248  61. *Studies*, 48, 70.

248  62. *Studies*, 109.

248  63. *Ker* I, 39.

248  64. *Studies*, 48.

248  65. *GDA* 303, pl. 60c.

248  66. E.g. *CBMW* 166 ff.; *BSA* 69 (1974) 231 ff.

249  67. *Fortetsa* 134, no. 1563 and 200; pl. 113.

249     68. Cf. e.g. *Chronologie* pl. 31, 5 and, more generally, pls 29, 33, pl. 60 (Bologna).

249     69. I have been greatly assisted in my study of this vessel by Mr. T. G. H. James, Keeper of the Department of Egyptian Antiquities in the British Museum who, in answering my inquiries concerning comparative material in his charge has drawn my attention to material and references of which I should otherwise have been quite unaware.

249     70. F. Halbherr and P. Orsi, *Antichita dell' autro di Zeus Ideo ei di altre localita in Crete con un Atlante* (1888) 38 and Atlas pl. 12:9 — only one of the five is illustrated.

249     71. *Fortetsa* 136, 1571 and 1572; 201 and pl. 113.

249     72. *CCO* 152, n. 5.

249     73. *PAE* 1933, 99.

249     74. *Cesnola Atlas* III, pl. LIX 3.

249     75. *Hand CC*

249     76. *MMA Bronzes* 241, illustrated 243.

249     77. *El Amrah and Abydos* (London, 1902).

249     78. Op. cit. 71.

249     79. Op. cit. 102 and pl. XLVI.

249     80. Op. cit. 102 and pl. XLVII.

249     81. Op. cit. 99. and pl. XLIV, where the group is labelled 'XVIII Dyn'.

249     82. *Stone and Metal Vases* 27, no. 17 and pl. XXXIX.

249     83. *Catalogue Général des Antiquités Egyptiennes du Musée du Caire: Nos. 3426–3587, Metallgefässe*, nos 3523 and 3524.

249     84. BM 54381, 38229, 124602 — see R. D. Barnett, *Catalogue of the Nimrod Ivories* (London, 1957) 94.

249     85. Op. cit. 27, no. 16 and pl. XXXIX.

249     86. *Matmar* 68 and pl. XLIX.

249     87. Von Bissing, op. cit. 52, no. 3533.

249     88. 'Phoenician Metalwork and Egyptian Tradition', *Revista de la Universidad Complutense* XXV, no. 101 (1976) 83–9. I am grateful to T. G. H. James for referring me to this paper.

250     89. Culican cites jugs from the tomb of King Aspelta (593–565 BC) at Nuri in Nubia and the mid-6th-century queen Anitalqa — Durham, Nuri, *The Royal Cemeteries of Kush* 11, fig. 55, pp. 132–6 and fig. 100, which I have not been able to consult.

250     90. Culican, op. cit. 86.

250     91. See Culican op. cit. fig. 13 for a wine service from (Egyptian) Thebes now in the Cincinnati Art Museum, no. 4352, bowl and jug, the bowl (with hieroglyphic inscription) apparently hemispherical.

250     92. *CBMW* 147 f., fig. 17 and pl. 19a. For a very large LC collection Karageorghis, *Kition* 1 contents of Tomb 9 — especially ibid. 90.

250     93. *GG* 32, 52.

250     94. *AM* 35 (1910) 29.

250     95. *Ker* IV, 48 and pl. 38, inv. M.1.

250     96. *Ker* V, 236 and 202, fig. 5; *DAG* 116, fig. 56.

250     97. The graves in question are Ker G.1 (*Ker* V, 209 and pl. 163), 2 (op. cit. 210), 7 (op. cit. 214, pl. 163), 13 (op. cit. 218, pl. 163), 38 (op. cit. 234, pl. 163), 41 (op. cit. 235), 43 (op. cit. 238), 74 (op. cit. 260, pl. 163) and 75 (op. cit. 261).

250     98. *EA* 1889, 178.

250     99. Courbin, *Tombes géométriques d'Argos* 1, 129 f. and references.

250     100. *Hesperia* xxi (1952) 287–8, fig. 4; 293 and pl. 77b.

251     101. *SCE* ii 26 and pl. XCV.

251     102. Following the higher chronology of Mrs. Birmingham.

251     103. *Corinth* XII, 69, fig. 1, no. 517.

251     104. *Fouilles de Delphes* II, 3. fig. 56.

251     105. Dunbabin in *Perachora* 1, 155 and pl. 55.1.

251     106. For references to bronze vases in early contexts note R. S. Young, *Hesperia Suppl.* 11 (1939) 223, note 5.

251     107. *Arch. Hom.* Band 1, E. I (Kriegswesen) (Göttingen, 1977), 87–96.

251     108. *AA* 1970, 441 ff.

251     109. *Troy* III, 297, fig. 297. Bittel in *Gnomon* 28 (1956), 251.

251        110. *AA* 1975, 209 ff.

251        111. *Alaas*. 6 f. and pls III and LII.

251        112. *SCE* iv²2, 132, fig. 20 and references cited.

251        113. 'A propos de la découverte d'écuilles d'armure en bronze à Gostria-Alaas (Chypre)', *AA* 1975, 209—22, and the references there cited.

252        114. *Samos* VIII (1972), 56—8 and pl. 50.

252        115. *Lindos* I, no. 664, pl. 26.

252        116. *AJA* 67 (1963) 22 where she cites *Olympia* IV pl. XXIV, 446—449.

252        117. *Ancient Persian Bronzes in the Ashmolean Museum* (1971), 92 f., nos 93 and 94 — ibid. 94, fig. 20 and pl. 10.

252        118. *Samos* VIII, 57 and notes 148—51.

252        119. Op. cit. 93.

252        120. Andrae, *Die Kleinfunde von Sendschirch*, pl. 42, fig. 107.

252        121. *SCE* II, pl. VII, 4; CLI, 17.

252        122. Op. cit. 139.

252        123. *AJA* 63, 22 ff.

252        124. *GGP* 318.

252        125. Loc. cit.

252        126. *Kypros, die Bibel und Homer* (Berlin 1893) 204 f.

252        127. For weapon dimensions as a guide to classification, see Gordon, *Antiquity* 27 (195).

252        128. Verdelis in *AM* 78 (1963) 10—24.

253        129. *Ker* I, 101 and pl. 31, bottom, right.

253        130. *Ker* I, 104 and pl. 32, right.

253        131. *Ker* IV, 47, pl. 38; *JdI*, 91, fig. 9:7 and p. 121; on the general significance of this weapon cf. *DAG* 222 ff.

253        132. Cf. *GDA* 314 ff.

253        133. Coldstream's reference — *GG* 42 — to a fragmentary iron sword in the SPG II tomb S 33 is incorrect.

253        134. Answering one of Desborough's questions — *GDA* 311.

253        135. E.g. Tiryns XXVIII (*AM* 78, 10 ff., and see below, p. 000)

253        136. Most recently 'Late Minoan Vases and Bronzes in Oxford', *BSA* 63 (1968) 89—131, especially 98—104 and Late 14.

253        137. *EGAW* 94, 106 ff.

253        138. E.g. the eleven weapons from cremations in the Halos tumulus — *BSA* 18 (for 1911—12) 1—29, especially 25 ff. and fig. 15. Cf. *GG* 87 f.

253        139. *Eretria* III, 16, 22, 32.

253        140. See Andronikos, *Vergina* I, 262—5, figs 101 and 102, Petsas in *ADelt* 17 (1961—2), especially p. 242 and pl. 146a, for the one bronze Type II sword of this type found in the cemetery.

253        141. *Hesperia* xxv (1956) 48, = *JdI* 77, 126, fig. 27.6.

254        142. *Ker* V, 234 f. and pl. 000; see also *JdI* 77, 125 and fig. 23, 1a—b.

254        143. *Ker* IV, 34 f., pl. 000; *JdI* 77, 122 and fig. 10, 1a—b.

254        144. *Hesperia* xxi (1952) 282, 286, fig. 75 and pl. 31; *JdI* 77, 127 and fig. 28, 1a—b.

254        145. For this feature, see, e.g. E. L. Smithson, *Hesperia* xliii (1974) 341.

254        146. *Ker* I, 106 f., fig. 8; *JdI* 77, 121 and diag. 9, 4a—b.

254        147. Cf. *CBMW* 115, fig.   .

254        148. *Eretria* III, 16, fig.   .

254        149. *Eretria* III, 16.

255        150. Kerameikos PG Graves A and B: *Ker* I, 101 and pl. 31; *JdI* 77, fig. 7, 2 and 4, and p. 120 and *Ker* I, 104 and pl. 32; *JdI* 77, fig. 8, 1 and p. 21.

255        151. Dörpfeld's Areopagus Tomb II; Smithson in *Hesperia* xliii (1974) 342 and pl. 71g.

255        152. In the west Cemetery; *Eretria* III, 16, fig. 3.

256        153. *AA* 1936, 232.

256        154. *EGAW* 115 ff.

256        155. *EGAW* 166 f.

256        156. *Ker* IV, pl. 38, M.9.

256        157. *Hesperia* xxi (1952) 280 ff., esp. p. 287.

256      158. Cf. e.g. *EGAW* 166.

256      159. *Fortetsa* 137, 1602–5, pl. 172.

256      160. *DAG* 274.

256      161. H. and E. C. include in the evidence the objects of deer antler, T Pyre 1, 5–6, which they interpret as possible remains of a composite bow. M.R.P. thinks this excluded by other fragments of finer antler, also perforated, and suspects remains of a lyre. See also discussion on p. 226.

257      162. H. G. Buchholz 'Der Pfeilglätter aus dem VI Schlacht grab von Mykene und die helladischen Pfeilspitzen' in *JdI* 77 (1962) 1–58.

257      163. *Ker* IV, 27, 35 and pl. 38, inv. M.34; *AAA* 1, 20–30 esp p. 21–2.

257      164. Weinberg in *Hesperia* xvii (1948) 206, pl. 72. Both the excavator's comment and the illustration of the object leave some uncertainty about the correctness of the identification.

257      165. *DAG* 217 on the technical explanation.

258      166. *Hesperia* xviii, 297, pl. 72; *JdI* 77, III, fig. 29, 4 and p. 127.

258      167. *Ker* IV, 35 f., pl. 38, M.52.

258      168. Notice a slightly smaller knife in Lapithos Tomb 420.46 (1.26), dated c. 1000 BC – *SCE* i, 238 and pl. LIII.

258      169. *Hesperia* xxi (1952).

258      170. *JdI* 77, 66.

258      171. Cf. e.g. R. M. Dawkins and others. *Artemis Orthia* 224 f. and pls CXXXII–CXXXIII.

258      172. *SG*.

258      173. See, for instance, *CBMW* 185 f.

259      174. *Thorikos* IV (1967) 38–42, figs 44–8; *GG* 70–1.

259      175. *DAG* 213–17.

259      176. *Hesperia* xxi (1952) 290, no. 10, pl. 75c and fig. 3.

260      177. *EGAW* 39.

260      178. Cf. e.g. *JdI* 77, 89–90, figs. 7–8.

260      179. *JdI* 77, 102–3, figs 20–1.

260      180. *JdI* 77 (1962) 59–124.

262      181. *Ker* I, pl. 000.

263      182. *Goulandris* 198–201.

263      183. *JdI* 77, fig. 3, no. 4.

## 12. FRAGMENTARY POTTERY AND A STONE MOULD

265      1. For the nature of this fill see p. 103. Two levels were distinguished, but there seems to be no stylistic difference (one join noted between the levels, 871 and 872), and the material is discussed as part of a single whole. The ratio of closed to open vases is rather more than two to one, with coarse hand-made ware contributing about 5%.

265      2. The whole or fragmentary vases, S SF 1–16, from disturbed tombs or pyres, are described in the main catalogue of the cemetery. SF 14 and SF 16 are illustrated with the material here discussed, on PLATE 273.

266      3. *Ker* I, pl. 65, no. 552, the oinochoe from tomb 4; *Ker* IV, pl. 4, no. 921, the lekythos from tomb 22.

266      4. See *PGP* 4.

266      5. The cup SF 16, though found in this fill, was not really of it. It must have come from a disturbed grave, and is the only undeniably SM piece. See n. 2.

266      6. The krater sherd depicting part of a ship, 918 = PLATE 284, 11 is discussed separately, p. 267.

266      7. It should be borne in mind that fragments belonging to an amphora will be more numerous than those e.g. from a cup or skyphos.

267      8. Belly handles are extremely rare, as is the case in the settlement.

267      9. One unillustrated sherd has a multiple triangle with the centremost triangle filled in, as P 31,4 (LPG).

267      10. Found on Attic oinochoai EG I–MG I: see *GGP* pls 1–3. As exported to Lefkandi they are so far confined to MG I, see T 31,1 and T 33,1. Another atticising instance, if from an oinochoe, is PLATE 275, 943.

267        11. There were no identifiable sherds of hydriai, lekythoi, amphoriskoi, or pyxides.

267        12. See Williams, *Greek Oared Ships* pl. 12 f.

268        13. A fragment of a similar type of vase, of LH IIIC date, was found on Xeropolis, *BSA* 66, 341, fig. 5, 7. Comparison may also, however, be made with the dish or tray from Marmariani, *BSA* 31, 29 and pl. 8, no. 126, which is most unlikely to be earlier than LPG.

268        14. See the section on the one-handled cup.

268        15. See the relevant section, p. 341. For our eighth-century knowledge of the plate see *AA* 1963, 205–6, figs 43–7, from Salamis in Cyprus, associated with Cypriot CG IIIB and Attic MG II pottery.

268        16. The material from the East Cemetery, though in the main catalogue its tombs are combined with those of Palia Perivolia, is discussed separately, pp. 273–5.

268        17. The sherds from the upper fill of Pyre 32 (PLATE 277, 1000–22, and PLATE 154) are noted and discussed in the catalogue, even though (as with the material from the fill of Toumba tomb 32) they do not belong to this pyre.

268        18. Similar amphorae were found in pyres 28 and 41, from the same square as this example.

269        19. See *GGP* 19.

270        20. In Attica the 'branch' ornament is purely PG, though confined to lekythoi and oinochoai: see *Hesperia* xxx, 158 and 161 f. See also the discussion of Area 3 South on Xeropolis.

270        21. See *GGP* pl. 3j.

270        22. For 935 see Kerameikos grave 2, *Ker* V, i, pl. 17, no. 935; for 950 and 957, see Kraiker, *Aigina*, no. 51.

271        23. See PLATE 27, 777 from the settlement; and perhaps T 7,1, PLATE 172.

271        24. See *GGP* pl. 3n.

271        25. Professor Coldstream informs me that the closeness of the meander to the neck suggests that it is more likely to be MG I than EG II.

271        26. 967 (note its slightly raised base, flat underneath) is a complete profile. PLATE 284, 7 is a restoration of 966.

272        27. 980 looks like a krater, but it is unpainted inside.

272        28. Nearly the same number of open as of closed vase sherds were kept, but amphorae provided the great majority of the discarded material.

272        29. Professor Smithson tells me that this is a typically Mycenaean feature. It is also found on the EPG trefoil oinochoe S 32,2 (PLATE 101).

273        30. There are two others: S 38,15 (PLATE 282B) and S Pyre 3,1 (PLATE 282A).

273        31. The fourth tomb, 43, was close to the surface, and may be disregarded in this context.

274        32. See *GGP* 116, 119, and pl. 246.

274        33. A large fragment of a similar skyphos was found near Chalcis, at Nea Lampsakos: see *GGP* 152.

275        34. I have earlier suggested a transitional date SPG I–II.

275        35. The one in the centre of the third row probably belongs to a jug, not to a cup.

275        36. Except for the one in the bottom right hand corner, which is from an oinochoe.

275        37. The 'open' semicircles cannot be used as a stylistic pointer.

275        38. V and VI, which adjoin each other (there is a dividing baulk 50 cm wide), could form part of a wide area at the NW perimeter of the cemetery where no burials occur – tomb 30, in square VI, is at its NE corner.

275        39. See PLATE 284, 1–6 for profiles of some from Toumba square V; other examples are noted in the Area 3 South deposit, and occur occasionally elsewhere.

275        40. As will be seen below, PSC skyphoi are similarly absent from squares V and VI.

275        41. The same motive, drawn by the same painter, and associated with languettes, appears on the shoulder of an amphora from square VI (1076–7).

276        42. There was one fragment, not illustrated, of a massive amphora of the type common in pyres. It has either two tiers of semicircles with hourglass filling, or one of semicircles, and one of circles below it.

276        43. Cf. T 7,1 (PLATE 172) for the decoration.

276        44. Insufficiently preserved in one or two cases for one to be sure that they were not semicircles, but it may be stressed that there was no recognisable instance of a PSC skyphos.

277    45. Other sherds of the same vase were found in the fill of tomb 27 and in the surface material (see above).

277    46. The circles skyphos sherd 1154 could be an import; it is micaceous, with pink-brown clay and black-brown paint.

277    47. The date of tomb 7 may also be linked with that of the stratigraphically earlier tomb 8. Tomb 8 was empty, but had about thirty-five sherds in its fill, mostly from cups or skyphoi. None of these needs be later than LPG; among the open sherds were five of circles skyphoi, and from gently outcurving lips of monochrome cups. If one be confident of an LPG date, it would be additional evidence of the early appearance of these two types — for the skyphoi see P Channel, lower fill and for the cups see above on square V.

277    48. The PSC skyphos does nevertheless appear before the end of LPG: see the Moulds Deposit and P 3,14 (PLATE 128). The absence of this type from the surface material has already been noted; the only other identified fragments from the cemetery are from Pyres 2 and 3.

278    49. *Ker* V, i, pl. 22, no. 1254 (Grave 43). See *GGP* 20, n. 7 for the date suggested — a much earlier date than Kraiker's.

278    50. Professor Coldstream has suggested that it may be from a chest, such as *Hesperia* xxxvii, pls 24–5 and 27.

278    51. Mr. Sackett has suggested that the 'rim' is in fact a clean break where the pattern had originally joined two separate pieces.

278    52. I have assumed that all sherds with the interior unpainted, even the most massive, are from amphorae.

278    53. Some belong with, but do not join, the illustrated fragments.

# 13. THE DARK AGE POTTERY

282    1. One basic assumption is made, that there is no Late Helladic IIIC material in the cemeteries, with the possible exception of the White Ware lekythos KT2, which was in any case not found in the excavated area, and that the earliest pottery is SM. See the remarks on the gap in occupation between the end of LH IIIC and a late stage of PG on Xeropolis, and the difference between the IIIC of Xeropolis phase 3 and the SM of the Skoubris cemetery, *BSA* 66, 348 f.

282    2. Instances where there is some doubt about the sequence have been omitted.

282    3. See, however, p. 110 for the probable connecting link between S 4 and S Pyre 1A.

282    4. See p. 44 f. The distinction between LPG and SPG I is one of the most difficult to make.

282    5. I am assuming that the vases associated with any one burial (the usual custom at Lefkandi) were normally made within a few years of one another and of the burial. One must naturally allow for exceptions (recognisable by wear or even by difference in style?), and there can be heirlooms.

282    6. EPG: S 16, twelve vases, LPG: P 3, twenty-four; P 22, twenty-seven; T 26, seventeen. SPG I: P 10, twenty (of which thirteen are kalathoi); P 13, twenty; P 39B, seventeen (of which ten are kalathoi). SPG I–II: P 47, sixteen, including seven pyxides, SPG II: S 33, thirteen. SPG III: S 59 + 59A, twenty-five, including both kalathoi and pyxides.

283    7. S 46 (EPG). Some of these tombs had neither any contents nor were related stratigraphically to any other tomb, and so are undatable. The concentration of cist tombs in Skoubris, however, together with the fact that neither Palia Perivolia nor Toumba has produced a tomb group earlier than MPG, strongly suggests that what is valid for most applies equally to all.

283    8. No doubt the amphora should be added to the list, but the few examples known are not enough to establish continuity.

283    9. For example, only two krater sherds (normally a settlement shape) are certainly earlier than LPG, and these were from the surface of Toumba (PLATE 279, 1058, 1091).

283    10. Two only, both from S 16: one appears to be SM, the other EPG.

284    11. Note a double wavy line, and a double arc, both enclosing dots: S 8,2; S 32,6. The cross-hatched triangle is also known.

284    12. The same applies to the bird vase, but that belongs rather to the transition from SM to EPG.

284        13. The EPG pedestal bowl and four-handled bowl of S 16 are exceptions to this, in already having unusually high conical feet. Oddly, the only example before SPG of a flat-based cup, P 6,1, probably belongs to this phase, as the tomb is stratified beneath P 9, which is MPG.

284        14. *BSA* 66, 348 ff. There are differences in fabric as well as in shape and decoration.

285        15. For reviews of SM material see Styrenius, *Submycenaean Studies*, and *GDA* 64 ff. Where there is adequate evidence, as in Attica and the Argolid, the links do not seem close enough to indicate that either series gave rise to the Lefkandian style.

285        16. For references, see the main analysis of vase types.

285        17. See Catling, *Cypriot Bronzework* 201 and pl. 31, f. Not, unfortunately, known to have come from Cyprus, but classed with others all of Cypriot origin.

285        18. Common in The Cypriot PG style (a style which precedes PG as found in Greece and the Aegan). See particularly the vases from the Alaas tombs — Karageorghis, *Alaas, passim*.

285        19. See *PGP* 47 and pl. 7.

285        20. *GDA* 54 f.

286        21. *Pr.* 1960, 259, pl. 195a. Tomb 12.

286        22. Andreiomenou, *ChO* pl. 48a (multiple vase).

286        23. *PT* 211, fig. 146 f. Tomb C (lekythos with hand-drawn semicircles).

286        24. For example the trefoil oinochoai with languettes and compass-drawn semicircles.

286        25. *GDA* 168. See p. 303.

286        26. No comparative ceramic material has been identified. Note, however, the necklace from P 25B.

286        27. Chalcis: *ChO* 248 ff., pls 45—7. Thebes: *AD* 3, 30 f., figs 28 (cup, tomb 8) and 29 (jug, tomb 9). Delphi: *BCH* 61, pls 5 and 6; see *GDA* 203 ff., pls 47—8. Iolkos: *Pr.* 1960, 55 f., pls 35—9; *Pr.* 1961, 49 f., pls 19—22; see *GDA* 209, pl. 49. Skyros: *PT* 208 f., and fig. 144; *AD* 1918, suppl. 43 f. and fig. 10 (note cup of Black Slip ware); *Stele* 55 ff., pls 11 and 12. Naxos: *PGRT* 55 and pl. 15, nos 7 and 8.

286        28. Included among them is a kalathos with impressed triangles from Iolkos, not known at Lefkandi so early, but one of the characteristic types of LPG and SPG I: *Pr.* 1960, pl. 38a.

286        29. The material is too slight for a similar conclusion to be drawn for earlier phases: see however nn. 21 and 22 for EPG from Naxos and Chalcis, and n. 23 for SM or EPG from Theotokou.

286        30. This whole area is what is meant when mention is made of 'the region' or 'the region in which Lefkandi is situated', etc. — it is impossible to describe in brief terms. The material from later periods permits us to add Andros and Tenos, even though until now they have produced no EPG or MPG material.

286        31. The other is between SPG and Late Geometric.

287        32. The change-over from cist tombs to shaft graves took place a little earlier.

287        33. In Lefkandian terms this is satisfactory for the upper limit, but highly unsatisfactory for the lower, for the potters continued to make use of Attic LPG ideas long after the style had disappeared in Attica. The result is that it is at times impossible to distinguish between an LPG and an early SPG I group. In spite of this problem I have felt it advisable to make the break where I have: first, it coincides with the time when the local potters ceased for a while to draw on Attic pottery for their inspiration; and second, it has by now become conventional to equate the beginning of SPG with the start of Attic EG (see Coldstream, *GGP* 330), and to change this could give rise to confusion.

287        34. See generally *Ker* I and IV.

287        35. *PGRT* nos 36—42, pl, 6, from Kapakli (all wheel-made); *BSA* 31, nos 1—9, fig. 4 (hand-made), and nos 31—47, pl. 3 (wheel-made), from Marmariani. The shoulder decoration is similar to that at Lefkandi, and a Thessalian origin is more likely than an ultimately Attic one. The decoration on the neck, found on several Thessalian jugs, is not imitated, at least on this shape, at Lefkandi.

287        36. See Adelman, *Cypro-Geometric Pottery* (*SIMA* vol. 47). The Lefkandians replaced the long spout, and the underbase decoration is not so elaborate.

287        37. *Ker* IV, pl. 25; *Hesperia* 30, pl. 28. Both LPG. The Attic flasks are themselves are of Cypriot inspiration, so one might argue for indirect transmission to Lefkandi; the body shape of P 31,6 is, however, closer to that of Cypriot flasks.

287    38. The earliest known example from Cyprus is of GGII date, *SCE* IV, 2, fig. XIII, 3; for Athens there is an MPG example (see *Hesperia* 38, 98, n. 51), but nothing yet known for LPG.

287    39. It is possible that the mainly monochrome MPG type of cup persisted, but the evidence is fragmentary and elusive. It may seem odd that there are no other known survivals, but it must be remembered (a) that the range of MPG types is small, and confined to tombs, and (b) that some of the familiar shapes, e.g. the skyphos, were modified in the light of external influence. Only the pedestal bowl seems to have disappeared completely — the absence of any hydria from any LPG context is surely accidental.

287    40. See *Hesperia* xxx, 166, under no. 43. Or else it is a regional type: see *GGP* 151.

288    41. The presence of one at Iolkos in an MPG context (*Pr.* 1960, pl. 38a) does not prove a Thessalian origin, but suggests that equally early ones may yet be found at Lefkandi.

288    42. This shape probably always had decoration on the body, see e.g. PLATE 279, 1091 from Toumba, with hand-drawn semicircles. The evidence from Attica is too slight for any valid comparisons to be made with the Lefkandian material — except presumably for the circles motive.

288    43. See pp. 348–50. Twelve Attic, two probably Attic, one Cypriot, one unknown.

288    44. Coldstream sets out the evidence in *GGP* 149 ff. In Thessaly, Marmariani and Kapakli are not mentioned, but some of their vases are most likely to be LPG — note the absence of lekythoi, kalathoi (but see the MPG example from Iolkos, n. 41 above), and vertical-handled amphoriskoi. The latter type is found in Theotokou tomb B (see *PT* 213, fig. 146, a–e). The tombs from Iolkos (Nea Ionia) might be SPGI rather than LPG (*Thessalika* 5, 47 ff.: both have PSC skyphoi). The tomb groups from Halos (*BSA* 18, 1 ff., tombs 4, 7 and 8) are LPG, and show Attic influence, but there is no sign there of the jug with cutaway neck — southern and northern Thessaly seem at this time to be ceramically separate. On Skyros one cannot tell how much of Papadimitriou's material is LPG, but there is enough on exhibit in the Skyros Museum for one to be confident that the LPG phase is represented, and is similar to what is found in Lefkandi. In Euboea, the Arethusa group from Chalcis (*ChO* 257 ff.), if from one tomb, may be SPG I — note the flat base of no. 15, pl. 48b — but the lekythos from another tomb, pl. 46g, is very close to Attic LPG. The apparently impressed-triangle kalathoi from a tomb near Eretria (*BSA* 52, 14) are either LPG or SPG I. In the North Cyclades the Tenos (Kambos) group, described in detail *GGP* 149, conforms with the Lefkandian series — note the highfooted skyphos with two sets of circles. For the bases from Zagora on Andros see below — one whole group could be LPG (see n. 73). The group from Rheneia noted by Coldstream need not, I believe, be LPG. The evidence from Naxos is insufficient for one to be able to relate it to the *koine* at this time.

288    45. See two vases (amphoriskos and oinochoe) from Paralimni, illustrated *AD* 27, II.2, pl. 268, c and e, especially the former, which is of pure Lefkandian type — see P 31. Did this area perhaps belong to the region?

288    46. See *Vergina* I, fig. 27 (one or two of the amphoriskoi), and 181, figs 30 and 31 (cups with zigzag on the lip).

288    47. *JHS* 77, 212 ff., fig. 4. High-footed skyphos and cup, maybe not from Lefkandi, but certainly of regional style. Found at Amathus in Cyprus.

       48. P 10,19—20. See *GGP* 159 and n. 13 for its appearance and distribution.

288    49. P 39B,17.

289    50. The tombs suggest a total disappearance, but statistics from the settlement, notably the SPG Pit and Levelling Material, seem to favour a gradual phasing out.

289    51. It is necessary to make this qualification, because in the settlement there are still numerous instances of shoulder decoration, almost always semicircles, on small closed vases.

289    52. This also depends chiefly on the cemetery evidence, but in this it is supported by the settlement, especially the Moulds and SPG deposits and the SL material. It may be noted that the suppression of the zigzag meant that the potter did not have to concern himself with making a lip high enough to accomodate this motive.

289    53. This is not the whole story, as will be seen by reference to the sections on amphorae and kraters. All kraters, and outsize amphorae, may have motives introduced during SPG: examples are the battlement and meander, often cross-hatched as are the large squares in a chequerboard pattern, and opposed diagonals with unfilled interstices. This apply to SPG as a whole, though I think mostly not earlier than SPG II.

289    54. There are, however, instances (not among the earliest) of monochrome amphoriskoi.

289    55. The account depends almost exclusively on the material from tombs and pyres, as the stratigraphical divisions in the settlement are usually too imprecise for valid conclusions to be drawn. The picture must be understood to be partial and provisional, as in many other cases. One tomb alone, P 47, seems to combine features of both SPG I and SPG II, and may be regarded as transitional.

290    56. The doubt arises because of the presence of one sherd in the SL material, which as a whole is not earlier than SPG II.

290    57. See p. 303. Not yet found in any tomb or pyre. It appears in the SPG Pit and in the Levelling Material, but not in the Moulds Deposit; it is also one of the two most common vase shapes in the SL groups, which do not seem to precede SPG II. One cannot be quite certain that it was not introduced in SPG I, but I shall assume that it was an SPG II (and later) type.

290    58. There are exceptions: necks may be monochrome, very occasionally the shoulder has semicircles. But it is the shape that matters.

290    59. The type is known throughout the settlement, from LPG onwards.

290    60. See *GGP* 151.

290    61. PLATE 15, 129–131, from the SPG Pit, skyphos sherds. The cup S Pyre 4,1, and the pyxis P 21,2: both late EG II, verging on MC I.

291    62. PLATE 274, 912, from a trefoil oinochoe with probable meander panel on the neck; PLATE 278,C top left, from the fill above P 47, a skyphos sherd, certainly atticising EG II. There are indeed other atticising sherds from the Levelling Material and elsewhere, but these are either certainly MG, or more likely to be MG than EG (see below).

291    63. See e.g. *GGP* pl. 2, f and g.

291    64. See *AJA* 67, pls 83 and 84 (Dirmil); *Ist. Mitt.* 7, pl. 36,4 (Miletus).

291    65. Two exceptions may be noted, the flask S 33,3 and the pedestal bowl T 24,1; but in neither case has the source been established.

291    66. See the excellent analysis by Coldstream, *GGP* 151–5 for SPG, and 158–60 for the rectilinear style of Marmariani (perhaps the decoration on the neck, and the double-axe or butterfly ornament, were inspired by the earlier local hand-made ware?). He gives reasons for equating SPG with Attic EG, and these I have accepted for SPG I and II.

291    67. There are three relevant settlements: Grotta on Naxos, *Pr.* for 1949, 1950 and 1951; Iolkos, *Ergon* for 1960, 58, and see *Archaeology* vol. 11, 18; and Ktouri in Thessaly, *BCH* 56, 170 ff., and see *PGP* 313. There are, however, only brief preliminary reports of these, with little pottery illustrated.

291    68. For example, if we relied on the tombs from Lefkandi, we would be unaware that either the circles skyphos, or the shallow bowl with strap handles, or the krater, belonged to the potter's repertoire.

291    69. Chalcis: *AD* 16, Chron., 150. One tomb, two vases – a PSC skyphos and an atticising EG II skyphos. Perhaps also the Arethusa group, see n. 44. Theologos: *AD* 16, Chron., 152, pl. 133d. One tomb, seven vases – note pyxides and what may be a straight-walled jug.

291    70. *BSA* 18, 4 f., fig. 3. Seven vases.

292    71. Marmariani: *BSA* 31; Kapakli, *PGRT*. No means of telling how many burials, but the number of vases attributable to SPG I and II is probably substantial. Theotokou: *PT* 212 f., and fig. 145. Tomb A, four burials, eighteen vases (some surely not earlier than SPG II to judge from what looks like an atticising EG II skyphos), markedly different from the Lefkandian series. For other sites see *PGP* 132 f., 313 f., and *GDA* 368–70 (Site Index with references). Of the types found both in Thessaly and at Lefkandi, there is only one example in Thessaly of the circles skyphos, the shallow bowl, and the globular pyxis (but see no. 68 for the similar absence of the first two from Lefkandian tombs).

292    72. Four tombs, with 150–160 vases, excavated by Stavropoullos: *BCH* 61, 473, and a summary of types and decorative system in *PGP* 165 f. See *GGP* 152 for a tentative attribution to this period. Many of the vases are on exhibit in the Skyros Museum, and it is perfectly clear from these, as well as from other vases found elsewhere, just how great the resemblance is to the Lefkandian style. There is a difference, however, in relative popularity of types – e.g. one-handled cups were far more commonly placed in tombs on Skyros than at Lefkandi (see *PGP* 166, about eighty cups).

292    73. Zagora: *PGP* 161–3 and pl. 16. Two tombs, contents now confused. Five pots (143–4,

148—9, 151) are assigned by Coldstream to MG, *GGP* 166, and could therefore belong to one tomb. Five of the remaining six, the shoulder-handled amphora 150 (surely LPG), the three circles skyphoi 45, 146 and 152 (note that this has a rectangular panel between the circles), and the PSC skyphos 145, by the same painter as 146, could all belong to the other tomb, and could be either LPG or SPG I, the former the more likely. The sixth vase, the vertical-handled amphoriskos, probably belongs to these rather than to the MG group.

292     74. *Ann.* 8—9, 203 ff. for the Kardiani tombs and one or two sporadic vases, especially no. 11, fig. 35, a PSC skyphos with atypical lip and zigzag on its outer surface. *GGP* 152 f., 165 f., pls 32, c, e, and 34, a—b, e, g—h, for Ktikados and two of unknown provenance. *CVA* Vatican, fasc. 1, pl. 1, 1—4, nos 1—5, and *PGP* 158 f., pl. 25a for the Vatican group.

292     75. The skyphos with panelled zigzag between the handles (*GGP* pl. 34a) is also paralleled at Lefkandi, see PLATE 15, 149—50 from the SPG Pit, and PLATE 25, 682—3 (Miscellaneous).

292     76. Vertical-handled amphoriskoi vary a lot in shape, but are a regional type (*GGP* 154). This type of cup is also found in Thessaly, at Theotokou tomb A and at Kapakli.

292     77. PLATE 20, 451 and 65/P44 (Levelling).

292     78. *GGP* 197 f. To the PSC skyphoi, cups, and amphoriskos, from Orchomenos and Vranesi, mentioned by Coldstream (p. 198) as Thessalo-Cycladic elements, should probably be added the circles skyphos from Thebes (*AD* 1917, 203 f., fig. 148). The globular pyxis from Thebes (*GGP* 197, n. 8) sounds similar to one or two found at Lefkandi. The evidence is very slight, but this district seems close to the region (as it is geographically) at least during SPG I.

292     79. Delphi. *Delphes* V, 17, fig. 74. See *PGP* 190 f. PSC skyphos fragments.

292     80. Probably several of the vases from Vergina described by Andronikos, *Vergina* I, 168 ff. (e.g. PSC skyphoi, circles skyphos, krater, oinochoai, feeders). Cf. also Petsas in *AD* 17, 218 ff. See *GDA* 217 for the likely date; and *PGP* 179 f., 190 f. for PSC skyphoi on other sites in Macedonia.

292     81. Larisa in Aeolis: *Larisa am Hermos* iii, 170, and pl. 57, 4. Sherd of PSC skyphos with high lip. Old Smyrna: several unpublished PSC skyphoi, with high or medium lip, and circles skyphoi from the Anglo-Turkish excavations of 1948—51.

292     82. The material from the surface deposits of the cemeteries need not contradict such an assertion. All three cemeteries have produced Attic and atticising MG I sherds (no later than this), admittedly not in any great quantity, but including some fine pieces; without stratification, however, there is no way of determining whether any of the local pottery of SPG type is contemporaneous with these.

292     83. See pp. 16 ff. It is not hermetically sealed: there are post holes and pits, which account for the presence of a few LG sherds.

292     84. The atticising shapes are principally skyphoi, but there are also kraters, oinochoai/jugs, amphorae, and a pyxis lid-knob.

293     85. See pp. 36 ff. It will be seen that (a) the circles skyphos is less well represented than in the SPG Pit, and so may not survived long into SPG III, (b) the continued presence of cup sherds with zigzag on the outer lip, even though in smaller numbers than in the SPG Pit and Moulds, might suggest persistence into SPG III (or the other hand, none appeared in the SL material, and (c) the opposed diagonals motive, as on amphorae, oinochoai, and kraters, is more common in the Levelling than in the SPG Pit.

293     86. Sherds from five plates, as opposed to none in the SPG Pit.

293     87. About a third of the total, as opposed to a negligible percentage earlier. There are just two or three examples of the swept-back lip, so characteristic of the later stages in other areas. It is also worth noting that the PSC skyphos remained as popular as ever, and there is no indication that the atticising skyphos ousted it.

293     88. There is therefore a substantial discrepancy between the evidence of the settlement and that of the tombs. If the settlement gives the truer picture, as it surely must, the question could then arise as to whether certain tomb groups classed as SPG II may not in fact be later. The question cannot be answered, but the possibility should be borne in mind.

294     89. Where there is decoration on the body, the handle is barred; otherwise it is monochrome. This rule is followed almost without exception (e.g. S Pyre 1A,4 of EPG date) throughout.

294     90. S 28,3 (PLATE 100), with a flat base, is an exception.

294     91. A system typical of many other shapes during this time, and already visible in SM.

294      92. P 14,4 (PLATE 134), of MPG date, is a Black Slip cup of similar type, one of the earliest specimens of this ware known at Lefkandi.

295      93. I have assigned T 7, which contained one of these cups, to LPG, but it is possible that a case might be argued for SPG I. The number of conical feet found in the SPG Pit might support the conclusion that there was an overlap into SPG I.

295      94. The fragmentary cups from P Channel, Lower Fill (PLATE 276, 964—6) could belong to this class.

295      95. Almost all monochrome: in the Area 2 deposits, for example, only nine handles out of a total of 148 were barred. See above, n. 89, for the cemeteries.

295      96. PLATE 14, 36—9 and 46—9.

295      97. PLATE 13, 2, 3, 12 and 14 (Moulds), and PLATE 31, 1 and 2 (SPG Pit).

295      98. See PLATE 28, 70/P5—7 for three cups of class V.

296      99. See PLATE 13, 18 (Moulds) and PLATE 18, 256 (Levelling). And if S SF 14 (PLATE 273), a stray sherd from Skoubris, is a cup and is local, it provides another example.

296      100. Particularly prominent in T Square V, see p. 276 and PLATE 284, 1—6. These might well be early, but it is not easy to assign them even to MPG; some or all must surely be later. For the settlement see PLATE 15, 103 (SPG Pit).

296      101. *BSA* 66, 344 and 348 f. This is one of the factors that leads to the conclusion of a break in time, if not in population, between the Mycenaean settlement and the cemeteries excavated.

296      102. See the references in Styrenius, *Submycenaean Studies*.

296      103. Only in Cyprus was there a similar popularity at about this time — see, e.g., Benson, *The Necropolis of Kaloriziki* (*SIMA* vol. 36), pl. 16. Cypriot cups are light ground with double wavy-line decoration, but have a fairly high conical or flaring foot.

296      104. *Pr.* 1961, 50, pl. 21b. As the excavator says, probably originally from a tomb.

296      105. Presumably implying the use of a faster wheel, for which some single origin should be inferred — Attica?

296      106. See perhaps the cup from Agora tomb V, transitional SM to EPG, illustrated in *Submycenaean Studies*, fig. 38. It is also possible that the increased height of the conical foot in MPG may reflect an increased awareness of, and sympathy with, Attic ideas.

296      107. Chalcis   *ChO*, pl. 45d. No known context. Has the reserved band typical of so many
                    Lefkandian cups. Probably EPG.
       Thessaly  *PT* 211, fig. 146e. Theotokou tomb B. Late MPG shape, LPG context? *Pr.* 1960,
                    pls 37 a—b, 38a. Iolkos tomb 12. Associated with a cup of class III (LPG) as
                    in Lefkandi T 17. *Pr.* 1961, pl. 21a (surface), pl. 21c (tomb 27), pl. 22b
                    (tombs 31 and 36), all from Iolkos. Those from tombs 27 and 36 probably
                    EPG; the cup from tomb 31 has compass-drawn circles on the body.
       Skyros    *AD* 1918, suppl. 43 f., fig. 10 = *PGP* 164 f. One is Black Slip.
                    *PGP* 166, under 'Miscellaneous'. All probably MPG.
       Naxos    *Ergon* for 1960, 187, fig. 209. High conical foot, and compass-drawn circles
                    on body; but associated with a lekythos with hand-drawn semicircles.
                    Probably EPG.

296      108. *Stele* (Athens 1977), 55 ff., pl. 11. MPG—LPG.

296      109. *Vergina* I, 180 f., fig. 31.

296      110. *Vergina* I, 180 f., fig. 30.

296      111. *PGP* 168 (Cup, type A) gives a summary of most of the known material; see also *GGP* 151 and 153, and for the thirty-nine from the Kapakli tomb, *PGRT* 33 ff. and pl. 11. It may be noted that the cup with high straight lip, handle attached wholly to the body, and alternating diagonals on the belly, found in other parts of the region, has not yet been identified at Lefkandi.

297      112. The shape is called a bowl before LPG, a skyphos thereafter.

297      113. The three with reserved band are S 3,2 (FIG. 8, A), S 55,2 (PLATE 107), both with dots on the band and zigzag on the body, and the monochrome S 43,3 (PLATE 104). S 60,1 (PLATE 111) has zigzag on the body, but no reserved band inside the lip.

298      114. The attribution to EPG is also dependent on the associated vases. S SF, 11 may also belong to this phase.

298      115. Mention may be made here of the fragmentary bowl P Pyre 40,1 (PLATE 155). Handles

and foot are missing; the body is bell-shaped, coming up to a low, slightly outcurved lip, mono-chrome except for a reserved band on the outer lip. Difficult to classify, it seems to fit more comfortably into EPG or MPG than into any later period.

299     116. *BSA* 66, 336; 339, fig. 4; 345, fig. 7,1.

299     117. Stressed in *BSA* 66, 349. See however Mycenae, *BSA* 25, 33, fig. 9b. The motive is known elsewhere, e.g. Cyprus.

299     118. See *GDA* 39. For Athens see *Ker* I, pls 22 and 23.

299     119. Note also a vase from Vergina, but its profile differs and it is much larger: *Vergina* I, 170, fig. 24, N15.

299     120. *BSA* 11, 78 ff.; *PT* 208, and 209, fig. 144c.

299     121. *Asine* 427, fig. 275. (The hemispherical bowl is reminiscent of S 2,4).

299     122. All three deposits are assumed to be not later than LPG in date, and are certainly predominantly LPG, though it is debatable whether some sherds may not be SPG I: see the relevant discussions.

299     123. PLATE 14, Moulds; PLATE 24 right, Area 3 South, under the yard floor; PLATE 276, P Channel, lower fill. Particularly prominent in the last mentioned, which contained many more examples than are illustrated.

299     124. There being no complete profile in these groups, the type of base is uncertain; from the evidence of other contexts it appears that a ring base was usual, but a conical or flaring foot cannot be ruled out — see the two skyphoi from Andros, *PGP* pl. 16, and the one from Amathus in Cyprus, *JHS* 77, 214, fig. 4a. FIG. 8, F is a reasonable reconstruction.

299     125. PLATES 14, 34–5, 44; 24, 612, 614, 621; 276, 971.

299     126. PLATE 14, 34 (note also the cross-hatched diamond of 35); PLATE 24, 606 and 613.

299     127. See *PGP* 82 ff., classes IIa and IIb.

299     128. On two sherds the lip is sharply everted but not carinated: PLATE 13, 23; and PLATE 276, 969. An important variation, as these are the only two in any context, and the latter, from the lower fill of P Channel, is the only PSC sherd found in the deposit.

299     129. Central filling: PLATE 13, 19, and P 3,14 (FIG. 8, G). Central panel: PLATE 13, 29–30.

300     130. Pointers to its late appearance are the solitary example in the cemetery, in a tomb which borders on SPG I, and the single (and atypical) sherd from the P Channel deposit.

300     131. *PGP* 85 f., class III. Note the vertical dots, recalling the 'branch' pattern of LPG oinochoai and lekythoi in Attica. The only one at Lefkandi of its type.

300     132. PLATE 15, 140 and 150 (SPG Pit); PLATE 25, 682–3 (various areas). See *PGP* 86 ff., class IVa, for comparative material from Attica and the Argolid.

300     133. PLATE 25, 684–5 are close.

300     134. PLATE 25, 670 (various areas) is the best example. See also PLATES 15, 107 (SPG Pit) and 18, 307 (Levelling). These are the only ones, and at least the first two could belong to LPG.

300     135. For example, four of the five sherds in the Moulds Deposit have a central filling, as opposed to five out of about forty-five from the SPG Pit, and one from the Levelling Material. The fine fragments PLATE 25, 664–5 are almost certainly LPG, from their similarity to the vase found at Amathus, associated with an LPG cup (*JHS* 77, 214, fig. 4).

300     136. PLATE 15, 125 (SPG Pit) is slightly carinated. But is it SPG?

300     137. See e.g. PLATE 31, 11. The distinction is not always as clear-cut as one would wish — the Lefkandian potter was not bound by hard and fast rules.

301     138. PLATE 18, 286 (Levelling); PLATE 22E, third row left (Area 4 South); PLATE 25, 658. This type, better known outside Lefkandi, belongs for the most part to eighth-century contexts (see below).

301     139. Note a single example of the use of three sets of semicircles between the handles, PLATE 25, 655.

301     140. In many instances one cannot tell whether the arcs shown come from circles or semi-circles.

301     141. See generally *PGP* 194 f. Andros: *PGP* 162 and pl. 16. Tenos: *Ann.* 8–9, 219 and fig. 22 (Kardiani tomb 2), and *GGP* 149 (from the Kambos group, and with high flaring foot). Rheneia: *Délos* XV, pl. XXVII, 20 and 21. Thebes: *AD* 1917, 203 f., and fig. 148 (Kolonaki tomb 27). Vergina: *Vergina* I, 171 f., and fig. 24a (E26). Skyros, Phthiotic Thebes, Cyprus: *PGP* 194 f. The examples from Old Smyrna, found in the Anglo-Turkish excavations, are unpublished. Note the

presence of only one from Thessaly (and even this may have had three sets of circles), suggesting that, as at Lefkandi, it was not a type of vase placed in tombs.

301     142. The skyphos from the Kambos group is likely to be LPG.

301     143. Much has happened since I discussed this type of skyphos in *PGP* 180 ff. Many of the skyphoi mentioned there have now been fully published and illustrated. Many new ones have been found, from several new sites, especially in Cyprus: some have been published, some not.

301     144. *BSA* 68, 101 f.; *Dialoghi di Archeologia* 8 (1974–5), 97, fig. D. Both from Veii. *Archaeological Reports* for 1976–7, 66 (Villasmundo in Sicily).

302     145. PLATE 24, 626 (Area 3 South, under yard floor) has a similar motive (LPG).

302     146. See p. 300 and n. 133. The type with panelled zigzag on the body may also still have been in use in SPG.

302     147. PLATE 20, 451 and 65/P64 (Levelling).

302     148. PLATES 20–1 for the sherds from the Levelling; for others, from various deposits, see PLATE 26, 728–754. One example from the tombs, T 31,5 (PLATE 185), with multiple zigzag, firmly dated to MG I by association with four Attic imports.

302     149. *GGP* 14 ff. for a general discussion of the development (p. 24 for the introduction of the multiple chevron).

302     150. Imports, PLATE 15, 129–31 (SPG Pit); atticising, the sherd with multiple zigzag panel from above P 47, PLATE 278 C, top left.

303     151. It is chiefly on the basis of this vase, with its relatively high conical foot, that I would class S 16 as an EPG rather than as an SM group.

303     152. There are comparable unpublished examples in the region.

303     153. *GDA* 168. Not yet published in detail; it provides one of the very few possible ceramic links between the Argolid and Lefkandi.

303     154. *CVA* Cambridge I, 1–2, pl. I, 13. LPG from the associated vases, thought to belong together and to constitute the contents of a single grave.

303     155. PLATE 29B: Area SL, group A. PLATE 273, 846: S Gully Fill.

303     156. The miniature P 28,11 (PLATE 144) is certainly of this type, but is handmade. For the deposits associated with the cemeteries see PLATES 273, 844–7 and 279, 1057.

303     157. PLATES 15, 18 and 25 (especially the complete example 65/P77).

303     158. PLATE 276 shows two joining sherds, 976–7, from the lower fill of the Channel in P, which is very strongly LPG (and earlier) in character. They are from a shallow bowl, but the handle and decoration differ from those of the type discussed. An earlier type, possibly.

303     159. PLATES 28, 70/P3–4, and 29, A.

303     160. *BSA* 31, 30 and pl. 8, no. 130. Black Slip ware. Note that the Kapakli tholos tomb has not produced any shallow bowls.

303     161. *PGP* 166. Not yet fully published.

304     162. The tomb also contained a hand-made shallow bowl, no. 16, with another variation on the lug handle.

304     163. The fabric is brown, and not the characteristic grey of Black Slip.

304     164. *BSA* 31, 30 and pl. 8, nos. 127–9. Flat-based; rectangular lug handles.

304     165. *Ker* V, i, pls 15 and 101, from tombs 3 and 75A. Lug handles.

304     166. Such as Catling, *Cypriot Bronzework* 201, no. 24, and pl. 31 f, a cast tripod of a group almost all of which came from Cyprus, and are dated in the twelfth and eleventh centuries B.C. This example has no known provenance, but Cyprus is an obvious possibility.

304     167. The vase is noted and illustrated in Hencken, *Tarquinia* 85, fig. 35d, where it is compared with a tripod from the Latian urnfields, op. cit. fig. 35c. For a similar idea see *Ker* I, pls 64–5 (Athens), and *AD* 27, II. 2, pl. 268e (Paralimni in Boeotia).

304     168. Imitation of metal at this period would not be surprising in view of the evidence for a bronze foundry in the settlement.

304     169. See the two Attic LPG pyxides, *PGP*, pl. 13, not only for the decoration but also for the handles. There are many other instances of panelled motives.

304     170. See *BSA* 31, 48, fig. 19, from Marmariani.

305     171. Largely due to the generosity of the donors in tombs S 59 + 59A, P 3, P 10, P 39B, and T 13. These five tombs contained a total of over fifty kalathoi.

305     172. One, P 24,9, is Black Slip to the eye, but analysis has shown the fabric to be the normal Lefkandian.

305      173. On P 7,3 and P 10,9 the wall of the lower body comes out in a slight convex curve before giving way to the concave curve which leads to the lip.

305      174. P 39B,6. Bands on the outer body.

306      175. Probably by the same potter. If so, note that the one is very shallow, the other very deep.

306      176. I have for obvious reasons not included tombs or pyres which contained only kalathoi. On the assumption that the distribution is chronologically significant, I have in the list at the end apportioned such groups as follows: LPG or SPG I, P 8 and P 42, impressed-triangle kalathoi only; SPG I, S 25A, P Pyre 28, both types; SPG I or later, S SF9, P 17, P 37, T 27, T 36.

306      177. Even though this seems to be a homogeneous collection of late SPG II/early SPG III date.

306      178. See Professor Smithson's full and masterly account in *Hesperia* 37, 98 ff. She notes, furthermore, that in almost every case in Attica, where a distinction is possible, kalathoi are associated with female burials, and that kalathoi 'like other grave furniture are deceptively conservative and show no consistent development'. The latter statement is certainly true of Lefkandi, and the former might provide a useful criterion.

306      179. I pass over the question of the origin of the openwork technique; it is highly likely that it derives from some material other than clay, but one cannot go further than that.

306      180. Note that the two earliest Lefkandian examples are from P 22, which contained both Attic and Cypriot imports.

     For Attica see *Hesperia* 37, 98 ff. The earliest is dated to MPG (op. cit. 98, n. 51 — from a well); there are seven from the rich Athenian lady's grave, of EG II/MG I date, and the latest are from the Isis grave at Eleusis (*CVA* Athens 1, pl. 6:10 and 11). There are no LPG examples yet known, but the cut-work technique was familiar to the Athenians at that time — see the two stands from Kerameikos tomb 48, *Ker* IV, pl. 25, nos 2028 and 2029.

     For Cyprus, where the technique is also found on other shapes, openwork kalathoi are known in CG II and CG III. See *SCE* IV.2, figs XIII,3; XVI,2; XXII,4–5.

306      181. Crete, Vrokastro. *Vrokastro*, pl. XXXI, 1–2, from chamber tomb 1. Difficult to date, but need not be as late as Geometric. Samos, the Heraeum. *AM* 58, 125 and fig. XXXVII. Date uncertain. Kos, Serraglio tomb 10. *PGP* 224 and pl. 30; cf. *GGP* 264. Probably very late LPG. (This vase has incised decoration).

306      182. *PGP* 165 and 172.

306      183. *Pr.* 1960, pl. 38a = *GDA* 209, pl. 49.

307      184. For its use in the make-up of the multiple vase see the next section.

307      185. S 16,7 (PLATE 96), S 32,3 (FIG. 11, B), S 53,1 (FIG. 11, A — the earliest, and pure SM). P 16,11 would also have been included if its vertical handle had not turned it into a hydria.

307      186. Wavy lines, careless on S 53,1, formal on S 32,3; vertical wiggly lines on S 16,7.

308      187. Furumark, *Analysis*, 37, fig. 9, shapes 59, 61, 64. *Perati* II, 198 ff. for a full discussion with references (223 were found in this cemetery).

308      188. *BSA* 66, 333 ff., pls 50,5; 51,4; 55,4.

308      189. *PGP* 2 f.; *GDA* 33 and 35. Note that there are a few SM amphoriskoi from Athens, not far in shape from the unusual S 16,2; see especially *Ker* I, pl. 20, no. 439 from tomb 19.

308      190. S 20,3 (PLATE 99) and S 31,2 (FIG. 12, C) share with S 16,4 the close zigzag line(s) on the shoulder and the unpainted lower body and foot. S 32,4 (PLATE 101) looks earlier: it has the lower area unpainted, but the rest is monochrome with one reserved band; more important, the handles still come up to the neck, and the body is more biconical.

308      191. To these may be added P 3,12 (PLATE 128) of Black Slip ware. So also may S Pyre 15,1 (PLATE 114), which for shape and decoration (hand-drawn PSC) stands in a class of its own.

308      192. See those from P 13, P 23, and P 31.

309      193. T 26, three; P 24, two; P 7 and P 39, one each. T 26,15 (FIG. 12, D) and P 24,3 (PLATE 142) have a scribble zigzag at the base of the neck, recalling earlier practice; T 26,15 has a narrow ladder panel separating the sets of semicircles (cf. P 31,2 below); T 26,16 (PLATE 183) and P 39,1 (FIG. 12, G) have a thick zigzag on the neck.

309      194. P 31, two; P tombs 3, 13, 23, 39B, and Pyre 14B, one each (FIG. 12, I shows P 13,12 and FIG. 12, E P 23,5). Note the unusual design of P 31,2 (PLATE 144) and P 39B, 3 (PLATE 146), and the narrow ladder panel of the former.

309       195. Monochrome: P 3,13; P 10,1; P 18,1; P 31,1. Reserved bands: P 44,1.

309       196. Zigzag on belly: P 13,2; P 18,2 and 3 (FIG. 12, H); P 44,5. Zigzag on neck: P 13,1.

310       197. Three small later vases (P 47,2–3; P 28,2) of superficially similar shape are classified as small amphorae with handles from shoulder to lip.

310       198. PLATE 19, 359 = PLATE 33,40.

310       199. *ChO* 253, 266 f., pl. 46a and b: nos 5 and 6.

310       200. Op. cit. 257 f., 267 f., pls 48b and 49c: nos 13 and 14.

310       201. *AD* 27, II.2, 316 and pl. 268c. The shoulder decoration is multiple triangles with the innermost one painted over — compare P 31,3 and for the painted inner triangle the lekythos from the same tomb, P 31,4.

310       202. Theotokou: *PT* 213, fig. 146a. Halos *BSA* 18, p. 5, fig. 3, no. 5. Marmariani: *BSA* 31, p. 26, pl. 6, nos 81–2. Retziouni: *PGRT* 11 and 52, pl. 3, no. 9. Kapakli area (probable) *PGRT* 11 f., no. 11. Unknown provenience: *PGRT* 11 f., nos 10 and 12.

310       203. No. 81 from Marmariani, with compass-drawn semicircle, presumably not earlier than LPG; so also *PGRT* no. 10, as the semicircles, though hand-drawn, are done with such care that the potter must surely be imitating the more advanced technique. The amphoriskos from Retziouni could be earlier than LPG but not, I think, as early as SM.

310       204. *PGP* 165; see *GGP* 152 for the likely date.

310       205. The Vatican group: *PGP* 158 f., pl. 25A; see *GGP* 152. Ktikados grave 1: *GGP* 152, pl. 32c. See P 31,2 for the shape, perhaps.

310       206. Tenos: *Ann.* 8–9, 220, fig. 20, and 225, fig. 27; Kardiani tombs 1, no. 2 and 2, no. 7. Rheneia: *Délos* XV, Aa 58–61; *PGP* pl. 19, A1452–4 — see *GGP* pl. 32 f for A1452; *GGP* 149, said to be of similar shape to Kardiani tomb 1, no. 2.
          For a discussion of these see *GGP* 154 ff.

310       207. Rheneia A1453 also has the opposed diagonals on the shoulder.

311       208. *Ann.* 31–2 (1969–70), 472 f., figs 12a, 13b. Possibly to be linked with Rheneia A1455, which Coldstream considers to be probably atticising MGI (*GGP* 156).

311       209. *AD* 24, Chron., 433 and pl. 439. Flat-based, as so often in Crete.

311       210. Nos 1–3, PLATE 137, and see p. 348 for references to vases found in Athens. As often on Attic vases, P 3,10 has a lid; although its decoration is not paralleled exactly in Attica, the opposed groups of diagonals with filled interstices are a well-known motive there in LPG. LPG.

311       211. It has string holes on the handles, so may have been meant to have a lid, as has P 3,10.

311       212. The unfilled interstices suggest this, though they are not unknown in LPG — see amphoriskoi P 23,6–7 (PLATE 141). The broad zone in which the diagonals are placed here, perhaps the barred rim top, and the associated pyxides would all support an SPG I date.

311       213. P 44,4 (PLATE 148) was found in an SPG I tomb group, but its battered and fragmentary condition suggests that it was a stray, and its whole style (note the poorly formed foot) is that of an SM vase.

312       214. S Pyre 1A,3 (PLATE 92), lattice; S 16,8 (FIG. 13, A), chevrons and cross-hatched triangle; S 19,2 (PLATE 98), hand-drawn semicircles and wavy lines; S 38,2, crude circles, thick wavy line.

312       215. For example, the body of S 16,8 is more globular than that of the belly-handled amphoriskos S 16,7.

312       216. S Pyre 1A,3.

312       217. Furumark, *Analysis* 69 f. and fig. 20, type 325. See *Perati* II, 213 and the relevant notes showing the distribution of the amphoriskos type.

312       218. *ChO*, p. 256, pl. 48a. A vertical-handled type, triple in line, basket handle, decoration very close to S 16,8. For an LPG example, based on lekythoi, see *PGP* pl. 30, Kos Serraglio tomb 10. See also Corinth VII, i, pl. 10, from Vello: miniature hydriai, context probably EG.

313       219. See *Ker* I, pl. 14, nos 490 and 512 (Athens); Styrenius, *Submycenaean Studies*, fig. 58 (Ancient Elis); Karageorghis, *Nouveaux Documents* 191, fig. 47 (Idalion in Cyprus). I know of no parallel for the triangle enclosing horizontal rough zigzags.

313       220. *BSA* 66, 344 f. Already current in Phase 2b, it increases in volume in Phase 3.

313       221. See the list at the end of the section. S SF 10 may be either SM or EPG: it is like S 46,2. S Pyre 1,3 is a sherd with hand-drawn semicircles, not certainly from a lekythos, but SM as associated with a stirrup jar.

313     222. It has a much broader base, the handle is attached to the lip instead of to the neck, and the shoulder motive is unusual, and slightly reminiscent of that on the bowl S 32,6 (PLATE 101). Nothing else like it at Lefkandi — see for shape the 'bottle' *Ker* I, pl. 37, but it would be rash to claim a connexion.

313     223. *Ker* I, pl. 13, tomb 84 (lekythoi only); pl. 37, Acropolis Slope tomb B (a remarkable association of hand-drawn and the typical PG compass-drawn semicircles, and two very early but certainly PG cups). It may be noted that the Lefkandian potters, though the lekythoi they made were generally similar to those of Athens and must be roughly contemporaneous, used a slightly different general system of decoration, avoided the vertical wiggly lines not uncommon in Athens, and did not until much later change over from hand-drawn semicircles.

313     224. *Pr.* 1960, 259, pl. 159a, a cup with compass-drawn circles. It is unfortunate that the lekythos with hand-drawn semicircles from tomb C at Theotokou (*PT* 211, fig. 146f) was the only vase of its tomb; should it be dated SM or EPG?

314     225. They may include one sporadic unillustrated one, S SF 15, either from a tomb or pyre; it has a biconical body, a banded neck, and three sets of chevrons on the shoulder.

314     226. Exceptions: P 13,11; T 3,1 and 4; T 26,6 and 8. P 13,11 could be described as light ground.

314     227. T 26,6 and T 3,1 are the only lekythoi on which the previously popular feature of leaving the lower body and the foot unpainted is found. Evidence for continuity?

314     228. Note the curious upward tapering of the neck, a feature common to P 31,5 and T 7,3.

315     229. For the neck see also T 15,3.

315     230. E.g. *Ker* IV, tombs 39 and 48; *Hesperia* 30, 159 ff., pls 25 and 26 (Nea Ionia). The Attic shape went out of use at the end of LPG: in Lefkandi it survived at least till the end of SPG I.

315     231. See T 7,3 and T 26,6.

315     232. The two tombs shared the centaur.

315     233. The chevron motive had already appeared in MPG, see P 16,4, and could suggest an MPG date when found on its own. This may be relevant for S Pyre 17: no. 2 has chevrons only; no. 1 has semicircles with three arcs, and the place where the compass point was to go was carefully painted over, possibly suggesting unfamiliarity with the technique, and thus earliness. But one cannot be sure.

315     234. Several fragments of a large belly-handled amphora of a type in use from LPG to SPG II and one sherd of a PSC skyphos.

315     235. Sherds of an amphora similar to that in S Pyre 15, and a fragmentary globular pyxis which seems to fit better into SPG I than into LPG.

316     236. *ChO*, 251 and pl. 46c; 255 f. and pl. 47d.

316     237. See *ChO*, 266, where an EPG date is suggested, but this seems too early, in the light of our present knowledge.

316     238. *Pr.* 1961, pl. 22a. Double wavy line on the shoulder, and a surprisingly high conical foot.

316     239. *BSA* 31, 23 and pl. 5.

316     240. *BSA* 11, 78 f., fig. 3a; the lower body and foot are unpainted. Note the bowl with high conical foot, very like those from S 18 and S 51; the other associated vase is a hand-made jug with cutaway neck. For a mention of another see *PGP* 170 (the one attributed to Papadimitriou's tomb is an error, see op. cit. 165).

318     241. See *GDA* 38 (the attribution of only one oinochoe to Lefkandi is incorrect).

318     242. The general tendency, now and later, is that the nearer a vase is to being completely monochrome, the more likely the handle is to be monochrome too.

318     243. But note the sherds with tiers of dogtooth decoration from a pit in S Trench A extension (PLATE 273, 823–5): probably from oinochoai, they seem to provide a link with the earliest Attic PG, see *Ker* I, pl. 65, no. 552.

318     244. T 12B,1 (PLATE 173), close in shape to P 25B,3, is probably contemporaneous with these; it still has the monochrome system, but there is a zigzag on the shoulder.

318     245. *Ker* I, pl. 68, no. 545 (MPG); *Ker* IV, pl. 13, no. 1070 (MPG) and no. 2091 (LPG). See *PGP* 49 f.

318     246. No. 13 is exceptional in retaining the monochrome and reserved-band system of the earlier period, but the shape imitates Attic.

247. The Attic shape is also imitated in the Black Slip ware: T 26,11 and S 56,2 (SPG I).

248. The other vases from P 44 are SPG I, but reference to the catalogue will make it clear that no. 7 was found in the fill, and not associated with them.

249. Coldstream's lekythos-oinochoe, see *GGP* 11. One should therefore perhaps define P 22 as SPG I, but I have found it difficult to call a group which contains so many Attic or probably Attic PG vases anything but LPG.

250. Height 35 cm. See also the discussion in *BSA* 65, 23 f.

251. *BSA* 31, pl. 4, no. 56.

252. See *GGP* 265; *AJA* 67, pls 83 and 84; *Ist. Mitt.* 7, pl. 36,4.

253. *BSA* 31, pl. 3, nos. 42 and 47; pl. 5, no. 74, from Marmariani. *PGRT* 15, fig. 6 and pl. 4, no. 22, probably from Kapakli.

254. This motive may provide a link with the slender SPG II oinochoai discussed below.

255. Used as a feeder, it differs from the rest in having cross-hatched triangles on the shoulder.

256. There are three hand-made oinochoai, of grey fabric and burnished, P 4,4 (PLATE 128, SPG I) and T 2,6—7 (PLATE 168, SPG II) of much the same shape.

257. *GGP* 11 (EG I) and 14 (EG II). See particularly op. cit. pl. 2g, from Kerameikos tomb 74, of EG II date.

258. The tombs show how popular the Attic oinochoai were — nine examples from T 19, T 31, and T 33. Imitations are far less prominent. T 33 has a hand-made local copy of the Attic model, but for wheel-made atticising we have to depend on a few sherds from the surface material, PLATE 274, 912 from S Gully, and PLATE 275, 943, 949, 953 and 961 from the surface or upper fill of P Channel and not all of these need be oinochoai.

259. PLATES 22, 485; 24, 592; 26, 765. As with the cemetery sherds, none in a stratified context, and one cannot be sure that the imitations are of Attic MG rather than of EG II.

260. I confine myself to the region around Lefkandi, which includes Thessaly, Skyros, the North Cyclades, and Euboea itself. The links with Attica have been dealt with, and there appears to be little other significant material, though note may be made of a small oinochoe with high handle, conical foot, and chevrons on the shoulder, found in a tomb at Paralimni in Boeotia, *AD* 27, II.2, 316 and pl. 268e.

261. The two from Pteleon, perhaps SM, are unlike Lefkandian of any phase. See *PGRT* 16, nos 25—6, and pl. 4, See also *Pr.* 1953, 120 ff., and *LMTS* 130.

262. *Pr.* 1960, pl. 36b and pl. 37a. See also *Pr.* 1961, 50 for an unillustrated oinochoe from tomb 43, probably of this period to judge from the date of the cemetery as a whole.

263. Marmariani: *BSA* 31, 21 ff., nos 48—69. Theotokou: *PT* 212 f. (two from tomb B, five from tomb A). Halos: *BSA* 18, 4 ff. (eleven). Kapakli (4), Kapakli area (1), Pherae (2), Sesklo (1), U.P. (1): *PGRT* 13 ff. Iolkos, Nea Ionia: *Thessalika* 5, 49 f. (two). Demetrias: Apostolides, *Ai Pagasai*, fig. 2; see *PGP* 153.

264. Only one, from Sesklo, *PGRT* no. 23.

265. For Thessaly, *PGRT* 16, pl. 4, no. 24.

266. *Stele* (Athens 1977), 55 ff., pl. 12.

267. *PGP* 165 f.

268. *ChO* 250 f. and pl. 47a.

269. There are, however, for the SPG III period (the equivalent of Attic MG) a number of atticising broad-based oinochoai: see *GGP* 168 f. These reflect the similar renewal of Attic links at Lefkandi, of which the most impressive manifestation is the nine Attic MG I oinochoai.

270. *Ann.* 8—9 (1925—6) 218 f.

271. Furumark, *Analysis* 602, type 111. Note in particular, for its close similarity to the earliest ones in the tombs, a jug from phase 2b of the LH IIIC settlement of Xeropolis, *BSA* 66, 341, fig. 5:6.

272. P 15,1 (PLATE 134), a feeder, is exceptional in having cross-hatched diamonds and intersecting triangles on the shoulder, and a double swastika at the base of the handle. I have assigned it to LPG, but the swastika might suggest SPG I.

273. T 13,3, with lower body and foot unpainted, is a surprising reversion to earlier practice. The bodies are flattened globular or globular rather than ovoid.

274. One, P 36,3 (PLATE 145), is unpainted. Note that P 36,1 and P 39A,1 (hand-made, PLATE 146) are feeders.

323      275. Two Black Slip examples, and one Red Slip, are fragmentary.

324      276. *GGP* 150 f. with the relevant notes. The sites or areas involved are Halos, Iolkos (including the Kapakli region, but not the tholos tomb), Chalcis, Skyros (one jug is of Black Slip ware), Tenos (Kambos, see *GGP* 149), and Naxos. Add the jug with circles on the shoulder from Palaiokastro in Thessaly (*BCH* 56, 99, fig. 17, no. 5; see *PGP* 313), and a further example from Skyros, of MPG/LPG date (*Stele*, 55 ff., pl. 12). The two from Marmariani, *BSA* 31, nos 72–3, are rather different, especially in the neck.

324      277. *AD* 1917, 25 ff., fig. 29. Note the two parallel rough zigzags. MPG?.

324      278. *BCH* 61, 44 ff., pls 5 and 6; see also *GDA* 203 f., pl. 47. Probably MPG.

324      279. *BSA* 18, 4 f., fig. 3:1–3.

324      280. *Vergina* I, 177, fig. 26, P 2 and AZ 3.

324      281. PLATE 23, 550, from the surface down to the floor.

324      282. P. 35 and PLATE 16, 194.

324      283. P. 35.

325      284. P. 58 f, and PLATE 40, 38. Monochrome, reserved shoulder.

325      285. To judge from the lekythoi. Probably not an early phase of SPG I, as the tomb overlay T 3, also of SPG I date. One sherd of a jug with cutaway neck was found in the Toumba surface material, PLATE 279, 1067.

325      286. For the Late Geometric development, see below.

325      287. See, e.g., *Vergina* I, 193 ff. 236 jugs, all hand-made; still current in the eighth century. Note, however, op. cit. 192, fig. 38 (AZ8) in relation to the double-necked P 23,1.

325      288. *BSA* 31, 20 f.; nos. 1–9 hand-made nos. 31–47 wheel-made.

325      289. Kapakli, *PGRT* 19 ff.; nos 36–42, all wheel-made, all wheel-made. (I am assuming that the Kapakli tholos was first used in LPG; the earlier tombs from Iolkos contained no jugs of this type). The shape is similar to that of our jugs, and one has horizontal grooves below the rim; all have low feet. The cross-hatched triangles on the shoulder recall the decoration of the examples from P 22, but there is no attempt at Lefkandi to reproduce (at least on this shape) the decoration on the neck. Compare however the neck motive of Kapakli no. 39 with the central motive of pyxis no. 20 from P 13 (PLATE 133), a tomb which also contained a jug with cutaway neck.

325      290. There are a few hand-made examples from Skyros, see *PGP* 164 f.

325      291. See PLATES 39 and 40 for Lefkandian jugs.

326      292. See *Perati* II, 241 ff. Iakovidis lists the few with spout at 90° on pp. 242–3 (the only one from Perati itself, 976, is of a rather different shape, as he stresses).

326      293. *Pr.* 1960, 259, fig. 195a; cf. *Ergon* for 1960, 187, fig. 209. Tomb 12. For others of post-Mycenaean date, see Knossos, *Fortetsa* 153, pl. 38 (EPG?) and Pherae in Thessaly, Béquignon, *Recherches Archéologiques à Phéres*, 53, 73, and pl. 22,7 (no date assignable).

326      294. Possibly taking the idea from the Cypriot side-spouted jugs? See Pieridou, *PG Style in Cyprus* 22.

327      295. Marmariani: *BSA* 31, 23 and pl. 5, no. 69. Trefoil oinochoe type, spout at right angle to handle.

327      296. Athens: *Hesperia* 6, 367, fig. 30; jug, LPG. Tiryns: *Tiryns* I, pl. 16, 10; trefoil oinochoe, LPG. Kos: *GDA*, pl. 34B, tomb 63; two jugs; pl. 35, tomb 10; two hand-made trefoil oinochoai – all four LPG. Kameiros: *JdI* 1, 136; jug, LPG? With the exception of the feeder from Tyryns, all have the spout at right angles to the handle.

327      297. A few pyxis sherds were found in the surface material of Toumba, and a rim in the fill of P 47; these do not add anything to our knowledge.

327      298. In Attica the globular pyxis made its first tentative appearance in MPG, but is essentially an LPG shape, surviving marginally into EG I: *Hesperia* xxx, 163 f. Note that pyxides were found in both male and female burials.

327      299. The closest in shape to the Attic model are not those in LPG contexts, but P 13,17 (FIG. 17, B)–19, early in SPG I.

327      300. P 22,22 (FIG. 17, A); P 23,12; P 39,2; T 23A, 3.

329      301. E.g. T Pyre 2,6 (LPG) and S 59,5 (SPG III).

329      302. P 13,17 (FIG. 17, B) and 18 are exceptions, as they have semicircles; this is a matter, though, more of a shoulder decoration than of a reserved zone, and comes into the experimental category.

329        303. E.g. P 21,7 (FIG. 17, E).

329        304. See T 23,7 (FIG. 17, C). In Attica the butterfly motive, as used on other types of vase, is not known before MG I, but it appeared earlier outside that district (see *BSA* 50, pl. 48e, from Mycenae: EG I), and Attic practice cannot be used here as a chronological criterion.

329        305. In both cases associated with EG II and MG I Attic pyxides.

329        306. Note the 'crossword' design of T 23,2, repeated in the experimental P 13,20; much the same technique is apparent in the swastika of P 47,15.

329        307. In three instances, P 12, T 23, and P Pyre 34, it was either the only type of vase, or accompanied by just one other.

329        308. PLATE 16. The restored pyxis, 69/P44: the wide belly zone has groups of vertical lines, a design not found in the tombs. Everted rim: 200 (the other not illustrated). For two lid knobs, 185 and 187. Lid rims: 184 and 192; different rims, both remarkable for a decoration of semicircles, one of which with a triangle central filling. The lids and knobs need not be from globular pyxides.

329        309. PLATES 23, 532–3; 20, 401; 26, 764. It is also possible that certain of the sherds with zigzag or opposed diagonal belly motives could be from pyxides.

329        310. *AD* 16, *Chronika* 152 and pl. 133d.

329        311. *PGP* 165.

329        312. *PGRT*, pl. 13, no. 145.

330        313. See *PGP* 109, and more recently *Europa* (Grumach Festschrift) 75 ff. For the pyxis from Corinth, of EG I date, not mentioned in either of the two above publications, see *Hesperia* xxxix, 16 and pl. 9.

330        314. The shape had a long survival, especially at Corinth. See Callipolitis-Feytmans in *AE* 1973, 1 ff.

330        315. *Ker* I, pl. 27, no. 507; Styrenius, *Submycenaean Studies* 134, fig. 52 (Mycenae).

330        316. Though no string holes on the pyxis, two were pierced in the knob of the lid; perhaps the string was taken through the handle loops.

330        317. The best comparisons are from Karphi, *BSA* 55, 18, fig. 12.

330        318. See *GDA* 57.

330        319. In addition to the two discussed there is a third, P 39,3, but it had disintegrated to such an extent that one can say of it only that it was a pyxis, and hand-made.

330        320. See Courbin, *La Céramique Géométrique de L'Argolide* 226 f., pl. 77, C2410 (Argos); *GGP* 116, pl. 23h (Mycenae). The suspension lug may have been an Argive innovation for the wheelmade pyxis (*GGP* 114), but the idea could have derived from bronze pyxides, see Bouzek, *Graeco-Macedonian Bronzes* 24 ff.

330        321. *GGP* 117. For another example at Lefkandi, see PLATE 26, 712.

330        322. See above, for panelled Lefkandian pyxides. For Thessaly, *PGRT* pl. 13, from Marmariani. The cross-hatched square design may be derived from Thessalian kantharoi, see *PGRT* pl. 15.

330        323. *PGP* pl. 13.

330        324. In addition to the Attic pyxides found in the tombs, sherds of others of MG date were found in the cemetery deposits and in the settlement.

331        325. See *Perati* II, 248 f.; the probable positioning of the handle on our flask is, however, different. No example was found in the LH IIIC settlement on Xeropolis.

331        326. *BSA* 63, 115 and 113, fig. 5.

331        327. Karageorghis, *Nouveaux Documents* 214 ff. for earlier ones. For contemporaneous examples, Yon, *Salamine* II, pls 26–8; *RDAC* 1967, 13, fig. 8; Benson, *The Necropolis of Kaloriziki*, pl. 20.

331        328. A remote echo of the motive on the EPG flask, not necessarily evidence for continuity.

331        329. *SCE* IV. 2, fig. XIII.

332        330. *Ker* IV, pl. 25, no. 2034 (tomb 48); *Hesperia* xxx, 163, pl. 28, no. 35 (Nea Ionia). The type is still found in Attica in MG I: *Pr.* 1939, 30, tomb 5 from Marathon, and see *GGP* 16.

332        331. *PGP* 119.

332        332. *Clara Rhodos* 3, 146 f., fig. 142, tomb 141. One-handled, trumpet mouth; early ninth century, see *GGP* 265.

332        333. *AE* 1891, 27 f., pl. 3, 1; see *BSA* 68, 99. Two-handled, compass-drawn circles. Date unknown.

332       334. *AD* 24, i, 86 f., fig. 1 and pl. 50. One-handled, trumpet mouth; perhaps early ninth century.

332       335. There is no reason why it should not have been used in the settlement, but none has been identified.

332       336. Furumark's types 128 and 129, *Analysis* 604. See *Perati* II, 237 f. for the general picture in LH IIIC; at Lefkandi the hydria was one of the standard storage vessels during this period (*BSA* 66, 334 ff.).

332       337. Note the thin-brush decoration on the shoulder of S 19,7.

333       338. The non-local masterpiece S 51,2 (see pp. 348 ff.: of MPG date from its associated vases, in spite of its astonishing shoulder decoration) is so close to it in shape that it must surely have been made somewhere in the region.

333       339. As also on the trefoil oinochoai of this phase.

333       340. Styrenius, *Submycenaean Studies* 120.

333       341. *BCH* 61, pl. 5,5; *GDA* 203 f., pl. 47 (EPG is suggested on the basis of the belly-handled amphoriskos).

333       342. *Pr.* 1960, pl. 37, tomb XII. See *GDA* pl. 49.

333       343. *BSA* 11, 79, fig. 3d.

333       344. Nothing certain from Athens. Note two from Mycenae, which could be MPG: *Tiryns* I, 157, fig. 21.

333       345. *PGP* 223 (it may be that one or two belong to EG). One of these is illustrated in *GDA* pl. 34B.

333       346. See *PGP* 43 ff. and pl. 14, and occasional references in *GGP* — six from Athens and Attica, three from Skyros, one each from Délos and Amyklai. At Knossos the shape did not develop till the early ninth century, but then became fairly popular, see *Fortetsa* 146 f., and the same is perhaps true of other Cretan sites.

333       347. *ChO* 254, pl. 47b.

335       348. Due to their size, amphorae do not normally appear in tombs; on the other hand, they are frequently connected with pyres, and will in many cases have protruded from them — and in the course of time been broken. They are one of the commonest shapes in the settlement deposits, where, however, it is exceedingly unusual for anything approaching a complete profile to be recovered. I distinguish between the small amphorae, 20 cm or less in height, the medium, up to 50 cm, and the large ones of over 50 cm. Examples of the two former will be found on FIG. 19; for the latter, mostly fragmentary, reference is made to the line drawings and illustrations in the PLATES volume.

          349. See *Ker* I, pls 26—7 for the amphora in Athens. Vertical wiggly lines are found on other SM shapes there.

335       350. For each only one belly handle and one vertical handle were recovered; the only doubt is whether the handle from shoulder to neck had a companion — if not, the vase would be a hydria.

335       351. It is the earliest piece from this deposit, in use into LPG but probably no later and thus appreciably earlier than anything found in the tombs or pyres of this cemetery.

335       352. For four-handled amphorae of LH IIIC date in Achaea see Vermeule in *AJA* 64, 4 ff., pls 1 and 2 (note the dot-fringed semicircles). Examples of single or double wavy lines on the belly are also known in LH IIIC: Achaea, op. cit., pl. 2, fig. 9; *Asine* 397, fig. 260; *Perati* II, 263, fig. 114, no. 590. The triple wavy line (which with the double wavy line was standard on belly-handled amphorae in Athens throughout the PG period) may, however, originate in Cyprus, where it was common during LC IIIB2 (Cypriot Protogeometric) and thereafter: Pieridou, 43 and pls 19—21.

335       353. PLATE 279, 1097.

335       354. The full circles are not a valid criterion for earliness. They would be in Athens (see *Ker* I, pl. 41 and 56, of EPG date), but there are later instances at Lefkandi. The amphora found by Miss Andreiomenou near Thebes (*AE* 1976, Chr., 14, pl. 11c) may be of about the same date as this one — it also has 'empty' circles.

336       355. T 14,1 is an import. Note the triple wavy line on the belly (see S Pyre 3,1 above), a motive which seems by LPG to have disappeared from the local potter's repertoire.

336       356. Associated with two Attic LPG vases.

336       357. Probably a close link with Attica, see Smithson, *Hesperia* xxx, 161 f.; she takes the

system of decoration on these outsize amphorae back to early SM, and cites for LPG *Ker* IV, pl. 33, no. 1074, tomb 39. To this may now be added Charitonides, *AD* 28, i, p. 11 and pl. 5, from a tomb south of the Acropolis.

336      358. See PLATES 14: 61–7, 70–7, 79–81, 84–5 (Moulds); 24: 635–644, 647–652 (Area 3 South); 276: 983–8, 991–5 (P Channel, lower fill). Many others, not illustrated.

336      359. No doubt there were small amphorae, but as one cannot distinguish the sherds from those of closed vases of other types, no useful comment can be made. It is equally possible, of course, that some of the sherds assumed to be from amphorae could have come from hydriai, or even from large jugs or oinochoai.

336      360. To judge from SPG examples, it is possible that the monochrome neck more often denotes a belly-handled amphora.

336      361. There were no instances of bars on the outer or top rim.

336      362. PLATE 24, 652. See p. 46 on this motive, not found in Attica before EG.

336      363. See p. 270.

336      364. In this section I separate, so far as is possible, the neck-handled and belly-handled amphorae, and subdivide according to size (see n. 359 above on the difficulty of identifying small amphorae in sherd deposits). Some of the pieces discussed may be LPG, due to the wide range covered by the deposits and the uncertainty in dating some tombs and pyres.

336      365. SPG Pit, PLATE 17; Levelling, PLATE 19; SL Area, pp. 50–1. Other areas and deposits as well, and much not illustrated.

336      366. Both in the SPG Pit and in the Levelling Material.

337      367. Note, e.g., the extreme rarity of PSC skyphoi.

337      368. The pyre contained a kalathos with impressed triangles, and lay under Pyre 42, which produced a fragmentary flat-based cup with zigzag rim.

337      369. Pyre 41 overlay tombs 39 and 39A, of which 39A is very likely early SPG I, so the pyre cannot be earlier than SPG I. Pyre 44 contained a pyxis and a lekythos (PLATE 156) of which the latter looks neither earlier nor later than SPG I.

337      370. See *Ker* IV, pl. 6, no. 910, tomb 28 (LPG) for the broad single encircling bands. There is one example of full circles on the shoulder, *Ker* IV, pl. 5, no. 915, tomb 25, but this is MPG. A similar development is found at Knossos (see e.g. *Fortetsa*, pls 9 and 16), but the material as a whole suggests a parallel offshoot from Attica, and there is no need to conclude that for this shape alone there was a link between Lefkandi and Knossos.

*[handwritten margin note: Banded / no circles]*

337      371. Verdhelis, *PGRT*, 5 ff., figs 1–2, pl. 1, nos 1 and 2. Note particularly the continuation of the handle design on to the body of no. 2.

337      372. SPG Pit, PLATE 17, 230–7, 239–47. Levelling, PLATE 19, 376–83. Others unillustrated; see under the relevant chapters. Also found in Area 3 South, PLATE 23, 551–3 and PLATE 24, 593, and elsewhere, see PLATE 27, 778–80, 792–3.

338      373. Verdhelis, *PGRT*, 9 ff., fig. 5 and pl. 2, nos 7 and 8. Both have the hourglass on the neck; 7 has semicircles on the shoulder, 8 opposed diagonals on the belly.

338      374. *BSA* 31, pl. 5, no. 74.

338      375. *Ann.* 8–9, 219 and fig. 23. Kardiani tomb 2. Zigzag round the belly — and as the height of the vase is 32 cm it means that this motive can appear on a relatively large vase (see above). Coldstream, *GGP* 152 ff. dates the tomb group to EG II.

338      376. Sherds of belly and lower body, with double handle of bull's head type. The circles on the belly are flanked by verticals. The amphora may not have been of this class.

338      377. PLATES 275, 958 (P Surface); 276, 992 (P Channel, lower fill); 280, 1128–30, 1134–5 (T 32 fill).

338      378. PLATES 17, 221 (SPG Pit); 19, 370 (Levelling); 23, 546 (Area 3 South); 27, 791 (various).

339      379. S Pyre 4,3b shows a fine flaring lip with rays on the neck below; unfortunately, it is from a different vase than the neck and shoulder fragment 3c.

339      380. On the basis of associated vases. In three instances an LPG date is possible: S Pyre 14,2, associated with a Red Slip jug; and T Pyre 4,2 and 3, in view of the 'branch' pattern on the amphora T Pyre 4,1, though this latter vase clearly need not be contemporaneous with 2 and 3 (see below), and the pyre is later than LPG Tomb 26, as dug into it.

339      381. The pyre contained sherds of another amphora with 'empty' circles, so establishing the continued use of this feature from LPG to SPG II.

339     382. This feature survived because the vase, in use for some while (note the mending holes)
was eventually broken, inverted, and adapted for use as a stand.

339     383. The shape, so far as we have it, is a familiar one to Attic PG: see *PGP* 24 and 27 ff., Class II.
For examples see *Ker* I, pl. 43, T 14—17 from the Grave Mound; and note pl. 44, from Andros.

339     384. The chief source is the fill of T 32, PLATE 280. See also PLATE 275.

339     385. See e.g. PLATE 280, 1122, 1126, 1140, 1144.

339     386. There are krater sherds in the surface material of the cemeteries, and these include two
with the hand-drawn semicircle motive (PLATE 279, 1058 and 1091), so presumably not later
than EPG, and a very few with thick compass-drawn circles, which might be MPG (e.g. PLATE
279, 1059 and 1093), but we have no real idea of what a Lefkandian krater looked like before
LPG.

339     387. Not more than twenty sherds from the Moulds Deposit, and a mere handful from the
underfloor deposit of Area 3 South.

340     388. The statistics for Area 2 may show that barred rims were more popular than monochrome in SPG III. The Moulds Deposit is of no help — one monochrome, one barred; but
while eleven of the thirty-seven lips from the SPG Pit are barred, the figures for the Levelling
Material are twenty-four barred and four monochrome.

340     389. The painter may place two rough zigzags below the monochrome outer lip area and the
main decoration (PLATE 26, 701—2, 705, 722; PLATE 279, 1062), but this is uncommon.

340     390. E.g. vertical cross-hatched diamonds between vertical lines: PLATE 16, 156 + 163;
PLATE 24, 585.

340     391. PLATE 28, 70/P1. PLATE 19, 343 may be another.

340     392. PLATE 24, 633.

340     393. This is not certain, but seems justifiable from sherds such as PLATE 26, 710 and 713;
PLATE 273, 871—2; PLATE 279, 1063.

340     394. PLATE 16, 177; PLATE 19, 337 + 353, 355 (these probably not earlier than SPG II).
Note also PLATE 16, 168, and probably PLATE 26, 711, showing alternating diagonals with
filled interstices.

340     395. PLATE 26, 723.

340     396. PLATE 274, 918. Note that a cross-hatched rectangle flanks it.

340     397. PLATE 16, 164; PLATE 24, 633.

340     398. PLATE 16, 156 + 163, 166; PLATE 19, 354; PLATE 26, 720; PLATE 279, 1064.

340     399. PLATE 26, 704 and 713 (neither quite certain); PLATE 279, 1060, 1063, 1092.

340     400. PLATE 26, 712; less certainly, PLATE 19, 350.

340     401. PLATE 273, 871—2.

340     402. To the motives which postdate LPG can be added the alternating diagonals with unfilled interstices (SPG II or later?), and presumably the ship.

340     403. Marmariani: *BSA* 31, 30 ff., pls 9—11 and fig. 13 on p. 33. Kapakli: *PGRT* 22 ff.,
figs 14—17 and pls 7—8. The tendency is for a high conical or pedestal foot with ridges — more
common than at Lefkandi, to judge from the available material (note that the foot of 70/P1 is
a reconstruction). Rope ridges are found, as at Lefkandi. The decoration is also of a very similar
type; note the kraters with alternating diagonals with unfilled (Marmariani 140, Kapakli 50)
and filled (Kapakli 43) interstices. The latest Kapakli kraters, incidentally, are atticising, a
development that took place, as Coldstream says (*GGP* 155), well before the end of MG II:
this may be a pointer to what could have happened at Lefkandi during SPG III (where are
imported Attic kraters, see PLATE 29C, PLATE 275, 944, 950 + 957, PLATE 280, 1112).

340     404. *PGP* 97.

340     405. *Fortetsa* 160 f. See now *BSA* 71, 117 ff. and pl. 16, and *AR* for 1976—77, 15 f. and
figs 33 and 34.

340     406. *BSA* 33, 37 ff. nos 56—70.

341     407. LPG: the only complete one is from Nea Ionia, *Hesperia* xxx, 167 f., pl. 29; many of
the best fragments illustrated on pl. 51 of *Ker* I. EG and MG: for sizable fragments see *Ker* V,
i, pl. 17 (grave 2, EG II); pl. 22 (grave 43, early MG I); pl. 20 (grave 22, MG II).

342     408. One type of panel, for example, the cross-hatched diamonds and triangles flanked by
verticals, is found in Ithaca, Crete, the Dodecanese, and Attica. Even the unusual motive of
alternating upright and pendent semicircles appears at Knossos (*BSA* 55, 130 and pl. 31) and
at Aetos in Ithaca (*BSA* 33, 43, pl. 3).

341     409. PLATE 15, 144 (catalogued with the SPG Pit, but in a contaminated context); PLATE 18, 329–36 and PLATE 33, 30–1 (Levelling Material), PLATE 23, 528 and 529 (complete profile) from Area 3 South, Surface to yard floor; PLATE 25, 677–81 from various areas, unstratified; PLATE 273, 852–3 (joining) from S Gully Fill; and PLATE 277, 1035–8 from P North Channel.

341     410. *AA* 1963, 205 ff., figs 43–7 and fig. 35, 30. Associated with Attic and PSC skyphoi and Cypriot vases.

341     411. The fabric is the same as that of the PSC skyphoi, neither Cypriot nor Attic nor, from the description, Euboean, but could be North Cycladic. Information from Professor Coldstream.

341     412. Two plates were found in the Kerameikos, neither of them in a datable context – *Ker* I, 130 and pl. 52; *Ker* IV, 46 and pl. 34. The clay of one of these is confidently stated to be Attic (*Ker* I, 130) but Attic and Lefkandian clay can be indistinguishable to the eye. For further material see now Mrs. P. Bikai, *Pottery of Tyre*, Pls. XI no. 20, XXIIA nos. 5–6 and XXIV. Other potential Euboean candidates are Pls. XXIIA no. 4, XXIV no. 6 (both ps. skyphoi)

341     413. *Perati* II, 209 ff. for a discussion of the LH III alabastra with tripod feet: none is closely similar to this vase. See also op. cit. 207, fig. 79A, for the body shape (without struts).

341     414. *Ker* I, pl. 27, no. 507.

341     415. A rather larger bowl, with two string holes, from Chalcis, *ChO* 251 and pl. 45c, is probably MPG. See also the two hand-made bowls from Asine, *Asine* 427, fig. 275, of LPG date, and 430, fig. 282, undatable.

341     416. Pieridou, *PG Style in Cyprus* 14, 101, and pl. 1: 6–11. *SCE* IV. 2, the relevant line drawings. Adelman, *Cypro-Geometric Pottery* (*SIMA* vol. 47) almost *passim*. See Karageorghis, *Alaas*, pls 32 and 75.

342     417. Athens: *Ker* V, i, 213, pl. 15, grave 3 (EGI). Marmariani: *BSA* 31, 29 and pl. 8, no. 126.

342     418. The only example of the shape in tomb or pyre, but in its wheel-made version well known in the settlement.

342     419. The last two have a sagging body; P 4, 4 is much more carefully made.

342     420. Analysis suggests that its fabric is not local and is similar to that of the duck vases P 22, 3–4.

342     421. *Ergon* for 1971, 175 and fig. 207. From a PG tomb.

342     422. See perhaps the dipper *Asine* 430, fig. 280 from PG tomb 35.

342     423. T Pyre 9 contained a handle of a probably similar pithos.

343     424. This section and its conclusions were written by M. R. P. at V. D.'s suggestion.

343     425. *BSA* 66 336 illustrates the LH IIIC type. For Athens, Styrenius, *Studies*, 101, 113 and charts for contexts: examples, *Ker* V, i, plates 154–5.

343     426. Clay analysis suggests they are not local to Lefkandi at least.

344     427. For the Mycenaean askos see Furumark's type 194, *Analysis* 67 f. and fig. 20. On the development of the bird vase see Bouzek, *Eirene* VIII, 110 ff. and my article in *Kretika Chronika* 1972, 245 ff. The Lefkandian vase may be compared for shape to one of EPG date from Athens, *Ker* I, 92, pl. 63, no. 535.

344     428. *AJA* 1960, 11 f., pls 4 and 6k, no. 44. LH IIIC context, but the style may have persisted for a long time in this region.

344     429. These, and their associations, are discussed in *Kr. Chr.* 1972, 266 ff.; I have suggested that they provide evidence of contact with Cyprus, and are probably or possibly to be linked with developments in Athens and Achea.

344     430. Op. cit., nos 43–54 and 58.

344     431. In the case of bird-headed vases, the only parallels are from Skyros (see n. 435 below) and from Cyprus: *CVA* Cyprus I, pl. 34 (Enkomi); *RDAC* 1967, 8 f. and fig. 10, no. 39 (Palaepaphos); *Alaas*, pl. 35, L2.

344     432. A familiar motive on the local EPG and MPG pottery. Also found on bird vases of Athens (*AM* 78, 152 and fig. 54, of SM date) and Knossos (*P of M* II, i, 136, fig. 69, see *Kr. Chr.* op. cit., no. 35: Subminoan).

344     433. See *RDAC* 1967, the vase cited in n. 431.

344     434. Spectrographic analysis confirms what was already suspected. The district of origin is unknown, but Cyprus appears to be ruled out.

344     435. I am much indebted to Miss L. Marangou and to Mrs. Goulandris (to whose collection it belongs) for permission to mention a further one, from Skyros. It has a long sleek body,

and well-moulded tail and head; it has a high flaring foot (see n. 431), and on the back a lekythos-type spout and neck, with handle attached to the neck base. The decoration is horizontal bands. It has no context, but looks distinctly later than those already mentioned.

436. The airholes, on the back of 29, and on the neck of 28 are presumably vents for the escape of gases in firing.

437. See an earlier example, from Lapithos: Ohnefalsch-Richter, *Kypros, the Bible and Homer* 425, pl. 98, 6. LC IIIB1. But this is a pouring vase.

438. Kerameikos: *Ker* IV, pl. 31 (two from tomb 33, two from tomb 48). Nea Ionia: *Hesperia* xxx, 172, pl. 30, no. 54. See Professor Smithson's full and masterly accounts in *Hesperia* xxx, 170 ff. and 37, 103 ff., which show that: the Attic doll was but one item in a large repertory of subjects of fine hand-made incised ware which appeared suddenly in LPG: that so far objects in this ware have, at least in Athens, been found only in cemetery contexts, and may have been restricted to women and children; that the ware continued in use in Athens until the beginning of MG I, with new shapes and patterns added during Early Geometric (see especially the material from the rich lady's grave, dated to the end of EG II, in *Hesperia* xxxvii); that the few dolls known are from LPG tombs; and that as yet there is no convincing evidence which would determine the place of origin of this ware.

439. Note also the appearance of seven incised beads, of very similar fabric to that of the doll, in P 3, a tomb probably contemporary with P 22. These are also paralleled in Athens — and elsewhere.

440. See *BSA* 65, 21 ff.

441. This may account for the absence of genitals on a statuette which is in other respects clearly male.

442. *BSA* 65, 21.

443. Op. cit. 26 ff.

444. Centaurs, sphinxes, or minotaurs: Nicholls believes they were sphinxes, and that they may have had a Mycenaean mainland origin. See also the discussion and references in Catling's article in *RDAC* 1974, 95 ff.

445. I am indebted to Dr. Karageorghis for the very interesting suggestion, based on the features of the hollow eyes, the large ears, and the painted face, that the Lefkandian centaur was shown as wearing a mask. He quotes in this connexion masks found in eleventh century contexts at Kition. Mention may also be made of a contemporaneous centaur (?) figurine from Kos (Higgins, *Terracottas*, pl. 6A,B; *GDA* 174, pl. 34), but it is quite unlike the Lefkandian statuette.

446. Auberson and Schefold, *Führer durch Eretria* 158.

447. See Kunze, 7 *Olympiabericht* (1961), 146 ff.

448. *Führer durch Eretria* 158.

449. *Bibliotheca* II. v.4. This, I believe, is the only extant tradition of centaur being struck in the knee; in other accounts the wound is in the hoof.

450. Note that the Lefkandian figurine's surviving right hand has been given six fingers: if this is not accidental (and I do not think that anything to do with the figurine was accidental), then it is worth emphasizing that there is a very ancient and widespread tradition that six fingers are an attribute of the magician, a man of great wisdom — I am much indebted to Dr. Barnett for drawing my attention to this.

451. See *BSA* 65, 21 ff.

452. Op. cit. 26.

453. Catling, *RDAC* 1974, 95 ff., pls 16—17.

454. Op. cit. 110, n. 6.

455. P 39B,17 has a brown-buff clay, T 26,10 is soft-fired. Nor is grey fabric always a criterion: for the kalathoi P Pyre 28,1—4 and S Pyre 10,1, this is the result of burning; kalathos P 24,9 also has grey clay, indistinguishable from that of Black Slip P 24,5, but analysis shows it to be of the normal local fabric. All these kalathoi are of the impressed-triangle type, but it is interesting that S Pyre 10,1 also has combed decoration, typical of Black Slip vases.

Note that at Marmariani, *BSA* 31, 30, n. 1, the fabric is called bucchero; but this term usually has a different connotation, and is avoided here.

456. A jug fragment P Pyre 32,3 is exceptional in having a red-brown slip.

344

344

344

344

344
344

344
344
345

345

345
345
345
345

345

345
345
345
346
346

346

346      457. Lekythos P 22,18.

347      458. Unless the three hand-made oinochoai P 4,4 (SPG I) and T 2,6—7 (SPG II), of grey fabric, burnished, are to be considered as related to this group.

347      459. PLATES 18, 322 (Levelling); 27, 813 (various areas).

347      460. Exceptions are P 39B,17 and P 22,17—18: of the latter 17 (FIG. 21, C) has a squat bioconical body and flat base, 18 is relatively straight-walled, and has a ring base.

347      461. *AD* 1918, suppl. 43 ff. and fig. 10: cup and jug.

347      462. Kapakli district: *PGRT* 16 and pl. 4, no. 24, MPG or LPG oinochoe. Marmariani: *BSA* 31, 26 and pl. 6, no. 31, cup with trigger handle; 30 and pl. 8, no. 130, shallow bowl with bracket handles. These two are probably SPG; they lack the combed and incised decoration, but are evidently Black Slip, see *PGRT* 40, n. 1.

347      463. *Ann.* 8—9, 221 and 224, fig. 26, Kardiani tomb III, 2, a kantharos with fabric 'simile a bucchero'.

347      464. All except one from Palia Perivolia; nothing from the settlement, to my knowledge.

347      465. All traditional local jugs before SPG I, bar T 12A,2, have low conical feet, but the tendency in SPG I and II is to have a flat base. It may be that the Red Slip jugs (and the Black Slip, see P 24,5) encouraged this development.

347      466. *BSA* 31, 29 and pl. 7, no. 125.

347      467. No imported vase has yet been identified in a Submycenaean context. The section deals with wheel-made vases only, and the bird vase S 16,10 is discussed in another section.

348      468. Tufnell, *Lachish* IV, especially pl. 78: 798—800. In the Bronze Age, however, juglets more commonly had a pointed base.

348      469. Tufnell, *Lachish* III, pl. 88: 282—302.

348      470. Loud, *Megiddo* II, pls 71:9,11; 81:10. Lamon, Shipton, *Megiddo* I, pl. 47:141.

348      471. See Kenyon, *Archaeology in the Holy Land* 229, fig. 56:2, 6, from Tell Fara.

348      472. Dothan, *Ashdod* II—III, fig. 76:2, Late Bronze or Iron I.

348      473. Hamilton, *QDAP IV*, 20, no. 57. On this and other dipper juglets see Amiran, *Ancient Pottery in the Holy Land.*

348      474. Riis, *Sukas* I, 35, fig. 10d. Mouth lost; dated within the tenth and ninth centuries.

348      475. Chapman, *Berytus* XXI, 118 and fig. 23:92. Not very close.

348      476. Saidah, *BMB* 19, 70 f, no. 32.

348      477. Spectrographic analysis shows that the fabric is close to that of the Black Slip and Red Slip wares, which are now thought to have been made at Lefkandi, though not of the fabric typical of the site.

348      478. The posture adopted, with each archer about to transfix the other, is hardly realistic, but makes a good composition.

348      479. See Benson, *Horse, Bird and Man.* Archers are depicted on both Mycenaean and Geometric pieces, see pls 12:8 and 36:3—9. An archer is also portrayed on an LH IIIC sherd from Iolkos, *Ergon* for 1960, 60, fig. 73b.

348      480. *GGP* 15.

348      481. In all cases fabric, paint and decoration are adjudged to be Attic. The results of spectrographic analysis will be published elsewhere.

348      482. *PGP* 41 f. Note that 'Group I' from which it comes is in fact Well K 12:1, see Smithson, *Hesperia* xxx, 177: she gives it a range from MPG to LPG.

348      483. *Ker* IV, pl. 8. All the motives are there, on the one or the other; 2012 is the closer in shape to P 22,3, and also has decoration on the neck. Tomb 40 is probably fairly early in LPG, see op. cit. pp. 13 and 24.

348      484. *Hesperia* 30, 165 f. (under Nea Ionia no. 42); 37, 94 ff. Add now *AD* 28, pl. 35b (S of Acropolis).

349      485. *Ker* IV, pl. 12. The shoulder decoration reflects that on the chest, and that on the belly (a zone of alternating cross-hatched and chequered diamonds) is exactly repeated on the lid of the chest (lost on the Nea Ionia example).

349      486. *BCH* 87, fig. 9; and 362, fig. 59 (= Karageorghis, *Cypriote Antiquities in the Pierides Collection,* 46 and 113, no. 33). The shape is the same in principle, and although the system of decoration is different, some of the individual motives are the same — note particularly the chequered diamond.

349     487. *Ker* I, pl. 73, no. 575; *Ker* IV, pl. 20; *Hesperia* xxx, 163 f., pl. 26; *AD* 28, pl. 16d. Smithson, in *Hesperia* xxx, 164, assigns one unpublished example from the Agora to the Ripe (Middle) phase.

349     488. From the Agora, *Hesperia* xvii, 284 f., fig. 3; *Hesperia* xxi, 292 f., pl. 74 c.

349     489. *GGP* 13; *Hesperia* xxx, 164. The two from EG I tombs, however, have a meander as the central zone, with formal zigzags above and below, whereas no. 20 has alternating diagonals in the centre, with dogtooth above and below.

349     490. P6683 from Grave 38, mentioned by Smithson in *Hesperia* xxx, 164.

349     491. *CVA* Karlsruhe 2, pl. 46:1; *CVA* Cambridge 1, pl. 1:12. The latter was associated with two cups with high conical feet, and a pedestal bowl; all bought together, they very probably belong to a group (and if so, an LPG one), and come from Athens or Attica.

349     492. *Ker* I, pl. 71, nos 577 (20) and 570 (16).

349     493. *Ker* V, i, pl. 15, grave G1.

349     494. *PGP* 102 ff., *GGP* 11.

349     495. *Ker* IV, pl. 21, no. 919, with ring base as at Lefkandi. Note also for similar body, handles, and decoration, *Ker* I, pl. 70, no. 730, from LPG tomb 20.

349     496. The only opening is a hole in the centre of one side, perhaps rather too large to be explained simply as an air vent. I am indebted to Professor Coldstream for the suggestion that the vase may have been an incense burner.

350     497. As will be seen, the two vases in this category have features not found in Athens. Furthermore, analysis has shown that the clay is not that characteristic of Athens. Nevertheless, the paint (and its manner of application) and the shape are fundamentally Athenian in nature, and it seems probable that they were made in Attica, though not in Athens.

350     498. Wells, *AIARS* 24:4:1 (*Asine* II), 17 f., fig. 23. Accepted as local.

350     499. *PGP* 45 ff. This shape survived into EG I.

350     500. Further support for this is the presence in the tomb of a locally made vase, no. 8, a lekythos-oinochoe, which probably imitates an Attic type first appearing in EG I — see *GGP* 11.

350     501. It is first known in Cypriot Protogeometric (= LC III B2): Pieridou, pls 8:10, 9:1–2. It then continued in use through Cypro-Geometric, and is still found in Cypro-Archai I (see the relevant line drawings in *SCE* IV.2).

350     502. Asked for their first impression without knowing its context, Professor Gjerstad was inclined to place the vase in Early Bichrome II, or the early stage of CG III; Mrs. Pieridou preferred a date early in Bichrome III (CG III), suggested *SCE* IV.2, fig. 22:6 as a good comparative piece and placed it chronologically at the beginning of CG III; Dr. Catling opted for CG II, and cited a WP II vase, *SCE* IV.2, fig. 13:9 and Ayia Anastasia *TZ*, 56 of CG I for comparative purposes. I am most grateful to these three for passing on their views to myself and to Mr. Popham.

350     503. See *Ker* I, pl. 56, no. 560 (tomb 18) and pl. 55, no. 561 (tomb 5) for the zigzag on the upper shoulder.

351     504. A slight overlap is suggested by the occurrence of both forms, old and new, in Areopagus tomb D 16:2. See *Hesperia* xvii (1949) 289 f. nos 3 and 2, pls 67–8; *GGP* pl. 1 g.h.

351     505. *PAE* 1939, 30 fig. 3a; H. 12.3, D. c. 15.9.

351     506. *Hesperia* XXVII, 89, no. 9, pl. 21.

    507. Sequence, all from well-documented tomb groups, giving the ratio of the maximum diameter to the height of the body:

| Tomb | Reference | Ratio of diameter to height | Date |
|------|-----------|-----------------------------|------|
| Areopagus D 16:2, no. 2 | (n. 504 supra) | 1.29 | EG I |
| Marathon 2 | (n. 505 supra) | 1.29 | EG II |
| Lefkandi T 21,2 | | 1.33 | EG II |
| Lefkandi S 59,4 | | 1.64 | MG I (beginning) |
| Areopagus I, 18:2, no. 7 | (n. 509 infra) | 1.85 | MG I (early) |
| Phinopoulos II, NM 15318 | (art. cit. n. 509 infra, pl. 79) | 2.06 | MG I |
| Kerameikos 20, no. 263 | *Ker* V. 1, pl. 52 | 2.11 | MG I (later) |
| Kerameikos 20, no. 265 | *Ker* V. 1, pl. 52 | 3.14 | MG I (later) |

As is already apparent in Kerameikos tomb 20, from late MG I onwards there is no consistent development in the shape of the flat pyxis.

351     508. cf. *GGP* 17.

351     509. *Hesperia* xiii (1974) 361, no. 7, pl. 77e.

351     510. *Ker* V. 1, pl. 71, nos 927 and 2139.

351     511. *Ker* V, 1, pl. 72, no. 870; *Hesperia* xliii (1974) 353, no. 1, pls 77a, 79a.

351     512. *Ker* V, 1, pls 72 and 109, no. 2149.

351     513. Smithson, *Hesperia* x/iii (1974) 353, no. 1, pls 76a, 77a.

351     514. P 22,9.

351     515. (a) An Attic export to Argos, C 54 from tomb 14/1 (EG II): P. Courbin, *La Céramique géométrique de l'Argolide* (Paris, 1966) 66, pl. 148. (b) Athens NM 15311, probably from Phinopoulos tomb 1: Smithson, *Hesperia* xliii (1974) 378 f., pl. 78e.

352     516. e.g. *GGP* pls 7e, 8g.

352     517. e.g. Brann, *Agora* VIII, 39, no. 72, pl. 5.

352     518. *Hesperia* xxxvii (1968) pl. 21, no. 4; *Ker* V, 1, pl. 83, no. 864.

352     519. *PAE* 1951, 120, fig. 38, centre (Palaia Kokkinia tomb lambda).

    520. T.L. Shear, *Hesperia* vi (1937) 365, fig. 30, lower row, centre; Smithson, *Hesperia* xxx (1961) 170, no. 53, pl. 30.

352     521. Painted wheel-made: *EA* 1898, 109, fig. 29 from the Isis tomb, Eleusis (bucket, MG II); *Bull. Met. Mus.* N.S. 19 (1960–1) 152, fig. 1 (bucket, LG); *AM* 43 (1918) pl. 5,1 and Corbett, *BMQ* 19 (1954) 65 ff., pl. 26 (skyphoi, LG); *CVA* Munich 3, pl. 119,6 (kantharos, LG). Handmade: Mylonas, The West Cemetery of Eleusis (in Greek, Athens, 1975) B, 267 ff., pl. 424a (jugs, LG); also *Corinth* VII, 1, pl. 14, no. 90 (trefoil oinochoe, LG).

352     522. Painted wheel-made: Smithson, *Hesperia* xxxvii (1968) 86 f., no. 5, pl. 21 (the Rich Athenian Lady). Hand-made: Smithson, *Hesperia* xliii (1974) 358, nos 17, 18, pl. 76 (Areopagus tomb I 18:1).

352     523. *Hesperia* xxxvii (1968) pl. 27.

352     524. *Ker* V, 1, pl. 29, no. 884.

352     525. E.g. *Ker* V, 1, pl. 112, no. 1252; *GGP* 18, n. 6.

352     526. E.g. *Ker* V, 1, pl. 46, no. 2146 (belly-handled amphora); *AJA* 44 (1940) pl. 19,2 (neck-handled amphora); *Hesperia* x/iii (1974) pl. 77c,8 (pointed pyxis).

352     527. Sequence from well-documented tomb groups, giving the ratio of the maximum diameter to the height:

| Tomb | Reference | Ratio | Date |
|------|-----------|-------|------|
| Kerameikos 2 | *Ker* V, 1, pl. 105 | 1.5 | EG II (early) |
| Areopagus H 16:6, no. 25 | *Hesperia* xxxvii, pl. 22 | 1.56 | EG II (late) |
| Areopagus H 16:6, no. 26 | *Hesperia* xxxvii, pl. 22 | 1.65 | EG II (late) |
| Marathon 2 | *PAE* 1939, 30 fig. 3d | 1.86 | EG II (late) |
| Lefkandi S Pyre 4,1 | | 1.74 | EG II/MG I |
| Phinopoulos I, no. 3 | *Hesperia* xliii pl. 78e. | 1.6 | EG II/MG I |
| Areopagus AR, V, no. 4 | *Hesperia* xliii pl.. 75d | 2.0 | MG I |
| Eleusis Theta 23, no. 759 | Mylonas op. cit. pl. 376 | 1.91 | MG I (late) |

353     528. Desborough, *PGP* 138 f.

353     529. *BSA* 31 (1930–1) 26 f., class 13, fig. 12 (Marmariani); *PGRT* 29 ff., pls 9, 10 (Kapakli).

353     530. *Vergina* I (Athens, 1969) pl. 59, 1.

353     531. Ibid. pl. 41, 13.

353     532. See, most recently, M. Yon, *Salamine de Chypre* II (1971) 47–50; V. Karageorghis, *Alaas* (1975) 72 shape 10, with references.

353     533. Attica: Smithson, *Hesperia* xxx (1961) 163, nos. 35–6, with references (EPG, LPG, EG). Rhodes: *Clara Rhodos* iii, fig. 142 bottom (EG). Skyros: Desborough, *PGP* 166, 'circular-bodied jug'. Crete: see below.

353     534. Adhromyli: *BSA* 12 (1905–6) 54 f., nos 3214–17, fig. 22. Kavousi: *AJA* 5 (1901) 135 pl. 2 top right. *Vrokastro* 102, fig. 57E and 149 f., fig. 89F, G. None of these flasks is adequately described or illustrated; but those from Adromyli are compared to the shape of a warming-pan,

and must therefore be lentoid rather than globular. The museum of Ay. Nikolaos exhibits an unpublished lentoid flask with trefoil lip and quatrefoil designs on each face, perhaps LG.

353        535. For later Cretan exports see *GGP* 382, nn. 1—4.


# 14. HISTORICAL CONCLUSIONS

355        1. The conclusions reached by our contributors in their individual sections have been of great help in composing this more general survey, though we have dared at times to offer a different interpretation for which they are in no way responsible. Much, too, is owed to frequent and detailed discussion with Vincent Desborough, while M. Popham is grateful also to those who participated at Oxford in a seminar in which these conclusions were discussed and constructively criticised.

Material from Lefkandi has already been considered in studies with historical conclusions by contributors to this volume: J. Boardman, *GkO* 62 f; J.N. Coldstream, *GG* 40—3, 63—5 and 191—201; V.R.d'A. Desborough, *GDA* 43 f., 67 f.,, 188 f. and 348; V.R.d'A. Desborough, *Euboean Participation*; P.G. Themelis, *Griechische Grabbanten*, especially 32 f., 37 f. and 69 f.

355        2. Differences are discussed in outline in *BSA* 66 (1971) 342, 348—9. This account could be expanded considerably. For instance, the latest IIIC deep bowl usually painted all over has a reserved band inside the lip with an unpainted lower body and base; in SM the reserved line and reserved lower body are absent, though they are reintroduced in EPG, whereas its wavy line decoration is a new feature. The SM small amphora with two neck-handles, the lekythos and the triple vase are absent in IIIC, whereas the IIIC scroll and 'whisker' decoration on amphoras and hydrias has disappeared in SM and is replaced by semicircles rare in the LBA settlement.

355        3. *PrelReport* 23.

355        4. The Khaliotis tombs, KT 2 (PLATE 255a) and Desborough's comments p. 313 above.

356        5. E.G. Desborough, *GDA* 107 and 307 where he, too, favours the restoration of SK 15B, 15 as a ring with spiral attachment.

356        6. See above, pp. 284—5 and note 15.

356        7. For possible interrelationships, see Catling, above, under Fibulae for S 40,5 and S 43,6. To MRP, vase S 19,4 (PLATE 255f) seems closely related stylistically to one from Mycenae, *GDA* 48, pl. 2A.

356        8. 23 SM burials compared with 19 LPG, or 29 LPG into early SPG.

357        9. S 16,3 (PLATE 207b) and S 46,3 (PLATE 270b) with the comments of Higgins and Desborough above.

357        10. Duck vase, S 16,1 (PLATE 254c); pyxis and flask, S Pyre 1a, 1 and 2 (PLATE 92) with Desborough's comments. He tentatively adds to possible Cypriot influence the tripod dish, S 4,1, and the introduction of the high conical foot in his conclusions.

357        11. On the lack of imports elsewhere, see Desborough, *Euboean Participation* 34; he opts for traders *from* the E. Mediterranean.

357        12. P 25B,5 (PLATE 233), and Higgins comments.

357        13. PLATE 210b—c, and Desborough's comments.

357        14. Desborough, *Euboean Participation* 31—2 and his comments above.

358        15. Desborough pp. 348 f. above on imports, and pp. 286 f. on details of influence.

358        16. E.g. in P 3 and P 22. Desborough might have preferred to include the trefoil-lipped
358    flask, p. 287 above and note 37.

358        17. Discussed pp. 200 f. above; warrior burial, T 14.

358        18. See above, for pottery pp. 287 f., for earrings p. 220 and note 30.

19. P 22,28—9 and 18.

358        20. P 22,19 (PLATE 270a) and discussion, pp. 287 and 350.

359        21. T 26 and comments p. 211 and 214.

359        22. The earlier cist grave had by now been completely superseded by the shaft grave, a gradual and understandable change for which no outside influence or innovatory impulse need be supposed.

359        23. The evidence from Xeropolis shows that the deep Attic skyphos with circle and panel

decoration was adopted and in fashion in LPG, so the Euboean pendent semi-circle shallower skyphos could have evolved from it. The Lefkandian potters, however, by MPG had modified the Mycenaean type deep bowl into a smaller and shallower version for which they seem to have had some liking, e.g. S 18,2 and S 51,3, and it is possible that it was this vase, further modified, to which was added the new form of decoration in a non-Attic way, which gave rise to this characteristic Euboean vessel.

359    24. Surface sherds from the escarpment N. of Xeropolis and from building foundations on the headland E. of the site include some fragments which probably date as early as this stage.

359    25. See Catling pp. 239 and 264 above.

359    26. While iron was available on Euboea and could have been exploited by this period, copper and tin, and of course precious metals were required from abroad.

360    27. See Desborough pp. 288 f. above.

360    28. Desborough, *Euboean Participation* 33—4. The Eretrian colony said to have been founded at Methone c. 733. It would be interesting to know the date of the earliest Euboean type pottery found yet further north, *PGP* 179—80.

361    29. *GDA* 196 and *JHS* 77 212 f.

361    30. *Euboean Participation* 33.

361    31. T 26, P 47 and T Pyre 1.

362    32. E.g. PLATE 248, 9—13 and Catling's comments above under Fibulae.

362    33. P 47 (PLATES 149—50) already referred to in the previous section, T Pyre 8 (PLATE 192) and P 13 (PLATE 215).

362    34. Desborough, p. 291 above.

362    35. Coldstream, *GC* 51 and *GGP* 343.

362    36. COLOUR PLATE 1 in this volume. Discussed above by Desborough and in greater detail in *BSA* 65, 21 f.

363    37. E.g. PLATES 218—19 with Higgin's comments, and PLATES 93 and 239*j—k* with Catling's comments on this mace-head and the bowl.

363    38. E.g. PLATES 220—3 with Higgins' comments.

363    39. E.g. PLATES 224—8 and PLATE 110 no. 39.

363    40. E.g. PLATE 229 with Higgins' comments.

363    41. E.g. T 31 and T 33, and the decorated fibulae in S 59 and T 13, with the comments above of Coldstream on the pottery and Catling on the fibulae.

364    42. T 27, T 32 and T 36.

364    43. Discussed at pp. 22—3 and 49—52 above.

364    44. The so-called 'Levelling Material', see pp. 36 f.

365    45. The recent construction of a building on the W. slope of Toumba revealed a small section of walling, containing LPG sherds, which appears to continue eastwards towards the summit of the hill. The author is grateful to Mrs. E. Touloupa, the Ephor, for permitting him to make this small investigation in 1977.

366    46. For the most recent publication of material relating to Eretria and its 'foundation', see A. Andreiomenou, *AE* 1975 206—29 and P. Themelis, *Ergon* 1976 16—9 and pl. 16 (= *AR* 1976—7 fig. 31), an Atticising vase of ?MG I. For Chalcis, see Desborough, *GDA* 200—1 and *Kharisterion eis A.K. Orlandon* 2, 248 f. where the material is published. To these should be added a chance find from Vasiliko, near Lefkandi, apparently vases from a tomb, *AD Chron* 27 (1972) 341 and pl. 292.

366    47. If it is accepted that the establishment of Pithecussae was a joint venture and that the reported Eretrian colony on Corcyra had the blessing of Chalcis. For a different possible interpretation, see Jeffery, *Archaic Greece* 63—70 with references.

367    48. See note 44 above.

367    49. Riis, *Sukas* I, remains the fullest survey of the N.E. imports. Those in Cyprus have been usefully assembled by E. Gjerstad *et al.* in *Greek Geometric and Archaic Pottery found in Cyprus*, Stockholm 1977. Pendent semicircle and full circle skyphoi in Italy, see *BSA* 68 (1973) 191 f.; *NdS* 1972 256 fig. 36; *Dialoghi* VIII 86 f.: that from Sicily has been reliably reported but not yet published.

A general account of trade with the Levant is given by Coldstream, *GC* 92 f. MRP differs from him in believing that most of the pendent semicircle skyphoi (including ones in Crete) are Euboean, and that the low-lipped variety are more frequent at Lefkandi than he (and Desborough in his account above) allow. It is hoped to consider this aspect and some of the examples of these skyphoi from Al Mina in a forthcoming article in *BSA*: they are not all low-lipped and some could well be earlier than 825 BC.

367          50. Dikaios, *AA* 1963 204 f.

367          51. Al Mina, Woolley, *JHS* LVIII (1938) 1 f. and 133 f., with discussion of erosion at pp. 7–8. See also Boardman, *GrO* 62 f. and Coldstream, *loc. cit.*

367          52. That from Tyre makes a considerable addition and includes examples of the Euboean plate, one of which was found at Troy. Blegen, *Troy* IV p. 279 and Pl. 303, 8; p. 233 and Pl. 278, 26 a skyphos rim. See Section 13, n. 412.

367          53. Corcyra with its reported Eretrian colony, expelled about 734 BC by the Corinthians, is one possibility: see Jeffery, *Archaic Greece* 64.

368          54. See Boardman's comments in Section 4.

368          55. Stone implements and loomweights, discussed in Section 5. The plain coarse pottery appears to be in a different tradition from that current throughout SM to SPG III.

368          56. Possible minor differences in pottery are discussed by Boardman at pp. 76 f. above, and differences in script by Jeffery on pp. 91 f. The two cities could well, however, have differed in their political institutions.

369          57. Seal of the Lyre-Player group, discussed with references in Section 5.

369          58. Published and discussed in *Eretria* III.

369          59. For bibliography, see Appendix B, note 1.

# Appendix  A

TABLES 1–3 are intended to make quick reference to dated tomb groups easier, and to facilitate further study of the cemetery materials. Only those tombs and pyres to which it has been possible to assign dates are included. TABLE 1 covers the periods SM–MPG, TABLE 2 LPG–LPG/SPG I and TABLE 3 SPG I–III.

Overall, the statistics are as follows: there are 147 tombs, including 59 cists, 72 shaft graves, 12 pit graves and 4 mud brick graves. Eighty pyres are known, but nine of these either could not be dug or else had been destroyed.

Of these totals, 31 tombs and 33 excavated pyres had no contents, and are not included here for this reason. Another 6 tombs and 19 pyres contained objects, usually fragmentary, which do not provide close enough dating criteria to warrant their inclusion. Of the 37 tombs not shown on the charts, 21 were cists, 14 were shaft graves and 2 were pit graves.

TABLE 4 is an index of tombs and pyres with suggested dates. These are arranged in numerical order within cemeteries for easy reference. All tombs and pyres which contained objects are listed in this table, including a few for which it has not yet been possible to give a date.

TABLE 5 is intended to summarise, in graphic form, all the available stratigraphic evidence from both cemeteries and settlement.

## TABLE 1. Dated tomb and pyre groups, SM—MPG

| TOMB/PYRE NO.[1] | TOMB TYPE[1] | CONDITION[2] | Cup | Bowl/Skyphos | Shallow bowl | Kalathos | Belly H. Amphoriskos | Vert. H. Amphoriskos | Stirrup jar | Lekythos | Trefoil Oinochoe | Jug | Pyxis | Flask | Hydria | Amphora | Other[3] | Black Slip Ware | Red Slip Ware | Imports[4] | TOTAL | pins Bronze | pins Iron | earrings Gold | earrings Bronze | Bronze rings | Bronze | Iron | Iron dirk/knife | Other[5] | Faience | Glass | Other[6] | Cloth | TOTAL | Bone (grammes) or Inhumation | Age/Sex[7] | DATE |
|---|---|---|---|---|---|---|---|---|---|---|---|---|---|---|---|---|---|---|---|---|---|---|---|---|---|---|---|---|---|---|---|---|---|---|---|---|---|---|
| S 3 | C | D | 1 | | | | | 1 | | | | | | | | | | | | | 2 | | | | | | | | | | | | | | - | | | SM |
| S 9 | C | D | | | | | | | | 3 | | | | | | | | | | | 3 | | | | | | | | | | | | | | - | | | SM |
| S 15B | C | D | | | | | | | | | | | | | 1 | | | | | | 1 | | | | | 1 | 4 | | 1 | | | | | | 6 | | | SM |
| S 17 | C | I | 1 | | | | | | | | | | | | | | | | | | 1 | | | | | | 2 | | | | | | | | 2 | | | SM |
| S 19 | C | I | 1 | | | | | 1 | 1 | | | 1 | | | | 1 | 2 | | | | 7 | | | | 1 | 2 | 4 | | | | | | 2 | | 9 | 2g | | SM |
| S 22 | C | I | 1 | | | | | | | | | | | | | | | | | | 1 | | | 2 | 1 | 2 | 2 | | | | | | | | 7 | | | SM |
| S 24 | C | D | 1 | | | | | | | | | | | | | | | | | | 1 | | | | | | | | | | | | | | - | | | SM |
| S 36 | C | D | | | | | | | | | | | | | | | | | | | - | 1 | | | | | | | | | | | | | 1 | 76g | | SM |
| S 37 | C | I | 1 | | | | | | | | | | | | | | | | | | 1 | | | | | | | | | | | | | | - | | | SM |
| S 38 | C | I | | | | | | 1 | 1 | | | | | | | | 1 | | | | 3 | 2 | 2 | 2 | | | 1 | 2 | | 1 | | | 1 | a | 11 | 7 frs. | | SM |
| S 40 | C | I | 1 | | | | | | | | 1 | 1 | | | | | | | | | 3 | | | | | 3 | 3 | | | | | | | | 6 | | | SM |
| S 41 | C | I | | 1 | | | | | | | 1 | | | | | | | | | | 2 | | | | | | | | | | | | | | - | | | SM |
| S 42 | C | D | 1 | | | | | | | | | | | | | | | | | | 1 | | | | | | | | | | | | | | - | | | SM |
| S 43 | C | I | 1 | 1 | | | | 1 | | | | | | | | 1 | | | | | 4 | | | | | | 3 | | | | | | | | 3 | | C | SM |
| S 44 | C | D | | | | | | | | | 1 | | | | | | | | | | 1 | | | | | | | | | | | | | | - | | C | SM |
| S 49 | C | I | 1 | | | | | | | | | | | | | | | | | | 1 | | | | | | | | | | | | | | - | | | |
| S 53 | C | I | | | | | | | | 1 | | | | | | | | | | | 1 | | | | | 1 | | | | | | | | | 1 | | | SM |
| S 54 | P | I | | | | | | | | | | | | | | | | | | | - | | | | | | 1 | | | | | | | | 1 | | | SM |
| S 55 | C | D | 1 | | | | | | | | 1 | | | | | | | | | | 2 | | | | | | | | | | | | | | - | | | SM |
| S 60 | C | I | 1 | 1 | | | | | | | 1 | | | | | | | | | | 3 | | | | | | 1 | | | | | | | | 1 | | C | SM |
| S 62 | P | I | | | | | | | | | 1 | | | | | | | | | | 1 | 2 | | | | | | | | | | | | | 2 | | | SM |
| KT 1 | C | R | | | | | | | | | 1 | | | | | | | | | | 1 | 2 | | | | | | | | | | | | | 2 | | | SM |
| S 2 | C | I | | | 3 | | | | | | 1 | | | | | | 1 | | | | 5 | | | | | | | | | | | | | | - | | C | EPG |
| S 4[8] | C | I | 1 | | | | | | | | | 1 | 1 | 1 | | | 2 | | | | 6 | | | | | | | | | | | | | | - | | | EPG |
| S 8 | C | D | 2 | | | | | | | | | 1 | 1 | | | | | | | | 4 | | | | | | 2 | | | | | | | | 2 | | | EPG |
| S 10 | C | I | 2 | | | | | | | | 1 | 1 | | | | | 1 | | | | 5 | 3 | 1 | | | | 3 | | | | | | | a | 7 | 1g | | EPG |
| S 16 | C | I | 1 | | | 1 | 1 | 2 | 2 | | | 1 | | | | 1 | 3 | | | | 12 | | 2 | | | 5 | 11 | | 1 | | | | | | 19 | | | EPG |
| S 20 | | I | 2 | 1 | | | | | 1 | | 1 | 1 | | | | | 1 | | | | 7 | | | | | 1 | 1 | 1 | | | | | | | 3 | | | EPG |
| S 27 | C | I | 1 | | | | | | | | 1 | | | | | | | | | | 2 | | | | | | | | | | | 1 | | | 1 | | F | EPG |
| S 28 | C | I | 3 | | | | | | | | | | | | | | | | | | 3 | | | | | | | | | | | | | | - | | C | EPG |
| S 31 | C | I | | | | | | 1 | | | 1 | | | | 1 | | | | | | 3 | | | | | 1 | 1 | | | | | | | | 2 | | | EPG |
| S 32 | C | I | | 1 | | | 1 | 1 | | | 1 | 1 | 1 | | | | | | | | 6 | | | | | 1 | | 1 | | | | | | | 2 | | | EPG |
| S 34 | C | I | | 1 | | | | | | | 1 | | | | | | | | | | 2 | | | | | | | | | | | | | | - | | | EPG |
| S 46 | | D | 1 | | | | | | | | 1 | | | | | | | | | 1 | 3 | | | | | 3 | 1 | 1 | | | | | a | 5 | | M | EPG |
| S 12 | C | I | | | | | | | | | 1 | | | | | | | | | | 2 | | | | | | | | | | | | | | - | | | MPG |
| S 18 | C | I | 2 | 1 | 1 | | | | | | 1 | | | | | | | | | | 5 | | | | | | | | | | | | | | - | | | MPG |
| S 29 | C | I | 2 | | | | | | | | 1 | | | | | | | | | | 3 | | | | | | | | | | | | | | - | | | MPG |
| S 51 | C | D | 1 | 1 | | | | | | | 1 | | | | | | | | | 1 | 4 | | | | | | | 1? | | | | | | a | 1 | 7g | | MPG |
| P 6 | P | I | 1 | | | | | | | | | | | | | | | | | | 1 | | | | | | | | | | | | | | - | | | MPG |
| P 9 | S | I | 1 | | | | | | | 1 | 3 | | | | | | | | | | 5 | | | | | | | | | | | | | | - | | C | MPG |
| P 14 | S | D | 1 | | | | | | | | | | | | 1 | | | 1 | 1 | | 4 | | | | | | | | | | | 1 | | | 1 | | C | MPG |
| P 16 | S | I | 1 | | | | | | | 1 | 1 | | | | | 1 | | | | | 5 | | | | | 1? | | 1 | | | | | | | 2 | | M | MPG |
| P 25 B | C | I | 1 | | | | | | | 3 | | | | | | | | | | | 4 | | | | | | | | | | | 1 | (1) | | 1 | | C | MPG |
| T 12 B | S | I | | | | | | | | | 1 | | | | | | | | | | 1 | 1 | | | | | | | | | | 2 | | | 3 | Inh | A | MPG |
| **PYRES** | | | | | | | | | | | | | | | | | | | | | | | | | | | | | | | | | | | | | |
| S 1 | | | | | | | 1 | | | 1 | | | | | | 1 | | | | 3 | | | | | | | | | | | | | | - | | | SM |
| S 3 | | | | | | | | | | | | | | | | | 1 | | | | 1 | | | | | | | | | | | | | | - | | | SM |

1. C = cist, S = shaft, P = pit, MB = mud brick, U = urn
2. I = intact, D = disturbed, R = robbed
3. Multiple vases, tripod, askos, bottle, alabastron, duck vases
4. Syro-Palestinian; or unknown
5. Spiral pendant, unidentified frs.
6. Shells, ivory fr., amethyst bead
7. A = adult, M = male, F = female, J = juvenile, C = child; letter abbreviation is italicised where anthropological evidence is available; other identifications are suggested by grave goods.
8. S Pyre 1A is included with S 4

| Tomb/Pyre No. | Tomb Type[1] | Condition[2] | Cup | Bowl/Skyphos | Shallow bowl | Kalathos | Amphoriskos | Lekythos | Trefoil Oinochoe | Jug | Pyxis | Flask | Amphora | Other[3] | Black Slip Ware | Red Slip Ware | Attic | Cypriot | Handmade | Animal/Human | TOTAL | Iron pins | Gold earrings | Gold rings | Bronze fibulae | Iron swords/spearheads | Iron knife/axe arrowheads | Other[4] | Clay (beads etc.) | Faience | Other[5] | Cloth | TOTAL | Bone (grammes) | Inhumation | Age/Sex[6] | Date |
|---|---|---|---|---|---|---|---|---|---|---|---|---|---|---|---|---|---|---|---|---|---|---|---|---|---|---|---|---|---|---|---|---|---|---|---|---|---|
| P 3 | S | I | | 1 | | 8 | 2 | 3 | 2 | 1 | 2 | 1 | 2 | 1 | | | | | | 1 | 24 | 2 | | 2 | | | | | 12 | | | | 16 | | cr | | LPG |
| P 19 | S | D | 1 | | | | | | 1 | | | | | | | | | | 1 | | 3 | | | | | | | | | | | | – | | | | LPG |
| P 22 | S | I | | | | 2 | | 2 | 7 | 1 | | | 2 | | | | 12 | 1 | | 3 | 30 | 1 | | 2 | | | | 2 | | | | | 5 | | cr | F | LPG |
| P 23 | S | D | | | | 2 | 4 | 2 | | 3 | 1 | | 2 | | | | | | | | 14 | 2 | | 1 | | | | | | | | 1 | 4 | | cr | | LPG |
| P 24 | S | I | | | 1 | 5 | 2 | | | | | | 1 | | | | | | 1 | 1 | 11 | 2 | | | | | | | | 1 | 1 | | 4 | | cr | J | LPG |
| P 31 | S | I | | | | 3 | 2 | | | 1 | | | | | | | | | | | 6 | | | | | | 1 | | | | | | 1 | | | M | LPG |
| P 35 | S | I | 1 | | | | | | 1 | | | | | | | | | | | | 2 | | | | | | | | | | | | – | | | C | LPG |
| P 41 | S | D | | | | | 1 | 1 | | | | | | | | | | | | | 2 | | | | | | | | | | | | – | | | | LPG |
| T 7 | S | D | 1 | | | | | | 2 | | | | | | | | | | | | 3 | | | | | | | | | | | | – | 25g | | A | LPG |
| T 12A | MB | I | | | | | | | 2 | | | | | | | | | | | | 2 | | | 1 | | | | | | 1 | | | 2 | | | | LPG |
| T 14 | U | I | | | | | | | | 1 | | | 1 | | | | | | | | 2 | | | | 1 | 1 | | | 1 | 1 | | | 4 | 3817g[7] | cr | M/F | LPG |
| T 17 | S | I | 3 | | | | | | | | | | | | | | | | | | 3 | | | | 1 | | | | 1 | | | | 2 | | | C | LPG |
| T 18 | U | I | | | | | | | | 1 | | | | | | | | | | | 1 | | | | | | | | | | | | – | 1168g | | M | LPG |
| T 26 | S | I | 1 | 1 | | 3 | 6 | 3 | 2 | | | | | | | 1 | | | | | 17 | | | | 1 | | 1 | 1 | | | | | 3 | | Inh | M | LPG |
| P 7 | S | I | | | | 4 | 1 | | 1 | | | | | | | | | | | | 6 | | | | | | | | | | 1 | | 1 | | | J | LPG–SPG I |
| P 8 | S | I | | | | 1 | | | | | | | | | | | | | | | 1 | | | | | | | | | | | | – | | | | LPG–SPG I |
| P 15 | S | I | | | | | | | 1 | | | | | | | | | | | | 1 | | | | | | | | | | | | – | | | C | LPG–SPG I |
| P 33 | S | I | | | | | 1 | | | | | | | | | | | | | | 1 | | | | | | | | | | | | – | | | | LPG–SPG I |
| P 42 | S | I | | | | 2 | | | | | | | | | | | | | | | 2 | | | | | | | | | 1 | | | 1 | | | | LPG–SPG I |
| T 9 | S | I | | | | | | | | | | | | | | | | | | | – | | | | 2 | | | | | | | | 2 | | | | LPG–SPG I |
| T 29 | S | D | 1 | | | | | | | | | | | | | | | | | | 1 | | | | | | | | | | | | – | | | C | LPG–SPG I |
| **PYRES** | | | | | | | | | | | | | | | | | | | | | | | | | | | | | | | | | | | | | |
| P 11 | | | 1 | 3 | | | 4 | 2 | | 1 | | | 1 | | | | | | | | 12 | | | | | | | | | | | | – | 41g | | | LPG |
| P 14B | | | | | | 1 | 1 | | 1 | | | | | | | | | | | | 3 | | | | | | | | | | | | – | 48g | | J | LPG |
| T 1 | | | | | | | | | | | | | | | | | | | | | – | | 1 | | 1 | 1 | 1 | | | | 2 | | 6 | | | M | LPG |
| T 2 | | | | | | | | | | 3 | | | 2 | | | | 2 | | | | 7 | | | | 4+ | | | | | | | | 4+ | 32g | | A | LPG |
| S 10 | | | | | | 1 | | | | | | | | | | | | | | | 1 | | | | | | | | · | | | | – | | | | LPG–SPG I |
| S 14 | | | | | | | | | 1 | | | | 2+ | | | | | | | | 3+ | 1 | | | | | | | | | | | 1 | | | | LPG–SPG I |
| P 14A | | | | | | | | | 1 | | | | | | | | | | | | 1 | | | | | | | | | | | | – | 234g | | A | LPG–SPG I |
| P 28 | | | | | | 4 | | | | | | | | | | | | | | | 4 | | | | | | | | | | | | – | | | F | LPG–SPG I |
| P 29 | | | | | | | | | | | | | | | | | | | | | – | | 2 | | | | | | 2 | | | | 4 | | | | LPG–SPG I |
| P 32 | | | | | | 2 | | | | | | | 2 | | | | 6 | 2 | | | 12 | | | | | | | | | 1 | | | 1 | 3g | | | LPG–SPG I |
| P 39 | | | | | | | | 1 | | | | | 1 | | | | | | | | 2 | | | | | | | | | 1 | | | 1 | 10g | | F ? | LPG–SPG I |
| P 42 | | | 1 | | | | | | | | | | | | | | | | | | – | | | | | | | | | | | | – | 63g | | | LPG–SPG I |
| T 4 | | | | | | | | | | | | | 4 | | | | | | | | 4 | | | | | | | | | 1 | | | 1 | 3g | | F ? | LPG–SPG I |

TABLE 2  Dated tomb and pyre groups, LPG and LPG–SPG I

1, 2. See TABLE 1, n. 1 and 2
3. Bowl, spouted bowl
4. Hair rings, unidentified frs., needle
5. Stone marbles, ivory frs., objects of antler
6. See TABLE 1, n. 7
7. T 14,1 = 1665g, T 14,2 = 2152g

## CONTENTS — POTTERY | METAL OBJECTS | OTHER

TABLE 3. Dated tomb and pyre groups, SPG I–III

| Tomb/Pyre No. | Tomb Type[1] | Condition[2] | Cup | Bowl/Skyphos | Shallow bowl | Kalathos | Amphoriskos | Lekythos | Trefoil Oinochoe | Jug | Pyxis | Hydria | Amphora | Other[3] | Black Slip Ware | Red Slip Ware | Attic | Other imports[4] | Handmade CP | Other | TOTAL | Pins Gilt | Pins Bronze | Pins Iron | Gold earrings | Rings Gold (*Bronze) | Fibulae Gold (*Gold) | Fibulae Bronze | Fibulae Iron (*Gold) | Bracelets Gilt | Bracelets Bronze | Gold diadems | Gold (*lead) attachments | Bronze vessels | Iron sword + spearhead | Iron knife/*axe | Other[5] | Clay (beads etc.) | Faience | Amber | Crystal | Glass | Other[6] (*Cloth) | TOTAL | Bone (g)/Inh | Age/Sex[7] | DATE |
|---|---|---|---|---|---|---|---|---|---|---|---|---|---|---|---|---|---|---|---|---|---|---|---|---|---|---|---|---|---|---|---|---|---|---|---|---|---|---|---|---|---|---|---|---|---|---|---|
| S 5 | U | D | | | | | | | | | | | 2 | | | | | | | | 2 | | | | | | | | | | | | | | | | | | | | 1 | | | 1 | 32g | M | SPG I |
| S 25A | [C] | D | | | | 3 | | | | | | | | | | | | | | | 3 | | | | | | | 2 | | | | | | | | | | | | | | | | 2 | | | SPG I |
| S 56 | P | – | | 1 | | 1 | | | | 1 | 1 | | 1 | | | | | | | | 5 | | | | | | | | | | | | | | | | | | | | | | | – | | | SPG I |
| P 4 | S | I | 1 | | | 1 | | | 1 | | | | 1 | | | 1 | 1 | | | | 6 | | | | | | | | | | | | | | | | | 1 | | | | | | 1 | | | SPG I |
| P 10 | S | | 1 | | | 13 | 1 | | 1 | 1 | | | 1 | 2 | | | | | | | 20 | | | | 1 | 1 | | | | | | | | | | | | | | | | | * | 2 | | F/C | SPG I |
| P 13 | S | I | | | | 3 | 5 | | 4 | 4 | | | | 4 | | | | | | | 20 | | | | | | | | | | | | | | 1* | | | | | | | | | 1 | | M | SPG I |
| P 18 | S | I | | | | 3 | | | | 2 | | | | | | | | | 1 | | 6 | | | | | | | | | | | | | | | | | | | | | | | – | | | SPG I |
| P 27 | S | I | | 1 | | | | | 1 | | | | | | | | | | | | 2 | | | | | | | | | | | | | | | | | | | | | | | – | | | SPG I |
| P 39(B) | | I | | 1 | 1 | 12 | 2 | 1 | | 1 | 2 | | | | | | | | | 2 | 22 | | | | | | | 2 | | | | | | | | | | | | | | | * | 2 | Frs. | F ? | SPG I |
| P 44 | S | D | | | | 1 | 2 | | (1) | 2 | | | 1 | 1 | | | | | | | 8 | | 1 | | | | | | | | | | | | | | | | | | | | | 1 | Frs. | C | SPG I |
| T 1 | S | I | | | | | 1 | 1 | | | | | 1 | | | | | | | 2 | 5 | | | | | 2 | 2 | | 2 | | | | | | | | | | | 1 | | 1 | | 8 | Frs. | | SPG I |
| T 3 | S | I | | | | | 5 | | | | | | 2 | | | | | | | | 7 | | | | | | | 1 | | | | | | 2 | | 1 | | | | | | 1 | | 5 | 4g | | SPG I |
| T 15 | S | D | 2 | | | 1 | 2 | 1 | 1 | | | | | | | | | | | | 8 | | 1? | 3 | | | 4 | | | | | | | | | 1 | | | 2 | | | | 11 | | C | SPG I |
| T 22 | S | I | 1 | | | 2 | | 2 | 1 | | | | | | | | | | | | 6 | | | | | | | 7 | 9 | | 2 | | | | | 1 | | | 2 | 3 | | 1 | 4 | 29 | 1g | C ? | SPG I |
| T 23A | S | D | 1 | 1 | | | | | 1 | | | | 1 | | | | | | | | 4 | | | | | | | | | | | | | | | | | | | | | | | – | | C ? | SPG I |
| T 25 | S | I | | | | 2 | | | 1 | | | | | | | | | | | | 3 | | | | | | | | | | | | | | | | | | | | | | | – | | | SPG I |
| T 37 | S | D | | | | | | | 1 | 1 | | | | | | | | | | | 2 | | | | | | | | | | | | | | | | | | | | | | | – | | | SPG I ? |
| P 12 | S | I | | | | | | | 3 | | | | | | | | | | | | 3 | | | | | | | | | | | | 1* | | | | | | | | | | | 1 | | | SPG I–II |
| P 17 | P | I | | | | 1 | | | | | | | | | | | | | | | 1 | | | | | | | | | | | | | | | | | | | | | | | – | | | SPG I–II |
| P 36 | S | | 1 | | | | | | 1 | 3 | | | | | | | | | | | 5 | | | | | | | | | | | | | | | | | | | 1 | | | | 1 | | C | SPG I–II |
| P 39A | P | | | | | | | | 1 | | | | | | | | | | | | 1 | | | | | | | | | | | | | | | | | | | | | | | – | | C | SPG I–II |
| P 47 | S | I | | | | | 5 | 1 | 7 | 3 | | | | | | | | | | | 16 | | | | | | | | | | | | | 1 | 1+1 | | | 1 | | | | 4 | Inh | M | SPG I–II |
| T 23 | S | D | | | | | | | | 1 | 12 | | | | | | | | | | 13 | | | | | | | | | | | | | | | | | | | | | | | – | | | SPG I–II |
| S 21 | [C] | R | | | | | | | | | | | | | | | | | 2 | | 2 | | | | | | | | | | | | | | | | | | | | | | | – | | | SPG II |
| S 25B | [C] | D | 1 | | | 1 | | | 1 | | | | | | | | | | | | 3 | | | | | | | | | | | | | | | | | | | | | | | – | | | SPG II |
| S 33 | P | D | 1 | 2 | | | | | | 5 | 3 | | | | | | 1 | 1 | | | 13 | | | | 3 | 1 | | 2 | | | | | | | | | | | | | | * | 6 | | F | SPG II |
| S 45 | S | I | 1 | 1 | | 4 | | 2 | | | | | 1 | | | | | | | | 10 | | | | | | | 1 | | | | | | | | | | | | | | | 1 | | F | SPG II |
| P 21 | S | I | | 1 | | | | | 8 | | | | | | 1 | | | | | | 10 | 1 | | | | | | | | | | | | | | | | 1 | | | | | 2 | | | SPG II |
| P 28 | P | I | 3 | | | 2 | 1 | | 3 | | | | 1 | 1 | | | | | | | 11 | | | | | | | | | | | | | | | | | | | | | | | – | | | SPG II |
| P 43 | P | I | 1 | | | 4 | | | 1 | | | | | | | | | | | | 6 | | | | | | | 1 | | | 2 | | | | | | | | | | | 1 | | 4 | | | SPG II |
| P 45 | S | I | | | | | | | | | | | | | | | | | | | – | | | | | | 2 | 2? | | | | | | | | | | | | | | | 4 | Inh | 2 A | SPG II |
| T 2 | S | D | 1 | | | 2 | | | | 1 | | | | | | | | | 1 | 2 | 7 | | | | | | | | | | | | | | | | | | | | | | | – | | | SPG II |
| T 4 | MB | D | | 1 | | 3 | | 1 | | 1 | | | 1 | | | | | | | | 6 | | | | | | | | | | | | | | | | | | | | | | | – | | | SPG II |
| T 5 | S | D | | 1 | | 4 | 1 | 2 | 1 | | | | | | | | | | | | 9 | | | | | 2 | 5 | 5 | 1? | | 2 | | | | | | | | | 2 | 1 | | 18 | 4g | C | SPG II |
| T 13 | MB | I | 1 | | | 10 | | | | 1 | 2 | | | | | | | | | | 14 | | | | | | 2 | 4 | 1 | 1* | | 2 | | | | | | | | 2 | | | 1* | 14 | | C | SPG II |
| T 28 | S | D | | | | | | | | 1 | | | | | | | | | 1 | | 2 | | | | | | | | | | | | | | | | | | | | | | | – | | F | SPG II |
| T 24 | S | I | | | | | | | | | | | | | | | | 1 | | | 1 | | | | | | | | | | | | | | | | | | | | | | | – | | | SPG II–III |
| T 27 | S | I | 1 | | | 1 | | | | | | | | | | | | | | | 2 | | | | | | 4 | 5 | 1 | | 2 | | | | | | | | 1 | | 1 | 1 | 1 | 16 | 2g | | SPG II–III |
| T 32 | S | D | | | | | | | | | | | | | | | | | | | – | 2 | | | | | 6 | 6 | | | | | | | | | | | 2 | | 1 | (2) | | 17 | 2g | | SPG II–III |
| T 36 | MB | D | | | | 1 | | | | | | | | | | | | | | | 1 | | | | | | 2 | 3 | | | 1 | 1 | | | | | 10? | 3 | 1 | 2 | 3 | 2 | 5 | 33 | Teeth | C | SPG II–III |
| S 59(A) | S | I | | 3 | | 14 | 1 | 1 | | 3 | 1 | | | | | | | 1 | | | 25 | 2 | | | 2 | | 7 | 9 | | | | | | | | | | 5 | 1 | | | | * | 26 | 17g | F | SPG III |
| T 19 | S | I | | | | 1 | | | | | | | | | | | 2 | 1 | | | 4 | | | | | | | | | | | | | 1 | | | | | 1 | | | | | 1 | | C | SPG III |
| T 31 | S | I | 1 | 1 | | | | 1 | 1 | | | | | | | | 4 | 1 | | | 9 | | | | | | 6 | 3 | | | | | 1 | | | | | 3 | | | | 1 | | 14 | Frs. | | SPG III |
| T 33 | S | I | | | | | | | 1 | | | | | | | | 4 | | | | 5 | | | | | | | 1 | 2 | 1 | 2 | | | | | 6 | | | 2 | 2 | 4 | * | 20 | | C | SPG III |
| P 2 | S | I | 1 | | | | | | | | | | | | | | | | | | 1 | | | | | | | | | | | | | | | | | | | | | | | – | | | SPG. |
| P 46 | S | I | | | | | | | | | | | | | | | | | | | – | | 2 | | | | | | | | | | | | | | | | | | | | 2 | 24g | J | SPG |
| **PYRES** | | | | | | | | | | | | | | | | | | | | | | | | | | | | | | | | | | | | | | | | | | | | | | | | |
| S 15 | | | 1 | 1 | | | | 1 | 2 | 1+ | | | 1 | | | | | | | | 7+ | | | | | | | | | | | | | | | | | | | | | | | – | 27g | | SPG I ? |
| P 15 | | | | | | | | | | 1 | | | | | | | | | | | 1 | | | | | | | | | | | | | | | | | | | 1 | | | | 1 | | F | SPG I |
| P 31 | | | 1 | | | | | | | | | | | | | | | | | | 1 | | | | | | | | | | | | | | | | | | | | | | | – | | | SPG I ? |
| P 34 | | | | | | | | | 4 | 1 | | | | | | | | | | | 5 | | | | | | | | | | | | | | | | | | | | | | | – | 10g | | SPG I |
| P 44 | | | | | | | | 1 | | 2 | | | | | | | | | | | 4 | | | | | | | | | | | | | | | | | | | | | | | – | 1g | | SPG I |
| T 8 | | | | | | | | | | 1 | 2 | | | | | | | | | | 3 | | | | | | | | | | | | | | 1+1 | | | | | | | | 1 | 3 | 30g | | SPG I |
| T 3 | | | 1 | | | | | | 1 | | | | | | | | | | | | 2 | | | | | | | | | | | | | | | | | | | | | | | – | | | SPG I–II |
| S 2 | | | | | | | | | | | | | | | | | | | | | – | | 2 | | | | | 1 | | | | | | | | | | | | | | | 3 | 68g | J | SPG II |
| S 4 | | | 1 | 1 | | | | | | 1 | 3 | 1 | | | | | | | | | 7 | 2 | | | 2? | 1 | 4 | 4 | 2 | | | | | | | | | 6 | | | | | | 21 | 96g | F | SPG II |
| P 41 | | | | | | | | 1 | | 2 | | | | | | | | | | | 3 | | | | | | | | | | | | | | | | | | | | | | | – | | | SPG |

**TABLE 3. Dated tomb and pyre groups, SPG I–III**

1, 2. See TABLE 1, n. 1 and 2
3. Dishes, plates, multiple vase, mug, kantharos, centaur, horse figurine
4. Of unknown provenience
5. Mace head, scale pans, scale plate, plaque, rivet, unidentified frs., beads, hair spiral, foil
6. Shells, bone, clay sealings, steatite seals, ivory
7. See TABLE 1, n. 7.

# TABLE 4. Index of dated tombs and pyres

**SKOUBRIS CEMETERY**

| | | |
|---|---|---|
| S 2 | – | EPG |
| S 3 | – | SM |
| S 4 | – | EPG |
| S 5 | – | SPG I |
| S 8 | – | EPG |
| S 9 | – | SM |
| S 10 | – | EPG |
| S 12 | – | MPG |
| S 15B | – | SM |
| S 16 | – | EPG |
| S 17 | – | SM |
| S 18 | – | MPG |
| S 19 | – | SM |
| S 20 | – | EPG |
| S '21' | – | SPG II |
| S 22 | – | SM |
| S 23 | – | ? |
| S 24 | – | SM |
| S 25A | – | SPG I |
| S 25B | – | SPG II |
| S 27 | – | EPG |
| S 28 | – | EPG |
| S 29 | – | MPG |
| S 31 | – | EPG |
| S 32 | – | EPG |
| S 33 | – | SPG II |
| S 34 | – | EPG |
| S 36 | – | SM |
| S 37 | – | SM |
| S 38 | – | SM |
| S 40 | – | SM |
| S 41 | – | SM |
| S 42 | – | SM |
| S 43 | – | SM |
| S 44 | – | SM |
| S 45 | – | SPG II |
| S 46 | – | EPG |
| S 49 | – | SM |
| S 51 | – | MPG |
| S 53 | – | SM |
| S 54 | – | SM |
| S 55 | – | SM |
| S 56 | – | SPG I |

S 59 ⎫
S 59A ⎭ – SPG III

| | | |
|---|---|---|
| S 60 | – | SM |
| S 62 | – | SM |
| S 63 | – | SM |
| KT 1 | – | SM |

| | | |
|---|---|---|
| S Pyre 1 | – | SM |
| S Pyre 1A | – | EPG |
| S Pyre 2 | – | SPG II |
| S Pyre 3 | – | SM |
| S Pyre 4 | – | SPG II |
| S Pyre 6 | – | LPG–SPG |
| S Pyre 8 | – | ? |
| S Pyre 10 | – | LPG–SPG I |
| S Pyre 12 | – | LPG–SPG |
| S Pyre 13 | – | ? |
| S Pyre 14 | – | LPG–SPG I |
| S Pyre 15 | – | SPG? |
| S Pyre 17 | – | MPG–LPG? |

**PALIA PERIVOLIA and EAST CEMETERIES**

| | | |
|---|---|---|
| P 2 | – | SPG |
| P 3 | – | LPG |
| P 4 | – | SPG I |
| P 6 | – | MPG |
| P 7 | – | LPG |
| P 8 | – | LPG–SPG I |
| P 9 | – | MPG |
| P 10 | – | SPG I |
| P 12 | – | SPG I–II |
| P 13 | – | SPG I |
| P 14 | – | MPG |
| P 15 | – | LPG–SPG I |
| P 16 | – | MPG |
| P 17 | – | SPG I–II |
| P 18 | – | SPG I |
| P 19 | – | LPG? |

| | | |
|---|---|---|
| P 21 | – | SPG II |
| P 22 | – | LPG |
| P 23 | – | LPG |
| P 24 | – | LPG |
| P 25B | – | MPG |
| P 27 | – | SPG I |
| P 28 | – | SPG II |
| P 31 | – | LPG |
| P 33 | – | LPG–SPG I |
| P 35 | – | LPG |
| P 36 | – | SPG I–II |
| P 39A | – | SPG I–II |

P 39 ⎫
P 39B ⎭ – SPG I

| | | |
|---|---|---|
| P 41 | – | LPG |
| P 42 | – | LPG–SPG I |
| P 43 | – | SPG II |
| P 44 | – | SPG I |
| [P 44,7 | – | LPG] |
| P 45 | – | SPG I–II |
| P 46 | – | SPG |
| P 47 | – | SPG I–II |

| | | |
|---|---|---|
| P Pyre 1 | – | ? |
| P Pyre 8 | – | ? |
| P Pyre 9 | – | LPG–SPG |
| P Pyre 11 | – | LPG |
| P Pyre 14A | – | LPG–SPG I |
| P Pyre 14B | – | LPG |
| P Pyre 15 | – | SPG I |
| P Pyre 16 | – | ? |
| P Pyre 17 | – | ? |
| P Pyre 19 | – | SPG |
| P Pyre 28 | – | LPG–SPG I |
| P Pyre 29 | – | LPG–SPG I? |
| P Pyre 31 | – | SPG I? |
| P Pyre 32 | – | LPG–SPG I |
| P Pyre 34 | – | SPG I |
| P Pyre 36 | – | LPG–SPG |
| P Pyre 39 | – | LPG–SPG I |
| P Pyre 40 | – | ? |
| P Pyre 41 | – | SPG |

| | | |
|---|---|---|
| P Pyre 42 | – | LPG–SPG I |
| P Pyre 44 | – | SPG I |

**TOUMBA CEMETERY**

| | | |
|---|---|---|
| T 1 | – | SPG I |
| T 2 | – | SPG II |
| T 3 | – | SPG I |
| T 4 | – | SPG II |
| T 5 | – | SPG II |
| T 7 | – | LPG |
| T 12A | – | LPG |
| T 12B | – | MPG |
| T 13 | – | SPG II |
| T 14 | – | LPG |
| T 15 | – | SPG I |
| T 17 | – | LPG |
| T 18 | – | LPG |
| T 19 | – | SPG III |
| T 22 | – | SPG I |
| T 23 | – | SPG I–II |
| T 23A | – | SPG I |
| T 24 | – | SPG II–III |
| T 25 | – | SPG I |
| T 26 | – | LPG |
| T 27 | – | SPG III |
| T 28 | – | SPG II |
| T 29 | – | LPG–SPG I |
| T 31 | – | SPG III |
| T 32 | – | SPG II–III |
| T 33 | – | SPG III |
| T 36 | – | SPG II–III |
| T 37 | – | SPG I? |

| | | |
|---|---|---|
| T Pyre 1 | – | LPG? |
| T Pyre 2 | – | LPG |
| T Pyre 3 | – | SPG I–II |
| T Pyre 4 | – | LPG–SPG I? |
| T Pyre 5 | – | ? |
| T Pyre 6 | – | ? |
| T Pyre 7 | – | ? |
| T Pyre 8 | – | SPG I? |

| DATE | S M | EPG | MPG | L P G | SPG I | SPG II | SPG III | S P.G III | L G |
|---|---|---|---|---|---|---|---|---|---|
| | | | | | LPG/SPG I | SPG I/II | =MG I | =MG II | |
| C | S 3 ----- S 2 ------------------------------------ S 5 | | | | | | | | |
| E | S 9 ----- S 10 | | | | | | | | |
| M | S 19 ---- S 20 | | | | | | | | |
| E | | | S 18 | | | | | | |
| T | S 36 ------------------------------------------------ S 33 | | | | | | | | |
| E | S 55 ------------------------------------------------ S 59 | | | | | | | | |
| R | ⌈( S4 ⌊( S pyr. la | | | | | | | | |
| I | S 46 ----------------------------------- S 45 | | | | | | | | |
| E | | | P 16 -- P pyr.14B -- 14A | | | | | | |
| S | | | T 12B ------------------ T 12A | | | | | |
| | | | P 25B --------------- P pyr.34 | | | | | |
| | | | | ⌈( T pyr.1 ⌊( T 17 | | | | | |
| | | | | ⌈( T 7 ⌊( T 12A | | | | | |
| | | | | T 26 ---- T pyr.4 | | | | | |
| | | | | P 24 -------- P 21 | | | | | |
| | | | | P 19 ----------- P12 | | | | | |
| | | | | T 14 -------------- T 5 | | | | | |
| | | | | ⌈( P pyr.28 ⌊( P pyr.42 | | | | | |
| | | | | P pyr.32 ----- P 28 | | | | | |
| | | | | T 29 ------------- T 27 | | | | | |
| | | | | T 1 ---- T 5 | | | | | |
| | | | | ⌈( T 3 ⌊( T 15 -- T 13 | | | | | |
| X | | | | AREA 2, PIT 1 -- AREA 2, PIT 2 -------------- AREA 2 ---- AREA 2 | | | 'LEVELLING' | YARD |
| E | | | | 'MOULDS' 'SPG PIT' | | | | | |
| R | | | | | | | | | |
| O | | | | AREA 3(S) ----------- AREA 3(S) | | | | | |
| P | | | | FILL YARD | | | | | |
| O | | | | | | | | | |
| L | | | | | | | | | |
| I | | | | | | | | | |
| S | | | | | | | | | |

TABLE 5. Stratified deposits from the cemeteries and settlement

In addition, six other tomb/pyres were stratified though in these three instances of superimposition the contents of the earlier tomb/pyres were insufficient to enable them to be dated. They are: S Pyre 13 (undated) above S Pyre 14 (LPG/SPG I), P 46 (undated) above P Pyre 34 (SPG I) and T Pyre 5 (undated) above T 29 (LPG/SPG I).

# Appendix B

# The Ancient Name of the Site[1.]

## M. R. POPHAM

We may start with the obvious alternative either that the name of the settlement was wholly forgotten in antiquity (and/or is not contained in any surviving literature) or that it was remembered and has been handed down in some form or other.

The latter alternative seems at least likely. Up to about 800 BC, to judge from present evidence, it was the most important city in Central Euboea. Although thereafter it yielded pre-eminence to Chalcis and Eretria, it still remained no mean settlement in contemporary terms. Two other factors give cause for hope. The ultimate hostility between Chalcis and Eretria gained a certain notoriety in antiquity: it was clearly no mean border clash, as indeed Thucydides emphasises,[2] so immediate participants and casualties in the struggle could well have been recorded; and we assume Xeropolis was such a casualty. Moreover, Strabo's account of Euboea is unusually long, detailed and seemingly well-informed despite several obvious errors and confusions: the surviving work of a local historian is likely to have been his prime source.[3]

Even so, it must be stated at the beginning that no city is specifically named by any of our sources as lying between Chalcis and Eretria, and the only battle casualty mentioned, Kerinthos, must, it seems be located elsewhere.

Recently two differing views have been put forward; that Xeropolis is old Eretria, favoured by the Swiss excavators of the 'new' town of that name, or that it is old Chalcis, advocated by Bakhuizen who has been principally interested in that city. Common to both solutions is the implied assumption that a site of such obvious importance as Xeropolis must have been well known. The two most famous cities in the region — in fact the only ones which attract any real attention from Homer on — are Chalcis and Eretria, so its name might be concealed in one or other of these.

## OLD ERETRIA

The arguments which can be adduced in favour of this solution appear at first the stronger. Their basis is Strabo's reference to an 'ancient' or 'old' Eretria, the ruins of which were said to be still visible. Grave difficulties, both chronological and geographical, however, arise when we turn to the details. The destruction of old Eretria is ascribed by Strabo to the Persians, while the distances he quotes to fix its situation, and the part of Attica from which they are measured, must mean that he envisaged it as lying to the east of Eretria. Where precisely it should be located is another problem: it could be the prehistoric and later site of Palaiokastri at Amarynthus.[4] This, however, is a surmise, but one closer to the text than to adopt Xeropolis, which involves rejection of Strabo's distances, direction and date, and assumes some faint recollection that Eretria was once elsewhere, at another location which Strabo (or his sources) has hopelessly confused.

Strabo is, then, no authority for the view that Xeropolis is the former abode of the Eretrians. Better support may lie in archaeological probability. More detailed argument on this point has been given above in the Historical Conclusions. In outline, Eretria has so far produced little evidence of Dark Age (or Late Bronze Age) occupation until about 750 BC, by which time it was a settlement of considerable extent; this makes it likely that it was 'founded' somewhat earlier, roughly about the time Xeropolis seems to be in decline. So, a movement of population from Lefkandi to the new site of Eretria is a quite feasible explanation. But, in itself, this gets us no nearer to the ancient name of Xeropolis, unless we assume that those who migrated (if they did) took the name of their settlement with them.

## OLD CHALCIS

There is no literary support for this alternative view, which relies on geographical and archaeological probabilities. It has been strongly advocated recently by Bakhuizen, and was floated as a possibility some time before in conversation by Miss Sylvia Benton who took an early interest in our excavations. On this point, too, more detailed discussion is included in the Historical Conclusions. The main point in the argument is that the Lelantine Plain, and Xeropolis on its eastern edge, belong geographically to Chalcis — a fact that the aerial view at PLATE 1a should vividly demonstrate.[5] It is held, therefore, to be inconceivable that a powerful Chalcis did not control and enjoy the resources of the Plain and hold its strategically placed main settlement. Again, an element in the argument is that, while there did exist a Protogeometric settlement at Chalcis, in the vicinity of the Arethusa Spring, the dominant city before and for some time after appears to have been Xeropolis.

Bakhuizen, it is true, does not propose Chalcis as the original title of Xeropolis; instead, on the slenderest of grounds, he selects Euboea, a city said to have been submerged by the sea and which enjoyed some mythological popularity.

Are there any other candidates? We turn first to Homer and the Catalogue of Ships, whether or not we believe in its Late Bronze Age basis, for Lefkandi was important in that period too and may be presumed to have retained its old name into the Iron Age.[6] Apart from Chalcis and Eretria, Homer lists Histiaea, Kerinthos, Dios, Karystos and Styra. Strabo is able to locate these, apparently without difficulty, the first three in the north, the remaining two in the south, and there is independent evidence to support this.

Kerinthos, however, remains an attractive candidate. For, as Xeropolis it would help make sense of an enigmatic passage of Theognis who links its otherwise unattested destruction with devastation of the Lelantine Plain, the flight of the (unspecified) city's aristocrats and the Cypselids of Corinth.[7] However, Strabo specifically states that Kerinthos was in the territory of Histiaea, adding the information that it was a small city, by the sea with the River Budoros nearby.

Other possibilities mentioned in later accounts are few, with little in their support. Oechalia, destroyed by Herakles, seems, if not myth, to belong to earlier days; Strabo places it in Eretrian territory (at a time when he ascribes the leading position to Chalcis) and calls it a village. There is also Strabo's 'Tamynae, sacred to Apollo', which could be linked with Apollo's landfall in the Lelantine Plain described in the Homeric Hymn to Apollo. But Apollo rejects the Plain as a place for his temple, while Strabo locates Tamynae in Eretrian territory. Moreover, there is epigraphical evidence to suggest that both places were 'demes' of Eretria in the 4th century and were probably located to the east of Eretria.[8]

This might seem to exhaust the possibilities, and lead to the conclusion that the assumptions made at the beginning were baseless and that the name of Xeropolis has not survived at all or, if so, in such a confused or vague recollection as to be valueless in our search. However, if we adhere to those assumptions, there remains one candidate which has been before us all the time.

## LELANTON

One name survives traditionally attached to the region – the Lelantine Plain, though Strabo is, in fact, the first to give us its location near Chalcis. For him, the Plain was the point at issue in the fighting between Chalcis and Eretria: precise authority for this, as Bakhuizen has pointed out, is late though to reject these references as fabrications, as he does, may be the wrong solution to the very real problem of how Eretria could ever have expected to keep control of the Plain which is so near to Chalcis. May the answer not be that Strabo and others did inherit a tradition that the conflict (or one phase of it) was 'about Lelanton', for this is the phrase used not only by him but also by Plutarch and a scholiast on Hesiod?[9] If so, the late scholarly invention would consist not in its fabrication but in its interpretation, in equating Lelanton with the Plain, Strabo's τὸ Λήλαντον καλούμενον πεδίον. In other words may the scholiast, who glossed Lelanton on a fragment of ?Euphorion with 'a mountain and a city' be correct in supplying us with the name of Xeropolis, whether by guesswork, or good information nowhere else preserved?[10]

However, one of our two earliest references would, as the text stands, appear unambiguously to support Strabo's view – and, of course, he may well have had it in mind. The Homeric Hymn to Apollo makes the god land in his travels on the Plain Lelanton, the two words being in apposition, though it might be argued that the region is envisaged by the poet as being yet uninhabited, so this is inconclusive.[11] Callimachus, who seems to be recalling this passage in his Delian Hymn, refers to the 'Lelantine Plain', making the name adjectival, a usage which occurs rarely elsewhere.[12]

Theognis, the other early authority, calls it the plain *of* Lelanton, which needed explanation: Hesychius hazards a Euboean king Lelantos and this, also, is put forward by a scholiast on Callimachus.[13]

Lelanton next appears on an inscription at Athens which is concerned with the confiscation and sale of the possessions of the Hermocopidae and is dated 415–3 BC. One of those convicted, Oeonias, had property in Euboea including some 'at Lelanton'. We have no evidence that Xeropolis was occupied at this time, so we must assume that a contemporary settlement existed nearby, unless the inscription refers to the Plain, in which case its name at Athens must have been well enough known to stand on its own.[14] Theophrastus, our next authority (around 300 BC) is unfortunately ambiguous when in referring to certain plants which prefer light rather than rich soil, he quotes as an example Euboea: there, he says, they do not occur 'at Lelanton' but they do around Kanethos.[15]

Two other references, earlier than Strabo, survive and he is himself responsible for preserving one of them, though we cannot be sure that he repeats the actual words of Archemachos. This Euboean historian, writing in the 3rd century BC, made the legendary Curetes settle at one stage at Chalcis where they are said to have been continuously at war with an unidentified enemy 'over the plain of Lelanton', which might have been another factor in influencing Strabo's interpretation of later events, if he is here quoting accurately.[16] Apart from this, there remains a fragmentary poem ascribed to Euphorion of Chalcis, roughly contemporary with Archemachos, in which 'of Lelanton' is preserved but not its subject.[17] Thereafter, as stated above, Lelanton is usually mentioned on its own, as being the cause of the war.[18]

We have seen that Hesychius explained the name Lelanton as being derived from a king Lelantos, which need not merit serious consideration. Another current view would derive the name of the plain from the river which passes through it, the Lelas. Lelas, however, has no ancient authority and may be a quite modern scholastic invention; it is not in Strabo, who curiously does not mention the river at all, nor is it named in any of our ancient sources except Pliny, who mentions the River Lelantus or Lelantum, 'flumine Lelanto', which merely adds more complication to the name, and may be suspected of being a simple confusion.[19]

Such, then, is the evidence about Lelanton: it is clearly not without ambiguity and in so far as it relates to the war, mostly late. It opens, however, the possibility that Lelanton was originally the name of our settlement to which the Plain was ascribed: with time, the settlement and its name became forgotten though some references to the cause of the war being 'about Lelanton' survived and required explanation. The early poetic references to a plain and Lelanton supplied a ready answer. If, however, this explanation was mistaken, and it was not the Plain but Xeropolis which was meant, a new area of speculation is opened up. It might well be argued, for instance, that while Eretria could never have expected to retain possession of the Plain and enjoy its produce from a distance without destroying Chalcis, it might have tried to hold Xeropolis as an outpost — one which some of its citizens may have regarded as their ancestral home.

This is speculation only, and it should again be emphasised that as a possible solution it relies basically on the assumption set out at the beginning, that the name of Xeropolis has survived in our ancient sources.

## APPENDIX B

1. For general background and the views mentioned in this account, see the following. On the Lelantine War, D. Bradeen, *TAPA* lxxvii (1947) 223 f.; G. Forrest, *Historia* vi (1957) 160 f.; S. Bakhuizen, *Chalcis-in-Euboea* (Chalcidian Studies III) and L.H. Jeffery, *Archaic Greece* 63–70. On the name of Xeropolis, Old Eretria, *Studies* 68; *Ant. Kunst* 9, 108 and 11, 105: Oechalia, *Archaeology* 25, 19 and Themelis, *AE* 1968 163 n. 5: 'Euboea', Bakhuizen, op. cit. 7–13. The main ancient source is Strabo, C 444–9 and 58–61.

2. Thuc. I 15 and comment by Jeffery *op. cit.* 65.

3. He specifically refers to one such local historian, Archemachus in C 466. His main confusion, for present purposes, is between the region of Aedipsos and the Lelantine Plain, ascribing to the latter mistakenly thermal springs, a mine and, in C 58, the eruption of lava after an earthquake.

4. As suggested also by Bakhuizen *op. cit.* 78 f.: for the site, see *Studies* 64, Site 62. Strabo's account and distances have been considered in detail by Themelis, *loc. cit.* 157 f. Themelis suggests a difference in meaning between ancient (παλαιά) Eretria, the Mycenaean site, and old (ἀρχαία) Eretria, destroyed by the Persians, and holds that while Strabo differentiates them, the Eretrians mixed them up. He concludes that ancient Eretria was roughly in the same location as the later, post Persian, city; but this would make the two distances given by Strabo, measured from different parts of the Attic coast, otiose to say the least.

5. A point emphasized by Boardman, *BSA* 52 (1957) 27, 'It is geographically Chalcidian territory and so must always have been for as long as Chalcis was any sort of power'.

6. Iliad II 536 f.

7. Theognis 891–3, a passage much discussed and debated on various grounds: the Cypsalids are an amendment. ... ἀπὸ μέν Κήρινθος ὄλωλεν | Ληλάντου δ᾽ ἀγαθὸν κείρεται οἰνόπεδον | ...

8. I am indebted to Dr. L.H. Jeffery here and in general for valuable help and suggestions. Pausanias IV 2,3 mentions that Hekataios ascribed an Oechalia to the Eretrian district called Skios: there were of course several rival claimants. Both Tamynae and Oechalia were seemingly 'demes' of Eretria in the 4th and 3rd centuries BC, Wallace, 'The Demes of Eretria' *AJA* xvi (1947) 115 f., where they are tentatively located to the NE of Eretria. The western limit of Eretrian territory is unknown but, if it reached to the river Lelas, then their claims become somewhat stronger. Oechalia was first suggested to the author by the late Prof. Marinatos: see also Themelis, loc. cit.

9. Plutarch, *Moralia* 153F ἐν ταῖς περὶ Ληλάντου μάχαις. Scholiast on Hesiod, *W and D* 649–56 ναυμαχοῦντα πρὸς Ἐρετρίεας ὑπὲρ τοῦ Ληλάντου the only reference to a naval engagement in the war.

10. *Oxyrh. Pap.* XXX 2526, a passage kindly brought to the author's notice by Prof. G. Huxley when the theory was first under consideration.

11. Line 220 στῆς δ᾽ ἐπί Ληλάντωι πέδιωι.

12. Delian Hymn 288–9 πέδιον Ληλάντιον. Scholiast on Thuc. I 15 ἐπολεμοῦν οὗτοι πρὸς ἀλλήλους περί τοῦ Ληλαντίου πεδίου. Also in the epitomy of Strabo and in Eustathius on Iliad 2 542 and Iliad 9 529. I am grateful to Mr. P.M. Fraser for his help and advice here and in general.

13. Theognis, see note 7. Hesychius, Ληλάντου πέδιον. τῆς Εὐβοίας ὠνομασμένου ἀπὸ Ληλάντου βασιλέως.

14. SEG XIII, 13 and Pritchett, *Hesperia* xxii (1953): Stele II lines 178 and 312, neither of which is quite complete but, together, leave no doubt that the text was ἐν Ληλάντῳ.

15. Theophrastus, De Causis Plantarum VIII 8,5 ἐν τῷ Ληλάντῳ.

16. Geogr. C 465 περὶ τοῦ Ληλάντου πεδίου πολεμοῦντας, see *FGH* 424 F9.

17. See note 10. ... ] κροκάλαις ὑπὸ κυμανθεῖσα | ...] σανήλυθε Ληλάντοιο.

18. An exception is Aelian, Var. Hist. VIII 1 who, in referring to the expropriation of Chalcidian lands and their apportionment as Athenian cleruchies, mentions the setting up of a shrine to Athena 'in the place called Lelanton', ἐν τῷ Ληλάντῳ ὀνομαζομένῳ τόπῳ.

19. Pliny *NH* IV ch. 21. Strabo's omission is curious in that the river is the largest in Euboea. The description in the Admiralty Handbook (1945) 75 is worth quoting. 'The western extension of Olimbos is penetrated by the river Lilas, which traverses the plain of Yidhes in a defile and has the largest river basin in Evvoia. It reaches the gulf just south of the narrows and its delta has provided Khalkis with most valuable fruit land and a water supply. The surrounding low hills are composed of limestone and serpentine, from which magnesite is obtained.'

Lelas as the name of the river, an intelligent surmise, seems to have been invented in the last century, and since then many places have had their ancient names 'restored' to them, including Eretria (Nea Psara), Amarynthus (Batheia) and Aedipsos (Lipso). Lelanton in Greek and Lilanto in Italian apparently survived.

# Appendix C

# The Human Remains from the Cemeteries[1]

## J. H. MUSGRAVE

## A. CREMATIONS

The majority of these burials were cremations rather than inhumations. Considerable literature exists on ancient cremations and this was helpful in the preparation of this report.[2]

The following points are of general application in any description of cremated remains; and since those from Lefkandi were, with one or two exceptions, sparse token offerings, space can be saved by treating these before individual cremations are described. Points of particular interest will be discussed in greater detail at the end of this report.

1. *Condition.* This was found to be fairly uniform. The number of white, brittle and warped pieces indicated that the bodies were consumed at a temperature of between 800° and 900°C, the temperature at which modern cremation furnaces operate.[3] The recovery of a fair number of blue-black, i.e. less well burnt, pieces suggested that the temperature did not exceed 900°C.

2. *Colour.* This is closely linked with condition. It ranges from black to dazzling white, depending upon the amount of organic material still remaining in each bone, in uncontaminated burials. The presence of metal objects and the chemical composition of the surrounding earth can introduce a wide range of additional hues. The Lefkandi material was mostly white, but included several green fragments that had lain near copper or bronze.

3. *Size, number and weight of the fragments.* The description of individual cremations will show that they were not distinguished by their size and volume. Most were simple token offerings.

4. *Evidence of pounding.* The small size of most pieces indicated that this practice was adopted generally. There is clear evidence for it in Toumba 14,1.

5. *Sex, age and number of individuals in each grave or urn.* Generally the evidence was inconclusive on these points.

6. *Signs of multiple cremations.* The Lefkandi series appears to represent a collection of individual cremations. Exceptions, where there is evidence for double cremations, are S Pyres 6 and 17.

7. *Pathology.* It was not easy to diagnose recognisable pathological lesions on such fragmentary material.

8. *Grave or urn goods.* These are obviously described and discussed fully elsewhere. Only those with any anthropological significance are mentioned in this section.

9. *Animal bones.* These were not common. Their occurrence too has been noted.

## B. INHUMATIONS

Five inhumations were recognised with certainty during excavation, three in the East cemetery (P 45, a double inhumation; and P 47) and two in Toumba (T 12B and T 26). In each case the bones were too badly eroded to make it possible to lift and re-assemble or restore a complete skeleton. Those traces which survived, whether as bone fragments, dust or just as a discoloration of the earth, were consolidated and lifted where possible. Very approximate dimensions of limbs and skeletons may be taken from the tomb plans (PLATES 123, 159 and 162). All were laid out in an extended position and the estimated heights of the individuals (in metres) were: 1.55 and 1.55 (P 45); 1.80 (P 47); 1.55 (T 12B); and 1.60 (T 26). P 47 and T 26 are warrior graves. We shall return to the problem of interpreting these and other unburnt bones later.

## THE SKOUBRIS CEMETERY

Few human remains were found in this cemetery. The majority of the graves contained cremations. Inhumations of unburnt bones are described as such in the text.

*S 5 c*. 50 frs, wt. 32 g; size range 8.0 x 2.0 to 74.2 x 17.6 mm. Found in base of cremation amphora 5,1 near surface. None easily identified. Coated with clay; no trace of pyre dust; weathered or washed before burial?

*S 10* 3 frs, wt. 1 g; size range 4.5 x 3.5 to 8.4 x 4.9 mm. Some green discoloration from proximity to bronze.

*S 19* One identifiable skull fr, wt. 2 g; 13.5 x 11.6 mm. Weathered or washed before burial.

*S 36* 76 g of *unburnt* rather than cremated bones. Remains comprised mainly limb bone frs. Some of considerable length, e.g. 112.5 mm. Two premolar teeth were also recovered with enamel deeply etched by acids in the soil. Four greenish frs indicated close proximity to bronze.

*S 38* 7 frs, light brown to green in colour; size range 9.0 x 2.7 to 37.4 x 14.8 mm. Found with a small iron pin. It is not clear whether these remains were cremated or not.

*S 51* 6 limb bone frs of unequal size, ranging from 19.6 x 4.9 to 57.1 x 19.2 mm. Found with bronze fibula SK 51,7; hence greenish colour. Wt. 7 g.

*S 59* 29 mixed frs; wt. 17 g; size range 14.9 x 6.2 to 34.7 x 11.8 mm. Only one identifiable piece: the head, neck and tubercle of a ? mid-thoracic rib. One bronze pin was found with the bones; hence their light green colour. It is not certain whether these bones were cremated or not.

*S 62* 2 limb bone frs measuring: 32.6 x 13.3 x 10.4 mm; and 21.1 x 11.0 x 1.6 mm. Both oval in cross-section. Could be parts of a rib or a thumb metacarpal. Found with bronze pin SK 62,3; hence green tinge. It is not certain whether these bones were cremated or not.

*S 63* 22 small frs, many of hand bones. Size range 1.9 mm (length only) to 31.0 x 8.5 x 6.3 mm. Found with a bronze pin and fibulae; hence dark green to brown colour. It is not certain whether these bones were cremated or not.

*S Pyre 2* 85 frs, wt. 68 g; size range 4.2 x 1.3 to 61.0 x 7.3 mm for a rib fr. Largest skull fr. (warped) measured 42.2 x 30.0 x 4.0 mm. Some identifiable frs: skull (10 +), mainly parietal, thickest 5.0 mm; ribs (3 +). In addition the distal half of the ? right humerus of a ? juvenile was restored from 5 separate frs; length 108.0 mm; shaft thickness (no landmarks) 15.9 mm; wt. 14.5 g.

S *Pyre 4A* (upper) 96 quite well cremated frs, wt. 126 g; size range 9.2 × 8.2 to 62.2 × 11.9 mm (limb); 63.0 × 47.1 mm (skull). One third of frs from skull. Small size of supraorbital region and left mastoid process suggested female sex. Also recovered were a fr. of shell and a small piece of copper or bronze.

S *Pyre 4B* (lower) 27 frs, wt. 16 g; size range 6.9 × 3.2 to 35.0 × 10.1 mm. One skull fr. measured 24.3 × 17.4 × 3.0 mm. Two limb bone frs were glued together to make a piece measuring 35.0 × 12.5 × 10.0 mm and vaguely triangular in cross-section; part of a forearm or fibula?

S *Pyre 6* (i). From *above* Pyre 6, disturbed by bulldozer. 4 frs, making up the distal end of the shaft of the ? left humerus of a juvenile, measuring 70.0 × 24.0 × 17.0 mm. Wt. 15 g. (ii). From Pyre 6 proper. 21 frs, wt. 31 g; size range 16.0 × 8.9 to 83.9 × 10.5 mm. Evidence of two individuals: (1) part of a ? *juvenile* ulna formed from two separate frs; and (2) a fr. of a thick *adult* limb bone, measuring 43.4 × 20.0 × 6.0 mm.

S *Pyre 7* 21 frs, wt. 27 g; size range 8.0 × 6.9 to 51.0 × 14.5 mm. With them was found a perforated boar's tusk. Also recovered from the pyre section in the *side* of the bulldozed trench were: 10 rather poorly cremated skull frs, wt. 24 g; size range 8.1 × 6.2 to 56.2 × 46.4 × 7.0 mm.

S *Pyre 9* Comprised: (i) 6 *not* very well cremated frs, wt. 6 g; size range 8.9 × 3.7 to 49.4 × 18.7 mm; and (ii) 33 *well* burnt frs, wt. 14 g; size range 11.0 × 6.8 to 58.0 × 12.5 mm. Total = 39 frs, wt. 20 g.

S *Pyre 12* One unidentifiable fr, measuring 13.9 × 10.2 × 2.9 mm. Nominal wt. 1 g.

S *Pyre 13* c. 143 well cremated frs, wt. 125 g; size range 3.0 × 1.0 to 63.6 × 12.9 mm. Mainly unidentifiable long bone frs.

S *Pyre 15* 27 frs, wt. 27 g; size range 12.6 × 2.6 to 44.6 × 18.9 mm. One small cranial fr. measured 29.7 × 18.9 mm. Probably also from this pyre: *c*. 24 frs, wt. 13 g; size range 5.8 × 3.2 to 32.3 × 18.9 mm. From them were restored: a tibial shaft fr. measuring 55.0 × 3.0 mm; and a portion of a rib 42.0 mm long.

S *Pyre 17* An informative cremation comprising 76 frs, wt. 76 g; size range 9.0 × 3.2 to 57.5 × 13.0 to 70.5 mm (longest). Rib frs seemed to predominate but remains of two individuals could be distinguished:

(1) *Adult* Part of a ? 10th rib 70.5 mm long; part of a clavicle 57.4 mm long; part of a femur 38.5 mm long with a wall thickness of 5.3 mm.

(2) *Child* 2 cranial frs, measuring 44.2 × 13.0 mm and 39.5 × 14.0 mm; an unsided zygomatic bone 23.5 mm long; part of a clavicle at least 53.3 mm long; part of a ?? rib 31.2 mm long. This child was not a baby.


## THE PALIA PERIVOLIA CEMETERY

The majority of the burials in this cemetery were of cremations. Inhumations of unburnt bones are described as such in the text.

P *34* c. 30 very crumbly *unburnt* limb bone frs, wt. 18 g. The largest measured 45.3 × 15.7 mm.

P *39* A few heavily encrusted and eroded *unburnt* frs. Among them were identified 2 lower limb bone frs, too fragile to weigh and restore:

(1) Middle $\frac{1}{3}$ of shaft of an un-sided femur. Gracile, with weak *linea aspera*. Female?

    Fragment length                          143.0 mm

    Maximum diameter: antero-posterior    24.5 mm

    Maximum diameter: transverse        23.5 mm

(2) Very distorted — almost rectangular in cross-section — fr. of shaft of tibia 185.0 mm long.

*P 45* Double inhumation; remains in very poor condition. The surviving frs, wt. 53 g, apparently belonged to an adult of unknown sex aged between 17 and 25 years at death. *Skull:* large part of right frontal region; trace of patent metopic suture; smallish frontal sinus; minimum frontal breadth *c.* 110.0 mm (= 2 × 55.0 mm); max. thickness (on metopic suture) 7.0 mm. *Teeth:* crowns of the following four were examined:

    1.  6⌋ or 7⌋. Wear stage 2.

    2. ⌊8 . Wear stage 2.

    3. 6⌉. Wear stage 2 to 3; caries distally; enamel pearl.

    4. 7⌉. Wear stage 2; caries buccally; enamel pearl; cusp pattern + 4.

*Rest of skeleton:* approximately a dozen other frs, incl. the heads of two hand proximal phalanges. The remains of a herbivore tooth were also recovered.

*P 46* *c.* 40 *unburnt* frs, wt. 24 g. The largest measured 61.0 × 20.0 mm. Also recovered was the crown of a molar tooth very tentatively identified as an unerupted lower 8. The remains could therefore have belonged to a young person.

*P 47* Inhumation. This grave contained extensive remains of a poorly preserved skeleton of an adult male (?). The skull was too friable to restore. It had been laid on its left side, which subsequently collapsed. The outline of the right side was clearly visible. A selection of 9 anterior and 6 cheek teeth (4 lower and 2 upper molars) was examined. Their state of preservation was poor but it was possible to observe that the upper 8s were not very worn, from which two inferences may be drawn: either (i) they had not erupted long before death; or (ii) the lower 8s had not erupted or were congenitally absent. Signs of unerupted or congenitally absent third molars (8s) were also noticed in Toumba 26 and in the occupants of two LH IIIC graves on Xeropolis (AA(s) digging levels 13 + 15 and CC level 16). The rest of the skeleton was well represented: pieces were examined of the vertebral column, ribs, shoulder girdle, arms, hands, pelvic girdle, legs and feet. Though some frs were large, e.g. a portion of the left femur 290.0 mm long, their condition generally was too poor for them to be very informative.

*P Pyre 1* *c.* 20 postcranial frs, wt. 14 g. The longest, though not the largest, was 49.6 mm long.

*P Pyre 11* *c.* 50 frs, wt. 41 g. The longest, though not the largest, was 42.6 mm long.

*P Pyre 12* 1 fr., wt. less than 1 g; length 29.0 mm.

*P Pyre 14A* Uncertainly distinguished from Pyre 14B. A comparatively large cremation: *c.* 151 frs, wt. 234 g. The largest, a fr. of a ? left tibia, measured 87.4 × 28.0 mm and weighed 19 g. Approx. 26 cranial frs were examined: largest measured 34.2 × 25.0 mm. The thickest was 6.0 mm thick. Some equivocal traces of increased trabeculation in the cranial diploë were observed. The remains probably belonged to an adult of average size.

*P Pyre 14B* 25 frs, wt. 48 g. The largest measured 58.5 × 21.4 mm. The appearance of a suture line on a skull fr. from the frontal region, measuring 43.2 × 38.2 × 3.5 mm, suggested that these were the remains of a young person. The robusticity of the limb bone frs, incl. a radius, indicated that they did not belong to a child.

*P Pyre 18* 5 well-cremated frs, wt. 15 g. The longest, a portion of a tibia (?), measured 63.9 mm.

*P Pyre 19* *c.* 17 very undistinguished frs, wt. 9 g. The longest measured 43.1 mm.

*P Pyre 20* 20 well cremated frs. wt. 20 g. The longest measured 59.5 × 15.5 mm.

*P Pyre 23* 8 smallish well cremated frs, wt. 12 g. The largest measured 37.4 × 16.0 mm.

*P Pyre 25* 42 quite well cremated frs, wt. 32 g. The largest measured 48.3 × 21.7 mm.

*P Pyre 26* *c.* 40 moderately well cremated frs, wt. 95 g. The length of the longest, though not the largest, was 67.1 mm.

*P Pyre 27* 8 frs, wt. 24 g. The longest measured 43.5 mm.

*P Pyre 28* 36 frs, wt. 57 g. The largest measured 54.4 × 17.7 mm.

*P Pyre 31* 4 very small frs, wt. 3 g.

*P Pyre 32* 3 small moderately well cremated frs, wt. 3 g. The longest measured 25.0 mm.

*P Pyre 33* 34 frs, wt. *c.* 40 g. The longest limb fr. measured 46.8 mm; the largest skull fr. 34.8 × 28.5 mm. Also examined was one black cranial (?) fr. measuring 26.0 × 18.8 mm, wt. *c.* 1 g. It is not certain whether this specimen is bone. If it is, its black and shiny appearance could be the result of incomplete combustion while it was saturated with or covered by blood.[4]

*P Pyre 34* 15 small frs, wt. 10 g. The longest measured 38.7 × 9.4 mm.

*P Pyre 37* *c* 18 well cremated cranial (1) and postcranial (17) frs, wt. 10 g. The longest measured 42.0 mm.

*P Pyre 38* *c.* 40 small frs, wt. 12 g. The longest measured 32.5 mm.

*P Pyre 39* 17 small, well cremated frs, wt. 10 g. The longest measured 41.2 mm.

*P Pyre 40* *c.* 115 frs, wt. 100 g. The longest, though not the largest, measured 59.0 mm. 3 small, uninformative cranial frs were also examined.

*P Pyre 42* 35 well cremated postcranial frs, wt. 63 g. The largest measured 59.8 × 18.0 mm.

*P Pyre 44* 2 small white frs, wt. 1 g. The longer measured 27.6 mm.


## THE TOUMBA CEMETERY

The majority of the burials in this cemetery were of cremations. Inhumations of unburnt bones are described as such in the text. The biggest and best cremations came from this cemetery.

*T 3* Fr. left clavicle (length 64.0 mm) and fr. 1st rib (?) recovered with large bronze fibula. Nominal wt. 4 g.

*T 5* 3 very small frs of limb bones of young child; the developing crowns of two permanent molar teeth: |6 and 6| . Nominal wt. 4 g.

*T 7* 25 g of *unburnt* remains comprising: *c.* 35 very small skull frs (largest measuring 21.7 × 20.5 mm); a lower ?4 and a lower ?6; proximal end of small right femur (measuring 54.0 × 26.3 mm); and 3 small frs of either burnt bone or stone (largest measuring 24.5 × 12.3 mm). Colour of remains ochre. Condition very poor. Teeth informative: enamel much eroded but still possible to detect some caries on occlusal surface of lower ?6; degree of wear — not great but with some pulp exposed — indicated an age at death of not more than 35 years.

*T 12B* 535 g of inhumed remains comprising: a very crushed skull and ten teeth (combined wt. 225 g); and a few vertebral and limb frs (longest measuring 94.5 mm; combined wt. 310 g). An interesting perforation was observed in the right frontal bone of the skull. It measured 14.0 x 11.0 mm on the outer surface and 12.5 x 5.0 mm on the inner, where it assumed a figure-of-eight outline. Skull wall thick (6.0 mm in centre). There seems little doubt that the hole was pathological. According to Dr. C.J. Hackett 'This perforation might have arisen by the coalescence of several small cavities resulting from an infection which the response of the bone had largely overcome. It could have arisen from a small penetrating wound giving entry to a pyogenic infection' (Hackett. personal communication). Dr. Calvin Wells thinks that the signs are 'characteristic of blood borne metastases from malignant growths' and wonders whether the hole was the result of 'a neoplasm of low malignancy — myeloma perhaps', but adds the cautious rider that 'Trauma in skulls can imitate almost anything' (Wells: personal communication). This perforation recalls a very similar one in the right frontal bone of the skull of skeleton FK 1836 excavated from a Classical tomb at Eretria by the Swiss Archaeological Mission.[5]

The teeth included the upper left 1, ?2, 3 and 4; the upper right 1; the lower left ?1 and ?6; and three unidentified premolars. The wear on $\overline{6}$ (stage 3 + to 4) suggested an age at death of 25 to 35 years. The rest of the teeth were similarly worn. No caries was observed.

*T 14 Urn cremation 1* T 14,1 is one of the three largest and best preserved cremations from Lefkandi. All three deserve to be described in detail.

(i) *General observations*
1. *Condition.* Brittle and warped.
2. *Colour.* Black through grey to yellow and white. A fairly large number of darker pieces indicated that the pyre did not reach a sufficiently high temperature to consume every scrap of organic matter. The back of the skull was not as well cremated as other areas indicating, as one might expect, that the body lay supine throughout most of the funerary rites.
3. *Size:* generally small; largest measured only 48.3 x 14.0 mm. *Number:* too numerous to count. *Weights:* dust 800 g; rest 865 g.
4. *Evidence of pounding* was provided by the small size of the pieces.
5. *Sex:* very difficult to assess: probably male. *Age:* under 40. *Number of individuals in urn:* one.
6. *Signs of multiple cremations.* None.
7. *Pathology.* Very slight traces of osteoarthritic lipping on vertebrae; and of *cribra orbitalia* in roof of right orbit.
8. *Urn goods.* None observed among bones.
9. *Animal bones.* None observed among human bones.

(ii) *Particular observations*
*Skull.* Of the skull approximately 30 fragments, weighing 40 g, were examined. The largest measured 45.0 x 27.0 mm. Quite a large portion of the right frontal bone in the region of the upper lateral corner of the orbit was preserved. The upper rim of the orbit was sharp, a trait common in but not confined to female skulls, in which the supraorbital region is not well developed. Small *cribra orbitalia* were noticed in the roof of the orbit. These cranial bones were thin and generally well cremated.

*Body size.* The following measurements indicate that these bones were part of a larger skeleton than that recovered from T 14,2 but smaller than the Classical adult male skeleton FK 1530 from Eretria. The scores in round brackets represent a rough and ready estimate of the value in the fresh, uncremated bone; the cremated score is taken to be 85% of the fresh one. Information on shrinking is scarce. Van Vark (1970) found that the critical temperature for shrinking was 800°C; little more took place above that temperature. The loss of 15% is somewhat arbitrary and extrapolated from Van Vark's valuable but limited figures, which were not intended to apply to all parts of the skeleton.

(a) *Talus: transverse diameter of superior articular surface*

| | | | |
|---|---|---|---|
| T 14,1 | Right (?) | 32.0 mm | (37.6 mm) |
| T 14,2 | | 25.5 mm | (30.0 mm) |

(b) *Metacarpal I: transverse diameter of the head*

| | | | |
|---|---|---|---|
| T 14,1 | Left (?) | 19.5 mm | (22.9 mm) |
| T 14,2 | approx. | 16.0 mm | (18.8 mm) |
| Eretria FK 1530 | Left | 25.0 mm | |
| Eretria FK 1530 | Right | 26.3 mm | |

(c) *Ulna: transverse diameter of the coronoid process*

| | | | |
|---|---|---|---|
| T 14,1 | Right | 21.8 mm | (25.6 mm) |
| Eretria FK 1530 | Right | 27.8 mm | |

*T 14 Urn cremation 2* T 14,2 is the best preserved and most complete of all the cremations from Lefkandi.

(i) *General observations*

1. *Condition.* Excellent. Hard, brittle, twisted and warped with many bones showing herring-bone breaks.

2. *Colour.* Almost pure white, indicating thorough cremation at high temperature. Body of a lumbar vertebra black: subject supine for most of cremation.

3. *Size:* ranged from minuscule fragments to a piece of the proximal one third of the left ulna measuring 125.3 × 27.7 mm. *Number:* too numerous to count. *Weights:* larger unsorted pieces 1190 g; sorted postcranial pieces 520 g; skull 165 g; jaws and teeth 37 g; dust 240 g.

4. *Evidence of pounding.* The overall size of these bone fragments and the fact that they were placed in an urn are sufficient grounds for believing that an attempt was made to reduce them to a uniform size.

5. *Sex:* very difficult to assess; thought to be female, perhaps lightly built. *Age:* under 35. *Number of individuals in urn:* one.

6. *Signs of multiple cremations.* None.

7. *Pathology.* None observed.

8. *Urn goods.* One piece of iron measuring 31.6 × 14.9 mm.

9. *Animal bones.* A femur of a small rodent or insectivore: an intrusion?

(ii) *Particular observations*

*Skull.* The fragments were weighed (165 g) but not counted. Three pieces were joined to form the glabella and supraorbital region which yielded the following information:

(a) Metopic suture still patent.

(b) Supraorbital notches, and for foramina, transmitted the supraorbital nerves and vessels.

(c) Superior rim of orbits sharp.

(d) Neither glabella nor supraorbital tori very pronounced.

(e) Frontal sinuses moderately pneumatised.

(f) Thickness of the frontal bone fragments ranged from 6.0 to 7.0 mm.

*Jaws and teeth.* The bones of the upper jaw (maxilla) were not recognised but remains of approximately fifteen upper teeth including all six molars were found. These lacked only enamel. Much of the lower jaw (mandible) was reconstructed from well-preserved pieces. Roots of all but $\overline{2|}$ and $\overline{|5}$ were found and replaced in their sockets. Traces of caries (??) were seen on $\overline{6|}$, but it is very difficult to distinguish between destruction by burning and that by caries.

*Rest of skeleton.* A wide range of identifiable pieces was available for study, including 40 to 50 recognisable hand and foot bone fragments. The general impression given by these pieces was that they were small and showed no signs of bone pathology. A score of 37.7 mm (44.4 mm in the fresh state) for the maximum diameter of the head of one femur fell within the range for females.

*T 18 Urn cremation* T 18 is the third most complete cremation from Lefkandi after T 14,1 and T 14,2.

(i) *General observations*

1. *Condition.* Generally excellent. Hard, brittle, twisted and warped.

2. *Colour.* Almost pure white except for blackened chin. An interesting observation indicating that the body lay prone throughout much of the proceedings.

3. *Size:* the largest fragment, from a thin femur (?), measured 105.6 × 26.0 mm. *Number:* too numerous to count. *Weights:* skull and mandible 58 g; rest of skeleton 800 g; dust 310 g.

4. *Evidence of pounding.* The overall size of these bone fragments and the fact that they were placed in an urn are sufficient grounds for believing that an attempt was made to reduce them to a uniform size.

5. *Sex:* very difficult to assess; thought to be male. *Age:* adult of unknown age. *Number of individuals in urn:* one.

6. *Signs of multiple cremations.* None.

7. *Pathology.* None observed.

8. *Urn goods.* None observed among bones.

9. *Animal bones.* One cockle shell.

(ii) *Particular observations*

*Skull.* The thirty or so fragments examined gave the impression of being thin and of having belonged to a small skull.

*Jaws and teeth.* Corpus of mandible from region of 6 on each side to symphysis preserved; alveoli (sockets) destroyed and missing. Genial tubercles and digastric pits well marked (male traits). Architecture of chin also male; outline straight transversely and concave inferiorly. Roots of four unidentified anterior teeth examined: adult. One fragment of molar enamel also examined: uninformative.

*T 22* 4 small frs weighing less than 1 g and making part of a small tubular bone measuring 40.3 × 10.5 mm. Wrong shape – too tubular – to have been part of an adult fibula or even metacarpal. Could easily have belonged to arm or leg of child. Greater precision impossible. Bone stained green; lain near copper or bronze. Found with small white faience disc (diam. 3.0 mm).

*T 26* The fragmentary and inhumed remains from this grave belonged to an adult aged between 25 and 35 years at death. Of the skull only very eroded frs, wt. 95 g, were recovered. Reconstruction not attempted. A good selection of loose teeth was preserved. They may be charted as follows:

R

L

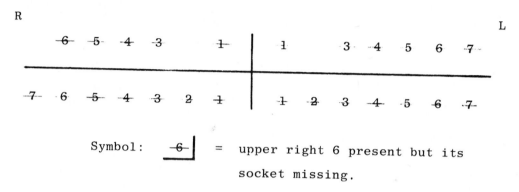

Symbol:    —6⌋    =   upper right 6 present but its

socket missing.

*Notes on teeth.* 1. With the exception of  7⌋  the missing teeth were all absent on both sides. This observation increases the probability that one or more of the 8s, top and bottom, either never erupted or failed to develop. The recovery of the unerupted crown of an upper 8 lends weight to the former suggestion. Attention has already been drawn to signs of congenitally absent third molars in P 47 and in the occupants of two LH IIIC graves on Xeropolis (AA(s) digging levels 13 + 15 and CC level 16). It is quite possible that both upper 2s of T 26 were also congenitally absent. 2. The wear on the molars ranged from stage 2 (⌊7 ) to 3 + ( 6⌋ and  6⌉), consistent with an age of 25 to 35 years. 3. No caries was observed.

Of the rest of the skeleton numerous eroded and compressed frs, mainly of long bones, were lifted. They were too friable to develop from their compact earth matrix.

*T 27* 2 unidentifiable frs, wt. 2.0 g; dimensions of larger 33.6 × 9.9 mm.

*T 31* 5 frs of ? *unburnt* bone.

(i) 3 very small frs of a ? finger bone; lengths 9.0; 6.3; and 2.4 mm.

(ii) 2 frs of a ? metacarpal or ? rib, measuring (1) 34.0 × 7.8 × 1.0 mm; and (2) 27.7 × 7.8 × 1.7 mm.

All frs bore dark and browny green stains indicating close proximity to copper or bronze object. In fact found near bronze vase T 31,6 and gold ring T 31,5.

*T 32* 8 small *unburnt* frs of limb bone or rib, wt. 2 g. Longest measured 24.5 × 8.5 mm; largest 21.0 × 11.2 mm. Brittle but not too eroded. Greenish hue (copper or bronze).

*T 36* Crowns of four teeth (three permanent and one ? deciduous): ⌊6 or ⌊7 ; 6⌋; 6⌉ ; and ?? ⌈d . Could have belonged to a six year-old child. Identified from a photograph; originals not examined. It is not certain whether these teeth were cremated or not.

*T Pyre 2*  c. 80 not too well cremated frs, wt. 32 g. Longest fr. 42.2 mm long. Also found were roots of  1⌉ and  ?2⌉ and an upper 5 of a fully adult subject.

*T Pyre 4* A solitary fr. measuring 37.7 × 17.0 mm, wt. 3 g. Impossible to identify but ridge ran obliquely down its length; could be part of a weak femur or even part of a tibia.

*T Pyre 5* Two small collections of bones were excavated separately from this pyre.

(i) From Pyre 5 proper. *c.* 60 small frs. wt. 36 g. Length of longest, but not largest, 62.0 mm. Not too well cremated; diploë of skull fr. very black. Interesting skull fr., measuring 59.0 × 47.0 mm, from ? parietal region: thin cortex; thickish diploë: max. thickness of parietal wall 6.0 mm. Sex: one fr. of sharp interosseous border of a radius or ulna, measuring 38.2 × 10.4 mm, appeared too gracile to have belonged to a male; therefore ?? female.

(ii) From Pyre 5 (North). 7 moderately well cremated limb bone frs, wt. 7 g. The two largest measured: (1) 28.6 × 18.5 mm; and (2) 24.8 × 22.6 mm; both from leg(?).

*T Pyre 6 c.* 22 small limb bone frs, wt. 13 g. Fr. of radius or ulna measuring 35.4 × 10.5 mm; one of fibula 29.4 × 10.6 mm. Both interesting: each tubular with patent lumen. Frs looked small; from a small person.

*T Pyre 8* 17 moderately well cremated limb bone frs, wt. 30 g. Slightly larger than many preserved from other cremations: largest measured 65.0 × 17.0 mm; probably from a humerus (position of nutrient foramen); if so perhaps belonged to a robust male.

*T Square VI* from depth 30 cm (1.50 S, 1.0 E)

2 *unburnt* frs of a ? left femur, wt. 46 g.

(1) Portion just below lesser trochanter.

| | |
|---|---|
| Fragment length | 56.0 mm |
| Subtrochanteric diameter: antero-posterior | ?21.5 mm |
| Subtrochanteric diameter: transverse | ?28.6 mm |
| Platymeric index | ?75.2% |

(2) Middle $\frac{1}{3}$ of shaft.

| | |
|---|---|
| Fragment length | 102.0 mm |
| Midshaft diameter: antero-posterior | ?26.0 mm |
| Midshaft diameter: transverse | ?25.0 mm |

Colour: light ochre; centre very white where broken.

Condition: dry crumbly, brittle and eroded.


## DISCUSSION

It was not easy to determine the *number* of individuals buried in the Lefkandi cemeteries. For example, when only a gram or so of bone was recovered (a topic we shall return to shortly), it seemed difficult to accept that this solitary fragment represented all the earthly remains of one individual. Moreover, when the material is so scanty to start with there is always the possibility that one or two token interments may inadvertently have been overlooked, as happened to S 16 and S 53. The following estimates of the number of individuals buried in each of the cemeteries must be regarded as extremely tentative. They are based entirely on the remains examined by this author and take no account of any tombs or pyres that yielded no human remains to be examined.

(a) *Skoubris.* Approximately 24 individuals, including perhaps 3 young people of indeterminate age. Also included in the estimate are S 16 and S 53, which were not seen by this author.

(b) *Palia Perivolia*. Approximately 28 individuals, including at least 1 young person.

(c) *Toumba*. Approximately 19 individuals, including perhaps 3 young people.

About the *ages* of these people it was equally difficult to obtain very much reliable information. However, the most complete burials confirmed that adults tended to die quite young. For example P 45, P Pyre 14B, T 7, T 12B, T 14,1, T 14,2 and T 26 all died in the prime of life, say between 17 and 40 years. The young persons recovered from all three cemeteries indicate that child mortality too was probably high (see S Pyres 2, 6, and 17; P 46; and T 5, T 22 and T 36). The evidence for such statements about child mortality is of necessity not particularly reliable. For example T 36 comprised, as we have seen, only the crowns of four teeth (3 permanent and 1 deciduous).

An attempt was made to determine the *sex* of both unburnt and cremated remains by means of a number of well-known techniques.[6] Despite these efforts it is impossible to say anything significant about the *sex ratios* of the occupants. All that can be said is that both males and females were buried in the cemeteries (males: P 47; T 14,1, T 18, T Pyre 8; females: T 14,2, T Pyre 5). In fact it was satisfying to observe such sex differences if for no other reason than that they indicate that these cemeteries were shared by both sexes. It is risky to assume that both men and women were always buried together in the same cemetery. For example, this author found that of the Minoan skeletons buried in a communal tomb at Myrtos Pyrgos, southern Crete, very few, if any, could be identified confidently as female.[7]

No complete limb bones were recovered. Hence no biological assessment of *stature* could be made. The heights of the occupants of P 45, P 47, T 12B and T 26, recorded above in metres, must therefore be regarded as estimates, albeit perfectly reasonable ones: P 45 ($5'1''$ and $5'1''$); P 47 ($5'10\frac{3}{4}''$); T 12B ($5'1''$); and T 26 ($5'3''$). With the exception of P 47 they were apparently not very tall.

The *health* of the Lefkandians buried in these cemeteries was probably not very robust. Obviously cremated bones, and fragmentary ones at that, are not very informative on this matter. However, we have already observed that life expectancy was generally rather low. We can also say that T 14,1 had begun to suffer from osteoarthritis, as had three people buried in the Settlement on Xeropolis.

One hotly debated question in Aegean palaeopathology is whether *malaria* was endemic in the region in prehistoric times. The evidence is indirect and is based on the observations that (1) the highest incidence of the blood disorder sickle-cell anaemia occurs in those parts of the world where malaria is endemic; (2) those who inherit sickle-cell anaemia in its most severe form die young; and (3) those who are afflicted less severely, though they are weakened by it, nevertheless acquire thereby some protection against malaria and can produce fertile offspring.[8] As sickle-cell anaemia is a blood dyscrasia it leaves its mark on those areas of the body where the production of red blood cells takes place, namely the marrow spaces in the bones and especially in the diploë of the cranial vault of young people. Consequently it has been argued that if a large number of human bones is recovered from an archaeological site displaying the signs of sickle-cell anaemia and even thalassaemia then malaria was endemic in the population.[9] There are flaws in this argument, not the least being the unreliability of observations based solely on the macroscopic examination of material which is frequently very poorly preserved. Nor is there evidence that it was universally distributed at a high level of incidence throughout the Eastern Mediterranean at this time as this author observed in his radiographic screening of the Minoan remains from Myrtos Pyrgos mentioned above and as Angel himself acknowledges.[10]

It is, however, worthwhile recording that four subjects from Lefkandi (3 from the Cemeteries; 1 from Xeropolis) did exhibit a few signs, all of them equivocal, of some form of blood disorder. They were:

1. P 14: increased trabeculation in the cranial diploë.
2. T 14,1: traces of *cribra orbitalia.* For a discussion of the possible connexion between this condition and haemoglobin disease see Steinbock.[11]
3. T Pyre 5: thickened diploë of cranial vault.
4. Xeropolis burial DD level 21, Nbk. find 18, p. 32: perforated right frontal bone with small *cribra orbitalia.*

One of the principal aims of a study such as this is to inquire whether the human remains themselves can tell us a little more about *the techniques employed to dispose of the dead.* In the case of cremations this anthropological investigation can be divided into sections dealing with the cremation itself and the subsequent interment.

The remains from the Lefkandi Cemeteries will probably not add very much to our knowledge in this interesting field. However, the recovery of a herbivore's tooth from P 45 and of shell fragments from S Pyres 4A and 7 and from T 18 may suggest either the provision of food for the journey to the next world, or a funeral feast or sacrifice on the part of the mourners.

However, few animal remains were found. For example the three most complete cremations (T 14,1; T 14,2; and T 18) yielded only one cockle shell and such evidence is too slight to justify any conclusion. The bones may have been collected carefully and distinguished from those of sacrifice or feast.[12]

The same three Toumba cremations tell us in what position each body lay for much of the period that it was being consumed by the flames. We have already observed that the back of the skull of T 14,1 and the body of one lumbar vertebra of T 14,2 were less well burnt than the rest of the skeleton, from which it is reasonable to infer that the bodies had remained supine for a long time. It was the chin however of T 18 that was similarly affected. His blackened chin does not necessarily indicate that he was placed on his pyre in a prone position: 'As the pyre began to collapse and shrink the body would tilt, perhaps turn right over, perhaps disintegrate into several parts . . .'.[13]

At this point we should perhaps consider the difficult problem of interpreting the small collection of apparently *unburnt* bones, and question whether in any case these indicate inhumation.

The first point to be borne in mind is that the presence of a few unburnt bones or even an almost complete skeleton does not prove that no attempt was made to cremate the body initially. This is especially true when the apparently unburnt bones in question are very few in number and very friable. Both Lisowski and Gejvall have drawn attention to the tendency of 'poorly combusted cremations' to 'crumble into unrecognizable dust owing to decay'.[14] Of greater relevance to this discussion of Greek cremations are the reports by Shear, Blegen and Iakovides of incompletely burnt bones from the Athenian Agora and from Perati.[15] Pertinent too are the following figures recorded by Robinson.[16] Of the 53 cremations that he excavated at Olynthus he found that 'skeletal remains' could be identified in 30 of them; that in 6 the orientation could be determined; and that in 5 of these 6 'the bones were not greatly disarranged'.

In the absence of any evidence to the contrary therefore one could argue that cremation was the order of the day at Lefkandi and that *all* the unburnt material came from rather badly organised cremations. This of course is far too rash a claim to make for 'as has often been pointed out, cremation was never universally practised in Greece but went alongside inhumation'.[17] Moreover, there is clear archaeological evidence that at least five of the burials in the Lefkandi Cemeteries were inhumations.

It may be prudent therefore to subdivide all this questionable material into four categories as follows:

1. Remains which certainly came from inhumations: P 45 (double), P 47; T 12B and T 26.
2. Remains which probably came from inhumations: S 36; P 39, P 46; T 7 and Toumba Square VI.
3. Unburnt bones almost certainly collected from cremations: S 38, S 59, S 62, S 63; T 31 and T 32.
4. Remains about whose disposal it is probably impossible to say anything precise: P 34; T 36 (and S 16 and S 53 — not seen by this author).

This anthropological classification agrees substantially with one prepared independently by Mr. Hugh Sackett, the main difference being the transfer of S 38, S 39, S 62, S 63 and T 32 from category 4 to category 3. We may safely conclude therefore that both inhumation and cremation were practised at Lefkandi; but that sometimes the mourners were content with collecting a few rather poorly combusted pieces of bone.

This brings us to a consideration of the subsequent interment, the second field in which the bones can cast some anthropological light. The mourners had the choice of either leaving the bones where they lay after the fire had gone out (or been extinguished); or they could gather together as many or as few of the bones as they wished for interment within or without a special receptacle.

Anyone who has read the descriptions of the individual burials might suspect that the Lefkandi cremations were distinguished by their scantiness. A study of some of the available literature on ancient cremations would confirm this suspicion. It would also reveal that while the Lefkandi cremations were particularly sparse, ancient cremations generally were rather light. For example Lisowski stated that whereas a substantial cremation might weigh about 2,000 g, 'weights of 10 g are quite frequent'.[18] Similarly Weiner observed a 'high fequency of burials below 400 gms in weight' among the cremations from Dorchester-on-Thames, with 72% (84 out of 117) weighing 800 g or less.[19] Of the cremations from the Oakley Cottage Romano-British cemetery near Cirencester, Gloucestershire, Wells found that no body was 'anything like completely retrieved' and few were more than 20% complete.[20] Of 212 Anglo-Saxon urns from Illington, Norfolk, that Wells examined only 104 contained cremated remains and the 'amount of surviving material varied greatly from one burial to another. Urn 153 contained only a single fragment; Urn 126 contained 2,863 and others perhaps even more'.[21] Finally we must mention the cremations from Olynthus and Perati. Of the 53 cremations from Olynthus 15 contained 'large coarse amphorae', of which many 'were found to contain ashes and a few even bones. . . . In no case were all the bones in the amphora.' These amphorae Robinson regarded as *osteothekai* to receive the bones after 'an attempt had been made to pick up the bones from the ashes'.[22] At Perati 'not more than a third (tomb 157) and sometimes as little as a fortieth part (tomb 36) of the skeleton . . . was collected'.[23] More will be said about the Perati cremations later.

The extreme scantiness of the Lefkandi material is emphasised dramatically when the

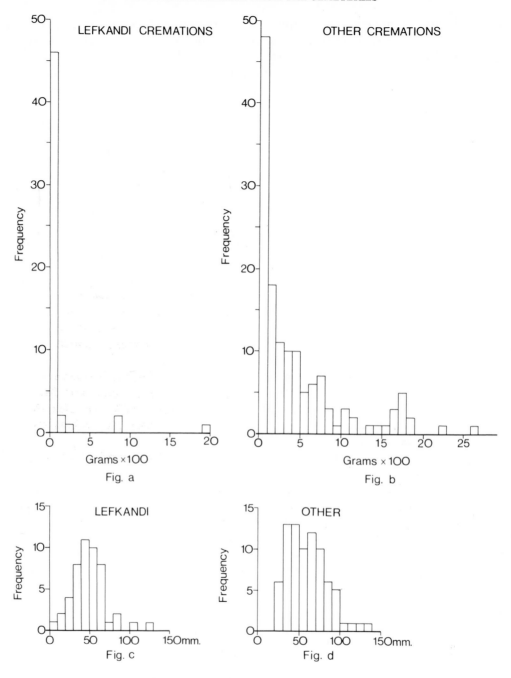

FIG. a. Weight frequencies of Lefkandi cremations.

FIG. b. Weight frequencies of cremations described by Denston,[41] Lisowski,[42] Lisowski & Spence,[43] Paidoussis & Sbarounis,[44] Spence,[45] and Musgrave.[46]

FIG. c. Frequencies of maximum lengths of postcranial fragments in Lefkandi cremations. Sample size = 49; mean = 50.98 mm; standard deviation = 21.71 mm.

FIG. d. Frequencies of maximum lengths of poscranial fragments in cremations described by Denston,[47] Lisowski,[48] Spence,[49] and Musgrave.[50] Sample size = 79; mean = 59.87 mm; standard deviation = 23.87 mm.

weights and their frequencies are expressed graphically on a histogram (Fig. a) and compared (Fig. b) with scores culled from cremation reports by Denston,[24] Lisowski,[25]
Lisowski and Spence,[26] Paidoussis and Sbarounis,[27] Spence,[28] and Musgrave.[29] This mode
of presentation is similar to that employed by Weiner in his report on the Dorchester
cremations.[30] The paucity of the 52 Lefkandi cremations plotted on Fig. a is further
emphasised when it is pointed out that 46 of them (88.46%) weighed less than 100 g. Of
the 139 comparative cremations plotted on Fig. b only 48 (34.53%) weighed less than
100 g. If the critical level is fixed at 50 g then the contrast becomes even starker: 76.92%
(40 out of 52) of the Lefkandi cremations weighed less than 50 g; whereas only 23.02%
(32 out of 139) of the comparative series weighed less than 50 g.

However, fuller cremated remains have been found in Geometric Greece. A collection
of 13 Geometric cremations from Lower Gypsades, Knossos, was quite substantial. Their
weight ranged from 150 g to 1,650 g, with a median of 500 g, a mean of 613.85 g and a
standard deviation of 393.64 g.[31] These cremations were apparently larger than the 12
from Perati described by Paidoussis and Sbarounis. Their weight ranged from c. 1 g to
1,741 g, with a median of 410 g, a mean of 498.67 g and a standard deviation of 502.92 g
(author's own statistics). The intact urn cremations from Lefkandi, T 14,1, T 14,2 and T 18
are comparable with these in volume.

Fragment length was also studied in case evidence should emerge which indicated that
attempts had been made to reduce the token burials in size as well as volume. Data on
fragment lengths have been collected and recorded for some years. For example, such
authorities as Weiner, Wells, Lisowski and Gejvall have shown that the bones recovered
from European cremations generally range in length from 'minute splinters'[32] to 'pieces
a couple of decimetres in length',[33] with an average size of about 15 to 20 mm. The
presence of a large number between 10 and 20 mm long is taken to indicate deliberate
pounding by the mourners to reduce all the bones to a uniform and convenient size, a
practice still carried out in modern crematoria.[34] It is of course easy to forget that bones
do not always crack and break into several pieces of their own accord. Indeed Denston
has reported the recovery of a complete radius 225 mm long from a Neolithic cremation on
the Isle of Man.[35] Several other very long fragments were also recovered from this site,
for example portions of a fibula 213 mm long and of a femur 204 mm long. Clearly these
had not been pounded.

No attempt was made to calculate the mean length of the bones from each cremation.
Such an endeavour would have been pointless given the enormous range in the lengths of
the individual fragments. A more informative way of comparing the lengths of the Lefkandi
remains with those from elsewhere was to take only the longest piece from each. These
frequencies are reproduced on Figs c and d. The comparative series was, with one or two
minor differences, the same as that used in the comparison of weights. It will be seen at
once that the longest bones of the Lefkandi cremations were not very much shorter than
those of the comparative series. The means and standard deviations recorded in the legends
to these Figures confirm this observation. It is perhaps interesting to record that the mean
maximum length of the 13 Geometric cremations from Lower Gypsades, Knossos,[36] was
considerably higher than that of the Lefkandi cremations: 71.38 mm (standard deviation
15.85 mm) as opposed to 50.98 mm (standard deviation 21.71 mm).

There is therefore every reason to believe that some of the cremated bones from
Lefkandi had been pounded, as were some from Perati.[37] For example the bones of T 14,1
were particularly small; whereas those from T 14,2 and T 18 were larger and may not have

been broken up so assiduously. In the case of T 14,2, however, it is interesting to recall that remains of all six upper molar teeth were found but all traces of their sockets had vanished. This indicates either that the skull was lifted from the pyre intact and subsequently smashed deliberately; or that the mourners sifted the ashes with exceptional thoroughness.

Relevant to the question of pounding the bones are the related ones of (i) how long was allowed to elapse between the cooling of the pyre and the collection of the bones; and (ii) whether any attempt was made to clean them before burial. As a lot of pyre dust was still clinging to most of the bones examined it is probably safe to conclude that bones were taken straight from the fire and buried without further ado.

The burial of minute quantities of grimy bones at Lefkandi would appear to accord with the contemporary beliefs in the fate of the body after death. As Mylonas has pointed out, 'the bones had no significance after they were deprived of the flesh which covered them'.[38] It could be argued that such a casual attitude towards the bones themselves is at variance with the provision of an eye-catching receptacle to contain them. But human nature can always be invoked to account for such apparent inconsistencies, for example 'the human frailty of wanting to impress others with costliness of offerings or to stress the superior status of the deceased'.[39] It may be significant that Homer described the costly gold urn which contained Patroclus' bones and the shroud of purple linen that covered it, but made no reference to any attempt being made to clean them beforehand. Perhaps it was not necessary: they were after all ὀστέα λευκά (Iliad XXIII, 252–254). However the discovery of traces of cloth *inside* metal urns from Attica[40] suggests that cremated bones were sometimes treated with touching respect.

## CONCLUDING REMARKS

The general conclusion to be drawn from a study of these cremations is that the Lefkandian men and women were not particularly long lived; and that when they cremated their dead they performed the rites with creditable competence. For the task of collecting the last remains they apparently had little enthusiasm, the volume of bone gathered being in most cases unusually small. There is every reason to believe that both men and women were buried in these cemeteries; and that children too were cremated, as they were elsewhere, for example at Perati.

## APPENDIX C

1. I would like to thank Mr. Hugh Sackett for inviting me to study these remains, and for his hospitality; Mr. Gordon Purdy for assisting me on my first visit to Eretria; Mr. C. B. Denston, Professor F.P. Lisowski, Mr. T.F. Spence and Professor J.S. Weiner for setting excellent examples in the writing of cremation reports for me to follow; Dr. C.J. Hackett and the late Dr. Calvin Wells for palaeopathological diagnoses; and the Calouste Gulbenkian Foundation, the Royal Society and the National Hellenic Research Foundation for financing two visits to Eretria, in 1972 and 1974.

2. E. Breitinger in W. Kraiker and K. Kübler *Kerameikos* I (1939) 223 ff.; N.G. Gejvall in D. Brothwell and E. Higgs *Science in Archaeology* (2nd ed.)(1969) 468 ff.; F.P. Lisowski in T. Bielicki *Anthropologie und Humangenetik* (1968) 76 ff.; D.M. Robinson *Excavations at Olynthus* XI (1942); T.F. Spence *PPS* 33 (1967) 70 ff.; G.N. Van Vark *Some statistical procedures for the investigation of prehistoric skeletal material* (2nd ed.)(Rijksuniversiteit te

Groningen, 1970); G.N. Van Vark *Ossa* 1 (1974) 63 ff.; J.S. Weiner in R.J.C. Atkinson, C.M. Piggott and N.K. Sanders *Excavations at Dorchester, Oxon* (1951) 129 ff.; C. Wells *Antiquity* 34 (1960) 29 ff.

3. Cf. Wells op. cit.

4. Cf. F.E. Camps *Medical and Scientific Investigations in the Christie Case* (1953); and D.R. Brothwell *Digging up Bones* (2nd ed.) (1972).

5. A study of the human remains from Tombs FK 1530, FK 1534, FK 1833 and FK 1836 at Eretria is in preparation by the present author.

6. J.D. Boyd and J.C. Trevor in K. Simpson *Modern Trends in Forensic Medicine* (1953) 133 ff.; D.R. Brothwell *op. cit.*; F.E. Camps and J.M. Cameron *Practical Forensic Medicine* (1971); G.A. Dorsey *Boston med. surg. J.* 137 (1897) 80 ff.; T. Dwight *Am. J. Anat.* 4 (1905) 19 ff.; N.G. Gejvall op. cit.; S. Genoves in D. Brothwell and E. Higgs *Science in Archaeology* (2nd ed.) (1969) 429 ff.; *Gray's Anatomy* (35th ed.) (1973); R.J. Harrison in F.E. Camps *Medical and Scientific Investigations in the Christie Case* (1953) 74 ff.; W.M. Krogman *The Human Skeleton in Forensic Medicine* (1962); F.P. Lisowski op. cit.; F.G. Parsons *J. Anat. Physiol., Lond.* 48 (1914) 238 ff.; K. Pearson and J. Bell *Drap. Co. Res. Mem. biom. Ser.* 10 (1919); T.D. Stewart in F.E. Camps *Gradwohl's Legal Medicine* (3rd ed.) (1976) 109 ff.; F.P. Thieme and W.J. Schull *Hum. Biol.* 29 (1957) 242 ff.; Van Vark op. cit.

7. A study of the human remains from the Middle to Late Minoan village at Myrtos, Pyrgos, in southern Crete is in preparation by the present author.

8. Cf. A.C. Allison *Br. med. J.* 1 (1954) 290 ff.; *Scient. Am.* 195 (1956) 87 ff.; *Cold Spring Harb. Symp. quant. Biol.* 29 (1964) 137 ff.

9. J.L. Angel *Am. J. phys. Anthrop.* 22 (1964) 369 ff.; *Science, N.Y.* 153 (1966) 760 ff.; in D.R. Brothwell and A.T. Sandison *Diseases in Antiquity* (1967) 378 ff.; *The People of Lerna* (1971).

10. J.L. Angel *The People of Lerna* (1971) 78.

11. R.T. Steinbock *Paleopathological Diagnosis and Interpretation* (1976) 239 ff.

12. Cf. Achilles' instructions for the cleaning of Patroclus' bones in *Iliad* XXIII, 238—42. For a discussion of the difficulty in reconstructing ritual from scanty remains, see G.G.E. Mylonas in A.J.B. Wace and F.H. Stubbings *A Companion to Homer* (1963) 478 ff.

13. Wells op. cit.

14. F.P. Lisowski op. cit.

15. Cf. T.L. Shear *Hesperia* 2 (1933) 451 ff.; C.W. Blegen *Hesperia* 21 (1952) 279 f; S.E. Iakovides *Perati* 2 (1970).

16. D.M. Robinson loc. cit.

17. G.G.E. Mylonas loc. cit.

18. F.P. Lisowski loc. cit.

19. J.S. Weiner loc. cit.

20. C. Wells *Trans. Bristol archaeol. Soc.* 81 (1963) 60 ff.

21. C. Wells *Antiquity* 34 (1960) 29 ff.

22. D.M. Robinson loc. cit.

23. *Perati* 2.

24. C.B. Denston *PPS* 31 (1965) 49 ff.; *Proc. Soc. Antiq. Scotland* 98 (1966) 73 ff.; 100 (1968) 96 ff.; 104 (1972) 59 ff., 133 ff.; *Trans. Dumfries. & Galloway nat. Hist. & antiq. Soc.* 46 (1969) 84 ff., 98 ff.; *Proc. Suffolk Inst.* 33 (1973) 43 ff.; *Cremation and inhumation remains from a Neolithic site at Ballaharra, Isle of Man*, unpublished MS; *Archaeol. J.* 131 (1974) 22 ff., 27ff, 93 ff.; *J. Northampton. Mus. & Art Gallery* 11 (1974) 56 ff.

25. F.P. Lisowski in T.G.E. Powell and G.E. Daniel *Barclodiad y Gawres* (1956) 62 ff.; *Proc. Soc. Antiq. Scotland* 89 (1956) 83 ff.; *J. Soc. Antiq. Ireland* 89 (1959) 26 ff.; in S. Piggott *The West Kennet Long Barrow* (1962) 90 ff.

26. F.P. Lisowski and T.F. Spence *Archaeologia Cambrensis* 120 (1971) 64 ff.

27. M. Paidoussis and Ch.N. Sbarounis *Opuscula Atheniensia* 11 (1975) 129 ff.

28. T.F. Spence *Trans. Birmingham archaeol. Soc.* 81 (1964) 139 ff.; *Trans. Dumfries. & Galloway nat. Hist. & antiq. Soc.* 42 (1965) 54 ff.; 44 (1967) 97 ff.

29. J.H. Musgrave *The cremations from the Geometric tomb on the Ephraimoglou Estate, Lower Gypsades, Knossos, Crete*, unpublished MS.

30. J.S. Weiner op. cit., fig. 32.

31. See n. 29 above.

32. J.S. Weiner op. cit., 129 ff.

33. N.G. Gejvall loc. cit.

34. Ibid.

35. C.B. Denston in unpublished MS on Ballahara, see n. 24 above.

36. See n. 29 above.

37. *Perati* 2; *Opuscula Atheniensia* 11 (1975) 129 ff.

38. G.G.E. Mylonas loc. cit.

39. S.A. Immerwahr *Agora Picture Book no. 13* (1973).

40. D.C. Kurtz and J. Boardman *Greek Burial Customs* (1971).

41. See n. 24 above.

42. See n. 25 above.

43. See n. 26 above.

44. See n. 27 above.

45. See n. 28 above.

46. See n. 29 above.

47. See n. 24 above.

48. See n. 25 above.

49. See n. 28 above.

50. See n. 29 above.

# Appendix D

# Analyses of Bronze and Other Base Metal Objects from the Cemeteries

R. E. JONES

This report forms a preliminary account of the results of analyses by X-ray fluorescence (XRF) of a representative number of base metal, principally bronze, objects from the three main cemeteries.[1] The aims of this study were (1) to examine the nature of the metals alloyed with copper and their range of contents within and between groups of similar objects, (2) to clarify the identification of some problematic objects composed either of bronze or iron or a combination of these metals and (3) to provide, where possible, independent evidence for archaeological/typological proposals regarding suspected imports and the grouping or matching of objects.

## METHOD

The analyses were made non-destructively by XRF using the Isoprobe.[2] The two sources of excitation were an Americium 241 gamma source for tin, silver and antimony fluorescence, and an X-ray source operated at 15 kV and 0.7 mA for the remaining elements. Quantitative determinations of the copper, tin, lead, arsenic, zinc and Ni contents were made by reference to calibrations prepared from standards of known composition. Operating conditions in the museum were such that the calibrations had to be checked at least twice each working day. The state of preservation of the bronzes varied considerably; some of the objects had received conservation treatment in the form of a coating of polyvinyl applied over the cleaned metal surface. The quality of the surface prepared for analysis was graded,[3] and the detection limits were tin (Sn) 0.5%, iron (Fe) 0.5%, zinc (Zn) 1%, nickel (Ni) 0.5%, lead (Pb) 1% and arsenic (As) 1%.

The problems and limitations associated with the determination of composition by this technique, such as the effects of surface enrichment and compositional heterogeneity, especially for tin and arsenic, have been discussed by many workers in this field;[4] the latter factor, through segregation effects, should especially be borne in mind. Reproducibility measurements of the tin content determinations were associated with a coefficient of variation of 10%; the overall error in the tin content (in the range of 0–15%) was estimated to be 15% of the given tin content for a prepared metal surface with little (B) or no (A) cuprous oxide present as corrosion contaminating product. Above 15%, and in those objects containing lead in excess of 10%, the error was approximately ±20%. The corresponding figures for lead and iron up to concentrations of 15 and 10% respectively were ±25%. A special problem arose with those bronzes containing particularly high tin, lead and iron contents for which none of the standards was appropriate. In this case, a semi-quantitative estimation of the contents of these metals was made by reference to calibrations obtained from standards prepared later in the laboratory consisting of copper, lead and iron oxides mixed together in varying concentrations with respect to each other in powder form. These standards covered the concentration ranges of these metals from 10–50%.

## RESULTS AND DISCUSSION

The analyses are presented by cemetery and according to type of object in Table 1 (a–c). Of the approximately 171 objects classed as bronze, 110 were analysed; breaking this figure down for each cemetery, the percentages of bronzes analysed to the numbers found were 73, 55 and 95 for Toumba, Skoubris and Palia Perivolia respectively.

The main features of the composition data are (a) the high proportion of tin bronzes.[5] The distribution of tin contents (Fig. 1) is wide with a peak in the 5–7% range, and only 4% of the analysed bronze objects are composed of copper alone or copper with less than 1% tin; (b) the high incidence of leaded bronzes (Fig. 2); 46% of the objects contain more than 1% lead; (c) the surprising feature of detectable amounts of iron, 30% of the bronze objects containing more than 1% of this metal (Fig. 3). That the presence of iron in these objects may be associated with a poor quality analytical surface, or may result from serious contamination due to burial conditions and/or proximity to iron objects merits serious consideration. The first objection may be discounted since examination of the grading of the surfaces (in Table 1) of the iron-rich bronze objects indicates that they are in no way inferior to those of the remainder. Secondly, the concurrence of both iron and iron-rich bronze objects

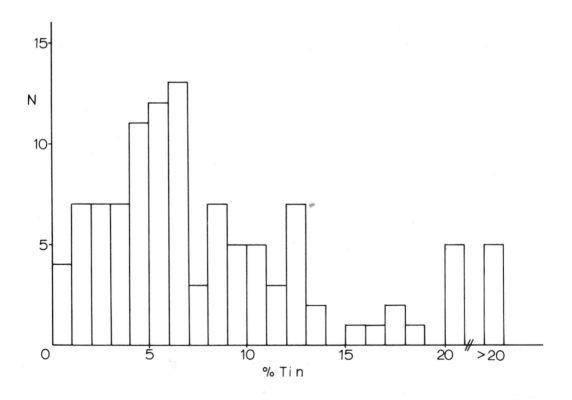

FIG. 1. The distribution of tin contents of all the bronze objects analysed.[6]

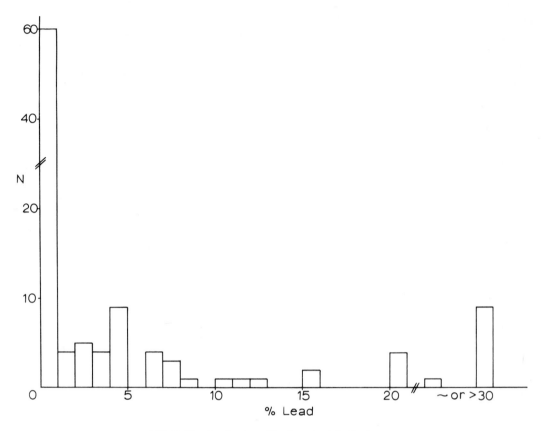

FIG. 2. The distribution of lead contents in the bronzes.

within a tomb is found to be limited in extent. Among these bronzes containing more than 1% iron, only seven (T 27,9, T 13,23 and 24, S 33,17, S Pyre 4,1, P 23,15 and P Pyre 4,5,1) were found in tombs which also yielded iron objects. The remainder in this category of bronzes were from contexts in which iron objects were absent. Conversely, there are several instances of the juxtaposition of iron objects and bronzes which lack iron in their compositions.

Table 1 includes the straightforward identification of a small number of the non-bronze objects.

Grouping the objects from all three cemeteries into the three main periods, (a) SM, (b) PG, and (c) SPG, the distributions for the tin contents may be examined. Some distinction between those for (a) SM and (b) PG on the one hand and (c) SPG on the other is apparent, the latter being very broad (Fig. 4). Those for lead are rather similar; the percentages of objects having more than 1% lead in the three periods are 39, 42 and 47% respectively, and the SPG period exhibits the broadest span of lead contents. These figures are higher than the corresponding value (31%) for decorative Geometric period bronzes mainly from N. Greece reported by Craddock.[7] There are two SM bronzes which contain iron (S 60.4 and S 22.5), but the incidence of iron in bronze is otherwise restricted to the LPG and SPG periods.

The bronze fibulae account for approximately 45% of the bronze objects from the

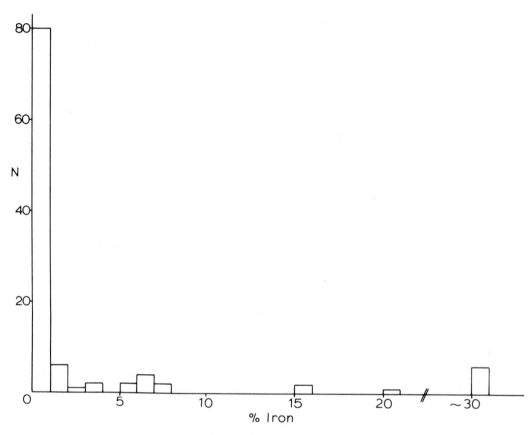

FIG. 3. The distribution of iron contents in the bronzes.

cemeteries, and 67 of these were analysed representing 61% of all the objects analysed; the corresponding figures are 66, 64 and 50% for the Toumba, Skoubris and Palia Perivolia cemeteries respectively. Examination of the tin contents of the fibulae according to cemetery reveals contrasting wide and narrow distributions in the Toumba and Skoubris examples (mean 9.7 and 5.3% tin) respectively (Fig. 5). The Palia Perivolia group is too small for direct comparison, but its distribution tends towards that of Toumba rather than Skoubris. This situation is paralleled, but to a lesser extent, in the lead content distribution (Fig. 6); five of the objects in the Toumba group have lead contents in excess of 25%, and in addition they all contain both tin (with one exception) and iron greater than 15%. The composition data for the fibulae may be summarised as follows:

| Cemetery | No. of bronze fibulae | % age with Pb | % age with Fe | % age with detectable amounts of Pb and Fe |
|---|---|---|---|---|
| Toumba | 27 | 56 | 44 | 41 |
| Skoubris | 34 | 35 | 15 | 9 |
| P. Perivolia | 6 | 83 | 67 | 67 |
| Total | 67 | 48 | 31 | 31 |

Table 1a. Composition data for bronzes and other metals in Skoubris (copper forms the remainder of the composition of the bronzes throughout Table 1: > = greater than)

| No. | Descr. | Tomb No. | % Sn | Pb | Fe | Other | Surface |
|---|---|---|---|---|---|---|---|
| 1 | Fibula | S 8,6 | 2.1 | — | — | | B |
| 2 | Fibula | S 15B,3 | 4.4 | — | — | | B |
| 3 | Fibula | S 15B,4 | 5.4 | 2 | — | | B |
| 4 | Fibula | S 15B,5 | 5.0 | 15 | 0.5 | | B |
| 5 | Fibula | S 16,18 | 2.3 | — | — | | A/B |
| 6 | Fibula | S 16,19 | 6.9 | — | — | | B |
| 7 | Fibula | S 16,22 | 8.0 | 20 | — | | A/B |
| 8 | Fibula | S 16,24 | 3.3 | — | — | | A/B |
| 9 | Fibula | S 16,26 | 3.0 | — | — | | B |
| 10 | Fibula | S 16,27 | 6.8 | 20 | — | | B |
| 11 | Fibula | S 16,28 | 6.2 | 7.5 | — | | B |
| 12 | Fibula | S 19,10 | 2.9 | 4 | — | | B |
| 13 | Fibula | S 19,12 | 5.6 | — | — | | B |
| 14 | Fibula | S 19,13 | 4.6 | — | — | | A/B |
| 15a | Fibula | S 20,8 | 6.7 | 4 | 0.5 | | B |
| 15b | Fibula | S 20,8 | 5.6 | — | — | | B |
| 16 | Fibula | S 22,8 | 3.4 | — | — | | A/B |
| 17 | Fibula | S 25A,5 | 9.6 | — | — | | B |
| 18 | Fibula | S 40,4 | 0.5 | — | — | | B |
| 19 | Fibula | S 40,5 | 3.9 | 2 | — | | B |
| 20 | Fibula | S 40,6 | 1.7 | — | — | | B/C |
| 21 | Fibula | S 43,5 | 3.4 | — | — | | B |
| 22 | Fibula | S 43,6 | 4.5 | 4 | — | | B |
| 23 | Fibula | S 46,5 | 6.6 | 6 | tr | | B |
| 24 | Fibula | S 54,1 | 1.7 | — | — | | A/B |
| 25 | Fibula | S 59,29 | 7.4 | — | — | | B |
| 26 | Fibula | S 59,30 | 10.0 | — | — | | B |
| 27 | Fibula | S 59,31 | 6.3 | — | — | | B |
| 28 | Fibula | S 59,32 | 9.0 | 3.5 | 6 | | B |
| 29 | Fibula | S 59,33 | 8.9 | — | — | | B |
| 30 | Fibula | S 59,34 | 8.5 | 3 | — | | B |
| 31 | Fibula | S 59,35 | 6.0 | — | — | | B |
| 32 | Fibula | S 60,4 | 5.5 | — | 6 | | B |
| 33 | Fibula | S Pyre 4,11 | 6.3 | — | — | | B |
| 34 | Fibula | S Pyre 4,13 | 4.3 | — | 5 | | B |
| 35 | Ring | S 15B,6 | 8.0 | — | — | | B |
| 36 | Ring | S 16,14 | 8.2 | — | — | | A/B |
| 37 | Ring | S 16,15 | 12.1 | — | 0.5 | | A/B |
| 38 | Ring | S 16,16 | 5.4 | — | — | | A/B |
| 39 | Ring | S 16,17 | 5.9 | 7 | — | | B |
| 40 | Ring | S 17,2 | 9.0 | — | — | | A/B |
| 41 | Ring | S 17,3 | 5.4 | — | — | | A/B |
| 42 | Ring | S 19,14* | 3.4 | 4.0 | — | | B |
| 43 | Ring | S 19,15* | 5.4 | — | — | | B |
| 44 | Ring | S 22,5 | 4.8 | — | 3.5 | | B |
| 45 | Ring | S 31,4 | 8.0 | — | — | | B |
| 46 | Ring | S 39,1 | 4.5 | — | — | | B/C |
| 47 | Ring | S 40,7 | 2.5 | — | — | | A/B |
| 48 | Pin | S 16,29 | Iron with tr. of Cu | | | | C/D |
| 49 | Dress Pin | S 36,1 | > 20 | 7.5 | | 2% Zn | A/B |
| 50 | Pin | S 62,2 | 4.5 | 30 | 1 | As pr | B |
| 51 | Pin | S 63,1 | 6.0 | 2.5 | — | | B |
| 52 | Macehead | S 5,3 | 20 | 2.0 | — | | B |
| 53 | Bead | S 33,17 | 2.4 | tr | 7 | 1% Zn | B |
| 54 | Plaque | S 59,38 | Lead | | | | |
| 55 | Scale plate | S 59,37 | 7.7 | — | — | | B |
| 56 | Scale pan | S 59A,11 | Lead | | | | |
| 57 | Scale pan | S 59A,12 | Lead | | | | |

## Table 1b. Composition data for bronzes and other metals from Toumba

| No. | Descr. | Tomb No. | % Sn | Pb | Fe | Other | Surface |
|---|---|---|---|---|---|---|---|
| 1 | Fibula | T 1,10 | 15 | 30 | > 30 | | B/C |
| 2 | Fibula | T 3,10 | 12 | 6 | 0.5 | | B |
| 3 | Fibula | T 5,17 | 6.1 | — | — | | B |
| 4 | Fibula | T 5,20 | > 20 | 6 | — | | B |
| 5 | Fibula | T 5,25 | Iron only | | | | D |
| 6 | Fibula | T 9,1 | 12.5 | 1 | 1.5 | | B |
| 7 | Fibula | T 12A,4 | 4.3 | — | — | | B |
| 8 | Fibula | T 13,22 | 1.2 | — | — | | A |
| 9 | Fibula | T 22,19 | 6.6 | 4 | — | | B |
| 10 | Fibula | T 22,21 | 0.5 | — | 0.5 | | B |
| 11 | Fibula | T 22,25 | 5.1 | 4 | 1 | | B |
| 12 | Fibula | T 22,26 | 1.9 | 4 | 2 | | B/C |
| 13 | Fibula | T 22,27 | 1.7 | 3 | 1.5 | | B/C |
| 14 | Fibula | T 27,9 | 7 | 30 | 30 | | B |
| 15 | Fibula | T 27,10 | 4.4 | 1 | — | | B |
| 16 | Fibula | T 27,11 | 4.3 | — | — | Zn tr | B |
| 17 | Fibula | T 31,23 | 11.7 | — | — | | B/C |
| 18 | Fibula | T 32,11 | > 20 | 25 | 15 | Zn tr | B/C |
| 19 | Fibula | T 32,12 | 20 | 30 | 30 | | B |
| 20 | Fibula | T 32,13 | 10.0 | — | — | | B/C |
| 21 | Fibula | T 32,14 | 8.0 | — | — | | B |
| 22 | Fibula | T 32,15 | 20 | 30 | 15 | | B |
| 23 | Fibula | T 32,16 | 17 | 12 | 6 | Zn tr | B |
| 24 | Fibula | T 36,23 | 10.2 | — | tr | | A/B |
| 25a | Fibula | T 36,24 | 11.6 | — | — | Zn 2% | A/B |
| 25b | Rivet | T 36,24 | 1.8 | — | — | | B |
| 26 | Fibula | T 36,25 | 4.9 | 1.5 | — | | B |
| 27 | Fibula | T Pyre 2,8 | 3.9 | — | — | Zn tr, Ni tr | B |
| 28 | Fibula | T Pyre 2,9 | 2.5 | — | — | | B |
| 29 | Bracelet | T 1,8 | 6.4 | 10 | 3 | | B |
| 30 | Bracelet | T 1,9 | > 20 | 15 | 0.5 | | B |
| 31 | Bracelet | T 13,23 | 20 | 30 | 30 | | A/B |
| 32 | Bracelet | T 13,24 | > 20 | 30 | 30 | | B |
| 33 | Bracelet | T 33,17 | 5.9 | — | — | Ni tr | B/C |
| 34 | Bracelet | T 36,26 | 17 | 30 | 20 | | B |
| 35 | Bowl | T 31,20 | 13.6 | 2 | — | | B |
| 36 | Bowl | T 33,16 | 20 | — | — | | A/B |
| 37a | Jug (body) | T 33,15 | 18 | — | — | | B |
| 37b | Jug (handle) | T 33,15 | 13.1 | — | — | | B |
| 38 | Cup | T 22,18 | 9.2 | — | — | | B |
| 39 | Pin | T 12B,2 | pr | pr | pr | Zn tr | C/D |
| 40 | Spearhead socket | T 14,3 | — | — | — | | C/D |
| 41a | Vessel (handle) | VII | 12 | 20 | tr | | B |
| 41b | Vessel (sheet) | VII | 12.8 | tr | — | | B |
| 42 | Rivets on Iron knife | T 3,11 | pr | — | — | | C/D |
| 43 | Rivets on Iron knife | T 14,4 | Iron only?? | | | | |
| 44 | Rivet on Fibula | T 22,26 | Iron with tr of Cu | | | | |
| 45 | 'Scrap of silver'? | T 14 | Iron only | | | | |
| 46 | Needle? | T 26,20 | Iron only | | | | |

## Table 1c. Composition data for bronzes and other metals in Palia Perivolia

| No. | Descr. | Tomb No. | % Sn | Pb | Fe | Other | Surface |
|---|---|---|---|---|---|---|---|
| 1 | Fibula | P 3,25 | 6.5 | 4 | – | | B |
| 2 | Fibula | P 3,26 | 2.5 | – | – | | B |
| 3 | Fibula | P 23,15 | 5.0 | 11 | > 30 | | B |
| 4 | Fibula | P 43,7 | 10.6 | 6.5 | 1 | | B |
| 5a | Fibula | P 45,1 | 16 | 4 | 5 | 1% Zn, 0.5% As | B |
| 5b | Paddlewheel | P 45,1 | 11.0 | 8 | – | tr Zn | B |
| 6 | Fibula | P 45,2 | 12.0 | 3.5 | 1 | | A/B |
| 7 | Bracelet | P 14,5 | – | 1.2 | – | | B |
| 8 | Bracelet | P 43,8 | 9.8 | tr | – | tr As | B |
| 9 | Roll top pin | P 21,11 | 1.3 | – | 0.5 | | B |
| 10 | Pin | P 46,1 | 12.0 | 30 | 6.5 | | B/C |
| 11 | Pin | P 46,2 | 10.0 | 20 | 7.5 | | B |
| 12 | Ring | P 10,21 | – | – | – | | A/B |

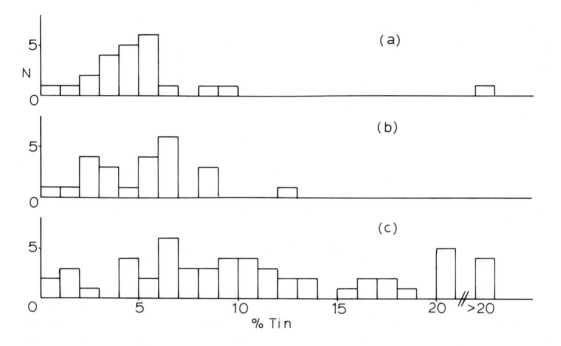

FIG. 4. The distribution of tin contents in (a) SM, (b) PG and (c) SPG.

The archaeological description of the fibulae has indicated some variation in their typology and development, but in relating the parameters which delineate their classification to their compositions, few correlations are evident. For example, five fibulae from Toumba characterised by high lead and iron and, with one exception, high tin contents (T 1,10, T 27,9, T 32,11–12 and T 32,15) divide themselves between types: II.19 (asymmetric, swollen bow), arched bow (? Italian type), abnormal (arched bow with three bosses) and arched bow (slightly swollen) respectively. Nevertheless, comparison between typological pairs of fibulae and their compositions has been more rewarding. Confirmation that the following sets of fibulae, which are confidently ascribed as pairs typologically, may be assured owing to the acceptable level of similarity in their compositions: T 22,26 and 27,

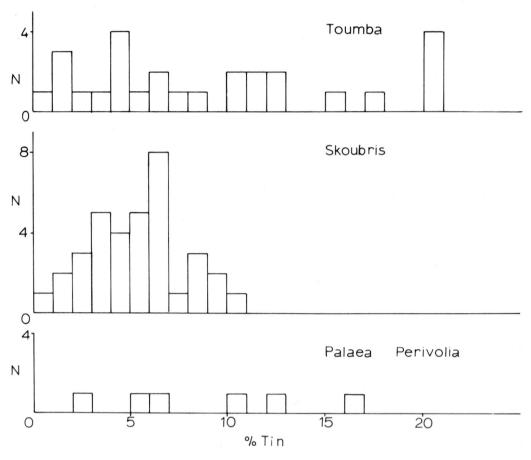

FIG. 5. The distribution of tin contents in the bronze fibulae from the three cemeteries.

T 32,11–12, T 32,13–14, T 32,15–16 and PP 45,1–2. Fibulae T 59,32–4 which are grouped as a triplet and T 16,27–28, however, while homogeneous in their tin contents, show marked discrepancies in their lead and iron contents and lead contents respectively. These results, in particular, serve to demonstrate a possible serious example of the segregation effects of these two metals in the bronze. The compositions of S 16,18 and 26 strengthen the evidence, which typologically was not entirely certain, that they form a pair; by contrast, there is sufficient dissimilarity in the compositions of T 22,21 and 25, another candidate for possible pairing, to suggest that they should not be so matched. T 27,9–10 are definitely not pairs in composition terms, but T 27,10–11 may be matched. The bracelets and rings may be treated in a similar manner, and the histograms indicate that their tin, lead and iron distributions form the same pattern within each cemetery as observed above with the fibulae. Of the two pairs of bracelets analysed, only one set, T 13,23 and 24 may be seen to match in composition, the other set, T 1,8 and 9 having grossly divergent compositions. Among the three possible pairs of rings, S 16,15 and 16, S 17,2 and 3 and S 19,14 and 15, there is poor matching throughout.

The discussion so far has taken no account of the probable presence of imported bronzes

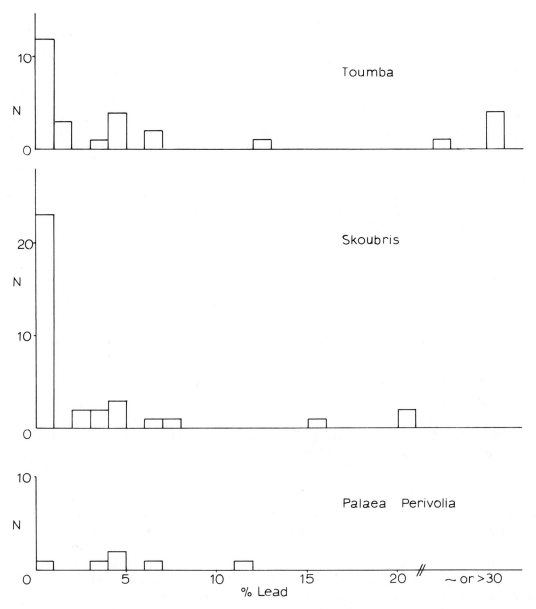

FIG. 6. The distribution of lead contents in the bronze fibulae from the three cemeteries

among the Lefkandi metal object assemblage, and the analytical data should now be considered in the light of this information. The bronzes suspected on archaeological grounds to be imports, and these include the most likely candidates, S 59,37, T 33,15 and S 5,3, have been grouped according to their tentative region of origin (Attic, 'Eastern' and 'Western') and their compositions compared. With one exception, no discernible trends or correlations are evident, and thus the composition evidence is purely equivocal with respect to provenience; S 59,37 and T 33,15 are tin bronzes with no lead and the macehead, S 5,3, has a high tin content (20%) and 2% lead. This may come as no great surprise since it is known, for example, that leaded bronzes occur in Egypt from the end of the new Kingdom and the Late period,[8] although few relevant analyses are available. The unique pair of fibulae, however, T 32,11—12, are very clearly distinguished in composition from the other two fibulae, T 5,17 and T 22,19, with possible Italian connexions; indeed the former pair is alone among the suspected imports in exhibiting the feature of high tin, lead and iron contents. The other bronzes belonging to this composition type, which are restricted primarily to the Toumba, but also the Palia Perivolia cemeteries and, chronologically, to the SPG period, bear no particular archaeological traits which mark them down as imports. Thus the strong implication must be that this unusual composition type represents a local 'anomaly'. But before proceeding with some comments on the nature of this 'anomaly', it is necessary to review the available information on the presence of iron in bronze generally. Firstly, it is recognised that this metal is normally associated with bronze as an impurity; for example, among the 8,000 analyses of early copper and bronze artefacts from Europe made by the Stuttgart group,[9] only a handful contain more than 1% iron the large majority having very considerably less than this amount. For the Aegean, the available analyses of bronzes of the Bronze Age and Geometric periods[10] indicate that iron is infrequently more than a minor impurity in bronze.

Craddock[11] analysed a wide variety of Late Bronze Age bronzes (tools, weapons and statuettes), 114 in all, 3 of which had more than 1% iron. There were 19 Subminoan statuettes, arrowheads and knives of which only 1 had more than 1% iron, 3 Protogeometric fibulae all with less than 0.2% iron and 165 Geometric bronzes (73 statuettes which included 2 with 4.6 and 3.8% iron and 2 with 1—2% iron; 92 decorated bronzes, mostly fibulae, pins and pendants, 1 of which contained iron in the 1—2% range.) At the Unexplored Mansion at Knossos (LM II), there was one example with 1% iron among the 80 bronze artefacts analysed.[12] XRF analysis of 63 bronzes from Nichoria, mainly of the LBA and Dark Age periods, gave eleven with detectable iron of which eight had 1% or more of iron.[13] Spectographic analyses of the prills, droplets and some artefacts from the same site and for the same time span, 71 in number, produced 6 examples with 1% or more of iron.[14] Stathis[15] has reported the analyses of 5 prehistoric copper objects from Eutresis in Boeotia, none of which contained iron. Twenty-three bronzes, mostly of post Bronze Age date, including 9 from the Argive Heraeum (rings and pins) of the Geometric period, were analysed by Davies, who, in an earlier study, examined a few prehistoric metal finds from Vardaroftsa in W. Macedonia (see footnote 26).[16] The most interesting composition in Davies' 1934—5 report was that of a piece of a bronze plate from Olympia containing 7% iron, 1.5% lead, a trace of tin, 0.93% nickel and 0.32% arsenic, the remainder being copper. It was the discovery of an iron-rich copper object of LH IIIA2 date from Nichoria and the presence of notable quantities of iron in copper 'lumps' from Sardinia (one of the 7/6th centuries and the other of the 13th century BC) which prompted Cooke and Aschenbrenner[17] to investigate the phenomenon in detail. The first problem to be tackled was the form of the iron in the bronze. Simple tests for magnetism on 193 copper objects of wide geographical distribution showed that in 27 examples the iron was metallic, and not, for example, in the form of magnetite, a common slag constituent. The results of metallographic studies on these iron-rich artefacts and on some laboratory prepared specimens suggested to Cooke and Aschenbrenner that the presence of iron could be explained in terms of the following smelting conditions in the furnace: the use of iron oxide as a flux, and strongly reducing conditions maintained by increases in the charcoal content of the furnace and the temperature. They proposed that iron rich copper/bronze artefacts are indicative of the use of low sulphur copper ores since the sulphur would be expected to prevent the formation of metallic iron. This is borne out by the extensive archaeological and metallurgical investigations of the copper smelting methods at Timna in south Israel,[18] the earliest evidence of which is of Chalcolithic date. It is clear, however, that malachite and other carbonate and oxide ores were also exploited there in later times (later Bronze Age, Iron Age and the Roman period). The improvement in furnace design and the use of higher temperatures which took place after the Chalcolithic period, while facilitating the separation of the copper from the slag, concomitantly caused the reduction of the iron flux. The prolonged contact between the resultant iron with the slag caused the introduction of iron into the copper. The presence of tin in copper does not apparently inhibit this process; Cooke and Aschenbrenner[19] had no difficulty in preparing a 10% tin bronze with 8% iron. Tylecote and Boydell[20] observed that the presence of 4.5% iron increased the hardness of copper by 76%. The Lefkandi bronzes containing iron may thus reasonably be interpreted within this scheme; 20 of these bronzes were selected with iron contents ranging from 2—30%, of which 18 gave positive tests for magnetism. There was a rough correlation between strength of attraction to the magnet and the iron content with one exception: the bead, T 33,17, whose estimated iron content was 7%, was more strongly attracted to the magnet than were the fibulae with 30% iron. A distinction should perhaps be made between those containing high tin and lead contents in addition to an excess of iron which were alluded to above as a local 'anomaly', and the remainder which may or may not contain lead and for which the tin content is variable but below 20%. At any rate, it is the frequency and extent of this phenomenon which is remarkable at Lefkandi. That iron ores were known and perhaps first exploited in Euboea during the 10th and 9th centuries BC seems likely, and certainly today there are several active iron ore (of residual type) mines in central Euboea.[21] Ancient sources have written of Chalkis as a metallurgical centre in early historical times,[22] a situation which Bakhuizen has hypothesised to be a factor in the early colonising movement of Chalkis.[23] The double mine of copper and iron described by Strabo[24] near Chalkis above the Lelantine Plain has been the subject of some discussion and speculation[25], but, geologically, there is no evidence in support of its existence. At this stage, satisfactory explanations for the existence of the iron-rich bronzes and their suggested division into the 'anomalous' group and the remainder are not feasible with the available data, and indeed will not be forthcoming until some metallographic examinations have been accomplished.[26] For the moment, they may best be seen as accidental bronzes, products of the metalsmith experimenting with bronze and lead, but failing to remove the iron from the former during smelting. Their appearance may not have been unusual (until or unless corrosion set in), and functionally, these objects, fibulae and bracelets, would have been at no disadvantage. In a more general sense, the Lefkandi base metal objects are expressions of the metalsmith's increasing awareness and interest in the use of iron alongside the repertoire of metals and techniques which were inherited from the preceding Mycenaean era. The paucity of bronzes from the excavations of the last phases of the Mycenaean settlement on Xeropolis, and the absence of analytical data for such bronzes, place the question of the extent to which the post-Mycenaean bronzes from the cemeteries were the products of the re-use of scrap metal into the realm of speculation. But in its own right, the present body of composition data provides evidence from a number of quarters that there was a ready availability of the base metals to the metalsmith at Lefkandi during the time span of the cemeteries, a situation aided perhaps by the site's geographical position. Firstly, there is the general use of tin throughout the SM and SPG periods for decorative objects which clearly did not require the strengthening properties imparted by this metal to copper. Rather, the advantages of the presence of tin in casting the bronze objects should be highlighted, and in a narrower sense the advantage of wearing a bronze, rather than a copper, ring may be borne in mind.[27] Secondly, the variability of the tin contents among the bronzes as a whole, pointing to a lack of concern in economising in the use of this metal and the finding of tin oxide in a SPG gold bead (see footnote 2 in Appendix E, on the gold analyses), suggest that the regular metalsmiths at Lefkandi were kept well supplied in this respect; the itinerant bronze worker travelling with his own supplies may perhaps have been in a more advantageous position to maintain his source of tin. Snodgrass[28] has hypothesised, primarily on the basis of the metal finds from Attica, that there may have been a temporary sharp reduction in the copper and tin trade in the Middle Protogeometric period which inevitably affected the Aegean. Although there are insufficient numbers of analysed bronzes in the individual E, M, and LPG periods at Lefkandi to test this hypothesis satisfactorily, there is nothing indicative in the tin distribution and the frequency of copper objects for the PG period as a whole to suggest that there was a shortage of tin at this time. But a note of caution should be sounded here since it is unwise to generalise on the basis of the analysed Lefkandi bronzes alone, which form a wide but nevertheless incomplete spectrum of the total bronze object output. The nature of grave goods precludes the presence of, for example, the more functional and utilitarian bronzes such as tools.

The relative scarcity of lead objects contrasts markedly with its presence in bronze. The present results have shown that lead was a frequent addition to the bronzes, this process facilitating the casting properties of the metal. The most likely source of the lead from Lefkandi was Laurion where the earliest evidence for the mining of argentiferous lead ores dates as early as the Middle Bronze Age.[29] Extraction of the metallic lead (and silver[30]) presumably took place at Laurion itself,[31] but in explaining the discrepancy between the occurrences of lead in metallic form and as a component of bronze it is possible to speculate that lead ore rather than metallic lead was transported to Lefkandi, the former being added directly to the molten copper. The main objection to this suggestion, however, is that it might have created unexpected and complex metallurgical problems. On the other hand, it is worth recalling the relevance here of the inlay of the gold pendant, P 22,34, which consisted of lead carbonate hydroxide (footnote 2 in Appendix E).

In conclusion, the chronological span of the Lefkandi cemeteries was a crucial and formative period in the development of later Greek metallurgy. To the Lefkandi metalsmith, the arrival of iron on the metallurgical scene, coupled perhaps with the inspiration and motivation gained by the examples of some fine imported bronzes, brought about a desire on his part, if not a need, to experiment. The present results have hopefully provided a framework for further study on the Lefkandi[32] and other early Iron Age sites' metal materials.

## APPENDIX D

1. I wish to acknowledge and to thank the Archaeological Service and Miss A. Andreiomenou for giving their permission for both this work and that described in Appendix E (gold analyses) to be carried out. I am indebted to Dr. H.W. Catling who has been a direct collaborator throughout this investigation. I also wish to thank Dr. G.J. Varoufakis and Dr. P.T. Craddock for their comments and discussion.

2. E.T. Hall, F. Schwizer and P.A. Toller, X-ray analysis of museum objects: a new instrument. *Archaeometry* 15 (1973) 53—78.

3. As described in H.W. Catling and R.E. Jones (1976), Analyses of copper and bronze artefacts from the Unexplored Mansion, Knossos, *Archaeometry* 18 (1976) 57—66.

4. See, for example, J.A. Charles, Heterogeneity in metals, *Archaeometry* 15 (1973) 105—114; S.R.B. Cooke, Analyses of copper/bronze samples, pp. 129—35, in McDonald et al., Excavations at Nichoria in Messenia: 1972—73, *Hesperia* 44 (1975) 69—141.

5. In a few instances, individual components of an object were individually analysed because it can be argued that they were made separately. Thus, the rivet of T 36,24 is considered as a separate sample to the fibula itself; the same applies to T 41a and b and P 45,1.

6. Three bronzes T 12b,2, T 14,3 and T 3,11 are also excluded here and from Figs 2—4.

7. P.T. Craddock (1976) The composition of the copper alloys used by the Greek, Etruscan and Roman civilisations: (1) the Greeks before the Archaic period, *Journal of Archaeological Science* 3, 93—113. The relative frequency of leaded bronzes among the Subminoan statuettes from the Dictean Cave should be noted.

8. J. Lucas, revised by J.R. Harris, *Ancient Egyptian materials and industries* (London, 1962) p. 244.

9. S. Junghans, E. Sangmeister and M. Schröder *Kupfer und Bronz in der frühen Metall zeit Europas* (SAM 2) (Berlin, 1968).

10. Craddock op. cit., Catling and Jones op. cit., and G. Rapp, R.E. Jones, S.R.B. Cooke and E.L. Henrickson, Analyses of the Metal Artefacts, ch. 10, pp. 166—81 in G. Rapp and S.E. Aschenbrenner *Excavations at Nichoria in Southwest Greece, Volume I: Site, environs and techniques* (1978).

11. Craddock op. cit.

12. Catling and Jones op. cit.

13. Rapp et al., op. cit.

14. Rapp et al., op. cit.

15. E. Stathis, *Praktika Akad. Athenon* 6 (1931) 418—20.

16. O. Davies, The Chemical composition of Archaic Greek bronze, 35, (1934—5) 131—7.

17. S.R.B. Cooke and S.E. Aschenbrenner, The occurrence of metallic iron in ancient copper, *Journal of Field Archaeology* 2 (1975) 251—66.

18. B. Rothenberg, R.F. Tylecote and P.J. Boydell, *Chalcolithic copper smelting, excavations and experiments*, Institute for Archaeometallurgical studies, monograph I (London, 1978).

19. Cooke and Aschenbrenner op. cit.

20. Rothenberg et al., op. cit. p. 47.

21. S.C. Bakhuizen and R. Kreulen; Chalkis-in-Euboea, Iron and Chalcidians abroad, *Chalcidian Studies III* (Leiden, 1976) Part II.2.

22. See Bakhuizen op. cit. 43—4.

23. Bakhuizen op. cit. Part II.4.

24. Bakhuizen op. cit. 48—9 and 58—9.

25. Bakhuizen op. cit. and L.H. Sackett et al., Prehistoric Euboea: contributions towards a survey, *BSA* 61 (1966) Appendix III.

26. The only published analysis of a bronze which approaches this 'anomalous' group in its iron content is that by Davies (op. cit.) of a blade fragment from Settlement 10 at Vardaroftsa. The corrected iron content was 24.5%, but the validity of the composition as a whole, which includes 7.28% antimony and 13.33% nickel, has been questioned by Craddock (op. cit.).

27. Rapp et al., op. cit. 174.

28. A.M. Snodgrass, *The Dark Age of Greece* (Edinburgh, 1971) 237.

29. H.F. Mussche, *Thorikos, A guide to the excavations* (Brussels, 1974), 59—66.

30. Silver was not encountered in any of the analysed bronzes at or above its detection limit in this study of 1%.

31. The earliest excavated areas at Laurion where the metallurgical processing of the ore was carried out date to the Archaic period.

32. The desirability of metallographic examinations of some of the Lefkandi bronzes has already been mentioned, and the new technique described by Varoufakis (Chemical polishing of ancient bronzes, *Archaeometry* (1976) 18, 219) may be most suitable in this connexion.

# Appendix E

# Analyses of Gold Objects from the Cemeteries

### R. E. JONES

## INTRODUCTION

Thirty-two gold objects from the three main cemeteries were analysed non-destructively by X-ray fluorescence. This number represents about a quarter of the total number of gold objects from the cemeteries, and consists of selected examples of all the major types of jewellery. The aim of this study was to examine the purity of the gold with respect to the most commonly occurring impurities, silver and copper.

## METHOD

The nature of the material necessitated the use of a non-destructive analytical technique, in this case the Isoprobe which was also employed in the base metal analyses. The two sources of excitation were obtained from an Americium 241 gamma source for silver fluorescence and a X-ray tube operated at 15 kV and 0.7 mA for gold, copper and lead fluorescence. Quantitative determinations of the gold, silver and copper contents were made by reference to calibrations prepared from standards of known composition. For gold and silver, calibrations were obtained from five binary alloys containing silver in the 0.5–40% range and the silver detection limit was approx. 0.25%. Estimation of the copper content was problematic owing to the presence of gold and silver diffraction lines, in particular those at approximately 7.7 and 8.4 KeV which lie close to the copper Kα line. Silver alloy standards containing copper up to a concentration of 20% and varying amounts of zinc and lead which together did not exceed 6% were employed. The limit of detection of copper was approximately 0.5%. The presence of other elements such as lead was noted qualitatively.

All the objects selected for analysis were in excellent condition. The texture of the surface was smooth, and the colour was homogeneous over the whole surface area of the object. The thickness of the object at the position of analysis varied considerably according to the type of object. It was estimated that those objects ('attachments' and diadems, in particular) referred to as gold foil had a thickness which did not exceed 0.1 mm. The effects of burial on the surface composition of gold and silver objects are visually less apparent than those of bronze or iron objects, but it is known that serious surface enrichment of the more noble elements can arise.[1] In such circumstances, the analysis of the surface of the object by X-ray fluorescence would lead to an estimated gold content which was higher than the true value. A more reliable estimate of the silver content would be expected in the case of the gold foil objects (due to the total penetration of the radiation) than in those with a greater cross-section if appreciable surface enrichment had taken place. Inspection of the analytical results in Table 1, however, indicates that there are no major differences in the silver content of the gold foil objects ('attachments', diadems and pins) on the one hand and the rings

461

## Table 1.

| Group | % Au | Ag | Cu | Group | % Au | Ag | Cu |
|---|---|---|---|---|---|---|---|
| *'Attachments'* | | | | *Spirals* | | | |
| T 3,8 | 91 | 9 | — | SK 33,14 | 98 | 1.5 | 0.5 |
| T 3,9 | 91 | 9 | — | SK 45,11 | 99 | 1 | — |
| T 36,6 | 91.5 | 8.5 | — | SK 59,17 | 93 | 7 | — |
| T 36,7 | 89 | 11 | — | | | | |
| T 36,10 | 87 | 13 | — | | | | |
| PP 47,17 | approx. 67 | 30 | 3 | *Bracelet* | | | |
| | | (Pb present) | | T 27,7 | 94 | 5.5 | 0.5 |
| *Rings* | | | | *Pins* (gilt iron) | | | |
| T 22,7 | 94 | 6 | — | SK pyre 4,9 | 95 | 5 | — |
| T 32,2 | 94 | 6 | — | SK pyre 4,10 | 97.5 | 2.5 | — |
| T 32,6 | 94 | 6 | — | | | | |
| T 32,11 | 98 | 2 | — | | | | |
| T 31,13 | 99 | 1 | — | *Fibula* | | | |
| SK 59,19 | 95 | 5 | — | T 13,15 | 97.5 | 1.5 | 0.5 |
| SK 59,24 | 93 | 7 | — | | | | |
| | | | | *Bead and pendant* | | | |
| *Earrings* | | | | T 31,19 | 97 | 3 | — |
| T 5,10 | 97 | 3 | — | Toumba VIII | 93.5 | 6 | 0.5 |
| T 5,11a | 98.5 | 1.5 | — | | | | |
| T 5,11b | 98 | 2 | — | *Gold rim round scarab* | | | |
| T 13,16 | 89.5 | 10.5 | — | T 36,20 | approx. 78 | 20 | 2 |
| T 13,17 | 97.5 | 1 | 1.5 | | | | |
| | | | | *Earring with inlay* | | | |
| | | | | PP 22,34 | 84 | 16 | — |
| *Diadems* | | | | | | | |
| T 19,5 | 96.5 | 3.5 | — | | | | |
| T 33,6 | 95 | 5 | — | | | | |
| T 33,7 | 95 | 5 | — | | | | |
| T 36,2 | 90 | 10 | — | | | | |

and earrings on the other. This suggests that, if surface enrichment has occurred among these samples, its effects have not been serious at least with respect to silver. But for copper, the determination of its content may be less reliable; this metal having a higher detection limit than silver is difficult to quantify accurately in electrum using the Isoprobe for reasons which have already been mentioned.

The proposed lack of serious surface enrichment was put to the test by analysing T 32,6 quantitatively, firstly using the two sources as described above, and secondly using the gamma source alone. In both cases it was possible to prepare separate calibrations from the standards. In the event of compositional heterogeneity through the cross-section of the object, a difference in the gold/silver ratio would be expected from the two determinations owing to the deeper penetration of the gamma rays (approximately $100 \mu$) with respect to the X-rays. The ratios were 10.8 (91.5% gold) and 8.1 (89% gold) respectively. This discrepancy can be accounted for by experimental error. For a given surface position, the reproducibility of the silver content determination was associated with a coefficient of variation of 10%. The overall error for silver was estimated to be ± 15% of the silver content; for copper it was estimated to be ± 20%.

## RESULTS AND DISCUSSION

The results of the analyses are given in Table 1 where the objects are grouped according to type.[2] T 5,11 (a) and (b) refer to the earring itself and the grains of one of the three mulberries respectively. The distribution of silver contents is shown in Fig. 1. Copper was detected in seven of the thirty-two samples, and iron was detected in the two gilt iron pins owing to the penetration of the radiation through the gold layer to the iron. It is clear that the quality of the gold is high, as indicated by the low silver contents and the relative infrequency of detectable amounts of copper. The mean silver content is 6.9%. Rings T 31,13 and T 32,11, earring T 5,11 and spirals S 33,14 and SK 45,11 have particularly low silver contents, a situation which contrasts somewhat with the 'attachments' as a group. One of these (P 47,17) and the gold setting of the scarab (T 36,20) contained approximately 30% and 20% silver respectively, and they may both be classed as electrum. The former had a noticeably lighter than average colour. Whether these two objects represent natural or deliberate alloys is a matter of speculation.

Three pairs of objects were analysed: T 36,6—7, T 5,10—11 and T 13,16—17. While the former two pairs have very similar compositions, there is a significant difference in the silver content in the latter which may simply be interpreted in terms of the use of different batches of gold to prepare the coils. There is as much variation in composition among the examples of one type of jewellery within a single tomb as there is between tombs or cemeteries. But, in general, the observed differences in silver content between groups of objects, and within the assemblage as a whole, may be taken to reflect no more than the natural variation in composition occurring in the starting material. It should be noted that the analysed samples all belong to SPG with the exception of P 22,34 which is somewhat earlier in date (LPG).

The lack of published analyses of gold objects of the Protogeometric and Geometric periods from the Aegean, and their paucity from other regions around the eastern Mediterranean of the same period, make an assessment of the significance of the present results difficult. Stos-Fertner and Gale[3] have published 160 analyses of gold, electrum and silver objects from Egypt (now in the Ashmolean Museum) of which a few are of the XXI and XXII dynasties. They noted wide variations in the silver and copper contents in the gold and electrum objects from 1% to more than 40% of silver. Their recent (unpublished) work has included analyses of Mycenaean, Minoan and Late Cyriot jewellery (again from the

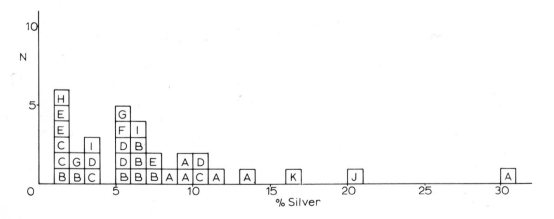

FIG. 1. Distribution of silver contents in the gold jewellery; A, 'attachments'; B, rings; C, earrings; D, diadems; E, spirals; F, bracelet; G, pins; H, fibula; I, bead with pendant; J, gold rim around scarab; and K, earring with inlay.

Ashmolean Museum) which reveal a broadly similar situation. Among eleven LH IIIA gold beads from Mycenae was one gold/copper alloy; the silver content of the remainder varied from 7 to 28.4% with a mean of 18.4%. The Cretan and Cypriot material contained an average silver content of 12.5 and 23.1% respectively. Other more isolated analyses of gold may be mentioned: Young[4] has reported the analyses of a gold Minoan double axe and a snake goddess containing 12% silver, 3% of iron and copper and a trace of iridium, and a similar silver content with some zinc respectively. He also analysed a gold bowl from Olympia containing 9% silver and a small amount of copper. By comparison, the gold from Lefkandi is rather surprisingly and consistently of high quality in terms of purity. The problem of whether the source of the gold for this jewellery was naturally pure or deliberately refined cannot at this stage be resolved. Furthermore, no information is forthcoming from the composition data presented here regarding its origin(s). It is noted that gold has been found in small amounts in mixed mineral deposits at the southern tip of Euboea.[5]

*Acknowledgements*

I wish to thank the Archaeological Service and Miss A. Andreiomenou for giving their permission for this investigation to be carried out. I am grateful to Dr. and Mrs. N. Gale for discussions and for allowing me to mention their analyses of Mycenaean, Minoan and Cypriot jewellery in advance of publication.

## APPENDIX E

1. E.T. Hall, Surface enrichment of buried objects, *Archaeometry*, 4, (1961) 62–6.

2. The friable light coloured material inside the earring, P 22,34 was analysed by X-ray diffraction (XRD) through the kindness of Dr. S.E. Philippakis at Demokritos Nuclear Research Centre, Athens. The material was found to consist of hydrocerussite (lead carbonate hydroxide) and a little calcite. This lead compound is an alteration product of lead slags, and has been identified as such at, for example, Laurion. The sample inside the bead, T 22,17, was examined and analysed by Miss M. Bimson at the British Museum Laboratory. This sample was a mixture containing white to light-brown fragments, one of which was identified by XRD as αquartz Four other fragments gave diffuse XRD patterns indicating small particle size, but the material was identified as cassiterite, tin oxide. The significance of this finding is discussed in the section on the base metal analyses.

3. Z. Stos-Fertner and N.H. Gale, Chemical and lead isotope analysis of ancient Egyptian gold, silver and lead, Archaeometry conference (Bonn, 1978).

4. W.J. Young, Technical examination of a gold Minoan double axe, *Boston Bulletin* LVII (1959) 17.

5. Institute for Geology and subsurface research. *Mineral resources of Greece* (Athens, 1973).